Praise For Previous Editions of Robert Cowart's *Mastering Windows*®

The first book I've read that does what it sa[ys]

Six years ago I bought my first computer. [...old days?] computers and applications came with docu[...] [...] [...]nally taught myself a little bit about computers by [...] Windows 3.*x* came with two of them. Not so with Windows 95 or 98. No matter how I struggled, it was difficult to learn the systems or to find the information I really needed. Then I bought *Mastering Windows 98*. I learned more about Windows 98 in the first one hundred pages than in all of the previous books I had read. My copy lies, dog-eared, beside my computer as a constantly ready source of easy to understand information. Next to my computer, it's the most important purchase I've made. It really does show you how to master Windows 98.

Steven Dean
Bullhead City, AZ

I've liked Cowart's books before, and this is no exception. As with previous versions of *Mastering Windows* by Cowart, this is well-written with clear explanations, useful asides, and seat-of-the-pants advice. He isn't afraid to say what works and what doesn't work with Microsoft's operating system, and how to work around obstacles.

Elaine
New York, NY
(reader comment courtesy of Amazon.com)

We use Cowart's books at the Center for Electronic Arts because, in addition to being complete, well-organized, and clearly written, they actually make the subject material humorous!

Harold Heddleman
Executive Director and Founder
Center for Electronic Arts, San Francisco, CA

This book has been a great help for me. Usually when my colleagues or I need to look for any Windows information we use this book. Last week I needed to link several Windows 98 machines in order to do a network rendering; we got all the information we needed from *Mastering Windows 98*. I strongly recommend this book for all Windows 98 users. No matter what they need to do, no matter what level they are, this book is the best single source for all Windows needs.

Francisco Rivera, 3D Animator
Anima Productions, Novato, CA

It was worth paying a little more for this book than for the cheaper competition. This one couldn't be clearer and easier to use, even to a new Windows user like myself; yet at the same time, it gives you useful depth and background if you want it. I prefer something more than a recipe—I'd like to know why one must do this or should do that, and this book always makes that clear. In fact, it is helping me understand how Windows and PCs work in general, not just how to use 98. But, for all that, it is eminently practical. I have yet to run into a difficulty it doesn't solve for me with clarity and directness (by contrast Microsoft's help files are often useless, in that they presuppose too much knowledge on the user's part). The book is also thorough—it has info on such useful things as how to use Outlook Express, or networking, or Kodak or Paint imaging, or multimedia. I strongly recommend this book for any user, whether a newcomer to Windows (like me) or an experienced one—even the latter might well get something out of it. Quite an achievement. And the writing is quite good, too, which is something you can't take for granted, but makes a crucial difference.

Barney Sherman
Fairfield, IA

I've been using computers for a long time. The Commodore 64, the Macintosh. The 286, 486. A P120, a P166, and now my new P2400 box.

Along the way I've seen a lot of software come and go and a lot of books come and go, too. I have read a lot of them, because no matter what you're trying to do, it seems the help file just doesn't have it.

I got this book for my friend, who is a computer novice, and it provided the kick that got him into his PC. On the other side of the coin, I use my computer every day, and I liked the book so much I got myself a copy.

It is rare that I come across a book that all types of users could benefit from. How does this book do it? It really is really, really big. But it is laid out well enough that you could just as easily read it from front to back as you could keep it on the shelf for a reference. It is a sort of book for all occasions.

Carl Lumma
Philadelphia, PA

MASTERING

WINDOWS ME

MASTERING™
WINDOWS® ME

Robert Cowart

SYBEX®

San Francisco • Paris • Düsseldorf • Soest • London

Associate Publisher: Richard J. Staron
Contracts and Licensing Manager: Kristine O'Callaghan
Acquisitions and Developmental Editor: Ellen L. Dendy
Editors: Rebecca Rider, Jim Gabbert, Donna Crossman
Production Editor: Kylie Johnston
Technical Editor: Scott Warmbrand
Book Designers: Patrick Dintino, Catalin Dulfu, Franz Baumhackl
Graphic Illustrators: Tony Jonick, Jerry Williams!
Electronic Publishing Specialist: Adrian Woolhouse
Proofreaders: Jennifer Campbell, Nanette Duffy, Molly Glover, Laurie O'Connell, Nancy Riddiough
Indexer: Ted Laux
CD Coordinator: Kara Eve Schwartz
CD Technicians: Kevin Ly, Keith McNeil
Cover Designer: Design Site
Cover Illustrator/Photographer: Sergie Loobkoff, Design Site

*This book is dedicated to
Sam Harris and the thousands
of other members of RESULTS,
the international grassroots
organization dedicated to
eliminating poverty, hunger, and
illiteracy around the world.*

ACKNOWLEDGMENTS

I am indebted to all the talented people at Sybex for their invaluable assistance in the production of this book. Special thanks to Ellen Dendy, the acquisitions and developmental editor, for her invaluable work on this project. Thanks go to editors Rebecca Rider, Jim Gabbert, and Donna Crossman, who spent long hours recasting my often ambiguous statements and keeping track of all my changes. Thanks also to Kylie Johnston, production editor; Adrian Woolhouse, electronic publishing specialist; Scott Warmbrand, technical editor; and Ted Laux, indexer.

A project as ambitious and time-pressured as this book required a team effort in the writing department, too. I am indebted to several people for their research, writing, and editorial contributions. Thanks to Faithe Wempen for her edits to this version of the book, incorporating Windows Me's features. For help in the networking section, thanks to Brian Knittel, Arthur Knowles, and Jim Blaney. For help with some aspects of Windows Me communications, my appreciation goes to John Ross, Gene Weisskopf, and Pat Coleman. And special thanks to my multitalented friend and writing colleague Dr. Steve Cummings, whose assistance was responsible for portions of the Accessories section.

The world of the Internet is so quickly evolving that no one person can keep up with it. Janine Warner and many friends and acquaintances in the San Francisco Bay area, on the Web, and in newsgroups provided me with additional information essential to the Internet section of this book.

Finally, I want to thank my friends and my family for their continued support during these seemingly endless writing projects.

CONTENTS AT A GLANCE

CONTENTS

6   WordPad and Paint Basics   145

7   Other Windows Accessories   189

17 Using Image Acquisition and Movie Maker   443

18 Working with Multimedia and Entertainment Hardware   477

INTRODUCTION

Thank you for purchasing (or considering the purchase of) this book! *Mastering Windows Me* is designed to help you get the most out of Microsoft's Windows Me (Millennium Edition) with the least amount of effort. You may be wondering if this is the right book for you. I've written this book with both the novice and the experienced PC user in mind. The intention was to produce a volume that would prove both accessible and highly instructive to all Windows users.

Based on my best-selling *Mastering Windows 98 Second Edition*, this new edition uses the same time-tested approach for teaching computer skills that has helped hundreds of thousands of beginners in many countries become Windows-literate. It covers the latest technology, incorporating changes based on Microsoft's release of a Windows Me.

What's New in Windows Me?

Windows Me is a natural extension of Windows 98; it updates the operating system to include support for all the latest hardware standards and improvements that have developed over the last few years. Now Windows Me fully supports such technologies as IEEE FireWire, USB, and Universal Plug-and-Play.

There are also a host of new or improved features:

Internet Explorer 5.5 Brings the latest in Web browsers to Windows Me. Internet Explorer 5.5 has the latest security and customization features, and the ability to display all the latest Web content.

Home Networking Wizard Walks you through the process of configuring a PC for network use, making a once complex process very easy.

Windows Media Player A brand-new, greatly enhanced version of this program offers MP3 and CD audio play, as well as Internet Radio and a variety of other audio and video formats.

Windows Movie Maker A handy utility for editing digitized video footage and for combining video or still pictures into multimedia shows with musical soundtrack and narration.

Internet Connection Sharing Allows you to share a modem or other Internet connection (such as cable modem or ISDN connection) with other PCs in your home. (This feature was included in Windows 98 Second Edition too.)

System Restore Provides a way to return to earlier Windows configurations to correct problems. For example, if you installed a program and then Windows started crashing frequently, you could restore your configuration to the way it was before you installed that program.

Games Windows Me comes with some new games for your enjoyment, including a challenging new solitaire variation called Spider and several Internet-based games such as Backgammon and Reversi.

Scanner and Camera Wizard Helps you acquire images from your scanner or digital camera more easily, in most cases allowing you to bypass any proprietary software that came with the device in favor of a standard Windows interface.

Who Should Read This Book?

What kind of background do I expect you to have to get the most out of this book? From the outset, this book doesn't require that you have a working knowledge of a previous version of Windows. All I assume is that you have a modicum of familiarity with a PC. So, whether you are new to Windows and are a bit PC-literate, or whether you already have a fair amount of experience with Windows computers but need to find out what makes this version and its newest features click, this book is a perfect choice. I think you'll find it easy to read and not over your head. There are everyday examples to explain the concepts, and all the accessory programs that come with Windows Me are explained in detail so you can do it all with nothing more than this book, your computer, and Windows Me itself.

For Beginning Users

I've written over 30 books at this point, spanning a range of computer topics over the past 15 years. A number of those books have been beginner books, so even though this book is thick, it doesn't mean it's impossible to read through, or that it's meant only for computer geeks. Nope—I know what beginners are looking for. After all, I haven't forgotten my friends who think you use a mouse like you use a TV remote control, and I know there are more of you out there! So in this book, I explain the basics and assume very little.

I have to admit that a lot of what's new in Windows Me is of particular interest to experienced Windows users who have been looking for some of Windows Me's latest features for years now. So as not to lose the experienced reader from the outset, I've used Chapter 1, "What Is Windows Me?" to introduce the beginning user and the experienced user to what they'll find once they start working with Windows Me. If, as a beginner, you find that Chapter 1 gets over your head rather quickly, don't despair. The true step-by-step introduction to using Windows begins in Chapters 2 and 3 ("Getting Your Hardware and Software Ready for Windows Me" and "Exploring the Interface"); if you want, you can skip Chapter 1 until after you get your feet wet.

TIP If you are new to computers, you should at least have some understanding of PC terminology. Though Windows Me takes much of the effort out of using your computer, it's still a good idea for you to understand the difference between things such as RAM and hard-disk memory, for example. And although I'll be covering techniques for performing typical tasks in Windows—such as copying files, formatting disks, and moving stuff from one folder to another—I'm assuming that you already understand why you'd want to do these things in the first place. (Of particular importance is a basic understanding of the differences between data files and program files.) I'll be describing these types of things briefly within the book, but you may also want to take some time out to study up on these topics if your knowledge is a little shaky.

What about Power Users?

If you're a power user, familiar with earlier versions of Windows and the intricacies of DOS, then the explanations and procedures here will quickly bring you up to speed with Windows Me and how it differs from its predecessors. For example, the first chapter (which can be skipped by novices) is a thorough analysis of what's new in Windows Me and how it compares to other members of the Windows family of operating systems. By quickly skimming the next several chapters, you'll learn how to use the features that may be new to you, such as System Restore, Windows Movie Maker, Windows Media Player, the Home Networking Wizard, and Internet Connection Sharing.

The advanced discussions in Parts II through V will be extremely useful whether you're an MIS professional, an executive, an instructor, or a home user. There's significant coverage of the increasingly important area of electronic communications from the Windows workstation, be it through the Internet, over a LAN, via services such as AOL and CompuServe, or through an independent Internet Service Provider. You will learn how to get onto the Internet: that is, how to choose the correct transmission medium (whether it be analog modem, cable modem, ISDN, DSL, or satellite dish); how to choose and install a typical modem; how to share an Internet connection over a network; and how to choose and sign up (immediately) with an Internet Service Provider. Soon, you'll be cruising the Web using Internet Explorer, reading newsgroups, sending e-mail with Outlook Express, and having live video chats with people around the world with NetMeeting.

A multimedia section (Part III, " Using Windows Me Multimedia") explores the possibilities for adding high-performance audio, video, CD-ROM, MIDI, and DVD elements to your Windows setup. With the right hardware, you'll be running 3-D games, watching DVD movies, and seeing streaming-video Web sites.

Local area networking is an essential part of corporate computer use. Even many homes are networked with several computers these days. So, several chapters toward the end tackle all the most salient aspects of Windows Me networking, from the initial planning stages through configuring file and printer sharing.

Customizing your computer by adding new hardware and software is something all users have to do from time to time. So extensive coverage of Control Panel, Plug-and-Play, dealing with "legacy" hardware, using the new Taskbar options, and how to add and manage typical items such as modems, new video boards, fonts, and Windows software modules (including the Accessibility options for folks who have bad eyesight or who are motor challenged) are all included in this tome. Technical tips and tricks are scattered liberally throughout.

Because Windows has become such a complex system, maintaining a Windows computer and keeping it working has become a specialty unto itself. Windows Me incorporates an extensive new set of maintenance and troubleshooting tools for system files, hard disks, and online communications, including the new System Restore feature you might have heard about in the press. I'll show you when and how to use them in Chapters 14 and 15 ("PC Health Features" and "Improving System Performance").

 NOTE Although for many users, Windows Me will be factory installed on the computer, this won't always be the case. If you're faced with installing Windows Me on your own, turn to Appendix A, "Installing Windows Me on Your Computer," for installation procedures and considerations.

This is just a sample of the topics you'll find between the covers of this book.

Why This Book?

As you know, there is built-in online Help with Windows Me. So why do you need a book? Well, it's because the Help system doesn't tell you what you want to know. True, great efforts have been made on Microsoft's part to simplify Windows Me and make it more intuitive and friendly in hopes that reference tomes like this one will no longer be necessary. The Help system has been revamped and is now a bit easier to use, as you'll see in Chapter 8, "Getting Help When You Need It." But until a computer can rap with you in everyday language, like the one on the *Starship Enterprise*, you will still need a good book, especially when you're talking about a computer program or operating system that is as all-inclusive (read "complex") as Windows Me.

If you happen to find some technical manuals from the manufacturer, explanations are often written in computerese, assuming too much knowledge. Other times they only give you the bare rudiments of how to unpack the box and how to call their Customer Assistance number. This is often true of trade books as well; they're either too technical or they speak only to the novice user, with no recognition that the majority of interested users are intermediate or advanced users. The beginner books, in particular, don't give the novice anything to grow into.

Here I've done the legwork for you: I've boiled down the manuals, tested each version of Windows long before they were released, had discussions with many Windows testers, and experimented on various machines from laptops to networked workstations. Finally, I sat down and wrote a book that was reviewed and revised by a whole group of critical editors, all with the goal of explaining Windows Me in normal, everyday English.

The writers who helped out with this book have a wide diversity of experience with both Windows Me and other PC software and hardware. By pooling their knowledge and working with both Windows 9*x* and Windows Me, I have come up with a thorough cross-section of useful information about this landmark operating system, and have condensed it into the book you see before you.

While researching this book, I tried to focus not just on the How To's but also on the Whys and Wherefores. Too many computer books tell you only how to perform a simple task without explaining how to apply it to your own work. In this book, step-by-step sections explain how to perform specific procedures, and descriptive sections explain general considerations about what you've learned. As you read along and follow the examples, you will not only become adept at using Windows, but you will also learn the most efficient ways to accomplish your own work.

Conventions Used in This Book

There are a few conventions used throughout this book that you should know about before beginning. First, there are commands that you enter from the keyboard and messages you receive from Windows that appear on your screen. When you have to type something in, the text will be boldface. For example, "In the text field, type **a:setup**."

When referring to files and folders, the text may be on its own line like this:

```
School Stuff\Sally's thesis on arthropods.doc
```

OR it might be included right in a line like this: "Now look for the folder named Letters to the Editor."

More often than not, responses from Windows will be shown in figures so you can see just what the screens look like. Sometimes, though, I'll skip the picture and just display the message in text.

Finally, there are many notes and tips in this book. They are generally positioned below the material to which they relate. Most are self-explanatory. The "Tech Tips" in particular, however, are directed at readers who may be interested in the behind-the-scenes workings of the program; you may safely skip them if you're not interested. Here's an example:

 TECH TIP Tech Tips are tips that are more technical in nature; they may be skipped by the non-technical reader.

Before You Begin...

Before you can begin working with Windows, make sure you have correctly installed Windows Me on your computer's hard disk. A large percentage of what appear to be software problems are often the result of incorrect installation. If your copy of Windows is already installed and operating correctly, you have no need to worry about this and can move ahead to Chapter 1. However, if you haven't installed Windows, you should turn first to Appendix A, which covers the Windows Setup program. If your copy of Windows is installed but appears to be operating significantly differently than what is discussed in this book, you might want to seek help from a computer professional or a friend who can determine whether your Windows Me system was installed correctly. For the purposes of this book, I installed all the options in my machine, so my setup might look a little different from yours. The chapters about the Control Panel and Internet Explorer explain how you can install options that may have been omitted when Windows Me was initially installed on your computer.

Happy reading! I hope this book helps you on your way to success in whatever line of work (or play) you use your computer for.

PART I

Up and Running

CHAPTER 1

What Is Windows Me?

FEATURING:

Windows Millennium Edition (Me) is Microsoft Corporation's latest upgrade to its phenomenally successful and ubiquitous software, which has been generically dubbed *Windows*. As of this writing, Microsoft's Windows remains the most popular family of computer operating systems in the world. Even if you've never used Windows before, you are probably well aware that it is a household term and that it has helped make Bill Gates the richest man in the world. No doubt Windows will be with us in some form for a good while.

There are many versions of Windows out there, and it can get a little confusing figuring out the differences among them. This chapter explains the various Windows versions, including Windows Me and helps you decide whether Windows Me is the best choice for your needs.

Please bear in mind that some terms or concepts may not make sense to you just yet. Don't worry; you'll begin to understand them as you work through the various chapters in the book. With that said, let's dive into the world of the latest and greatest graphical operating system for IBM-compatible PCs.

Defining Windows

Windows is an *operating system*—that is, a program whose primary purpose is to serve as the interface between you and your PC. You tell Windows what you want to do— open a program, delete a file, and so on—and it makes sure that your wishes get carried out. Programs such as word processors, spreadsheets, and databases run *on top* of an operating system.

Windows is also in a class of software called a GUI (Graphical User Interface). How you interact with your computer to do things like writing a letter, entering data into a mailing list, playing games, or doing simple housekeeping tasks, such as backing up or organizing your important files, is determined by the *interface*. On most computers, the hardware part of the interface consists of your screen and the keyboard. But the software part of the interface determines what things look like on the screen, how you give commands such as "check the spelling" or "print this report" to the computer, how you flip between pages of text, and so forth.

In days of old, before Windows, these kinds of chores were all done with keyboard commands, and often very cryptic ones at that. With the advent of Windows, many everyday computer tasks—such as running programs, opening files, choosing commands, changing a word to italic, and so forth—can be done using a graphical approach that is much more intuitively obvious to people who are new to computers. Also, because all Windows programs (even ones from different software manufacturers) use essentially the same commands and graphical items on the screen, once you've mastered your first Windows program, learning others is much easier.

Windows Versions

In all, there have been over a dozen versions of the Windows operating system released since it began with version 1.0 back in the 1980s. At first, it can be a bit intimidating to have all these version numbers being bandied about, so here's a quick synopsis to help you get it all straight in your head.

By the way, the following sections use the term *platform* to describe the various operating systems; it's simply another term for *operating system*. You can think of the operating system as the basis on which all the other programs on your PC run—it's the *platform* that supports everything. This is where the term platform comes from.

Windows 3.*x*: The Obsolete Platform

Some very old desktop computers (five years old or more) still have the original Windows version they came with—something in the 3.*x* platform. The "*x*" is a generic placeholder, so 3.*x* includes Windows 3.0, Windows 3.1, and Windows 3.11 for Workgroups. People refer to this group as 3.*x* because all of these versions were similar. None of these versions is sold in stores anymore.

 NOTE   Earlier versions of Windows included Windows 1.0, Windows 2.0, Windows 286, and Windows 386.

Windows 3.0 was the first commercially successful version and the first to have major applications written to run with it. Windows 3.1 corrected many of the problems in Windows 3.0 and added some nifty new features, such as support for TrueType fonts. In response to the requests from corporate users who wanted stronger networking capabilities, Windows 3.11 for Workgroups was released. It's basically the same thing as Windows 3.1 but with extra networking capability.

Windows 9*x*: The Home Platform

Most desktop and laptop PCs for home and small-office users run on the Windows 9*x* platform. 9*x* is a term used to refer to any of the following versions of Windows: Windows 95, Windows 98, or Windows 98 Second Edition (SE). Windows Me is the most current version of this platform and the only one still sold in stores. In this book, 9*x* usually is used to refer to Windows 95/98, comparing these versions to the current version—Windows Me.

Windows 95 was the original 32-bit operating system from Microsoft. It replaced Windows 3.*x* as the operating system of choice on new PCs, and it offered significant improvements, including easier Internet connection and better hardware support. Windows 98 improved on Windows 95, making the operating system more robust (and less crash prone), adding support for the newest devices (such as USB), and providing more utilities for keeping the system healthy. Windows 98 SE was a minor update, adding just a few new utilities. Most of the improvements between Windows 98 and Windows 98 SE can be downloaded for free from the Microsoft Web site.

Windows Me further improves upon Windows 98 SE by adding additional system tools, more multimedia support, and some improvements to the Internet Explorer Web browser. Is it important—or even useful—to upgrade to Windows Me if you already have Windows 98? I'll answer that question in detail later in this chapter.

Windows NT/2000: The Business Platform

Microsoft also offers network operating systems, known as Windows 2000 and its predecessor, Windows NT (the most recent version of which is 4.0). Both NT and 2000 provide the features and functions required to run medium- to large-sized networks, and indeed, both of them come in different "flavors." Windows NT *Workstation* and Windows 2000 *Professional* are the client versions, designed for use on the individual PCs in the network. Windows NT *Server* and Windows 2000 *Server* have the industrial-strength features it takes to run large enterprise networks—they are built to run on a server machine as opposed to desktop machines. Features important to network operating systems include reliability, performance and administrative scalability, network administration tools, security, and failure recovery.

 NOTE Windows 2000 was introduced in February of 2000, but many companies are choosing to migrate from NT to 2000 slowly. Because of the sheer amount of money and effort it takes to install and deploy a new network operating system, some companies (especially smaller firms) are opting not to switch from Windows NT to 2000, as long as Microsoft continues to support NT.

Later in this chapter, I'll discuss who of you out there should consider switching from Windows Me to Windows 2000 Professional (or Windows NT Workstation).

Windows CE: The Pocket PC Platform

Many handheld computing devices, called Pocket PCs, run a diminutive version of Windows called Windows CE, which was in version 3.0 at the time of this writing. A variety of hardware vendors—including Casio, Hewlett-Packard, and Compaq—manufacture Pocket PC devices that run Windows CE.

NOTE Pocket PC devices are direct competitors to the popular device known as the Palm, from 3Com. The Palm runs a proprietary operating system, not Microsoft's Windows CE.

Pocket PC devices and the software that runs on them are designed to interface with a desktop PC running Windows, so you can transfer files to the handheld device to take with you as you travel. The Windows CE operating system includes pocket versions of Outlook, Excel, Word, and many other Microsoft Office applications, and it lets you play music files and games, record memos, and more.

NOTE For more information on Pocket PCs, Windows CE, and Pocket PC–compatible software, visit www.microsoft.com/mobile/pocketpc/.

In the next several years, there will probably be other versions of Windows developed for devices that you wouldn't normally think of as computers. We'll likely see refrigerators that have their own built-in version of Windows, televisions, clock radios, and who-knows-what else. Windows will be everywhere—at least if Microsoft has its way.

Is It Worth It to Upgrade to Windows Me?

With all that said, let's look at Windows Me. Is it really new? Why should you care? If you're already happy with Windows 98, should you upgrade? All good questions.

Analyzed bit by bit, Windows Me is not a big deal, certainly not as big a deal as the upgrade from Windows 3.*x* to 95 or 98 was. But taken as a whole, it's certainly worth the hassle of upgrading. It sports a truckload of refinements, add-ons, conveniences, and some important networking and administrative enhancements. It integrates with the Internet really well, is more reliable, and lets you do cool stuff, such as playing MP3 music files on your computer. And then there's Internet Explorer thrown into the package. There's quite a collection of terrific new utility programs, such as a System Restore feature and Wizards that walk you step-by-step through complex procedures like setting up a home network and sharing an Internet connection. That's it in a nutshell. If you want to know the details, read the rest of this chapter. If you'd rather get right into using it, skip to Chapter 2, "Getting Your Hardware and Software Ready for Windows Me."

Here are the most notable features of Windows Me:

Windows Media Player You've probably heard a lot lately in the press about MP3s and other digital music formats. Well, Windows Me has you covered. It includes a great multimedia player, called Windows Media Player, that plays almost all audio and video clip formats in one handy utility. Earlier versions of Windows came with a Media Player program, but let me stress that this is *not* the old version; this puppy is brand-new, and chock-full of features. You'll learn all about it in Chapter 16, "Using the Windows Media Player."

Windows Movie Maker   Movie Maker helps you pull in video clips from a video camera, or still images from your scanner or from files on your hard disk, into a full-fledged show, complete with narration, soundtrack, and fade-out transitions. It's similar to PowerPoint in that you're assembling a presentation out of individual pieces, but the focus is on motion and sound. This is not a professional-quality video-editing tool, but it's more than adequate for your home movies or your organization's fund-raising drive.

Scanner and digital camera support   Windows Me provides direct support for many models of scanners and digital cameras. This means that you don't have to install the driver software for these devices—you can use the built-in interface that Windows provides. It also means that the interface is standardized, so if you get a new scanner or camera, you don't have to relearn the software.

Gaming improvements   Windows now comes with a variety of multiplayer games, such as Backgammon and Hearts, that you can play over the Internet through Microsoft's Gaming Zone. It also features a technology called DirectPlay Voice that lets you chat using a microphone during some online gaming sessions.

Internet Explorer 5.5   Windows Me comes with the latest version of the popular Web browser, Internet Explorer. It's only slightly different than the previous version, but a Print Preview feature has been added that earlier versions lacked.

Windows Help and Support   The Help system is now easier and more intuitive to use, and it contains a whole slew of tours and tutorials for learning basic tasks. It is also more integrated with the online Help information, and it automatically remembers the help topics you've looked at recently so that you can recall them with ease.

System Restore   Most people who have used Windows a lot have messed up their system Registry at least once. It's the configuration file (actually two files working together) that stores all your Windows settings, including which programs are installed and which system files are used for various tasks. Sometimes, while installing or removing a program or shutting down your PC incorrectly, you can introduce errors that can cause your PC to malfunction.

The System Restore feature enables you to go back in time, to an earlier version of the Registry, to correct a problem. For several years, there have been Windows add-on programs you could buy that did this, but now Windows has the feature built-in. See Chapter 14, "PC Health Features," for all the details.

AutoUpdate   Ever wonder if you have the latest versions of all your important system files? Well, wonder no more in Windows Me. If you have an Internet connection, Windows can periodically connect to the Windows Update Web site, check for updates, and automatically download them to your PC. Then it lets you know that an update has arrived, and you can choose whether to install it or not.

Home Networking Wizard   Have you ever wanted to network the PCs in your home but were intimidated by the technical aspect of the project? Windows Me comes with a great new Home Networking Wizard that walks you step-by-step through the configuration of each PC. Just install the network cards in each PC, run the cables, and then let the Wizard handle the rest. It's covered in Chapter 24, "Building a Peer-to-Peer Network."

MSN Messenger Service   MSN Messenger Service enables you to exchange instant messages with your friends who are online at the same time. You can download this feature for free from Microsoft. You don't have to upgrade to Windows Me to get it, but if you do upgrade, the MSN Messenger Service software is automatically installed for you.

Personalized Start menu   The Start menu in Windows Me remembers what programs you select from it most frequently and displays only those programs when you initially open it. You can click the down-arrow at the bottom of a menu to expand it to see the full listing. Over time, this personalized menu system can save you time and effort, because the programs you never use are not displayed until you call for them. You'll learn more about this in Chapter 4, " Getting Down to Business: Running Your Applications."

Behind-the-scenes improvements   In addition to the obvious improvements you've just read about, Windows Me contains some great features that you won't even know are there. One example is System File Protection. This feature guards your system files against corruption and other programs copying over them when they install themselves. Also, because Windows Me relies less on the old MS-DOS way of doing things, it is free to run your Windows-based programs better. And it has some networking and Internet-connection improvements that make those features run more smoothly, too.

Windows Me versus Other Operating Systems

You just learned what makes Windows Me better than earlier versions of Windows, but what if you currently use some other operating system? Let's review some of the most common competitors of Windows.

Windows Me versus Windows 2000

Because there are two Microsoft operating systems that will run on a PC (Windows 2000 and Windows Me), which should you choose?

NOTE It has been reported that Microsoft is eventually planning on releasing a single version of Windows that combines the best features of both Windows Me and Windows 2000. At the time of this writing, this new operating system's launch date has not yet been set.

A rather simplistic way of looking at the question is by asking, "Are you a business user or a home user?" Generally speaking, Windows 2000 is better for business use because it's more robust and less crash prone. People using their computers for business can ill afford to have a system error and lose their work-in-progress. However, Windows Me remains the favorite for home use because of its enhanced entertainment features and direct support of popular add-on devices like scanners and digital cameras.

What about networking? Windows Me can be used to set up a simple peer-to-peer network that connects a few PCs for file and printer sharing, and Windows 2000 Professional can do the same thing. However, Windows 2000 Professional has better network security capabilities—that is, more capability to prevent one PC from freely accessing another PC on the network. If you need to set up a network that includes a server (that is, a PC dedicated to running the network), you'll want Windows 2000 Server for the PC functioning as the server. The other PCs on the network (the clients) can use either Windows Me or Windows 2000 Professional, but the network will be the most secure and have the most capabilities if the client PCs are running Windows 2000 Professional.

Windows 2000 also requires higher-end hardware in order to operate at a decent speed than Windows Me does. You might find that Windows Me runs much better on an older PC (say, a 200MHz Pentium) than Windows 2000 does.

The bottom line? If the computers you are considering upgrading aren't top-of-the-line, if having a full 32-bit operating system with high-level system security is nothing more than academic to you, if you'd like to have the widest diversity of new technology available and supported and you'd like to enjoy the widest variety of software compatibility, Windows Me is the clear winner.

 NOTE If you own an expanding business and are in doubt about which network operating system route to take, don't worry. You can start with all Windows Me workstations connected to one another in a peer-to-peer fashion (see Part V, "Networking," for more about peer-to-peer networks) and then add a Windows 2000 Server station later if you want more network security and performance. And if you have been using or are still using a NetWare network, 32-bit NetWare client support is built-in.

Windows Me versus Macintosh

Macintosh is both a line of computers and the operating system that runs on them. Both are manufactured by Apple Corporation. You can't use the Macintosh operating system on the same type of PC that runs Windows, so your choice of hardware effectively dictates your choice of the Macintosh operating system or not.

Macintosh systems look and operate very similarly to Windows PCs, and many of the most popular programs are available for both. If you are working in the field of professional graphics, you will probably want a Mac because it's the standard for that industry. Otherwise, a PC is probably the better choice. Why? It's not because there's anything wrong with the Mac. On the contrary—on the Macintosh's tombstone it will probably say, "This machine ran a superior operating system." Since the Mac is less popular, however, fewer programs are written for it, so you have fewer software choices (especially in the game arena).

Apple has encountered considerable success recently with the stunning new iMac, thanks primarily to its ease of use, attractive design, and grocery list of standard features. But the iMac is still regarded as overpriced and not well suited to "power" users, so it is not poised to replace Windows PCs just yet.

Windows versus Linux

Besides the iMac, one of the most popular alternative operating systems to emerge today is Linux. Based heavily on Unix, programmer Linus Torvalds first released Linux in 1994, and it has grown substantially since. Linux is touted as an "open source" operating system, meaning that the basic source code can be freely distributed by anyone. Essentially, Linux can run on all of the same hardware as Windows.

Initially, Linux users operated solely by typing command lines at system prompts, much like DOS users did in the days before Windows. Since then, several individuals and software companies have stepped up to produce graphical user interfaces for Linux, including KDE and GNOME.

To put it bluntly, the main selling point of Linux right now seems to be that it is not Windows. The Linux operating system shows real promise, especially when used as a network or Web server, but for the average PC user, it still requires a great deal more time and mental effort to learn and maintain. Furthermore, the list of software available for Linux pales in comparison to what is available for Windows 9x/Me (although that list is growing). Unless you have a serious grudge against Microsoft and Bill Gates, you might find it easier to stick with Windows for now.

Test-Driving Windows Me

Not sure whether Windows Me is for you? Give it a try and see.

Windows Me comes with an Uninstall feature that you can use to remove it and revert to your previous version of Windows if you decide at any time that you don't like it. When running the Windows Me setup program, it asks whether you want to keep backups of your old system files. Just make sure you answer Yes to that question so that you'll be able to uninstall Windows Me just as you would uninstall any other program (from Add/Remove Programs in the Control Panel). See Chapter 9, "Customizing Windows with the Control Panel," for details about uninstalling programs.

Some people have commented that the Uninstall feature in Windows doesn't always work perfectly, though, so you might want to take greater precautions if you think you might want to remove Windows Me later. To do that, use a program like Norton Ghost or DriveImage to back up your entire hard disk to another drive, such as a writable CD-ROM. Then, if you don't like Windows Me, you can restore that backup and have things exactly the way they were before.

If you have enough space on your hard disk(s), you can set up multiple operating systems on a single PC—each on its own partition—and choose at start-up which operating system you want to work with. (A partition is a logical disk drive, such as C or D. A single hard disk can be divided into multiple partitions, each with its own drive letter.)

Does your system have what it takes to run Windows Me? Do you need any hardware or software upgrades before installing? The next chapter addresses this very issue.

CHAPTER **2**

Getting Your Hardware and Software Ready for Windows Me

FEATURING:

Assuming you made it through the last chapter unscathed, you should now have a pretty good idea of what Windows Me is all about. Our mission with this book is not only to teach you how to use Windows, but also what it has to offer you, what benefits you will gain from it, and how to prepare yourself for it.

TIP If you are learning to use Windows for the first time and have recently purchased a computer with Windows Me preinstalled, the information in this chapter will not be essential to getting started, so you can move ahead to Chapter 3, "Exploring the Interface." But if you're migrating to Windows Me from a previous incarnation of Windows, or if you simply find this stuff interesting (is it my deathless prose?), you should read on.

What's the minimum base system you'll need to run Windows Me, really? And, beyond the minimum requirements, what can you do to upgrade your system to capitalize on Windows Me's coolest features, like its 32-bit operating-system underpinnings, advanced processing features, multimedia and Internet stuff, cool display options, gaming, and networking? Beyond Windows Me itself, what new software will you have to (or want to) buy to really take advantage of what Windows Me now makes available to you? (And what software will you have to jettison or pass on to Uncle George?) In this chapter, I'll try to cover all these considerations because knowing what you're getting into may help ease your transition to Windows Me.

NOTE In this chapter, I'm assuming that you're upgrading from Windows 9*x*, rather than the earlier Windows 3.1. If your PC uses Windows 3.1, it is probably a very old PC that won't be capable of running Windows Me (at least not very well!). Rather than trying to upgrade a piece or two of it, you will probably find it most cost-effective to get a whole new PC, or to stick with Windows 3.1.

Evaluating Your Existing Software

To prepare for upgrading to Windows Me, assuming you *are* upgrading (versus simply purchasing a new computer that comes with Windows Me on it), you'll have to consider some things about your existing software. So, let's look at software compatibility first.

Windows Me was designed with backward compatibility in mind. It should be compatible with most existing 16-bit DOS and Windows applications. It's also compatible with 32-bit programs that were designed for Windows 9x and Windows NT. So, the good news is that compatibility with your existing PC software is likely to be high. Because of this, you should not need much new software. If you are upgrading from Windows 98, you probably won't need any at all.

 NOTE 16-bit programs are older programs that work on the older Windows 3.x platform as well as Windows 9x/Me. 32-bit programs are designed to work only with Windows 9x/Me or Windows NT/2000, which are true 32-bit operating systems.

However, if you still have some old programs that you've been using through several upgrades of MS-DOS and Windows, consider whether now might be the time to retire them. Here are some critical questions to ask about old programs:

Does it still run under Windows Me? Most Windows-based programs will run, but some MS-DOS–based programs will not. You might be able to adjust the program settings to make it run (see Chapter 4, "Getting Down to Business: Running Your Applications"), but in the end, the program might not work well enough under Windows Me to entice you to keep it. You won't know until you try, unfortunately.

Will running it potentially harm my system? Some older utility programs, such as older versions of Norton Utilities, are designed for a specific operating system. Running such programs with an operating system other than the one they were built for can sometimes cause problems.

Does Windows Me include this program's capability, making it redundant? Many of the utilities in earlier versions of the Norton Utilities and other utility suites were great ideas at the time because Windows lacked any built-in features of the kind. Windows Me now contains utilities that handle tasks (such as defragmenting a disk and checking it for errors, cleaning up unwanted files, and reverting a system back to earlier configurations) that make most third-party utilities unnecessary.

Does the program perform well and do everything I need it to do? If the program still works fine and you don't wish for faster performance or more capabilities, go ahead and use it. Nobody said you had to have the latest and greatest of every type of program!

Which programs can you run, and which ones can't you run? Well, providing an actual list here wouldn't be meaningful because it changes every day as more companies release Windows versions of their software. When you go to purchase new software, just be sure to check the box for the Windows Me or Windows 98 logo, or ask the dealer. (Generally speaking, any program designed for Windows 98 will probably work just fine with Windows Me, because they are so similar.)

Most utilities designed for Windows 9*x* should continue to work well under Windows Me, because 9*x* and Me are similar, 32-bit operating systems. If you have a 32-bit file system, however, some older Windows 95 utilities might not function because they are designed to work only with FAT16, the 16-bit file system (which was the only game in town back when Windows 95 was released). Nowadays most PCs use FAT32, the 32-bit file system that Windows 98 and later versions support.

Dealing with DOS Programs

As I've mentioned before, any well-behaved Windows application or utility program is likely to run under Windows Me without incident. However, some DOS programs, especially hard-disk utilities, may have trouble running. Chapter 4 covers some tweaks you can do to a DOS program's PIF file (a shortcut that contains settings for running a DOS program under Windows) that might help it run; you can play around with these to see if any of them help.

You probably will not want to run DOS-based utility programs under Windows Me anyway because Windows Me has the same or better capability in one of its own utilities. Besides, such programs might mess up your system. Typically, these programs don't recognize long file names or the FAT32 file system, two of Windows Me's standard file organization features.

 NOTE Windows 9*x* had an MS-DOS mode that you could use to restart your PC without loading Windows; this made it possible to run stubborn MS-DOS programs that wouldn't cooperate with Windows. This mode is not part of Windows Me; however, Windows Me is better at handling MS-DOS programs than its predecessors, so you should not need it. If you absolutely must boot to a plain MS-DOS prompt, use your emergency boot disk that you made when you installed Windows Me. Chapter 14, "PC Health Features," explains how to create another emergency boot disk, if you've misplaced yours.

Why Old Utilities Can Damage Your System

The sections above discussed why programs might not run. Consider now why you might not *want* to run a particular program.

First in this category are "shell replacement" programs for Windows 3.*x*. These programs were designed to improve on the confusing aspects of Windows 3.1, and they included a number of useful utilities that Windows 3.1 lacked. Such programs will probably run—at least in a limited way—with Windows Me, but you should not use them because they tie into the operating system intimately. Because of this, they could cause system problems when they find that the files present are not the ones that they expected to find.

These shells are only one class of popular Windows utilities. There are scads of other utility programs for Windows, some of which you may rely on daily. Will you still be able to run them, and will they work under Windows Me?

One class of utility that will *certainly* run into trouble on Windows Me (if it doesn't bomb altogether) is composed of Windows 3.*x* system optimization (tune-up) programs. Tune-up utilities (for example, WinSleuth and System Engineer, among others) are popular among power users who want to squeeze every last drop of performance from their Windows systems. By examining your computer's hardware and then thoroughly checking out its Windows configuration settings, these programs recommend changes, and some of them actually go ahead and make the changes. They churn through the `config.sys`, `autoexec.bat`, `win.ini`, and `system.ini` files, examining their contents, rearranging entries when necessary, deleting items as necessary, and so forth. They also typically optimize disk caching and virtual memory settings.

The problem with running these programs under 32-bit versions of Windows (like Windows Me) is as follows: The configuration files that these programs fiddle with are either not actually used by Windows Me or they are used very differently by Windows Me than by DOS and Windows 3.*x*. Thus, many of the changes such a utility would make would not be appropriate or wouldn't make a difference in Windows Me's operation.

As mentioned in Chapter 1, "What Is Windows Millennium Edition?" the Windows Registry provides a centralized, easily managed repository of system and applications settings. The Registry replaces (or augments, in certain cases) the following Windows 3.*x* files.

- `autoexec.bat`, which stores start-up information for the DOS operating system pertaining to some device drivers and TSR programs, declares the system search path, and executes any start-up programs
- `config.sys`, which loads device drivers and memory managers and sets up system variables

 NOTE   Windows Me checks for `autoexec.bat` and `config.sys` at startup, and if it finds any commands there that aren't in its Registry, it adds them to the Registry. That way, if you install an older program that requires a certain setting in one of those files, that setting becomes part of the Windows startup, although in an indirect way.

- `win.ini`, which stores information about the appearance and configuration of the Windows environment
- `system.ini`, which stores software and hardware information that pertains directly to the operation of the operating system, its device drivers, and other system-specific information

- other .INI files, comprising various initialization files, which store user preferences and start-up information about specific applications (for example, win-file.ini for File Manager, clock.ini for the clock.exe program, and control.ini for Control Panel)

Windows Me will run 16-bit Windows 3.*x* applications, which expect to find information in win.ini or system.ini files telling them how they should run, but it does so by tricking those applications into reading the information from the Registry instead of from the .INI files. Some programs use their own special .INI files, and Windows allows them to continue to do so, but any requests to the general Windows .INI files are redirected to the Registry.

Some Windows 3.*x* utility programs conceived to fine-tune Windows 3.*x* do so by tweaking the SmartDrive, virtual memory, drivers, and other base system settings. Windows Me not only incorporates the 32-bit drivers for disk caching and virtual memory management that would not be affected by these alterations, but it dynamically and intelligently scales many resources to take the best advantage of the hardware and software mix on which it's running. Therefore, for example, a utility that adjusts the permanent swap file size will have no effect, because the swap file in Windows Me is temporary and changeable in size.

The upshot of all this discussion is that if you are upgrading from Windows 3.*x* and you're attached to your system utilities, you should check to see if you can obtain a newer version of those utilities aimed at Windows Me, or at least at Windows 9*x*.

16-Bit versus 32-Bit Applications

As Windows 9*x*/Me and Windows NT/2000 have taken hold in the market, software developers have recompiled their applications into 32-bit versions. This has provided them a performance edge over their previous editions, satisfying the needs of users for faster, more reliable, and more efficient programs. Windows Me's compatibility with older 16-bit applications is really only a stopgap measure on Microsoft's part, allowing users to gracefully upgrade to Windows Me and Windows 2000 while still using their existing applications.

Some of the decisions you'll make about what programs to keep or do away with (as discussed above) will become moot because the attractive new features and faster performance of 32-bit applications will spur you to upgrade. Over the last few years, many software makers have offered various upgrade incentives, pushing their Windows 9*x* (and now Windows Me) versions.

⚠ **TIP** Don't waste your hard-earned bucks. Before you replace your Windows 9*x* software packages with ones supposedly "made for Windows Me," check to see if they're actually something new! Windows 9*x* and Windows Me both run 32-bit applications, so chances are good that you can continue using your current version because only the boxes and manuals have been changed for the Windows Me version.

In the long run, though DOS and Windows 3.*x* applications support will be built into successive iterations of Windows for some time, the impetus really is toward the Windows 32-bit design model. In fact, Microsoft developers are already pushing Windows 2000 into the 64-bit realm, utilizing cutting-edge processors from Intel and Compaq. As 64-bit computing becomes a reality in the coming years, the mainstream migration to 32-bit PCs is inevitable.

In the coming year or two, we're going to see a lot more video teleconferencing for the average user, more sophisticated multimedia CDs, interactive groupware and gaming on the Internet, fancy computer-based video-editing systems for your home movies, CD-ROM and DVD-ROM burners, and virtual-reality games. Software is a sort of virtual reality in and of itself, and developers' ideas seem limited only by the box with which they have to work.

These developments will affect not only the way we work (and play) but our buying decisions and purchasing patterns. The desire for more functionality in software will lead more software writers to market their software on DVD because they can "bundle" video-based tutorials with the application. Already, some CD-ROM–based programs, such as Quicken Deluxe, have short video and audio training lessons built in. My point is that there are many incentives for you to purchase the latest 32-bit software, just as there were reasons why you bagged your WordPerfect 5.1 in favor of a Windows word processor.

A little word of warning, though. Just because a program is 32-bit doesn't guarantee that it will be better than its 16-bit predecessor. For example, it might not run any faster. A program's speed of execution is dependent on the efficiency of the code the programmer writes. Some 16-bit programs run faster than their newer 32-bit cousins because the code was tighter and better thought-out. However, whether the 16-bit version is faster or not, it's very likely you'll get more features in a newer 32-bit version of a program.

Evaluating Your Existing Hardware

Does your hardware have what it takes to run Windows Me? Generally speaking, if you ran Window 98 successfully on your PC, Windows Me will be no problem. But let's look at the specifics.

The Box

Let's start with the basic box: the computer itself, if you will. Windows Me is going to run its fastest, of course, on fast Pentium II and Pentium III machines. The minimum system requirements reported by Microsoft are a Pentium 150 MHz processor and 32MB of RAM.

If you can lay your hands on a real Plug-and-Play machine (it needs a Plug-and-Play BIOS built in) that has ACPI (the new power management scheme) *and* a fast processor, such as a Pentium II or III or an equivalent processor from Cyrix or AMD, you will have the basis for a Windows Me powerhouse. This machine will require little effort to upgrade when it comes time to stuff in a new card or two.

If you're interested in running Windows Me on an existing machine, here are some notes about what kind of performance you can expect. For sluggish to modest performance using productivity applications such as word processors (assuming you use a slim word processor, not something huge like the entire Microsoft Office suite), even an old 90 MHz Pentium machine will prove marginally adequate for Windows Me. For more demanding application mixes, such as graphics, computer-aided design, or heavy database use, the faster the better. The same goes for networked machines that will serve as printer and communication servers.

If you're planning to buy a new machine, it doesn't make sense to buy anything new short of a Pentium III (or equivalent, such as a Athlon running at 700Mhz or above—what with the price of systems dropping like lead balls off the Tower of Pisa. If you shop around, you should be able to get a 933 MHz Athlon or Pentium III for only a tad more money than a bargain-basement system.

RAM

Just as with Windows NT and 2000, Windows Me scales automatically and intelligently to avail itself of any extra RAM you throw its way. 32MB is a bare minimum for running the operating system (and probably you will need more like 64MB if you are looking for decent performance).

System RAM is only one consideration and only about half the story when it comes to deciding what kind of memory to get for your computer. A hotly discussed topic in the computer magazines is the amount and kind of *cache RAM*. Cache RAM is very fast RAM used by the CPU to temporarily store data as it is sent to and from system RAM, speeding up memory fetches. RAM caching has been shown to increase system speed considerably.

When shopping for a notebook or desktop computer, go for 128K L2 cache minimum if you are buying an Intel Celeron processor, and at least 512K for the Pentium II, Pentium III, or AMD Athlon. With the Celeron 300A and faster, the L2 cache is integrated into the CPU itself, which means it runs much faster. This is why 128K is adequate only for Celerons.

Hard Disk

You'll need approximately 295MB of free hard disk space to install Windows Me. You will also want to have lots of additional free disk space for the dynamically sized virtual-memory paging (the *swap file*). The good news is that drives are *cheap* now. If you know where to shop, you can buy a 15 gigabyte (GB) drive for less than $100 these days.

 NOTE The Windows Me files do not have to be installed on the boot drive. If you have a two-drive system, drive D can hold everything except the boot files. The Setup program sleuths around for a drive with enough space to handle the install process and suggests a drive and folder.

You'll want to use a fast hard disk. So what else is new, you ask. Well, not everyone knows that the hard disk and video card are the two most likely bottlenecks in a system. You'll want a drive with a fast access time: around 12ms (milliseconds) average access time. (*Average access time* is a specification that will likely be advertised along with the drive's price and refers to how long it takes the drive to locate and retrieve data.)

Monitor/Video-Card Support

Windows Me is packaged with 32-bit driver support for many devices, including a wide variety of video cards. Support for all generic VGA cards and the more popular cards based on chip sets (such as the Cirrus Logic, ATI Mach, NewMagic, Chips and Technologies, S3, ET-x000, Western Digital, various 2-D and 3-D accelerators, and AGP [Accelerated Graphics Port] adapters) is also on board. In fact, Setup will run around and look at your hardware, and as it does, it will investigate the video card's identity and do its best to load the appropriate drivers. In all four of my systems, this has worked reliably.

Windows will probably work well with your existing video card, but there's always room for video performance improvement. Most video cards sold today work in the AGP slot of a motherboard. The AGP slot is the fastest bus available, and it is definitely preferable. Video cards for the PCI bus are also very good, if an AGP slot is not available on your system. An inexpensive PCI video card should be fine for business use, but if you're a serious gamer, you'll want a high-end video card with 3-D support.

The amount of RAM on a video card determines its maximum resolution and color depth. Those two factors both require memory, so, for example, for the same amount of RAM use, you could have a lower resolution with a higher number of colors or vice versa. Today, most video cards come with 16MB of RAM or more, which should be plenty unless you have a huge monitor that you want to run at a very high resolution and color depth. (The monitor size doesn't have anything to do with the amount of video-card RAM needed, but larger monitors are easier to read at higher resolutions, so higher resolutions get used with them more often.)

Speaking of monitors, any size will work with Windows, but bigger is often better. Most people prefer a 17″ monitor or larger these days, although just a few years ago, 15″ was the norm. The monitor quality is measured in either dot pitch or stripe pitch, depending on the type. Lower numbers are better; the minimum you should accept is .27mm. The monitor should also be capable of at least a 72MHz refresh rate (higher is better) at the resolution you will be running it most often (perhaps 800×600).

Flat-panel displays are becoming more popular, even though their cost is still high. Their display is similar to that on laptops, but in a stand-alone frame. These flat monitors offer outstanding quality and color, as well as convenience.

 TIP Laptop and other flat-panel screens look very good at only one resolution—the so-called *native resolution*. Other resolutions may be displayable, but they'll look blocky.

Plug-and-Play Items

Plug-and-Play (or *PnP*, as it is commonly abbreviated) is a technology that seems too good to be true. With PnP, you just plug in a board, reboot your computer, and you're off and running. All existing peripherals, sound boards, video boards, network cards, and so forth, are automatically configured for you as the operating system boots up. No DIP switches to set, no IRQ conflicts, no hassles. Sounds impossible, right? Well, in the last few years since Windows 95 hit the streets, a plethora of PnP devices have shown up.

 NOTE You don't have to buy PnP devices for your Windows Me machine. Non–Plug-and-Play cards will work fine in a PnP-enabled computer. You just give up the autoconfiguring features of the device. Also, in many cases, Windows Me's hardware installation program is pretty intelligent about detecting and correctly installing non-PnP cards.

For PnP to work, three areas of technology must coordinate:

- the system BIOS
- the operating system
- possibly some related hardware drivers

That leaves out all *legacy computers* (which in this case, would include any computer that doesn't have PnP specifically built into the BIOS). In regard to the first point, most older computers that do *not* have PnP-aware BIOS chips in them are probably so slow that they are not ideal for running Windows Me anyway.

In regard to the second item in the preceding bulleted list, Windows Me itself, of course, is PnP-aware, so the operating-system angle is covered.

In regard to the third bullet point, you should note that you can't expect to get PnP convenience with any existing 16-bit drivers from Windows 3.*x* or with the large number of older plug-in cards (with the exception of credit-card PC cards used in laptops). But PnP drivers and applications have been making a strong appearance in the last few years and they are now the norm.

So, when you prepare to install Windows Me, you should consider buying PnP boards, PnP display monitors, PnP printers, PnP mice, PnP scanners, and PnP computers only. The majority of new systems are now PnP-ready. Ditto for add-in cards. Purchasing systems and boards that currently comply with the PnP specification will save you precious time and Excedrin headaches later.

 NOTE To be permitted to display the "Windows-98 compatible" or "Windows-Me compatible" logo, hardware and software must be PnP capable. Look for this logo when making a purchase.

When you're shopping, be aware that new equipment must sport the full *Plug-and-Play* moniker (the whole term spelled out, with capital *P*s) to be truly compliant. Also, keep in mind that, like other evolving industry standards (ADSL, SCSI, ACPI, PCMCIA, AGP, and PCI, just to name a few), the spec for PnP continues to fluctuate as bugs or oversights become evident over time. We're all held hostage on that account. With Windows Me, we're now into the third generation of PnP, so at least we can feel a little more confident that we're not shelling out good money for what a couple of years ago might have turned out to fit the description "Plug-and-Pray" more than it fit the term "Plug-and-Play."

Scanners and Digital Cameras

Windows Me includes a new technology that drives certain scanners and digital cameras, but not all brands and models. It works only with scanners and cameras that are on Microsoft's Hardware Compatibility List (HCL). You can find this list at www.microsoft.com/hcl. Windows Me can operate these compatible devices through its Scanner and Camera Wizard feature.

Even if your scanner or camera isn't on this list, it will still work in Windows Me, just as it always has in earlier versions of Windows, by using its own drivers and software. This is no big hardship since the software that the device manufacturer provides is probably perfectly adequate. However, if you are buying a new scanner or digital camera, and you can find one that you like that's also on the HCL, all the better.

Other Items

What else is there to consider when looking for sound cards, SCSI controllers, CD-ROM drives, DVD drives, USB ports, or network boards? Well, some of this is hard to predict because the hardware is always evolving. But here are a couple of tips.

For starters, if your existing hardware works with the version of Windows you're upgrading from, they'll operate correctly within Windows Me. If drivers for your cards aren't supplied initially by Windows Me, you can use your old ones. As mentioned in Chapter 1, eventually every hardware manufacturer will supply 32-bit NT-style (WDM) drivers for their hardware. In the meantime, either your old Windows 3.*x*-style 16-bit drivers or your Windows 9*x* drivers will do the job.

Second, get a machine that is *ACPI compliant*. As I mentioned in Chapter 1, ACPI is the new power conservation specification developed in 1997. Windows Me's *OnNow* capability and smartest battery management (for longer computing on batteries) require ACPI. OnNow lets you power down your computer without closing all your apps, and it then lets you turn it on again, continuing right where you left off. It's a real timesaver. If you like this idea, check to see that any new computers you purchase meet the latest ACPI specification.

The hardware specifications I've explained in this chapter are only suggestions. Your old computer will probably be fine running Windows Me, even if it doesn't exactly match the recommendations. The most important factors are the processor speed and the amount of memory (RAM), followed closely by the type of video card and the size of the hard disk.

CHAPTER **3**

Exploring the Interface

In this chapter, I'll begin explaining Windows so you can start using your computer to get your work done. If you're an experienced Windows user, you can skim this chapter just to get the gist of the new features of Windows Me. If, on the other hand, you're new to Windows, you should read this chapter thoroughly. It will introduce you to essential Windows concepts and skills that you'll need to have no matter what your line of work is or what you intend to do with your computer. A solid grasp of these concepts will also help you understand and make best use of the rest of this book.

Windows 101

Windows owes its name to the fact that it runs each application or document in its own separate *window*. A window is a box or frame on the screen. Figure 3.1 shows several such windows.

You can have numerous windows on the screen at a time, each containing its own program and/or document. You can then easily switch between programs without having to close one down and open the next.

FIGURE 3.1
Windows are frames that hold information of some sort on the screen.

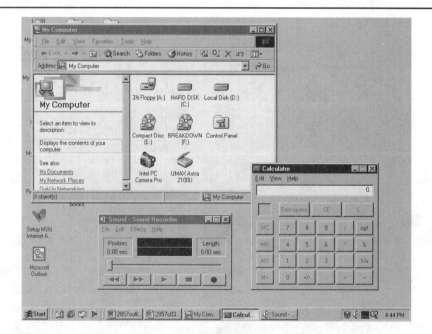

Windows also has a *Clipboard* that lets you copy material between dissimilar document types, making it easy to cut and paste information from, say, a spreadsheet into a company report or a scanned photograph of a house into a real-estate brochure. Windows provides the means for seamlessly joining the capabilities of very different application programs. Not only can you paste portions of one document into another, but by using an advanced document-linking feature, such as OLE, those pasted elements remain *live*. That is, if the source document (such as some spreadsheet data) changes, the results will also be reflected in the secondary document (such as a word-processing document) containing the pasted data.

Windows also comes with quite a handful of its own little programs. For example, there's a word-processing program called WordPad, a drawing program called Paint, an e-mail program, Internet connectivity programs, several games, utilities for keeping your hard disk in good working order, and a digital music and video player, just to name a few.

Before Moving Ahead...

Before going on in this book, make sure you've read the introduction and installed Windows correctly on your computer. (Installation is explained in Appendix A, "Installing Windows Me on Your Computer".)

While reading this chapter, if you ever have to quit Windows to do other work or simply because you want to turn off your computer, just jump to the end of this chapter and read the section called "Exiting Windows." Also, if, you ever find that you don't understand how to use a Windows command or perform some procedure, use the Help system, as described in Chapter 8, "Getting Help When You Need It."

If you truly get stuck and don't know how to escape from some procedure you're in the middle of, the last resort is to reboot your computer and start up Windows again. Though this isn't a great idea, and you may lose part of any documents you're working on, it won't actually kill Windows or your computer. There are several ways to do this, but always try this one first: Click the Start button and choose Shut Down. Then choose Shut Down from the list of shut-down options.

If that doesn't work, try pressing the Ctrl, Alt, and Del keys simultaneously. (In other words, press and hold Ctrl and Alt, then tap Del.) A box appears, offering you a Shut Down button to click. If your computer is really stuck, sometimes you might have to press Ctrl, Alt, and Del again (that is, twice in a row). Most likely, this will restart Windows.

The most drastic but surefire way to reboot the computer is by pressing the reset switch on your computer or turning your computer off, waiting about five seconds, and then turning it on again. This will almost invariably get you out of what you were doing, and make the computer ready to use again. When your computer restarts, it will probably run ScanDisk to correct any errors that you caused by shutting down this way.

WARNING All but the first method (using the Shut Down command on the Start menu) are last resorts to exiting Windows, and can result in losing some of your work! It's better to follow the instructions at the end of this chapter (in the section entitled "Exiting Windows").

Starting Windows

To start up Windows and get to work, follow these steps:

1. Remove any floppy disk from the computer's floppy disk drives.

2. Turn on your computer, monitor, and any other peripherals you're likely to use (for example, an external CD-ROM drive or external modem).

3. Wait. Windows typically takes about a minute to load.

   If you see an Enter Windows Password or Enter Network Password box that prompts you for your username and password, enter them and click OK. If you don't want to be prompted in the future for a Windows password, do not enter a password (in other words, leave the Password box blank). To start Windows without logging in, click Cancel.

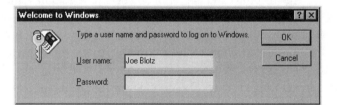

 NOTE *Clicking* means positioning the mouse pointer on the item in question and then clicking the *left* button once (or, if you've custom configured your pointing device, whichever button you've assigned as the *primary* button). The middle and right (or secondary) mouse buttons won't cut it unless I mention them specifically—they are used for other things! *Double-clicking* means clicking an item twice in quick succession.

Depending on your computer and whether it is connected to a network or not, you might see a Windows logon box, an Enter Network Password logon box, both, or neither. Your Windows logon connects you to your computer itself, establishing any special settings. (If you are using the multiuser feature, discussed in Chapter 9, "Customizing Windows with the Control Panel.") Your Network logon connects you to your network.

PART

I

Up and Running

4. Now the Windows Desktop appears, looking approximately like that in Figure 3.2. Take a look at your screen and compare it to the figure. Your screen may look a bit different, but the general landscape will be the same.

FIGURE 3.2
The Windows Desktop, the starting point from which you'll work

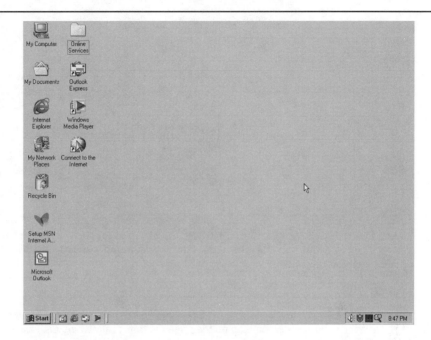

If this is the first time you have started Windows Me on this PC, you'll see a Welcome to Windows Millennium Edition video and hear some jazzy music; just wait for it to quit, and then when you get to the screen shown in Figure 3.3, click Exit to get out of there.

FIGURE 3.3
The Welcome to
Windows screen, which
appears the first time
you run Windows Me
on a PC (after an
introductory video has
finished playing)

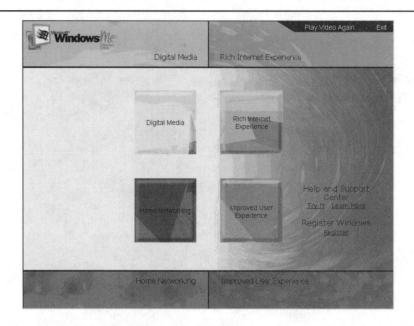

NOTE   If you or someone else has used Windows already on this PC, it's possible that some open windows will come up on the screen automatically when Windows boots (starts up). It's also possible that you'll see more icons on the Desktop than what's shown in Figure 3.2.

Parts of the Windows Screen

Now let's take a quick look at the basic parts of the Windows start-up screen: the Desktop, icons, and the Taskbar. Once you understand these three essential building blocks, you'll begin to get a feel for how Windows works.

The Desktop

The *Desktop* is your overall work area while in Windows. It's called the Desktop because Windows uses your whole screen in a way that's analogous to the way you'd use the surface of a desk. As you work in Windows, you move items around on the Desktop, retrieve and put away items (as if in a drawer), and perform your other day-to-day tasks. You do all of this using graphical representations of your work projects called *icons*.

Icons

An *icon* is a graphical symbol that represents something in your computer. To get your work (and play) done, you interact with these little graphics. Notice the icons along the left side of your desktop. The icons have names under them. Windows Me uses icons to represent folders, documents, and programs when they are not currently open and running. Below are a couple of icons.

My Computer   Research for
                  Thesis

Some of the icons on your desktop are programs or utilities you can run by double-clicking them. Internet Explorer is one such icon; double-clicking it opens the Internet Explorer Web browser program. Other icons, such as My Computer, open up a list of drives on your system from which you can browse your files.

Internet   My Computer
Explorer

Notice that some icons, such as Windows Media Player icon shown below, have little arrows in their bottom left corners. Such icons are shortcuts. In other words, they are pointers to a file, rather than the original file itself. In the case of Windows Media Player, the real program file is stored in your C:\Windows folder; the shortcut on the Desktop merely provides a shortcut for running it. You can delete shortcuts without deleting the original file.

Windows
Media Player

Some icons, such as My Documents and Online Services, look like folders. They represent—you guessed it—folders on your hard disk. Just like in a file cabinet, folders help keep your files organized. You can even have folders within folders, a useful feature for really organizing your work from the top down. My Documents is a folder in which you can store the documents you create in various applications such as word processors and spreadsheet programs. It's a special-purpose folder that actually lives right on the Desktop. Online Services, on the other hand, is a normal folder, and so its icon looks a bit plainer.

My Documents   Online
                Services

Taskbar

The *Taskbar* is the bar running along the bottom of the screen. It contains the Start button at the far left, followed by a group of four small icons. Then there's a big blank expanse, and at the right end are some more icons and a clock.

By clicking the Start button, you can enter a menu system from which you can start programs, run utilities, find files, and shut down your PC. You'll learn more about it in Chapter 4, "Getting Down to Business: Running Your Applications."

The icons to the immediate right of the Start button are on what is called the *Quick Launch toolbar*. Each of the icons is a shortcut for opening a program or performing an action. From left to right, they are as follows: Show Desktop, Internet Explorer, Outlook Express, and Windows Media Player. The latter three are all programs you will learn more about later, but the first one, Show Desktop is different. When you have windows open that obscure the Desktop fully or partially, you can minimize them all at once by clicking the Show Desktop button. Don't worry if you don't understand windows yet, or don't know what minimizing is; that's all covered in the next section.

That blank expanse in the middle of the Taskbar is reserved for buttons representing each open window or running program. (You'll see a lot of examples of this portion of the Taskbar in Chapter 4, when we talk about programs.) You can switch among open windows by clicking the button for that program's window in the Taskbar. Here's an example of a button that would appear on the Taskbar if a Microsoft Word document were open:

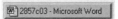

At the other end of the Taskbar is an assortment of other icons. You'll probably have different ones than the ones shown here. This area is called the System Tray, and those icons represent programs that are running in the background, such as a virus protection program or a volume controller. Finally, at the far right end, is your system clock. If you point at it, a ScreenTip box appears telling today's date, too. If the date and/or time aren't right, you can double-click the clock to open a box where you can change them.

Understanding Windows

Just in case this whole "windows" thing is eluding you, here's the scoop on what a window is and the various types of windows. Because there are different types, people can get somewhat confused when looking at a bunch of windows on the screen.

It's actually simple. When you want to do some work, you open up a program or document, and a window containing it appears on the Desktop. This is similar to pulling a file folder or notebook off the shelf, placing it on the desk, and opening it up. In Windows, you do this for each task you want to work on.

Just as with a real desktop, you can have a number of project windows scattered about, all of which can be in progress. You can then easily switch between your projects, be they letters, address lists, spreadsheets, games, or whatever, as you can see in Figure 3.4. This approach also allows you to copy material from one document to another (by cutting and pasting between them) more easily.

FIGURE 3.4
Windows let you see documents simultaneously.

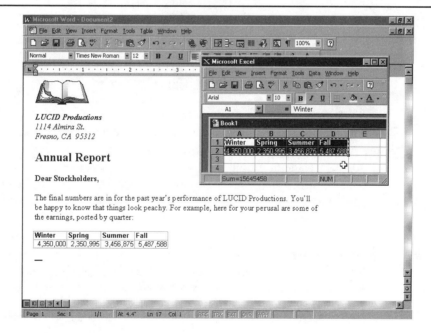

Types of Windows

There are three types of windows that you'll encounter while working: *application windows, document windows,* and *folder windows.*

TIP If you want to place a window on the screen that you can play with a bit as you read the next section about window sizing, double-click the My Computer icon.

Application windows are those that contain a program that you are running and working with, such as Microsoft Word, Excel, Paint, WordPerfect, and so on. Most of the work that you do will be in application windows.

Figure 3.5 shows a typical application window.

FIGURE 3.5
An application window is a window in which a program is running.

Some programs let you have more than one document open within them at a time. What does this mean? Well, take the spreadsheet program Microsoft Excel, for example. It allows you to have several spreadsheets open at once, each in its own document window. Instead of running Excel several times in separate application windows (which would use up too much precious RAM), it just runs once and opens several document windows within Excel's main window. Figure 3.6 shows Excel with two document windows open inside it.

 NOTE Notice that each document has its own rectangular button on the Taskbar. Microsoft Office 2000 programs work that way to make it easier for you to switch among multiple open documents in the same program. Some programs show only one button in the Taskbar for a running program, regardless of the number of documents you have open within it.

FIGURE 3.6

Two document windows within an application window

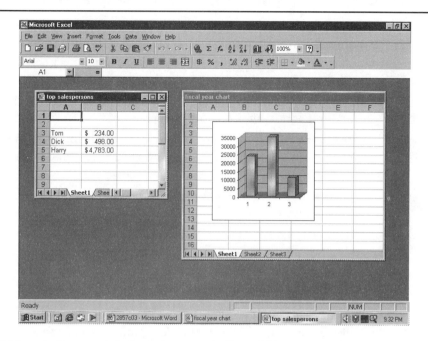

Folder windows are windows that contain lists of files contained in a particular folder. For example, if you double-click the C drive icon in My Computer, a list of folders on the C drive appears. You'll work extensively with folder windows in Chapter 5, "Organizing Files, Programs, and Disks."

Title Bar

The name of the program or document appears at the top of its respective window, in the *title bar*. In Figure 3.6, notice the application window's title bars read Microsoft Excel, while the two document windows are top salespersons, and fiscal year chart.

If the document window is maximized so that it fills the entire application window, then they share a common title bar and it reports both the name of the application and the name of the document. For example, here Notepad's title bar shows the name of the document currently open:

The title bar also serves another function: It indicates which window is *active*. Though you can have a lot of windows on the screen at once, there can be only one active window at any given time. The active window is the one you're currently working in. When a window is made active, it jumps to the front of other windows that might be obscuring it, and its title bar changes color. You make a window active by clicking anywhere within its border.

Minimizing, Maximizing, and Closing Windows

At the far right end of a window's title bar are its window control buttons: Minimize, Maximize/Restore, and Close. Maximize and Restore are actually two different buttons, but only one or the other appears at any given moment. Each of these buttons is described below:

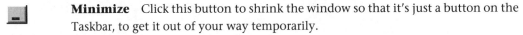

Minimize   Click this button to shrink the window so that it's just a button on the Taskbar, to get it out of your way temporarily.

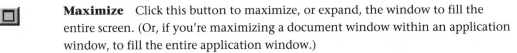

Maximize   Click this button to maximize, or expand, the window to fill the entire screen. (Or, if you're maximizing a document window within an application window, to fill the entire application window.)

Restore   If a window is already maximized, the Restore button appears. Click it to return the window to its non-maximized size.

Close   Click this button to close the window entirely. If it's an application window, the program closes down. If it's a document window, the document closes.

Resizing or Moving a Window

Sometimes you'll want to adjust the size or position of a window. You might want to arrange several windows side by side, for example, so you can easily see them both, copy and paste material between them, and so forth. You can't move or resize a maximized window, of course, because there's nowhere for it to go.

TIP   Clicking and dragging a window's corner allows you to change both the width and height of the window at one time.

NOTE   *Dragging* simply means keeping the mouse button depressed while moving the mouse.

You manually resize a window using these steps:

1. Carefully position the cursor on any edge or corner of the window that you want to resize. The mouse pointer changes to a two-headed arrow.

    The lower-right corner on some windows (it looks like a little triangular tab) is designed just for resizing.

2. No matter whether you click an edge or corner, the next step is to press the left mouse button and hold it down.

3. Drag the window edge or corner to the desired position and then release the mouse button. While you were dragging, you probably noticed a *ghost* of the window's outline that moves with the arrow. This is used to indicate that you are resizing the window and to show you what the shape of the window will be when you release the mouse button (see Figure 3.7).

FIGURE 3.7
Change a window's size by dragging its corner.

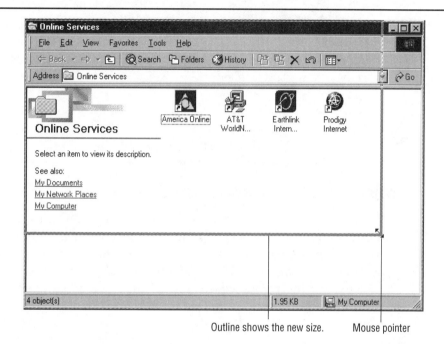

Outline shows the new size.   Mouse pointer

To move a window without resizing it, drag it by its title bar. Release the mouse button when it's where you want it.

Using the Control Box

Every title bar has a little icon at its far left side. This is the Control box. It has two functions. First, clicking it opens a menu, called the Control menu. Figure 3.8 shows a Control box with its Control menu open. This is the same menu you get when you right-click a minimized window in the Taskbar.

FIGURE 3.8

Single-clicking the
Control box brings up
the Control menu.

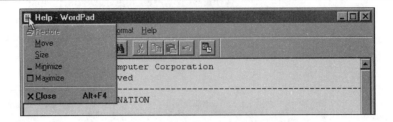

FIGURE 3.8

Second, you can double-click the Control box to close the window (terminate the program or close the document).

 TIP Pressing Alt+Hyphen opens the Control box of the active document window; Alt+ spacebar opens the Control box of the active application window.

Scroll Bars, Scroll Buttons, and Scroll Boxes

On the bottom and right edges of many windows, you'll find *scroll bars*. These are used to "pan across" the information in a window: up, down, left, and right. This is necessary when there is too much information (text or graphics) to fit into the window at one time. For example, you might be writing a letter that is two pages long. Using the scroll bars lets you move around, or scroll, within your document to see the section you're interested in since two full pages of text won't be displayed in a window at one time. Figure 3.9 illustrates this concept.

FIGURE 3.9

Scrolling lets you work
with more information
than will fit on your
screen at one time.

A window's scrolling feature consists of the scroll bar itself, a scroll box within the bar, and scroll arrows at each end (see Figure 3.10).

FIGURE 3.10
A window with scroll bar, scroll box, and scroll arrows

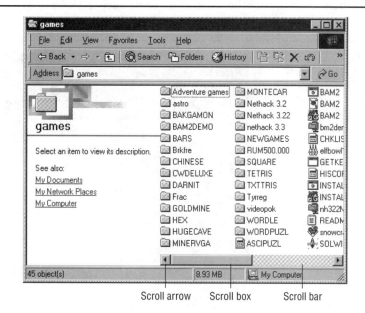

Scroll arrow   Scroll box   Scroll bar

There are several ways to use a scroll bar, depending on how much you want to scroll and how quickly (or with how much precision):

- You can scroll the display bit-by-bit by clicking a scroll arrow, or you can scroll faster by holding down the mouse button while pointing it at a scroll arrow.

- You can drag the scroll box to scroll very quickly. This is useful when you need to move all the way to one side or to the top or bottom quickly.

- You can click the scroll bar above or below (or to the left or right of) the scroll box to scroll one screen in that direction.

In some windows and programs, the size of the scroll box tells you how much of the window's contents are not currently displayed. For example, in Figure 3.10, the scroll box takes up about half of the scroll bar, meaning that there is about twice as much content as is currently displayed. In other programs, the scroll box remains a small rectangle no matter what.

All about Menus

The *menu bar* is a row of words that appears just below the title bar. (It appears only on application windows. Document windows do not have menu bars.) Each of those words is a menu name. Click a menu name to open a menu; then click a command on the menu to select it.

For example, in Figure 3.11, I have clicked the word File, opening the File menu. I'm now ready to click the command I want (such as Open or Rename).

FIGURE 3.11
A typical menu in a file management window

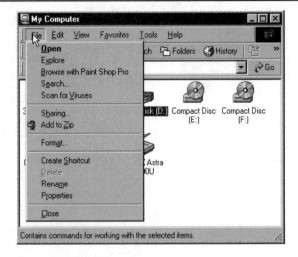

> **TIP** I could have also held down the Alt key and pressed F to open that menu. Each command and each menu name has an underlined letter called a selection letter that, in conjunction with the Alt key, activates it.

If a menu has a command that appears in bold, it's the default command. The default command is the one that's issued if you double-click on the selected object. For example, in Figure 3.11, the icon for the D drive was selected before opening the menu, and the Open command is bold. That means that I could have double-clicked the D drive's icon as a shortcut for opening the File menu and choosing the Open command. Not all menus have a default command. (In fact, most don't.)

If a command on a menu appears dimmed, it means that command is not available at the moment. For example, in Figure 3.11, the Delete command is unavailable because I can't delete the selected drive.

Commands with an ellipsis after their names (three dots) open dialog boxes that prompt you for additional information. You'll learn more about dialog boxes later in this chapter.

Here are a few special menu features you might encounter:

- Commands with a check mark next to them are on/off toggles for a particular feature.

- Commands with a right-pointing arrow next to them open a submenu.

- Some menu commands have a key combination next to the name. You can press that key combination instead of opening the menu and choosing that command.

- Commands with a dot next to them are part of an option group, a set of mutually exclusive commands. When you select one, the previously selected command becomes deselected.

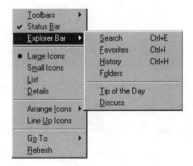

Once a menu is open, you can move your mouse to the right or left to open a different menu instead, or you can press the right or left arrow key on your keyboard. To select from a menu, you can click the command you want, type the command's selection letter, or use the up or down arrow keys to highlight the command and then press Enter.

You can cancel a menu (that is, make the menu disappear without selecting any commands) by simply pressing the Esc key or by clicking anywhere outside of the menu.

Right-Clicking in Windows

As I mentioned earlier in the chapter, right-clicking objects throughout the Windows interface brings up a shortcut menu with options pertaining to the objects at hand. The same options are typically available from the normal menus but are more conveniently reached with a right-click.

Right-clicking isn't merely part of the Windows interface; it has been incorporated into many Windows programs, too. For example, Microsoft Office programs such as Word and Excel have had right-click menus for some time. Some of the accessory programs supplied with Windows Me have context-sensitive right-click menus, too. In general, the contents of the right-click menus change depending on the type of object. Options for a graphic will differ from those for a spreadsheet cell, text, a Web page, and so on.

TIP I suggest you start using the right-click button whenever you can. You'll learn through experimentation which of your programs do something with the right-click and which don't. Some older Windows programs won't even respond to the click; others may do the unexpected. But in almost every case, right-clicking results in a pop-up menu that you can close by clicking elsewhere or by pressing Esc, so don't worry about doing anything dangerous or irreversible.

A good example of a right-clickable item is the Taskbar. Right-click an empty place on the Taskbar, and you'll see this menu:

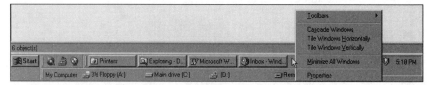

Now right-click the Start button, and you'll see this menu:

Right-click the Desktop, and you'll see the following menu.

Try right-clicking as many of the icons and elements on your Desktop as possible in order to see the wide variety of right-click menus that are available. Click away without selecting a command to close each one, or simply right-click something else.

Right-clicking isn't only part of the Windows Me interface; it has been incorporated into recently written Windows programs, too. For example, Microsoft Office programs, such as Word and Excel, have had right-click menus for some time. Some of the accessory programs supplied with Windows Me have context-sensitive right-click menus, too. In general, the contents of the right-click menus change depending on the type of object. Options for tables will differ from those for spreadsheet cells, frames, text, graphics, and so on.

Here are a few other right-clicking experiments to try:

- Right-click My Computer and notice the menu options.

- Right-click a document icon. If you right-click a DOS batch file (any file with a .bat extension), you'll have an edit option on the menu. What an easy way to edit a batch file!

- Right-click a program file, such as Pbrush.exe in the Windows directory or on a fill with a .dll (Dynamic Link Library) extention. The Quick View option (available only if you have the Quick Viewers installed) lets you read information about the program, such as how much memory it requires to run and when it was created. A Properties option may tell you even more.

- When you right-click a printer in the Printer's folder, you can quickly declare the printer to be the default printer or to work offline (not actually print yet, even though you print to it from your applications) or go online with accumulated print jobs. Right-click the Desktop to set the screen colors, screen saver, and so forth.

- Right-click any program's title bar and notice the menu for resizing the window or closing the application.

- Right-click a minimized program's button down in the Taskbar. You can close the program quickly by choosing Close.

- Right-click the time in the Taskbar and choose Adjust Date/Time to alter the date and time settings for your computer.

Many objects such as folders, printers, Network Neighborhood, and Inbox have a right-click menu called Explore that brings up the item in the Windows Explorer's format (two vertical panes). This is a super-handy way to check out the object in more detail. You'll have the object in the left pane and its contents listed in the right pane. In some cases, the contents are print jobs; in other cases, they are fonts, files, folders, disk drives, or computers on the network. (File management through Windows Explorer is covered in Chapter 5.)

Sharable items, such as printers, hard disks, and fax modems will have a Sharing option on their right-click menus. The resulting box lets you declare how an object is shared for use by other users on the network. (See Chapter 24, "Building a Peer-to-Peer Network," for networking information.)

Using Property Sheets

Just as most objects have right-click menus, many also have property sheets. Properties pervade all aspects of the Windows user interface; they provide you with a simple and direct means for choosing settings for everything from how the screen looks to whether a file is hidden or what a shared printer is named.

Virtually every object in Windows—whether a printer, modem, shortcut, hard disk, folder, networked computer, or hardware driver—has a *property sheet* containing such settings. These settings affect how the object works and, sometimes, how it looks. And property sheets not only *display* the settings for the object but usually allow you to easily *alter* the settings as well.

You've probably noticed that many right-click menus have a Properties command. This command is often the quickest path to an object's property sheet—not that there aren't other ways. Many dialog boxes, for example, have a Properties button that will bring up the object's settings when clicked. And the Control Panel is used for setting numerous properties throughout Windows. Still, as you become more and more comfortable with Windows, you'll find that the right-click approach is most expedient.

Properties can provide information about a program, feature, or document. Suppose, for example, that you're browsing through some folders (or the Windows Explorer) and come across a Word document. Wondering what it is, when it was created, and who created it, you just right-click and choose Properties. The file's property sheet pops up, as shown in Figure 3.12. There are several tab pages on the sheet because Word specifically stores additional property information in its files.

FIGURE 3.12

A typical property sheet for a document file. This one is for a Word file, so it has several pages listing its editing history, who created it, keywords, title, and so forth.

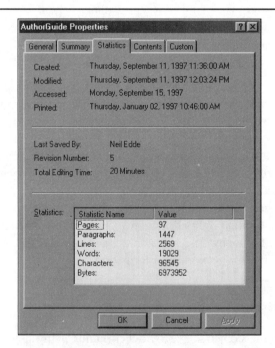

The parts of the Windows Desktop itself also have properties. For example, if you right-click the Desktop and choose Properties from the menu, the Display Properties dialog box shown in Figure 3.13 appears. This is the same Display Properties dialog box that you would see if you went through the Control Panel (covered in Chapter 9).

FIGURE 3.13
The property sheet for the Desktop enables you to customize your display settings.

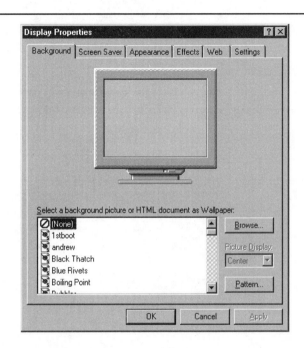

Working with Dialog Boxes

As I said earlier, a *dialog box* appears when you select a command with an ellipsis (...) after it. Dialog boxes pop up on your screen when Windows or the Windows application program you're using needs more information before continuing. Some dialog boxes ask you to enter information (such as filenames), while others simply require you to check off options or make choices from a list. The list may be in the form of additional sub–dialog boxes or submenus. In any case, after you enter the requested information, you click OK, and Windows or the application program continues on its merry way, executing the command.

Though most dialog boxes ask you for information, other boxes are only informative, alerting you to a problem with your system or an error you've made. Such a box might also request confirmation on a command that could have dire consequences, or it might explain why the command you've chosen can't be executed. These alert boxes sometimes have a big letter *i* (for "information") in them, or a question mark (?).

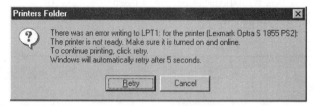

Of course, most dialog boxes are more complicated than that—much more compli-cated. Some of them even have *tab pages* with each page containing a different set of options. Tab pages keep a dialog box to a reasonable size while still letting you adjust a lot of settings from it. To get to the page of settings you want, just click the tab with the correct name. Figure 3.14 shows a multitabbed dialog box from Microsoft Word.

FIGURE 3.14
Some dialog boxes have multiple tabs that organize the available settings. Click a tab, and a new set of options appears.

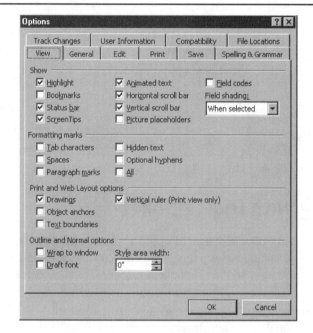

Entering Information in a Dialog Box

Most dialog boxes have several text boxes, check boxes, option button groups, and other elements with which to make your selections. You can move between the sec-tions in three ways:

- The easiest way is by clicking the section you want to alter.

- If you are using the keyboard, you can press the Tab key to move between sec-tions and then press the Spacebar to select them.

- You can also use the Alt key with the underlined letter of the section name you want to jump to or activate. Even when you are using a mouse, the Alt+key combinations are sometimes the fastest way to jump between sections or choose an option within a box.

In the following sections, let's briefly look at the various kinds of controls in dialog boxes and how to work with them.

Text Boxes

You enter text (or other keyboard characters) into a *text box*. For example, you'd click in the text box, then enter the name of a file you want to save or open.

Sometimes a text box contains a default value that you can either leave or change. If the text box already contains text and you would like to change it, you can select the existing text (by double-clicking it) and typing in your own. Another way to edit existing text in a text box is by clicking it once. An insertion point (a vertical line) will appear, and then you can use Backspace or Delete to remove the parts you don't want and type new text as needed to edit.

Some text boxes have a down-pointing arrow at the right, which you can click to select from previous text you have typed into this dialog box in the past. That can save you time if you find yourself repeatedly entering the same text in a text box time after time.

Check Boxes

Check boxes are the small square (or sometimes diamond-shaped) boxes. They are used to indicate nonexclusive options. When the box is empty, the option is off; when you see a ✔ in the box, the option is on. Click the box to turn the option on, or off.

Option Buttons

Unlike check boxes, which are nonexclusive, option buttons are exclusive settings. Sometimes called radio buttons, these are also round rather than square or diamond shaped, and only one option can be set on at a time. Clicking the desired button turns it on (the circle will be filled) and turns any previous selection off. If you are using keyboard shortcuts, first jump to the section by pressing Tab, and then use the arrow keys to select the option.

Increment Buttons

When a text box must contain a numeric value (such as a number of copies, as shown below), little up and down increment arrows appear next to the box. You can enter a number the same as with any text box, or you can click the arrow buttons to increment the number up or down.

Command Buttons

Command buttons are like option buttons except that they are used to execute a command immediately. They are also rectangular rather than square or circular. An example of a command button is the OK button found on almost every dialog box. Once you've filled in a dialog box to your liking, click the OK button, and Windows or the application executes the settings you've selected. If you change your mind and don't want the new commands on the dialog box executed, click the Cancel button.

There is always a command button that has a thicker border; this is the command that will execute if you press Enter. Likewise, pressing the Esc key always has the same effect as clicking the Cancel button (that's why there's no underlined letter on the Cancel button).

Some command buttons are followed by ellipses (...). As you might expect, these commands will open additional dialog boxes for adjusting more settings.

Other command buttons include two >> symbols in them. Choosing this type of button causes the particular section of the dialog box to expand so you can make more selections.

List Boxes

List boxes are like menus. They show you a list of options or items from which you can choose. For example, when choosing fonts to display or print text in, WordPad shows you a list box. You make a selection from a list box the same way you do from a menu: by just clicking it. From the keyboard, highlight the desired option with the arrow keys, and then press Enter to choose it. Notice that this list box has its own scroll bar.

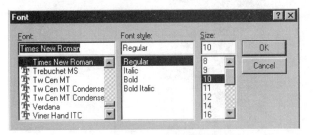

To save space, some list boxes are drop-down lists. You click the down-pointing arrow to their right to open up the list, and then click your choice.

 TIP You can quickly jump to an option in a list box by typing the first letter of its name. If there are two choices with the same first letter and you want the second one, press the letter again, or press the down-arrow key.

Using Open or Save As Dialog Boxes

A dialog box like one of the three shown in Figure 3.15 often appears when you're working in Windows programs. This type of box is called a *file dialog box* or simply a *file box*. Though they are used in a variety of situations, you're most likely to run into file boxes when you want to open a file or when you save a document for the first time. For example, choosing File ➢ Open from almost any Windows program will bring up such a box asking which document file you want to open.

FIGURE 3.15

A file dialog box lets you scan through directories to open or save a document. Here you see three typical file dialog box types.

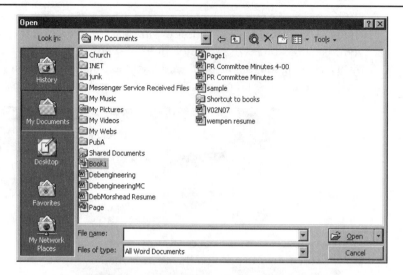

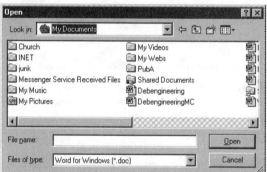

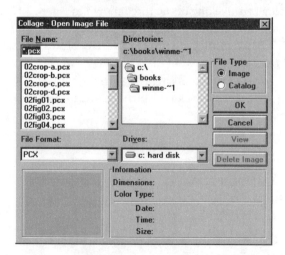

NOTE If you're new to Windows, you may want to mark this section of the book with a paper clip and refer back to it when you have to save or open a file for the first time.

File dialog boxes vary somewhat from program to program, even though they perform the same job.

First, you choose the location in which you want to look for files to open, or in which you want to save. To do so, choose the drive first. If there's a Drives list, select the drive you want from there. If not, open the Look in or Save In list and choose the drive. Next, select the folder you want by double-clicking it.

Next, if you are opening a file, find it on the list of files in that folder and double-click it. The dialog box goes away, and the file opens.

If you are saving a file, you enter a file name in the File Name box. Some programs give you the option of saving in a particular format; choose a different format if desired. Then click the OK or Save button to save.

Exiting Windows

When you're finished with a Windows session, you should properly shut down Windows before turning off your computer. This ensures that Windows saves your work on disk correctly and that no data is lost. Even if you are running an application in Windows and you close that application, you *must* also exit Windows, before turning off your computer.

 WARNING Exiting Windows properly is very important. You can lose your work or otherwise foul up Windows settings if you don't shut down Windows before turning off your computer. If you accidentally fail to do so, the computer probably won't die or anything, but the hard disk will be checked for errors the next time you turn it on.

Here are the steps for correctly exiting Windows:

1. Close any programs that you have running.

   This can almost always be done from each program's File menu—choose Exit from the menu—or by clicking the program's Close button.

   If you forget to close programs before issuing the Shut Down command, Windows will attempt to close them for you. This is fine unless you were working on a document and didn't save your work. In that case, you'll be prompted by a dialog box for each open document, asking you if you want to save your work.

NOTE If you have a non-Windows program running, such as an MS-DOS–based game, you'll have to close it manually before Windows will let you exit. You'll also be reminded if this is the case by a dialog box telling you that Windows can't terminate the program and you'll have to do it from the DOS program. Quit the DOS program and type **exit** at the DOS prompt, if necessary.

2. Next, click the Start button and choose Shut Down. You'll now see a dialog box like that in Figure 3.16.

FIGURE 3.16
Use the Start ➤ Shut Down command to safely end your Windows session.

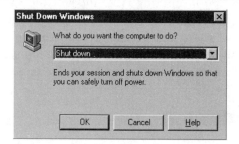

3. Choose Shut Down from the drop-down list if it is not already selected.

 NOTE Standby is an option only on computers that support the Suspend to Disk feature (mainly laptops). It allows you to shut down to conserve power but retain your work in all your Windows programs so that you don't have to do a full restart when you are ready to work again. See your computer's documentation for details.

4. Click OK.
5. Wait for Windows to tell you it's okay to turn off your computer. This can take up to about fifteen seconds. Then turn off the computer, printer, monitor, and other stuff you have attached. You're home free.

 NOTE Some computers turn themselves off automatically after step 4, so you don't need step 5.

CHAPTER 4

Getting Down to Business: Running Your Applications

This chapter is all about running programs in Windows. That's probably why you bought Windows in the first place, right? If you've just upgraded from Windows 9*x*, you already know a lot about how to use Windows and Windows applications. A few things will be different with Windows Me, but you'll probably pick those up quickly.

Running Programs

As with many of the procedures you'll want to do while in Windows, starting up your programs can be done in myriad ways. Here's the complete list of ways to run programs:

- Choose the desired application from the Start button's menus.
- Add the application to the Quick Launch tool toolbar and click it to run.
- Open My Computer, navigate your way through the folders until you find the application's icon, and double-click it.
- Run Windows Explorer, find the application's icon, and double-click it.
- Find the application with the Search command and double-click it.
- Locate a document that was created with the application in question and double-click it. This will run the application and load the document into it.
- Right-click the Desktop or in a folder and choose New. Then choose a document type from the resulting menu. This creates a new document of the type you desire, which, when double-clicked, will run the application.
- Open the Documents list from the Start button and choose a recently edited document. This will open the document in the appropriate application.
- Choose Run from the Start menu and enter the name of the file you want to run.
- Enter command names from an MS-DOS window within Windows. In addition to the old-style DOS commands that run DOS programs and batch files, you can run Windows programs right from the DOS prompt.
- Double-click a shortcut icon on the Windows Desktop. Many programs place shortcut icons on the Desktop to make launching them easy, and you can also create your own Desktop icons.

In deference to tradition, I'm going to cover the approaches to running applications in the order listed above. That is, application-centric first rather than document-centric. Realize, however, that all the approaches are useful while using Windows, and you will probably want to become proficient in each of them.

Running Programs from the Start Button

When you install a new program, a shortcut to the program is almost always added to the Start button's menu system. When this is the case, you just find your way to the program's shortcut on the menu, choose it, and the program runs.

For example, suppose you want to run Notepad:

1. Click the Start button.

2. Point to Programs. The following menu appears.

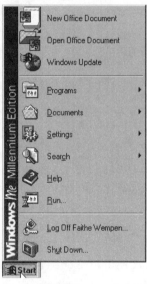

This menu contains two types of items: shortcuts to programs, and folders. Notepad isn't here, so let's continue.

3. Point to Accessories. A submenu swings out, displaying more shortcuts (and more folders too).

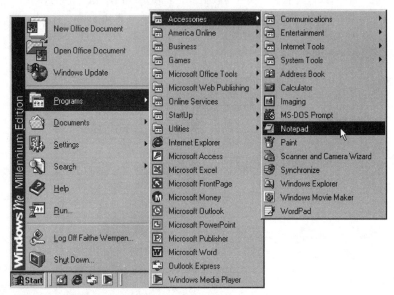

4. Click Notepad. The Notepad program starts.

If Notepad doesn't appear on the Accessories list, look for the down-pointing arrow at the bottom of the list and click it to display additional menu options. This feature is called Personalized Menus, and I'll tell you about it shortly.

You've now successfully opened Notepad. It's sitting there with a blank document open, waiting for you to start typing. Chapter 7, "Other Windows Accessories," covers the ins and outs of using Notepad, so I won't discuss that here. For now, just click the Close button, or open the File menu and choose Exit.

As you may have already noticed with this exercise, sometimes spotting a program in a list is a visual hassle. Computers are smart about alphabetizing, so notice that the items in the lists are in order from A to Z. Folders appear first, in order, then programs after that. This ordering is something you'll see throughout Windows. To make things even simpler, you can press the first letter of the item you're looking for, and the highlight will jump to it. If there are multiple items starting with that letter, each key press will advance one in the list. This works fairly reliably unless the pointer is sitting on an item that has opened into a group.

PART

I

Up and Running

TIP When you first install a program, its shortcut or submenu appears at the bottom of the menu. When you restart the PC, it usually takes its alphabetical place in the menu, but if it doesn't, you can always realphabetize all the menus. Just right-click the Taskbar and choose Properties. Then click the Advanced tab, and then the Re-sort button. Then click OK.

Sometimes you might accidentally open a list that you don't want to look at—say, Documents. Just move the pointer to the one you do want (Programs, for instance). The Document list will close and the Programs list will open. It takes a little getting used to, but you'll get the hang of it. Another way to close unwanted program lists is by pressing the Esc key. This has the effect of closing open lists one at a time. Each press of Esc closes one level of any open list. To close down all open lists, just click anywhere else on the screen, such as on the Desktop or another window, and all open Start button lists will go away.

If you see a double down-pointing arrow at the bottom of a menu, it means that the Personalized Menus feature of Windows Me has been turned on. This feature hides the menu commands and folders that you have not used recently until you click that down-pointing arrow to expand the full menu. Windows remembers each program you start, and over time, the initial list on each menu becomes customized for your usage so that you don't have to wade through lots of programs you never use.

When you initially open a menu with Personalized Menus turned on, it looks like this:

Click here to see the
rest of the commands.

Then, when you click the down-arrow at the bottom, it expands like this, with the previously hidden programs appearing pressed in:

You can turn the Personalized Menus feature off if you don't like it. To do so, right-click the Taskbar and choose Properties from the menu that appears. Then clear the Use Personalized Menus check box and click OK.

Since the personalized menus are just that—personalized—initially, each person's screen will show different commands on the various menus. So, for the illustrations in this book, I'll show the Personalized Menus feature turned off, to avoid confusion.

Running Programs from My Computer

There are times when you might want to do a little sleuthing around on your hard disk using a more graphical approach as opposed to hunting for a name in the Start list. The My Computer icon lets you do this. My Computer is usually situated in the upper-left corner of your Desktop. Double-clicking it reveals an interesting entry point to all the elements of your computer.

The My Computer icon is the entry point into the file system, and other parts of your computer, including each of your drives, the Control Panel, and any scanners or cameras you have attached, Dial-up Networking, and Printers. You may find that moving around in My Computer is very Mac-like, if you're familiar with the Macintosh operating system. Getting to a program you want can be a little convoluted, but if you understand the folder tree structure or if you've used a Mac, you'll be able to grasp this fairly easily. Try it out by following these steps:

1. Get to the Desktop by minimizing any windows that are currently on your screen. You can do this by clicking each window's Minimize button, but the fastest way is by clicking on the Show Desktop icon to the right of the Start Button.

TIP Yet another way to minimize all your windows in order to see the Desktop is to right-click the clock in the Taskbar and choose Minimize All Windows.

2. Double-click My Computer. A window appears, looking something like this:

3. Typically, Drive C is where your programs will be located. Double-click the drive icon, and your hard drive's contents will appear, as shown in Figure 4.1.

 NOTE Depending on how Windows is configured, the contents of the C drive might appear in their own window or in the same window. In Chapter 5, "Organizing Files, Programs, and Disks," you'll learn how to set file management options such as this.

FIGURE 4.1
Clicking a drive icon displays its contents. Here you see a portion of what I have on my C drive. Folders are listed first. Double-clicking a folder will reveal its contents.

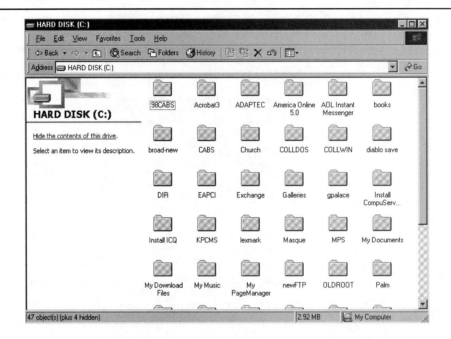

 TIP Pressing Backspace while in any folder window will move you back one level. While in the C drive window, for example, pressing Backspace takes you back to the My Computer window. Or, if you're looking at a directory, Backspace will take you up to the root level. The Up button on the toolbar works, too. (It's the one that looks like a folder with an up arrow in it.) The Back button takes you back to the previously viewed folder.

4. Double-click the folder containing the program you want to run. Keep double-clicking folders until you find the file for the program.

5. When you see the program you want to run, click it. For example, in Figure 4.2, I've found America Online.

PART

I

FIGURE 4.2
*Run a program by
double-clicking its icon.*

AOL icon

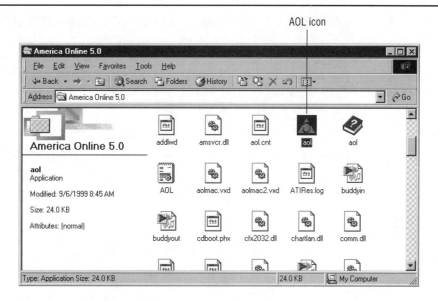

Keep in mind some of the things you should know about running programs this way:

- Program files usually have an `.exe` or `.com` file extension; that's how to determine which file in a particular folder is the one that starts the program. A *file
  extension* is a code (usually 3 characters) following a period in the file's name
  that indicates the file's type. By default, Windows does not show file extensions
  for file types that it recognizes, so it can be difficult to tell which file to double-
  click to start the program. Usually, the program file has a unique icon, like the
  one for AOL in Figure 4.2. You can also turn on the display of file extensions by
  doing the following: From My Computer, open the Tools menu and choose
  Folder Options. Click the View tab, and deselect the Hide File Extensions for
  Known File Types check box.

- The standard Large Icon view shown in Figures 4.1 and 4.2 can be annoying
  because it doesn't let you see very many objects at once. To change the view,
  open the View menu and choose a different one (List is good, for example.) You
  can also click the Views button on the toolbar to open a list of views. Small Icon
  view is just like Large Icon view but the icons are tiny and sit next to the filename rather than above it. List is just like Small Icons except they're arranged in
  columns rather than rows. And Details shows the file size, date and time last
  modified, and the file type. Figure 4.3 shows the same window as Figure 4.2, but
  in List view.

FIGURE 4.3
List view makes each file take up less space in the window so you can browse with less scrolling.

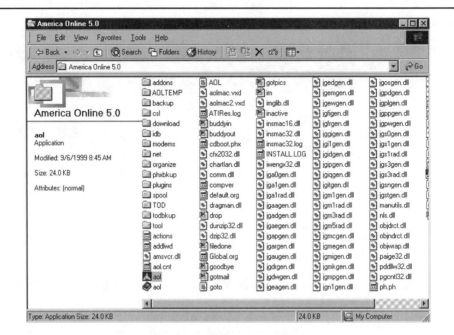

FIGURE 4.3
List view makes each file take up less space in the window so you can browse with less scrolling.

Running Programs from Windows Explorer

Working your way through a lot of folder windows, as you did in the preceding section, can get tedious. You might find it more efficient to work your way through the folder structure using a folder tree view, which is what Windows Explorer offers. Remember, to switch to Windows Explorer from a My Computer window (like the ones in Figure 4.1 through 4.3), just click the Folders button on the toolbar.

 NOTE To use My Computer or Windows Explorer to run a program, you must know in what folder that program resides. This can be tricky to determine. Many programs, however, are in subfolders within the Program Files folder, so you might look there. These program running techniques, of finding and double-clicking the program file, are useful chiefly for situations in which a program's shortcut is not on the Start menu. When the Start menu method is available, it's usually faster and easier to use than using My Computer or Windows Explorer.

Here's how to use Explorer to run your programs:

1. If you're already in a My Computer window, click the Folders button on the toolbar. Or, click Start, point to Programs, point to Accessories, and click Windows Explorer. Figure 4.4 shows what Windows Explorer looks like.

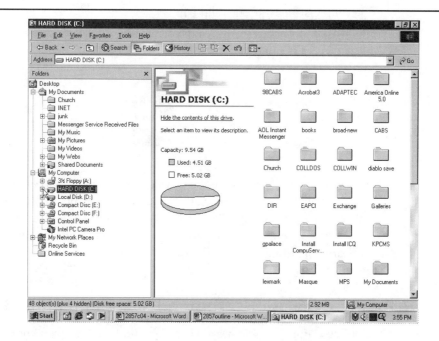

FIGURE 4.4
*Windows Explorer is
like My Computer but
with an additional pane
to the left that displays
the folder tree.*

 TIP   Another way to run Explorer is to right-click My Computer, or a drive's icon in the My
Computer window, and choose Explore.

2. When the Explorer window comes up, adjust the view as desired. For example,
you might choose to maximize the window or to choose a different view (such
as Small Icons or List).

3. The items on the left side are folders. Scroll down to the folder that contains the
program you're looking for (folders are listed in alphabetical order). If a folder
has a + sign next to it, it has subfolders. Clicking the + sign displays the names
of any subfolders.

4. Click the folder containing the program you want to run. When you do this, its contents appear in the right pane.

5. Then double-click the program you want to run. Here, I'm about to run Vppro, a video poker game.

Just as when you were using folders, you can change the appearance of listed items by clicking the View button, using the little list next to the View button, or opening the View menu and choosing Large Icons, Small Icons, List, or Details. It's easier to see which file is a program when the display is set to Large Icons (because you can see the icon clearly) or Details (because the third column will say *application* if the file is a program).

Running Applications from the Search Command

The Search feature in Windows Me helps you find the file if you know the filename of the program you're looking for but don't know where it's located. It can even cut you some slack if you don't know the whole name because you can specify just part of it. When you provide Search with a program (or other file, such as a document) name, it will begin looking through a specific disk or the whole computer (multiple disks in order to find the program in question. Once Search accumulates the results, you can double-click the correct program from the resulting list, and it will run. Pretty spiffy.

 NOTE In Windows 9x, this feature was called Find instead of Search, but it worked basically the same way.

Here's an example. I have a backgammon game called Pcgammon somewhere on my computer. It's a program that doesn't have its own setup program, so it never got added it my Start menus. I could do that manually, as you'll learn how to do later, but I'm too lazy to do that for all the programs I have. So I use the Search command, as shown in Figure 4.5.

FIGURE 4.5
The Search feature in Windows helps find a file when you aren't sure where it is stored.

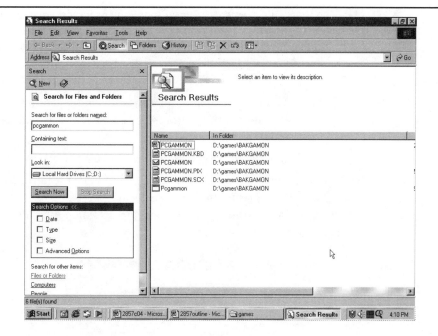

 NOTE From here on out, I'm going to rely more heavily on the shorthand notation to describe making multiple menu choices. Instead of "Click the Start button, choose Programs, then choose Accessories, and then choose Paint," I'll say, "Choose Start ➢ Programs ➢ Accessories ➢ Paint."

To find a file on your system, follow these steps:

1. Choose Start ➢ Search ➢ For Files or Folders. The Windows Explorer window appears with a Search pane to the left.

 TIP If you are already in My Computer or Windows Explorer, you can open the Search pane by clicking the Search button on the toolbar.

2. Enter the file's name in the Search for Files or Folders Named text box. If you don't know the exact name, enter as much of it as you do know.

> **TIP** The Search utility accepts wildcard specifications for filenames. An asterisk stands for any number of characters; a question mark stands for a single character. So, to find all files that begin with W, you would search for W*. Or, to find all files that begin with W and have exactly three letters in the name, you would search for W??.

3. (Optional) If you are searching for a data file and you know it contains certain text, enter that text in the Containing Text box. This is especially useful if you don't remember the filename at all.

4. Open the Look In drop-down list and choose the drive(s) on which to search.

5. (Optional) Click the Search Options hyperlink and enter any additional criteria in the boxes that appear. These options include searching by date and time, by file size, or by file type, and specifying whether to search subfolders and whether the search should be case-sensitive.

6. When you are done selecting Search options. Click Search Now. In a few seconds, any files or folders matching the search request show up in the right pane, as shown in Figure 4.5. Note that several Pcgammon files were located, but that only the last one is an application (a program). You can tell by looking at its icon. An MS-DOS–based program icon looks like a white window with a blue title bar.

7. Double-click the found application and it runs.

Be careful not to double-click too slowly (that is, don't pause too long between clicks). If you do, Windows thinks that you want to change the file's name. You know this has happened when a little box appears around the name of the file, like shown in the graphic below.

If you do find yourself in this position, just press Esc to get out of editing mode. To be safe, it's better to click on any item's icon (the picture portion) when you want to run it, open it, move it around, and so forth.

Starting a Program Using a Data File

As I mentioned above, some documents will open up when you double-click them—if they are *registered*. Windows has an internal Registry (basically just a list) of file extensions that it knows about. Each registered file type is matched with a program that it works with. When you double-click any document, Windows scans the list of registered file types to determine what it should do with the file. For example, clicking a file with a .bmp extension will run Paint and load the file (unless you have installed some other graphics editing program that has usurped the .bmp file extension for itself).

The upshot of this is that you can run an application by double-clicking a document of a known registered type. For example, suppose I want to run Word. All I have to do is spot a Word document somewhere. It's easy to spot one, especially in Large Icon view, because all Word documents have Word's telltale identifying icon. Unregistered documents have a generic-looking icon. Check out Figure 4.6. In this figure, I'm about to double-click a Word document I came across in a folder. Notice that the icon next to it is what an unregistered data file's icon looks like.

FIGURE 4.6
Double-clicking a file of a registered type runs the program that created it.

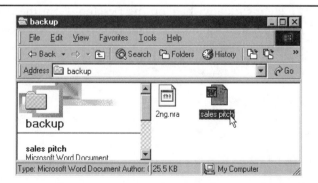

Once the program runs, you may decide you don't want to work with the actual document that you used to get the program going. That's OK because most programs will let you close the current document (try choosing File ➢ Close) and then let you open a new document (usually via File ➢ New) or an existing one with File ➢ Open.

TIP Try clicking the Start button and choosing Documents to see a list of the files you've recently edited. Depending on what's on the list, you may be able to run the program you're looking for without first opening the application.

Running an Application by Right-Clicking the Desktop

When you don't want to bother finding some favorite program just to create a new document, there's an easier way. How often have you simply wanted to create a To Do list, a shopping list, a brief memo, a little spreadsheet, or what have you? All the time, right? Microsoft figured out that people often work in just this way—they don't think "Gee, I'll root around for Excel, then I'll run it, and then I'll create a new spreadsheet file, save it, and name it." That's counterintuitive. On the contrary, it's more likely that they think "I need to create a 'Sales for Spring Quarter' Excel spreadsheet."

You can just create a new *empty* document of the correct type on the Desktop and name it. Then, by clicking it, you will be able to run the correct program. Windows takes care of assigning the file the correct extension so that the whole setup works internally. Try an experiment to see what I'm talking about.

1. Minimize open windows so you can see your Desktop area.

 TIP Remember, you can click the Show Desktop button in the Taskbar to minimize all the open windows. You can reverse the effect and return all the windows to view by clicking the button again.

2. Right-click anywhere on the Desktop. From the resulting menu, choose New. You'll see a list of possible document types. As an example, Figure 4.7 shows the types in my computer.

FIGURE 4.7
You can create a variety of new document types by right-clicking the Desktop. This creates a blank document that you then name and run.

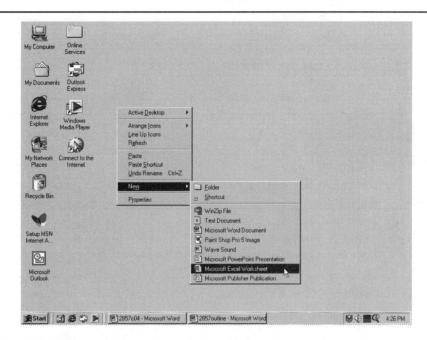

3. Click a document type from the list. A new document icon appears on your Desktop, such as the one below, which appeared when I chose Microsoft Excel Worksheet.

4. The file's name is highlighted and has a box around it. This means you can edit the name. As long as the whole name is highlighted, whatever you type will replace the entire name. When you create a new document this way, you don't have to worry about entering the extension. For example, an Excel file normally has an .xls extension, but you could just type in **Shopping List** for the name and press Enter (remember, you have to press Enter after typing in the name to finalize it). The actual filename will be Shopping List.xls because Windows adds a hidden file extension for you.

5. Double-click the icon and its associated program will run. In the case of the Excel file, the Excel program will run, open the new workbook, and wait for you to start typing in your shopping list.

Using the Start ➤ Documents List

As I mentioned earlier, choosing Start ➤ Documents lists the documents you've recently created or edited. It's an easy way to revisit projects you've been working on. This list is maintained by Windows and is *persistent*, which means it'll be there in subsequent Windows sessions, even after you shut down and reboot. Only the last 15 documents are remembered, though, and some of these won't be things you'd think of as documents. Some of them might actually be more like programs or folders. Check it out and see if it contains the right stuff for you. Figure 4.8 shows my list the day I wrote this section.

Notice the My Documents choice at the top of this list. This is a shortcut to the My Documents folder on the Desktop. That's a folder that some programs use to store documents you've created. Office 2000, for example, defaults to storing your documents in the My Documents folder.

FIGURE 4.8
The Document list from the Start button provides a no-brainer path to ongoing work projects, but only the last 15 documents you viewed or edited are shown.

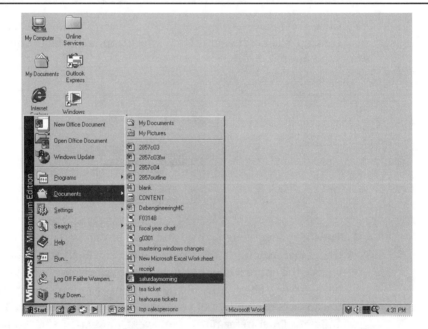

Many Windows programs have a similar feature that lists your most recently edited documents at the bottom of their File menus. Because many of my favorite programs sport this feature, I tend to rely on that more than on the Documents list.

> **TIP** You can clear off the items in the Documents list and start fresh if you want to. Right-click the Taskbar and choose Properties, click the Advanced tab, and click the Clear button.

Running a Program with the Run Command

The Run command on the Start menu enables you to type in the name of a program you want to run, much like you would type a command in at an MS-DOS prompt (for those of you who still remember MS-DOS!). This is useful for quickly starting a Windows utility that doesn't have a shortcut on the Start menu (Sysedit, for example, or Msconfig), or for running an MS-DOS program that requires startup parameters or switches.

It's less common these days than it used to be, but some programs allow you to run them in certain special modes by adding additional commands after the filename when you type it in at a command prompt. For example, suppose you want to play a DOS-based game called Nethack. You can play it in a special cheat mode if you type **Nethack /w** at the DOS prompt, but if you run it from within Windows, you don't have the opportunity to enter any special switches like that. With the Run command, however, you can type in anything you want in addition to the command name before letting it rip.

Follow these steps to use the Run command:

1. Choose Start ➤ Run. The Run dialog box opens.
2. Type the filename and any extra parameters in the Open text box. See Figure 4.9.
3. Click OK.

FIGURE 4.9
The Run command offers a way to include extra parameters when running a program.

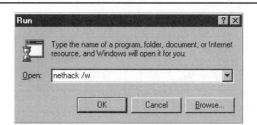

One snag you might run into is that the Run command can't find the file. This can happen if the folder in which the file is located is not in the *system path*. The path is the group of folders in which the system looks for files. If you see a message that the file was not found when trying the Run command, enter the complete path in the Open box. For example, if my Nethack file is in a folder called Games, I would enter **C:\Games\Nethack /w**.

Running DOS Programs

These days, you'd be hard-pressed to find a new program that runs under MS-DOS. But 10 years ago, MS-DOS ruled, and almost all programs were DOS- rather than Windows-based. Windows Me has less support for DOS-based programs than earlier versions of Windows did, simply because the DOS system is dying out and there's not much demand anymore for it.

Windows Me will run most MS-DOS–based programs adequately, and there are some tweaks you can perform to make them run a little bit better. But the MS-DOS mode support of Windows 9x is gone, as is the ability to write custom configuration files for MS-DOS mode. In the following sections, I'll show you what you can do to make an MS-DOS program run as well as possible under Windows Me.

Techniques for Running DOS Programs

You can run most MS-DOS programs using most of the same techniques that were explained earlier in the chapter:

- Click the program's name in a folder (pretty good method) in Windows Explorer.
- Enter the program's name at the Run command (an acceptable method, but cumbersome since you will probably need to type the complete path).
- Choose Start ➢ Programs ➢ Accessories ➢ MS-DOS Prompt and then type in the program's name at the command prompt.
- Double-click a document file with an extension that you've manually associated with the DOS program.

I explained the first two of these techniques earlier. The only difference between running Windows programs and DOS programs using those techniques is that DOS programs don't normally have an identifying icon, such as a big "W" for Word. Instead, they tend to have a boring, generic icon that looks like the one below.

Therefore, you have to rely on the icon's name alone. This one is for XTREE Gold, but because the actual program's name on disk is xtgold.exe, that's what you see. Well, actually, you don't see the .exe part, because as I mentioned earlier, .exe extensions are normally hidden from view.

Because the last two approaches in the above list differ from running Windows programs and haven't been covered, let's check those out. Then, I'll tell you a bit about how DOS programs operate in Windows and what you can quickly do to modify their behavior.

First, consider the option of running a DOS program from the good old DOS prompt.

To run a DOS session, do the following:

1. Choose Start ➢ Programs ➢ Accessories ➢ MS-DOS Prompt.

2. The result will be what's called a *DOS box*—a window that operates just like if you were using a computer running DOS. Try typing in **DIR** and pressing Enter. You'll see a listing of files on the current drive, as shown in Figure 4.10. Note that short and long filenames are both shown in this new version of DOS. Long filenames are in the rightmost column, with corresponding short filenames over on the left.

3. Type **exit** and press Enter when you are finished running DOS programs or executing DOS commands. This will close the DOS window and end the session.

 NOTE   If no DOS program is actually running, clicking the DOS window's Close button will also end the DOS session. If a DOS program is running, trying this results in a message prompting you to quit the DOS program first.

FIGURE 4.10
The DOS box lets you enter any standard DOS commands and see their output. Here you see the end of a DIR listing and the DOS prompt that follows it.

Options While Running a DOS Session

While running a DOS session, there are several easy adjustments you can make that are either cosmetic or actually affect the performance of the program. You can easily do any of the following:

- Toggle the DOS session between full screen and windowed.
- Turn the toolbar on or off.
- Adjust the font.
- Resize the DOS box.
- Allow the DOS session to work in the background.

Let me briefly discuss each of these options. Refer back to Figure 4.10 for toolbar buttons.

First, if the DOS window is taking up the whole screen (all other elements of the Windows interface have disappeared) and you'd like to have the DOS program running in a window so that you can see other programs, press Alt+Enter to switch it to a window. Once windowed, you can return it to full-screen mode, either by clicking the Full Screen button or pressing Alt+Enter again.

Next, you can turn on the toolbar if you want easy access to most of the nifty features. Then you won't have to use the menus. If you don't see the toolbar shown in Figure 4.10, click the control icon for the DOS window and choose Toolbar. (Choose the same command again, and the toolbar will turn off.)

Full Screen button

Once the toolbar is showing, you can set several useful options. One of these is the font drop-down list. This list includes a list of adjustable fonts you can use in a DOS box, one of the nice features in Windows. Using this drop-down list is the easiest way to change the font.

 NOTE You can also click the A button on the toolbar to open a dialog box from which you can select a font, but that's the rather long way around.

In this list, fonts are listed organized by the size of the character matrix (in pixels) that comprises each displayed character. The larger the matrix, the larger the resulting characters (and consequently the DOS box itself) will be. Setting the size to Auto has the effect of scaling the font automatically if you resize the DOS box from its lower-left corner. When resizing, don't be surprised if the mouse pointer jumps around a bit wildly. The box is not infinitely adjustable as Windows programs are, so, as you're adjusting, the outline of the window jumps to predetermined sizes.

 NOTE The A button on the toolbar lets you choose whether only bit-mapped fonts, True-Type fonts, or both will show in the Fonts listing on the left. By default, both types are available, giving you more size choices.

The Background button determines whether the DOS program will continue processing in the background when you switch to another program. By default, this setting is on. You can tell it's on because the button looks indented. You can turn it off if you want your DOS program to temporarily suspend when it isn't the active window (i.e., when it isn't the window in which you're currently working).

Background button

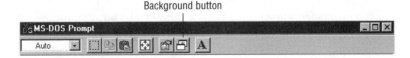

TIP You can have multiple DOS sessions running at the same time in separate windows. This lets you easily switch between a number of DOS programs that can be running simultaneously.

 NOTE You can copy and paste data from and to DOS applications, using the Windows clipboard. See "Sharing Data between Applications" later in this chapter for details.

Additional Property Settings for DOS Programs

Though you can run more than one DOS window simultaneously, as mentioned above, DOS programs were designed to run one at a time, and they are usually memory hogs. They often need as much as 560K of free conventional memory, and some may require some additional expanded or extended memory to perform well. Since DOS programs think they don't have to coexist with other programs simultaneously, they are often written specifically to claim all available system resources for themselves unless told otherwise. That's why you might need to adjust the properties for a DOS program to make it run nicely under Windows. This usually involves faking out the DOS program into believing that the system resources it is receiving constitute all that the PC has to offer, when in fact the PC is apportioning out resources to several programs at once.

In most cases, Windows Me does pretty well at faking out DOS programs without your help by using various default settings and its own memory-management strategies. However, even Windows isn't omniscient, and you may occasionally experience the ungracious locking up of a program or see messages about the "system integrity" having been corrupted.

 TIP In reality, what Windows is doing when running DOS programs is giving each of them a simulated PC to work in called a *VDM* (Virtual DOS Machine).

If a DOS program doesn't run properly under Windows, or if you wish to optimize its performance, you must modify its PIF (Program Information File), declaring certain settings that affect the program within Windows. Here's how it works: The first time you run a DOS program, a PIF is automatically created in the same directory as the DOS program. It has the same name as the program but looks like a shortcut icon. Examining the properties of the icon will reveal it has a `.pif` extension.

To adjust a program's PIF settings, simply open the Properties box for the DOS program and make the relevant setting choices. This can be done by running the DOS program in a window and clicking the Properties button on the toolbar, or, without running the program, by right-clicking its PIF icon and choosing Properties. When you close the Properties box, the new PIF settings are saved. From then on, those settings go into effect whenever you run the program from within Windows.

Consider the following to fine-tune the DOS environment for running a program:

- If the program will run at all under Windows Me without crashing:

  1. Run it as explained earlier in the chapter.

  2. If it's not in a window, press Alt+Enter to run it in windowed mode.

  3. Click the Properties button if the toolbar is showing, or, if it isn't showing, click the Control Box in the upper-left corner of the window and choose Properties.

Properties button

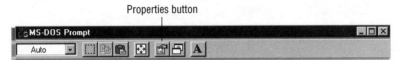

- If the program *won't* run without crashing:

  1. Navigate with My Computer or Explorer to the folder containing the DOS program.

  2. Find the program's icon and click it.

  3. Choose File ➢ Create Shortcut. A new icon will appear in the folder, called Shortcut to *program*.

  4. With the new shortcut highlighted, choose File ➢ Properties.

Now you'll see the DOS program's Properties sheet, from which you can alter quite a healthy collection of settings (see Figure 4.11).

FIGURE 4.11

The Properties box for the program Pcgammon

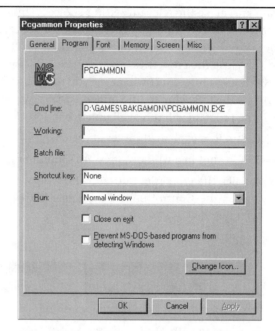

After you have spent some time looking through the tabs and exploring your options, simply select your settings as necessary. When you're happy with them, click OK to save them. The next time you run the program by double-clicking the shortcut or the program's icon, these settings will go into effect.

What settings should you change? Good question. It's a complex procedure to determine what settings will make a particular MS-DOS program run better. Fortunately, the Windows Help system offers a very good MS-DOS Programs Troubleshooter; you can use this to walk step-by-step through the process. To use it, open the Help system (Start ➤ Help) and search for MS-DOS Programs.

Here's a quick rundown of some of the more common fixes:

- If the program can't find some of its data files as it runs, enter the program's folder path in the Working text box on the Program tab.

- If the program is designed so that it won't run if it detects that you're running it within Windows, mark the Prevent MS-DOS Based Programs from Detecting Windows check box on the Program tab.

- Set the font that the program uses on the Font tab.

- Allocate a specific amount and type of memory to the program on the Memory tab.

- Choose between full-screen and windowed operation on the Screen tab.

- Try turning off Fast ROM Emulation on the Screen tab if you are having problems with the program writing text to the screen. Be aware that this slows down the program's performance, however.

- Try turning off Dynamic Memory Allocation on the Screen tab if you are having display problems switching back and forth between Windows and this program.

- Turn off Allow Screen Saver on the Misc tab if problems occur when the screen saver kicks in when the program is running.

Using Desktop Shortcuts

When it comes to running your programs, Windows has a spiffy feature called *short-cuts*. Shortcuts are alias icons (that is, icons that represent other icons) that you can add almost anywhere, such as in folders or on the Desktop, on the Taskbar's Quick Launch toolbar (later for that), or on the Start menu. (As a matter of fact, all the entries on the Start menu are actually shortcuts to the corresponding programs.)

The neat thing about shortcuts is that since they're really only a link or pointer to the real file or application, you can have as many as you want, putting them wherever your heart desires, without duplicating your files and using up lots of hard disk space. So, for example, you can have shortcuts to all your favorite programs right on the Desktop. Then you can run them from there without having to click the Start button, walk through the Program listings, and so forth, as we've been doing.

Many of the icons that are automatically placed on your Desktop when you install Windows are actually shortcuts. The icon for Outlook Express is a good example.

Notice the little arrow in the lower-left corner of the icon. This indicates that the icon is actually a shortcut to the program file for Outlook Express. Double-click it to open the program. This isn't an infallible way to distinguish a shortcut from a "real" file, however, because some shortcuts don't have the arrow, and there are utility programs (such as TweakUI) that will remove the shortcut arrows from shortcut icons.

In Chapter 5, I'll explain how you make, copy, and place shortcuts. I'll also cover how you can dump shortcuts of your favorite programs onto the Start button so they are right there on the first menu when you click Start.

Switching between Applications

Remember, Windows lets you have more than one program open and running at a time. You can also have multiple folders open at any time, and you can leave them open to make getting to their contents easier. Any folders that are open when you shut down the computer will open again when you start up Windows again.

People often think they have to shut down one program before working on another one, but that's really not efficient nor is it true. When you run each new program or open a folder, the Taskbar gets another button on it. As you know from Chapter 3, "Exploring the Interface," simply clicking a button switches you to that program or folder. For the first several programs, the buttons are long enough to read the names of the programs or folder. As you run more programs, the buttons automatically get shorter, so the names are truncated.

You can resize the Taskbar to give it an extra line or two if you want to see the full names. Position the cursor on the upper edge of the Taskbar so that it turns into a double-headed arrow (this takes some careful aiming). Then drag it upward a half inch or an inch and release. Here I've added two additional lines for my current set of buttons:

Obviously, as you increase the size of the Taskbar, you decrease the effective size of your work area. On a standard 640 × 480 VGA screen, this means you'll be cutting into your work area quite a bit. On higher-resolution displays screens, the impact will be less.

Another nice feature is that you can set the Taskbar to disappear until you move the mouse pointer down to the bottom of the screen. This way, you sacrifice nothing in the way of screen real estate.

 TIP If you prefer, you can also position the Taskbar on the right, left, or top of the screen. Just click any part of the Taskbar (other than a button) and drag it to the edge of your choice.

Here's how to set the Taskbar options:

1. Choose Start ➤ Settings ➤ Taskbar and Start Menu.

2. You'll now see the dialog box shown in Figure 4.12. Click *Auto hide* to turn that option on—this is the one that makes the Taskbar disappear until you move the pointer to the edge of the screen where you've placed the Taskbar.

TIP A quick way to get to the Taskbar's Property settings is to right-click an empty area of the Taskbar and choose Properties.

3. Click OK.

   Once you do so, the Taskbar will disappear. Try out the Auto Hide setting: Move the pointer down to the bottom and see how the Taskbar reappears.

FIGURE 4.12
You set the Taskbar options from this box. The most likely choice you'll make will be Auto Hide.

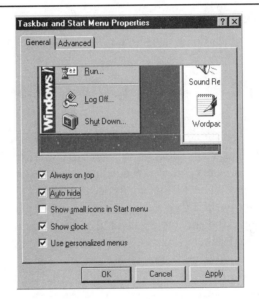

 TIP Even when set to Auto Hide, the Taskbar still uses one or two pixels (a very small area) at the edge of the screen to indicate where it is and to act as a trigger zone to pop up the Taskbar when the pointer touches it.

Switching with Alt+Tab

Don't like the Taskbar? Are you a habituated Windows 3.x user? Okay. As you may know, there's another way to switch between programs and folders—the Alt+Tab trick. Press down the Alt key and hold it down. Now, press the Tab key (you know, that key just above the Caps Lock and to the left of the Q). You'll see a box in the center of your screen showing you an icon of each program or folder that's running, like this:

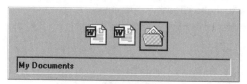

Each press of the Tab key will advance the outline box one notch to the right. The outline box indicates which program you'll be switched to when you release the Alt key. If you want to back up one program (i.e., move the box to the left), you can press Alt+Shift+Tab. Note that the name of the program or folder is displayed at the bottom of the box, which is especially useful when choosing folders, as all folders look the same.

Sharing Data between Applications

One of the greatest features of Windows is the ability to share pieces of information between your programs. You have the ability to mix and match a great variety of document types, such as text, sound, graphics, spreadsheets, databases, and so forth. This lets you construct complex documents previously requiring physical cutting and pasting and possibly the aid of an art department.

Windows offers three internal vehicles for exchanging data between programs: the Windows Clipboard, Object Linking and Embedding (OLE), and Dynamic Data Exchange (DDE). I'll concentrate on using the Windows Clipboard here because it's the concept you will use most.

 NOTE Many of my examples in this chapter refer to Microsoft products. This isn't necessarily my endorsement of Microsoft products over other competing products! Competition in the software marketplace is a healthy force, ensuring the evolution of software technology, and I highly support it. But, because so many of you are bound to be familiar with the Microsoft product line, I use products such as Word, Excel, Graph, and Access in my examples in hopes of better illustrating the points I'm trying to make here.

Using the Windows Clipboard

Though it's not capable of converting data files between various formats, such as between Excel and Lotus 1-2-3 or Word and WordPerfect, the Windows Clipboard is great for many everyday data-exchange tasks. Just about all Windows programs support the use of the ubiquitous cut, copy, and paste commands, and it's the Clipboard that provides this functionality for you.

Clipboard makes it possible to move any kind of material, whether text, data cells, graphics, video, audio clips, and OLE objects between documents—and since Windows 95, between folders, the Desktop, Explorer, and other portions of the interface. The actual form of the source data doesn't matter that much, because together, the Clipboard utility and Windows take care of figuring out what's being copied and where it's being pasted, making adjustments when necessary—or at least providing a few manual options for you to adjust. The Clipboard can also work with non-Windows (DOS) programs, albeit with certain limitations that I'll explain later.

How does the Clipboard work? It's simple. The Clipboard is built into Windows and uses a portion of the system's internal resources (RAM and virtual memory) as a temporary holding tank for material you're working with. For example, suppose you have cut some text from one part of a document in preparation for pasting it into another location. Windows stores the text on the Clipboard and waits for you to paste it into its new home.

The last item you copied or cut is stored in this no-man's-land somewhere in the computer until you cut or copy something else, exit Windows, or intentionally clear the Clipboard. As a result, you can paste the Clipboard's contents any number of times.

You can examine the Clipboard's contents using the Clipboard Viewer utility supplied with Windows. (It isn't installed by default, but you can add it with Add/Remove Programs in the Control Panel.) You can also use the Clipboard Viewer to save the Clipboard's contents to disk for later use or to share specific bits of data for use by others on your network.

To place information in the Windows Clipboard, you simply use each application's Edit menu (or the Edit menu's shortcut keys) for copying, cutting, and pasting (see Figure 4.13).

Here are the steps for cutting, copying, or pasting within a Windows program:

1. First, arrange the windows on screen so you can see the window containing the source information.

2. Select the information you want to copy or cut, such as text, a graphic, a few spreadsheet cells, or whatever. In many programs, simply clicking an object, such as a graphic, will select it. Other programs require you to drag the cursor over objects while pressing the left mouse button.

3. Once the desired area is selected, open the application's Edit menu and choose Copy or Cut, depending on whether you want to copy the material or delete the original with the intention of pasting it into another location.

4. If you want to paste the selection somewhere, first position the cursor at the insertion point in the destination document (which may or may not be in the source document) you're working in. This might mean scrolling up or down the document, switching to another application using the Taskbar, or switching to another document within the *same* application via its Window menu.

5. Open the Edit menu and choose Paste. Whatever material was on the Clipboard will now be dropped into the new location. Normally, this means any preexist-

ing material, such as text, is moved down to make room for the stuff you just pasted.

 TIP There may be some shortcuts for cut, copy, and paste in specific programs, so you should read the manual or help screens supplied with the program. Generally, Ctrl+X, Ctrl+C, and Ctrl+V are shortcuts for cutting, copying, and pasting, respectively.

FIGURE 4.13
Copying and pasting in a Windows program

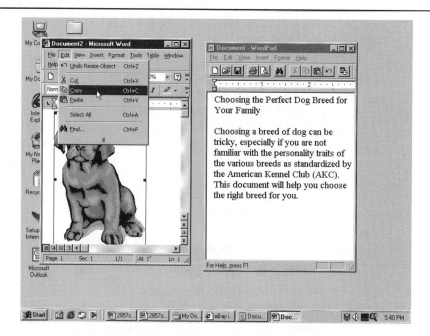

Right-Click Shortcuts for Cut, Copy, and Paste

As mentioned earlier, the cut, copy, and paste scheme is implemented throughout Windows Me, even on the Desktop, in the Explorer, in folder windows, and so forth. This is done using right mouse-button shortcuts. Many applications offer this feature too.

Right-clicking a file in a folder window and choosing Copy puts a pointer to the file on the Clipboard. Right-clicking another location, such as the Desktop, and choosing Paste drops the file there. Try clicking the secondary (normally the right) mouse button on icons or on selected text or graphics in applications to see if there is a shortcut menu. Figure 4.14 shows an example of copying some text from a Word document using this shortcut.

FIGURE 4.14
Shortcuts for cut, copy, and paste are built into much of Windows via the right-click menu. Windows applications are beginning to implement this feature, too, as you see here in Word.

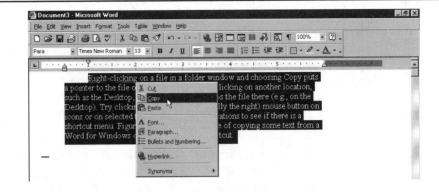

Up and Running

Enhanced Clipboard in Office 2000

Microsoft Office 2000 comes with an enhanced Clipboard that can store up to 12 different clips at once, rather than only one. When you copy or cut something to the Clipboard in one of those programs, and then copy or cut something else before you paste the original item, the Clipboard toolbar appears, showing each clip as a separate icon. From there, you can select the clip you want to paste. For more information, see the Help system in one of the Office 2000 programs.

Copying Text and Graphics from a DOS Window

Copying selected graphics from MS-DOS programs is also possible. This is a pretty nifty trick for lifting material out of your favorite DOS program and dropping it into a Windows document. There's only one caveat: The DOS program has to be running in a window, not on the full screen.

When you cut or copy selected material from the DOS box, it gets dumped into the Clipboard as text or graphics, depending on which mode Windows determines the DOS window was emulating. Windows knows whether the application is running in character mode or graphics mode, and it processes the data on the Clipboard accordingly. If text mode is detected, the material is copied as characters that could be dropped into, say, a word-processing document. If the DOS application has set up a graphics mode in the DOS window (because of the application's video requests), you'll get a bit-mapped graphic in the destination document when you paste.

NOTE As you may know, some fancy DOS programs may look as though they are displaying text when they're really running in graphics mode. For example, WordPerfect for DOS can run in a graphics mode that displays text attributes such as underline, italics, and bold, rather than as boring block letters displayed in colors that indicate these attributes. When you copy text from such a program and then paste it into another document, you'll be surprised to find you've pasted a graphic, not text. This means you can't edit it like text because it's being treated like a bit-mapped graphic. The solution is to switch the DOS application back to Text mode and try again. Refer to your DOS program manual for help.

Because of the DOS box's toolbar, the procedure for copying is simple to learn. You can use the menus or the toolbar almost as if you were using another Windows program. Figure 4.15 illustrates the simple technique. Here are the steps:

1. First, switch to the DOS application and display the material you want to work with.

2. Make sure the application is running in a window, rather than running full screen. If it's not, press Alt+Enter. (Each press of Alt+Enter toggles any DOS window between full and windowed view.)

FIGURE 4.15
Copying text from an MS-DOS box is now a simple procedure. Click the Mark button, click and drag across the desired text, and click the Copy button.

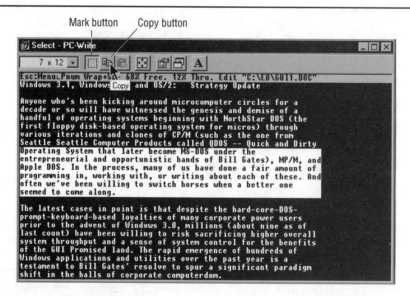

3. If the DOS box's toolbar isn't showing, turn it on by clicking in the upper-left corner of its window (on the MS-DOS icon) and choosing Toolbar.

4. Click the Mark button (the one that looks like a dashed square).

5. Holding the mouse button down, drag the pointer over the desired copy area, dragging from upper left to lower right. As you do so, the color of the selection will change to indicate what you're marking.

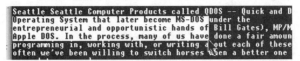

6. Release the mouse button. The selected area will stay highlighted.

7. Click the Copy button. The information is now on the Clipboard.

 NOTE Notice that there isn't a Cut button because you can't cut from a DOS application in this way. Cutting has to be done using the DOS program's own editing keys, and it won't interact with the Windows Clipboard.

 TIP As soon as you click the Mark button, the DOS box's title bar changes to read *Mark*. Once you start marking the selection, the word *Select* precedes the program's name in the title bar, indicating that you're in select mode. Typing any letter on the keyboard terminates the selection process.

That's all there is to copying information from an application that's running in the DOS box. Of course, the normal procedure will apply to pasting what was just copied. You just switch to the destination application (which, incidentally, can be a DOS *or* a Windows program), position the cursor, and choose Edit ➢ Paste to paste in the Clipboard's contents at the cursor position. (For a DOS application as the destination, you'd use the Paste button on the DOS box's toolbar.

Working with the Clipboard Viewer

Once pieces of data are on the Clipboard, you may not want to paste them immediately, or you might want to see what's there. There's a program supplied with Windows that makes this really easy. Clipboard Viewer can be found in the Accessories folder (choose Start ➢ Programs ➢ Accessories ➢ System Tools ➢ Clipboard Viewer). This program lets you do some useful Clipboard-related things, such as the following:

- View the Clipboard's contents.
- Save and retrieve the Clipboard's contents to/from a file.
- Clear the Clipboard's contents.
- Set up pages of the Clipboard, each storing things you plan to use later or want to make available to networked colleagues.

NOTE If you don't see the Clipboard Viewer in your System Tools menu, you might need to install it from Add/Remove Programs in the Control Panel. See Chapter 10, "Customizing the Desktop, Taskbar, and Start Menu," to learn how.

Let's look at each of these simple tasks in order.

Viewing the Clipboard's Contents

Sometimes you'll simply forget what information is on the Clipboard because you won't remember what you cut or copied last. Before you go ahead and paste it into an application (especially if that application doesn't have an Undo command), you might want to check out what's going to get pasted. Another time when viewing is useful is when you're trying to get a particular item into the Clipboard and don't know how successful you've been. Bringing up the Viewer and positioning it off in the corner of the screen can give you instant feedback as you cut and copy.

Here's how to view the Clipboard's contents.

1. Click the Start button and choose Programs ➤ Accessories ➤ System Tools ➤ Clipboard Viewer.

2. The Clipboard Viewer window comes up, displaying the Clipboard's current contents. Figure 4.16 shows typical Clipboard contents—in this case, a portion of an image I just copied from a graphics program.

Notice that the image in Figure 4.16 doesn't look particularly good. It's rather mottled and distorted. Don't worry; the copy on the clipboard is fine. It's just that the Clipboard Viewer has limited display capabilities.

FIGURE 4.16
The Clipboard's contents being displayed

When you first view the Clipboard's contents, the Viewer does its best to display the contents so that they look as much as possible like the original. However, this isn't a fail-safe method, so there may be times when you'll want to try changing the view. To do this, follow these steps:

1. Open the Display menu in the Clipboard Viewer.

2. Check out the available options. They'll vary depending on what you've got stored on the Clipboard. Choose one option and see how it affects the display. The Default setting (called *Auto*) returns the view to the original display format in which the material was first shown. However, none of them will affect the Clipboard contents—only its display.

 NOTE When you actually go to paste into another Windows application, the destination program tries to determine the best format for accepting whatever is currently on the Clipboard. If the Edit menu on the destination application is grayed out, you can safely assume that the contents are not acceptable. (Changing the Clipboard's view format as described above won't rectify the situation, either. In fact, it doesn't have any effect on how things actually get pasted.)

Storing the Clipboard's Contents in a File

When you place new material onto the Clipboard, reboot, or shut down the computer, the Clipboard contents are lost. Also, because the Clipboard itself is not *network aware* (meaning it can't interact with other workstations on the network), you can't share the Clipboard's contents with other networked users. However, there is one trick left. You *can* save the Clipboard's contents to a disk file. Clipboard files have the extension .clp. Once the Clipboard's contents are stored in a disk file, they function just like any other disk file—you can later reload the file from disk. If you do a lot of work with clip art and bits and pieces of sound, video, text, and the like, this technique can come in handy. Also, if you give network users access to your .clp file directory, they can, in effect, use your Clipboard.

 TIP The Clipboard CLP files use a proprietary file format that is readable by virtually no other popular programs. So, to use a CLP file, you have to open it in Clipboard and *then* paste it where you want it to appear. This might seem like a hassle, and it is.

In any case, here's how to save a Clipboard file:

1. First make sure you have run the Clipboard Viewer, as explained above.

2. Choose File ➢ Save As. A standard Save As dialog box appears.

3. Enter a name. As usual, you can change the folder, name, and extension. Leave the extension as CLP because Clipboard uses this as a default when you later want to reload the file.

4. Click on OK. The file is saved and can be loaded again as described below.

As I mentioned, once the file is on disk, you can reload it. Use these steps.

1. Run Clipboard Viewer.

2. Choose File ➤ Open. The Open dialog box will appear.

3. Select the file you want to pull onto the Clipboard. (Only legitimate CLP files can be opened.)

4. If there's something already on the Clipboard, you'll be asked if you want to erase it. Click OK.

5. Change the display format via the View menu if you want to (assuming there are options available on the menu).

6. Paste the contents into the desired destination.

WARNING   When you reload a CLP file, anything currently on the Clipboard will be lost.

CHAPTER **5**

Organizing Files, Programs, and Disks

FEATURING:

n this chapter, you'll learn how to organize your own work within Windows Me. I'll tell you how to use the Desktop, the Taskbar, the file system, and Windows Explorer in order to arrange your programs and documents so that you can get to them easily. With the techniques I'll show you in this chapter, you'll be ready to set up new folders and move your work files into them—just like setting up a new filing cabinet in your office. You'll also learn how to put your programs and projects on the Start menu as well as on the Desktop so that they are within easy reach.

Using Windows Explorer

To run Windows Explorer, click the Start button and choose Programs ➢ Accessories ➢ Windows Explorer. Windows Explorer will load.

> **TIP** If you use Windows Explorer often, add a shortcut icon on the Quick Launch toolbar or at the top of the Start menu. See "Putting Programs on the Start Menu" in Chapter 10, "Customizing the Desktop, Taskbar, and Start Menu," for details.

Maximize the window and it will look something like Figure 5.1. Of course, the folders in your window will be different from those shown in this figure.

FIGURE 5.1
The basic Explorer screen, showing the folder tree on the left and the contents on the right

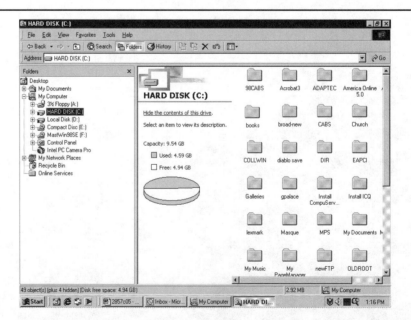

PART

I

Up and Running

Before we get too deep into Windows Explorer, let's clear up one potential source of confusion. My Computer is another way of working with the files and folders on your system. When you double-click My Computer on the Desktop, a list of drives appears; you can double-click a drive icon to display that drive's contents, then double-click a folder to display its contents, and so on. All of this happens in a single pane, with the new content replacing the previous content each time you change levels in the organizational structure (see Figure 5.2).

FIGURE 5.2
The My Computer window shows your files and folders in a single pane.

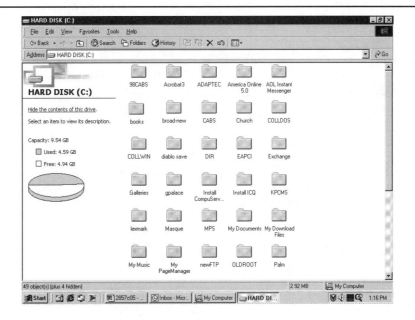

 TIP You can make My Computer open up separate windows for each file/folder display by changing the Folder Options setting. Choose Tools ➤ Folder Options, then choose the Open Each Folder in Its Own Window button, and then click OK.

In earlier versions of Windows, My Computer and Windows Explorer were separate. In Windows Me, however, they are basically the same window, except for the presence or absence of the folder tree pane. Click the Folders button on the toolbar to toggle the folder tree pane off or on from either window.

Because of this change, you can now access Windows Explorer by double-clicking My Computer on the Desktop and then clicking the Folders button. And there is still another way: Right-click the My Computer icon and choose Explore from the shortcut menu.

Displaying the Contents of Your Computer

When you run Windows Explorer, all the objects appear in the folder tree on the left. Some of those objects may have a plus sign (+) next to them, which means the object is *collapsed*—in other words, it contains sub-items that aren't currently showing. For example, my hard disk drive, shown in Figure 5.1, is collapsed. So are My Network Places (which you won't see unless you have network options installed) and the floppy drive (drive A). Here's how to check out the contents of such an item:

1. Click the item itself, not on the + character. For example, click your C drive's icon. Now its contents appear in the right pane as a bunch of folders.

 TIP You can change the view in the right pane just as you do in any folder. Click the Toolbar icons over to the left or use the View menu to display large icons, small icons, list view, or details.

2. Another approach is to click directly on the plus sign (+). This opens up the sub-levels in the left pane, showing you the relationship of the folders in a tree arrangement. The tree is a graphical representation of your disk layout. Here's a multiple-level folder structure, all completely open.

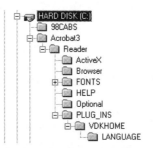

3. Notice that the plus sign is replaced with a minus (–), indicating that the object's display has been expanded. Click it again, and it collapses.

4. To collapse everything, click the minus sign next to My Computer.

5. Click the Desktop icon up at the top of the tree. Notice that all the objects on your Desktop appear in the right pane.

If you have more folders than can be seen at one time, the window will have a scroll bar that you can use to scroll the tree up and down. Notice that there are two scroll bars—one for the left pane and one for the right. These scroll independently of one another, a feature that can be very useful when you are copying items from one folder or drive to another. Also notice the toolbar; it's just like the ones you saw in Chapter 3, "Exploring the Interface."

TIP You may or may not see a status line at the bottom of the window, displaying information about the item(s) you have selected in the right or left panes. You can turn this on or off with the View ➢ Status Bar command. Turning it off frees up a little more screen space for displaying folders and files, though having it on gives you some useful information, such as how much free disk space you have. Choose View ➢ Toolbars to choose which toolbars will display. Turning off button text and/or the Address bar are options I sometimes use to see more files at one time.

Selecting the Correct Drive and Choosing a Folder

To select the drive whose contents you want to work with, follow these steps:

1. Scroll the left pane up or down until you see the drive you want. If the drive you want isn't showing, you may have to expand the My Computer icon by clicking its plus sign. At least one hard drive (and probably a floppy) should be visible.

2. Click the name or icon of the drive whose contents you want to work with. The right pane then displays its contents. On a hard disk, you'll typically see a bunch of folders there followed by a list of any files that are stored in the top-level folder of the drive. If you scroll the list a bit, you'll reach the files. Remember, at this point you are in the root, or top-level, folder of the selected drive. You have to find a specific folder before you get to see what's in it.

3. If the drive has folders on it, you now have a choice. You can double-click one of the folders in the right pane, or you can expand the drive's listing in the left pane by clicking its plus sign.

   Which option you choose doesn't really matter. You can get to the same place either way. The advantage of expanding the drive in the left pane is simply that it gives you a more graphical view of how your disk is organized, and it also lets you drag items from the right pane into destination folders. Go ahead and click the drive's plus sign if it's showing, this will display its folders in the folder tree.

4. Now suppose you want to see which fonts you have in your Fonts folder. The Fonts folder is a subfolder of the Windows folder. If necessary, scroll the left pane down until you see the Windows folder.

5. Because the Windows directory has subfolders, click the plus sign. Its subfolders now show.

6. Fonts is one of the subfolders under the Windows directory. Click the Fonts folder to see the font files displayed in the right pane (see Figure 5.3).

FIGURE 5.3
The Font folder's
contents displayed

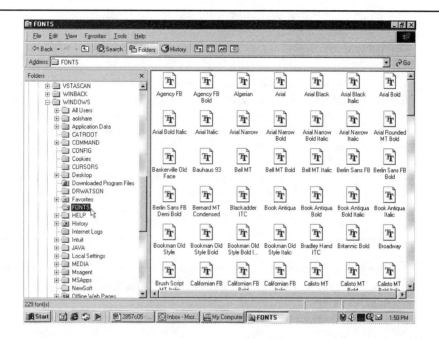

Up and Running

Try clicking the Desktop folder (in the Windows folder) to see the list of items on your Desktop, or click the Help folder to see all the Windows Help files. (There are quite a few!)

Here are a few tips when selecting folders:

- Only one folder can be selected at a time in the left pane. If you want to select multiple folders, click the parent folder (such as the drive icon), and select the folders in the right pane.

- When a folder is selected in the left pane, its icon changes from a closed folder to an open one.

- You can move to a folder by clicking it, typing the first letter in its name on the keyboard, or moving the highlight to it with the arrow keys. When selected, the folder icon and name become highlighted.

- You can jump quickly to a folder name by typing its first letter on the keyboard. If there is more than one folder with the same first letter, you can press the key again to advance to the next choice that starts with that letter.

- Click the plus sign to expand a folder tree one level down. Click the minus (–) sign to collapse a folder's tree up a level.

- The fastest way to collapse all the branches of a given drive is to click that drive's minus sign.

Notice that every time you select a folder, its contents are displayed in the folder-contents side of the window. The contents will include subordinate folders (listed first and looking like little folders just as they do in the left window), followed by the list of files.

 WARNING When selecting folders and files, be careful not to drag them accidentally! The icons are small, and this is easy to do, especially in the left pane. Dragging one folder on top of another folder will dump the first one into the second one (complete with all of its sub-folders, if it has any), thus rearranging the directory tree. This could make programs and files hard to find; worse, some programs might not work. In short, it will generally be an annoyance. If you think you have accidentally dragged a folder into the wrong place, open the Edit menu immediately. The first choice will probably read *Undo Move*. Choose it and the folders or files you dragged will be returned to their previous locations. You can also use the keyboard short-cut for Undo: Ctrl+Z.

 TIP You can easily move between folders you have visited by clicking the toolbar's Back and Forward buttons.

Refreshing the File Listing

Sometimes other programs will affect the contents of an open drive window. For example, you might switch away from Explorer into an application window such as Word, Excel, or whatever, and create a new document in a folder that's displaying back in the Explorer. Or you might edit a file that's also displayed in the folder's window, changing its size (in bytes). Normally, Windows takes care of updating the informa-tion in the display; however, there are times when this doesn't happen reliably. Win-dows may have trouble detecting that a folder's contents have changed, particularly when you are connected to a network. This will also be an issue if you change floppy disks and want to see the folder on the new disk. If you suspect that a folder may have been changed in some way that isn't reflected in the folder pane, just choose View ➤ Refresh or press F5.

Selecting Files

Before you can work with the files in a folder, you have to select one or more of them. As with other objects in Windows, you select files by highlighting them. Here are vari-ous methods of selecting (and deselecting) files:

To select one file Click the file once. Notice that the status bar (if shown) indi-cates that one object is selected.

To select multiple nonconsecutive files Click the first file to select it and hold down the Ctrl key as you click additional files.

To select a group of consecutive files (This is easiest in the List or Details view because objects are in a list.) Click the first file in the series, then hold the Shift key as you click the last item you want to select. As an alternative, you can draw a box around the files you want to select.

To select several groups of consecutive files Select the first group as described above. To select the second group, hold down the Ctrl key and click the first file in the second group. Hold down Shift and Ctrl keys simultaneously and click the last file in the second group. Repeat for each additional group.

To select all the files in a folder Choose File ➢ Select All. You can then deselect specific files by Ctrl-clicking.

To invert the selection of files Select the files you want to omit from the selection. Then choose Edit ➢ Invert Selection.

Once highlighted, a file or group of files can be operated on by using the mouse or by using the commands on the File and Edit menus. For example, you can drag a group of files into another folder, delete them, copy and paste them somewhere else, or print them (assuming they are documents). Here's a quick recap of some of the commands and clicks you can use here:

- *Run* a program or *open* a document by double-clicking it. Alternatively, highlight a file and press Enter.

- *Print* a document by choosing File ➢ Print. Alternatively, right-click it and choose Print.

- *Send* selected file(s) to a floppy drive or your Desktop (or to other programs that you can add to the Send To menu) with File ➢ Send To or by right-clicking and choosing Send To.

- Create a *new* document or shortcut or certain types of registered documents with File ➢ New or by right-clicking and choosing New. You can also create a new shortcut for the selected item(s) with File ➢ Create Shortcut. Then you can copy or move the resulting shortcut to wherever you like (e.g., the Desktop, Start button, or Quick Launch bar).

- *Paste a shortcut* for the selected item(s) by first copying the item(s). Then move to the destination and choose Edit ➢ Paste Shortcut. Alternatively, right-click-drag and choose Shortcut from the pop-up menu when you release the mouse button. Yet another way to create a shortcut is to drag the icon with the Alt key held down and drop it where you want the shortcut.

- *Delete* the selected item(s) with File ➢ Delete, the Del key, or by right-clicking and choosing Delete. This sends items to the Recycle Bin. Clicking the X button in the Toolbar has the same effect.

- *Rename* items with File ➤ Rename, by right-clicking and choosing Rename, or by clicking again on the selected file or pressing F2. Edit the name, and then press Enter to finalize the new name.

- Check a file's Properties by clicking the Properties button on the toolbar. Or, as a quicker way, select the file and press Alt+Enter. You could also choose File ➤ Properties or right-click the file and choose Properties from the menu that appears. (Properties are covered in Chapter 3.)

- *Copy* a file by clicking the toolbar's Copy To button. A dialog box appears in which you select the location you want to copy to. (This is a new feature in Windows Me.) You can also copy the file to the clipboard with Edit ➤ Copy or Ctrl+C and then paste it in a new location with Edit ➤ Paste or Ctrl+V. Yet another way of copying is to drag the file to a new location with the Ctrl key held down.

- *Move* selected item(s) from one location to another with the Move To button on the toolbar. Or, you can choose Edit ➤ Cut followed by Edit ➤ Paste, or drag-and-drop with the Shift key held down.

- *Undo* your last action with the Edit ➤ Undo command.

 TIP In Explorer and in My Computer folders, pressing Backspace always moves you up a level in the folder hierarchy. This is an easy way to move back to the parent directory of the current folder. After several presses, you'll eventually end up at the My Computer level, the top level on any computer. At that point, Backspace won't have any effect.

When moving files around, keep these points in mind: The new destination can be a folder window that you opened from My Computer, a folder in the left pane of Explorer, or a folder in the right pane. Many programs that support drag-and-drop will let you drag from Explorer into them, too. To open a Word file in an existing Word window, for example, drag the file onto the title bar of the Word window. You can even drag a document onto a printer's window, icon, or shortcut. The general rule is this: If you want to move it, try selecting it and dragging it to the new location. If the action isn't allowed, Windows will inform you and no damage will have been done. If you're trying to move the item and get a shortcut instead, right-drag the item and choose Move from the resulting menu.

Organizing Files and Folders

Now I'll show you a bit more about how you work with folders.

Making New Folders

As you may recall from the last chapter, you can create new documents simply by right-clicking the Desktop, choosing New, then choosing the type of file you want and naming it. Then you double-click it to start entering information into the document. Or, as you probably know, you can create documents from within your programs and save them on disk using commands in the programs.

In either case, you're likely to end up with a lot of documents scattered around your hard disk, or worse yet, a lot of documents lumped together in the same folder with no sense of organization. In interviewing users and teaching people about Windows over the years, I've found that most people haven't the foggiest idea where their work files are. They know they're on the hard disk, but that's about it.

 TECH TIP To some extent, Windows will exacerbate this problem because every document or folder that's on the Desktop is actually stored in the SystemRoot\Desktop folder on the disk. Typically, this will be the C:\Windows\Desktop folder. Even though each folder the user has on the Desktop will be a subfolder of the Desktop folder, it still means that wiping out the C:\Windows\Desktop folder or doing a clean install of Windows by wiping out everything in the \Windows folder and below would wipe out anything on the Desktop. Normally, this won't be a problem for most people because this kind of willy-nilly removal of whole folders or folder trees is something only power users are likely to do. If you are the kind of computer user who is going to be poking around on the hard disk, handle your Windows\Desktop folder with due respect.

Saving all your files in one directory without sorting them into folders makes creating backups and clearing off defunct projects that much more confusing. It's difficult enough to remember which files are involved in a given project without having to sort them out from all of Word's program and support files, not to mention all the other writing projects stored in that directory.

There's no excuse for bad organizing. And there are plenty of reasons to organize your files: You'll know where things are, you'll be more likely to make backups, and you'll be less likely to accidentally erase your doctoral dissertation because it was in the WordPerfect directory that you deleted so you could install a new word-processing program.

Probably the most intuitive way for most people to organize their work is to do it right on the Desktop. You can create as many folders as you like right there, name them what you like, and voila, you've done your homework.

If you want to get really tidy, you can pull all your subfolders into a single folder called something like My Work. To show you how to create folders and then move them around, I'm going to consolidate mine. First I'll create a new folder.

1. Right-click the Desktop. Choose New from the resulting menu, then Folder.

2. A new folder appears, called New Folder. Its name is highlighted and ready for editing. Whatever you type will replace the current name. I'll enter the name **My Work.**

3. Now I'll open the folder by double-clicking it.

So much for creating a new folder on the Desktop.

Incidentally, you're not limited to creating new folders only on the Desktop. You can create new folders within other folders (such as My Documents) using the same technique. That is, open the destination folder's window. Then right-click an empty area inside the folder's window and choose New ➤ Folder.

Moving and Copying Items between Folders

Now that I've got a new folder on the Desktop, I can start putting stuff into it. Let's say I want to pull several of my existing Desktop folders into it to reduce clutter. It's as simple as dragging and dropping.

1. Open the destination folder. (Actually you don't even have to open the destination folder, but what you're about to do is more graphically understandable if you do.)

2. Size and position the destination folder's window so you will be able to see the folder(s) you put in it.

3. Drag folders from the Desktop into the destination folder's window.

Now all I have to do is close the My Work folder, and there's that much less clutter on my Desktop.

NOTE You can drag-and-drop most objects in Windows using this same approach. Every effort has gone into designing a uniform approach for manipulating objects on the screen. In general, if you want something placed somewhere else, you can drag it from the source to the destination.

WARNING When dragging and dropping, aim carefully before you release the mouse button. If you drop an object too close to another object, it can be placed *inside* that object. For example, when moving folders around, or even when repositioning them on the Desktop, watch that a neighboring folder doesn't become highlighted. If something other than the object you're moving becomes highlighted, that means it has become the target for the object. If you release at that time, your object will go inside the target. If you accidentally do this, just open the target and drag the object out again, or, if the incorrect destination was a folder, open any folder and choose Edit ➤ Undo Move or right-click the Desktop and choose Undo Move from the pop-up menu. Also, if you press Esc before you drop an object, the process of dragging is canceled.

Moving versus Copying

When you drag an item from one location to another, Windows does its best to figure out if you intend to copy it or move it. As you might surmise, *copying* means making a replica of the object. *Moving* means relocating the original.

In the procedure above, Windows assumed I wanted to move the folders from one location to another. This makes sense because it's not likely you'll want to make a copy of an entire folder. But you could.

The general rule about moving versus copying is simple. When you *move* something by dragging, the mouse pointer keeps the shape of the moved object.

Design Jobs

But when you *copy*, the cursor takes on a + sign.

Design Jobs

To make sure you are copying, no matter what the destination, hold down the Ctrl key as you drag. Or, to make sure you are moving regardless of the destination, hold down Shift.

But Isn't There an Easier Way?

Here's a little technical tip you'll need to know regarding dragging. The easiest way to fully control what's going to happen when you drag an item around is to right-click-drag. Place the pointer on the object you want to move, copy, or make a shortcut for, then press the right mouse button (or left button if you're left-handed and have reversed the buttons) and drag the item to the destination. When you drop the object, you'll be asked what you want to do with it, like this:

Being able to create a shortcut this way is pretty nifty. Often, rather than dragging a document file (and certainly a program) out of its home folder just to put it on the Desktop for convenience, you'll want to make a shortcut out of it. There are important considerations when using shortcuts, however, so make sure you understand what they do. See "Using Desktop Shortcuts" in Chapter 4, "Getting Down to Business: Running Your Applications," for details.

Organizing Document Files

Once you've thought out how to name and organize your folders, naturally, you'll want to start stashing your documents in their rightful folders.

As you might expect, moving and copying documents works just like moving and copying folders—you just drag and drop. When you want to copy files, you press the Ctrl key while dragging. If you want to create a shortcut, drag with Alt held down, or right-click-drag and choose Shortcut from the resulting menu. Here's an example you might want to try.

1. Clear off the Desktop by clicking the Show Desktop icon in the Quick Launch toolbar.

2. Create a new folder on the Desktop by right-clicking the Desktop and choosing New ➢ Folder. Name it **My Test Folder**.

3. Now create a couple of new documents by right-clicking the Desktop, choosing New, and then choosing a document type. Name the documents whatever you like.

Now let's say you want to put these three files into the new folder. You could just drag them in one by one. But there's a faster approach: Selecting multiple objects at once. This can be useful when you want to move, copy, delete, or make shortcuts out of them in one fell swoop.

1. First, we're going to *snap a line* around the items we want to drag. Move the pointer to an empty area on the Desktop at the upper-left corner of the three documents and press the left mouse button. Now drag the mouse down and to the right. This draws a box on the screen, outlining the items you are selecting. You know which items you've selected because they become highlighted.

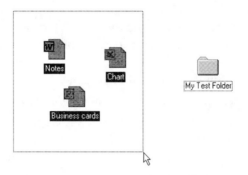

2. Once the documents are selected, you can perform a number of tasks on them. For example, you could right-click one and choose Open, which would open all three documents in their respective programs. In this case, though, we want to move them. So while they are all selected, just drag one of them. The whole group will move.

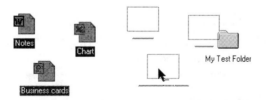

3. Using this method, drag the items over the destination folder and release when the folder becomes highlighted.

 TIP Not all the outlines of the items you're moving need to fit into the destination folder before you release the mouse button. If just a single document's outline falls within the boundary of the target, all the selected items will move to the target folder.

Deleting Items

Of course, there will be times when you'll want to delete items, like that old report from last year. Deleting files regularly is very important if you don't want to become like everyone else—strapped for disk space. The same techniques will apply to deleting other objects as well, such as printers and fax machines you have installed, because all objects in Windows Me are treated much the same way, regardless of their type or utility.

Deleting a File

So how do you delete a file? Let me count the ways. Because Windows Me has a Recycle Bin, using it is one of the easiest ways to get rid of files, assuming you can arrange things on your screen to find the Recycle Bin. But there are other ways that are even easier though less graphically pleasing than dragging an item over the Recycle Bin and letting go.

Use the following steps to delete a file:

1. Select the file in its folder, on the Desktop, in the Search box, or wherever.

2. Drag the item on top of the Recycle Bin, press the Del key on your keyboard, or right-click the item and choose Delete from the resulting menu. Unless you drag to the Recycle Bin, you'll be asked to confirm the deletion.

3. Choose appropriately. If you choose Yes, the item goes into the Recycle Bin.

If you want the file to be immediately deleted, rather than going to the Recycle Bin, hold down the Shift key at step 2. This is useful, for example, if you're deleting a lot of really large files in order to clear off space on your hard disk. Until files are flushed from the Recycle Bin, they still take up space on the drive. Bypassing the Recycle Bin frees up the space immediately.

 TIP If you throw something away in the Recycle Bin, you can still get it back, at least until you decide to empty the trash.

To Delete a Folder

Deleting a folder works much the same way as deleting a file. The only difference is that deleting a folder deletes all of its contents. When you drag a file over to the Recycle Bin, or delete it with one of the other techniques, you'll see a confirmation message warning you that all the contents—any shortcuts, files, and folders (including files in those folders) will be deleted. Take care when deleting folders because they may contain many objects.

WARNING Before deleting a folder, you may want to look carefully at its contents. Open the folder and choose View ➤ Details to examine what's in it, to check on the dates on which the files were created, and so forth. Check the contents of any folders within the folder by opening them; you might be surprised by what you find.

Putting Items on the Desktop

The Desktop is a convenient place to store items you're working on regularly. Each time you boot up, the same files and folders you left there are waiting in easy reach. So how do you put things on the Desktop? You have probably figured out already that you simply drag them there from any convenient source such as a folder or the Search box.

 TIP You can also drag files and folders to the Desktop from Windows Explorer. See "Using Windows Explorer" earlier in this chapter for more details.

However, there are a few details to consider when using the Desktop that aren't immediately obvious. First, some objects can't actually be *moved* to the Desktop—only their shortcuts can. For example, if you open the Control Panel (Start ➤ Settings ➤ Control Panel) and try pulling one of the icons (called Control Panel *applets*) onto the Desktop, you'll see this dialog box.

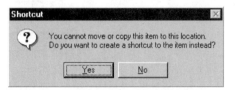

In the case of the Control Panel, setting up a shortcut is your only choice because Windows won't let you move it. As you drag an icon from the Control Panel onto the Desktop or into a folder, the icon turns into a shortcut icon (it has a little arrow in it). But in some other cases, you'll have the choice of moving, copying, or creating a shortcut. How do you choose? Here's a little primer about shortcuts.

Because a shortcut will work just as well as the real thing (the program or document file itself), in general shortcuts are a good idea. As I've said before, you can have as many shortcuts scattered about for a given item as you want. For example, suppose you like to use a particular set of programs. You can have shortcuts for them on the Start button menu, on the Quick Launch toolbar, on the Desktop, and in some folder such as, say, My Favorite Programs. You still have only one copy of the program, so you haven't used up a lot of disk space, but the programs are easily available from multiple locations.

TIP Shortcuts do consume *some* disk space. Each shortcut file has the .1nk (for Link) extension and contains information about where the program, folder, or document it represents is stored. Files with the .1nk extension will typically use up the smallest amount of space that the disk operating system (DOS) will allow. Most of these files consume 1K, though you'll find some to be 2K.

The same holds true for other objects, such as folders or documents that you use a lot. You can have shortcuts to folders and shortcuts to documents. For example, try dragging a folder (the folder must be displayed as an icon) onto the Start button, and you'll see that a shortcut to the folder is created. A good way to create a shortcut to a document is, as I mentioned earlier, to right-drag it somewhere and choose Create Shortcut(s) from the resulting menu.

I have to warn you of a few things when using shortcuts, however. Remember, shortcuts are *not* the real McCoy. They are *aliases* or pointers to an object only! Therefore, copying a document's shortcut to a floppy disk doesn't copy the document itself. A colleague will be disappointed if you copy only the shortcut of a document to a floppy and then give it to them because there will be nothing in it. When you are in doubt about what is getting copied, look at the icon that results from the procedure. If it has a little arrow in it, it's a shortcut.

Shortcut to
Bart Simpson
portrait

If no arrow, then it's (usually) the actual file.

Bart Simpson
portrait

NOTE I say "usually" above because the arrow is not a 100-percent reliable indicator of a shortcut. Some shortcuts don't have them (such as the shortcut to Internet Explorer on your Desktop), and the arrows can be turned off using a program like TweakUI.

And consider this: When you move the real McCoy around—whether a program, folder, or document—it may disable some shortcuts that point to it. For example, assume you've set up a bunch of shortcuts that expect your Annual Budget to be located in folder X. Then you move the budget document to folder Y. What happens? Nothing, until you try clicking those shortcuts. Then you'll get an error message. Windows will try to find the missing object to which the shortcut is pointing.

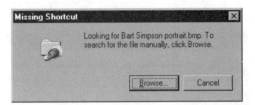

If the object is found, then the shortcut will be repaired and will work next time. If it's not found, Windows does its best to find something *like it*, but usually suggests something pretty bogus. You can click the Browse button and use the resulting Browser box to poke around and find the file, fixing the link. If neither you nor Windows finds the target, the shortcut remains useless, and will do the same rigmarole next time you try it.

 WARNING Programs that are *installed* into Windows using setup programs don't like to be moved around. Almost any program that you actually install with an Install or Setup program will register itself in Windows Me's *Registry*, informing Windows of the folder in which it is located, what kinds of files it uses, and other details. Moving the program around after that (i.e., actually moving it rather than moving the shortcuts that point to it) will mess up something somewhere, unless the program actually comes with a utility program for relocating it. There are also some third-party utility programs that will enable you to move programs around without having to reinstall them.

Saving Files on the Desktop from a Program

One of the features I like best about Windows is the ability to use the Desktop as a sort of temporary holding tank. Here's one example. Suppose you want to copy some files from the floppy disk. It's as easy as opening the floppy disk window from My Computer, then dragging the desired file onto the Desktop. Voila, it's on the hard disk!

(Technically, it's in a Desktop subdirectory of your Windows Me directory, but for all intents and purposes it's simply on "the Desktop.")

You can use the same kind of approach to move or copy items from one folder to another. Rather than having to open both folders and adjust your screen so you can see them both, you can just open the source folder and drag the items onto the Desktop temporarily. When you find or create the destination folder, you can later copy the items there.

But what about using the Desktop from your favorite programs? Although the Desktop is actually a subdirectory of your Windows directory, it's fairly easy to save a file to the Desktop. The newest programs such as those in Office 2000 use Save As and Open dialog boxes with a Desktop button that really makes this easy (Figure 5.4).

FIGURE 5.4
Saving a file to the Desktop is easy in Office 2000 programs. Just click the Desktop button.

Some Windows programs have a file box that doesn't have the button but at least lets you open a list and choose Desktop, as in Figure 5.5.

FIGURE 5.5
Some Windows File dialog boxes require you to open the drop-down list here, scroll up, and choose Desktop.

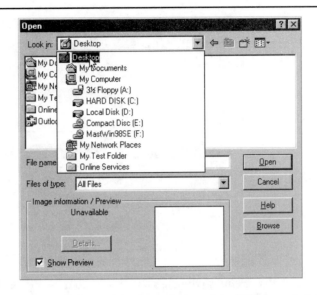

File boxes for 16-bit programs (like those designed for Windows 3.*x*) don't have a direct way to get to the Desktop. Sorry. It's because the Desktop didn't exist in older versions of Windows. Anyway, as a result, saving a file to (or opening one from) the Desktop from a 16-bit program takes a little more doing. Still, you can do it. The following steps show you how:

1. Open the Save, Save As, or Open dialog box from the File menu as usual.

2. In the dialog box, select the drive that contains Windows. This is probably your C drive.

3. Switch to the Windows folder. Then look for the Desktop folder. Figure 5.6 shows an example.

FIGURE 5.6
Opening a file from
Collage Complete,
a 16-bit program

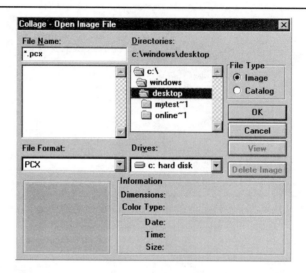

4. Enter or choose the file's name or open one of the subfolders on the Desktop.

NOTE When your computer is set up for multiple users, there may be multiple Desktop directories, one for each user. They're located in subdirectories under Windows\Profiles. There will be one for each user who has an account. For example, for Joe, there will be a directory named Windows\Profiles\Joe\Desktop. These directories are *not* normally hidden and can be accessed from any program without modification.

In a 16-bit program, subfolders that have long names will show up in the 16-bit file boxes with shortened names. For example, if you look again at Figure 5.6, you will notice that the folders on the Desktop that end with the ~ (tilde) character. For older programs, Windows removes any spaces that occur in the filename, shortens any names that are longer than eight characters (it shortens them to six characters), and for characters 7 and 8 Windows inserts a ~ and a number. The number is helpful, because if the first six characters of two filenames are the same (for example, "Joe's resume" and "Joe's resume revised"), the number is incremented for each file. So those files would appear as joe'sr~1 and joe'sr~2. A later file named "Joe's rock collection" would show up as joe'sr~3.

Copying Files and Folders to and from Removable Media

Whether you're sending a file to a colleague around the world, "sneaker-netting" some work down the hall, or simply making a backup of some important files, copying to and from removable disks such as floppies or Zip disks is one of those recurring computer-housekeeping chores.

NOTE As you might expect, there are multiple ways to copy files to and from removable disks. I'll show you the most common methods in the following sections. You can also copy files at the MS-DOS prompt, which can come in handy if you ever need to work from your emergency boot disk because of a system malfunction. Refer to a book on DOS if you need help copying files by typing in copy commands at the DOS command prompt. Or open a MS-DOS window and type **copy /?** to read some help information about the Copy command.

Copying to and from a Removable Disk with My Computer

Earlier in the chapter, I explained how to copy and move files between folders. It works the same way from disk to disk.

So far we've mostly focused on Windows Explorer in this chapter, so let's try the disk-to-disk copying with My Computer instead. Remember that My Computer is exactly the same as Windows Explorer except it doesn't have the folder tree at the left.

Your computer's floppy disk drives simply appear as icons in the My Computer window. Some disk drives—such as an Iomega Zip drive—have special icons on them. Open a disk drive icon and it brings up the contents of the disk, displayed in the same format as a typical folder on your hard disk.

To display the contents of a floppy disk using My Computer:

1. Double-click My Computer on the Desktop.

2. Insert a floppy disk into your disk drive, and then double-click that drive's icon in the My Computer window. A list of the current files on the floppy disk appears.

TIP If you want the floppy disk's contents to open in its own window, hold down Shift as you double-click the floppy drive icon.

Once the floppy drive's window opens, you can easily work with it just as you do with other folders. Drag items from the window to other folders you might have opened on the Desktop, or vice versa.

TIP When you replace one disk with another, the computer doesn't know about it automatically, as it does on the Mac. After you change the disk, the contents of an open floppy disk window will still be the same, even though the disk holds a completely different set of files. To update the contents of the floppy disk's window, press the F5 key. (This same technique is needed with Explorer, incidentally, whenever you change a floppy or other removable disk.)

If you see a message like this one while trying to move files, then the disk is probably write-protected:

On diskettes, there's a little tab on the back of the disk that must be in the closed position for the disk to be written onto (new files put on it). Figure 5.7 shows the tab. If this tab is in open position (so you can see through the hole), the disk is write-protected. In some programs, such as Word, that create temporary or backup files while you are editing, you cannot even read a file from a write-protected floppy.

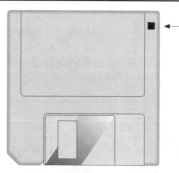

FIGURE 5.7
Location of write-protect slider on 3½" floppies

Write-protect notch. Open the notch (so you can see through the hole) to prevent accidental erasure of the diskette. Or make sure it's closed if you want to store something on the disk.

If you see a message saying that the disk isn't formatted, then it is either brand-new or was formatted for use in another kind of computer or device, such as a Mac.

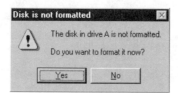

Check to make sure it is not a Macintosh disk that contains anything you want to keep, and then format it by clicking Yes in the message box. You can also format a floppy from one of the following:

- Explorer or My Computer by right-clicking the floppy drive's icon and choosing Format
- Any floppy-disk shortcut icon by right-clicking it and choosing Format
- The DOS prompt's Format command

I'll cover formatting later in this chapter, in the section "Formatting Disks."

NOTE   To see how much room is left on any disk drive, including a floppy, select the drive in My Computer and check out the information that appears to the left of the file listing. You can also right-click the drive in My Computer and choose Properties. You'll see a display of the disk's free and used space. Another approach is to open My Computer and set the view to Details. All drives' statistics will be reported.

Copying Files to a Disk with Send To

Realizing that people wanted an easy way to copy a file or folder to a floppy disk, Microsoft has provided a cute little shortcut to the interface that copies to a floppy from almost anywhere.

1. Just right-click any file or folder icon.
2. Then choose the Send To option.

TIP   The Send To option is very handy. You can customize the Send To list for other purposes, such as sending a file to a viewer program, to the Desktop, a file compression program, a network destination, and so on. Just add the destination shortcuts to the \Windows\SendTo directory, and they'll show up in the Send To list.

Copying Files to a Disk's Shortcut

Because a shortcut works just fine as a drag-and-drop destination, one convenient setup for copying items to a floppy is this:

1. Place a shortcut of the floppy drive on the Desktop. You can do this by opening My Computer and dragging the desired floppy drive to the Desktop.
2. Now, whenever you want to copy items to the floppy drive, insert a diskette in the drive, adjust your windows as necessary so you can see the drive's shortcut, and simply drag and drop objects on it. They'll be instantly copied to the disk.

And, of course, opening the shortcut icon will display the disk's contents.

Using the Cut, Copy, and Paste Commands with Files and Folders

You're probably well acquainted with the Cut, Copy, and Paste commands as they pertain to programs such as word processors. These commands let you remove, replicate, or move bits of data around while working on your documents. You can also use them with files and folders.

NOTE If you're *not* familiar with these concepts as applied to programs, don't worry. They'll be explained in Chapters 6 and 7, "WordPad and Paint Basics" and " Other Windows Accessories," which cover the supplied accessory programs.

Here's how it works, using a real-life example. Today, I downloaded a file from CompuServe called editschd.doc. My e-mail program dumped the file in my Download folder, but I want it in my Mastering Windows Me folder instead. Well, I could open both folders, arrange them on screen, and drag the file from one to the other. Or I could drag the file first to the Desktop, then to the destination folder. But instead of either of these, I used the Cut and Paste commands to accomplish the same task more easily. Here are the steps I used:

1. First, I opened the source folder—which in this case was the Download folder.

2. Next, I located the file in question, right-clicked it and chose Cut (not Delete, because that command actually trashes the file instead of preparing to put it somewhere else).

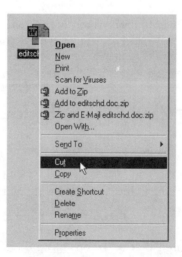

3. This turns the icon into a shadow of its former self, but it's still there in a ghostly form, which means it's waiting to be pasted into another location.

editschd.doc

TIP At this point, failing to paste the file into a destination or pressing Esc will abort the cutting and copying process. Nothing will be lost. The file will remain in its original location.

NOTE If, when you go to paste, the Paste command is grayed out, it means you didn't properly cut or copy the object. You must use the Cut or Copy command on a file or other object *immediately* before using the Paste command, or it won't work. That is, if you go into a word processor and use the Cut or Copy commands in a *document*, then the Paste command for your *files* or other objects will be grayed out and won't work.

Now, a few points about cutting, copying, and pasting objects in this way. First, if you want to make a copy of the file rather than move the original, you'd choose Copy rather than Cut from the menu. Then, when you paste, a copy of the file appears in the destination location.

Second, you can cut or copy a bunch of items at once to save time. The normal rules of selection apply:

- Draw a box around them as I described in "Organizing Document Files" earlier in this chapter.

- Or, press the Ctrl key and select each additional object you want to work with.

- Or, select the first of the items you want to select, hold down the Shift key, and click the last of the items you want to select. This selects the entire *range* of objects between the starting and ending points.

Once a number of items is selected (they will be highlighted), right-clicking any one of the objects will bring up the Cut- Copy- Paste menu. The option you choose will apply to *all* the selected items. Also, clicking anywhere outside of the selected items will deselect them all.

TIP Take a look at the Edit menu in any folder window. There are two commands at the bottom of the menu—Select All and Invert Selection. These can also be useful when you want to select a group of files. Suppose you want to select all but two files; select the two you *don't* want, then choose Edit ➤ Invert Selection.

Finally, remember that you can cut, copy, and paste complete folders, too, just by choosing the folder's icon and then choosing the Cut or Copy command. When you paste the folder somewhere new, you get all of its contents, including any other folders within it.

 TIP What if you accidentally goof and realize that you didn't want to move an object or objects to the new location after all? After you perform the Paste, simply open the Edit menu in any folder and choose Undo. This is a great feature! Often I'll accidentally drag some folder somewhere due to a slip of the wrist or finger or something, and I do not even realize what I've done. Suddenly a folder is gone. Before doing anything else, I choose Undo, and the damage is undone.

Windows Me comes with a new feature in addition to the traditional copy, cut, and paste commands. Your toolbar includes Move To and Copy To buttons that accomplish a cut-and-paste or copy-and-paste more quickly.

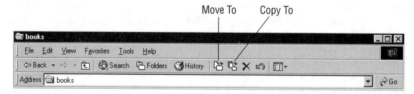

Here's how to use these buttons:

1. In a file management window, select the files or folders to be moved or copied.

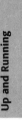

2. Click the Move To or Copy To button. A Browse for Folder dialog box opens.

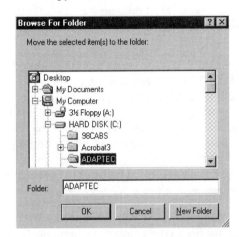

3. Select the location where you want to move or copy the file or folder.

4. Click OK. The move or copy operation is complete.

Working with the Recycle Bin

When right-clicking an object, you may have noticed the Delete command in the menu.

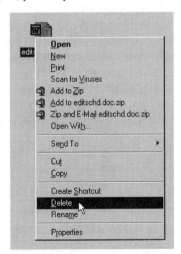

This command isn't the same as the Cut command. Delete sends the selected files, folders, or other objects to the Recycle Bin (essentially the trash can), while the Cut command puts the file on the Clipboard for pasting to another location. The shortcut for the Delete command is the Delete key on the keyboard (pretty obvious, eh?).

When you delete a file, folder, or other item, it gets put into the Recycle Bin, which is actually a special folder on your hard disk. This folder or directory is called, as you might expect, Recycled, typically on your C drive.

 TECH TIP Each logical drive (drive with a letter name) has a Recycled directory on it. So, if you have a C and D drive, you'll have two Recycle Bins. Recycled folders are hidden, so they don't normally show up in Explorer or folders. You'll just have a Recycle Bin on the Desktop, which provides access to them as a group. If you have access to the top-level folder of a networked drive, whether mapped to a logical drive on your machine or not, it too will have a Recycled folder. CD-ROM drives, even though given a logical drive letter, do not have Recycled folders for the obvious reason that you can't delete their files or folders.

The Recycle Bin temporarily holds things that you delete. Because items are not actually *erased* from your computer when you delete them with the Delete command, you can get them back in case you made a mistake! Even better than the Undo command discussed above, this is a terrific feature. How many times have you accidentally erased a file or directory and realized you goofed? For most people even a single accidental erasure was too much. Now, with the Recycle Bin, all you have to do is open its folder, find the item you accidentally deleted, and choose the File ➤ Restore command to undelete it.

Well, actually there's a caveat here. The Recycle Bin will hang onto your deleted items only until you empty the bin. Once you empty the bin, anything in it is *gone*. At that point, your only hope is one of the undelete programs like those from PC Tools, Norton, or the Undelete program supplied with MS-DOS versions 5 and above (if you upgraded to Windows from MS-DOS). When you're doing your hard-disk housecleaning, merrily wiping out folders and files in hopes of regaining some needed disk space, you should be aware of one thing: Because files aren't actually erased until you empty the Recycle Bin, you won't increase your available disk space until you do just that.

Restoring a File or Folder You Accidentally Trashed

If there's one single thing you'll want to know about using the Recycle Bin, it's how to get back something you accidentally put there. (This page alone may make this book worth your investment!)

1. Get to the Desktop one way or another.

 TIP You can also reach items in the Recycle Bin via any folder window, using the drop-down list in the Address bar. Just scroll down to it. The Windows Explorer is another way.

Up and Running

2. Open the Recycle Bin icon. The folder will list all the items you trashed since the last time the Recycle Bin was emptied. Figure 5.8 shows an example.

FIGURE 5.8
A typical Recycle Bin
before emptying

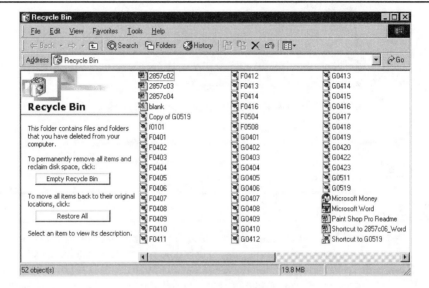

3. Hunt around for the thing(s) you accidentally trashed. When you find it, highlight it by clicking it. (You can select multiple items using the techniques I described earlier in this chapter.)

If you want to know more about an item, click it and choose File ➤ Properties. A dialog box displays when the item was created and when it was deleted. (Or, if you are in the Details view, a column appears displaying the deletion date of each item.)

TIP You can also restore an item in the Recycle Bin or Windows Explorer by right-clicking the item and choosing Restore.

4. Right-click the item and choose Restore (or choose File ➤ Restore, or click the Restore button to the left of the file listing). This will move all selected item(s) back to their original locations.

Emptying the Recycle Bin

You've probably already noticed the command that empties the Recycle Bin. It's on the File menu in the Recycle Bin window. When you want to free up some disk space and are sure that all the contents of the Recycle Bin can be dispensed with, go ahead and empty it. It's always a good idea to have plenty of free disk space for Windows Me and your programs to work with, so regularly emptying the trash, just like at home, is a good practice.

Here's the easiest way to empty the Recycle Bin:

1. Get to the Desktop.

2. Double-click the Recycle Bin.

3. Examine its contents to make sure you really want to jettison everything.

4. Choose File ➤ Empty Recycle Bin.

5. You'll be asked to confirm the process; click Yes.

 TIP You can quickly empty the Recycle Bin by right-clicking it from the Desktop and choosing Empty Recycle Bin.

 NOTE We all love to accumulate junk on our hard disks. It doesn't matter whether the disk holds only 400 megabytes or a nine gigabytes. It will fill up. When your hard disk can gets too crammed, Windows Me starts to strangle. At that point, a dialog box reporting the sorry state of your disk housekeeping will pop up on your screen. If there is stuff in the Recycle Bin, the box will have a button you can click to empty the trash for you, reclaiming some precious space. You'll also have the option of dumping Internet temp files that may have accumulated as you browsed the Web. To delete lots of non-essential files at once, use the Disk Cleanup program that comes with Windows, described in Chapter 15, "Improving System Performance."

Setting the Recycle Bin's Properties

If your hard disk is modest in size or it is getting crammed, decreasing the size of the Recycle Bin might be in order. In other cases, you might even want to *increase* its size. The options in the Recycle Bin's property sheet are therefore worth a quick look-see.

To get to the setting, right-click the Recycle Bin icon, either on the Desktop or in Explorer, and then choose Properties.

There will be a tab for each of your local hard disks. If you choose Configure Drives Independently, you'll use those tab pages to make individual drive settings. Otherwise you'll just use the Global page.

If you don't want to be able to reclaim deleted files, check the Do Not Move Files... option. This will speed up deletion. It will also free up disk space immediately after the files are gone.

As a default, 10 percent of each drive is used for the Recycle Bin. When you delete a file on drive C, it goes to drive C's Recycle Bin until you empty the bin. When you delete from drive D (if you have a second hard drive), it goes into drive D's Recycle Bin. As a Recycle Bin reaches capacity, newly deleted files will push older files off the bottom of the list, deleting them permanently. In practical terms, the Recycle Bin's size simply determines how long a file will be recoverable before it's pushed off the list. It also determines the maximum size file that will be recoverable after an accidental deletion. If a file is larger than the maximum size of the Recycle Bin, then it just won't be recyclable. You will be warned of this when you try to erase some humongous item.

If you want to alter the size of your Recycle Bins, use the percentage slider. As a rule, the default of 10 percent works just fine. If you work with very large files, you may want to increase this percentage to accommodate them. If you're short on disk space and don't tend to make deletion mistakes, decrease it.

 NOTE When you empty the Recycle Bin, all bins are flushed. You can't empty them on a drive-by-drive basis unless you use a file-management program other than Explorer. You *can* use Explorer to delete specific files from the Recycle Bin, by selecting and deleting them individually, however.

The final check box (Display Delete Confirmation Dialog) is normally set on, requiring you to confirm before Windows will empty the bin. If you find the confirmation boxes annoying, turn off this check box.

Renaming Documents and Folders

As you work with your files, folders, and other objects, you may occasionally need to rename them, either to more easily identify them later or because their purpose has changed and the current name is no longer valid. In any case, it's easy enough to change an object name.

In general, renaming objects works similarly throughout Windows Me. The surest, though not necessarily the quickest, way is this:

1. Right-click the object you want to rename and choose Rename from the resulting menu.

   At this point, the name will be highlighted and the text cursor (small vertical bar) will be blinking.

2. Here's the tricky part. Because the whole name is highlighted, whatever you type now will replace the whole name. More often than not, this isn't what you want to do. Typically, you'll just want to add a word or two, fix a misspelling, or something. So, just press ← (the left arrow key). This will deselect the name and move the cursor one space to the left. Now use the normal editing procedures with Backspace, Del, arrow keys, and regular typing to modify the name.

3. Click outside the little text box encircling the name (or press ← once) when you're through; that will store the new name.

 NOTE A shortcut for editing a name is to do a *slow* double-click the name. This puts the name into edit mode, with the cursor blinking away and the name highlighted. Be careful not to double-click quickly, or this will run the application or open the document.

If, when renaming a file, you see an error message about how changing the extension of the file may make it unworkable, you'll typically want to choose No.

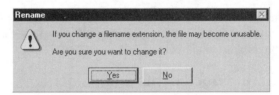

This message just means you forgot to give the filename an extension by typing in a period and the same three-letter extension it had before. So just rename it again, making sure to give it the same extension that it had before.

 WARNING This typically occurs only if you have chosen to show file extensions for known file types, or if the file does not have a known file type. That's because when a file's extension is hidden, Windows uses the same extension when you rename the file without your having to type the extension at all. In fact, if you type an extension when renaming the file, Windows makes it part of the name. For example, suppose I have file extensions hidden and I rename the file `mytext.doc` using the above procedure to `mytext.txt`. The file looks like it's renamed, but if you turn on the display of extensions, you'll see that the file is now called `mytext.txt.doc`. Windows kept the extension and simply tacked on your `.txt` to the end of the filename before the extension.

So for example, let's say the file is named
`Budget for Winter 1999.wks`
and you change it to
`Budget for Spring 1999`

You'll probably see an error message when you press the ← key. Renaming the file to

    Budget for Spring 1999.wks

would prevent the error message.

As I discussed earlier, extensions for registered file types are normally hidden. So a Word for Windows file named Letter to Joe, for example, will simply appear as

    Letter to Joe

not

    Letter to Joe.doc

which is the name that's actually stored on the disk. When you change the name of a file that doesn't have an extension showing, you don't have to even think about what the extension is or about accidentally typing in the wrong one.

Setting File and Folder Options

There are several kinds of customization you can set for managing your files and folders in Windows:

- You can arrange and sort files and folders on the Desktop or in file management windows.
- You can control the look of individual folders.
- You can set global options that affect all file management.

I'll discuss each of these customizations in the following sections.

Sorting Files, Folders, and Shortcuts

The icons on the Desktop start out arranged in a neat column or two along the left side of your screen, but as you create and delete shortcuts, your Desktop can become cluttered.

To straighten them up, do the following:

1. Right-click the desktop and choose Arrange Icons. A submenu appears.

2. Choose how you want the icons ordered: By Name, By Type, By Size, or By Date.

By Name	Sorts the display of objects alphabetically based on the name. Folders always appear first in the listing.
By Type	Sorts the display of objects according to type. (The type is only visible when you list the objects' details.) Folders always appear first in the listing.
By Size	Sorts the display of objects in increasing order of size. Folders always appear first in the listing.
By Date	Sorts the display of objects chronologically, based on the date the object was last modified.

If you want to keep the icons permanently arranged, right-click and choose Arrange Icons ➤ AutoArrange. From then on, any icons you place on the Desktop, or move around on it, will snap back into their proper place immediately. To turn the feature off, issue the same command again.

 NOTE If the icons get just a little bit out of alignment and you want to straighten them up without really moving anything, right-click the Desktop and choose Line Up Icons.

To use these same sorting options in a file window, you can choose them from the View ➤ Arrange Icons menu or you can right-click for a shortcut menu containing the Arrange Icons command.

Right-clicking menus in certain specialized windows may give you additional Arrange options. For example, in the Recycle Bin window you'll see this:

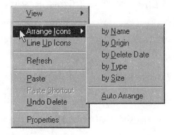

And in the My Computer folder you'll see this:

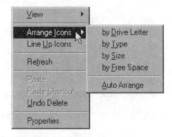

There's another way to sort the files, but it works only in Details view. Change to Details view (View ➤ Details); then click the column heading by which you want to sort. For example, to sort files by type, click the Type column:

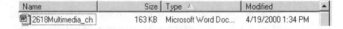

Clicking the heading once sorts in ascending order (A to Z, 0 to 9). Clicking a second time sorts in descending order. This is particularly useful in the Size and Modified columns, letting you easily bring to the top of the list the files you've modified most recently *or* those you modified ages ago; or you can quickly find which files in a folder are very large and might be taking up significant space on your hard disk.

Customizing a Folder

Individual folders can be customized in a variety of ways, using the Customize This Folder Wizard. Although previous versions of Windows included some folder customization, Windows Me is much stronger in this area. You can format certain folders based on formatting templates, and apply the same formatting to some or all folders on your system.

Follow these steps to customize a folder:

1. Display the folder that you want to customize.

2. Choose View ➣ Customize This Folder, or right-click in the folder and choose Customize This Folder. The Customize This Folder Wizard starts.

3. Click Next to begin.

4. If it's not already selected, choose the Customize option button.

(If you have previously customized the folder and now want to remove the customization, you would choose the other option button, Remove Customization.)

5. Mark any of the checkboxes under Customize for features you want to set:

- Choose or edit an HTML template for this folder.

- Modify background picture and filename appearance.

- Add folder comment.

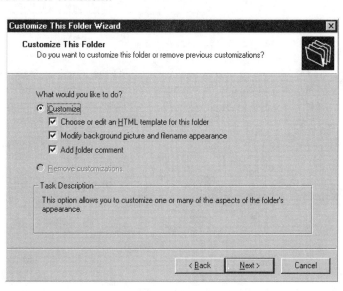

For the purpose of these steps, I'll assume you've marked all three of these. If you don't mark one or more of them, you can skip the steps in this procedure that pertain to those customizations.

6. Click Next to continue. The list of HTML templates for the folder display appears.

7. Select the template you want to use, and then click Next.

The Classic (Icons Only) template, for example, omits the extra information about the selected file or folder that often appears in the left side of the window and takes up lots of space.

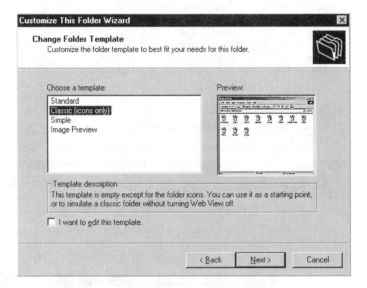

TIP Advanced users might want to edit the template. Mark the I Want to Edit This Template check box, and then when you click Next, an HTML editing window appears with the code in it. Make your changes to the code, close the window, and then go on to step 8.

8. (Optional) Select a background image to use for the folder.

The images listed are those in the Windows folder, but you can use an image located anywhere else by clicking Browse and locating it.

9. Choose a foreground and background color for the filename appearance. The foreground color will be the color of the text; the background color will be behind it.

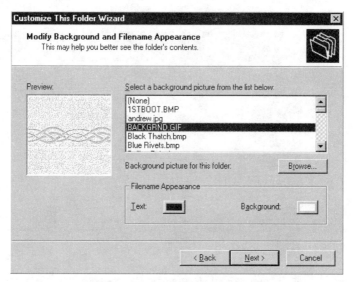

10. Click Next to continue.

11. Type a comment in the Folder Comment text box. Then click Next.

    This comment will appear when the folder is selected in the information pane to the left of the listing—provided, of course, that the folder that's one level up from this one in the folder tree does not use a template that omits that pane, such as Classic (Icons Only) or Simple.

12. Click Finish. The folder appears with its new appearance. Figure 5.9 shows an example.

FIGURE 5.9
*A customized
folder view*

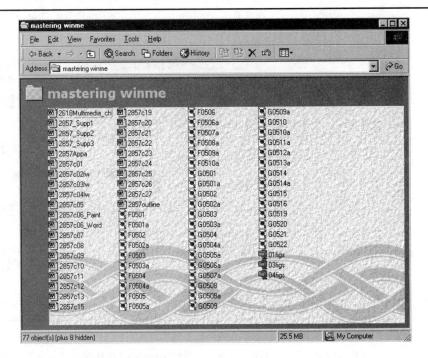

Note that when you are viewing the folder's contents, you won't see the comment. You must go up one level and then select the folder (by clicking it once) to see the comment, as in Figure 5.10.

FIGURE 5.10
The folder's comment is visible from one level up.

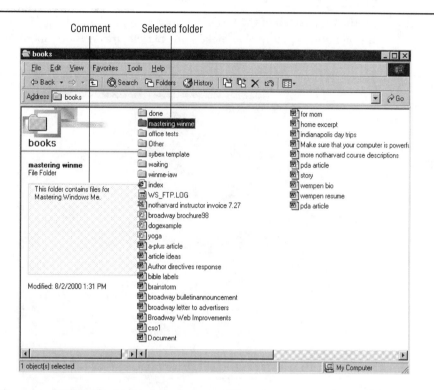

Once you get a folder looking the way you like, you can opt to have all other folders use the same display arrangement:

1. Choose Tools ➢ Folder Options.

2. Click the View tab.

3. Click the Like Current Folder button.

4. Click OK.

You will work more with this Folder Options box later in the chapter.

Setting Global Folder Options

In Windows Explorer or My Computer, you can choose Tools ➢ Folder Options to set the global options for working with files and folders on your system. Except where indicated, these settings will apply to all file listings, as well as to your Desktop where applicable.

Setting General Folder Options

On the General tab of the Folder Options dialog box (Figure 5.11), you'll find some option buttons that let you make some big-picture decisions about file management.

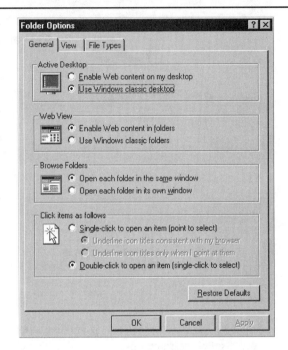

Here are the features you'll encounter on the General tab:

Active Desktop   The default setting is Use Classic Desktop. The alternative, Enable Web Content on My Desktop, allows you to place active controls on your Desktop that automatically update themselves with information from the Internet. For more information about this feature, see "Using the Active Desktop" in Chapter 10.

Web View   The default is Enable Web Content in Folders. This is what gives you that extra pane to the left of the file listing that describes the selected file or folder. The alternative, Use Windows Classic Folders, is like setting all folders to the Classic (Icons Only) HTML template in individual folder customization.

Browse Folders   The default is Open Each Folder in the Same Window. In other words, in My Computer when you double-click a drive icon, the drive's contents appears in the same window, replacing the drive icons. The alternative is Open Each Folder in Its Own Window, which clutters up your screen faster but makes it easier to drag-and-drop between locations.

Click Items as Follows The default is Double-Click to Open an Item (Single Click to Select). And that's the way I've been instructing you throughout this whole book. The alternative, Single Click to Open an Item (Point to Select), makes Windows work more like a Web page.

Setting File and Folder Viewing Options

The View tab of the Folder Options dialog box contains a long list of check boxes for turning on/off individual characteristics and features. Table 5.1 lists them, and provides some advice as to what to choose. (If in doubt, the default is usually a good setting.)

TABLE 5.1: THE FOLDER OPTIONS VIEW SETTINGS

Setting	Meaning
Automatically search for network folders and printers.	Determines whether Windows will periodically look on the network for shared printers, drives, and folders and add them to My Network Places. Recommendation: leave this on unless you are often disconnected from the network (such as with a laptop).
Display all control panel options and all folder contents.	When on, this setting bypasses the simple version of the control panel and all the extra warnings about not modifying system files when opening folders like Windows. Recommendation: turn on for advanced users; leave off for beginners.
Display the full path in the address bar.	When on, the entire path of an open folder appears in the address bar. For example, a full path name might be C:\joe's work\budgets\1998, whereas the folder name alone would display as 1998. Recommendation: turn on for advanced users; leave off for beginners.
Display the full path in the title bar.	Same as above, except for the title bar. Recommendation: leave turned off.
Hidden files and folders.	When set to Do Not Show Hidden Files and Folders (the default), this omits these files from folder listings. When set to Show Hidden Files and Folders, this setting shows all files, including hidden ones, but shows the hidden ones slightly ghosted so you can tell they are special at a glance. Recommendation: Leave at the default for beginners, turn on the display of hidden files for advanced users.
Hide file extensions for known file types.	When set on, files with recognized extensions won't have their extensions showing. Unrecognized (unregistered) file types will still show their extensions. Turn this off to see all extensions, even if they are registered in Windows Me. Recommendation: Leave on for beginners; turn off for everyone else.
Hide protected operating system files.	Hides essential files that must not be modified or deleted in order for Windows to work. Recommendation: Leave on for everyone, except if you are an advanced user doing troubleshooting.

Continued ▶

PART

I

Up and Running

TABLE 5.1: THE FOLDER OPTIONS VIEW SETTINGS (CONTINUED)

Setting	Meaning
Launch folder windows in a separate process.	Slightly increases system stability by opening each folder window in a separate memory address space. Turning it off may speed up system performance slightly, but may make Windows crash. Recommendation; leave turned on.
Remember each folder's view settings.	When turned on (the default), Windows remembers your view settings for a window after you close it. Recommendation: leave turned on.
Show My Documents on the Desktop.	When on (the default), the My Documents icon appears on the Desktop; when off it does not. Recommendation: leave turned on.
Show pop-up description for folder and Desktop items.	When not viewing a folder as a Web page (see View menu option), this enables a pop-up menu displaying the same info that's normally displayed in the left-hand pane of a folder when you highlight an icon in a folder or on the Desktop. Recommendation: leave on.

Click the Restore Defaults button if you have doubts about what you've done or if, at a later date, you want to return the behavior of the system to its original state.

Controlling Toolbar Buttons

You might have noticed a setting on the View ≻ Toolbars menu called Customize. This opens a Customize Toolbar dialog box, in which you can choose what buttons appear on the toolbar in your file management windows. You can also choose the size of the buttons and whether text appears on them or only the pictures (see Figure 5.12).

FIGURE 5.12
Use this box to customize your file management window's toolbar.

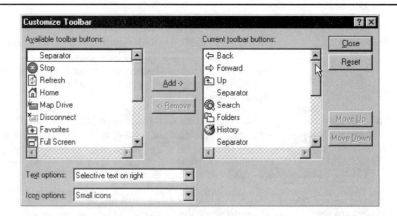

To add or remove a button from the toolbar, click it and then click the Add or Remove button.

To change the appearance of buttons in general, open the Text Options drop-down list and choose one of these:

Show Text Labels   Shows the button names beneath the icons. Results in large buttons.

Selective Text on Right   Shows button names to the right of the icons, but only for certain icons where the meaning may not be immediately apparent from the picture.

No Text Labels   Omits all text from buttons.

You can also choose the icon size from the Icon Options drop-down list: small or large.

Working with Disks

Windows Explorer has a few features that apply specifically to managing your disks, particularly floppy disks. These commands make the process of formatting disks and copying disks a bit simpler. There's also a way to easily change the volume label of a disk, the optional name that each floppy or hard disk can be assigned (typically for archival purposes).

 WARNING   Most of the popular large-capacity storage devices, such as the Iomega Zip drive or Imation LS-120, come with their own utility for formatting. Check with the drive's documentation to see what the best formatting method is.

Formatting Disks

As I mentioned earlier, floppy disks must be formatted before they can be used in your computer. Many disks you buy in the store are preformatted, so this isn't an issue. Some are not, however. Also, more than likely you have many disks with old defunct programs and files on them that you'd like to reuse. To gain maximum room on such a disk, you'll want to erase all the old files, something you can most efficiently achieve with a "quick format" procedure.

 WARNING   Formatting erases all data from the disk! Reversing the process is difficult, if not impossible.

Here's how to format a disk:

1. Put the disk to be formatted in the floppy drive.

2. Open the My Computer window or Windows Explorer. Right-click the floppy disk and choose Format.

   The dialog box shown in Figure 5.13 appears.

3. Select the disk capacity from the Capacity drop-down list. In almost all cases the capacity should be 1.44Mb. Only very old 3.5" disks will be 720Kb capacity.

TIP There is an easy way to tell a 1.44Mb disk from a 720Kb one: look at the holes in the corners. A 1.44Mb disk has two holes. One is covered with a sliding panel; the other is open. A 720Kb disk has only the hole with the sliding panel.

4. For Format type, choose one of the following:

   Quick   Simply deletes the file-allocation table and root folder of the disk, but the disk is not scanned for bad sectors. It doesn't actually erase the whole disk and reinitialize it or check for errors in the disk medium itself. Quick formatting can only be done on a disk that has been formatted in the past, and for a PC. You can't quick-format a Mac disk, for example, though you could do a full format on it.

   Full   Checks the entire disk's surface to make sure it's reliable. Any bad spots are omitted from the directory table and won't be used to store your data. This kind of format isn't fast, but it better ensures that valuable data are stored properly on the disk.

NOTE Disks can actually lose some of their formatting information with time. If you are going to use an old disk, it's best to full-format it to prevent data loss down the road. And if you do not know where it has been, it's a good idea to full format it to prevent any possible viruses from spreading. If the disk has been around some strong magnets, such as electric motors or unshielded loudspeakers, it is best to full-format then, too.

5. (Optional) Enter a label if desired in the Label box.

NOTE All floppy and hard disks can have a volume label. This is not the paper label on the outside, but a name encoded into the folder on the disk. It shows up when you type **DIR** at the DOS prompt and in some other programs. The label really serves no functional purpose other than to identify the disk for archiving purposes. You can change the label from the disk's Properties box at any time.

6. (Optional) If you don't want a label, and you want to clear any existing label from the list, mark the No Label check box.

7. (Optional) To see a summary of the formatting process when finished, mark the Display summary when finished check box.

8. Click Start. You may see a confirmation message. A gas gauge at the bottom of the dialog box will keep you apprised of the progress of the format. A typical full format will take a minute or so.

FIGURE 5.13
Right-click on a floppy drive and choose Format to reach this dialog box. A disk must be formatted before you can store files on it.

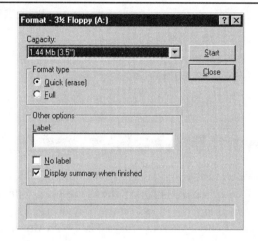

Copying Disks

If you receive valuable data on a floppy disk, you might want to make a copy of the disk just to be on the safe side. (You can also copy the disk's content to a folder on your hard disk, for further security.)

 NOTE You cannot copy a hard disk using the following steps. To *clone* a hard disk, in other words, to make an exact copy of it on another hard disk, use a program such as Drive-Copy or Norton Ghost.

To copy a floppy disk, follow these steps:

1. Make sure you have a blank floppy disk ready, or one that contains nothing you want to keep.

2. Insert the disk to be copied in your floppy drive.

3. Right-click the floppy drive's icon and choose Copy Disk. A dialog box pops up asking for the destination drive. If you only have one drive, that's okay.

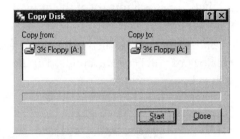

4. Click Start.

5. When prompted, remove the disk being copied, insert the blank disk, and then click OK to continue.

6. When the disk is finished copying, click Close to leave the Copy Disk dialog box.

Using Network Drives, Files, and Disks

As explained further in Part V, "Networking," Windows Me can be used on either *peer-to-peer* or *client/server* networks. The first type, usually found in smaller businesses, is much simpler and can be maintained by its users. Client/server networks are usually the responsibility of administrators; if you are on such a network, you probably don't have to worry too much about connecting to or disconnecting from network drives, or sharing resources, as described in this section, though you may still have such options. (Some network administrators can be very controlling about such operations.) In either case, networked drives will be visible in Windows Explorer just as if they were part of your own computer.

 TIP If you need to network the computers in your home or small office, refer to Chapter 24, "Building a Peer-to-Peer Network."

Many everyday tasks, such as using a document or program on a network file server or another workstation's hard disk can be done right from Windows Explorer without any fancy footwork. You just open My Network Places from the Desktop or from Windows Explorer (open the drop-down list in Explorer or any folder and choose My Network Places) and browse your network just as you would the contents of your own computer (see Figure 5.14).

FIGURE 5.14

Notice that the My Documents folder from another computer on the network is expanded in the folder tree.

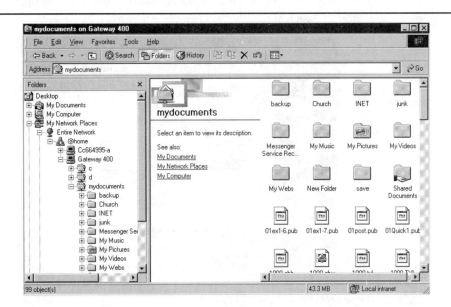

If the network is operational and people are sharing stuff on their workstations, there will be computers listed in the right pane, as in Figure 5.14. Click one of them and start browsing. Examining someone else's drives and folders is exactly like looking at your own.

Note that you'll only see *shared* items on any networked computer, not *everything* on that computer. This scheme allows users to protect confidential items. Password protection is another option, limiting access of shared objects to specific users. All of the folders in Figure 5.14 were intentionally shared. (See the following section to learn how to share your system's content.)

Virtually all 32-bit Windows programs will let you use networked drives and folders with no hassle. For example, say I wanted to open a Notepad file that's stored on someone else's computer. I simply find the file and double-click, just as if it were on my computer. If I'm already in, say, WordPad and I want to use its File ➢ Open command to open a file, no problem. I would simply open the Look In drop-down list and choose My Network Places, and then navigate to the desired file or folder. Of course, the same approach applies to saving a document with File ➢ Save.

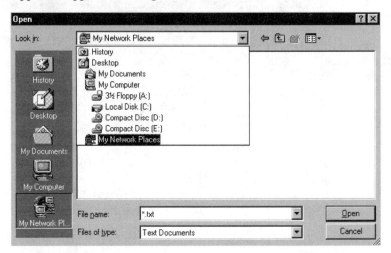

Sharing Folders and Drives

You can share drives and folders on the network for others to use. When you run the Home Networking Wizard, you specify whether you want your My Documents folder to be shared, as well as your printers. But you can also share any other drives or folders too.

Shared items can have passwords, and they also can have specific privileges (read-only or read-write). If you have a bunch of files that you want people to be able to see but not alter, just put them into a new folder and share it as read-only. If you want only specific people to be able to alter the files, share them protected by a password. Take the following steps to share your drives and folders.

1. In My Computer or Explorer, right-click the folder or drive you want to share.

WARNING Because sharing a hard disk itself (from the root level) allows network users into all directories on the disk, doing so can be dangerous. Clicking a disk icon in the Explorer or My Computer and sharing it is certainly the easiest way to share all files and folders on your computer. However, it allows any connected user to alter or erase everything you have on your hard disk. Your only defenses are to share files and folders with password protection or marked "read only" via their Properties box.

2. Choose Sharing. The Properties box for that drive or folder appears with the Sharing tab displayed.

3. Click Shared As.

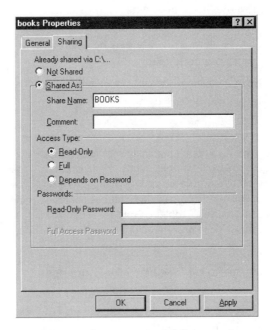

4. Set any sharing options desired (described following these steps).

5. Click OK. The icon of the folder or drive will change to include a little hand under it, a suggestion of sharing.

books

Here are the options you can set for sharing:

- The Share Name is, by default, the same name as the directory itself. This should be limited to a DOS 8.3-character name if others on the network will be using an operating system that doesn't display long file names, such as Windows 3.11 or DOS.

 TIP Even if you choose to limit the Share Name to the DOS 8.3 file-naming convention, you might want to elaborate on the directory name a bit. For example, while still conforming to DOS file-naming conventions (spaces and some characters are illegal), you could lengthen Reports to Reports.98.

- You can add a comment line that network users will see, perhaps explaining who the file is for or what is in the shared folder. This will show up when someone checks out your computer in Network Neighborhood or Explorer in the Details view. This line can be approximately 50 characters long and include spaces and punctuation.

- Next, you have the option of setting specific permissions to restrict the use of the directory by others.

 NOTE If you don't manually set the permissions, although anyone can access the directory, nobody will be able to edit the files in it or make other changes that an application might require, such as recording changes to a style sheet or creating a temp file in the directory. If you are sharing a folder that has applications in it for use by workers on the Internet, this could cause a problem. Consider carefully whether you should share the directory with Full permission to prevent potential application or document problems.

- Set the Access Type by clicking the appropriate button. You have three choices:

  Read   Enables viewing file names, copying information, running applications in the directory, and opening document files.

  Full   All permissions listed above, plus the ability to delete files, move files, edit files, and create new subdirectories.

  Depends on Password   The type of access will be determined by which password option is chosen and which password is entered by the person attempting to use the disk or folder.

 WARNING   Be careful not to share directories that have subdirectories unless you want those to become accessible with the same level of restriction. A user has the same rights to all the subdirectories as they have to the shared parent directory.

- Finally, there are the password settings. With Read-Only or Full selected, you can enter a password in the appropriate spot. Anyone trying to use the folder will be prompted to enter a password. If you choose the Depends on Password option, the level of access the remote user is granted (Read-only or Full) is determined by the password they enter.

 NOTE   Access to shared objects can be further controlled from the Network applet in the Control Panel. Using this applet, you can control whether access is granted on a user-by-user basis or on a group basis. Group access control is discussed in Part V of this book.

This concludes our discussion of files, folders, and drives. In the next chapter, you'll learn about WordPad and Paint, two of the most useful Windows Me accessory programs. And in the process of learning about these programs, you will also learn how to perform common tasks in nearly any program, including printing and opening/saving document files.

PART

I

Up and Running

CHAPTER **6**

WordPad and Paint Basics

This chapter introduces two of the most important accessory programs that come with Windows Me: WordPad and Paint. WordPad is a simple word processing program that you can use to compose letters, memos, reports, and other text-based documents. Paint is a program that creates artwork out of lines and shapes. You also can use Paint for simple diagrams and illustrations, and it's also great fun for kids to play with.

Not only does this chapter show you how to use these two programs, but it also eases you into some essential skills that will carry over into other programs, including saving and opening files and printing your work.

Working with WordPad

If you're like most people, you'll end up using your computer for writing more than for any other task. Writing letters, memos, and reports with your computer is much more efficient—and much more fun—than banging them out on a typewriter. To get you started, Windows Me comes with a simple yet capable *word processor*, called WordPad, for editing and printing text documents.

WordPad lacks the frills of the hefty word processing programs like Microsoft Word for Windows, WordPerfect, or Word Pro, but it works fine for most everyday writing chores. WordPad gives you all the essential tools you'll need for editing word processing documents of virtually any length; it is limited only by the capacity of your disk drive. Like the high-end programs, it even lets you move text around with the mouse, a feature called *drag-and-drop editing*. WordPad accepts, displays, and prints graphics pasted to it from the Clipboard; it also lets you edit those graphics right in your document. WordPad may not offer all the bells and whistles of the market leaders, but it's no toy—and besides, the price is right.

Exploring the WordPad Window

To start WordPad and create a new document, choose Start ➤ Programs ➤ Accessories ➤ WordPad. The WordPad window will appear with a new, empty document window open (see Figure 6.1).

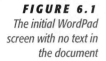

FIGURE 6.1
The initial WordPad screen with no text in the document

Standard toolbar Formatting toolbar Ruler

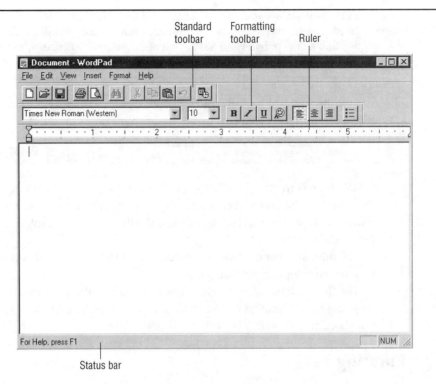

Status bar

As usual, up at the top of the WordPad window, you see the menu and title bars. The menu bar offers options for writing, editing, and formatting text. Notice that in Figure 6.1, the title bar shows Document as the filename because you haven't named it yet.

Just below the menu bar you should see a row of buttons, each with a small graphical icon. This is the *Standard toolbar,* shown below. If you don't see the toolbar, someone has turned it off. Display it by choosing View ➤ Toolbar.

Clicking the toolbar buttons gives you one-step access to some of the most common WordPad commands. For instance, the first button (on the far left) shows a single sheet of blank paper. Clicking this button creates a new, blank document. About halfway across the row of buttons, the Find button—the one showing a pair of binoculars—lets you search for specific passages of text.

TIP In WordPad, you don't need to memorize what each button does. Just position the mouse pointer over the button and wait for a few seconds. WordPad will display a small text box with a one- or two-word description of the button's function. In addition, the Status bar at the bottom of the screen displays a longer help message.

Like the Standard toolbar, the *Formatting toolbar* offers a set of graphical buttons, but it also contains (at the far left) two drop-down list boxes for selecting font and type size.

All of the Formatting toolbar's controls affect aspects of your document's appearance. Besides the font and type-size controls, various buttons let you set such characteristics as type style (such as boldface and italics) and paragraph alignment (such as left-aligned or centered).

The *ruler*, another control bar available from the View menu, lets you see and modify paragraph indents and tab stops.

The *Status bar* is a thin strip at the very bottom of the WordPad window. It displays messages from WordPad on the left. On the right are indicators showing when the CapsLock and NumLock keys are depressed.

Entering Text

Notice the main document area of the WordPad window. Because you haven't typed in anything yet, the only item to look at here is the blinking cursor in the upper-left corner. This *insertion point* indicates the place where new text will appear when you type.

Now begin creating a document. Of course, you're free to type in anything you want. However, to establish a consistent text to refer to later on in this chapter, try entering the text shown in Figure 6.2. (For later steps in the tutorial, keep the two misspelled words, *Pizza* and *sight*, as they are.) Press Enter only to start a new paragraph, not to end a line within a paragraph; WordPad automatically wraps text to the next line as needed.

If you make mistakes while you are typing, use the Backspace key to back up and fix them. If you don't see an error until you have typed past it, leave it for now. You'll learn how to fix any mistakes later.

FIGURE 6.2
*The WordPad window
after you've entered the
sample text*

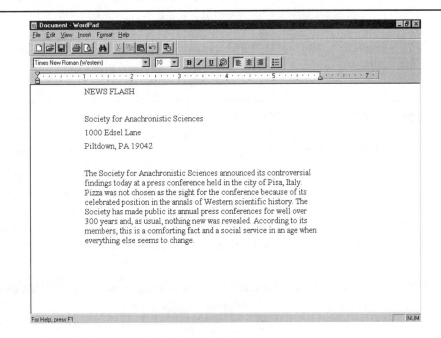

 WARNING Don't insert two spaces (that is, don't press the spacebar twice) between sentences as you would with a typewriter. WordPad will automatically add enough space to clearly separate each sentence. If you add two spaces, your text will print with unsightly gaps between sentences.

Editing Your Text

The first step in editing is learning how to move around in the text. If you followed the instructions above, you moved the cursor only by pressing Enter and, perhaps, by pressing Backspace to delete a character or two after you made a mistake. For the most part, you left the cursor alone and it moved along by itself as you typed. But now you'll want to move up and down to fix misspelled words and make other changes. After all, it's the ability to move around freely in your document and make changes at will that makes a word processor so much more capable than a typewriter.

Moving the Cursor

The *cursor* marks the position where letters appear when you type. As noted before, this is the insertion point. Editing your text involves moving the cursor to the correct location and then inserting text, removing words, fixing misspellings, or marking blocks of text to be moved, copied, or deleted.

The easiest way to move the cursor is just to point and click. When the mouse pointer is over the document window, it looks like a large letter I or a steel beam (this shape is often called the *I-beam pointer*). Move the I-beam pointer so that the vertical line is over the place in the text where you want to begin editing or typing. When you click, the blinking insertion point will jump from wherever it was to this new position.

 NOTE After positioning the cursor with the mouse, don't forget to click; otherwise, you'll end up making changes in the wrong place.

You can also use the arrow keys to move the cursor. This is often quicker than using the mouse when you need to move the cursor by only a few characters or lines.

Because writing relies heavily on the keyboard, WordPad provides several keyboard combinations that can be used to move the insertion point. These are listed in Table 6.1, along with the single keystrokes for moving the cursor.

TABLE 6.1: KEYS FOR MOVING THE INSERTION POINT IN WORDPAD

Key Combination	Moves the Insertion Point...
↑	Up one line
↓	Down one line
←	Left one character
→	Right one character
Ctrl+←	Left one word
Ctrl+→	Right one word
Ctrl+Home	Beginning of document
Ctrl+End	End of document
Ctrl+PgUp	Top left of current window
Ctrl+PgDn	Bottom right of current window

Selecting Text

Much of editing with a word processor centers around manipulating blocks of text. A *block* is a section of consecutive text characters (letters, numbers, punctuation, and so on). Blocks can be of any length. Many of the commands in Windows programs use this idea of manipulating blocks of information.

You must *select* a block before you can work with it. When you select a block, it becomes the center of attention for WordPad. As shown in Figure 6.3, WordPad highlights the block. Until you deselect it, WordPad treats the block differently than the rest of the document. For example, some menu commands will affect the selection and nothing else.

FIGURE 6.3
The highlighted passage is a selected block of text.

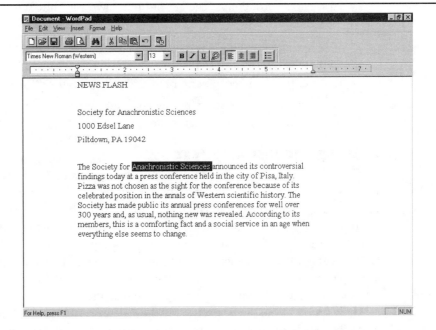

There are two main ways to select a text block: with the mouse, by dragging over the area you want to select, and with the keyboard, by holding down the Shift key while you move the cursor. We'll cover both methods in detail in a moment. You *deselect* by clicking elsewhere, selecting elsewhere with the mouse, or moving the cursor after releasing the Shift key.

Once you've selected a block, be careful about the keys you press. If you type **A**, for example, the text of the whole block (the *selection*) will be replaced by the letter A. If this happens accidentally, choose Edit ➢ Undo or click the Undo button on the toolbar *before doing anything else*, and your text will be returned to its previous state.

After selecting a block of text, you can manipulate it in any number of ways: You can cut or copy it, change its font size, alter the paragraph formatting, and so forth.

To select text with the mouse, drag the cursor across it while holding down the left mouse button. To select with the keyboard, move the insertion point where you want to start, and then hold down the Shift key as you use the arrow keys to expand the selection area. (Hold down the Ctrl key too to expand the selection one word at a time.)

Here are some shortcuts for selecting various parts of a document:

- To select an entire line or a series of entire lines, move the mouse pointer to the left of the text. Then click to select the entire line, or click and drag up or down to select multiple lines.

- To select a word, double-click it, or hold down the Shift key as you single-click the word.

- To select a paragraph, triple-click it, or move the mouse pointer into the left margin next to the paragraph and double-click.

- To select the entire document, press Ctrl+A or choose Edit ➤ Select All.

- An alternative way of selecting the entire document is by pressing Ctrl+click or by triple-clicking in the selection area.

Deleting and Inserting Text

To modify text, position the insertion point where you want it, and then use the Delete key to remove the character to the right or Backspace to remove the character to the left. If you typed the text in Figure 6.2 earlier in the chapter, you can practice deleting now. Find the word *sight* and delete the "gh" from it so that it reads *sit*. Then position the insertion point at the end of the word and type an **e** so it reads *site*.

Notice that the line opened up to let the *e* in. Unlike on a typewritten page, lines on a computer screen are flexible. You may have noticed that WordPad rewraps all the lines of the paragraph almost instantly as you insert text.

Many simple errors can be fixed using the Delete or Backspace key. But suppose you wanted to delete an entire word, sentence, or paragraph. You could do this by moving to the beginning or end of the section that you wanted to erase. You would then need to hold down Delete or Backspace, respectively, until the key is repeated and has erased all the words, letter by letter. But this is a slow and potentially risky method. If you're not careful, you may erase more than you intended to. You can do this more easily by selecting the text you want to delete; you would then press Delete or Backspace to get rid of it, or simply start typing the replacement text in order to delete the selected text and enter the replacement at the same time.

For more practice, find the word *not* in the second sentence of the sample text from Figure 6.2, the one that now begins "Pizza was not chosen." So that the paragraph makes more sense, delete the *not* by double-clicking the word to select it and then by pressing Delete. Then double-click the word Pizza and type Pisa, replacing it.

 TIP If you delete some text accidentally, you can retrieve it by choosing Edit ➤ Undo or clicking the Undo button before you make any other changes. And if you want to remove a word but save it on the Clipboard for later use, you cut it instead of deleting or clearing it. You'll learn how to cut selected blocks next.

Using Cut, Copy, and Paste

The editing process often involves moving large portions of text, such as sentences and paragraphs, within a document. Rather than inserting a block of text by retyping it, you can do it by picking it up and moving it from one place to another with the Cut, Copy, and Paste commands.

Moving Blocks with Cut and Paste Commands

To move a block of text, select it and then use the Cut command to move it to the Clipboard. Then reposition the insertion point where you want to paste it, and issue the Paste command.

There are several ways of issuing these commands. To cut, you can do any of the following:

- Open the Edit menu and choose Cut.
- Click the Cut button on the toolbar.
- Press Ctrl+X.

To paste, you can do any of these:

- Open the Edit menu and choose Paste.
- Click the Paste button on the toolbar.
- Press Ctrl+V.

Here's an example of how you can use the Paste command to reverse the order of the first two paragraphs in our sample letter. Select the "News Flash" line (this is a one-line paragraph) with whatever technique you prefer, and carefully select the blank line immediately below the paragraph, too, because you want a blank line between the paragraphs after the move. This second line is also a *paragraph* as far as WordPad is concerned. If you're selecting by dragging, just drag the mouse a little further down. If you double-clicked in the margin to select the first paragraph, press Shift to retain the paragraph selection and then double-click to the left of the blank line. You'll know the blank line is also selected when a thin strip at the left margin becomes highlighted (this is the normally invisible *paragraph mark* associated with the blank line).

 TIP Every paragraph has a paragraph mark. Paragraph attributes such as alignment, tab settings, and margins are contained in it. Copying this mark is an easy way of copying attributes from one place to another.

Now it's time to cut the block. Use any of the methods I just told you about. Then move the insertion point to the place where you want to insert the paragraph, which happens to be just before the *T* of the word *The* in the first main paragraph. Finally, paste the paragraph back into your document. Use any of the paste methods explained in the preceding list.

Sometimes, after moving paragraphs around, you may need to do a little adjusting, such as inserting or deleting a line or some spaces. You can always insert a line by pressing the Enter key. If you have extra blank lines after a move, you can delete them by putting the insertion point on the first space of a blank line (the far left margin) and pressing the Backspace key.

 NOTE Just a reminder: once you've placed text (or any other information) on the Clipboard, you can reuse it as many times as you like because it stays on the Clipboard until you replace it with new information by using the Cut or Copy commands.

Moving Blocks Using the Right Mouse Button

In WordPad, clicking the right mouse button over the document pops up a shortcut menu offering immediate access to the most common editing commands, as shown in Figure 6.4.

FIGURE 6.4
WordPad's pop-up menu is displayed when you click the right mouse button.

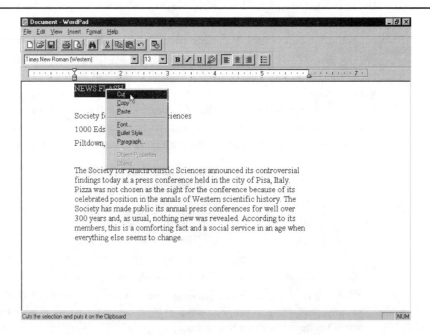

To use the shortcut menu to cut and paste, select the text to be cut, and then right-click it to open the menu, and choose Cut. Then reposition your insertion point where you want to insert, right-click that spot, and choose Paste from the shortcut menu.

For practice, use this method to move the NEWS FLASH text back to its original position in your sample document.

Copying Blocks of Text

When you want to move existing text to a new location without deleting the original, you need the Copy command. After selecting a block of text, use Copy instead of Cut to place a copy of the text on the Clipboard. Then move the cursor to the spot where you want the copy and paste it in. As usual, you have several alternatives for copying a selected block to the Clipboard:

- Click the Copy button.
- Click the right mouse button, and then choose Copy from the pop-up menu.
- Choose Edit ➢ Copy.
- Press Ctrl+C.

After you've copied the text to the Clipboard, you paste it in just as you would when moving a text block.

Formatting Paragraphs

Paragraphs are the most essential division of your text when it comes to *formatting*, which simply means controlling the appearance of your document. A paragraph is defined by WordPad as any text terminated by pressing the Enter key. So even a single letter, line, or word will be treated as a paragraph if you press Enter after typing it. For that matter, pressing Enter on a completely blank line creates a paragraph, albeit an empty one.

WordPad handles each paragraph as a separate entity, with its own formatting information. The press release you created early in the chapter uses a standard block-paragraph format typical of many business letters. In that format, a paragraph's first line is not indented, so you separate paragraphs with an empty paragraph. Also notice that the right margin is *ragged*, rather than aligned evenly—or *justified*—as it is on the left margin.

These, and other qualities affecting the appearance of your paragraphs, can be altered while you are entering text or at any time thereafter. As you change the format settings, you immediately see the effects. Bold letters will look bold, centered lines centered, italic letters look slanted, and so forth.

For most documents, you may find that you are satisfied with WordPad's default format. WordPad applies the standard default format for you, carrying it from one paragraph to the next as you type. If you decide you would rather use a different format for a new document, just alter some settings before typing anything. Then everything you type into the new document will be formatted accordingly until you change the settings again.

Adjusting Alignment

Alignment refers to where the text in a paragraph sits within the margins. *Left* is the default, causing text to be flush with the left margin (and ragged along the right margin). *Center* centers every line of the paragraph. *Right* causes text to be flush with the right margin (and ragged along the left margin).

To display or modify the settings for a given paragraph, click anywhere on it and then view or change the setting, either from the Formatting toolbar or from the Format Paragraph dialog box. Anytime you position the insertion point in a paragraph, the rulers and menu will reflect that paragraph's current settings.

NOTE WordPad does not permit you to create fully justified paragraphs; that is, paragraphs with text that is flush along both the right and left margins. If you want justified paragraphs, you'll need to use another word processor.

To see the current paragraph alignment setting, move the insertion point to the paragraph in question and click. If the Formatting toolbar is visible, you can simply look at the bar to see the alignment. The alignment buttons will indicate the current setting—the button for that setting looks like it has been pressed, as shown below. Click a different button to change the alignment.

Left aligned   Centered   Right aligned

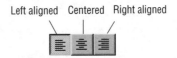

To change the setting for multiple paragraphs at once, select them first, and then change the alignment.

You can also see and change the current settings for a paragraph by displaying the Format Paragraph dialog box, shown in Figure 6.5. To open the Format Paragraph dialog box, choose Format ➢ Paragraph, or click the right mouse button with the pointer over the paragraph and then pick Paragraph from the pop-up menu. At the bottom of the Format Paragraph dialog box, you'll see the current paragraph's alignment setting. Change it if you desire.

FIGURE 6.5
The Format Paragraph dialog box, like the buttons in the Formatting toolbar, indicates the settings for the current paragraph.

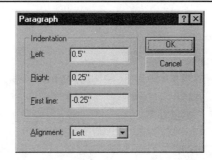

Creating Bulleted Paragraphs

One of the most common conventions in business and technical writing is the use of *bullets* to set off the items in a list. The standard bullet—and the one WordPad uses—is a heavy circular spot. But a bullet can be any symbol offset to the left of a paragraph. Bulleted text is useful for, and illustrated by, the following items:

- Calling attention to the individual benefits or features of a product or service

- Listing a set of options

- Itemizing the parts or supplies needed for a given job

WordPad can automatically add a bullet to any paragraph or to each paragraph in a selected block of text. WordPad places the bullet at the original left indent of the paragraph, shifting the rest of the paragraph to the right (the position changes are accomplished by adjusting the left indent and first-line indent settings, as you can see on the ruler).

To apply bullets to an unbulleted paragraph or group of paragraphs, place the cursor in the paragraph to be bulleted, or select a group of paragraphs and choose Format ➤ Bullet Style, or if the Formatting toolbar is visible, click the Bullet button shown here.

The Bullet Style command works as a toggle—if the paragraph already has a bullet, the Bullet command removes the bullet.

Formatting Characters

WordPad includes commands for altering the look of the individual letters on the printed page. This is called *character formatting*. You can use character formatting to emphasize a section of text by making it bold, underlined, or italicized, or you may want to change the size or the font.

NOTE As with all Windows programs, WordPad measures character sizes in *points*. Typical point sizes are from 9 to 14 for ordinary text. Newspaper headlines may appear in anything up to 60 points or so.

Just as with paragraph formatting, WordPad starts you off with a standard character format: a conventional, unobtrusive font (Times New Roman) at a standard size (10 points). But you can change character formatting to your heart's content. WordPad gives you three ways to modify character formatting:

- From the Formatting toolbar
- From the Fonts dialog box
- With shortcut Ctrl+key combinations to change type styles

You can change the formatting of individual characters, selected blocks of text, or the whole document. Character formatting applies to paragraphs as a whole only if the paragraphs are actually selected.

Formatting Existing Characters

To change the formatting of characters you've already typed, begin by selecting the text character(s) to be altered. You can select a single letter, a sentence, a paragraph, the whole document, or any arbitrary sequence of characters. Now you have three choices:

- Use the controls on the Formatting toolbar to alter individual format characteristics (font, size, and so forth). This is a quick way to control any aspect of character format.
- Use keyboard shortcuts to modify the text style (boldface, italics, or underlining). This is the quickest way to change these particular styles.
- Use the Fonts dialog box to set all the format characteristics from a single window. This lets you see a sample of how your text will look as you experiment with different formatting choices.

Here's how to use the Formatting toolbar to change character formatting:

1. If the Formatting toolbar isn't already visible, choose View ➤ Format Bar to display it.

2. To change the font of the selected text, choose the new font name from the drop-down list at the left side of the Formatting toolbar.

NOTE The icon next to the font name tells you whether it is a TrueType or Printer font. Note that the type of font you choose affects the range of available sizes. Scalable fonts, such as TrueType and PostScript (Type 1) fonts, can be used in virtually any size; other fonts have a set number of specific font sizes available.

3. To change the text size, pick a new size from the next list box or type in the size you want (WordPad only allows integer font sizes; fractional values won't work).

4. To turn styles (boldface, italics, or underlining) on or off, click the appropriate button. When the style is active, the appropriate button looks like it has been pressed.

5. To change the color of the selected text, click the button that displays an artist's palette and pick your color from the list that appears.

You can also use keyboard shortcuts (these are also toggles) to modify the character styles (bold, italics, and underlining) of a selected block, as follows:

- Ctrl+B for bold

- Ctrl+I for italics

- Ctrl+U for underlining

Note that you can change these settings in any combination. For example, a single selection can be italicized, underlined, and displayed in fuschia—if you're willing to take some serious liberties with typesetting etiquette.

After you've returned to your document and deselected the block, the Formatting toolbar shows you the current formatting of the character or selection. If the character or selection has been italicized, for example, the button for italics appears pushed.

 TIP You can see at a glance if a selected block contains more than one style, font, or font size. For example, if only part of the block is set to bold, the Formatting toolbar button for bold appears translucent. If the block contains two or more different fonts, the entry in the box for fonts will be blank.

The Fonts dialog box (Format ➤ Fonts) lets you see a sample of your character-formatting choices before you apply them. Otherwise, if your formatting experiments prove unsuccessful, you'll need to reset each setting for the selected block individually.

To modify character formatting with the Fonts dialog box, follow these steps:

1. With the text selected, choose Format ➤ Fonts or right-click and choose Fonts. You'll see the Fonts dialog box (see Figure 6.6).

2. In the dialog box, you can make changes to any of the character-formatting settings you wish.

3. When you're finished setting character formats, click OK.

FIGURE 6.6
Use the Fonts dialog box to change the character formatting for selected text.

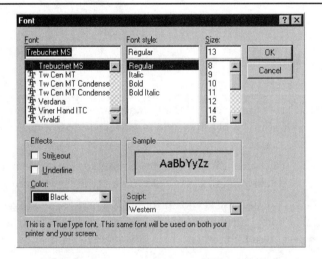

Formatting Characters as You Type

You can also change the appearance of text as you type. Subsequent characters will be entered with the new settings, and the settings will remain in effect until you change them.

For instance, you would press Ctrl+B once to start typing bold characters, and then you would press it again when you were ready to type more unbolded text. The same procedure applies to the other character formats.

Using Undo to Reverse Mistakes

WordPad makes allowances for our imperfections via the Undo command. In a split second, a slip of the mouse—choosing Clear instead of Cut—can send a large block of text to oblivion instead of to the Clipboard.

 Undo is, quite understandably, the first selection on the Edit menu. But you can access Undo even faster if the toolbar is visible. Just click the button showing an arrow with a curved stem.

Undo can reverse the following:

- Block deletions made with the Delete command from the Edit menu or the Delete key on the keyboard.

- Individual or multiple letters that you erased using the Delete or Backspace keys. Unfortunately, it will return only the last letter or series of letters erased. Once you move the cursor to another location using any of the cursor-movement keys and delete again, the text in the previous deletion is lost.

- Selected blocks directly deleted and replaced by typing new text on the keyboard.

- New text that you typed in. This can be undone back to the last time you issued a command.

- Character- and paragraph-formatting changes (if you select the Undo command immediately after making the change).

When you realize you've done something that you regret, select Edit ➢ Undo or click the Undo button on the toolbar. But remember, the Undo command can recall only the last action. If you decide you have made a mistake, either while entering or deleting, you must undo the damage before using any other editing or formatting commands.

Saving Your Work

WordPad stores your document in memory while you work on it. However, memory is not a permanent storage area; you will lose your work when you turn off your computer unless you first save it to disk.

You save your documents with two commands: File ➤ Save and File ➤ Save As. The first time you save a document, WordPad will ask you for a name to give your document—in this situation, the Save and Save As commands work the same. After the initial save, WordPad assumes you want to use the current name unless you indicate otherwise by using the Save As command.

Remember to save your work frequently. Nothing hurts like losing forever an afternoon's inspired writing. Taking a few moments to save your document every five or ten minutes is much easier on the psyche.

There are three ways to save a file: File ➤ Save, the Save button (the one with the picture of a floppy disk, shown here) and the Ctrl+S key combination.

No matter which of these methods you use to start the process, the Save As dialog box, shown in Figure 6.7, appears because this is the first time you've saved this file.

FIGURE 6.7

The Save As dialog box appears when you choose to save a file. After making sure the drive and folder are correct, type in the filename.

WordPad has assigned a generic name, Document, but you can change it. Finish saving your file as follows:

1. Type in a more descriptive name in the File Name box.

2. Ensure that the correct drive and directory are selected.

3. If you wish to change the type of file you'll be saving, do so by picking a new choice from the Save as Type drop-down list box.

4. Click OK.

The Save as Type drop-down list box is normally set to store your document in the Word for Windows 6.0 format. Different programs use different coding systems, or *formats,* to store the document's text, its character and paragraph formatting, any graphics or other objects, and other miscellaneous information. You shouldn't alter this setting unless you want to create a document that other word processors or other types of programs can read.

NOTE There are two distinct uses for the term *format*: It can refer to the way a document is stored in a disk file or to the appearance of text in a document.

Opening Other Documents

Once a WordPad document has been saved on disk, you can come back to it at any future time. To *open* a document—moving the information stored on disk into RAM so you can work with it again—use the Open command.

Keep in mind that in WordPad, unlike fancier word processors, you can only work with one document at a time. When you open a document, it replaces the one you were working with, if any. If you want to keep the changes you made in a document, you must save that document before opening a new one. But don't worry—WordPad will remind you to save before it lets you open another document.

 As usual, you have several options for opening existing documents: choose File ➣ Open, press Ctrl+O, or click the Open button (the one with a picture of a file folder opening) on the toolbar.

Regardless of which technique you use, you'll see the Open dialog box (Figure 6.8). After listing any subfolders, this dialog box shows you all the files in the current directory matching the setting in the Files of Type drop-down list box. Unless someone has changed the entry, you'll see a list of all files stored in the Word for Windows format, WordPad's preferred format.

FIGURE 6.8
The Open dialog box enables you to select a file to open in WordPad.

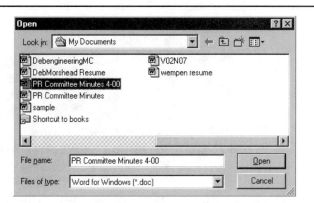

To open a document, double-click it in the list or click once on the document and then click Open. At this point, if you haven't already saved the previous document, WordPad asks if you want to do so. Choose Yes or No, as you prefer.

Although WordPad's standard format for storing documents on disk is the Word for Windows 6.0 format, WordPad can also open documents stored in several other formats including the following:

- Windows Write format (Write was a simple word processor included with earlier versions of Windows)

- Rich Text Format

- Text-only files (regular, MS-DOS Text, or Unicode Text)

If you know the format of the document you want to open, select that format in the Files of Type drop-down list box. If you're unsure of the format, choose All Files instead, and WordPad will display all the files in the current directory. Once you locate the correct document in the list, double-click it to open it.

Changing Display Options

You have some choices about the way the WordPad window looks and works. As you learned earlier, the View menu lets you turn on or off any of the individual control bars: the Standard toolbar, the Formatting toolbar, the ruler, and the Status bar. Other display options are available via the Options dialog box.

To open the Options dialog box, choose View ➢ Options. You'll see the dialog box shown in Figure 6.9.

The Options dialog box is tabbed. One tab covers general options; the remaining tabs apply to the various document types (file formats) that WordPad can handle.

FIGURE 6.9
The Options dialog box lets you set measurement units for the ruler and for spacing settings, among other choices.

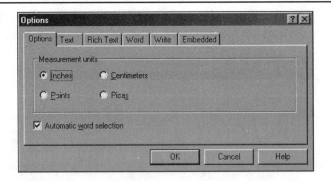

Aside from the tab labeled Options, the other tabs in the Options dialog box pertain to the various types of documents that WordPad can open—Word for Windows 6.0, Windows Write, Rich Text Format, and text-only files, as well as WordPad documents embedded via Object Linking and Embedding (OLE) in other documents. Each of these pages offer identical choices, as shown in Figure 6.10.

FIGURE 6.10
The Options dialog box offers these choices for each type of file WordPad can handle.

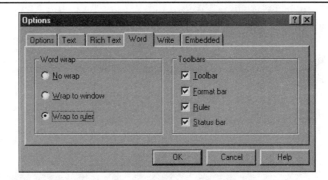

The check boxes on the right let you select which of the control bars (the toolbar, Formatting toolbar, ruler, and Status bar) WordPad will display automatically when you open a document of the type indicated by the tab.

On the left side of each tabbed panel are radio buttons for selecting the way Word-Pad wraps your text from line to line on the screen. Note that none of these choices affects the way your document prints:

No Wrap   If this button is selected, WordPad doesn't wrap your text at all. As you add text anywhere within a line, the line keeps expanding toward the right, regardless of the right indent and right margin settings. On printed copies, the text still wraps according to the indent and margin settings.

Wrap to Window   With this button selected, WordPad wraps the text to fit within the document window, ignoring the right indent and margin settings. Choose this setting to see all your text, even when the WordPad window is narrower than the paragraph width set by the ruler. Again, this doesn't affect printed documents.

Wrap to Ruler   When this button is selected, the displayed text wraps according to the right indent and right margin settings as shown on the ruler (whether or not the ruler is visible).

Printing Your Documents

Generally speaking, the ultimate goal of all your typing and formatting is a printed copy of your document. Printing a WordPad document is a straightforward process. Like the major-league word processors, WordPad lets you see a preview of your document as it will appear in print, and you can fix your mistakes before they appear on paper.

Previewing a Document

Instead of wasting paper on a document with an obvious layout mistake, use Word-Pad's Print Preview command to inspect your work before you print. This command displays your document on screen just as it will look when printed. You can look at entire pages to check the overall layout or zoom in on a particular portion to check details.

To see a preview, choose File ➢ Print Preview, or click the Print Preview button in the toolbar—it's the button with the picture of a magnifying glass over a sheet of paper, shown here.

The WordPad window fills with a mock-up of your document, fitting two full pages into the available space, as shown in Figure 6.11. A special toolbar offers quick access to a number of special commands, and the mouse pointer becomes a magnifying glass.

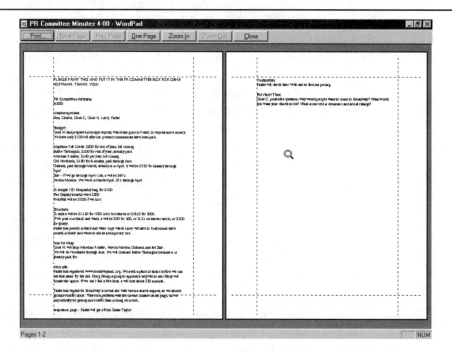

At this level of magnification, you can't read ordinary-size text, but you can check for problems with page margins, paragraph alignment, and spacing. Clicking anywhere on the document window changes the magnification, cycling through the three available levels. Starting from the full-page view, the first click zooms you in on the portion of the page you clicked on, the second gives you a life-size close-up of a still smaller area, and the third click returns you to the full-page view. You can also change the magnification by clicking the Zoom In or Zoom Out buttons in the toolbar.

To page through the mock-up of your document, click the Next Page button. You can move back toward the beginning with the Prev Page button. To display only a single page of the document instead of two, click the One Page button. You can switch back to the two-page view by clicking the same button, which will now read Two Page. You can also page through the mock-up with the PgUp and PgDn keys.

When you're satisfied that the document looks as you expected, click the Print button to begin the actual printing process, covered in the next section. On the other hand, if you find mistakes, click the Close button to return to editing the document.

Printing

When you are about ready to print, don't forget to save your file first just in case the computer or the printer goes berserk in the process and you lose your file. If you want to print only a portion of your document, select that portion. And don't forget to turn on the printer and make sure it has paper and is ready to print (in other words, that it is *online*).

First, choose File ➢ Page Setup, and check that paper size and paper source are correctly set (as shown in Figure 6.12). Notice that you can print envelopes via this setting.

FIGURE 6.12
Set your page margins in the Page Setup dialog box.

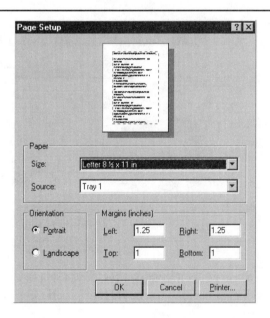

Then choose File ➢ Print, press Ctrl+P, or click the Print button from the Print Preview window. You'll be presented with a dialog box asking you about the following options, as shown in Figure 6.13:

Name (of Printer)   If the printer you plan to use isn't already chosen in this box, choose it from the drop-down list of your installed printers.

Properties This button takes you to the Printer Properties dialog box for the selected printer. From this dialog box, you can choose the paper orientation (portrait or landscape), paper size and feed, print quality (for text) and resolution (for graphics), and other options available for your printer. See the discussion of printer properties in Chapter 11, "Printers and Printing," for details.

Print Range If you want to print all the pages, click All. If you want to print specific pages only, click Pages and type in the range of page numbers you want to print in the From and To boxes. If you want to print only text that you selected, click Selection.

Copies Specify the number of copies of each page to be printed.

Collate Choose whether each complete copy should be printed one at a time, in page order (more convenient but slower), or all copies of each page should be printed before moving onto the next page (quicker but requires you to hand collate). This option applies only if you're printing more than one copy of the document.

FIGURE 6.13
Select printing options in the Print dialog box.

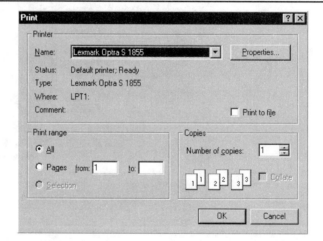

When you've made your choices, press Enter or click OK. If the printer is connected and working properly, you should have a paper copy of your document in a few moments.

 TIP If you're sure the settings in the Print dialog box are already correct and you want a copy of the entire document, you can streamline the printing process via the toolbar's Print button—it's the one showing the picture of a printer ejecting a page. When you click the Print button, WordPad immediately begins sending your document to the printer.

Creating Simple Artwork with Paint

Paint is a program for the artist in you. It's a simple, but quite capable, program for painting and drawing images on your computer screen, and, optionally, printing them out. You can brush on colors free-form, draw lines and geometric shapes, and even add text to your pictures. A variety of nifty special effects are at your command, too.

Here are some ideas for things you can do with Paint:

- Create printed signs.
- Create illustrations for printed matter.
- Create images for use in other Windows programs.
- Design invitations.
- Enhance digitized images or photographs.
- Draw maps.
- Make wallpaper images for your Windows Desktop.
- Edit clip art (pre-drawn images you can buy in collections).
- Clean up "digital dust" from scanned images.

Starting Paint

To bring up Paint, choose Start ➢ Programs ➢ Accessories ➢ Paint. The Paint window appears. Figure 6.14 shows the Paint window. You will probably want to maximize the window if it is not maximized already.

The *work area* is the main part of the window where you do your painting. Along the left side, the *Tool Box* provides a set of buttons for activating the tools you use to paint. You choose colors from the *Color Box* at the bottom of the window. The Status bar offers help messages on menu choices and displays the coordinates of the mouse pointer.

FIGURE 6.14
The Paint window

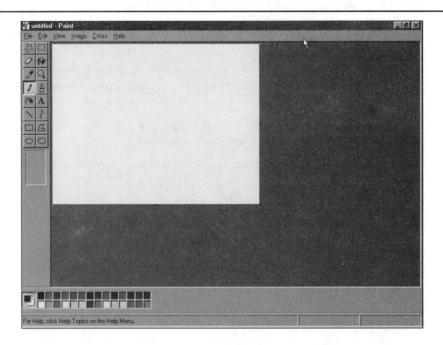

Setting a Picture's Basic Characteristics

Before you actually start painting, decide whether you want to change any of Paint's standard settings governing the picture's basic characteristics: its size and whether it's a color or black-and-white image. To change the settings for either of these characteristics, choose Image ➢ Attributes to display the Attributes dialog box shown below.

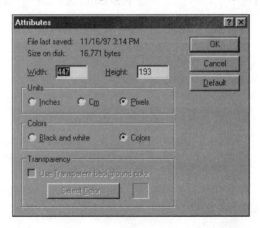

The first thing you should decide when starting a new picture is how big it should be. If you're creating a picture to fit snugly into another document, or if you have an idea of how much room you'll need to express your ideas, defining the picture's size now may save you some work down the road. It's easy to change the size of a picture, so don't spend much time on this decision.

Keep in mind that the size of the image you see is tied to the resolution of your screen. Actually, the size settings control only the number of dots in the picture (even though you can set the size in inches or centimeters in the Attributes dialog box). If you increase the resolution of your screen (see Chapter 10, " Customizing the Desktop, Taskbar, and Start Menu"), the picture will look smaller because each component dot is smaller.

Likewise, the image will almost certainly print smaller than it appears on your screen because most printers have much higher resolution than even an SVGA monitor.

 NOTE When you change the size of a picture, Paint remembers the new dimensions. From then on—until you make further size changes—Paint uses these dimensions whenever you choose File ➢ New to create a new picture. This is true even if you open other larger or smaller pictures in the meantime.

You can resize a picture with the mouse or by typing entries in the Attributes dialog box. Using the mouse is easier if the entire picture fits in the work area, but many pictures are bigger than that. Besides, whereas the mouse isn't very accurate, you can type exact dimensions. At any rate, you use the same resizing techniques whether you're working with a brand new picture or an existing one.

To set the size of your picture with the Attributes dialog box:

1. Choose Image ➢ Attributes. The Attributes dialog box appears.

2. Decide on the measurement units you want to use and click the corresponding radio button. Pixels (screen dots) is the standard unit, but you can choose inches or centimeters instead.

3. Type in new width and height values. You can return at any time to the standard size values—equal to the size of your screen—by clicking Default.

4. Click OK to return to Paint. The size of your canvas will change according to your entries, though you can only see this if the entire canvas fits within the work area.

Take these steps to resize a picture with the mouse:

1. Find the picture's sizing handles, the small squares at the bottom-right corner of the picture and along the bottom and right edges. If the picture is larger than the work area, you'll have to scroll down or to the right to see the sizing handles. (The handles at the other three corners and along the other edges do nothing.)

2. To change the picture's width, drag the handle on the right edge to the left (to make the picture narrower) or to the right (to make the picture wider). To change the height, drag the bottom-edge handle up or down. To change both dimensions simultaneously, drag the handle at the lower-right corner.

Opening an Existing Picture

To open an existing picture for editing, do the following:

1. Choose File ➤ Open.

2. Select the picture by name in the Open dialog box. Windows Me comes with several BMP files scattered around through various folders. I used the Start ➤ Search ➤ For Files or Folders command to find one. I entered *.BMP as the "named" section of the Find box and found 953 BMP files. I found the file open in Figure 6.15 in my C:\Windows folder.

Now you can edit the picture and save it again or copy any part of it to the Clipboard for use with other programs.

 NOTE Paint remembers the last four pictures you've opened or saved, listing them by name at the bottom of the File menu. To open one of these pictures without slowing down for the Open dialog box, just choose the picture from the File menu.

FIGURE 6.15
A picture file opened and displayed in the work area

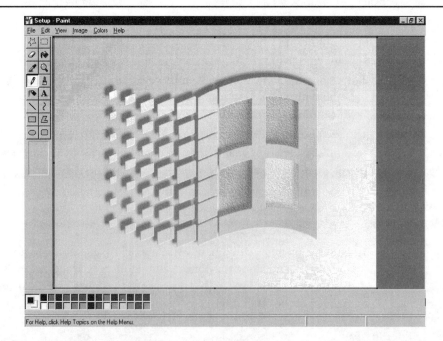

Paint can open pictures stored in its own format (also known as the BMP format), and also in JPG and GIF format. If you want to open pictures stored in other formats, such as PCX or TIF, you'll have to translate them to the BMP format with conversion software first. Paint can save only in BMP format.

Setting the Foreground and Background Colors

The *foreground* or *drawing* color is the main color you paint with. For example, when you add strokes with Paint's paintbrush, draw lines or shapes, or even when you type text, these items appear in the currently selected foreground color.

 NOTE The term *color* describes either a color or a colored pattern selected from the Color Box. If you are using a black-and-white screen, colors in the Color Box may appear as shades of gray or varying densities of dot patterns.

The *background* color is somewhat different. Once you have a picture on your screen, many of the tools (such as the Brush, Pencil, and the shape tools) let you paint with the so-called background color just as you would with the foreground color. All you have to do is hold down the *right* mouse button instead of the left one as you paint. The background color also determines the fill color for circles, squares, and other enclosed shapes, the fill color inside text frames, and the color with which you erase existing parts of the picture. If you select a section of the picture and drag it to another location, the resulting "hole" will be filled with the background color. You can change the background color as many times as you like.

The current settings of the foreground and background colors are shown in the area at the left side of the Color Box. In this area, the box on top, toward the upper left, shows the foreground color. The box in back, toward the lower right, shows the background color. The default colors are a black foreground on a white background, and they always come up that way when you open a new or existing picture.

To set the foreground color, click the left mouse button on the color you want. To set the background color, click the right mouse button on a color.

 WARNING You can't change the color of an existing picture's actual background by changing the background color with the Color Box.

TIP If you want to start a new picture with a certain color as the "canvas," here's how. Before painting anything on the picture, choose the correct background color and click anywhere over the work area with the Paint Can tool, described below. The entire picture area will change to that color. Now start painting. Alternatively, after choosing the desired background color, draw anything in the work area, then choose Image ➤ Clear Image.

An alternative technique for selecting colors is the Eyedropper tool. The Eyedropper lets you "suck up" a color that already appears in the picture. That color becomes the new foreground or background color for use with any of the painting tools. Here's how to use the Eyedropper:

1. Click the Eyedropper tool in the Tool Box.

2. In the picture, click over the desired color with the left button to select it as the foreground color; use the right button to make it the background color. The Color Box display changes accordingly.

You can now paint with the chosen color using any of the painting tools as detailed in the next section.

Using the Painting Tools

Here's a brief description of how each of the tools in the Tool Box works:

1. Click the tool you want to use.

2. Position the pointer in the work area where you want to start painting, selecting, or erasing, and then click and hold the mouse button.

3. Drag to paint, select, or erase. Release the mouse button when you are through.

Paint's Tool Box offers a slew of useful controls to help you realize your artistic vision. Here's the Tool Box with the Air Brush button selected:

To choose a tool, you simply click its button in the Tool Box. The tool is then activated (and highlighted), and the pointer changes shape when you move back into the work area. In most cases, the tool stays selected until you choose another one.

When some of the tools are selected, the area below the grid of buttons provides options for the selected tool. The options are different for each tool. For example, if you're drawing with the Line tool, you can choose how thick the line should be by clicking an icon in this area. Or, with the Airbrush tool, shown above, the width of the spray can be selected. If there are no options associated with a tool, this area is empty.

The following sections will describe each of the painting tools.

Brush

The Brush is the basic painting tool. It works like a paint brush, pen, or marker. Use this tool to create freehand art.

With the Brush, you can paint in either the foreground or the background color, switching between the two by simply changing which mouse button you press. All of the painting tools that add lines, strokes, or enclosed shapes work this way.

Here's how to use the Brush:

1. In the Color Box, select the foreground and background colors you want to paint with by clicking them with the left button and right buttons, respectively.

2. Choose the Brush tool in the Tool Box.

3. Pick a size and shape for your brush from the tool options area in the bottom of the Tool Box. The diagonal brush shapes produce lines that vary in width depending on which direction you move the brush—it's a calligraphic pen effect.

4. Move the pointer over the work area so it becomes a crosshair. Press and hold the left button to paint with the foreground color, the right button to paint with the background color. Paint by dragging the mouse around in the work area. Release the button when you want to stop painting. Repeat the process as often as you like.

In Figure 6.16, you can see a simple design created with the brush.

FIGURE 6.16

A freehand design made with the brush

TIP The status bar reports the location of the cursor while you draw. This can be useful for doing precision work. A second readout farther to the left is only active when you're drawing shapes such as boxes, ellipses, and polygons or when you're selecting an area of the picture. This set of coordinates tells you where the mouse pointer is relative to the location where you started drawing the shape or where you began selecting.

Pencil

The Pencil works much like the Brush for freehand art, except that it only paints lines that are one dot (pixel) wide.

You can produce essentially the same effect with the Brush by choosing the smallest circular shape for the Brush (at the top right of the Brush-shape display), but the Pencil is often a convenient way to draw fine lines freehand while leaving the brush for wider swaths.

You can force the Pencil to draw straight vertical, horizontal, or diagonal lines, something you can't do with the Brush. After selecting the Pencil tool, hold down the Shift key while you drag the mouse. The direction you initially move establishes the line's direction—as long as you hold down Shift, you can only lengthen the line, not change directions (this is different from the way the Line tool works, as described below).

Eraser

The Eraser works like the eraser on a pencil—only you don't have to rub. Just drag it across an area (with the left mouse button held down), and it erases whatever it touches, leaving nothing but the background color behind. Use the Eraser whether you want to obliterate a major section of your picture or just touch up some stray dots or lines.

You can change the size of the eraser by clicking one of the squares below the toolbox when the Eraser tool is selected.

 TIP Even the smallest Eraser size covers more than a single dot in your picture. To erase (change) individual dots, use the Pencil tool (see the next section), setting the foreground color to the desired erasure color.

Airbrush

Here's a tool that's a legal outlet for repressed graffiti artists.

The Airbrush works like the real thing, or like a spray can, spraying a mist of paint that gets thicker the longer you hold it one place. Think of the mouse button as the button on the top of the spray can. Just set the foreground and background colors, click the Airbrush tool, move into the picture area and start spraying. You can choose a spray width below the toolbox.

 TIP Moving the mouse quickly results in a finer mist, while letting it sit still or moving very slowly plasters the paint on.

Line

Use the Line tool to draw straight lines (and only straight lines). You have five line widths to select from.

 TIP Hold the Shift key down to force the line to be vertical, horizontal, or at a 45-degree angle.

Below is an example of a drawing made up only of lines.

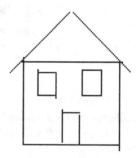

Curve

Use the Curve tool for drawing curves, of course. But don't expect to master this tool quickly—it will seem downright strange at first. Start by laying down a straight line, just like you would with the Line tool. Then you get two chances to "stretch" that line into a curve—once from one location and once from another. The result might be an arc, an *S* curve, or even a pretzely shape. You do this by clicking any part of the line and dragging the crosshair cursor around. The line will stretch like a rubber band. Release the button when the bend is correct.

Rectangle

The Rectangle tool draws boxes. You can draw three types of boxes: hollow boxes with borders only; filled, bordered boxes; and solid boxes without borders. Choose the option from the toolbar after you click the tool. Here are the steps to follow in order to create a box:

1. Click where you want one corner of the box to start. This sets the anchor.
2. Drag the crosshair down and to one side. As you do, a rectangular outline will appear.
3. Release the mouse button when the size is correct.

TIP If you draw with the right button instead, the border and interior colors are reversed. This applies to the other tools for drawing enclosed shapes as well.

TIP To constrain boxes to be perfect squares, hold down the Shift key as you draw. This applies to filled boxes as well as to hollow ones.

Rounded Rectangle

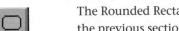

The Rounded Rectangle tool works exactly like the regular Rectangle tool described in the previous section, but it creates boxes with rounded corners, rather than crisp right angles.

Ellipse

This tool also works just like the Rectangle tool, except that it creates ellipses (ovals).

Use the same basic drawing technique. The rules regarding the fill and border colors of boxes apply to ellipses, too. Here are some bubble-like objects created with the Ellipse tool. The perfect circles were created by holding down the Shift key while drawing with the Ellipse tool.

Polygon

With the Polygon tool you can create an endless variety of polygonal shapes.

As with the Line tool, you manually draw straight lines—the difference being that you keep adding endpoints until you complete the polygon's edges.

TIP To constrain any line of the polygon to be vertical, at 45 degrees, or horizontal only, hold down the Shift key as you draw.

Here are the steps to follow to make a polygon:

1. If you're drawing a bordered polygon, select the Line tool and choose a line width for the border.

2. Then choose the polygon tool and choose the type of polygon you want to draw (border only, filled and bordered, or solid with no border).

3. Click and hold the button down. Drag the mouse pointer to the endpoint for the side and release the button. The line you've drawn defines the first side of the polygon.

4. Press and hold the mouse button again as you drag to the endpoint of the next side (or just click over this next endpoint). Paint draws the second side. Continue adding sides in this way, but *double-click* to mark the endpoint of the next-to-the-last side (for example, the fourth side of a pentangle). Paint connects this endpoint with the original anchor point, filling in the polygon if appropriate.

 NOTE A polygon's sides can cross. You can haphazardly click all over the screen, and, until you double-click, Paint will keep connecting the dots regardless.

You can create a cubist artistic effect with this tool because of the way Paint calculates an enclosed area. It starts at the top of the screen and begins filling areas. If your polygon has a lot of enclosed areas from multiple lines overlapping, Paint alternates the fills. Thus adjacent enclosed areas will not all be filled. Using the tool with the cut-out tools and the Invert command can lead to some rather interesting geometrical designs.). Figure 6.17 shows an example of the possibilities.

FIGURE 6.17
A geometric design created with the Polygon tool using filled polygons

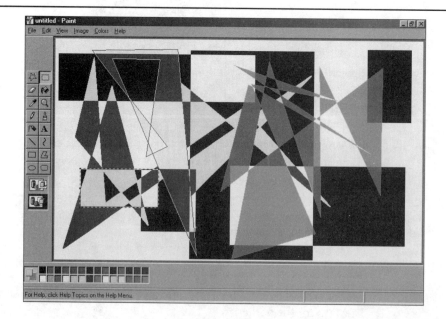

Paint Can

The Paint Can will fill in any enclosed area with the foreground color. An *enclosed area* can be defined by any lines or curves in the work area. So three separate lines set up to form a triangle constitute an enclosed space just as much as a box's border does. Because the entire work area is also considered an enclosed space, you can use the Paint Can to change the background of the picture. Letters you create with the Text tool (discussed next) can be filled, too. Just point the tip of the spilling paint into the area to be filled and click. The enclosed area will be filled with the foreground color if you click with the left button, with the background color if you click with the right.

Note that the color flows to fill the entire enclosed area. If there is a "leak" in what you thought was an enclosed area, the paint will seep through the crack, so to speak, and fill everything until it is stopped by a complete boundary. You may accidentally fill the entire work area. If this happens, just choose Undo.

Text

The Text tool lets you add words to your pictures, which is great when you're designing flyers, invitations, maps, instructions, and the like. This is a good tool for annotating pictures created in other programs. (Kodak Imaging is good for this, too.)

You can add text in two ways: as text only, so that only the characters you type are added to your picture; and as text on a solid rectangular background that covers up whatever was there in the picture. These two styles are also called *transparent* and *opaque*. Follow these steps to insert text into your Paint file:

1. Choose the color for the text by clicking in the Color Box with the left button (text always appears in the selected foreground color). If you plan to add opaque text (on a solid-color background), choose the color for the background by clicking it with the right button.

2. Choose the Text tool in the Tool Box.

3. In the tool-options area at the bottom of the Tool Box, choose the icon for opaque or transparent text. The top one turns on the opaque style.

4. Draw your text frame using either mouse button. When you let go, handles appear on the dashed rectangular frame at the corners and along the edges, and, if you chose the opaque text style, the frame fills with the background color. The Fonts toolbar (also known as the Text toolbar) appears. Figure 6.18 shows a text frame and the Fonts/Text toolbar.

TIP You can resize or reposition this frame, change color, or change the font type and size at any time until you finalize your text entry by clicking outside the text box.

FIGURE 6.18
The Paint Fonts toolbar,
which serves as the Text
tool's toolbar.

5. Choose the font, size, and styles for your text from the Text toolbar. You can use bold, italic, and underline in any combination.

 TIP If the Text toolbar isn't visible, choose View ➤ Text Toolbar to restore it to the screen.

6. Click again over the new text frame to make the insertion-point cursor reappears. Now type whatever you like. When your text reaches the right edge of the text frame, Paint wraps down to the next line. You can use standard Windows text-editing techniques to move the insertion point, select characters or words, and cut, copy, and paste.

7. As long as the rectangular outline of the text frame remains on the screen, you can change its size and location and the colors of the text and the frame background, and edit the text:

To resize the frame   Drag any of the handles, the little squares at the corners and along the sides of the frame. The mouse pointer becomes a double-headed arrow when it's directly over a handle, indicating that you can move the handle.

To move the frame   Drag any part of the frame outline that isn't a handle. The mouse pointer becomes an arrow when it's over the outline. As you drag, a solid gray rectangle represents the moving frame, which appears at the new location when you release the button.

To change colors   On the Color Box, click the left button to change the color of the text, and click the right button to change the frame background's color. You can also switch between a transparent and opaque text frame by clicking the appropriate icon in the tool-options area or by choosing Image ➤ Draw Opaque.

8. Click outside the text frame to finalize your text entry. You can no longer edit the text.

Selecting an Area

The Tool Box offers two tools for selecting specific portions of a picture for further manipulation. Appropriately enough, they're collectively called the *selection tools*.

They are the top two buttons on the Tool Box. The one on the left with the star-shaped outline is for selecting irregular shapes; it's called the Free-Form Selection tool. The one on the right with the rectangular outline, the Select tool, is for selecting rectangular areas.

Once you've selected an area with either tool, you can cut, copy, and paste it, or drag it around in the picture. You can also perform many other manipulations on a selection, such as inverting its colors or rotating it.

Selecting Rectangular Areas

The easiest way to select an area—or define a cutout, if you prefer—is with the Select tool, the one with the dotted rectangular outline at the top right of the Tool Box.

All you have to do is take the following steps:

1. Select the Select tool (how's that for computerized English?).

2. Move to the upper-left corner of the boxed area you want to select. Click and hold down the left mouse button.

3. Drag the mouse down and to the right. As you draw, a dotted rectangular outline indicates the selection area.

4. Release the button. After a moment, the dotted outline appears, indicating the selection.

> ⚠ **TIP** Don't use the handles to redefine the selection area—they're for resizing the image within the area.

Once you've selected an area, it remains selected until you click outside the dotted outline around it (the *selection rectangle*) or until you choose another tool.

Selecting Irregular Areas

The Free-Form Select tool lets you select any area of the picture by drawing a line free-hand around the area.

It allows you to select exactly the part of the picture you're after, hugging the edges of the element that interests you, and avoiding others you want to leave unaffected. As you hold the mouse button down, draw a line completely around the area. If you make a mistake in defining the selection, press the right mouse button and make the selection again. When you're through, Paint displays a dotted rectangular outline large enough to contain the entire selection, even though the irregular shape is all that is selected.

Moving a Selected Area

Once you've selected an area, the simplest thing you can do with it is to move it elsewhere in the picture. All you have to do is drag it where you want it to go: Press the left mouse button down anywhere within the selection or cutout, move to the new location, and release the button. Below, I've adjusted the letters in the word Plain:

Even after dragging, an item remains selected until you click outside the selection rectangle; this is so you can move it again or perform other manipulations.

 TIP If you previously changed the background color for an interim operation, be sure to change it back to the "real" background color, or you'll get a shape of an unwanted color in your picture left behind when you drag the selection.

To move a *copy* of the selection, leaving the original in place, just hold down the Ctrl key while you drag the cutout to its new home. This is a good trick for duplicating any shape quickly.

Opaque vs. Transparent Placement

When you move a selection by dragging it, you can choose between *opaque* and *transparent* placement at the new location. In opaque placement, the selection will completely replace whatever you place it on top of in the picture—nothing of what was previously there will show through.

In transparent placement, the selection's background disappears, so only the foreground elements in the selection appear at the new location. But this only works if you select the background color of the selection as the background color in the Color Box (by clicking in the Color Box with the right button). Select the correct background color before you move the selection.

Sweeping

Sweeping a selection is a neat trick that deposits multiple copies of the cutout (selection) across the picture as you move the mouse. You can use this technique to suggest motion of an object or to create interesting artistic effects:

Just as when you move a single copy of a selection, you can do opaque or transparent sweeping. Again, the background color of the cutout and the current background color have to be the same for transparent sweeping to work as you'd expect. Just drag the selection while holding the Shift key down. Copies of the cutout are made as you drag the cursor around.

Using the Clipboard with Selections

Paint uses the Windows Clipboard just like any other program does. You can copy and paste stuff to and from a Paint picture. You can also move parts of your picture around using the Windows Clipboard as an alternative to dragging it around. It's usually easier to drag, but if you want to paste the item a number of times, or cut a design from one picture, then open another picture and paste it in, use the Clipboard.

To cut or copy a selection to the Clipboard, define the area with one of the Selection tools, then choose Edit ➢ Cut or Edit ➢ Copy, or just press the standard Windows keyboard shortcuts for these commands (Ctrl-X and Ctrl-C, respectively). Paste the contents with Edit ➢ Paste, or Ctrl-V. It appears in the upper-right corner of the screen as a selection. Then drag it where you want it.

 NOTE When you cut a selection to the Clipboard, Paint fills in the space left behind with the currently selected background color.

Saving and Retrieving a Selection

You can save a selection as a disk file for later use. Using this technique, you can create a stockpile of little graphics (like clip art) that you can call up from disk to drop into new pictures. Here are the steps to save and retrieve a selection:

1. Define the selection with either of the selection tools.

2. Choose Edit ➢ Copy To. A file box pops up. Name the file as you wish.

3. When you want to reload the cutout, choose Edit ➢ Load From and click the picture file containing the selection from the file box. It will appear in the upper-left corner of the current picture on screen.

4. Reposition the selection by dragging it.

Saving Your Work in Paint

If you're painting for posterity—or at least have some use in mind for your work other than doodling—remember to save your work to disk regularly. Of course, you can open pictures you've worked on before for further editing—or just to admire them.

You can save pictures as disk files in several formats, all of them variations of the basic Paint (BMP) format. Normally, you can just let Paint choose the correct format for you. But there may be times when knowing which format to use comes in handy.

Here are the available formats and their descriptions:

Monochrome bitmap Use when you have only two colors (black and white) in your picture.

16-color bitmap Use when you have 16 colors or fewer in your picture.

256-color bitmap Use when you have more than 16 and fewer than 257 colors in your picture.

24-bit bitmap Use when you have more than 256 colors in the picture.

Why change a picture's format? Here's the most common reason: you have a picture and you like its design, but it looks cartoonish because it has too few colors. By saving it in a format with more colors, you'll be able to modify it with a much richer, more realistic color palette. But this only works if your screen can display the additional colors and is set up in Control Panel to do so (see Chapter 10 for instructions). Note that the more colors you save, the larger the files become and the more disk and RAM space they'll need.

 WARNING Saving a picture with a format that has fewer colors may ruin it. When you save (for example, if you save a picture with 16 colors as a monochrome bitmapped file), Paint translates each color in the original picture into the closest match in the new format. Clearly, you're likely to lose a significant amount of detail, especially when going to the monochrome format—the picture may well come out looking like a sea of black with a few white dots, or vice versa.

TIP After you've saved a new picture, or if you're working with a picture you opened from disk, Paint can tell Windows to use the picture as wallpaper. From then on, the picture will appear as the backdrop for your Windows Desktop. Just choose File ➢ Set as Wallpaper (Tiled). If want the whole screen filled with multiple copies of the image. Choose File ➢ Set as Wallpaper (Centered) if you want a single copy of the image centered on the Desktop.

Printing in Paint

Finally, you might want to print out your artwork! Here's how you do it:

1. Open the picture document, if it's not already open.

2. Turn on the printer and get it ready to print.

3. If you want to change the page margins or paper orientation, choose File ➢ Page Setup and make the necessary entries in the dialog box.

4. To see how the picture will look on the printed page, choose File ➢ Print Preview. You'll see a mock-up of the printed page on your screen. This works exactly like the Print Preview function in WordPad.

5. When you're ready to print, choose File ➢ Print, or, from Print Preview, click the Print button. The standard Windows Print dialog box will appear, allowing you to choose the correct printer, specify which pages should print and how many copies, and change the printer's settings (by clicking the Properties button).

CHAPTER 7

Other Windows Accessories

The last chapter covered WordPad and Paint, two of the most popular accessory programs in Windows Me. In this chapter, you'll learn about the other accessories included with Windows. These accessories are fairly modest programs, but each is genuinely useful in its special niche. If you take the time to acquaint yourself with their basic functions, you'll know where to turn when you need help with a problem they can solve.

 NOTE As you may have noticed by now, quite a few programs and utilities came along with Windows Me. Clicking Start ➤ Programs ➤ Accessories and then choosing Communications, Entertainment, Accessibility, Internet Tools, or System Tools will reveal many selections. The number of selections you have depends on what's been installed on your machine from the Windows Me CD. (See Chapter 13, "Adding and Removing Hardware and Software," for how to add Windows components.)

Accessory Roundup

Once you've learned the basic navigation in Windows—running programs, managing files, and so on—you are finished "learning Windows." I'll bet you didn't know it was as simple as that, eh? All that remains in your Windows education is to master the accessory programs.

However, mastering all the accessories is not as simple as it sounds. Windows comes with a wide variety of accessory programs; in fact, almost all of the remainder of this book is devoted to accessories of one type or another. There are accessories that configure hardware, accessories that entertain you, accessories that perform system maintenance, and many more types.

This chapter starts the ball rolling by discussing some of the more common, general-purpose accessories (in addition to WordPad and Paint, of course), but it's only the beginning. The following directory shows where in the book each accessory program is covered.

- This chapter covers the following general accessories:
  - Notepad
  - Imaging
  - Calculator
  - Character Map
  - Clipboard Viewer

- Phone Dialer
- Games
- System accessories are covered in Part II:
  - ScanDisk—Chapter 14
  - System Information—Chapter 14
  - Resource Meter—Chapter 14
  - System Monitor—Chapter 14
  - System Restore—Chapter 14
  - Disk Cleanup—Chapter 15
  - Disk Defragmenter—Chapter 15
  - DriveSpace—Chapter 15
  - Maintenance Wizard—Chapter 15
  - Scheduled Tasks—Chapter 15
- Multimedia accessories are covered in Part III:
  - Windows Media Player—Chapter 16
  - Scanner and Camera Wizard—Chapter 17
  - Windows Movie Maker—Chapter 17
  - Sound Recorder—Chapter 18
  - Volume Control—Chapter 18
- Internet accessories are covered in Part IV:
  - HyperTerminal—Chapter 19
  - Internet Connection Wizard—Chapter 20
  - Internet Explorer—Chapter 21
  - Outlook Express—Chapter 22
  - Web Publishing Wizard—Chapter 23
  - NetMeeting—Supplement 1 on the accompanying CD-ROM
- Networking accessories are covered in Part V:
  - Home Networking Wizard—Chapter 24
  - Direct Cable Connection—Chapter 24
- Accessibility accessories are covered in Appendix B:
  - Accessibility Wizard
  - Magnifier
  - On-Screen Keyboard

Using Notepad

Like WordPad, Notepad lets you type and edit text. But the two programs have different missions. Notepad is a tool for text editing *only*, while WordPad can be used to make the text you type look good (that is, to *format* your text). To use the appropriate jargon, Notepad is a *text editor,* while WordPad is a *word processor.* (WordPad is covered in Chapter 6, "WordPad and Paint Basics.")

In Notepad, you can type text, but you can't change the fonts, add bold, italics, or color, modify the tab settings, center a paragraph—well, you get the point. So why bother with Notepad? After all, you could type your text in WordPad and simply not use that program's formatting features.

Notepad's main advantage over WordPad is that it's *lean*—it takes up much less memory than WordPad, and it starts up faster, too. It's small enough to keep open all the time so that you can jot down quick notes whenever you need to. And it's a perfect tool to call up whenever you need to view a text file, such as a readme file that comes with a new program you've just downloaded from the Internet.

Notepad opens and saves *text-only* files—files that contain only text characters. That is, text-only files *don't* contain any of the formatting codes used by word processors to store information about the look and layout of a document. Text-only files are also known as plain-text files, ASCII files, plain-ASCII files, or simply *text files*, which is what Windows calls them.

 Windows recognizes a text file as such only if it is stored on disk with the filename extension `.txt`. Files having the `.txt` extension appear in your folders with the text-file icon, shown to the left. Text files often have other extensions, however. For example, a shareware game might come with a file called `read.me` that is actually a text file. To read it in Notepad, you could rename it as `readme.txt` or open it manually in Notepad, or associate the extension `.me` with Notepad.

Though text files look fairly boring, they do have some important advantages over fancier, formatted text documents. The most important one is their universality: Text files provide the lowest common denominator for exchanging text between different programs and even between different types of computers. Every system has a way to create and display text files. That's why they remain the medium for most of the e-mail messages passed back and forth on the Internet and other information services, as well as those posted to electronic bulletin boards.

Text files are also good for storing the "source code" used to generate computer programs. When a programmer writes the source code, he or she types it in using a text editor such as Notepad, saving the work in a text file. That way, the instructions needed to create the final program aren't mixed up with extraneous formatting information that would confuse the *compiler* or *interpreter* (software that converts the source code into a working program).

You may not be a programmer, but you may sometimes deal with program files of a sort—your system-configuration files, including win.ini, sys.ini, and protocol.ini. These text files qualify as programs because they tell your system how to operate. You can edit them with Notepad.

 TIP You can also edit certain system files using the Notepad-like interface in sysedit.exe. Run it from the Run command; it's just like Notepad but with several important system-configuration text files preopened.

Running Notepad

To run Notepad, choose Start ➤ Programs ➤ Accessories ➤ Notepad. Notepad will appear on your screen, and you can immediately begin typing in the empty work area. Figure 7.1 shows a sentence already entered.

FIGURE 7.1
The Notepad window

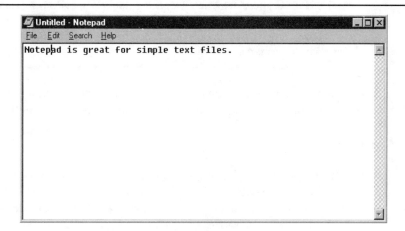

Alternatively, you can double-click any document that Windows recognizes as a text file. As it starts up, Notepad will open that file automatically, and you'll see the text in the work area.

Opening Files

Once Notepad is up and running, opening another text file is as simple as choosing File ➤ Open and selecting the file you want from the Open dialog box—just as you learned in Chapter 6.

NOTE Of course, you can choose File ➢ New to start a new file at any time. If you've made changes in the previous file, Notepad gives you the expected opportunity to save it before creating the new file.

Keep in mind, though, that Windows may not recognize the file you want to open as a text file. When you initially bring up the Open dialog box, it's set to display only files stored with the .txt extension (note the setting in the *Files of Type* area). To locate a text file with another extension, open the Files of Type drop-down list and choose All Files.

If you try to open a file that is too large, Notepad will warn you with this message:

This file is too large for Notepad.

Would you like to use WordPad to read this file?

Clicking Yes will automatically run WordPad, which will open the chosen file.

 WARNING Be careful about opening non-text files with Notepad. While it's fine to browse through a non-text file to see if you can make sense of it, don't make any changes and, above all, *don't save the file*. If you do, the file may be unusable even by the program that originally created it.

Notepad will go ahead and open any file you specify, even if it doesn't contain only text. If you open a non-text file, it will probably look like unintelligible garbage.

Entering and Editing Text

To enter text in Notepad, just start typing. The insertion point will move, just as it does in WordPad. When you reach the right edge of the window, the text wraps to the next line so you can see it. However, this line break is only for display purposes; it's not stored in the file. If you resize the window, the text will re-wrap. If you want to turn off automatic wrapping, choose Edit ➢ Word Wrap to toggle it off.

 NOTE Certain types of program files, such as .bat, .ini, and config.sys files, are line-oriented and are better edited with Word Wrap turned off. This allows you to distinguish more clearly between one line and the next in the case of long lines.

To edit your text, just move the cursor to the point you want to change. You can select, cut, copy, and paste text with the mouse, using the same techniques described in Chapter 6. To select all the text in the file, choose Edit ➢ Select All.

To move around in the text, you can use the scroll bars, of course. You can also use the following keys:

Key	Moves Insertion Point To
Home	Start of the line
End	End of the line
PgUp	Up one window
PgDn	Down one window
Ctrl+←	Start of previous word
Ctrl+→	Start of next word
Ctrl+Home	Start of the file
Ctrl+End	End of the file

Searching for Text

If you're working with a very long readme file, or some other documentation file provided with a program, you might want to search it for a particular word or phrase.

Follow these steps to search:

1. Choose Search ➤ Find. The dialog box appears.

2. Type in the text you want to search for, as shown in the example below.

3. Check the Match Case box if you want to find only text having the same capitalization as your text. If you want the search to ignore capitalization, leave the box clear.

4. Click Up if you want to search the portion of text above the current insertion point. Down is the default setting—Notepad searches from the insertion point to the end of the file and stops. Unlike WordPad, Notepad does not wrap around to the top of the file and continue the search down to the insertion point.

5. If you want to search again for the same word, choose Search ➤ Find Next or, better yet, press F3.

Printing a Notepad File

To print a Notepad file, choose File ➤ Print. Notepad immediately starts the printing process and always prints the entire document—you don't have an opportunity to select which pages will print or how many copies.

Notepad's Limitations

Just so you won't use Notepad for the wrong tasks, here's a summary of its limitations:

- It has no paragraph- or character-formatting capability. It can, however, wrap lines of text to fit the size of the window, which is a nice feature.

 NOTE New in Windows Me: Notepad now wraps lines of text to fit the display window by default. In earlier versions of Windows, you had to choose Edit ➤ Word Wrap each time you opened or created a document.

- Files are limited to text only. Notepad can't open formatted documents created with WordPad, Microsoft Word for Windows, WordPerfect, or any other word processor. (Actually, it can open the files, but they won't look right).
- Files are limited in size to about 50K. This is fairly large, accommodating approximately 15 pages of solid, single-spaced text, or about 20 pages of regularly spaced material.
- It doesn't have any fancy pagination options, though it will print with headers and footers via the Page Setup dialog box.

Annotating Pictures with Imaging

Ever since Imaging arrived in Windows 98 Second Edition, people have been wondering what to make of it. It isn't really a full-featured graphics program, and it doesn't take the place of a general-purpose graphics editor like Paint. It has a rather odd assortment of tools, including some surprisingly powerful annotation features, but no drawing and painting tools. You can acquire images from a scanner directly from Imaging, but you can't color-correct or apply visual effects to the scanned images the way you can in other scanner-related programs like Adobe PhotoDeluxe.

So what's it good for? Well, primarily it's good for annotating images. In other words, it places captions over the top of photographs and other pictures. It also enables you to load multiple pages at the same time and sort them or view them in thumbnail view.

To start Imaging, choose Start ➤ Programs ➤ Accessories ➤ Imaging.

Opening a Graphic

Imaging will open graphics in lots of different graphics formats, but some of its main features, such as annotation, are not available unless you're working with a .TIF or .AWD format image. In addition, you can save your work only in .TIF, .AWD, or .BMP format. .TIF and .BMP are standard graphics formats, and .AWD is a fax graphic format. Open a file with File ➤ Open, just as with any other program.

Scanning a Graphic

You can also scan directly from Imaging if you have a compatible scanner. The first time you do so, you need to make sure the correct scanner or imaging device is selected, so choose File ➤ Select Scanner. Choose the scanner you want to acquire from and click OK.

Then, when you're ready to scan:

1. Choose File ➤ Scan New or click the Scan New button. The Scan dialog box appears.

2. Place the picture to be scanned in the scanner, and then click Preview to do a test scan.

3. Drag the red squares to adjust the scan area, and set any other scan options desired. (I won't go into Windows's scanner controls here because they're covered in detail in Chapter 17, "Using Image Acquisition and Movie Maker.")

4. Click Scan to scan the picture and send it to Imaging.

Working with a Graphic

Once the picture is in Imaging, you can use the buttons on the toolbar to modify it. I won't get into every single button and feature here, because you can easily try them out on your own; but here are a few highlights:

Select Image   Lets you define an area of the image by dragging a rectangle around it.

Drag   Lets you move a selected part of the image by dragging it.

Rotate Left   Rotates the entire image (or the selected portion) 90 degrees to the left.

Rotate Right   Rotates the entire image (or the selected portion) 90 degrees to the right.

Annotating a Graphic

The Imaging program really shines in its ability to annotate—that is, to superimpose on the top of an image. You can add explanatory text to a picture, such as writing the names of the various relatives in an old photo underneath each person.

Annotation is so important that it has its own menu and toolbar. (The toolbar buttons correspond one-to-one with the menu commands, so you can use either one.)

> **TIP** If the commands on the Annotation menu are unavailable, it's probably because the image isn't in the right format. Save your work in .TIF format, and they'll appear.

If the Annotation toolbar doesn't appear at the bottom of the program window, click the Annotation Toolbar button to turn it on, or choose View ➤ Toolbars and select it from the Toolbar dialog box.

Here are the annotations you can use:

- Freehand Line

- Highlighter

- Straight Line

- Hollow Rectangle

- Filled Rectangle

- Typed Text

- Attach-a-Note

- Text from File

- Rubber Stamp

To apply one of the annotation effects, click the button you want (or choose one from the Annotation menu) and then click the image or drag across it. The exact procedure depends on the annotation chosen. For example, if you choose the Typed Text annotation, click the image and then type the text. Figure 7.2 shows some of the annotations in place.

FIGURE 7.2
Some annotations done in Imaging

Attach-a-note (solid background)

Typed text (clear background)

After typing your annotation, you can do the following to format it:

- Use the Annotation Select tool to select an annotation, placing a black dotted frame around it. You can then drag the black squares on the frame to resize the annotation area.

- Delete an annotation by selecting it (with the Annotation Select tool) and pressing Delete.

- Move an annotation by selecting it and dragging it by any part except one of the black squares.

- Right-click the annotation and choose Edit to move the insertion point back into the annotation's box for further text editing.

- Right-click the annotation and choose Properties to open a Text Properties dialog box, in which you can choose different settings for the annotation. For example, for a text annotation, you can choose a different font, size, and text attributes.

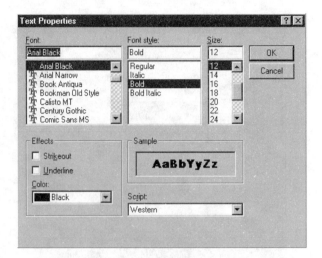

Performing Calculations with the Calculator

You can use the Calculator to perform simple or complex calculations. There are really two calculators in one—a Standard Calculator and a more complex Scientific Calculator for use by statisticians, engineers, computer programmers, and business professionals.

To run the Calculator, choose Start ➢ Programs ➢ Accessories ➢ Calculator. A reasonable facsimile of a handheld calculator will appear on your screen, as shown in Figure 7.3. If your Calculator looks larger, it's the Scientific one. Choose View ➢ Standard to switch back to the basic calculator. The program always remembers which type was used last and comes up in that mode.

FIGURE 7.3
The Standard
Calculator

TIP For quick tips on how to use any Calculator button, just click the right mouse button over the Calculator button of interest. A little *What's This* button appears. Click this, and you'll see a pop-up Help window. Of course, you can also choose Help ➢ Help Topics to display the main Help text.

Performing a Calculation

To perform a typical calculation, follow these steps:

1. Clear the Calculator's display by pressing Esc on the keyboard or clicking the C (clear all) button. (This is not necessary if you just opened the Calculator.)

2. Enter the first value in the calculation by clicking the numbers or using the keyboard.

   You can use the Backspace key to fix mistakes, click C (clear all) to clear the Calculator and start again, or click CE (clear entry) to clear only the current entry but preserve the previous result.

 TIP If you set the keypad's Num Lock setting on, you can use it to enter the numbers and the four mathematical operators. This is easier than using the number keys across the top of the keyboard.

3. After entering the first number, click the mathematical operator you want to use. (The asterisk represents multiplication, Sqrt calculates the square root, and $1/x$ calculates the reciprocal. The others are self-evident.)

4. Enter any additional numbers followed by the desired operators. In this way, you can perform a sequence of operations using the result of each computation as the beginning of the next one.

5. Press Enter or click the Calculator's equals (=) button. The answer appears in the display.

 TIP To add up a series of numbers or to find their mean, you may prefer to use the statistical functions on the Scientific Calculator. This way, you can see all the numbers in a list before you perform the calculation instead of having to enter them one at a time. And don't let the idea of statistics make you nervous—the technique is very simple.

Most of the operations on the Standard Calculator are self-explanatory, but a couple of them—square roots and percentages—are just a bit tricky. They are explained later in this chapter, as are the functions of the Scientific Calculator.

Copying Your Results to Other Documents

To enter the number displayed in the Calculator readout into another document, just use the standard Windows Copy and Paste commands. Use the Calculator for your computations, and then, when the result you want is in the display, choose Edit ➤ Copy (or press Ctrl+C). The value will be copied to the Clipboard. Then switch back to your document, position the cursor where you want the result, and paste it in.

Using the Memory Keys

The memory keys work just like those on a standard calculator. MS stores the displayed number in memory, MR recalls the memory value to the display for use in calculations, M+ adds the current display value to the existing memory value, and MC clears out the memory, resetting it to zero.

When the Calculator's memory contains a value, an *M* appears in the small area just above the MC button. If no value is in memory, this area is empty.

Copying Calculations from Other Documents to the Calculator

Although the Calculator doesn't keep records of your computations for reference or reuse, you can get around that limitation via the Clipboard and a text editor, such as Notepad or your word processor. Here's what to do:

1. In the text editor, type in the entire equation using the special symbols listed in Table 7.1.

2. Copy the equation to the Clipboard.

3. Switch to Calculator.

4. Click the C (clear all) button to clear the Calculator, then press Ctrl+V or choose Edit ➤ Paste.

If you've written out the equation correctly, the Calculator will compute the answer for you.

TABLE 7.1: KEYBOARD SHORTCUTS FOR THE CALCULATOR

Calculator Button	Equivalent Keyboard Key
%	%
(	(
)	)
*	*
+	+
+/−	F9
−	−
.	. or ,
/	/
0–9	0–9
1/x	r
=	= or Enter
A–F	A–F
And	&
Ave	Ctrl+A
Bin	F8
Byte	F4
Back	Backspace
Clear All	Esc
CD	Del
Cos	o
Dat	Ins
Dec	F6
Deg	F2
Dms	m
Dword	F2
Exp	x

Continued ▶

TABLE 7.1: KEYBOARD SHORTCUTS FOR THE CALCULATOR (CONTINUED)

Calculator Button	Equivalent Keyboard Key
F–E	v
Grad	F4
Hex	F5
Hypo	h
Int	;
Inv	I
In	n
Log	l
LSH	<
M+	Ctrl+P
MC	Ctrl+L
Mod	%
MR	Ctrl+R
MS	Ctrl+M
n!	!
Not	~
Oct	F7
Or		
PI	p
Rad	F3
S	Ctrl+D
Sin	s
Sqrt	@
Sta	Ctrl+S
Sum	Ctrl+T
Tan	t
Word	F3

Continued ▶

TABLE 7.1: KEYBOARD SHORTCUTS FOR THE CALCULATOR (CONTINUED)	
Calculator Button	**Equivalent Keyboard Key**
Xor	^
x^2	@
x^3	#
x^y	y

Here's how a simple calculation might look, ready for copying from the text editor to Calculator:

((2+4)+16)/11=

or

(2+(4+16))/11=

Note that you must surround each pair of terms in parentheses to indicate the calculation sequence. This is true even if you would have gotten the right answer had you typed in the numbers into the Calculator without the parentheses.

If you don't like the parentheses, you can try this format instead:

2+4=+16=/11=

Note that this time you have to insert an = after each arithmetic operation; the Calculator gets confused if you don't.

You can use the following special characters in an equation to activate various Calculator functions:

:c   Clears the Calculator's memory.

:e   If the Calculator is set to the decimal system, this sequence indicates that the following digits are the exponent of a number expressed in scientific notation; for example, 1.01:e100 appears in the Calculator as 1.01e+100.

:m   Stores the number currently displayed in the Calculator's memory.

:p   Adds the number currently displayed to the number in memory.

:q   Clears the Calculator.

:r   Displays the number stored in the Calculator's memory.

\   Places the number currently displayed into the Statistics box, which must already be open.

Computing Square Roots and Percentages

To find a *square root*, just enter the number whose square root you want and click the Sqrt button. That's all there is to it—the only thing to remember is that this is a one-step calculation. You don't need to click the = button or do anything else.

Percentages are a little trickier. Let's say you want to know what 14 percent of 2,875 is. Here's how to find out:

1. Clear the Calculator of previous results. This is a key step—you won't get the right answer if you leave a previous result in memory when you start.

2. Enter the number you're starting with, **2875** in this case.

3. Click or type ***** (for multiplication) or *any* of the arithmetic operators. It actually doesn't matter which one you use—this step simply separates the two values you're entering.

4. Enter the percentage, **14** in this case. Don't enter a decimal point unless you're calculating a fractional percentage, such as 0.2 percent.

5. Now click or type **%**. The Calculator reports the result.

Using the Scientific Calculator

In the Standard view, the Calculator may seem a fairly simple affair, but wait until you see the Scientific view—this is an industrial-strength calculating tool that can handle truly sophisticated computations. Figure 7.4 shows how the Scientific Calculator appears on your screen. To display it, choose View ➢ Scientific.

The term *scientific* is somewhat misleading because the functions available here cover programming and statistics as well as the operations traditionally used by scientists. With the Scientific Calculator, you can do the following:

- Perform complex computations, grouping terms in up to 25 levels of parentheses.

- Display and perform calculations on values expressed in scientific (exponential) notation.

- Raise numbers to any power and find any (*n*th) root.
- Calculate logarithms and factorials.
- Perform trigonometric functions, such as sine and cosine, displaying values as degrees, radians, or gradients.
- Insert the value of pi into your calculations.
- Perform calculations in four bases (hexadecimal, octal, and binary, in addition to decimal) and translate values between the bases.
- Perform bitwise operations (logical and shift operations on individual bits in a value) such as And, Or, Not, and Shift.
- Calculate standard deviations and other statistical computations.

Details on the individual functions of the Scientific Calculator are beyond the scope of this book—if you're enough of a rocket scientist to use them, you probably don't need me to explain them to you. An introduction to operating the program is in order, however.

Accessing Additional Functions with the Inv and Hyp Check Boxes

The Inv check box at the left side of the Scientific Calculator functions something like the Shift key on your keyboard: Checking it alters the function of some of the Calculator's buttons. This means you have access to additional functions that aren't obvious from the button labels.

For example, to find the arcsine of the value currently displayed in the readout, you would check the Inv box, then click the Sin button. Similarly, to find a cube root, enter the number, check the Inv box, and then click the *x*^3 button. Instead of raising the value to the third power, you've calculated the cube root.

As you can guess, Inv stands for *inverse*, and it causes most buttons to calculate their inverses. With some buttons, though, checking the Inv box simply accesses a related function.

The Inv box is automatically cleared for you after each use.

Immediately to the right of the Inv box is the Hyp (for *hyperbolic*) check box, which works similarly. Its function is to access the corresponding hyperbolic trigonometric function when used with the Sin, Cos, and Tan buttons.

Working with Scientific Notation

To enter a number using scientific (exponential) notation:

1. Begin by entering the significant digits (the base number).
2. When you're ready to enter the exponent, click the Exp button. The display changes to show the value in exponential notation with an exponent of 0.
3. If you want to enter a negative exponent, click the +/– button.

4. You can now enter the exponent. The Calculator accepts exponents up to +/– 307. If you enter a larger number, you'll get an error message in the display and you'll have to start over.

You can switch back and forth between exponential and standard decimal notations for numbers with absolute values less than 1,015. To do so, just click the F-E button.

Working with Different Number Bases

The Scientific Calculator lets you enter and perform calculations with numbers in any of four commonly used number base systems: decimal (base 10), hexadecimal (base 16), octal (base 8), and binary (base 2). To switch to a different base, click the appropriate radio button from the group at the upper left. The value currently in the display will be translated to the new base.

Many of the Scientific Calculator's operators and buttons work only while the decimal numbering system is active. For example, you can use scientific notation only with decimal numbers. The letter keys (A–F) at the bottom of the Scientific Calculator's numeric button pad are for entering the hexadecimal digits above 9, and they work only in hexadecimal mode.

You have three display options when each number base system is active. The choices appear as radio buttons at the right side of the Calculator.

When the decimal system is active, you can display values as degrees, radians, or gradients. These are units used in trigonometric computations; for other work, you can ignore the setting.

 NOTE If the display is set for Degrees, you can use the Dms button to display the current value in the degree-minute-second format. Once you've switched to degrees-minutes-seconds, you can translate back to degrees by checking the Inv box, then clicking the Dms button.

The following choices are those for the other three bases:

Dword   Displays the number as a 32-bit value (up to 8 hexadecimal places).

Word   Displays the number as a 16-bit value (up to 4 hex places).

Byte   Displays the number as an 8-bit value (up to 2 hex places).

When you switch to an option that displays fewer places, the Scientific Calculator hides the upper (more significant) places but retains them in memory and during calculations. When you switch back, the readout reflects the entire original number, as modified by any calculations.

Grouping Terms with Parentheses

You can use parentheses to group terms in a complex calculation, thereby establishing the order in which the various operations are performed. You can *nest* parentheses inside other parentheses to a maximum of 25 levels.

Aside from the math involved, there's nothing tricky about using parentheses—except keeping track of them as your work scrolls out of the display area. In this regard, the Scientific Calculator does provide one bit of help: It displays how many levels "deep" you are at the moment in the small area just above the right parenthesis button.

Performing Statistical Calculations

The Scientific Calculator can also perform several simple statistical calculations, including standard deviations, means, and sums. Even if you're not savvy with statistics, the statistical functions provide a good way to add or average a series of values. You get to enter the numbers in a list, where you can see them all, and then click a button to get the result.

You access the statistical functions via three buttons at the left of the Scientific Calculator: Ave, Sum, and S. These buttons work only when you display the Statistics Box, as detailed in the general instructions below. The functions of each button are listed after the instructions.

Now you're ready for the general method for performing any statistical calculation:

1. Click the Sta button to display the Statistics Box, shown here:

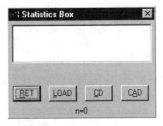

2. Position the Statistics Box and the Calculator on your screen so you can see the box and have access to the Calculator buttons and readout.

3. Place each value in the Statistics Box by entering the value in the Calculator and clicking Dat. Repeat this for all the values you want to perform the calculation on.

4. To delete an entry in the Statistics Box, highlight it, then click CD (clear datum). You can delete all the entries by clicking CAD (clear all data).

5. When you've entered all the correct values, click any of the three statistics buttons to perform the selected calculation. The answer appears in the Calculator's main readout.

Each of the statistical function buttons performs two functions: one "regular" function and a second function if you check the Inv box above before clicking the button. Here are the buttons' functions:

Button	Normal function	Function with Inv
Ave	Calculates the mean	Calculates the mean of the squares
Sum	Calculates the sum	Calculates the sum of the squares
S	Calculates the standard deviation	Calculates the standard deviation using n–1 as the population parameter

Never heard of the population parameter? You're not alone....

Entering Special Symbols with Character Map

The Character Map program lets you choose and insert into your documents those oddball characters such as foreign alphabetic and currency symbols and characters from specialized fonts such as Symbol and Wingdings. With Character Map, you can easily view and insert these symbols even though there aren't keys for them on your keyboard.

Here are some everyday examples. Suppose that instead of the standard straight quotes (like "this") you'd prefer to use real open and close quotes (like "this") for a more professional-looking document. Or perhaps you regularly use the symbols for Trademark (™), Registered Trademark (®), Copyright (©); Greek letters, or the arrow symbols ↑, →, ←, and ↓ that we use in this book. These, as well as fractions and foreign-language accents and the like, are included in your Windows fonts and can most likely be printed on your printer.

Character Map is a small dialog box that displays all the symbols available for each font. You select the symbol(s) you want, and Character Map puts them on the Clipboard for pasting into your document. Figure 7.5 displays some examples of special characters.

FIGURE 7.5
Sample characters inserted into a WordPad document using Character Map

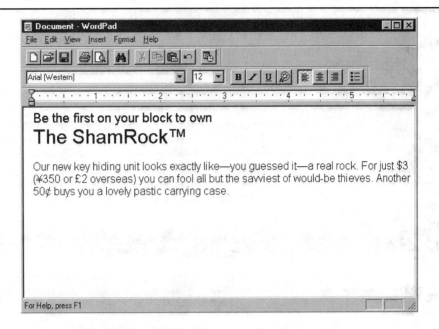

Here's how to use Character Map:

1. Choose Start ➢ Programs ➢ Accessories ➢ System Tools ➢ Character Map. The Character Map table appears, showing all the characters included in the font currently selected in the Font list. (A font can contain up to 224 characters.)

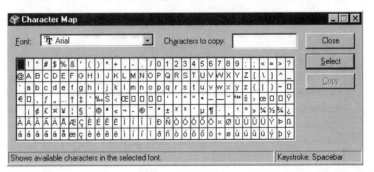

2. In the Font list, choose the font you want to work with. Most of the fonts have the same characters, but some special fonts have completely different *character sets*. For example, the Symbol font includes all sorts of special math and Greek symbols, while the Wingdings font consists of a wacky set of little pictures.

3. To make it easier to see the individual characters, you can click a character box and hold the mouse button down to magnify the symbol. You can accomplish

the same thing with the keyboard by moving to the character using the arrow keys. With this technique, each character is magnified as you select it.

4. Double-click a character to select it, transferring it to the Characters to Copy box. Alternatively, once you've highlighted a character, you can click the Select button or press Alt+S to place it in the Characters to Copy box.

 NOTE You can change fonts at any time. Just be aware that this will affect the characters you previously placed in the Characters to Copy box, not just new characters.

5. If you want to grab more than one character, keep adding them in the same way. Each new character is added to the end of the string in the Characters to Copy box.

6. Click the Copy button. This places everything that's in the Characters to Copy box onto the Clipboard.

7. Switch back to your destination application and use the Paste command (typically on the application's Edit menu) to insert the characters into your document. You may then have to select the inserted characters and choose the correct font to format the characters correctly.

Of course, once you've entered a character in this way, you're free to change its font and size as you would any character you typed in.

Entering Alternate Characters from the Keyboard

Notice that the bottom of the Character Map dialog box includes a line that reads
Keystroke:
When you click a character in Character Map, this line displays the keys you would have to press to enter the character directly from the keyboard rather than from Character Map. For the characters in the first three lines—except the very last character on the third line—the keystroke shown will be a key on your keyboard. If you're working with a nonstandard font such as Symbol, pressing the key shown will enter the selected symbol into your document. With Symbol, for example, pressing the *j* key enters the cheery symbol shown here:

For all the other characters, Character Map instructs you to enter a sequence of keys in combination with the Alt key. For example, say you wanted to enter the copyright symbol (©) into a Windows application document. Note that with a standard text font like Arial or Times New Roman selected in Character Map, the program lists the keystrokes for the copyright symbol as Alt+0169. Here's how to enter the character from the keyboard:

1. Press Num Lock to activate the numeric keypad on your keyboard if the keypad is not already active.

2. Press Alt and as you hold it down, type **0 1 6 9** (that is, type the 0, 1, 6, and 9 keys individually, in succession). When you release the Alt key, the copyright symbol should appear in the document.

Not all Windows application programs accept characters in this way, but it's worth a try as a shortcut to using Character Map.

Using the Clipboard Viewer

In Chapter 6, you learned to cut, copy, and paste text and other objects using the Clipboard. One way to find out what's on the Clipboard currently, in case you've forgotten, is to paste its contents into whatever program you happen to have open at the moment. (You can always use Edit ➤ Undo or delete the pasted item after your curiosity has been satisfied.)

Another way to find out what's on the Clipboard is to use the Clipboard Viewer. This handy utility not only shows the current contents of the Clipboard but also enables you to save it in a file (in a proprietary .CLP format) and to reopen it later so that you can place the selection on the Clipboard again. For example, suppose you have copied a large amount of important data to the Clipboard; but before you can paste it into another application, you realize it's time to rush off to an important meeting. You might use the Clipboard Viewer to save the Clipboard content to a file; that way, if something happens while you're gone that causes the PC to lose power or restart, the contents of your Clipboard will be safe. Another use for the Clipboard Viewer is simply to keep it open at all times, for quick reference if you forget what's on the Clipboard.

Open the Clipboard Viewer with Start ➢ Programs ➢ Accessories ➢ System Tools ➢ Clipboard Viewer. If it's not there, it's not installed. (See Chapter 13 for help adding and removing Windows programs.)

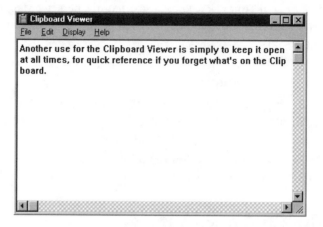

 NOTE Did you notice above how the word *Clipboard* is broken without hyphenation? On the Clipboard, you might see some odd line breaks, even breaking in the middle of words. Don't worry about it; the text will be fine after you've pasted it.

To save the Clipboard contents to a file, use File ➢ Save As, just as in any other program. And to open a saved clip, use File ➢ Open.

Using the Phone Dialer

Phone Dialer is a simple application that places outgoing voice telephone calls through your modem. You can tell Phone Dialer what number you want to dial by typing the number, choosing it from a Speed Dial list, or clicking numbers on an on-screen keypad. After you've called a number, you can select it from a list of recent calls. After it dials the call, Phone Dialer connects the line through to the telephone set plugged into the phone jack on your modem so you can pick up the handset and start talking.

You'll have to decide for yourself whether pressing keys on your computer keyboard is any improvement over pressing buttons on a telephone, but the speed-dial feature can be quite convenient for frequently called numbers. Of course, you're out of luck if you normally use separate telephone lines for voice and data.

PART

I

Up and Running

Phone Dialer is in the Windows Accessories menu, so you can start it by clicking the Start button and then choosing Programs ➣ Accessories ➣ Communications ➣ Phone Dialer. If you use Phone Dialer frequently, you can create a shortcut for this application.

When you start the program, the main Phone Dialer screen appears. To make a call, either type the number or click the numbers on the on-screen keypad. Figure 7.6 shows a number entered and ready to dial.

If you want to call a number you've called before, you can display recently dialed numbers in a drop-down menu by clicking the arrow at the right side of the Number to Dial field. When the complete number you want to dial is in this field, click the Dial button.

FIGURE 7.6
The Phone Dialer screen offers several ways to enter a telephone number.

Dialing a number with Phone Dialer is exactly like dialing the same number from your telephone. Therefore, you must include all the prefixes required by the phone company for this kind of call, such as a **1** for prepaid long-distance calls or a **0** for operator-assisted calls. On the other hand, if you're using an office telephone that requires **9** or some other access code for an outside line, you can use the Dialing Properties dialog box to add the code for all calls. You can open the Dialing Properties dialog box from Phone Dialer's Tools menu.

Programming the Speed Dial List

The eight entries in the Speed Dial list are push buttons. Click one of the names in the list to dial that person's number. When you click an unassigned button, the Program Speed Dial dialog box in Figure 7.7 appears. Type the name you want on the button in the Name field and the complete telephone number in the Number to Dial field. Click the Save button to save the new number and return to the main Phone Dialer screen, or click the Save and Dial button to call the number from this dialog box.

FIGURE 7.7
*Use the Program
Speed Dial dialog box
to assign names and
numbers to the
Speed Dial list.*

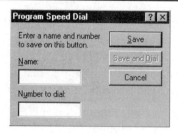

You can program several Speed Dial buttons at one time or change the name or number of a previously assigned button by choosing Edit ➤ Speed Dial. When the Edit Speed Dial dialog box in Figure 7.8 appears, click the button you want to change and then type the name and number you want to assign to that button. After you have configured as many of the eight buttons as you want to use, click the Save button.

FIGURE 7.8
*Use the Edit Speed Dial
dialog box to add
or change Speed
Dial items.*

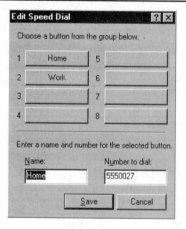

Placing a Call

When you place a call through Phone Dialer, the Dialing dialog box in Figure 7.9 appears. If you entered the number from the Speed Dial list, the dialog box will display the name of the person you're calling. Otherwise, it will report the call destination as *unknown.* If you wish, you can type the recipient's name and a few words about the call to keep a record of this call in the Phone Dialer log.

FIGURE 7.9
This dialog box appears when you place a call with a Phone Dialer.

As Phone Dialer places the call, you'll hear the dialing tones (or pulses) and the ringing signal or busy signal through the modem's speaker. A Call Status window will let you know when the call has gone through. To transfer the call to your telephone set, click the Talk button and pick up the handset, or click Hang Up to break the connection. If the modem detects a busy signal, you will see a Call Failed window instead.

After you pick up the receiver and click the Talk button, your call passes through the modem to your telephone set. At this point, there's no real difference between a Phone Dialer call and one placed directly from the telephone itself. To end the call, hang up the telephone.

Playing the Games

Windows Me's games are not installed by default, so you might miss out on them entirely. Choose Start ➤ Programs ➤ Games. If there's nothing there, turn to Chapter 13 to learn how to add Windows components, and add them in.

There are two kinds of games provided with Windows Me: regular games and Internet games. The regular games are Classic Hearts, Classic Solitaire, Freecell, Spider Solitaire, Minesweeper, and Pinball. All but the last two are card games. Each of the games is fairly easy to figure out; use the Help menu to get a description of the game rules and playing options.

The Internet games are new in Windows Me. If you have an Internet connection, you can use them to play games with other people all over the world, in total anonymity. To use them, you must sign up for the MSN Gaming Zone, but doing so is fast, free, and anonymous. Just follow the prompts the first time you play an Internet game to sign up.

Just as an example, here's how the Internet Backgammon would work:

1. Choose Start ➢ Programs ➢ Games ➢ Internet Backgammon. A MSN Gaming Zone introductory box appears.

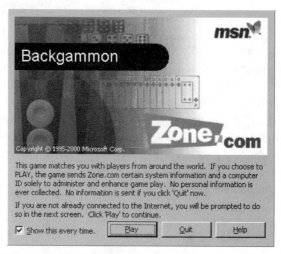

2. Click Play. If you are not currently connected to the Internet, a prompt appears from which you can connect. Do so if needed.

3. The system looks for another player to match you with; when one is found, a Backgammon board opens and the game begins.

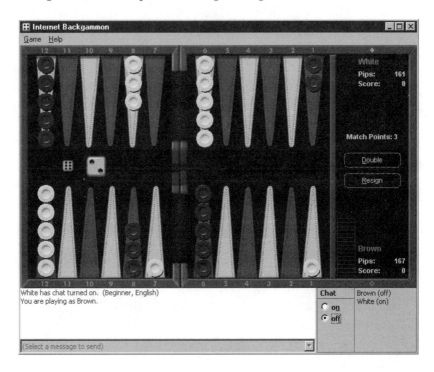

Had enough accessories yet? I hope not, because there are still lots more to cover. The next chapter, "Getting Help When You Need It," introduces you to the Windows Help and Support system. Then, in Part II of the book, we'll start delving into some of the other accessories I mentioned at the beginning of this chapter.

CHAPTER **8**

Getting Help When You Need It

No matter how much you know about computers, there will be times when you don't remember or understand how to use an operation or command, or even what a particular element on the screen is for. Luckily, you don't always have to drag out a book or manual to get some quick help. The people at Microsoft have done an exceptional job of developing built-in Help for this version of Windows. Once you learn how to use it, it'll answer many of your questions.

 NOTE My two cents on books: Many computer users still find books useful, which is lucky because it keeps writers like me employed and publishers, such as Sybex, in business. Books are sources of information and style that can't be rivaled by computers. With books, you can see how many pages of material there are on a given topic, batteries are *not* required, and they don't break if you drop them. Using them doesn't really take much know-how (except the ability to read), and you can skim through a book very easily to search for a given topic. In my opinion, books are pretty great and are bound (no pun intended) to be with us all for a long, long time.

Despite my probably biased stance on the superiority of books, let's face it: We don't always have a book with us or want to pore over an index to find the right reference. So online help (as it's called in the computer world)—especially *context-sensitive* help, in which the computer guesses what you're trying to do—can be a great boon. Windows Me has such a Help facility, as do virtually all Windows programs up until this point. Some online help is useful; some is downright lousy, telling you no more than the obvious. The good news is that because there is a standard for how programs are supposed to dish out help, once you learn how to get help with one program, you'll be equipped to take on others.

Along with Windows itself, the Windows *Help engine* (the program that puts help up on the screen and lets you search for a topic) has evolved over the years. Windows 98's Help was getting pretty good actually; it even let you search through every word of a Help file for topics that might not be listed in the table of contents, and it let you jump from topic to topic with Internet-style hyperlinks. But Windows Me's Help system leaps ahead of even those features, with integrated multimedia tours, tutorials, and seamless links to online support.

Most of the applications you use in Windows, however, employ the older-style Help window used in Windows 95 or Windows 98 (depending on the age of the program). New programs coming out in the future will likely integrate themselves with the Windows Help system, but for now, you'll have to learn to find your way around at least a couple of different types of Help systems. The good news is that (1) Help systems are, by nature, pretty easy to figure out, and (2) the differences are mostly cosmetic.

⚠ **TIP** To get help with an application, you need to have the application running, and it has to be in the *active* window (see Chapter 3, "Exploring the Interface").

The Windows Me Help System

To open the Help and Support window, shown in Figure 8.1, choose Start ➢ Help. In keeping with Windows Me's Internet focus, the Help and Support window is designed to look very much like a Web page and includes familiar Web-like elements such as hyperlinks and a Search box.

FIGURE 8.1
The redesigned Help and Support system for Windows Me

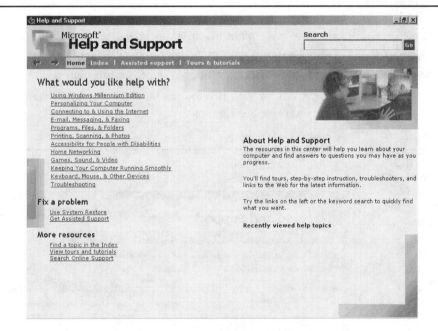

There are three main ways to look up a topic in Help and Support:

- Browsing with hyperlinks
- Looking up topics alphabetically in the Index
- Searching with the Search feature

I'll show you each of these methods, plus several other special features of the Help and Support system.

Browsing the Windows Me Help System

The opening Help and Support screen contains a series of hyperlinks that provide Help topic suggestions for browsing. For example, in Figure 8.1, under What Would You Like Help With, you can choose among several common activities.

Try it out with the following steps:

1. Click the Using Windows Millennium Edition hyperlink. Another list of hyperlinks appears, this time more targeted.

2. Click the What's New in Windows Me hyperlink. Another list of hyperlinks appears. On this list, however, the hyperlinks have icons next to them, indicating their purpose.

   • A Help article you can read

   • A Web page requiring Internet access to view, or an interactive trouble-shooter (more about these later in the chapter)

   • A multimedia tour or tutorial (more on these later)

3. Click the What's New in Windows Me hyperlink, and that article appears in the right-hand pane. See Figure 8.2.

FIGURE 8.2
The chosen article appears on the right, with the list of hyperlinks remaining on the left so you can make another choice.

Selected article

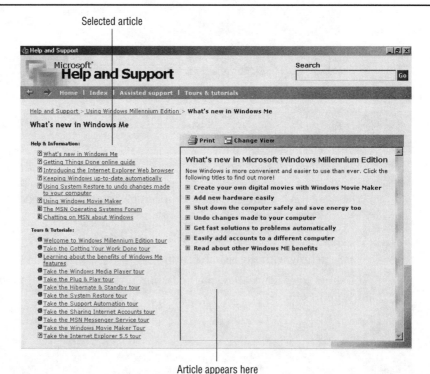

Article appears here

4. The chosen article happens to have several sections. Click the plus sign next to Add New Hardware Easily. A paragraph appears below it, along with a hyperlink that reads Tell Me More about Plug and Play.

5. Click the Tell Me More about Plug and Play hyperlink. Several paragraphs of text appear describing the feature.

6. Click the Print button above the article to print it. A Print dialog box opens; click OK.

7. Click the Back button on the Help and Support window's toolbar. It works just as in Internet Explorer (covered in Chapter 21, "Browsing the World Wide Web with Internet Explorer 5.5"). You return to the main What's New in Windows Me article.

8. Click the Welcome to Windows Millennium Edition Tour hyperlink. A tour window opens, separate from the regular Help system. See Figure 8.3.

FIGURE 8.3
A Windows Me tour window

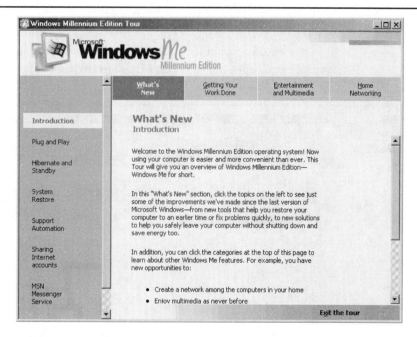

9. Explore the tour window if you like, and when you're finished, close the tour window by clicking Exit the Tour.

10. Click the Home button on the toolbar. You return to the initial Help and Support screen where you started.

Now you have a general idea of what the Help and Support system in Windows Me is about. You just click, click, click your way around until you find what you want.

"But wait a minute," you might be thinking. "That doesn't seem very efficient to me, just wandering around like that hoping to stumble upon the topic I'm looking for." Well, you're right. It's not the most efficient system. But luckily for all you down-to-business types, there are two other ways of using the Help system: Index and Search.

Using the Help Index

If you want to look up a certain term or concept, the Index is the perfect place to start. Just as in a book, the Index can help you more quickly locate just the piece of information you need to get the job done.

To use the Index, complete the following steps:

1. Open the Help system if it's not already open (Start ➤ Help).

2. Click the Index button on the toolbar. The Find a Topic in the Index screen appears.

   The left pane displays an alphabetical listing of topics. Notice that there is a scroll bar to the right of the list, so you can scroll the list to search for a topic. But the quicker way to find a topic is simply to start typing it in.

3. Type the word you want to look up. The list immediately jumps to the word you typed. For example, in Figure 8.4, I typed **printing**.

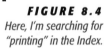

FIGURE 8.4

Here, I'm searching for "printing" in the Index.

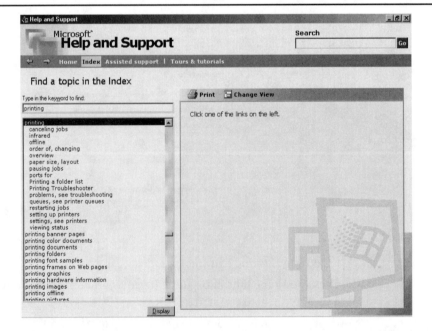

4. Find the exact phrase on the list you want, and double-click it. You'll now see some useful (you hope) information in the right-hand pane.

In some cases, before actually getting the Help information, you'll be presented with a list of articles to choose from. You simply double-click the one you want, or highlight it and click Display.

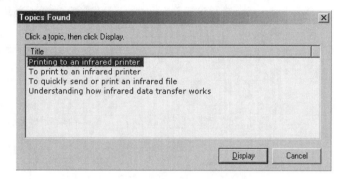

 TIP Remember, when a Help topic is being displayed, you can always get back to the main Help screen by clicking the Home button.

Once you find the article, tour, or tutorial you want, you can read it, print it, and so on, just as you learned earlier in this chapter.

Searching for Help

What if you want to look something up, but you aren't sure of the correct name for it? Answer: You use Search. The Search feature searches every word of every Help article, looking for the term you enter so that even if that term is not in the article's name, you can still find the article you need to read.

Here's how to do a Search:

1. If Help is not already open, choose Start ➤ Help.

2. Click in the Search box in the top-right corner, moving the insertion point into it.

3. Type the word you're looking for, and press Enter or click Go.

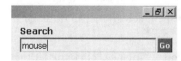

4. If no topics are found, you'll be alerted. If topics are found, their hyperlinks appear in the left pane, just as when browsing, and you can click the article that matches your interest. For example, Figure 8.5 shows the result when searching for "mouse."

FIGURE 8.5
Searching for "mouse"
found the articles
shown here.

Articles containing "mouse"

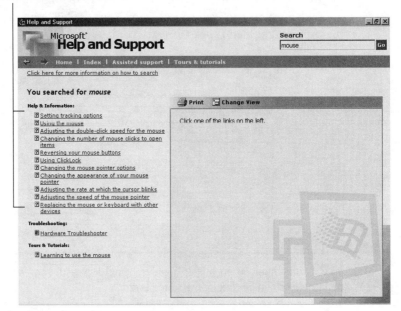

Exploring the Tours and Tutorials

As you've seen in the preceding sections, Windows Me's Help and Support provides not only articles but also Tours and Tutorials. Tours are separate windows, with their own controls, that give you an intensive lesson about a specific feature. Tutorials are interactive, step-by-step guides that teach you how to use a feature. You can run a tour or tutorial by selecting it from the list of hyperlinks when you browse or search for a topic, or you can choose from the full list of Tours and Tutorials as described in the following steps:

1. From the Help and Support window, click the Tours & Tutorials button on the toolbar. A list of hyperlinks for all the tours and tutorials appears.

2. Click the tour or tutorial you want to run. It opens in its own window. (Look back at Figure 8.3 for an example.)

3. Follow the on-screen instructions, or simply click various parts of the window to explore.

4. When you're finished, click the Exit the Tour hyperlink.

PART
I

Up and Running

Getting Assisted Support

Assisted support is Help that connects you to other people, groups, or companies, rather than simply relying on the Help information stored on your PC. To check out the Assisted Support options in Windows Me, do the following:

1. From the Help and Support window, click the Assisted Support button on the toolbar.

2. Click the link for the type of support you want:

   Microsoft Corporation This takes you to a form where you can formally request help from a Microsoft technical support person. First, you'll need to go through a registration process, and then jump through some other hoops; just follow the prompts.

 TIP On the first screen that appears, after you click Microsoft Corporation, there is a hyperlink for Searchable Knowledge Base. This is an online resource primarily for intermediate- and advanced-level users who are looking for information about known problems and bugs in Microsoft products. You might want to explore the Knowledge Base before you contact a support representative.

   MSN Computing Central Forums This takes you to a list of Microsoft Web sites such as Hardware Forum, Software Forum, and so on. Click the one you want to visit. Each site is packed with information about Microsoft products, and you might be able to find the answer you seek there.

   MSN Computing Central Message Boards This takes you to a list of user-to-user message boards (i.e., newsgroups), where you can interact with your fellow Windows Me users to discuss your Windows Me problems and solutions.

To return to the regular Help and Support system, you can click Home at any time, or click the Back button (the left arrow) to move back screen-by-screen.

At the bottom of the Assisted Support page are three special-purpose hyperlinks. The first one, Check Status, lets you check on the status of any formal help requests you've made. Review Resolved Incidents lets you see any formal help requests you've made in the past that have been resolved. And View System Information opens the System Information utility (which you'll learn more about in Chapter 14, "PC Health Features").

Getting Help in Windows Programs

As I mentioned at the beginning of the chapter, each Windows-based program offers its own Help system. The Help information might appear differently depending on the program you are using; however, the differences are largely cosmetic.

For example, let's look at the Help window for Windows Media Player 7, a free utility that comes with Windows Me. I chose Help ➤ Help Topics to open the Help window (see Figure 8.6).

FIGURE 8.6

The Help system in a Windows application has many of the same features as the Windows Me system, but in a different format.

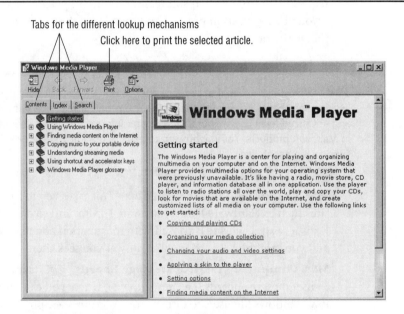

Tabs for the different lookup mechanisms

Click here to print the selected article.

Just like the Windows Me Help and Support screen, it contains three options for looking up information:

The Contents tab   Is roughly equivalent to the hyperlink system in Windows Me's Help. Click the Contents tab, and you'll see a series of books. Click the book you want to open, and subordinate books appear. Keep moving through levels of books till you find the topic you want.

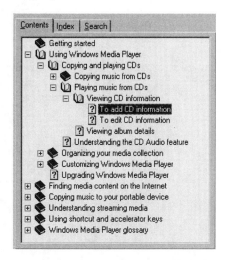

The Index tab   Works just the same as the Index feature in Windows Me's Help. You type the word to jump to that portion of the list, and then double-click the article you want.

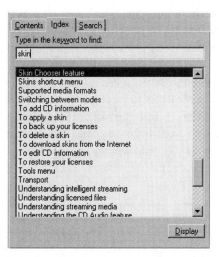

The Search tab Works the same as the Search box in Windows Me's Help. Enter the word and press Enter, and a list of articles containing that word appears.

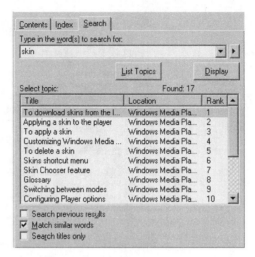

Using Windows 95–Style Help Files

Windows Help has evolved over the years, both for Windows itself and for Windows-based programs. If you have an older program, its Help interface probably looks a little different from the one you saw in the preceding section. Even in newer programs, Help screens come in many styles and formats, varying even between two programs created by the same manufacturer. What I can do is to briefly introduce you to the variety of elements you are likely to run into and let you take it from there.

The good news is that the word "Help" almost always appears at the far right side of any Windows program's menu bar. Clicking this menu brings up some choices pertaining to Help built into whatever program you're using. Figure 8.7 shows a potpourri of such Help menus.

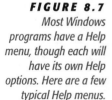

FIGURE 8.7
Most Windows programs have a Help menu, though each will have its own Help options. Here are a few typical Help menus.

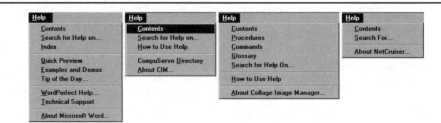

The majority of Help menus have a Search for Help On command or Help Topics command to help you narrow the topic search. Often, choosing one of these commands will present you with an Index box like the one described earlier. Other options (such as Help with Procedures) are pretty self-explanatory.

 TIP If, while looking at an application's Help screen, you can't remember how to use Help, just press the F1 key. You'll then usually see a list of topics explaining how to use the Help system.

The Help interface for programs written for Windows 95 looks much like the Help system I showed you for Windows Media Player earlier in the chapter, except that there isn't the two-pane system. Instead, there are multiple windows.

A typical Help window looks like what you see in Figure 8.8, a single pane—until you choose a topic.

FIGURE 8.8
This Help window is from Microsoft Word 97. It uses the older, Windows 95–style Help interface.

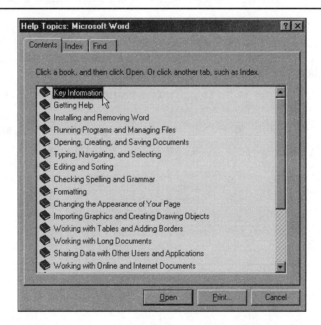

Notice the three tabs, Contents, Index, and Find (instead of Search). They work pretty much the same way as in the other Help interfaces you've seen. When you double-click a topic to read, however, you'll get a second window displaying the Help information. Figure 8.9 shows an example.

FIGURE 8.9
*Choosing a topic
produces a new
window with the Help
text in it.*

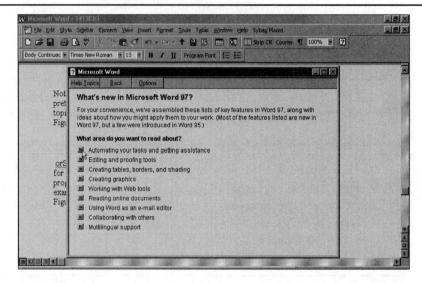

Sometimes the second window will have *hotspots* (a hotspot is any item in the Help screen text that does something special if you click it) or other buttons that do things if you click them, such as expand to show additional subtopics. In Figure 8.9, the little buttons in the central window are links. If the arrow pointer changes to a pointing hand, you know the thing you're pointing to is a hotspot. Click and something will happen.

Figure 8.10 shows NetCruiser's (an older Internet program from Netcom) opening Help screen.

Up and Running

FIGURE 8.10
*A typical Help screen.
Read the topic by
clicking an underlined
word or phrase. Click a
word underlined with a
dotted line to see its
definition.*

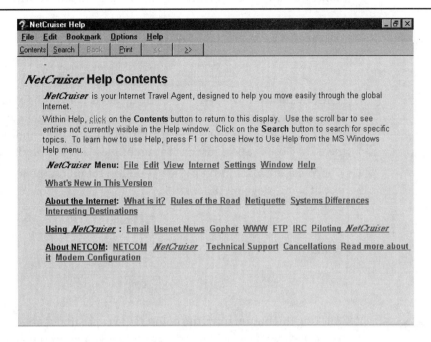

Notice the underlined words and the buttons just below the menu bar. These are just some of the elements to look for on Help screens. The following list describes these and other common Help-screen elements.

- Any word or phrase in a list that appears lighter (or green, on a color monitor) and is underlined with a solid line is a *topic*. Clicking a topic jumps you to the section in the online Help that's relevant to that word or procedure. You'll then see a new Help window with information about that topic.

- Occasionally you'll encounter hotspots that are graphics rather than words. They don't look any different from other graphics in the Help windows, but the pointer turns into the hand icon when it's positioned over them. You can activate this kind of hotspot by simply clicking it, as you do other hotspots. There are a few key combinations that highlight the hotspots in a Help window, making it easy to locate and select them. Pressing Tab advances to the next hotspot, Shift+Tab moves to the previous hotspot, and Ctrl+Tab highlights all the hotspots for as long as you hold both keys down.

- Some words appear lighter (or green) and are underlined with a dotted line.

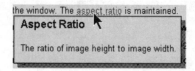

Clicking the word will typically bring up a box containing a definition. To see the definition, position the pointer on the term (once again, the cursor changes to the hand icon) and click. The definition pops up in a window like that shown here. To close the box, just click again or press any key on the keyboard.

- The What Is This? button is the "?" button found on the toolbar or in the title bar of some programs. It looks like this:

or like this:

Clicking this button turns the pointer into a question mark. Once that happens, you can click an element on the screen that you're curious about, and you'll see an explanation of the element. For example, you could open a menu and choose a command, like this:

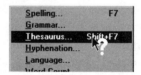

The result would likely be a screenful of information explaining the ins and outs of the highlighted command.

- The menu gives you a list of options you can choose from, such as Annotate, Print Topic, Copy, Font, and Keep Help on Top.

  Annotate   Lets you make notes or place bookmarks to customize the Help system.

  Print Topic   Prints the currently displayed topic on your printer. Just set up your printer and click this option. You'll then have a paper version of the Help topic at hand.

  Copy   Puts the current page of help information on the Clipboard so you can paste it into another document. This is useful for anyone writing documentation about a program, letting them easily import Help material into their own document. (Of course, you'll want to be careful about copyright infringement.)

Font   Lets you increase or decrease the size of the lettering in the Help boxes to get more text in the window or to increase visibility.

Keep Help on Top   Prevents the Help window from being obscured by other windows on the screen as they are selected or as you open new documents or applications.

Copying Help Information

In both Windows Me and older Help systems, there may be occasions when you will find it useful to copy information from Help topics into a document or another application. For example, if you're preparing a training manual for employees in your company who are learning Microsoft Word 2000, you may find useful guidelines within Word's Help utility that you want to incorporate rather than retyping it all.

Copying is done by way of Windows' Clipboard. You can copy an entire Help topic or only selected portions of it. For a complete discussion of Clipboard and text-selection techniques, see Chapter 6, "WordPad and Paint Basics." I'll briefly outline here the steps for copying to the Clipboard from Help.

1. Within the active Help topic window, use the mouse to select the text you want to copy.

2. If there is an Edit menu in the Help system, open it and choose Copy. Otherwise, press Ctrl+C to copy.

3. Switch to the document where you want to paste the information, open its Edit menu, and choose Paste. (If the program does not have an Edit menu, you can use Ctrl+V to paste.)

 NOTE   Selecting text works the same way throughout Windows and in most Windows applications; it's explained thoroughly in Chapter 6, which covers WordPad. The easiest way is to position the selection cursor—the blinking bar—at the beginning of the text. Then, keeping the mouse button depressed, move the mouse. Release the button when all the text you want to copy is highlighted.

Printing a Help Topic

Most Help systems, including Windows Me's and the ones in your programs, have a Print capability. Depending on the Help system, you might see a Print button on the toolbar, or there might be a Print command on a menu. Look around.

When you find the Print button or command, choosing it might print the selected article immediately, or a Print dialog box might open, inviting you to select a page range, a printer, and the number of copies. Again, go with the flow.

Using the Troubleshooters

Windows Me's Help includes many *troubleshooters*, which are Wizards that can help you diagnose and troubleshoot the most common problems with your Windows PC. There is no readily available list of the available troubleshooters, but you can pull up an impromptu list by using Search to search for "troubleshooter." You can also browse through the Troubleshooting hyperlink on the initial screen of Help and Support.

The troubleshooters ask you a series of questions and provide information based on your answers. For example, in the Modem Troubleshooter, you're first asked about the general nature of your problem:

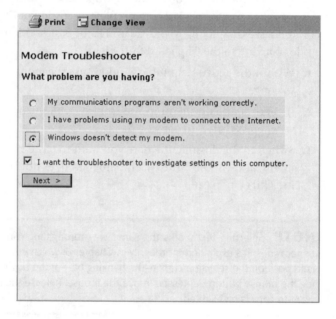

Make your selection and click Next, and the troubleshooter provides some suggestions:

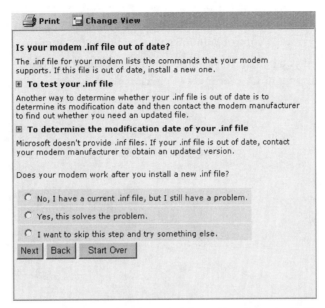

Answer the questions, and try the proposed fixes. For example, in the troubleshooter shown above, there are plus signs next to a couple of suggestions. Click the plus sign to expand a detailed, step-by-step explanation of how to accomplish the suggested activity. After trying the suggestions, choose an option button and click Next, or click Start Over to try another troubleshooter.

When Help Doesn't Help

If you can't find the information you need in the Help system for Windows Me or for the program you're using, don't despair. Here are some suggestions:

- Try the Assisted Support links in Windows Me's Help system to access the Internet and possibly locate information on MSN's forums or message boards.
- Go to Assisted Support ➤ Microsoft Corporation ➤ Searchable Knowledge Base to look up a problem or question in the Microsoft Knowledge Base.
- Visit the Web page for a particular device's manufacturer to see whether troubleshooting help is available there.
- Post a question on a Usenet newsgroup, as described in Chapter 22, "Communicating with Outlook Express News and Mail."
- Attend a computer users' group in your local area, if one is available. Perhaps one of the experts there can help you answer your question.

- Try calling the technical support phone number for the product or device you have questions about. The phone number is probably in the documentation that came with the product. The Windows Me technical support phone number for individual home users is (425) 635-7222. You get two no-charge calls for each copy of Windows Me you purchase; after that, you must pay.

If you bought the product at a retail store, that store might offer telephone technical support. It never hurts to check.

PART II

Optimizing and Customizing

CHAPTER 9

Customizing Windows with the Control Panel

FEATURING:

There are numerous alterations you can make to customize Windows to your liking—adjustments to screen colors, modems, mouse speed, passwords, key repeat rate, fonts, and networking options, to name just a few. They all contribute to making Windows work in a comfortable and intuitive way for you, the individual user.

Most customization is done through Windows Me's Control Panel. Once you change a setting with the Control Panel, alterations are stored in the Windows configuration Registry. The settings are reloaded each time you run Windows and stay in effect until you change them again with the Control Panel.

 TIP Many of the Control Panel options can also be accessed from other locations in Windows. For example, you can right-click the Desktop and choose Properties to get to the same Display Properties box that the Control Panel offers, and you can see Network Properties by right-clicking My Network Places and choosing Properties.

Each of the Control Panel's many icons opens a Properties dialog box for a particular class of devices or a particular program. You already saw some of them in action earlier in this book, where we talked about the Display Properties, the Taskbar, and the Start Menu Properties, for example.

In this chapter, we'll continue that exploration by looking at several other Control Panel categories. Upcoming chapters will discuss several others yet; for example, printers are covered in Chapter 11, "Printers and Printing," and fonts in Chapter 12, "Using Fonts Effectively." See the guide in the following section to find out which chapter to look to for information about a particular Control Panel category that interests you.

Opening the Control Panel

You open the Control Panel by clicking the Start button, choosing Settings, and choosing Control Panel. The Control Panel window then opens, as shown in Figure 9.1. Besides the standard set of Control Panel icons, you might have some extra icons, placed there by application software you have added or by the setup program for a particular device. For example, in Figure 9.1, the following items are not part of the standard Windows Me install: AudioHQ (placed there by my sound card installation program), Disc Detector (placed there when I installed Adaptec Easy CD Creator), Find Fast (installed with Microsoft Office 2000), LiveUpdate (installed with Norton AntiVirus 2000), and RealPlayer (placed there when I installed RealPlayer 7). In this chapter, I'll cover only the items that are native to Windows Me itself.

Not all of the Windows Accessories are installed by default, so you might be missing the Accessibility Options and/or Desktop Themes icons if those features have not been installed on your PC. (You can use Add/Remove Programs to add them from the Windows Me CD, as explained later in the chapter.)

Another possible difference: If your mouse came with custom software and you installed it, your mouse icon might look different, and the options for controlling the mouse might be different, too. (I'll remind you of that again later in the chapter, when it comes time to discuss mouse settings.)

 TECH TIP The Control Panel can also be reached from My Computer or from the Explorer. From the Explorer, scroll the left pane to the top and click on the My Computer icon. Then click the Control Panel in the right pane.

PART

II

FIGURE 9.1
Each item in the Control Panel window opens a window from which you can make adjustments.

Optimizing and Customizing

In new installations of Windows Me, the default setting is to show only the most commonly used items in the Control Panel, so your Control Panel window might look like Figure 9.2 instead. If so, click the View All Control Panel Options hyperlink at the left to arrive at the full version shown in Figure 9.1.

FIGURE 9.2

*An abbreviated version
of the Control Panel
might appear at first.*

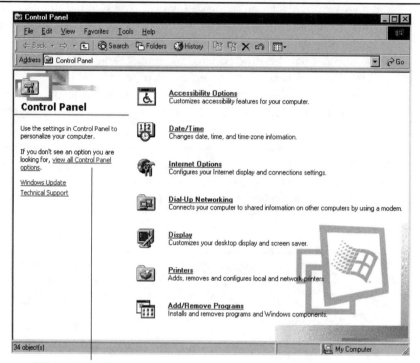

Click here for the full version.

 TIP   To change the default setting so that the full Control Panel appears every time, choose Tools ➢ Folder Options, click the View tab, and mark the Display All Control Panel Options and All Folder Contents check box.

Each icon in the Control Panel runs a little program (called an *applet*) when you open it, typically bringing up one or more dialog boxes for you to make settings in. Below is a list of all the standard Control Panel applets and what they do in alphabetical order (which is also the order in which they appear in the Control Panel).

Accessibility Options   Lets you set keyboard, mouse, sound, display, and other options that make a Windows Me computer easier to use by those who are visually, aurally, or motor impaired. See Appendix B, "Windows Me Accessibility Features."

Add New Hardware   Installs or removes sound, CD-ROM, video, MIDI, hard- and floppy-disk controllers, PCMCIA sockets, display adaptors, SCSI controllers, keyboard, mouse, printers, ports, and other device drivers. See Chapter 13, "Adding and Removing Hardware and Software."

Add/Remove Programs   You can add or remove modules of Windows Me itself and sometimes add or remove other kinds of programs. This applet will also let you create a startup disk, which is used to start your computer in case the operating system on the hard disk gets trashed accidentally. See Chapter 13.

Automatic Updates   Controls the settings for the Automatic Update feature, which is new in Windows Me. The Automatic Updates applet downloads the latest versions of important Windows drivers and utilities and installs them automatically. See Chapter 14, "PC Health Features."

Date/Time   Sets the current date and time, as well as the time zone you're in. You'll learn to set the date and time later in this chapter.

Desktop Themes   These combine custom sounds, color schemes, screen savers, and cursors into easily chosen settings groups. See Chapter 10, "Customizing the Desktop, Taskbar, and Start Menu."

Dial-Up Networking   A shortcut to the Dial-Up Networking folder available on the Start menu (Start ➣ Settings ➣ Dial-Up Networking), in which you can set up and modify dial-up networking connections such as to your Internet provider. See Chapter 26, "Extending Your Reach with Dial-Up Networking."

Display   Sets the colors (or gray levels) and fonts of various parts of Windows' screens, title bars, scroll bars, and so forth. Sets the background pattern or picture for the Desktop. Also allows you to choose the screen saver, display driver, screen resolution, and energy-saving mode (if your display supports it). See Chapter 10, "Customizing the Desktop, Taskbar, and Start Menu."

Folder Options   Displays the same options that you get when you choose Tools ➣ Folder Options in any file management window. These options let you control how Windows Me handles files and folders. They were covered in Chapter 5, "Organizing Files, Programs, and Disks."

Fonts   Adds and deletes typefaces for your screen display and printer output. Allows you to look at samples of each of your fonts. Fonts are discussed at length in Chapter 12.

Gaming Options   Adds, removes, and adjusts settings for joysticks and other types of game controllers and lets you enable Voice Chat for any games that support the feature. See Chapter 18, "Working with Multimedia and Entertainment Hardware."

Infrared   Configures and monitors infrared (wireless) communications. If your PC doesn't have an infrared port, you won't have this item in your Control Panel.

Internet Options   Settings for all Internet-related activities, such as Web, mail, newsgroups, your home page location, etc. This applet opens the same dialog box as when you choose Tools ➤ Internet Options in Internet Explorer. See Chapter 21, "Browsing the World Wide Web with Internet Explorer 5.5," for details.

Keyboard   Sets the rate at which keys repeat when you hold them down, sets the cursor blink rate, determines the language your keyboard will be able to enter into documents, and lets you declare the type of keyboard you have. See Chapter 13 for details.

Mail   Lets you add and customize the e-mail accounts on your PC. Similar to choosing Tools ➤ Accounts ➤ Mail in Outlook Express. See Chapter 22, "Communicating with Outlook Express News and Mail," for details.

Modems   Lets you add, remove, and set the properties of the modem(s) connected to your system. Covered in Chapter 19, "Introduction to Windows Communications."

Mouse   Sets the speed of the mouse pointer's motion relative to your hand motion and how fast a double-click has to be to have an effect. You can also reverse the functions of the right and left buttons, set the shape of the various Windows Me pointers, and tell Windows that you've changed the type of mouse you have. Mouse settings are covered later in this chapter.

Network   Function varies with the network type. Typically, this applet allows you to set the network configuration (network card/connector, protocols, and services); add and configure optional support for Novell, Banyan, Sun network support, and network backup hardware; change your identification (workgroup name, computer name); and determine the manner in which you control who gains access to resources you share over the network, such as printers, fax modems, and folders. See Part V, "Networking," for details.

ODBC Data Sources   If you are connected to a network and use an ODBC (Open Database Connectivity)–compliant database program such as Oracle or Access, this applet allows you to control your connections and modify driver settings. You can also specify data sources on your own machine for sharing on the network.

Passwords   Sets up or changes logon passwords, allows remote administration of the computer, and sets up individual profiles that go into effect when each new user logs on to the local computer. Passwords and security are covered in Chapter 26.

PCMCIA   Lets you stop PCMCIA cards before removing them, sets the memory area for the card service shared memory (very unlikely to be needed), and disables/enables the beeps that indicate PCMCIA cards are activated when the computer boots up. This icon only appears on laptops or on desktop machines configured with PCMCIA slots.

Power Options   If you have a battery-powered portable computer or an energy-efficient desktop machine, this applet provides options for setting the Advanced

Power Management details and viewing a scale indicating the current condition of the battery charge. Power options are covered later in this chapter.

Printers Displays the printers you have installed on your system, lets you modify the property settings for those printers, and lets you display and manage the print *queue* for each of those printers. Use this applet to install *printer drivers*. Installing new printer drivers and managing the print queue are covered in Chapter 7, "Other Windows Accessories."

Regional Settings Sets how Windows displays times, dates, numbers, and currency. These are covered in Chapter 13.

Scanners and Cameras Windows Me includes direct support for a variety of scanners and digital cameras, and this applet lets you test and configure the installed devices. Chapter 17, "Using Image Acquisition and Movie Maker," covers scanners and cameras.

Scheduled Tasks If you have used the Maintenance Wizard or Task Scheduler to set up programs to run automatically at certain times, you can control that schedule here. See Chapter 14 for details.

Sounds and Multimedia Turns off and on the computer's beep or adds sounds to various system events if your computer has built-in sound capability. Lets you set up sound *schemes*—preset collections of sounds that your system uses to alert you to specific events. See Chapter 18 for more information.

System Displays information about your system's internals—devices, amount of RAM, type of processor, and so forth. Also lets you add to, disable, and remove specific devices from your system, set up hardware profiles (for instance, to allow automatic optimization when using a docking station with a laptop), and optimize some parameters of system performance such as CD cache size and type. This applet also provides a number of system-troubleshooting tools.   You'll learn more about the System Properties in Chapter 13.

Taskbar and Start Menu Lets you control the properties for the Taskbar and the Start menu, such as size, placement, item arrangement, and the content of the Documents menu. This is the same Properties box you get when you choose Start ➢ Settings ➢ Taskbar and Start Menu. It's covered in Chapter 5.

Telephony Lets you delete your location, your dialing prefixes for an outside line, and other attributes relating to telephone-dependent activities that rely on the TAPI interface. Refer to Chapter 19 for more details.

Users Enables your computer to be set up for use by other people, allowing each user to have their own Desktop icons, background, color choices, and other settings. You'll learn how to set up multiuser operation in Chapter 13.

NOTE All the Control Panel setting dialog boxes have a ? button in their upper-right corner. You can click this button and then click an item in the dialog box that you have a question about. You'll be shown some relevant explanation about the item.

I'll now discuss the Control Panel applets in detail. Aside from the Accessibility settings, the applets here are the ones you're most likely to want to adjust.

Setting the Date and Time

The Date/Time icon lets you adjust the system's date and time. The system date and time are used for a number of purposes, including date- and time-stamping the files you create and modify, scheduling fax transmissions, and so on. All programs use these settings, regardless of whether they are Windows or non-Windows programs.

This applet doesn't change the format of the date and time—just the actual date and time. To change the *format*, you use the Regional applet, discussed later in this chapter.

To check and/or change the date and time, complete the following steps:

1. Double-click Date/Time in the Control Panel. The Date/Time Properties dialog box in Figure 9.3 appears.

 NOTE You can also open the Date/Time Properties dialog box by double-clicking the clock on the Taskbar.

2. Adjust the time and date by typing in the corrections or clicking the arrows. Note that you have to click the hours, minutes, seconds, or the~A.M./~P.M. area directly before the little arrows to the right will modify the correct value.

3. Next, you can change the time zone you are in. Choose a time zone from the drop-down list.

4. Click OK to accept your changes.

 NOTE Who cares about the time zone, you ask? Good question. For many users, it doesn't matter. But because people fax to other time zones and some programs help you manage your transcontinental and transoceanic phone calling, it's built into Windows Me. These programs need to know where in the world you and Carmen Sandiego are. So, use the Time Zone drop-down menu to select the time zone that you are in.

FIGURE 9.3

Adjust the date, time, and local time zone from this dialog box. A shortcut to this box is to double-click the time in the Taskbar.

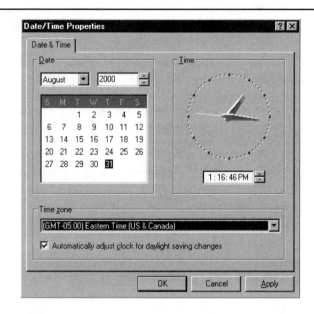

Selecting Regional Settings

The Regional settings customize Windows for use in other countries. If you're using Windows in English in the United States, don't bother making any changes.

The settings made from this box pertain exclusively to Windows and Windows applications; other programs won't take advantage of them. (Actually, even some Windows applications won't.) You should do some experimenting with the settings to see if they make any difference, or read the application's manual for information about how to set the formats for it.

Choosing Regional Settings from the Control Panel displays the dialog box you see in Figure 9.4. To change the settings, simply click the appropriate tab page and then click the drop-down list box for the setting in question. Examples of the current settings are shown in each section, so you don't need to change them unless they look wrong.

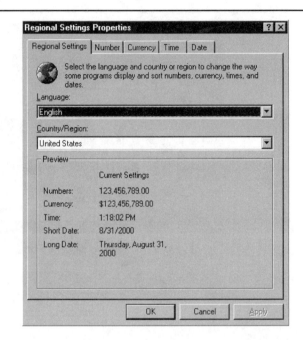

These are the tabs in the Regional Settings Properties dialog box:

Regional Settings   Use this tab to identify which country you're in. All other settings change in accordance with the accepted practices in that country. Normally, then, you'd need to bother with changing settings on the other tabs only if your settings differ from the settings that Microsoft has determined are standard for your country.

Number   This tab's settings are for displaying numbers with or without decimals, commas, or leading zeros, and with different decimal separators. It also determines whether to display measurements in metric or English units, and what your *list separator* should be. For example, in the phrase "Well, it's one, two, three, four, what are we fighting for...," the list separator is a comma. In other languages, items listed in a sentence are separated by other punctuation marks.

Currency   Set the currency indicator and the location and number of decimal digits.

Time   Allows for 12- or 24-hour time indication, ~A.M. or ~P.M. indicators, choice of separators, and leading zeros.

Date   Sets dates from a myriad of formats, such as 3/6/53; 03/06/53; 3/6/1953; 06-03-1953; March 6, 1953; and others. This is useful for programs that pop the date into text at the touch of a key or translate dates from one format to another.

Adjusting the Mouse

You can adjust seven aspects of your mouse's operation:

- Button configuration
- Double-click speed
- ClickLock
- Look of the pointers
- Pointer speed
- Snap To
- Pointer visibility

Wheel Mouse Support

Windows Me includes support for the Microsoft *wheel mouse* (the Intellimouse), which is a mouse with a little wheel sticking up between the mouse buttons. When you spin the wheel with some newer programs, it scrolls the contents of the active window; it relieves you of having to position the pointer on the scroll bar. Spinning the wheel one increment causes text to scroll several lines (default: three) per wheel detent.

Just because a window has a scroll bar doesn't mean it will work with the wheel. The program has to be wheel aware. Some wheel-aware programs, including the programs in Office 2000, will zoom in or out (i.e., cause the document to be displayed larger or smaller) if you rotate the wheel and hold down Ctrl at the same time.

Some wheel-aware applications (such as Internet Explorer or an Office 2000 program) also offer panning mode; you press down on the wheel to enter this special mode. When in panning mode, the mouse cursor changes to a special panning cursor, and just moving the mouse forward or backward will start the document scrolling in its window. The scroll speed is determined by how far you pull the mouse away from the position where you activated panning mode. When you want to exit the panning mode, simply press any mouse button.

Reversing Button Configuration

If you're left-handed, you may want to switch the mouse around to use it on the left side of the computer and reverse the buttons. The main button then becomes the right button instead of the left one. If you use other programs outside of Windows that don't allow this, however, it might just add to the confusion. If you use the mouse only in Windows programs and you're left-handed, then it's worth a try. Follow these steps to make the switch:

1. Open the Control Panel and double-click Mouse. Then click the Buttons tab if it is not already on top (see Figure 9.5).

2. Click the Left-Handed option. Then click Apply to check it out. Don't like it? Revert to the original setting and click Apply again.

FIGURE 9.5

Here you can reverse the buttons for use by left-handed people. You can also adjust the double-click speed.

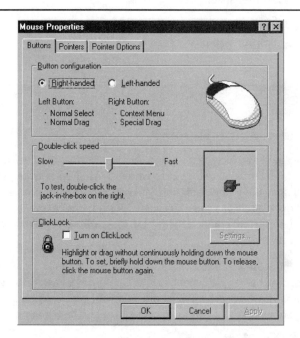

Adjusting the Double-Click Speed

The double-click speed setting can also be found on the Buttons tab (Figure 9.5). Double-click speed determines how fast you have to double-click to make a double-click operation work (that is, to run a program from its icon, to open a document from its icon, or to select a word). If the double-click speed is too fast, it's difficult for your fingers to click fast enough. If it's too slow, you end up running programs or opening and closing windows unexpectedly. Double-click the Jack-in-the-box to try out the new double-click speed. Jack will jump out or back into the box if the double-click registered. If you're not faring well, adjust the slider and try again.

NOTE You don't have to click Apply to test the slider settings. Moving the slider instantly affects the mouse's double-click speed.

Using ClickLock

ClickLock is a new feature in Windows Me. It's part of the Accessibility features, and it enables you to drag without continuously holding down the mouse button. Turn it on with the Turn on ClickLock check box on the Buttons tab (refer back to Figure 9.5).

To use ClickLock, simply hold down the mouse button for a second or two without moving the mouse, and it becomes locked down, as the Caps Lock key locks the Shift key down. To release it, hold it down again.

You can control how long you have to hold before ClickLock kicks in with the Settings button next to the ClickLock check box. Click the Settings button to open the Settings for the ClickLock box, and drag the slider to increase or decrease the amount of time.

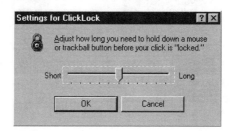

Selecting Your Pointers

Your mouse pointer's shape changes depending on what you are pointing to and what Windows Me is doing. If you are pointing to a window border, the pointer becomes a two-headed arrow. If Windows Me is busy, it becomes an hourglass. When you are editing text, it becomes an I-beam, and so on.

You can customize your cursors for the fun of it or to increase visibility. You can even install animated cursors that look really cute and keep you amused while you wait for some process to complete.

To change the cursor settings, do the following:

1. Click the Pointers tab of the Mouse Properties dialog box (see Figure 9.6). The list shows which pointers are currently assigned to which activities.

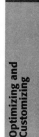

FIGURE 9.6

Choose pointer shapes or various activities here.

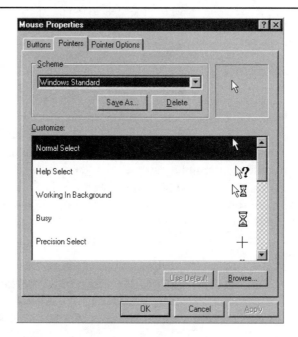

2. To choose a whole different set of pointers, open the Scheme drop-down list and choose a different pointer scheme.

TIP If there are only a couple of pointer schemes on the list, Cancel out of here and install the additional schemes from Microsoft's Windows Me CD (for instruction on how to add these, see Chapter 13). Then come back, and more schemes will be available.

3. To change an individual pointer, double-click an item in the list. In the Browse box that appears, select a different pointer and click Open.

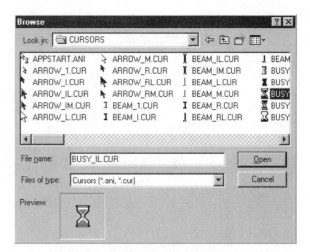

When you click a cursor in the Browse box, it will be displayed at the bottom of the box for you to examine in advance—a thoughtful feature. Even animated cursors will do their thing right in the Browse box. (Cursors with the .ani extension are animated ones.)

 TIP The extra cursors are kept in C:\Windows\Cursors. If there aren't many to choose from, install the additional pointer schemes in Windows (for instructions see Chapter 13).

 NOTE If you've changed the shape and want to revert, click Use Default to go back to the normal pointer shape that came with Windows Me.

4. If you would like to save changes you've made to the current pointer scheme, click Save As. Enter a name for the new scheme to be saved and click OK.

At this point, you can click OK to close the Mouse Properties, or you can go on to the next section to set more properties for your mouse.

Setting the Pointer Motion

On the Pointer Options tab of the Mouse Properties dialog box (see Figure 9.7), you control the way the pointer moves on-screen.

FIGURE 9.7
*You can adjust the
speed at which the
mouse pointer moves,
plus several other
specialized pointer
options.*

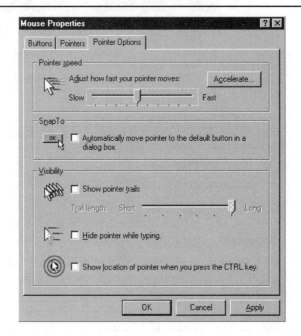

Pointer speed is the speed at which the mouse pointer moves relative to the movement of the mouse. Believe it or not, mouse motion is actually measured in *Mickeys*. (Somebody out there has a sense of humor!) A Mickey equals 1/100 of an inch of mouse movement. The tracking-speed setting lets you adjust the relationship of Mickeys to pixels. If you want to be very exact in your cursor movement, you'll want to slow the tracking speed, requiring more Mickeys per pixel. However, this requires more hand motion for the same corresponding cursor motion. If your desk is crammed and your coordination is very good, then you can increase the speed (fewer Mickeys per pixel).

If you use the mouse with MS-DOS programs that use their own mouse drivers, you might want to adjust the Windows mouse speed to match that of your other programs so that you won't need to mentally adjust when you use such non-Windows programs.

 TIP Incidentally, if you think the mouse runs too slowly in your non-Windows applications, there may be a fix. Contact your mouse's maker. For example, if you're using a Logitech mouse, a program called Click that is supplied with the Logitech mouse lets you easily control its tracking. See the Logitech manual for details.

Snap To

Snap To moves the mouse pointer to the default button whenever a dialog box is open. Some people find this feature very helpful; others think it's annoying. You decide.

Visibility

The Visibility settings consist of three options that make it easier to find your mouse pointer on-screen, especially if you have a visual disability:

Show Pointer Trails   This option creates a shadow of the mouse's path whenever you move it. Some people find it annoying, but for those who have trouble finding the pointer on the screen, it's a blessing. Mouse trails are particularly helpful when using Windows on passive-matrix or dual-scan laptop computers, where the pointer often disappears when you move it.

Hide Pointer While Typing   This option does just what the name says; when you press a key on the keyboard, the pointer disappears until you move the mouse again.

Show Location of Pointer When You Press the Ctrl Key   The option also does just what the name says. When this is on and you press Ctrl by itself, the pointer flashes to draw your attention to its position.

Setting Keyboard Options

Your keyboard probably works just fine without any modification of its settings, but there are a couple of adjustments you can make to its properties if you'd like.

Double-click Keyboard in the Control Panel to display the Keyboard Properties box. The main keyboard adjustments are found on the Speed tab, shown in Figure 9.8. They include the following:

Repeat Delay   Controls the interval between the time you hold down a key and when it starts to repeat (that is, to type its character very quickly on-screen).

Repeat Rate   Controls the rate at which the character repeat occurs once it gets started.

Cursor Blink Rate   Controls the speed at which the insertion point in text boxes (the vertical line) blinks on and off.

 NOTE   The Repeat Rate setting not only controls the rate for normal keys, but also affects the rate at which the spacebar, arrow keys, and Page Up and Page Down keys work.

PART

II

Optimizing and
Customizing

Drag the sliders to the left or right to adjust each setting. To test the first two, click in the text box provided and hold down a key.

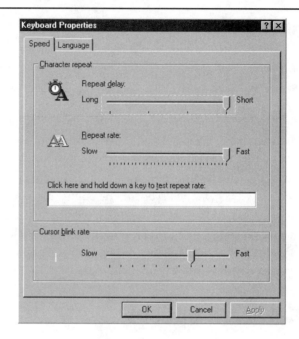

The second tab in the Keyboard Properties dialog box, Language, allows you to set up Windows to use a keyboard for a different language other than English.

Because of differences in language and alphabet, computers marketed abroad have different key assignments than your computer. Windows can't automatically detect what language a particular keyboard is for—that is, if you plug in a Spanish language keyboard, Windows simply sees it as a keyboard and doesn't know what symbols are on the tops of the keys. Therefore, you must use the Language tab in Keyboard Properties to specify the keyboard's language in order to get the pictures on the keys to match the letters that appear on-screen when you press them.

Typically, you'll have only one driver showing when you display the Language tab. To add a new one, click Add and choose a language from the resulting list. You may be prompted to insert a disk or CD-ROM so the applet can locate the proper driver. Then you'll have a second listing in the installed languages box. Here I've installed Spanish (Mexico) in addition to English:

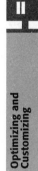

If you switch between languages as you type, you can use shortcut keys in Windows to switch between the language layouts for your keyboard. In other words, you don't have to have a Spanish-language keyboard plugged in to type in Spanish; all you need is one of the Spanish keyboard layouts loaded on the Language tab (and of course, the knowledge of which keys to press on the keyboard to get the characters you want). As you can see above, the default for switching is Left Alt+Shift, but you can choose Ctrl+Shift or None.

If you check Enable Indicator on Taskbar, your Taskbar will indicate which language driver is active at any one time. Clicking it brings up a menu that lets you easily switch between languages:

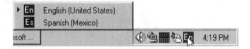

If you want to remove a language driver, select it in the dialog box and click Remove. Likewise, setting the default language is as easy as clicking Set as Default. This determines which language will be used when you start up your computer.

Controlling Passwords

The Control Panel's Password applet lets you change logon passwords, allow remote administration of the computer, and set up individual profiles that go into effect when each new user logs on to the local computer. The Passwords Properties dialog box is shown in Figure 9.9.

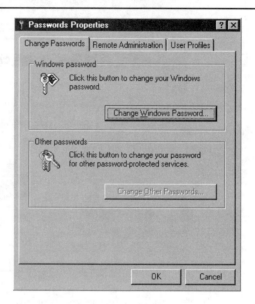

The Change Passwords Tab

On most PCs, the Change Windows Password is the only available option on the Change Passwords tab. You can click the Change Windows Password button to open a dialog box allowing you to enter a new password for logging on to Windows itself. If you do not currently see a logon box for Windows when you start your PC, then your password is probably set to nothing. If you enter a password here, you will see the logon box in the future.

Conversely, if you currently have a password but want to eliminate the Windows logon screen at startup, set your new password to nothing. Notice that you must know the old password in order to change it.

 NOTE Windows logon passwords can be as long as 127 characters, although that's a bit more than anyone would want to bother with. You may use letters, numbers, and punctuation marks. The maximum password length on other networks may be different. For example, NT and Novell passwords must be shorter. If there's any chance that your machine will eventually be logging in to a network using one of those servers, be sure to check the documentation with those networks before you start relying on extra-long passwords.

The Change Other Passwords button will be available only if your system is set up for other passwords, such as a network password.

The Remote Administration Tab

The Remote Administration tab page of the Passwords dialog box (refer back to Figure 9.9) is used for setting up passwords to allow someone at another workstation to access your computer. As discussed in various chapters in Part V, a network administrator can manage shared folders and printers on this computer and see who connects to them. Settings on this page determine which password the remote administrator has to enter remotely in order to create, change, or monitor shared resources on your computer. To set up the computer for remote administration, you have to enable it first by checking the box. Then enter the password you want to require for remote administration of your shared resources. Remember to inform your network administrator of the password.

The third tab in the Passwords dialog box is for user profiles, which is the subject of the following section.

The User Profiles Tab

Windows NT introduced the concept of multiple users on a given computer workstation (the PC), each with their own settings. In NT, such an arrangement is necessary because NT's security model necessitates that each user be given a set of security privileges controlling the use of network-shared resources. Windows Me isn't based on as ambitious a security model, but it still includes a decent functional subset of NT's user-by-user customizability. By creating an entry in the Configuration Registry for each user on the system, Windows Me can accommodate any number of people on the same computer, each having different settings. When a user signs in, the Registry is accessed, and the appropriate settings go into effect.

What does all this mean for the average person? Well, it means that each person in your family can choose their own screen colors and font settings, and they can customize the Start menu and the Desktop without worrying about messing up anyone else's settings. The only drawback to this feature is that it requires a significant amount of hard disk space because each person's settings must be saved separately. If you do not have at least 500 megabytes free on your hard disk, you might want to skip this feature.

The collection of settings each user creates is called a *user profile*. A typical user profile might include Desktop colors, screen saver, Quick Launch bar shortcuts, IE history and cookies, Outlook Express address book, and program groups. It does not create any Desktop folders or a My Documents folder, so users will have to share those.

As it comes from the factory, Windows Me is set up in single-profile mode. Each user who logs on will get the same settings regardless of the username and password they enter. To enable Windows to use multiple user profiles, you must turn the feature on and then configure at least one user. You can then add more users at your leisure.

Setting Up for Multiple Users

One way to set up for multiple users is to turn on the Users Can Customize Their Preferences... option on the User Profiles tab of the Passwords Properties dialog box.

 NOTE Another way of setting up for multiple users is to double-click the Users icon in the Control Panel. If multiple-user access is not yet configured on the PC, a Wizard runs that walks you through the process of setting it up. The method in the following steps is faster, though.

Here's how that works:

1. Start with an ordinary setup. Any settings that are currently in effect, such as icons on the Desktop, colors, etc., will be cloned into all subsequent profiles that get created.

2. Open the Passwords Properties dialog box (choose Passwords from the Control Panel) and click the User Profiles tab.

3. Click the second option (Users Can Customize...) to activate the lower portion of the dialog box, as seen in Figure 9.10.

PART

II

Optimizing and Customizing

FIGURE 9.10

The first step in configuring user profiles is to enable the feature in the Passwords Properties box.

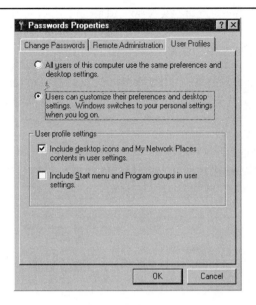

4. Select or deselect the check boxes as desired. The options declare which settings are stored in your new profile when you make changes from the Control Panel, property sheets, and so forth. If you elect *not* to turn on an option, you'll *share* the current setting of that item with other users.

 WARNING Turning on both check boxes will make the feature use more disk space; deselecting both will result in less disk space usage but less customization ability for each user.

5. Click OK. When prompted to restart your computer, click Yes.

Once you're set up for multiple users, Windows works just as you would expect. You have to sign in as usual. If you (or someone else) signs in with a name not recognized by the system, the following dialog box pops up:

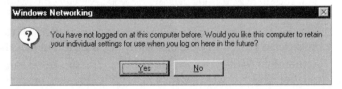

Click Yes, and Windows makes a copy of all the user-customizable elements you specified back in step 4. Then a box appears asking the new user to verify the password entered, which becomes that user's Windows logon password.

A copy of the settings currently in effect is made and assigned to the new user's environment, so the Desktop and all the other settings will appear as if nothing new had happened. But any changes the new user makes to the settings I listed above should have *no effect* on other user's settings.

Each additional new user now gets prompted for a password, and upon logging in the first time, is asked if they want the system to remember individual changes they make, such as Control Panel settings or the installation of new programs. If the user answers Yes, the settings will be stored individually from now on. Windows then clones the Start Button menus, Outlook Express and Internet Explorer settings, and some Registry settings for the new user. If you look carefully (using Explorer), you'll notice in the Profiles folder that some new folders are added under the Windows folder for each new user:

There's one ramification of all this multiple customization that you might bump into. Having separate profiles on the machine might tip off certain programs that there are additional users around. Programs that previously assumed you were the only user may now ask you for some identification, such as a password, before performing a task that requires security. Here's an example: Microsoft Exchange, even if set to remember your password automatically, will now prompt you to reenter the password when you attempt to log on to services such as the Microsoft Network. This prevents other users of the computer from logging on under your name, running up a bill, and reading your mail.

 WARNING Even though certain system settings that other users make on the computer won't affect yours, this doesn't mean other users can't affect your data files, folders, hard disks, and so forth. Unlike the password protection, you can assign to printers or folders that you share with users over the network, you can't password protect or specify user permissions for resources that are on your computer. Thus, once a user logs on to the system, they are able to gain access to any files on your hard disk. If you want to protect individual disks, folders, and files more thoroughly, you'll have to use another operating system such as Windows NT/2000.

Switching Users without Rebooting

You may have noticed that, in addition to shutting down Windows, from the Start button you have the option of logging on as a different user.

Choosing this option is an easy way to switch to another user's settings without having to wait for shutdown and reboot. It is the preferred approach, especially if resources on your machine are in use by other networked users.

Reverting to Single-User Operation

You can disable the multiuser option if you decide you want to revert to a single default profile for all users. Then the logon name and password a person enters affect only logging on to the network, not the local settings on the PC.

To revert to single-user operation, follow these steps:

1. Open the Passwords Properties box from the Control Panel.

2. Choose the User Profiles tab.

3. Select the first button, which will turn off the multiple-user setting.

4. Click OK and reboot.

Now, regardless of whom you log in as, you'll get the same settings. This won't erase any user folders created previously, though. This could cause a little havoc since previous users may lose individual settings, address book entries, IE histories, and so forth. Once individual settings are stored, it's preferable to use the User applet in the Control Panel to manage user profiles (or remove them). This is described in the following section.

 NOTE Even after turning off the multiuser option, all the subfolders for individual users will still be in the \Windows\Profiles folder (in case you later reactivate the multiuser setting). I once "lost" my Outlook Express mail folders after reverting to single-user mode. The only way that I could regain them was to reactivate multiuser mode and sign in using my old username and password.

Adding, Removing, and Changing User Profiles

Adding new profiles is easy enough. You just enable the feature as explained above, and let someone log in and enter a password of their choice. But you can also set up user profiles manually on the PC, as well as remove profiles and make changes to them.

To configure user settings, click Start ≻ Settings ≻ Control Panel and double-click the Users icon. You'll see the User Settings box shown in Figure 9.11.

FIGURE 9.11
Windows Me has user settings similar to those in Windows NT.

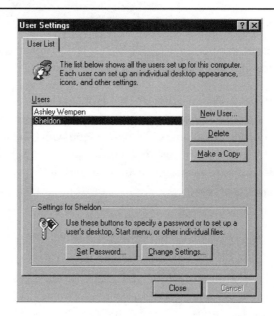

 NOTE Notice that in Figure 9.11, one user has a first and a last name, while another has only a first name. This happens because Windows allows users to set themselves up on-the-fly by entering a new username. Some people will enter their full name, while others will enter only their first name or a nickname. Windows accepts all equally.

All the users (anyone who has logged on since multiuser passwords were enabled) are listed. Each account can be removed, copied, or adjusted. You can add new accounts easily from this location, too. When you create new accounts from here, you have more options regarding which aspects of Windows are customized than you did when you initially enabled the feature in Passwords Properties. You can also customize the settings for users that are already created.

Creating a New User Profile

To create a brand-new user, instead of logging off and having someone new log on, just click New User and fill in the resulting boxes. You can set up multiple new users quickly this way.

Clicking New User runs an Add User Wizard that walks you through the process. After entering the name and password, you're presented with this box (incidentally, this is the same box you see when you click the Change Settings for an existing user):

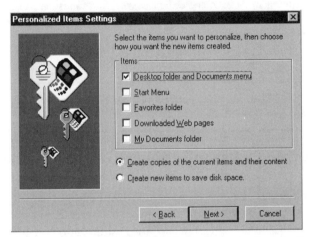

Mark the check boxes for the elements that you want to be customizable for this user. All unmarked items will use the default user settings, and whenever this user makes changes to those settings, those changes will be applied to the settings for all users (except those who have that particular feature marked as customizable).

An example will make this clearer. Suppose you mark the Favorites Folder check box for this new user you are setting up (let's call him Bob). A new copy of the current Favorites folder will be created for Bob, and any additions or changes Bob makes to the Favorites folder will appear only when he is logged in. Further, suppose that you *don't* mark the My Documents folder for Bob. Bob will use the general My Documents folder on the PC, rather than having his own copy. When Bob adds a file to My Documents, it will be placed in the general My Documents folder. Now, suppose there is another user, Alice, whom you set up with My Documents marked as customizable. The My Documents shortcut on Alice's Desktop will point to her own customized copy of My Documents, and she won't see Bob's document there (because it's stored in the general My Documents folder, not in Alice's copy).

After deciding which elements should be customizable, decide whether you want Windows to (a) create copies of the existing generic elements and let the new user customize his own copy of the current settings, or (b) create new, blank versions of the elements for the user. The latter saves disk space. However, it also denies the user access to any of the current "for all users" settings. For example, suppose you have marked the

Favorites folder for customization for Bob and you choose to create new items to save disk space. When Bob logs on, his Favorites menu will be empty. In contrast, if you choose to create copies of the existing settings, Bob's Favorites menu would have on it whatever was on the Favorites menu when you created Bob's user profile.

WARNING If you choose to have a new Start menu built, it will not include items for all the usual Windows accessories (or any other installed programs, for that matter). Thus, this is typically not a good choice, unless you *want* to restrict a user's easy access to programs.

Finish up the Wizard by clicking Next and then Finish.

NOTE Oddly, the Quick Launch bar will be shared by all users, regardless of the settings for an account.

Copying a User's Settings to a New Profile

You can use the Copy button as a shortcut to create a new user account based on all the settings of an existing account. Just highlight the one you want to copy and click Make a Copy. Then enter the new username and password. This is an easy way to create a new user profile based on the customization settings of another, without going through the whole rigmarole of creating the new user.

Changing a User's Password

The Set Password button is the easiest means for changing a user's password. Administrators or users might want to do this on a regular basis (every month or two) if network security is a concern and you are using passwords extensively (such as on a Novell or NT Server–based system).

Deleting a User Profile

Obviously, to delete a user profile, you simply highlight the account name and click Delete. But what happens when you do that? Are all the folders removed? Are all the files and folders on the user's Desktop and files in their My Documents folder trashed? Try it; you'll see this message:

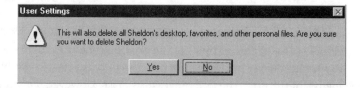

Fortunately, Windows prevents you from deleting yourself:

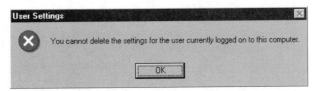

If you want to get rid of all user profiles, delete all the profiles except the one you are logged in as, and then turn off the User Profiles feature from the Passwords Properties box.

Choosing Power Options

Power options control how long after your computer starts being idle until your monitor shuts itself off, your hard disk stops spinning, and the system goes into Standby mode. On desktop PCs, such settings reduce power consumption and cut your electric bill, especially in a computer that's left on 24/7. On a laptop running on battery power, the settings are even more important, because they help make the battery last longer before it needs recharging.

Double-click Power Options in the Control Panel to open the Power Options dialog box. The tabs in the dialog box depend on the type of computer and the power management features supported by its BIOS. However, all computers at least have the Power Schemes and Advanced tabs.

PART
II

Optimizing and
Customizing

Setting a Power Scheme

Windows Me comes with three power schemes: Home/Office Desk, Portable/Laptop, and Always On. You can customize any of these schemes, or you can create your own schemes. (As always, a *scheme* is a group of settings saved under one name.) To choose a scheme, open the Power Schemes drop-down list and pick the one you want to use now.

Each scheme has three settings you can customize: Turn Off Monitor, Turn Off Hard Disks, and System Standby. On laptops, there are separate drop-down lists for each of these settings for two different operating modes: Plugged In and Running on Batteries. On desktop PCs there is only one drop-down list for each. Figure 9.12 shows a laptop, and Figure 9.13 shows a desktop PC.

 NOTE System Standby is a mode in which almost the entire computer is powered down but it's not turned off. Enough power is expended to keep the RAM active, so when you wake it up, the computer does not have to reboot and Windows does not have to restart.

FIGURE 9.12

A laptop PC has two operating modes: Plugged In and Running on Batteries.

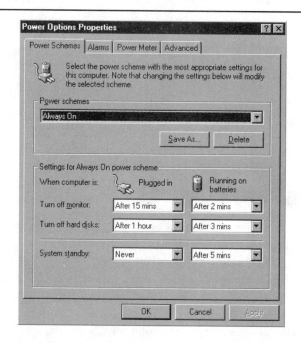

FIGURE 9.13

A desktop PC has only one operating mode and one set of drop-down lists.

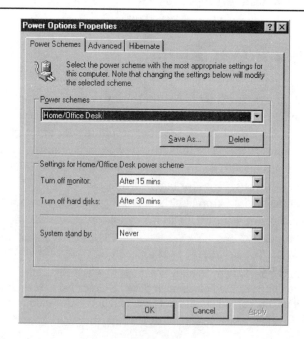

You can save your settings as a new scheme by clicking the Save As button, entering a name, and clicking OK. This works just the same as the other schemes in Windows, as you've seen in this chapter and as you will see in upcoming ones. You can delete a scheme you've created with the Delete button, but you can't delete the three schemes that come with Windows.

Setting Advanced Options

All computers show the Advanced tab, but the options available there may vary. The common options that everyone has are the two check boxes at the top:

Always Show Icon on the Taskbar   Places an icon in the System Tray that you can double-click to open a window showing battery status.

Prompt for Password When Computer Goes off Standby and Hibernate   Displays the Windows Logon dialog box when the computer wakes up after being in Standby or Hibernate mode.

 NOTE   Hibernate is a feature that uses part of the hard disk (about 100MB) to save the current contents of RAM. Then it shuts down the PC completely. When it wakes up again, it copies the data off the hard disk and back into RAM, and operation continues just as it was, including any open programs and data files. Not all computers support hibernation; if yours does, you will have a Hibernate tab in the Power Options dialog box.

Some computers will also have a Power Buttons area in the Advanced tab. This area allows you to control the behavior of the Power buttons on your PC. For example, the default behavior of the Power button is to turn the power off—obviously. But you can choose Standby as the Power button behavior so that when you press the Power button, the system goes into Standby mode instead. (If you do that and then you later want to really power off the system, hold the power button down for five seconds rather than just pressing and releasing.)

Enabling Other Power Options

Depending on the PC, you might have one or more of these tabs:

Alarms   On a laptop PC, the Alarms tab lets you control what will happen when the battery gets low. You can specify an audible or visual warning and/or an action such as automatically placing the computer in Standby mode.

Power Meter   On a laptop PC, you can view the current battery status and choose whether to show details for each battery (if you have more than one installed).

Hibernate   On a PC with support for the Hibernate feature, you can enable Hibernate support here. This claims a portion of the hard disk for Hibernate's use. After enabling this feature, an additional command appears on the Shut Down menu (Start ➤ Shut Down) for Hibernate.

Ready for more customization? In the next chapter, you'll learn how to customize the Desktop, the Taskbar, and the Start menu, three of the most important and often-used areas of Windows.

CHAPTER **10**

Customizing the Desktop, Taskbar, and Start Menu

FEATURING:

Customizing your Desktop and display can make a big difference in the overall usability of your PC. In this chapter, you'll learn how to change the display settings to make your Desktop look different and how to add and arrange shortcuts on the Desktop, on the Taskbar, and on the Start menu in a way that makes sense for your work habits.

Customizing the Display

The Display applet packs a wallop under its hood. For starters, it lets you choose colors, backgrounds, and other decoration for prettying up the general look of the Windows screen. It also includes the means for changing your screen driver and resolution.

 TIP The Display icon is accessible either from the Control Panel or from the Desktop. Right-click an empty area of the Desktop and choose Properties.

Here are the functional and cosmetic adjustments you can make to your Windows Me display from this applet:

- Set the background and wallpaper for the Desktop.
- Set the screen saver and energy conservation.
- Set the color scheme and fonts for Windows elements.
- Set the display device driver and adjust resolution, color depth, and font size.
- Change the icons you want to use for basic stuff on your Desktop, such as My Computer and the Recycle Bin.
- Set color management compatibility so that your monitor and your printer output colors match.
- Decide which Web goodies you want alive on your Desktop, such as stock quotes, news, and so forth.

Let's take a look at this dialog box page by page. This dialog box is a fun one to experiment with and will come in handy if you know how to use it.

Choosing a Wallpaper or Pattern

The Pattern and Wallpaper settings let you decorate the Desktop with something a little more festive than the default screen. *Patterns* are repeating designs, such as the woven look of fabric, that appear in black over the top of your chosen Desktop color. *Wallpaper* places a graphic image or Web page on the Desktop.

NOTE You must have the Show Web Content feature turned on in order to use wallpaper. If it's not turned on, when you choose a wallpaper, a prompt will appear asking whether you want to turn the feature on. You'll learn more about Show Web Content later in this chapter, when we discuss the Active Desktop feature.

Applying a Desktop Pattern

By default, there is no pattern on the Desktop. The Desktop appears in a solid color. (You'll learn how to change that color later in this chapter.) You can choose a pattern by following these steps:

1. Right-click the Desktop and choose Properties, and then click the Background tab.

2. Click the Pattern button. The Pattern dialog box appears.

3. Click the pattern you want to use. It appears in the Preview area.

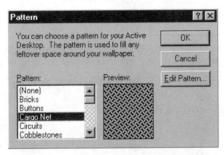

4. (Optional) To modify the pattern, do the following:

    a. Click Edit Pattern. The Pattern Editor dialog box opens.

    b. Click the pattern to turn each individual pixel of the pattern on or off as desired. You'll see your changes previewed in the Sample area.

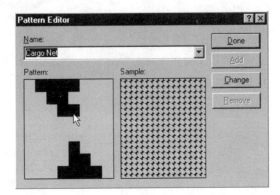

    c. Type a new name for the pattern in the Name box. Click Add to add the new pattern name to the list of patterns; then click Done.

PART

II

Optimizing and
Customizing

5. Click OK to accept the chosen pattern.

6. Make other changes to the display in the Display Properties dialog box, as described in the next sections, or click OK to close it if you are finished.

 TIP To preview the pattern without closing Display Properties, click the Apply button.

Applying a Wallpaper

A wallpaper image resides in a layer behind the Desktop icons but in front of the Desktop and pattern (if used), such that it partially or fully obscures the Desktop color/pattern but does not obscure any icons. Figure 10.1 shows a Desktop with both a pattern and a wallpaper image. Notice how some icons sit on top of the wallpaper, and how the Desktop pattern runs behind the wallpaper. You can use any image as wallpaper (BMP, JPG, PNG, DIB, or GIF format) or any Web page.

FIGURE 10.1
A Desktop with wallpaper and a pattern

The image in Figure 10.1 is centered, which means one copy of it appears in the center of the Desktop. You can also choose Tile, which places as many copies of the picture as needed in order to completely fill the screen, or Stretch, which stretches a single copy of the picture to fill the screen.

To apply a wallpaper, follow these steps:

1. Right-click the Desktop and choose Properties, then click the Background tab.

2. Choose the file you want to use from the list. The pictures on the list are the pictures and Web pages in the C:\Windows folder, plus any other pictures you have added to the list.

   To use a picture that doesn't appear on the list, click Browse, locate it, and click OK to select it.

3. Open the Display drop-down list and choose Center, Tile, or Stretch to position the chosen item.

4. Click OK to close the Display Properties, or continue making display changes as described in the next sections.

 TIP You can quickly download any image you find on a Web page to your PC and set it as your wallpaper by right-clicking it in your Web browser and choosing Set as Wallpaper. When you do so, the image is saved in the C:\Windows folder, under the name Internet Explorer Wallpaper. However, it is not permanently saved. When you do the same thing to another picture, the older picture is overwritten. To permanently save a picture to your hard disk from a Web page, right-click it and choose Save Picture As.

Setting the Screen Saver

A screen saver will blank your screen or display a moving image or pattern if you don't use the mouse or keyboard for a predetermined amount of time. Screen savers can prevent a static image from burning the delicate phosphors on the inside surface of the monitor, which can leave a ghost of the image on the screen for all time no matter what is being displayed. They can also just be fun.

 NOTE The monitors built these days are not as susceptible to burn-in as early models were, so you don't really need to use a screen saver. Most people use them just for the fun of it.

The screen-saver options allow you to choose or create an entertaining video ditty that will greet you when you return to work. You also set how much time you have after your last keystroke or mouse skitter before the show begins. And a password can be set to keep prying eyes from toying with your work while you're away.

To select a screen saver and set its options, do the following:

1. If the Display Properties dialog box is not already open, right-click the Desktop and choose Properties.

2. Click the Screen Saver tab.

3. Open the Screen Saver drop-down list and choose a screen saver. It appears in the preview window, as in Figure 10.2.

 TIP Want to see how it will look on your whole screen? Click Preview. Your screen will go black and then begin its antics. The show continues until you hit any key or move your mouse.

FIGURE 10.2
Setting up a screen saver

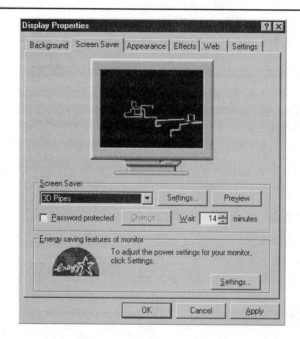

4. If you want to change anything about the selected screen saver, click Settings. You'll see a box of settings that apply to that particular screen saver. For example, for the 3D Pipes screen saver, this is the Settings box:

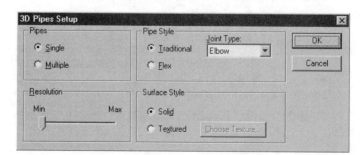

Most of the option boxes have fun sliders and stuff you can play with to get an effect you like. Depending on which screen saver you chose, you'll have a few possible adjustments, such as speed, placement, and details pertinent to the graphic. Play with the settings until you're happy with the results, and then click OK in the Settings box.

5. Back at the Screen Saver page, the next choice you might want to consider is using a password. Click the Password Protected check box if you want protection, and go on to the next two steps. Otherwise skip them.

 NOTE If you turn Password Protection on, every time your screen saver is activated, you'll have to type your password into a box to return to work. This is good if you don't want anyone else tampering with your files or seeing what you're doing. It can be a pain, though, if there's no particular need for privacy at your computer. Don't forget your password, either, or you'll have to reboot to get back to work. Of course, anyone could reboot your computer to get to your files, so this means of establishing security is somewhat bogus.

6. Click the Change button to define or change your password. In the dialog box that appears, type your new password.

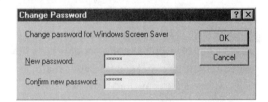

You won't see the characters—just an asterisk for each character (to preserve confidentiality). For confirmation that you typed it correctly, type it again in the Confirm New Password text box. (Don't copy the first password and paste it, because a mistake in the first one can result in your being locked out of your computer.) If there is a discrepancy between the two, you'll get an error message. In that case, reenter the password. (If you're changing the password, the steps will be approximately the same. Enter your old password first, then the new one and its confirmation.) When it's correct, click OK.

7. Back at the Display Properties dialog box, set the number of minutes you want your computer to be idle before the screen saver springs into action. Either type in a number in the Wait text box or use the Up and Down arrows to change the time incrementally.

PART

II

Optimizing and
Customizing

8. (Optional) If you want to set the power options now (which are the same as you learned about in Chapter 9, "Customizing Windows with the Control Panel"), click the Settings button at the bottom of the dialog box. Otherwise, go on to step 9.

   When you click Settings, the Power Options dialog box opens. Since I covered this thoroughly in Chapter 9, I won't go over it again.

9. When all the settings are correct, click OK to close the dialog box, or click Apply to apply your settings and leave the dialog box open for the next section.

Adjusting the Display Appearance

The Appearance tab of the Display Properties dialog box lets you change the way Windows assigns colors and fonts to various parts of the screen.

Windows sets itself up using a default color scheme called Windows Standard, which is fine for most screens—and if you're happy with your colors as they are, you might not even want to fool around with them.

However, the color settings for Windows are very flexible and easy to modify. You can modify the color setting of just about any part of a Windows screen. For those of you who are very particular about color choices, this can be done manually, choosing colors from a palette or even mixing your own with the Custom Colors feature. Once created, custom colors and color setups can be saved on disk for later use or automatically loaded with each Windows session. For more expedient color reassignments, there are a number of supplied color schemes to choose from.

After you click the Appearance tab, your dialog box will look like that shown in Figure 10.3. The various parts of the Windows graphical environment that you can alter are shown in the top portion and named in the lower portion. As you select color schemes, these samples change so you can see what the effect will be without having to go back into Windows proper.

FIGURE 10.3

*The dialog box for
setting the colors, font,
and metrics of the
Windows environment*

Loading a Color Scheme

Before customizing individual screen elements, first try loading one of the supplied
color schemes; you may find one you like:

1. If the Display Properties dialog box is not already open, right-click the Desktop
   and choose Properties. Then click the Appearance tab.

2. Open the drop-down Scheme list box and choose a color scheme.

   The colors in the dialog box will change, showing the scheme. Try them out.
   Some are garish, others more subtle. Adjusting your monitor may make a difference, too. (You can cycle through the different supplied color schemes without
   selecting them from the drop-down list: With the Color Schemes space highlighted, just press the ↑ and → keys. The sample screen elements will change to
   reflect each color scheme as its name appears in the Scheme box. There is an
   amazing variety!)

3. Click Apply or OK to apply the settings to all Windows activities.

Note that some color schemes not only apply different colors but also apply different fonts for common elements such as title bar text and menu text. In the following
section you'll learn how to select any font installed on your system for these elements
and others that involve text.

TIP Microsoft has incorporated a few color schemes that may enhance the operation of your computer. On the LCD (liquid-crystal display) screens that you'll be using in bright light, you might try the setting called High-Contrast White. If your eyes are weary, you may want to try one of the settings with the words *Large* or *Extra Large* in the name. These cause menus, dialog boxes, and title bars to appear in large letters.

Customizing the Colors and Fonts Used On-Screen

If you don't like the color schemes supplied, you can make up your own. It's most efficient to start with a scheme that's close to what you want and then modify it. Once you like the scheme, you may save it under a new name for later use. Here are the steps:

1. From the Appearance tab, select the color scheme you want to modify.

2. In the preview area at the top of the dialog box, click the Windows element whose color or other attributes you want to change. Its name should appear in the Item box. You can click menu names, title bars, scroll bars, buttons—anything you see. You can also select a screen element from the Item drop-down list box rather than by clicking the item directly.

3. Click the Color button to open up a series of colors you can choose from.

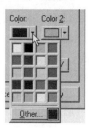

4. Click the color you want. This assigns it to the item.

5. If the Color 2 drop-down list is available, choose from it a second color for the selected item.

   Color 2 is available only if you are using High Color (16-bit) or True Color (24-bit) color depth, and if the particular screen item you have selected supports two color choices. Window title bars support this, for example. If you choose two colors, one color gradually fades into the other across the item's surface.

 TIP Want more colors? Click the Other button. This pops up another 48 colors to choose from. Click one of the 48 colors (or patterns and intensity levels, if you have a monochrome monitor) to assign it to the chosen element.

6. If the chosen item has an adjustable size (such as Active Window Border, for example), the Size text box is available. Enter a size, or use the up/down increment buttons to change the size.

7. If the chosen item contains text, the Font drop-down list is available, along with a Size and Color control for it. Choose a font, a font size, a font color, and font attributes (Bold and/or Italic). These controls will not be available if you have chosen an item that does not involve text.

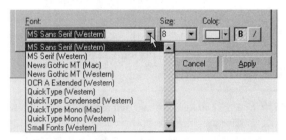

8. Repeat the process for each color you want to change.

9. If you want to save the new color/font combination as a new scheme, click Save As. Type a name for the new scheme and click OK.

Choosing from a Wider Selection of Colors

If you don't like the colors that are available, you can create your own. There are 16 slots at the bottom of the larger color palette for storing colors you set using another fancy dialog box called the color refiner. Here's how:

1. When choosing a color, click Other. The Color dialog box opens.

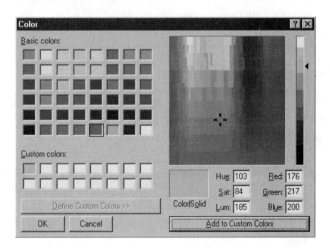

2. Do one of the following:
   - In the Basic Colors area, click a color you want, and then skip to step 4.
   - Click in the color palette (the rainbow area) to the right, picking a precise color.
   - To adjust the chosen color's intensity (light/dark), click the vertical bar to the right of the color palette.
   - To enter a precise color by HSB number, enter numbers (0 through 255) in the Hue, Saturation, and Lum (Brightness) boxes.
   - To enter a precise color by RGB number, enter numbers (0 through 255) in the Red, Green, and Blue boxes.

NOTE HSB and RGB are two different methods of defining a color. Both have their proponents, so Windows includes both as alternatives for you.

3. If you did anything in step 2 besides clicking one of the Basic Colors, click the Add to Custom Colors button, moving your new color choice to a rectangle below the Basic Colors area. You can then choose this color again in the future.

4. Click OK. You return to the Display Properties box, with the new color chosen.

NOTE If you use 16- or 256-color depth rather than one of the higher ones, some of the colors might appear as patterns of two colors blended together to approximate the color. This is called *dithering*, and it happens at low color depths when a color is chosen that isn't part of the set of colors available at that depth. When possible, avoid using dithered colors for your display because they are harder to look at for long periods of time.

Setting Display Effects

The Effects tab offers two features: It lets you choose the icons for the permanent residents on your Desktop such as My Computer and Recycle Bin, and it lets you turn on or off certain visual special effects.

NOTE Another way to change the icons is to apply a Desktop theme, covered later in this chapter.

1. Click the Effects tab in the Display Properties dialog box (see Figure 10.4).

FIGURE 10.4

*Change the look of your
Desktop icons from
here.*

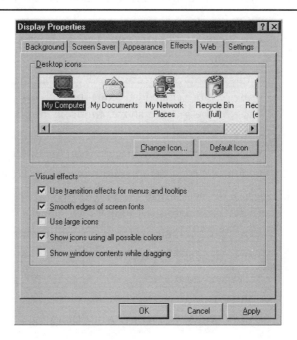

2. Click the icon you want to alter.

 NOTE To return an icon to its default appearance, click Default Icon.

3. Click Change Icon. The Change Icon dialog box appears, showing a few
alternatives.

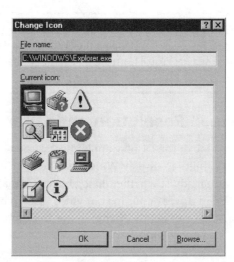

4. If you don't like any of the icons shown, click Browse and find another icon. You can find icons in several ways.

- One is to locate an ICO file. This is a little graphic designed specifically to be an icon.

- Another source of icons is EXE and DLL files. Most executable files contain one or more embedded icons that you can "borrow" as needed. For example, in the graphic above, the icons displayed are the ones embedded in `Explorer.exe`.

- You can also download icons from the Internet. Just search for *Icons* or *.ico*.

When finished, click OK to return to the Display Properties box.

5. Select or deselect any of the Visual Effects check boxes as desired (which are all fairly self-explanatory because of their names):

- Use Transition Effects for Menus and Tooltips
- Smooth Edges of Screen Fonts
- Use Large Icons
- Show Icons Using All Possible Colors
- Show Window Contents While Dragging

NOTE *Transition effects* are fade-ins and other visual effects that are there purely for aesthetics. Turning them off can speed performance slightly on a slower computer.

6. Click OK to accept your settings and close the Display Properties dialog box, or click Apply to leave the box open.

NOTE So far, we've been covering the tabs in the Display Properties dialog box in left-to-right order. However, I'm skipping the Web tab for the moment because it contains rather specialized settings. You'll learn about it in the "Using the Active Desktop" section later in this chapter.

Setting Screen Resolution and Color Depth

The Settings tab of the Display applet tweaks the video driver responsible for your video card's ability to display Windows. These settings are a little more substantial than those that adjust whether dialog boxes are mauve or chartreuse, because they load a different driver or bump your video card up or down into a completely different resolution and color depth, changing the amount of information you can see on the screen at once (see Figure 10.5).

NOTE When you change the color depth, you will be asked whether you want to restart your PC. If you don't restart after changing color depth, everything might be okay, or you might see some strange effects on-screen, such as missing or wrong icons. Such problems can be fixed by restarting, and are not critical.

FIGURE 10.5
The Settings page of the Display Properties controls the video card's device driver.

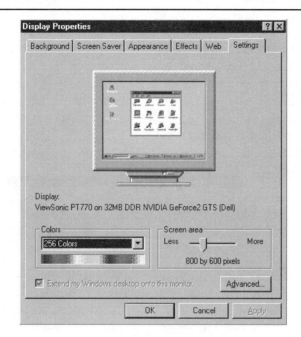

Optimizing and Customizing

Let's start with the Colors setting, which sets the color depth for your screen—the number of unique colors it can display. Open the Colors drop-down list, and you're ready to make your selection.

Assuming your video card was properly identified when you installed Windows Me, this drop-down list box will include all the legitimate options your video card is capable of. Your monitor is not the limiting factor here (with the exception of color LCD screens like those on laptops or flat-panel monitors, which do have limitations); the limitations have to do with how much RAM is on your video card. All modern analog color monitors for PCs are capable of displaying 16 million colors, which is dubbed True Color, or 24-bit color. Other choices are High Color (16-bit), 256 colors (8-bit), and 16 colors (4-bit). The higher the color depth you choose, the better photographs will look on-screen. However, on slow PCs, you can get better overall performance with a lower color depth. In addition, some games work best at a particular color depth, and will inform you of this if you try to run them at a too-high or too-low color depth.

TIP If you increase the Screen Area setting (discussed below) and the Colors setting decreases, your video card does not have enough memory to display both the higher color depth and the higher screen area setting. You'll have to make choices that represent a balance of the two.

The Screen Area setting controls your Desktop area. Drag the slider to the left or right to adjust it.

The higher the resolution you choose, the smaller the icons, windows, text, and everything else will appear on-screen. (The Desktop background will expand to fill in the full screen area.) Some jobs—such as working with large spreadsheets, databases, CAD, or typesetting—are much more efficient with more data displayed on the screen. Because higher resolutions require a trade-off in clarity and make on-screen objects smaller, some people prefer a low resolution, such as 640 × 480, where everything appears larger on-screen.

When you change the resolution (but not the color depth), you'll see this message:

Go ahead and click OK to try the setting. If your screen looks screwy and you can't read anything, don't worry. It will return to normal in about 15 seconds. If, on the other hand, you like what you see, there will be another dialog box asking you to confirm that you want to keep the current setting. Click Yes. Confirming that box makes the new setting permanent until you change it again.

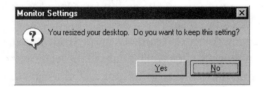

Changing the Video and Monitor Driver Options

The Advanced... button on the Settings tab leads you to a dialog box for your specific video card (shown in Figure 10.6), which allows you to actually change a bunch of nitty-gritty stuff, such as the type of video card and monitor that Windows thinks you have, the refresh rate, and some performance factors. Normally, these settings will be correct already, but if you install a new video card or monitor, you might want to check them.

FIGURE 10.6
You can adjust the
driver settings for your
display here.

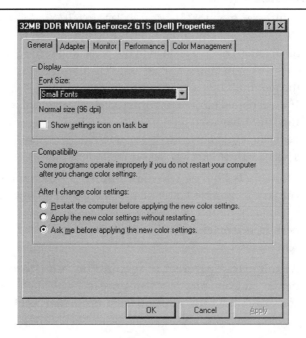

The General tab, shown in Figure 10.6, includes the option Show Settings Icon on Taskbar. Turn this check box on, and you'll get a little monitor icon next to the clock in the Taskbar. Click the icon, and you're able to immediately choose the color depth and Desktop area from a pop-up menu. It also has a Compatibility setting, in which you choose what happens when you change the color depth. Some systems are better than others at accepting color depth changes without rebooting, so experiment and then choose the best setting here for your situation.

Adapter Options

The main thing on the Adapter tab is a Refresh Rate drop-down list. The *refresh rate* is the number of times per second the display is repainted, or refreshed, by the light gun(s) inside the monitor. Higher is better, but your monitor and video card must both support the chosen resolution, or your monitor can be damaged. For best results, set the Refresh Rate to Optimal, allowing Windows to determine the highest available setting that the video card and monitor share.

On the Adapter tab, you see your current video card listed. If it's wrong, click the Change button and choose a different video driver. (See Chapter 13, "Adding and Removing Hardware and Software," for more information about changing and updating device drivers.)

Monitor Options

Bought a new monitor? Here's the place to tell Windows Me about it. It's important to tell Windows what monitor you have because it uses that information to calculate the optimal refresh rate, explained in the preceding section. If Windows thinks you have a Standard VGA or Standard Plug-and-Play monitor, it's probably not taking advantage of the monitor's best available refresh rate.

If the reported monitor is wrong, click Change and work through the Wizard to change the driver used for it. (Again, see Chapter 13 for details about working with driver changes/updates.)

There are three check boxes on the Monitor tab:

Monitor Is Energy Star Compliant   If your monitor fits this description, set this. It affects other Power Management settings in your computer (explained in Chapter 9). If this check box is unavailable, perhaps the Energy Star features have been turned off elsewhere, either in Power Options (see Chapter 9) or in your system BIOS setup.

Automatically Detect Plug-and-Play Monitors   Windows runs around and detects Plug-and-Play hardware once in a while (when booting up, for example). In some cases this can cause PnP monitors to flash wildly. If yours does this, try turning off this check box.

Reset Display on Suspend/Resume   Does your computer have the ability to go into a suspended state (low-power state)? I mean the whole computer, not just the screen. If it does, and your screen flickers or freaks out when your computer "wakes up," turn this check box off. It may help.

Performance Options

The Performance tab has only one feature: a Hardware Acceleration slider. If speed is your concern (and who isn't concerned with their computer's speed?), make sure the slider is set to Full. This is recommended for most computers. Occasionally, a computer/card combo (the monitor has nothing to do with this) won't be able to take advantage of all the graphics speed-up routines that Windows is capable of for things like moving lots of graphics around the screen quickly (known as *bit blitting*) and such. If you're seeing display anomalies, you might try slowing this setting down a bit, clicking OK, and closing the Display Properties box. Then see if anything improves.

 NOTE Depending on your video card, you might have other tabs in the dialog box, such as Color Management. Consult the documentation for your video card for details.

Using the Active Desktop

The Active Desktop was introduced in Windows 98, and it was supposed to be the next big thing. When turned on, it treats your Windows Desktop as though it's a Web page, and you can add Web components to it (called active controls) such as weather maps and stock tickers that update themselves from the Internet automatically. You can also place programmable objects on the Active Desktop, built from Java applets or ActiveX controls.

The Active Desktop feature places an HTML layer on the Desktop, which lies beneath (or behind) the traditional icon layer. It is on this layer that you can place active controls and HTML objects. You can also assign a Web page to be the Desktop's wallpaper, just as you can assign colors to the traditional background. (Colors and wallpaper were covered earlier in this chapter.) Figure 10.7 shows a Web-updated stock ticker in action, for example.

PART II

FIGURE 10.7
You can place HTML and active content objects on the Active Desktop, such as this stock ticker.

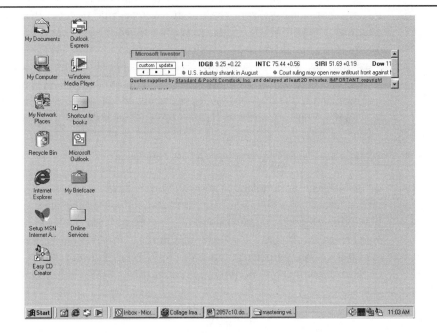

Optimizing and Customizing

 NOTE If several users share one computer, each can have their own customized Active Desktop, because the Desktop is part of each user's personal profile. See the section on user profiles in Chapter 9 for details.

When you're connected to the Internet in the usual way, you can work in any HTML Desktop object as though you were working within Internet Explorer (or some other Web browser). For example, you can click links, download files, fill out forms, copy data from the page and paste it into another document, and so on.

Even though Active Desktop was much hyped when Windows 98 came out, the feature never really caught on with the average Windows user. This was partly because at that time, most people didn't have high-speed or always-on Internet access, so the usefulness of active controls updated from the Web was limited. In Windows Me, the feature is offered, but not as a significant part of everyday operation.

Enabling the Active Desktop

To check whether the Active Desktop is enabled, right-click the Desktop and choose Active Desktop. A submenu appears. If no check mark is next to Show Web Content, click it to place one there.

When turning on Show Web Content, you probably won't notice any immediate difference in your Desktop. The real difference is that now your Desktop is ready to accept active controls. See the next section to learn how to add them.

 NOTE In Windows Me, Show Web Content must be turned on in order to use wallpaper of any kind on the Desktop. You learned about wallpaper earlier in this chapter. If you try to choose a wallpaper image while Show Web Content is off, you'll be prompted to enable it.

Enabling an Active Control

By default, there are no active controls in Windows Me, even when Show Web Content is turned on. You'll add content to the Active Desktop via the Web tab in the Display Properties dialog box, shown in Figure 10.8. There are several ways to get there. You can go through the Display applet in the Control Panel, or you can right-click the Desktop, choose Properties, and click the Web tab. However, the easiest way is to right-click the Desktop and choose Active Desktop ➤ Customize My Desktop.

FIGURE 10.8

*Here's where you add
and select active
controls for your
Desktop.*

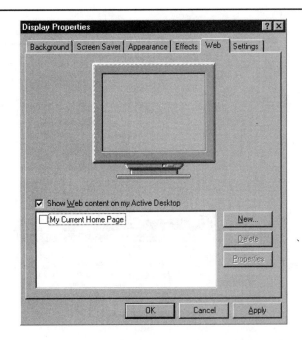

A list of the available active controls appears. To enable one, mark its check box. By default there is only one: My Current Home Page. This places the Web page specified as your starting page in Internet Explorer on the Desktop as wallpaper, as shown in Figure 10.9. (See Chapter 21, "Browsing the World Wide Web with Internet Explorer 5.5," for details.) It makes it very handy to use the Internet, but it does significantly reduce the amount of available Desktop space. Since the HTML layer is beneath the icon layer on the Desktop, you can drag icons from the Desktop on top of the Web page, but that makes them hard to see.

FIGURE 10.9

Turning on My Current Home Page as an active control results in a Desktop like this.

 NOTE The entire Active Desktop is defined within the single file `desktop.htt`, which resides as a hidden file in the same Internet Explorer folder where the Quick Launch folder is located.

All active controls, including the Web page shown in Figure 10.9, have their own title bar that you can use to move or close the control. It doesn't show by default, however. Click at the top of the active control, and a thin gray bar appears. Drag that bar to move the control around on-screen, click its Maximize button to maximize it (as with any other window), or click its Close (X) button to close it. (Closing it is the same as deselecting its check box on the Web tab shown in Figure 10.8.)

Adding More Active Controls

You can create your own active controls using HTML, ActiveX, or Java, but most of us aren't that technical. A better way to get active controls is to download them from Microsoft's Web site for free. Here's how:

1. Start your Internet connection if it's not already running.

2. If you are already in the Web tab of the Display Properties box, click the New button.

   Or, if Display Properties is not on-screen, right-click the Desktop and choose Active Desktop ➢ New Desktop Item.

   The New Active Desktop Item dialog box opens.

3. Click Visit Gallery. Internet Explorer starts and a Web page appears with various categories of active controls.

 NOTE If you see a message asking whether you want to install and run Investor Ticker, click Yes. This is a sample control that appears on the initial Active Desktop Gallery page. You can add it to your Desktop by clicking the Add to Active Desktop button underneath it when it appears on the Web page.

4. Click a button for the category you want (such as Weather, for example). A list of the available active controls in that category appears.

5. Click the control that you want more information about. A preview of it appears, along with an Add to Active Desktop button. See Figure 10.10.

PART

II

Optimizing and
Customizing

FIGURE 10.10

Select the active control you want. In this case there is only one control in the category.

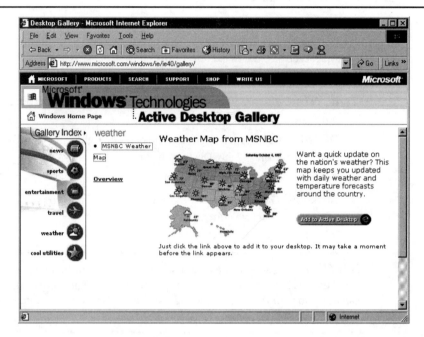

6. Click Add to Active Desktop. A prompt appears, asking whether you want to add an item to your Active Desktop.

7. Click Yes. A box appears, letting you know what you have chosen to do.

8. Click OK. The control downloads, along with the latest version of its content. It might take several minutes. When the download is finished, the control appears on the Desktop.

9. Continue adding more controls, or close Internet Explorer. Figure 10.11 shows the Weather Map from Figure 10.10 on the Desktop.

FIGURE 10.11
Here, the Weather Map control has been added to the Desktop.

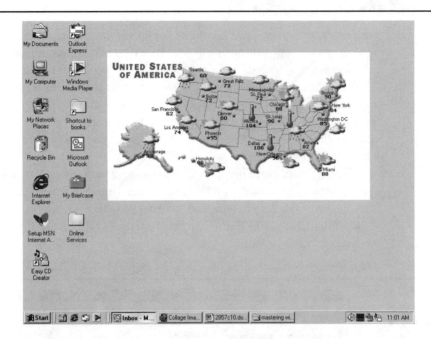

10. To move or resize an active control, click it to activate its title bar; then drag a border to resize the active control, or drag the title bar to move it.

Besides the fancy active controls available from Microsoft, you can also add other types of content to your Active Desktop. For example, you might place a Web page there, or a picture. (To add a picture to the Desktop, use the Wallpaper feature described earlier in the chapter.) To do so, perform steps 1 and 2 of the preceding steps to start the New Active Desktop Item Wizard, and then type the address of the Web page or picture in the Location box. Then click OK twice, and the Web page or picture will appear on the Desktop, just like any other active control.

Removing Active Controls

You can remove Web items or pictures from the Active Desktop in two ways: Hide them or actually delete them. To hide one, deselect its check box on the Web tab of Display Properties (Figure 10.8), or click it to make its title bar visible and then click its Close (X) button.

To delete an active control, go back to the Web tab of Display Properties, select the control, and click the Delete button.

Using Desktop Themes

The Desktop Themes applet combines sound schemes, color schemes, screen savers, and cursors for your Windows Me system. It isn't very different from what you can achieve using the Sounds, Display, and Mouse applets from the Control Panel. The advantage of Desktop Themes is that settings from these areas are pulled into one applet called Desktop Themes, making it easy to recall many settings at once. If you've installed Desktop Themes (use Control Panel's Add/Remove Software applet, then choose Windows Setup), you'll have several preset themes to choose from, some of which are fairly artistic.

Desktop Themes isn't just a tool for organizing your own settings into groups. You also get some great sounds and Desktop backgrounds along with cute new icons for My Computer, the Recycle Bin, and Network Neighborhood.

Running the Desktop Themes applet from the Control Panel brings up the dialog box shown in Figure 10.12.

FIGURE 10.12
Desktop Themes provide a means for coordinating various elements of the Windows Me environment and saving them under a single name.

You can create your own schemes by setting up the screen saver, sounds, cursor, and Desktop the way you like and then saving them using the Save As button at the top of the box. However, you might find that the supplied themes give you all the variation you need. Choose a theme from the drop-down list box to see what it looks like. You can preview the screen saver, pointers, and sounds using the two Preview buttons in the upper-right corner.

TIP Because some of the visuals are actually photo-realistic, some of the schemes may look pretty bad on your monitor, even in 256 colors, if you don't switch to a high-color or true-color setting. High-color themes are marked as such. If you *don't* have a high-color video driver, you might as well remove these schemes; it will save a significant amount of disk space (about 9MB).

In the Settings portion of the box, you'll see eight check boxes for things like Screen Saver, Sound Events, and so on. Each scheme includes settings for all these options. However, you might not want to load all these features when you change schemes; for example, you might like the sounds you already have but want everything else from one of the Desktop Themes. To do this, turn off the Sound Events option before clicking Apply or OK.

To switch back to the ordinary Windows Me settings, choose the Windows Default master theme at the bottom of the list of themes.

Using Toolbars on the Taskbar

The Taskbar, in addition to its other duties, can display a variety of toolbars containing shortcuts for helping you launch programs and work with files. In the following sections, you'll learn something about these toolbars.

Customizing the Quick Launch Toolbar

The Taskbar, by default, shows the Quick Launch toolbar at its left end, next to the Start button. This toolbar consists of four icons: Show Desktop, Internet Explorer, Outlook Express, and Windows Media Player.

You can add your own shortcuts to the Quick Launch toolbar by dragging and dropping them there. For example, here's a shortcut for Microsoft Money being dropped onto the Quick Launch toolbar. Notice that a vertical line appears showing where the new shortcut will be dropped in.

PART
II

Optimizing and
Customizing

To remove a shortcut from the Quick Launch toolbar, right-click the icon and choose Delete from the shortcut menu; then click Yes to confirm.

 TIP Items on the Quick Launch bar don't have text names, so how do you remember what they do? Folders are especially confusing since they all look identical. Just let the mouse rest over the icon for a moment, and its name will appear. Then click once if you're sure it's the one you want.

Displaying Other Toolbars

Quick Launch is not the only toolbar available for display on the Taskbar; there are these others as well:

Address   Adds an address area in which you can type in Web addresses or local resource addresses (for files, folders, or even network resources). This serves the same purpose as the Address bar in a folder window or a Windows Explorer/Internet Explorer window. A window will appear when you enter a resource name and press Enter. Typically, you'll use this for Web page addresses, but you could enter **My Computer** to see your My Computer folder; **command.com** to get a DOS box; **printers** to see the printers folder; or **c:** to see the contents of your hard disk.

Links   Adds a toolbar containing the same quick links that are currently set up in your Internet Explorer's Links bar. Clicking a link brings up or switches you to IE, then connects to the predetermined Web site.

 NOTE If you see a double right-pointing arrow at the right end of a toolbar, as above, it means there are more buttons than will fit on the screen at once. Click that arrow to see the others in menu form.

Desktop   Shows shortcut icons for everything on your Desktop (My Computer, My Network Places, and so on).

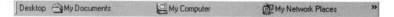

To display or hide one of these toolbars, right-click the Taskbar and point to Toolbars; then click the name of the toolbar that you want to display or hide.

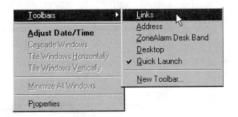

Creating Your Own Toolbars

You can also create your own toolbars to display on the Taskbar. To do so, you must already have an existing folder from which to create the toolbar; you can't create it out of thin air here. Then the content of that folder appears as a new toolbar. If you want to change what's on the toolbar, change the folder content. For example, you might place shortcuts for some programs or documents in a folder, and then specify that folder for the toolbar.

Why is this better than simply adding the shortcuts to the existing Quick Launch toolbar? Well, it isn't necessarily better. It's simply another way.

Use the following steps to create a toolbar:

1. Right-click the Taskbar and choose Toolbars ➢ New Toolbar. A New Toolbar dialog box opens.

2. Select the folder that you want to make into a toolbar.

3. Choose OK.

Of all the toolbars, the Quick Launch and Address are among the best, in my opinion. Also, I find that adding the Control Panel (via the New Toolbar option) is useful since I do lots of system tweaking and access the Control Panel frequently.

Adjusting the Toolbar Position

Each toolbar has its own "thumb tab" at the left, a ridged-looking vertical bar. You can move the toolbar around by dragging it by that tab.

You can slide it to the right or left, for example, to change the amount of space allocated for that toolbar on the Taskbar. To do so, position the mouse pointer over the tab so that the mouse pointer changes to a double-headed arrow, and then drag.

Mouse pointer

PART

II

Optimizing and
Customizing

To move a toolbar onto the Taskbar, point the mouse at any blank area of it (but not the tab) and hold down the mouse pointer so that the pointer turns into a four-pointed arrow. Then drag the toolbar where you want it.

You can even drag the toolbar off the Taskbar, making it a floating toolbar in its own window.

Controlling Taskbar Size, Positioning, and Options

With all the toolbars turned on, everything is all scrunched up on the Taskbar; so nothing is very readable.

Fortunately, you can give the Taskbar extra rows, so that each toolbar can have its own line (or even multiple lines). To do so, position the mouse pointer at the upper edge of the Taskbar and drag upward. Figure 10.13 shows a really huge Taskbar with many different toolbars displayed.

FIGURE 10.13
You can add new rows to the Taskbar by dragging its top edge upward.

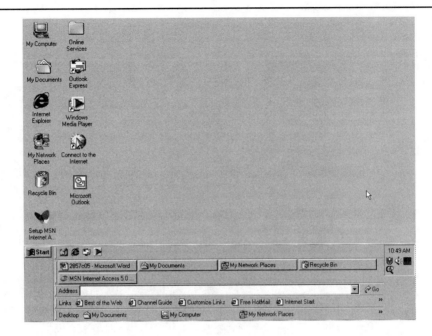

To resize the Taskbar back to normal, drag its top border back down where you want it.

The Taskbar can also be moved to other sides of the screen if you don't want it at the bottom. To drag it, simply point to any empty area of the Taskbar and drag it where you want it. Figure 10.14 shows it at the top, for example.

PART
II

Optimizing and
Customizing

FIGURE 10.14
*You can drag the
Taskbar to position it
wherever you want it.*

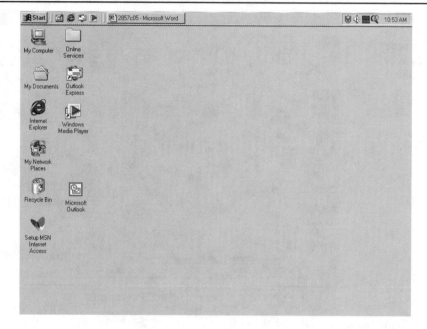

You can "auto hide" the Taskbar, too, so that it appears only when you point the mouse pointer at the bottom of the screen (or wherever you have placed the Taskbar). This saves space on the screen. Auto Hide is one of the Taskbar's options you can set through the Taskbar and Start Menu Properties:

1. Right-click the Taskbar and choose Properties. The Taskbar and Start Menu Properties dialog box opens, as shown in Figure 10.15.

TIP If you prefer, you can choose Start ➤ Settings ➤ Taskbar and Start Menu instead of right-clicking and choosing Properties.

FIGURE 10.15
*Choose the basic
appearance options for
the Taskbar and Start
menu here.*

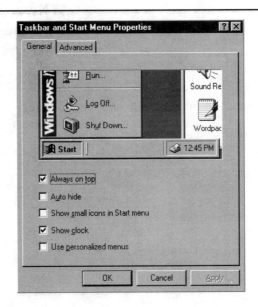

2. Select or deselect any of the check boxes as desired:

   Always on Top   Prevents a window from obscuring the Taskbar. Leave this on.

   Auto Hide   Makes the Taskbar disappear until you point to the area on-screen
   where it should be; then it appears.

   Show Small Icons in Start Menu   Makes the icons next to each shortcut
   on the Start menu small, rather than the default large size, to save space.

   Show Clock   Shows or hides the clock in the right corner of the screen.

   Use Personalized Menus   Turns on or off the Personalized Menus feature
   described in Chapter 4, "Getting Down to Business: Running Your Applications."

3. Choose OK.

Windows Me has even more abilities to further customize the way the Start menu
and Taskbar operate. Check out the Advanced tab of the Taskbar and Start Menu Properties dialog box, shown in Figure 10.16.

FIGURE 10.16
Some advanced options for the Taskbar and Start menu

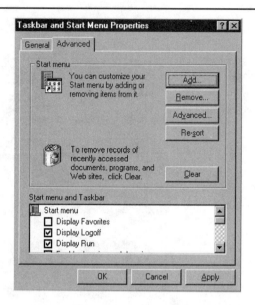

The top portion of the Advanced tab deals with adding and removing programs and shortcuts on the Start menu; let's leave that alone for the moment because you'll be working with it later in the chapter.

The Clear button erases Windows' memory of which menu commands you have issued (for the Personalized Menus feature), as well as erases the shortcuts on the Documents menu and some Internet browsing history information. Use this to "cover your tracks" if you are concerned about privacy.

The Start Menu and Taskbar section at the bottom of the dialog box contains a series of check boxes for various features. Turn them on or off as desired. For example, you have the option of removing the Log Off command from the Start menu, to prevent anyone from logging you off while you are away from your desk. There is also a series of "Expand" check boxes on this list. Marking one of them makes the item function as a submenu when you select it from the Start menu. For example, choosing Expand Control Panel makes the control panel icons into a submenu like this:

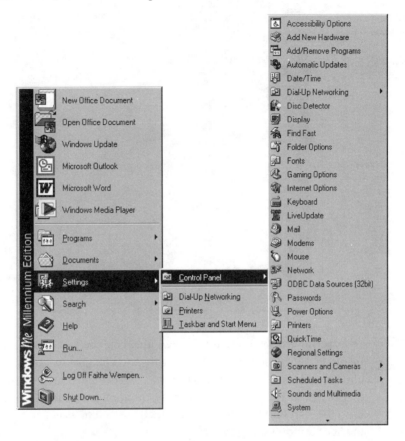

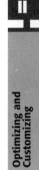

Putting Programs on the Start Menu

Every Windows user is bound to benefit from knowing how to put their favorite programs and documents right on the Start menu. That way, you can start programs by clicking the Start button and then clicking the program you want. No muss, no fuss, no wading through submenus. Figure 10.17 shows a Start menu with several program shortcuts at the top.

FIGURE 10.17
You can easily add your
favorite projects and
programs to the top of
the Start menu.

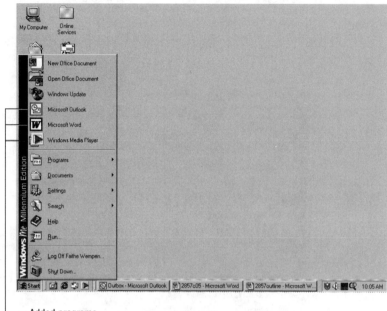

Added programs

As with most activities in Windows, there are several ways to add items to the Start menu. I'll show you the two that are the most straightforward: dragging onto the Start button, and using the Start ➤ Settings ➤ Taskbar and Start Menu command.

The first technique is simply to drag the application, folder, or document's icon onto the Start button. Windows will then create a *shortcut* and place the shortcut on the Start button's opening menu.

NOTE As mentioned in Chapter 4, a shortcut is not the application, folder, or document's *real* icon; it's a pointer to that icon. The result is the same either way. Clicking a shortcut has the same effect as clicking the object's original icon. In the case of the Start button's menu, choosing the shortcut item from the menu will run the application, open the folder, or open the document.

Here are the steps:

1. First, you'll need to find an icon that represents the object you want to put on the menu. The icon can be a shortcut icon or the original icon, either in a folder, on the Desktop, in the Search box, in Windows Explorer, or displayed in any other window that supports drag-and-drop techniques.

   The Search box is probably the easiest: If you know the name of the file or document you're looking for, just do a search using Start ➤ Search ➤ For Files or Folders.

2. Once you've located the object you want to add, drag it over the Start button and then release the mouse button.

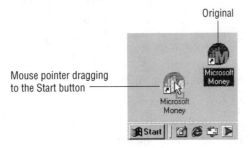

3. Now when you open the Start menu, you'll see that the object has been added at the top of the list.

That's the easiest way to add new items to the Start button. You can also drag objects *off* the Start menu, but it follows a slightly different approach (see "Removing an Item from a Menu or Toolbar" later in the chapter).

Modifying the Start Menu

You can add a shortcut to any of the submenus on the Start menu, not just on the first-level menu itself. To do so:

1. Drag the shortcut onto the Start button, just as you did in the preceding section, but don't release the mouse button yet. The Start menu opens.

2. Still holding down the mouse button, drag up to the menu you want to open. It opens.

3. Keep opening levels of submenus until you see the spot where you want to drop the shortcut.

4. Position the mouse pointer where you want the shortcut to appear; a horizontal line shows the selected position.

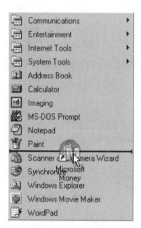

5. Release the mouse button, dropping the shortcut there.

There's also a more formal way of adding shortcuts to the Start menu:

1. Choose Start ➢ Settings ➢ Taskbar and Start Menu. The Taskbar and Start Menu Properties dialog box appears .

2. Click the Advanced tab and then click Add. A Create Shortcut dialog box opens.

3. Type the path to the program you want to create a shortcut for, or click Browse to locate it, select the file, and click Open. See Figure 10.18. Then click Next to move on.

FIGURE 10.18
Fill in the name and path of the item or use the Browse button. Browse is probably easier.

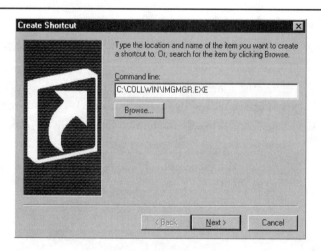

NOTE What if, instead of adding a *program* or *document* to a Start menu, you want to add a *folder*? Doing this can give you a shortcut to that folder as one of the options on your Start menu. The only catch is that you can't do it from the Browse box. If the Browse box is open, close it by clicking Cancel. Then enter the full path name of the folder.

4. Next, you're asked to choose the folder (that is, submenu) on the Start menu where you want the shortcut added. See Figure 10.19. Select the folder you want, and click Next.

 NOTE You can use the New Folder button to create a new folder (submenu) on the fly. If you're going to create a new folder, you have to decide where you want it to be added. For example, if you wanted to add a subfolder under Accessories, you'd first click Accessories, then click the New Folder button. A new folder would appear, waiting for you to edit its name. You'd type the name and then press Enter.

FIGURE 10.19
Choose which group or other location where the new shortcut will be added.

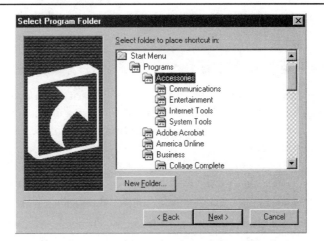

5. Now you're asked to name your shortcut, as shown in Figure 10.20. This is thoughtful because it's more informative to have a menu item called Collage Image Manager than IMGMGR.EXE. (When you just drop an icon on the Start button, incidentally, you're stuck with whatever name the icon has.) Enter the name you want, but don't make it incredibly long, because that will widen the menu appreciably, possibly making it difficult to fit on the screen.

PART
II

Optimizing and
Customizing

FIGURE 10.20

Assign a name to the shortcut.

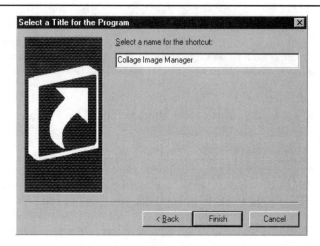

6. Click Finish. Then, back in the Taskbar and Start Menu Properties dialog box, click OK.

You can add more than one item at a time to your lists. Rather than closing the Taskbar Properties box in step 6, just click Add and do the whole thing over again for your next item.

Removing an Item from a Menu or Toolbar

There will no doubt be times when you'll want to remove an item from your Start button, such as when you no longer use a program often enough to warrant its existence on the menu. To remove a shortcut from the Start menu or from the Quick Launch toolbar, you can do any of the following:

- Drag it off the toolbar or menu and onto the Desktop. Then drag it from the Desktop into the Recycle Bin. Click Yes to confirm.

- Right-click it and choose Delete. Then click Yes to confirm.

- Use the following steps to remove it using the Taskbar and Start Menu Properties dialog box:

  1. Choose Start ➢ Settings ➢ Taskbar and Start Menu.

  2. Click the Advanced tab.

  3. Click Remove. The Remove Shortcuts/Folders dialog box appears.

4. Locate and select the shortcut or folder you want to remove. (Remember, clicking a plus sign opens up a folder.)

5. Click the Remove button.

6. Repeat steps 4 and 5 for other programs, or click Close when finished.

7. Click OK to close the Taskbar and Start Menu Properties dialog box.

 NOTE Removing a shortcut from the Start button menu does not remove the actual item from your hard disk. For example, if you remove a shortcut to Word for Windows, the program is still on your computer. It's just the shortcut to it that is being removed. You can always put the shortcut back on the menu.

Rearranging Shortcuts on the Start Menu

There are several ways to change a shortcut's location on the Start menu.

The easiest is simply to drag the shortcut where you want it, holding down the mouse button all the while. You can open submenus with the mouse button down, dragging the shortcut with you, until you find the spot where you want to drop it. Then just release the mouse button. See Figure 10.21.

PART

II

Optimizing and
Customizing

FIGURE 10.21
*Drag a shortcut from
submenu to submenu
on the Start button's
menu system.*

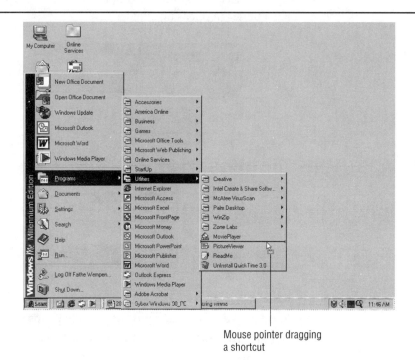

Mouse pointer dragging
a shortcut

You can also browse the Start menu's content as if it were a regular folder on your hard disk (which indeed it is!) by right-clicking it and choosing Explore from its shortcut menu (see Figure 10.22). In the resulting window you can drag shortcuts from folder to folder to move them. You learned about moving files in Windows Explorer in Chapter 5, "Organizing Files, Programs, and Disks."

FIGURE 10.22

You can browse the Start menu in Windows Explorer and modify its content by moving shortcuts from folder to folder.

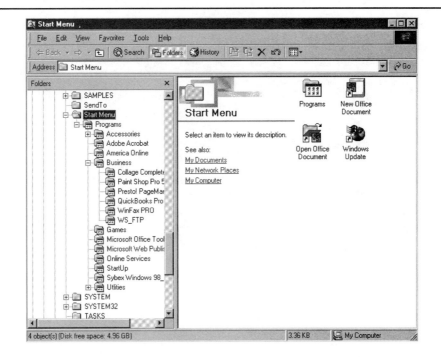

Another way to get to this same Windows Explorer window for the Start menu is this:

1. Choose Start ➢ Settings ➢ Taskbar and Start Menu.

2. Click the Advanced tab.

3. Click the Advanced button. The same file management window as shown in Figure 10.22 appears for your use.

 TIP To realphabetize all your menus, click the Re-Sort button on the Advanced tab of the Taskbar and Start Menu Properties dialog box.

From this file management window, you can do anything to the shortcuts that you can do with normal files—delete, rename, move, copy, and so on—as you learned earlier in this chapter.

PART

II

Optimizing and
Customizing

CHAPTER **11**

Printers and Printing

FEATURING:

If your printer is of the Plug-and-Play variety, Windows probably already recognizes it as the default printer. This means you'll be able to print from any Windows program without worrying about anything more than turning on the printer, checking that it has paper, and choosing the File ➢ Print command. If your printer isn't Plug-and-Play compatible, wasn't plugged in at the time of installation, or requires its own software to operate, you'll have to manually set up your printer before you can print. This chapter tells you how to do that and how to manage the use of your printer to get your work done.

As with Windows 3.1, Windows 9*x*, and Windows NT/2000, unless you specify otherwise, programs hand off data to Windows Me, which in turn spools the data to a specified printer. *Spooling* means temporarily putting information on the hard disk that's really headed for the printer. Your document then gets sent out to the printer at the speed at which the printer can receive it. This lets you get back to work with your program sooner. You can even print additional documents, stacking up a load of jobs for the printer to print. This stack is called a *queue*. Some printers come with their own print software that contains a separate print spooler; if that's the case, Windows hands off the print job to the printer's own software spooler, which in turn feeds it to the printer.

 TECH TIP Unlike Windows NT/2000, Windows Me doesn't always prevent a program from writing directly to the printer port. (In Windows NT, any such attempt by programs to directly write to hardware, such as an LPT port, is trapped by the security manager.) Windows Me offers less security in this regard. Applications can directly access a port. Also, if you shell out of Windows Me and run MS-DOS mode, direct port access is allowed.

 NOTE MS-DOS programs can also be spooled so that you can get back to work with your DOS or Windows programs while printing happens in the background.

When you print from a Windows program, the built-in Print Manager in Windows receives the data, queues up the jobs, routes them to the correct printer, and, when necessary, issues error or other appropriate messages to print-job originators. You can browse the printer's queue to see where your job(s) is in the print queue relative to other people's print jobs. You may also be permitted to rearrange the print queue, delete print jobs, or pause and resume a print job so that you can reload or otherwise service the printer.

Each printer you've installed appears in the Printers folder, along with an additional icon called Add Printer that lets you set up new printers. Printer icons in the folder appear and behave like any other object: You can delete them at will, create new ones, and set their properties. Deleting a printer icon from the Printers folder removes that printer's driver from your system. Double-clicking a printer in the folder displays its print queue and lets you manipulate the queue. Commands on the menus let you install, configure, connect, disconnect, and remove printers and drivers.

This chapter explains these features, as well as procedures for local and network print-queue management. Some basics of print management also are discussed, providing a primer for the uninitiated or for those whose skills are a little rusty.

Adding a New Printer

If your printer is already installed and seems to be working fine, you probably can skip this section. In fact, if you're interested in nothing more than printing from one of your programs without viewing the queue, printing to a network printer, or making adjustments to your current printer's settings, just skip to "Printing from a Program," later in this chapter. However, if you need to install a new printer, modify or customize your current installation, or add additional printers to your setup, read on.

Before running the Wizard, let's consider when you'd need to add a new printer to Windows Me:

- You didn't tell Windows Me what kind of printer you have when you first set up Windows.

- You're connecting a new printer directly to your computer.

- Someone has connected a new printer to the network, and you want to use it from your computer.

- You want to print files to disk that can later be sent to a particular type of printer.

- You want to set up multiple printer configurations (preferences) for a single physical printer so you can switch between them without having to change your printer setup before each print job.

Notice that a great deal of flexibility exists here, especially in the case of the last item. Because of the modularity of Windows Me's internal design, even though you might have only one physical printer, you can create any number of printer definitions for it, each with different characteristics.

 TECH TIP These printer definitions are actually called printers, but you can think of them as printer names, aliases, or named virtual devices.

PART

II

Optimizing and
Customizing

For example, you might want one definition set up to print on legal-sized paper in landscape orientation while another prints with normal paper in portrait orientation. Each of these two "printers" would actually use the same physical printer to print out on. While you're working with Windows Me's online help and this book, keep this terminology in mind. The word *printer* often doesn't really mean a physical printer. It usually means a printer setup that you've created with the Wizard. Typically, it's a collection of settings that points to a physical printer, but it could just as well create a print file instead.

About Printer Drivers

A printer can't just connect to your computer and mysteriously print a fancy page of graphics or even a boring old page of text. You need a *printer driver.* The printer driver (actually a file on your hard disk) translates your text file to commands that tell your printer how to print your file. Because different brands and models of printer use different commands for such things as *Move up a line, Print a circle in the middle of the page, Print the letter A*, and so on, a specialized printer driver is needed for each type of printer.

NOTE Because some printers are actually functionally equivalent, a driver for a popular brand and model of printer (for example, an Epson or a Hewlett-Packard) often masquerades under different names for other printers.

TECH TIP DOS programs require a print driver for the application, too. For instance, WordPerfect 5.1 running in a DOS session under Windows will use a DOS printer driver and a Windows Me printer driver to work under Windows Me.

When you add a printer, unless you're installing a Plug-and-Play–compatible printer, you're asked to choose the brand and model of printer. With Plug-and-Play printers, if the printer is attached and turned on, Windows queries the printer and the printer responds with its make and model number. Virtually all new printers are Plug-and-Play compatible, but if yours isn't, you'll have to tell Windows what printer you have so it will install the correct driver.

A good printer driver takes advantage of all your printer's capabilities, such as its built-in fonts and graphics features. A poor printer driver might succeed in printing only draft-quality text, even from a sophisticated printer.

If you're the proud owner of some offbeat brand of printer, you may be alarmed when you can't find your printer listed in the box when you run the Wizard. But don't worry; the printer manufacturer might be able to supply one. The procedure for installing manufacturer-supplied drivers is covered later in this chapter.

TIP Some printers now come with special software to replace the Windows print queue or to perform special maintenance procedures like cleaning or print head alignment. Check your printer's documentation to ensure it doesn't require a different installation procedure from what is described here.

 NOTE If your printer isn't included in the list, consult "When You Don't Find Your Printer in the List," later in this chapter.

Running the Add Printer Wizard

Microsoft has made the previously arduous chore of adding a printer something that's much more easily mastered by a majority of computer users. Here's what you have to do:

1. Open the Printers folder by choosing Start ➤ Settings ➤ Printers. You can also access it from the Control Panel.

 TECH TIP Depending on the type of access control you stipulate from the Access Control tab of the Network applet in the Control Panel, you may want to password-protect your printer when you share it on the network. By doing this, you help guard against a printer being continually tied up with print jobs from an unauthorized user somewhere on the network. Just share your printer with password protection as discussed later in this chapter, or if part of an NT domain, restrict access to your resources via the Control Panel applet mentioned above.

2. Double-click Add Printer. The Add Printer Wizard runs.

3. Click Next in the first dialog box that appears.

4. You're asked whether the printer is *local* or *network*. Because I'm describing how to install a local printer here, choose Local, and then click Next.

5. You're presented with a list of brands and models. In the left column, scroll the list, find the maker of your printer, and click it. Then, in the right column, choose the model number or name that matches your printer. Be sure to select the exact printer model, not just the correct brand name. Consult your printer's manual if you're in doubt about the model. What you enter here determines which printer driver file is used for this printer's definition. Figure 11.1 shows an example for an HP LaserJet 4.

PART

II

Optimizing and
Customizing

FIGURE 11.1

Choosing the printer make and model. Here I'm choosing a Hewlett-Packard LaserJet 4.

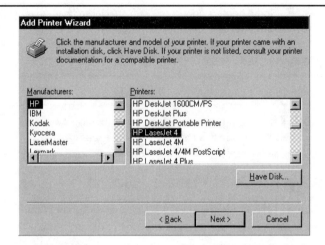

6. Click Next. Now you'll see a list of ports. You have to tell Windows which port the printer is connected to. (A *port* usually refers to the connector on the computer—but see Table 11.1 for the "file" exception.)

   Most often, the port will be the parallel printer port called LPT1 (Line Printer #1). Unless you know your printer is connected to another port, such as LPT2 or a serial port (such as COM1 or COM2), select LPT1 as in Figure 11.2.

FIGURE 11.2

Choosing the port that the printer is connected to is the second step in setting up a local printer.

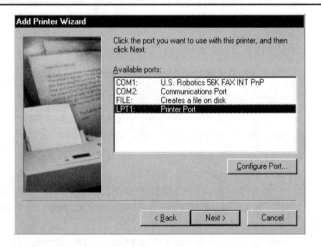

7. Select the port you want to use and click Next.

8. Enter a name for the printer. This name will appear in any printer listing and under its icon.

NOTE If the printer will be shared with DOS and 16-bit Windows users (such as people running Windows for Workgroups 3.11), you might want to limit this name to 12 characters because that's the maximum length those users will see when they are browsing for printers.

9. Choose Yes or No to specify whether the printer will be the default printer for Windows programs. Then click Next.

10. Finally, you're asked if you want to print a test page. It's a good idea to do this. Turn on the printer, make sure it has paper in it, and click Finish. If the driver file for your printer is in the computer, you'll be asked if you want to use it or load a new one from the Windows Me CD-ROM or floppy disks. It's usually easier to use the existing driver. If the driver isn't on your hard disk, you'll be instructed to insert the disk containing the driver.

11. The test page will be sent to the printer. It should print out in a few seconds, and then you'll be asked if it printed OK. If it didn't print correctly, click No, and you'll be shown some troubleshooting information containing some questions and answers. The most likely fixes for the malady will be described. If the page printed OK, click Yes, and you're done.

When the printer has been installed, an icon for the printer will show up in the Printers folder.

TABLE 11.1: PRINTER PORTS

Port	Notes
LPT1, LPT2, LPT3	The most common setting is LPT1 because most PC-type printers hook up to the LPT1 parallel port. Click Configure Port if you want to turn off the ability to print to this printer from DOS programs.
LPT3 Infrared printing port	If your computer is equipped with an infrared port, you may have this option.
COM1, COM2, COM3, COM4	If you know your printer is of the serial variety, it's probably connected to the COM1 port. If COM1 is tied up for use with some other device, such as a modem, use COM2. If you choose a COM port, click Configure Port to check the communications settings in the resulting dialog box. Set the baud rate, data bit, parity, start and stop bits, and flow control to match those of the printer being attached. Refer to the printer's manual to determine what the settings should be.
File	This is for printing to a disk file instead of to the printer. Later, the file can be sent directly to the printer or sent to someone on floppy disk or over a modem. When you print to this printer name, you are prompted to enter a filename. (See "Printing to a Disk File" later in this chapter.)

PART

II

Optimizing and
Customizing

When You Don't Find Your Printer in the List

When you're adding a local printer, you have to supply the brand name and model of the printer because Windows Me needs to know which driver to load into your Windows Me setup in order to use the printer correctly. (When you are adding a network printer, you aren't asked this question because the printer's host computer already knows what type of printer it is, and the driver is on that computer.)

What if your printer isn't on the list of Windows Me-recognized printers? Many off-brand printers are designed to be compatible with one of the popular printer types, such as the Apple LaserWriters, Hewlett-Packard LaserJets, or the Epson line of printers. Refer to the manual that came with your printer to see whether it's compatible with one of the printers that *is* listed. Some printers require that you set the printer in compatibility mode using switches or software. Again, check the printer's manual for instructions.

 TECH TIP Windows Me remembers the location from which you installed Windows Me originally. If you installed from a CD-ROM, it's likely that the default location for files is always going to be the CD-ROM drive's logical name (typically some higher letter, such as E or F). If you have done some subsequent installs or updates from other drives or directories, those are also remembered by Windows Me and will be listed in the drop-down list box.

Finally, if it looks like there's no mention of compatibility anywhere, contact the manufacturer for their Windows Me-compatible driver. If you're lucky, they'll have one. It's also possible that Microsoft has a new driver for your printer that wasn't available when your copy of Windows was shipped. Contact Microsoft at (425) 936-6735 and ask for the Windows Me Driver Library Disk, which contains all the latest drivers, or, better yet, check the Microsoft Web site at support.microsoft.com/support/printing.

 NOTE All existing printer setups should actually have been migrated from Windows 9x to Windows Me when you upgraded, so if it was working under Windows 9x, it will probably work fine under Windows Me. This is true for other types of drivers, too, such as video display cards, sound boards, and so on.

Also remember that Windows Me can use the 16-bit drivers that worked with Windows 3.x. So, if you had a fully functioning driver for your printer in Windows 3.x (that is, your printer worked fine before you upgraded from Windows 3.x to Windows Me), you should be able to use that driver in Windows Me.

If you have a driver that came on a disk with the printer, or if you have downloaded a driver from the Internet, here's how to use it to set up the printer in Windows Me:

1. Follow the instructions above for running the Add a Printer Wizard.

2. Instead of selecting one of the printers in the Driver list (it isn't in the list, of course), click the Have Disk button. You'll see this box:

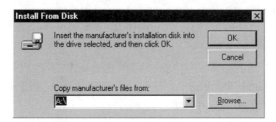

3. The Wizard is asking you to enter the path where the driver is located (typically a floppy disk). Insert the disk (or make sure the files are available somewhere), enter the path, and click OK. Enter the correct source of the driver. Typically, it'll be in the A or B disk drive.

 TECH TIP Incidentally, the Wizard is looking for a file with an .inf extension. This is the standard file extension for manufacturer-supplied driver information files.

4. Click OK.

5. You might have to choose a driver from a list if multiple options exist.

6. Continue with the Wizard dialog boxes as explained above.

 TECH TIP If none of the drivers you can lay your hands on will work with your printer, try choosing the generic text-only driver. This driver prints only text—no fancy formatting and no graphics. But it will work in a pinch with many printers. Make sure the printer is capable of or is set to an ASCII or ANSI text-only mode; otherwise your printout may be a mess. PostScript printers typically don't have such a text-only mode, but you can use a generic PostScript driver with them.

Altering the Details of a Printer's Setup—The Properties Box

Each printer driver can be fine-tuned by changing settings in its Properties dialog box. This area is difficult to document because so many variations exist due to the number

PART

II

Optimizing and
Customizing

of printers supported. The following sections describe the gist of these options without going into too much detail about each printer type.

The settings pertaining to a printer are called *properties*. As I discussed earlier, properties abound in Windows Me. Almost every object in Windows Me has properties that you can examine and change at will. When you add a printer, the Wizard makes life easy for you by giving it some default properties that usually work fine and needn't be tampered with. You can change them later, but only if you need to. It may be worth looking at the properties for your printer, especially if the printer's acting up in some way when you try to print from Windows Me.

1. Open the Printers folder (Start ➤ Settings ➤ Printers).

2. Right-click the printer's icon and choose Properties. A box such as the one in Figure 11.3 appears.

 TIP You can also press Alt+Enter to open the Properties box. This is true with many Windows Me objects.

3. Notice that there is a place for a comment. This is normally blank after you add a printer. If you share the printer on the network, any text that you add to this box will be seen by other users who are browsing the network for a printer.

4. Click the various tab pages of your printer's Properties box to view or alter the great variety of settings. These buttons are confusing in name, and there's no easy way to remember what's what. But remember that you can get help by first clicking the ? in the upper-right corner and then clicking the setting or button whose function you don't understand.

FIGURE 11.3
Each printer has a
Properties box such as
this, with several tab
pages. Options and
tabs differ from printer
to printer.

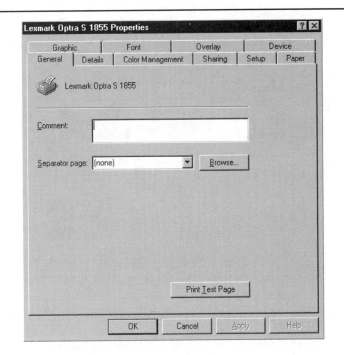

Deleting a Printer from Your Printers Folder

You might want to decommission a printer after you've added it, for several reasons:

- You've connected a new type of printer to your computer and you want to delete the old setup and create a new one with the correct driver for the new printer.

- You want to disconnect from a network printer you're through using.

- You've created several slightly different setups for the same physical printer, and you want to delete the ones you don't use.

In any of these cases, the trick is the same:

1. Open the Printers folder (Start ➤ Settings ➤ Printers).

2. Click once on the icon to select it and press Delete, or right-click it and choose Delete.

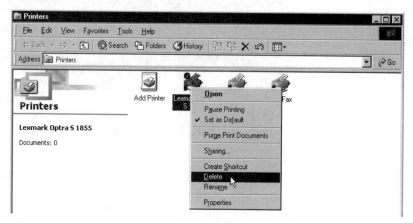

You will see at least one confirmation box before the printer is deleted. You may see another warning if there are print jobs in the queue for the printer.

NOTE If you have stipulated that the computer can keep separate settings for each user (via Control Panel ➤ Passwords ➤ User Profiles), the removal process removes only the printer setup from Windows Me's Registry for the currently logged-in user. Also note that the related driver file and font files are not deleted from the disk. Therefore, if you want to re-create the printer, you don't have to insert disks, and you won't be prompted for the location of driver files. This is convenient, but if you're tight on disk space, you might want to remove the printer fonts and drivers. To remove fonts, use the Fonts applet in the Control Panel, as described in Chapter 12, "Using Fonts Effectively."

Printing Documents from Applications

By now, your printer(s) is(are) added and ready to go. The procedure for printing in Windows Me is simple. Typically, you just open a document, choose File ➤ Print, make a few setting choices such as which pages to print, and click OK. (You might have to set the print area first or make some other setting choices, depending on the program.) If you're already happy with the ways in which you print, you might want to skim over this section. However, there *are* a couple of conveniences you might not know about, such as using drag-and-drop to print or right-clicking a document to print it without opening the program that created it.

About the Default Printer

Unless you choose otherwise, the output from Windows programs is routed to the print queue for printing. If no particular printer has been chosen (perhaps because the program—for example, Notepad—doesn't give you a choice), the default printer is used.

 NOTE The default printer can be set by right-clicking a printer icon and choosing Set as Default.

Exactly how your printed documents look varies somewhat from program to program because not all programs can take full advantage of the capabilities of your printer and printer driver. For example, simple word processing programs like Notepad don't let you change the font, while a full-blown word processing program such as Ami Pro or Word can print out all kinds of fancy graphics, fonts, columns of text, and so forth.

When you print from any program, the file is actually printed to a disk file instead of directly to the printer. The print queue then spools the file to the assigned printer(s), coordinating the flow of data and keeping you informed of the progress. Jobs are queued up and listed in the print queue window, from which their status can be observed; in this window, they can also be rearranged, deleted, and so forth.

Printing from a Program

To print from any program, including Windows 3.x and Windows 9x programs, follow these steps (which are exact for Windows programs but only approximate for other environments):

1. Check to see that the printer and page settings are correct. Some program's File menus provide a Printer Setup, Page Setup, or other option for this. Note that settings you make from such a box temporarily (sometimes permanently, depending on the program) override settings made from the Printer's Properties dialog box.

2. Select the Print command on the program's File menu and fill in whatever information is asked of you. For example, in WordPad, the Print dialog box looks like that in Figure 11.4.

FIGURE 11.4

When you choose Print from a Windows program, you often see a dialog box such as this that allows you to choose some options before printing. This one is from WordPad, a program supplied with Windows Me.

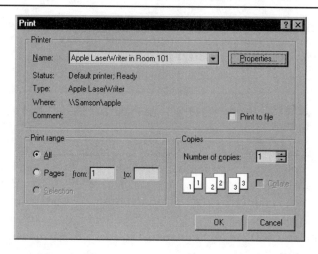

Some programs have rather elaborate dialog boxes for choosing which printer you want to print to, scaling or graphically altering the printout, and even adjusting the properties of the printer. Still, you can normally just make the most obvious settings and get away with it:

• Choose the correct printer

• Choose the correct number of copies

• Choose the correct print range (pages, spreadsheet cells, portion of graphic, etc.)

• For color printers, choose which ink cartridge you have in (black and white or color)

3. Click OK (or otherwise confirm printing). Windows Me intercepts the print data, writes it in a file, and then begins printing it. If an error occurs—a port conflict, the printer is out of paper, or what have you—you'll see a message such as this:

Check the paper supply, and check to see that the printer is turned on and that it's online (there may be a switch on the printer for this). If it's a network printer, make sure it's shared and that the computer it's connected to is booted up and has shared the printer for use.

TIP When printing commences, a little printer icon will appear in the Taskbar next to the clock. You can double-click this icon to see details of your pending print jobs.

Printing with Drag-and-Drop

You can quickly print Windows program document files by dragging them onto a printer's icon or window. You can drag from the Desktop, a folder, the Search window, or the Windows Explorer window. This will only work with documents that have an association with a particular program. (See Chapter 3, "Exploring the Interface," for a discussion of associations.) To check if a document has an association, right-click it. If the resulting menu has an Open command on it (not Open With), it has an association.

To print with drag-and-drop, follow these steps:

1. Arrange things on your screen so you can see the file(s) you want to print as well as either the printer's icon or its window (you open a printer's window by double-clicking its icon).

 TIP You can drag a file into a shortcut of the printer's icon. If you like this way of printing, keep a shortcut of your printer on the Desktop so you can drag documents to it without having to open up the Printers folder. By double-clicking a printer shortcut icon, you can easily check its print queue, too.

2. Drag the document file(s) onto the printer icon or window (Figure 11.5 illustrates this). The file is loaded into the source program, the Print command is automatically executed, and the file is spooled to the print queue. The document isn't actually moved out of its home folder; it just gets printed.

FIGURE 11.5
You can print a document by dragging it to the destination printer's icon or window.

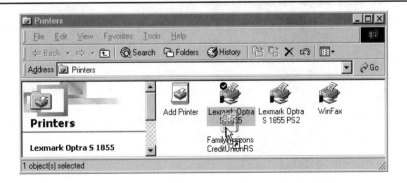

PART

II

Optimizing and
Customizing

If the document doesn't have an association, you'll see an error message:

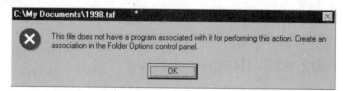

Also, a nice feature of this approach is that you can drag multiple files onto a printer's icon or open window at once. They will all be queued up for printing, one after another, via their source programs. You'll see this message asking for confirmation before printing commences:

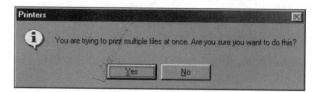

One caveat about this technique: As you know, some programs don't have a built-in facility for printing to a printer other than the default one. Notepad is a case in point: Try to drag a Notepad document to a printer that isn't currently your default printer, and you'll see this message:

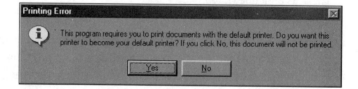

 TIP The drag-and-drop method can be used with shortcuts, too. You can drag shortcuts of documents to a printer or even to a shortcut of a printer, and the document will print.

 TIP In addition to using drag-and-drop, you can also right-click many documents and choose Print from the context menu that appears.

Working with the Print Queue

If you print more than a few files at a time, or if you have your printer shared for network use, you'll sometimes want to check on the status of a printer's print jobs. You also might want to see how many jobs need to print before you can turn off your local computer and printer if others are using it. Or you might want to know how many other jobs are ahead of yours.

You can check on these items by opening a printer's window. You'll then see the following columns:

Document Name   Name of the file being printed and possibly the source program.

Status   Whether the job is printing, being deleted, or paused.

Owner   Who sent each print job to the printer.

Progress   How large each job is and how much of the current job has been printed.

Started At   When each print job was sent to the print queue.

Figure 11.6 shows a sample printer with a print queue and related information.

FIGURE 11.6
A printer's window
with several print
jobs pending

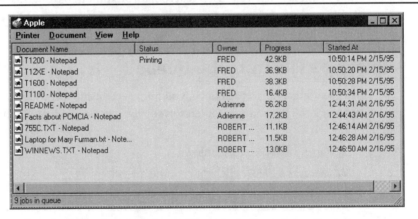

Complete the following steps to see the queue on a printer:

1. Open the Printers folder.

2. Double-click the printer in question.

3. Adjust the window size, if necessary, so that you can see all the columns.

NOTE If the print job originated from a DOS program, the document name will not be known. It will appear in the Document Name column as Remote Downlevel Document, meaning that it came from a workstation that doesn't support Microsoft's RPC (Remote Procedure Call) print support. Additional examples of programs that this may happen with are Windows for Workgroups, LAN Manager, Unix, and NetWare.

 TIP If the printer in question is a network printer and the printer is offline for some reason—such as its computer isn't turned on—you'll be forced to work offline. An error message will alert you to this, and the top line of the printer's window will say User Intervention Required—Work Offline. Until the issue is resolved, you won't be able to view the queue for that printer. You can still print to it, however.

Refreshing the Network Queue Information

Often the network cabling connecting workstations and servers is quite busy, so Windows usually doesn't bother to add even more traffic to the network by polling each workstation for printer-queue information. This is done when necessary, such as when a document is deleted from a queue. So, if you want to refresh the window for a printer to get the absolute latest information, just press F5. This immediately updates the queue information.

Deleting a File from the Queue

After sending a file to the queue, you might reconsider printing it, or you might want to rework the file and print it later. If so, you can simply remove the file from the queue.

1. Open the printer's window.
2. Select the file by clicking it in the queue.

 NOTE I have found, especially with PostScript laser-type printers, that after deleting a file while printing, I'll have to reset the printer to clear its buffer or I will at least have to eject the current page by pressing the page eject button (not all printers have a page-eject button). To reset, you'll typically have to push a button on the printer's front panel or turn the printer off for a few seconds and then back on again.

3. Choose Document ➢ Cancel Printing, press Delete, or right-click and choose Cancel Printing. The document item is removed from the printer's window. If you're trying to delete the job that's printing, you might have some trouble. At the very least, the system might take some time to respond.

NOTE   Of course, normally you can't delete someone else's print jobs on a remote printer. If you try to, you'll be told that this is beyond your privilege and that you should contact your system administrator. You can, however, kill other people's print jobs if the printer in question is connected to your computer. But, if you want to be able to delete jobs on a remote computer, someone has to alter the password settings in the remote computer's Control Panel to allow remote administration of the printer. Remote administration is covered in Part V.

 NOTE   Pending print jobs will not be lost when computers are powered down. Any documents in the queue when the system goes down will reappear in the queue when you power up. When you turn on a computer that is the host for a shared printer that has an unfinished print queue, you will be alerted to the number of jobs in the queue and asked whether to delete or print them.

Canceling All Pending Print Jobs on a Given Printer

Sometimes, because of a megalithic meltdown or some other catastrophe, you'll decide to bail out of all the print jobs that are stacked up for a printer. Normally you don't need to do this, even if the printer has gone wacky. You can just pause the queue and continue printing after the problem is solved. But sometimes you'll want to resend everything to another printer and kill the queue on the current one. It's easy:

1. Select the printer's icon or window.

2. Right-click and choose Purge Print Documents, or, from the printer's window, choose Printer ➢ Purge Print Documents. All queued jobs for the printer are canceled.

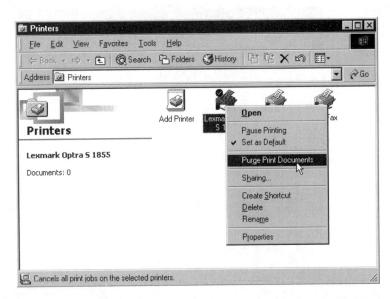

WARNING Make sure you really want to cancel the jobs before you do this. This is a good way to make enemies if people on the network were counting on their print jobs being finished anytime soon.

Pausing (and Resuming) the Printing Process

If you're the administrator of a printer with a stack of jobs in the print queue, you can pause a single job temporarily or you can pause all jobs on a particular printer at any time. This can be useful when you need to take a minute to add paper, take a phone call, or have a conversation in your office without the noise of the printer in the background. The next two sections explain the techniques for pausing and resuming.

Pausing or Resuming a Specific Print Job

You can pause documents anywhere in the queue. Paused documents are skipped and subsequent documents in the list print ahead of them. You can achieve the same effect by rearranging the queue. When you feel the need to pause or resume a specific print job, follow these steps:

1. Click the document's information line.

2. Choose Document ➤ Pause Printing (or right-click the document and choose Pause Printing as you see in Figure 11.7). The current print job is temporarily suspended, and the word "Paused" appears in the status area. (The printing might not stop immediately because your printer might have a buffer that holds data in preparation for printing. The printing stops when the buffer is empty.)

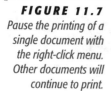

FIGURE 11.7

Pause the printing of a single document with the right-click menu. Other documents will continue to print.

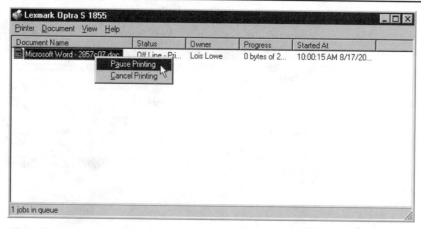

3. To resume printing the document, repeat steps 1 and 2 to turn off the check mark next to Pause Printing.

Pausing or Resuming All Jobs on a Printer

In similar fashion, you can pause all jobs on a given printer temporarily. You might want to do this for a number of reasons including the following:

- To load paper or otherwise adjust the physical printer
- To alter printer settings from the printer's Properties dialog box

Follow these steps to pause or resume all jobs for a printer:

1. Deselect any documents in the printer's window; press the spacebar if a document is selected.

2. Choose Printer ➢ Pause Printing. The printer window's title bar changes to say "Paused."

3. To resume all jobs on the printer, choose Printer ➢ Pause Printing again to turn off the check mark next to the command. The "Paused" indicator in the title bar disappears, and printing should resume where the queue left off.

Printing to a Disk File

There are times when you may want to print to a disk file rather than to the printer. When you print to a disk file, the codes and data that would normally be sent to the printer are shunted off to a disk file—either locally or on the network. Typically, the resulting file isn't just a copy of the file you were printing; it contains all of the special formatting codes that control your printer.

Why would you want to create a disk file instead of printing directly to the printer? Printing to a file gives you several options not available when you print directly to the printer:

- Print files are sometimes used by programs for specific purposes. For example, printing a database to a disk file might allow you to work with it more easily in another application.

- You can send the file to another person, either on floppy disk or over the phone lines with a modem and a communications program such as HyperTerminal. That person can then print the file directly to a printer (if it's compatible) with Windows or a utility such as the DOS copy command. The person doesn't need the program that created the file and doesn't have to worry about any of the printing details—formatting, setting up margins, and so forth.

- It allows you to print the file later. Maybe your printer isn't hooked up, or there's so much stuff in the queue that you don't want to wait. Later, you can use the DOS copy command or a batch file with a command such as copy *.prn lpt1 /b to copy all files to the desired port. Be sure to use the /b switch. If you don't, the first Ctrl+Z code the computer encounters will terminate the print job because the print files are binary files.

In some programs, printing to a disk file is a choice in the Print dialog box. If it isn't, you should modify the printer's configuration to print to a file rather than to a port. Then, whenever you use that printer, it uses all the usual settings for the driver but sends the data to a file of your choice instead of to the printer port.

To set up a printer to print to a file, follow these steps:

1. In the Printers folder, right-click the printer's icon and choose Properties.

2. Select the Details tab page.

3. Under Print to the Following Port, choose FILE:

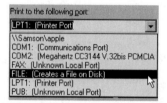

4. Click OK. The printer's icon in the Printers folder will change to indicate that printing is routed to a disk file.

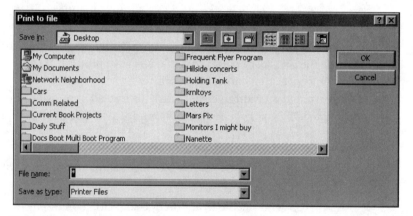

Now, when you print a file from any program and choose this printer as the destination for the printout, you'll be prompted for a filename.

CHAPTER 12

Using Fonts Effectively

Fonts are highly desirable to most users. Suddenly having the Gutenbergian power to lay out and print aesthetically sophisticated correspondence, books, brochures, and newsletters is one of the great joys of computerdom.

One of the most compelling characteristics of Windows—possibly even the single ability that most ensured the acceptance of Windows as *the* PC standard GUI (Graphical User Interface)—is the convenience of having a single system for displaying and printing text that works with all Windows programs. MS-DOS and versions of Windows prior to 3.1 could display and print high-quality fonts, but they had to rely on a bewildering hodgepodge of different printer drivers and font formats to achieve any success in this arena. Worse yet, each program solved font dilemmas in its own way, not sharing its wealth of fonts or font-management utilities with other MS-DOS programs.

By contrast, Windows programs starting with Windows 3.1, when TrueType fonts were introduced, need only a single printer driver and one pool of fonts. Thus, Lotus 1-2-3 for Windows, Ami Pro, Microsoft Access, Excel, Word, and PowerPoint on a Windows system can all share the same fonts and print with them to a number of printers without difficulty. Because fonts are so readily available at this point—in shareware packages, on the Internet, or on those economy CD-ROM packages down at the local computer discount store—getting your paws on some interesting fonts is a cinch.

Like other Windows versions, Windows Me comes with a set of stock fonts such as Courier New, Times New Roman, and Arial. You may be happy with these relatively banal, though useful, choices and possibly never feel the need to add to them. More likely, though, you'll want to augment these rudimentary fonts with a collection of your favorites to spruce up your documents. In this chapter I'll explain how to add and remove fonts from your system, how to choose and use fonts wisely, ways to procure new fonts, and even how to create fonts of your own.

Font Management in Windows Me

Fonts in Windows Me are managed from one convenient location: the Fonts applet in the Control Panel. From there, you can add fonts, remove them, sort them by type and similarity, and even display a sample of each of them.

Double-clicking Fonts from the Control Panel or selecting the Fonts folder in Windows Explorer will present a number of options for displaying your fonts (see Figure 12.1).

FIGURE 12.1

*The Fonts folder
(accessible from the
Control Panel) displays
and manages the
installed fonts.*

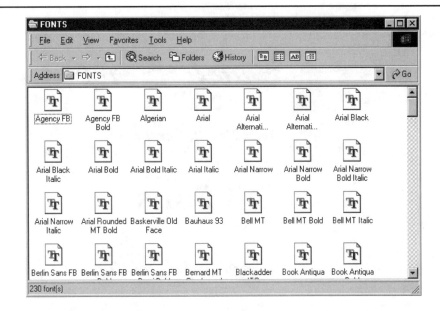

Some programs, such as word processors, may have additional fonts supplied with them—fonts not included with Windows—that you may want to use. Fonts can also be purchased separately from companies that specialize in typeface design, such as Bitstream, Adobe Systems, and Microsoft. Font packages usually come with their own setup programs, which will automatically install the fonts into your Windows system for you.

General Classes of Fonts

Fonts are the various type styles that you can use when composing a document, viewing it on the screen, or printing it on paper. Fonts add visual impact to your documents to help you express your words or numbers in a style that suits your audience. They can also increase readability.

As an example of some fonts, Figure 12.2 shows several popular type styles. Fonts are specified by size as well as by name. The size of a font is measured in *points*. A point is 1/72 of an inch. In addition, font styles include **bold,** *italic*, and <u>underlining</u>.

FIGURE 12.2
Various fonts and point sizes

Times New Roman

12 point

Brush Script

33 point

Times New Roman Italic

12 point

Gill Sans

28 point

Shelley Allegro

30 point

Casper Open Face

20 point

Windows comes supplied with a reasonable stock of fonts, some of which are installed on your hard disk and integrated into Windows during the setup procedure. The number and types of fonts installed depend on the type of screen and printer you have. When you install a printer into your Windows setup (see Chapter 11, "Printers and Printing"), a printer driver is installed. The printer driver includes a set of basic fonts for your printer.

There are several basic classes of fonts that are used in Windows, and an understanding of them will help you manage your font collection. Windows fonts break down into the following groups:

Screen Fonts   Control how text looks on your screen. They come in predefined sizes, such as 10 points, 12 points, and so forth.

Printer Fonts   Are stored in your printer (in its ROM), stored on plug-in cartridges, or downloaded to your printer by Windows when you print. Downloaded fonts are called *soft fonts*.

Vector Fonts   Use straight-line segments and formulas to draw letters. They can be easily scaled to different sizes. These are primarily used on printing devices that only draw lines, such as plotters.

TrueType Fonts   Are generated either as *bitmaps* or as soft fonts, depending on your printer. The advantage of TrueType fonts is that they will print exactly as seen on the screen. (TrueType fonts were introduced with Windows 3.1 to solve problems associated with differences between how fonts appear on screen and how they print.)

TrueType Fonts

With the addition of TrueType fonts in Windows several years ago, typefaces could be scaled to any size and displayed or printed accurately on virtually all displays and printers—without the addition of any third-party software. And because of the careful design of the screen and printer display of each font, TrueType fonts provide much better WYSIWYG (What-You-See-Is-What-You-Get) capabilities than previous fonts. Furthermore, you no longer have to ensure that you have fonts in your printer that match the fonts on your screen.

With TrueType any printer that can print graphics can print the full range of True-Type fonts—all orchestrated by Windows. And the results will look more or less the same, even on different printers. TrueType also allows users of different computer systems to maintain compatibility across platforms. For example, because TrueType is also integrated into Mac System 7 and higher (the Macintosh operating system), a document formatted on a Macintosh using TrueType fonts will look exactly the same on a Windows-equipped PC.

Finally, because TrueType is an integrated component of Windows, any Windows program can make use of TrueType fonts. These fonts can be easily scaled (increased or decreased in size), rotated, or otherwise altered.

Special Characters

Each TrueType font contains a number of special characters, like trademark (™) and yen (¥), punctuation such as the em dash (—) and curly quotes (""), and foreign (æ) and accented (ñ) characters. But Windows Me also includes a couple of special fonts you should become familiar with: Symbol and Wingdings.

Symbol contains a number of mathematical symbols, such as not-equal-to (≠) and plus-or-minus (±). It also contains a complete Greek alphabet for scientific notation.

Wingdings is quite a bit more versatile. It contains a wide range of symbols and characters that can be used to add special impact to documents. Instead of printing *Tel.* next to your phone number, why not place a telephone symbol? Wingdings includes several religious symbols: a cross, a Star of David, and a crescent and star, as well as several zodiac signs. Figure 12.3 displays the characters of these two fonts.

PART

II

Optimizing and
Customizing

FIGURE 12.3

Symbol and Wingdings are two TrueType fonts worth checking out. They contain characters you might find useful in your documents. You may even want to use one of these for your personal or corporate logo.

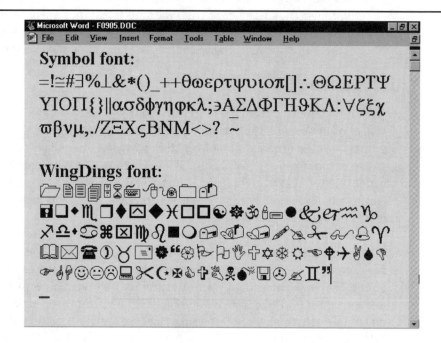

Bitmapped and Vector Fonts

So much for TrueType fonts. Now let's consider other types of fonts, namely bitmapped and vector fonts. First let's see how these two kinds of fonts work as screen fonts. Then I'll discuss printer fonts.

NOTE Recall from the list above that printer fonts are those built into the printer or those sent to the printer by the computer to print a document. Screen fonts are the fonts Windows uses to display text on the screen.

There are two types of screen fonts: bitmapped and vector. Each is quite different from the other and serves a distinct purpose.

Bitmapped Fonts

Bitmapped fonts are essentially a collection of bitmaps (pictures), one for each character you might want to type. These bitmaps cover the entire character set and range of styles for a particular typeface in a limited number of sizes. Examples of bitmapped fonts in Windows are Courier, MS Serif, MS Sans Serif, and MS Symbol. When you install Windows, these fonts are automatically copied to the appropriate Windows folder by Setup. Windows comes with a number of versions of these fonts. Based on the resolution of your video adapter, Windows chooses the font files that take best advantage of your particular display. Figure 12.4 shows a character map of a bit-mapped font (MS Serif).

 NOTE Some of your programs may not display the list of bitmapped fonts in their Font boxes. They may only show a list of TrueType fonts. This doesn't mean they aren't there, only that your program isn't displaying them. If you try other programs, such as MS Paint (when using the Text tool), you'll see a larger list, including such bitmapped fonts as MS Serif.

FIGURE 12.4
Map of a
bitmapped font

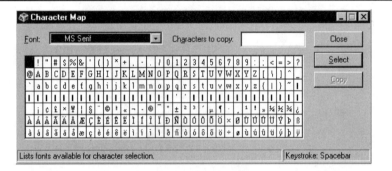

Because bitmapped fonts are dependent on the bitmaps included in their font files, you are limited to displaying these fonts in the sizes provided or in exact multiples of their original sizes if you want the font to look good. For example, MS Serif for VGA (Video Graphics Array) resolution includes bitmaps for display at 8, 10, 12, 14, 18, and 24 points. Opening the Size box for a bitmapped font will display a limited list of sizes, such as this list for Courier:

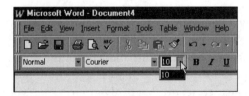

Even though the list of sizes for a bitmapped font is usually limited, you can type in any number you want. Windows will do its best to scale the font to the approximate size you asked for, but it will likely look pretty icky. There's one exception to this: Bit-mapped fonts can scale acceptably to exact multiples. So if 10 is on the list (as in the example above), you can get decent-looking 20-, 30-, or 40-point renditions, although the results will not look as good as a TrueType font at the same size.

NOTE Some programs don't allow you to use bitmapped fonts at all for your documents (or vector fonts either, described in the following section); they limit you to TrueType fonts only.

Vector Fonts

Vector fonts are more suitable for devices like plotters that can't use bitmapped characters because they draw with lines rather than dots. Vector fonts are a series of mathematical formulas that describe a series of lines and curves (arcs). They can be scaled to any size, but because of the process involved in computing the shape and direction of the curves, these fonts can be quite time consuming to generate. PostScript fonts are actually vector fonts, but because the PostScript printer itself is optimized to do the computing of the font sizes and shapes, performance is fairly good. Examples of vector fonts are Modern, Roman, and Script.

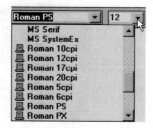

Procuring Fonts

The explosion of interest in typography generated by desktop-publishing technology has, in turn, resulted in a proliferation of font vendors. Even Microsoft is offering free TrueType fonts on the Internet. You can search for "free truetype fonts" using your favorite search engine, or go to the site `www.microsoft.com/truetype/fontpack/win.htm`.

Many other leading font vendors, including Bitstream and SWFTE, have brought out TrueType versions of their font collections. You can find these in most software stores. Shareware sources of TrueType fonts abound. Be aware, though, that not all TrueType fonts will look as good as fonts from the more respectable font foundries. Also, some users report that badly formed TrueType fonts can sometimes wreak havoc on your system.

If you're looking for fonts on the cheap side, check your favorite Internet directory like Yahoo!, Excite, or HotBot for Web sites that offer free font downloads. The Windows sections of these sites hold a number of free fonts that are yours for the taking. Many of the fonts are PostScript Type 1 fonts that have been converted to TrueType. The quality of these fonts is generally not as good as the commercial fonts, but in most cases you'll be hard-pressed to notice the difference. In several computer stores, I've seen numerous cheapie CD-ROMs that pack hundreds of TrueType fonts on them.

 TIP Here's a great source for typefaces: www.microsoft.com/truetype/links. This Web site links to a couple hundred sources of fonts, font-related shareware, "type-o-zines" (Web-based magazines about fonts), and tips about using fonts; it also links to numerous type designers.

Adding and Removing Fonts Using the Control Panel

Now that you have the basics of fonts under your belt, let's get down to the business of managing and maintaining your font collection. As mentioned earlier, the Control Panel's Fonts applet (also available from Explorer if you display the \Windows\Fonts directory) is the tool for the job. The Fonts applet lets you do the following:

- Add fonts to your system so that your programs can use them.
- Remove any fonts you don't use, freeing disk space.
- View fonts on-screen or print out samples of each font you have.
- Display groups of fonts that are similar in style.

Adding Fonts

If no installation program came with your fonts or if you want to add some TrueType fonts to your system that you downloaded from the Internet or otherwise acquired, here's how to do it:

1. Choose Start ➢ Settings ➢ Control Panel and double-click the Fonts icon.

   A Fonts window appears, as shown in Figure 12.5. All your installed fonts appear in a folder window that looks like any other folder. You can choose the form of the display from the View menu as with any other folder. There are a couple of extra menu options, though, as you'll see.

 NOTE If you have installed special printer fonts for your particular printer, these fonts may not appear in the Fonts folder. They will still appear on font menus in your programs. They just won't show up in the Fonts folder because they probably aren't stored in that folder.

NOTE Bitmapped and vector fonts are stored on disk in files with the extension .fon; TrueType font files have the extension .ttf. You won't see the extensions, however, unless you have modified your folder options to show the extensions for registered file types.

FIGURE 12.5

All of your installed fonts are displayed when you choose Fonts from the Control Panel. Because fonts are actually files, they appear the same way other files on your disks do. The TrueType fonts have the TT icon. The fonts with the A icon are bitmapped or vector fonts.

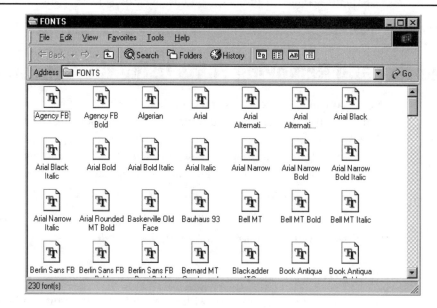

2. Choose File ➢ Install New Font.

An Add Fonts dialog box appears, as shown in Figure 12.6. Choose the correct drive and folder where the fonts are stored. Typically, the fonts you'll be installing are on a CD-ROM or a floppy disk drive, so you'll have to select the correct drive by clicking the drive selector.

3. Choose the fonts you want to add. If you want to select more than one, extend the selection by Shift-clicking (to select a range) or Ctrl-clicking (to select individual, noncontiguous fonts). Notice that I have selected several fonts to install at once. If you want to select them all, click Select All.

PART

II

Optimizing and
Customizing

FIGURE 12.6
Choose the drive,
folder, and fonts you
want to install.
Consider whether you
want the fonts copied
into the Windows font
directory, typically
\Windows\Fonts. You
can select multiple fonts
to install at once, using
the Shift and Ctrl keys.

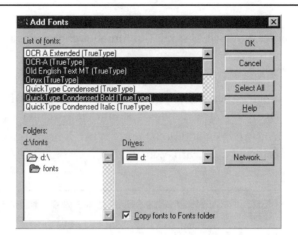

 NOTE   If the fonts you want to install are on a network drive, you have to choose the correct network drive from the Drives list. If the drive isn't on the list, this means you have to map the network drive to a local hard-disk name (D, E, F, and so forth) by clicking Network and filling in the resulting box.

4. When fonts are installed, they're normally copied to the \Windows\Fonts directory. However, font files are pretty large. If the fonts you're installing are already on your hard disk in another folder, you might want to leave them in their current home, especially if your hard disk is low on space. If this is the case, turn off the Copy Fonts to Fonts Folder check box. The fonts will still be installed, but they'll be listed in the Fonts folder with shortcut icons rather than normal font file icons.

 TIP   You should not deselect this check box if the files are being installed from a CD-ROM, a floppy, or another computer on the network (unless the network drive is always going to be available). You'll want the fonts on your own hard disk so they'll always be available.

5. Click OK. The font(s) will be added to your font list, available for your Windows applications.

If you try to install a font that's already in your system, the installer won't let you; so don't worry about accidentally loading one you already have.

Displaying and Printing Font Samples

Once you have a large selection of fonts, it can be difficult to remember what each looks like. Windows Me's built-in font viewer provides an easy way to refresh your memory.

1. Open the Fonts folder.

2. Double-click any icon in the folder. The font will open in the font viewer. In Figure 12.7, I've displayed a font called Arial Italic and maximized the window.

   You can open additional fonts in the same manner and arrange the windows to compare fonts with each another.

FIGURE 12.7

The font viewer kicks in when you double-click any font in the Fonts folder. The small numbers in the left margin indicate what point size is displayed to the right. Information about the font's maker appears in the upper portion of the window.

3. Sometimes it's useful to have a printout of a font. You can compile a hard-copy catalog of all your fonts for easy reference if you work with a healthy stable of fonts regularly. To print a single font, double-click it and then click Print (or right-click it and choose Print).

TIP To print all your fonts (or multiple fonts) in one fell swoop, select them in the Fonts window with Edit ➢ Select All. Then choose File ➢ Print (or right-click one of the selected icons and choose Print). You'll get a one-page printout for each font.

TIP The font viewer will work from any folder. So if you have a floppy containing some fonts you're thinking about installing but you want to see each font first, just open the floppy disk folder and double-click the fonts one at a time.

 TIP Like other objects in Windows Me, fonts have properties. Right-click a font's icon and choose Properties to view details about the font's size, creation date, location, type, DOS attribute settings, and so forth.

Viewing Font Families

Each variation on a typeface is stored in a separate file. That means that separate font files are required for normal, bold, italic, and bold italic versions of each font.

When you're viewing the contents of the Fonts folder, it can be helpful to see only one icon per font family instead of four. This way, you can see more clearly and quickly just which fonts you have. To do this, choose View ➤ Hide Variations.

Try it with your fonts and notice how it clears up the display. Unless all four files required for a complete font family are installed, a name won't appear in the listing now. For example, if you've installed only Garamond Bold but not Garamond, Garamond Italic, and Garamond Bold Italic, you won't see Garamond listed at all. You'll still see an icon for the one type you installed, but such icons won't be named. Double-clicking an unnamed icon will still display the font in the font viewer so that you can identify it.

To return the view to showing all font files listed separately, choose the Hide Variations command again to toggle the check mark off in the menu.

Viewing Fonts by Similarities

Many TrueType fonts contain within them something called *Panose* information. Panose information helps Windows Me classify a font by indicating a font's general

PART

II

Optimizing and Customizing

characteristics, such as whether it's a serif or sans-serif font. Based on this information, Windows can group together fonts that will appear somewhat similar on screen and when printed. It can be a boon to have Windows list the fonts that are similar in look to, say, Arial, in case you're looking for an interesting sans-serif font that everyone hasn't seen already.

 NOTE Some older TrueType fonts, as well as all bitmapped and vector fonts, won't have Panose information stored in them. This is also true of symbol fonts, such as Wingdings and Symbol. The Fonts folder will simply display No Panose information available next to the font in this case.

To list fonts according to similarity, follow these steps:

1. Open the Fonts folder, one way or another. You can do this most easily from the Control Panel, as described earlier, or from Windows Explorer.

2. Choose View ➢ List Fonts by Similarity. If the folder's toolbar is turned on, you'll have a button that will render the same effect.

3. The folder window will change to include column headings and a drop-down list. The list box is for choosing which font will be the model to which you want all the others compared. Open this list box and choose the desired font. The font must be one endowed with Panose information; otherwise, Windows will have nothing with which to compare other fonts. The results will look like Figure 12.8.

FIGURE 12.8
Font listing by similarity. Notice three categories of similarity: very similar, fairly similar, and not similar.

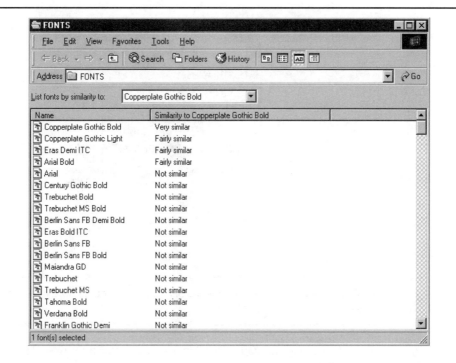

Removing Fonts

Fonts consume space on your hard disk. A typical TrueType font consumes between 50KB and 100KB of disk space. Deleting individual fonts or font sets also increases the available memory in your computer, letting you run more programs and open more documents simultaneously. If you're having memory-limitation problems, you could gain some room by eliminating fonts you never use. If you never use the italic versions of some fonts, for example, you might want to remove the Italic and Bold Italic versions specifically, leaving the normal version installed. A little-known fact is that even if an italic or bold font has been removed, Windows can still emulate it on the fly. It won't look as good as the real thing, but it will work.

To remove a font, follow these steps:

1. Open the Fonts folder. All the installed fonts are displayed.

2. To remove an entire font family (normal, bold, italic, and bold italic), turn on the View ➢ Hide Variations setting. If you want to remove individual styles, turn this setting off so you can see them.

3. Select the font or fonts you want to remove.

4. Choose File ➤ Delete, or right-click one of the selected fonts and choose Delete.

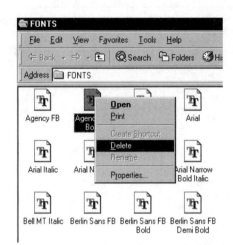

 WARNING Don't remove the MS Sans Serif font set; it's used in all the Windows dialog boxes.

5. A dialog box asks you to confirm the removal. Choose Yes. The font is moved to the Recycle Bin.

 WARNING You shouldn't remove or install fonts just by dragging them to and from the Fonts folder. Using the Install New Font command from the File menu ensures that the fonts will be registered properly in the Windows Registry and in the internal list of fonts that applications draw on for displays in their menus and dialog boxes. Always use the Install New Font command to add fonts and the Delete command to remove them.

Basic Guidelines for Using Fonts

Whether you rely on the fonts supplied with Windows or put together a sizable font collection, you should follow a few simple guidelines when formatting your documents. Attractive fonts by themselves aren't enough—the chief goal is readability.

- Allow plenty of space between lines. The space between two lines of text should be about 20 percent greater than the size of the font. Thus, if you're using a 12-point font, you should set the line spacing, or *leading*, to 14 points. This guideline doesn't hold true for headings, in which the line spacing should usually be about the same as the font size.

- Don't mix too many fonts in one document. It's often best to stick with one font for the main body of your text and a larger, bold version of the same font for headings. If you want to mix fonts, use a serif font for the body of your text and a sans-serif font for the headings, or vice versa. You can get away with using a third font for sidebar text, but you'll run the risk of clashing font designs.

- If you use two or more font sizes, be sure they contrast adequately. If your main text is in 12-point Times New Roman, use at least 14-point type for the subheadings.

- Use italics or boldface type to indicate emphasis. Avoid underlining and capitalizing letters, both of which make your text harder to read.

- Make your margins generous. One of the most common mistakes that causes an amateurish-looking document is text that crowds too closely to the edge of the paper. Allow plenty of space between columns as well.

- Following these few guidelines will help you avoid the most glaring errors of document layout. For more detailed advice, consult your bookstore or library for treatises on the topic of desktop publishing or graphic and printing design.

PART

II

Optimizing and
Customizing

CHAPTER 13

Adding and Removing Hardware and Software

FEATURING:

This chapter is all about adding and removing. Whether it's the latest 3-D game you've just bought or a brand-new modem, you need to take certain steps to set up the new item in Windows, and this chapter shows you how. It also shows you how to remove software to free up disk space and how to delete a hardware driver from Windows when that hardware no longer exists on your system.

Adding New Hardware

Windows Me fully supports the Plug-and-Play standard, which detects and attempts to automatically set up any new hardware you plug into your system. To work, however, (1) the computer must support Plug-and-Play (most computers made in the last five years do), and (2) the new piece of hardware must support Plug-and-Play (again, most devices made in the last five years do).

 NOTE Printers can also be Plug-and-Play compatible and automatically set up in Windows. However, some printers work best when you use the Setup program that comes with them to install additional drivers and utilities. See Chapter 11, "Printers and Printing," for more information about printers.

If both your computer and your new hardware support Plug-and-Play, Windows will probably detect the new device the first time you start up after installing it and will either automatically install a driver for the device or prompt you to insert the driver disk that came with it. You just follow the prompts, doing as you're told, and the new device is painlessly installed.

However, if you have an older computer or are trying to install some antique hardware, Plug-and-Play might not work. In such cases, you might need to set a *jumper* on the new hardware (a little black, plastic block that goes over two tiny pins on a circuit board) for a particular resource setting, and/or you might have to run a Setup program for the new hardware to tell Windows that it's there.

 NOTE Windows has two levels of Plug-and-Play. First, it detects any true Plug-and-Play devices; then it goes through a process in which it attempts to detect hardware that is not Plug-and-Play compatible. So, even if a device does not fully support Plug-and-Play, Windows Me might still be able to detect and configure it.

Setting Up an Automatically Detected Device

When Windows starts, you might see a box on-screen saying something like "Windows has detected new hardware and is installing the needed drivers." Just wait, and let Windows do its thing. If the box goes away and Windows continues loading, you're all set! Pretty painless, eh?

The other thing that could happen is that Windows displays the Add Hardware Wizard, telling you that it's getting ready to search for the best driver for the device. At this point, you have two choices:

- (Recommended) You can click Cancel and let Windows continue starting up. Then when Windows has started, you can insert the disk that came with the device and run its Setup program.

- You can insert the disk that came with the device, and then click Next and work through the Wizard to let Windows find the device driver on the disk and install it. This method is the quickest, but any utility programs that might have come with the device don't get installed.

Sometimes Windows will detect a new device, but it won't be able to identify it. When that happens, the device is placed in the Other Devices section of Device Manager. You can usually bring it to full operation by running the Setup program that came with the device or by using the Update Driver feature in the device's properties (from Device Manager) to install a driver for it. More on that later in the chapter.

Detecting Hardware with the Add Hardware Wizard

If Windows doesn't automatically detect your new device at startup, you can ask it to look for new devices using the Add Hardware Wizard in the Control Panel. The Add Hardware Wizard does the same standard check for new Plug-and-Play devices that happens at startup, plus it goes through a special routine for detecting non-Plug-and-Play devices.

 NOTE If you have a device that you are sure is Plug-and-Play compatible, but Windows didn't see it at startup, the Add Hardware Wizard is not likely to help Windows find the device. There is probably a problem with the way you installed it physically, or there's a resource conflict—or you need to run the software that came with the device. Running the Add Hardware Wizard manually from the Control Panel is useful chiefly for setting up older devices that don't conform 100 percent to the Plug-and-Play standard.

Follow these steps to run the Add Hardware Wizard:

1. Close any programs you have running. You're probably going to be rebooting the machine, and it's possible that the detection process will hang up the computer, possibly trashing work files that are open.

2. Look up or otherwise discover the precise brand name and model number/name of the item you're installing. You might need to know it somewhere during this process.

3. Open the Control Panel and double-click the Add New Hardware applet. The Add New Hardware Wizard opens.

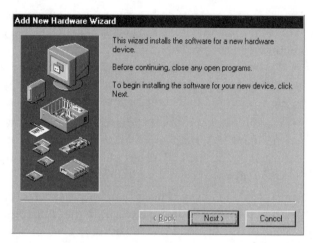

4. Click Next, and then Next again. The Wizard searches for new Plug-and-Play devices.

   If it finds any, it prompts you to complete the Wizard without having to go through the rest of these steps; follow the prompts to do so. If it didn't find any Plug-and-Play devices, continue to step 5.

5. It then asks whether you want to search for non-Plug-and-Play devices. Click Yes, and then click Next, and then Next again.

6. Wait for the results to appear.

If you see a message that it didn't find any new hardware, click Cancel. It didn't work. For help, see "Troubleshooting Device Problems" later in this chapter.

If you see a message that it found new hardware, click the Details button. A list of the detected devices appears.

7. To install the device(s) listed, click Finish. Or, if the device(s) found are not the devices you thought you were installing, click Cancel and see "Troubleshooting Device Problems" later in this chapter.

 NOTE The Add New Hardware applet in the Control Panel is intended only for adding new hardware, not for removing hardware and associated driver files. Removing drivers is done through the Device Manager portion of the System applet and is covered later in this chapter.

Manually Configuring Hardware with the Add Hardware Wizard

If you're the more confident type (in your own abilities, rather than the computer's), you might want to take the surer path to installing new hardware. Option two in the previous Wizard box lets *you* declare what the new hardware is. This option not only saves you time but even lets you install the hardware later, should you want to. This is because the Wizard doesn't bother to authenticate the existence of the hardware—it simply installs the new driver.

Here are the steps for using this option:

1. Close any programs you have running.

2. Look up or otherwise discover the precise brand name and model number/name of the item you're installing.

3. Open the Control Panel and double-click the Add New Hardware applet. The Add New Hardware Wizard opens.

4. Click Next, and then Next again. The Wizard searches for new Plug-and-Play devices.

5. When asked whether you want to search for non-Plug-and-Play devices, choose No, I Want to Select the Hardware from a List. Then click Next.

6. A list of device types appears. Click the type you want and then click Next.

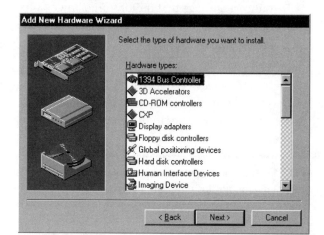

7. Depending on the device type you chose, a Wizard might start for the device type chosen. If so, work through the Wizard by following the prompts. Or a list of device manufacturers and models might appear. Choose the model you want to set up, and click Next.

8. Follow the prompts that appear to install the drivers for the device. You might be asked some other questions or be asked to insert the Windows CD-ROM or to reboot.

In some cases, you'll be shown the settings that you should adjust your hardware to match. (Often, add-in cards have switches or software adjustments that control the I/O port, DMA [direct memory access] address, and other such geeky stuff.) For example, I got this message when installing a SoundBlaster card:

"Windows can install your hardware using its default factory resource settings. To continue installing the software needed by your hardware, click Next. To view the factory default resource settings, click Details."

When I clicked Details, the screen shown in Figure 13.1 appeared. I can use this data to make sure any jumpers or switches on the sound card are set to match those settings.

FIGURE 13.1
For hardware that has address or other adjustments on it, you may be told which setting to use to avoid conflicts with other hardware in the system.

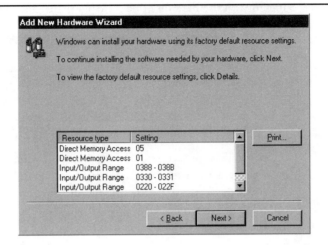

When Your Hardware Isn't on the List

Sometimes your new hardware won't be included in the list of items the Wizard displays. This means that Microsoft hasn't included a driver for that device on the Windows Me CD. Perhaps it's brand new and wasn't around when the disk went out the door from Microsoft. Or it could be that the manufacturer didn't bother to get its product certified by Microsoft and earn the Windows "seal of approval."

It's worth the few extra bucks to buy a product with the Windows 95, 98, or Me logo on the box rather than the cheaper clone product. As mentioned above, Microsoft makes new drivers available to users through several channels. However, manufacturers often supply drivers with their hardware, or you can get hold of a driver from the Internet.

TIP Microsoft maintains a Windows Me driver library that contains new, tested drivers as they are developed for printers, networks, screens, audio cards, and so forth. You can access these drivers through the Microsoft Web site, CompuServe, GEnie, or the Microsoft Download Service (MSDL). You can fax MSDL at (425) 936-6735. You can also order the entire library on disk by calling Microsoft at (800) 426-9400.

If you're in this boat, you can just tell the Add New Hardware Wizard to use the driver on your disk. Here's how:

1. Perform steps 1–5 of the preceding procedure.

2. When you see the list of manufacturers and models, click the Have Disk button. The Install from Disk dialog box appears.

3. In the box, enter the location of the driver (you can enter any path, such as a directory on the hard disk or a network path), and click OK.

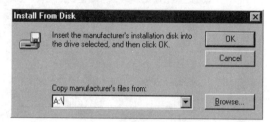

Often you'll be putting a disk in drive A, in which case you'd use the setting shown here. However, don't type the file name for the driver, just its path. Usually this will be just A:\ or B:\. If the driver is on a hard disk or CD-ROM and you don't know which letter drive or which directory it is, use the Browse button and subsequent dialog box to select the source drive and directory.

4. Click Next.

5. Assuming the Wizard finds a suitable driver file (it must find a file called oem-setup.inf), choose the correct hardware item from the resulting dialog box and follow the on-screen directions.

Removing Hardware

Windows Me is fairly aware of what's going on with your hardware. When you remove some Plug-and-Play–compatible devices, such as USB (Universal Serial Bus) devices, Windows automatically removes them from the Device Manager, freeing up its resources. (Well, actually, individual USB devices don't use system resources, but you get the idea.)

However, with other devices, the drivers for the device might remain installed even after the physical hardware is long gone. For example, suppose you have an ISDN (Integrated Services Digital Network) terminal adapter, and then you get a cable modem instead. Windows Me might continue to load the driver for the ISDN device every time you start Windows. This doesn't really hurt anything, but it's somewhat wasteful of system resources because that driver occupies space in memory and on the hard disk, and perhaps claims an IRQ (interrupt request) as well. To keep things tidy, it's a good idea to remove the drivers for devices you no longer have.

Some devices have their own software in addition to device drivers. For example, if you have a fax modem, it probably came with a faxing program as well as a driver to run the modem portion of the device. You'll want to remove the device's software before you remove the device through Device Manager because some software uninstall routines also uninstall the hardware drivers automatically. See "Removing Existing Programs" later in this chapter for details.

To remove a device driver from Windows, follow these steps:

1. Right-click My Computer and choose Properties. (Or go to the Control Panel and double-click System.)

2. Click the Device Manager tab.

3. Locate and select the device on the list. To do so, click the plus sign next to the device's category.

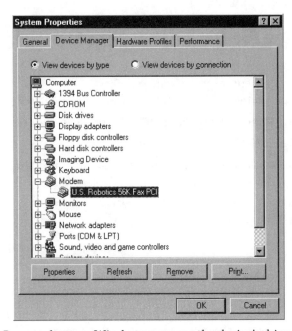

4. Click the Remove button. Windows removes the device's drivers.

5. Click Close to close the System Properties box.

You can also remove specific device types from their own applet in the Control Panel. For example, in the Modems applet you can remove modems, in the Printers applet you can remove printers, in the Network applet you can remove network cards and protocols, and so on.

Troubleshooting Device Problems

If you are trying to install a new device but Windows won't recognize it, or Windows sees it but it won't work, it's probably due to one of these situations:

- There is a resource conflict between the device and some other device.
- You need to run some setup software or install a driver for the device.

- You need to download a patch from the device manufacturer's Web site to make it work with Windows Me.

- The device is defective.

I've listed these in the order that I usually troubleshoot. Don't assume the device is defective until you have ruled out all the other possibilities.

The following sections walk you through the general process of troubleshooting a device.

Checking the Device in Device Manager

The Device Manager in Windows can tell you whether Windows sees the device and whether there are any resource conflicts.

To look for the device in Device Manager, follow these steps:

1. Right-click My Computer and choose Properties.

2. Click the Device Manager tab.

3. Locate the device on the list. You might need to click the plus sign next to a category to expand it.

If the device appears in the correct category, and no special symbols are shown next to it, then Windows sees it.

If a yellow circle with an exclamation point appears next to it, the device has a resource conflict. See the following section for help with that.

If the device has a red X next to it, the device has been disabled, either in Windows or in the BIOS program. Double-click the device to open its properties, and then make sure the Disable in this hardware profile check box is not marked. Then check in your BIOS setup to make sure the device has not been disabled there. Most BIOS programs allow you to enable or disable serial and parallel ports, for example, and people sometimes do that to free up the IRQs.

If the device is not on the list in the expected category, look in the Other Device category. If it appears there, you need to install (or reinstall) the drivers for it, or run its Setup program. See "Installing or Updating a Driver for a Device" later in this chapter.

Fixing a Resource Conflict

If there is a yellow circle and exclamation point next to a device, a resource conflict exists. This is rare in Windows Me because it does a better job of managing resources than earlier versions of Windows did, but a conflict does occasionally occur.

Resources are the memory addresses, IRQs, and DMA channels that the device uses to communicate with the processor. Windows dynamically assigns these through

Plug-and-Play each time you start your PC. However, some devices are quirky and will work only with certain settings, and other devices are not Plug-and-Play compatible and must have their IRQ set with jumpers on the device.

If you have a conflict between two devices, one of them needs to change. Do the following to change it:

1. Locate the device in Device Manager and double-click it. Its Properties box appears.

2. Click the Resources tab and check the Conflicting Device List at the bottom. If a conflict is listed, note whether it is an Input/Output Range conflict or an IRQ conflict.

3. Deselect the Use Automatic Settings check box.

4. Open the Settings Based On drop-down list and choose a different configuration. Keep trying different ones until you find one that reports No Conflicts.

5. Click OK to close the dialog box.

If you can't find a configuration with no conflicts, you can change the specific resource setting. To do so, click the resource (for example, Interrupt Request) and then click the Change Setting button. One of two things will happen: You might see a message that the setting cannot be modified, or you might see a box containing alternative settings, as in Figure 13.2. Try a different setting if you see the latter. Repeat until you find a setting that produces no conflicts.

Optimizing and
Customizing

FIGURE 13.2
If Windows allows it,
change the assignment
for a particular
resource to avoid a
conflict.

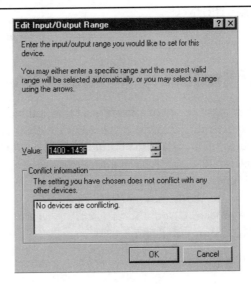

Installing or Updating a Driver for a Device

If the device doesn't work and/or it shows up in the Other Device category instead of the one it's supposed to be in, Windows has partially detected it but can't figure out what to do with it. You can help by running the Setup program that came with the device.

 TIP If you don't have a disk for the device, or you've tried the drivers on your disk but they don't appear to work for Windows Me, try going to the device manufacturer's Web site and downloading the latest setup software or drivers. Then use them instead of the disk in the following procedure.

If the device came with a disk but there's no Setup program on it, the disk probably contains bare drivers and INF files. INF files are configuration files containing information for setting up the hardware. They're crude, but usable. To install them, do the following:

1. From Device Manager, select the device and click Properties.

2. Click the Driver tab and then the Update Driver button. The Update Device Driver Wizard opens.

3. Choose Automatic search for a better driver.

4. If you have a disk for the device, insert it in your floppy or CD-ROM drive and then click Next.

5. Follow the recommendation that appears, depending on what Windows finds.

Adding and Removing Windows Components

Now let's look at the software side of adding and removing. First, there's the collection of applications that come with Windows Me itself. You can add and remove these at will. Adding them installs them from the Windows CD to your hard disk; removing them deletes them from your hard disk, but you can always reinstall them from the CD later if needed.

You use the Add/Remove Programs applet from the Control Panel to add or remove Windows programs. Double-click Add/Remove Programs and then click the Windows Setup tab, as shown in Figure 13.3.

FIGURE 13.3

*The Windows Setup tab
displays a list of
program categories.*

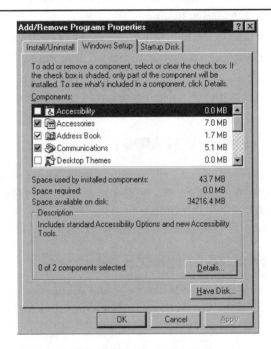

When you add or remove Windows components, you choose a category and then
choose programs within that category. For example, if you wanted to add or remove
Calculator, you would find it in the Accessories category. On the category list, each
category has a check box. An empty box means that none of the programs in that category are installed. A marked check box with a gray background means that some, but
not all, are installed. A marked check box with a white background means that all are
installed.

To add or remove a Windows component, follow these steps:

1. From the Control Panel, double-click Add/Remove Programs.

2. Choose the Windows Setup tab.

3. To add or remove the entire category, click its check box and skip to step 7.

   Or to add or remove a specific program, click the name of the category containing it and go on to step 4.

 NOTE If you don't know what programs are in what categories, feel free to browse.

4. Click Details. A list of the programs in the chosen category appears.

5. Place check marks next to the programs to install, and remove check marks next to the ones to remove.

6. Click OK. Repeat the process for other categories if desired.

7. Click OK to close the dialog box. If prompted, insert the Windows CD and then click OK.

8. If prompted, choose Yes to restart the computer.

Installing New Programs

Almost every program requires you to run a Setup utility that copies the needed files to your hard disk and sets the program up in the Windows Registry.

New programs can come from a variety of sources. You might download one from the Internet or buy a program in a store on a CD-ROM or floppy disk.

Installing a Downloaded Program

Many Web sites provide demo versions of commercial software, or totally free programs for the taking. When you click a hyperlink for a download, a dialog box appears, asking what you want to do with the file.

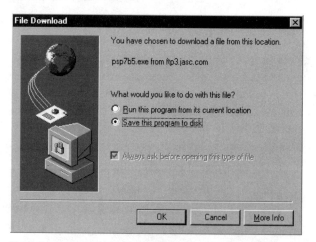

Choose Save This Program to Disk, and click OK. A Save As dialog box appears. In it, navigate to the drive and folder in which you want to save the file. I usually download everything into a folder called Incoming, with each download in a separate subfolder. When the correct location appears in the Save In box, click Save to move on.

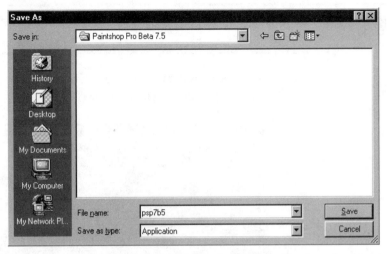

A progress meter shows the download in process. When the download is complete, this box appears:

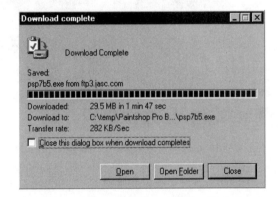

Click Open to start the Setup program; or choose Open Folder and then, after the folder opens, double-click the icon for the file you just downloaded.

Installing a Program from a CD-ROM

On most systems, when you insert a CD-ROM in your drive, it begins playing automatically. That means that the Setup program runs by itself, and you don't have to do anything except follow the prompts to complete the installation.

If for some reason, the Setup program on the CD doesn't start automatically, or if you're installing from a floppy disk, use the following procedure:

1. From the Control Panel, double-click the Add/Remove Software applet.

2. Click the Install button. A box appears, prompting you to insert the disk or CD-ROM.

3. Make sure the disk is inserted, and click Next.

NOTE Windows searches for programs named Setup or Install that have a `.bat`, `.pif`, `.com`, or `.exe` extension.

4. Windows presents the program it found by searching your disk drives. To accept it and run the Setup program, click Finish.

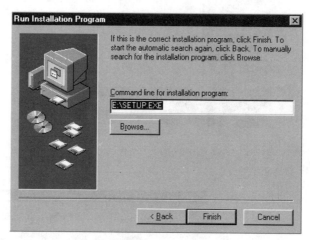

5. Follow the instructions on-screen to install the program.

Removing Existing Programs

This might be obvious, but you should not uninstall a program simply by deleting its folder on your hard disk. True, this does get rid of most of the program's files; but many programs also place files in the C:\Windows folder when they install, and you don't have any way of knowing which files from that folder need to be deleted. Also, the Windows Registry will still contain references to that program, and leaving that information in the Registry is bad, bad housekeeping. Do that enough times and you'll get sluggish performance and tough-to-troubleshoot errors.

Before removing a program through Windows Me itself, you should always check the program's disk or program group (from the Start button) for the possible existence of its own uninstall program. Such programs are frequently more thorough than the Windows Add/Remove Software approach.

NOTE When you remove a program, sometimes remnants of it are left in your Windows Registry. Over time, this can cause tough-to-troubleshoot problems, with multiple programs leaving conflicting, useless lines there. Fortunately, Windows Me includes a System Restore feature that can take you back to an earlier version of the Registry, before you installed that program. For details, see Chapter 14, "PC Health Features."

If there is no uninstall program, the next-best thing is to uninstall the program through Windows Me itself. You can remove most Windows-based programs with the Add/Remove Programs applet in the Control Panel. It's fairly straightforward; just follow these steps:

1. From the Control Panel, double-click Add/Remove Programs.

2. On the Install/Uninstall tab, locate the program that you want to remove, and select it.

3. Click the Remove button.

4. Answer any warnings about removing an application as appropriate.

NOTE Once a program is removed, you'll have to reinstall it from its source disks to make it work again. You can't just copy things out of the Recycle Bin to their old directories because settings from the Start button—and possibly the Registry—will have been deleted.

Now that you know how to work with hardware and software, let's move on to a particular class of utility program in Windows: those that help you keep your PC healthy. That's the subject of Chapter 14.

PART

II

Optimizing and Customizing

CHAPTER **14**
<u></u>

PC Health Features

FEATURING:

There are two sides to PC health: hardware and software. There's not much you can do about a hardware problem, other than replace the device. However, most problems that people encounter with their PCs are actually *software* problems, even if the end result is a hardware problem. For example, if something happens to corrupt your video drivers, your display will probably look awful, even though there's nothing physically wrong with your monitor or video card.

In this chapter, I'll provide you with the information and skills you need to monitor and troubleshoot whatever comes up that prevents your PC from working at its peak.

Keeping an Eye on PC Health

A big part of keeping your PC healthy is simply being aware of your PC's health on a day-to-day basis, just as you would with yourself or your child. Watch for changes. The occasional lockup or error message might not mean anything, but look for patterns of behavior that can signal a problem. The following sections outline some of the Windows Me tools that are designed to help you monitor your PC.

Viewing System Information

The System Information utility is a powerful control center for system analysis, configuration, and troubleshooting. It displays detailed information about your hardware and software, and its Tools menu provides easy access to a variety of helpful utilities. All in all, the System Information utility is a one-stop shop for the system technician or troubleshooter.

To run System Information, choose Start ➤ Programs ➤ Accessories ➤ System Tools ➤ System Information. Figure 14.1 shows its initial screen.

FIGURE 14.1
System Information
provides detailed data
about your hardware
and software
configuration.

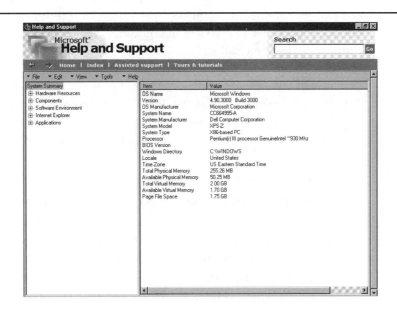

The System Information window has a folder tree on its left, just like in Windows Explorer. Click a plus sign to expand a category, then click an item in that category to see the detailed information for it. For example, Figure 14.2 shows detailed information about IRQ usage.

FIGURE 14.2
Selecting a category on
the tree brings up a
specific type of
information. Here, IRQ
usage is shown.

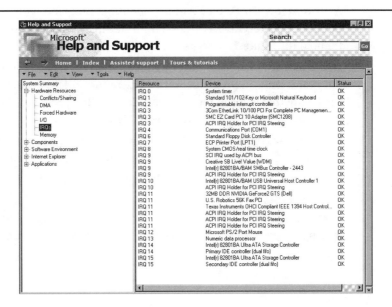

PART

II

Optimizing and
Customizing

All these techie details might not mean much to you at the moment, but if you are ever troubleshooting a problem over the phone with a technical support person, they might ask you about your system specifications. System Information will provide you with the needed information.

The Tools menu in System Information provides access to a variety of useful utilities. Most of these are not terribly useful for the average end user, but there are a few especially useful items in the bunch that I'll be describing later in this chapter and in Chapter 15, "Improving System Performance." These utilities include the following:

System Restore   Launches the System Restore program described later in this chapter.

Fault Log   Provides an error log for use in troubleshooting.

Network Diagnostics   Runs a utility for diagnosing problems connecting to a network.

DirectX Diagnostic Tool   Runs a utility for diagnosing video problems involving DirectX (a common video feature in games).

Update Wizard Uninstall   Helps you uninstall updates that you have downloaded using Windows Update (which is covered in Chapter 15).

Signature Verification Tool   Helps you diagnose Windows problems by verifying that certain critical Windows files have not been modified since they were installed.

Registry Checker   Checks the Registry for errors that could be causing system problems.

Automatic Skip Driver Agent   Identifies problems with drivers loaded at startup that have prevented Windows from starting in the past and allows you to skip them in the future.

Dr. Watson   Loads a monitoring program in the background that watches for errors and faults in programs. When one occurs, it logs detailed information about the failure that you can send to the company that produced the software to help them create a patch that solves the problem.

System Configuration Utility   Controls how Windows starts up and what drivers and programs it loads. You'll learn more about it in Chapter 15.

ScanDisk   Checks your hard disk for physical and logical errors. It's covered later in this chapter.

WMI Control   Is a control board for Windows Management Implementation, which lets you take control of remote PCs on a network for maintenance and security.

Using the Resource Meter

The Resource Meter is a little utility that constantly monitors the amount of free system resources. There are three measurements: system resources, GDI resources, and user resources. If any of them fall to a low level (say, 25 percent free or so), the likelihood of program crashes and other problems increases. The most common cause of system resource levels being low is a poorly written program hogging too large a chunk of resources for itself, or a program crashing and failing to release the resources it was using.

To run the Resource Meter, choose Start ➤ Programs ➤ Accessories ➤ System Tools ➤ Resource Meter. If it's not there, you'll need to add it with Add/Remove Programs (see Chapter 13, "Adding and Removing Hardware and Software"). When you start the Resource Meter, it appears only as an icon in the system tray. Double-click that icon, however, and a dialog box appears with exact percentages for each of the resource categories.

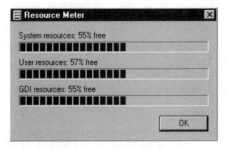

So what do you do with this information? Mostly you just keep an eye on it, and if one of the levels drops below 25 percent or so, you close all your applications and restart your PC.

Using the System Monitor

The System Monitor is a more complex version of the Resource Meter. Instead of a single numeric percentage in a few categories, it shows you a graph of various system statistics. The default one is Kernel Usage, shown in Figure 14.3, but you can also show other graphs for items such as File System, Memory Manager, and Microsoft Network Client.

FIGURE 14.3

The System Monitor graphs system usage so that you can watch the effect of opening or closing a specific application.

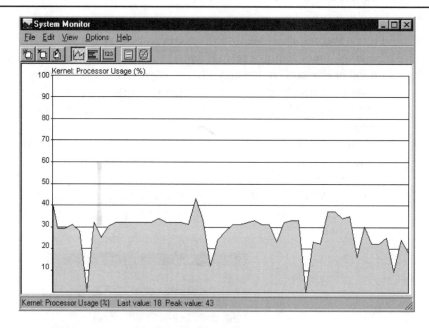

To add another graph to the display, choose Edit ➤ Add Item and select another statistic to graph.

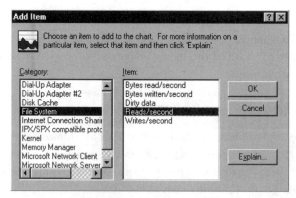

Note that you can also remove items from the display area using the Edit menu.

So what do you *do* with this information? If you're an average user, not much. But if you're a programmer or a PC technician, you can use the data to track down problems.

Keeping Your System Up-to-Date

Windows works best when it has the latest versions of everything, including any patches or updates that prevent or fix problems with Windows Me and Internet Explorer. There are a couple of ways you can get those latest versions. One of them,

Windows Update, has been around since Windows 98 and still works beautifully. The other, AutoUpdate, is new in Windows Me and automates the process of checking for, retrieving, and installing the latest updates. Both require Internet connectivity, so start your Internet connection before using either one.

Using Windows Update

Windows Update connects you to a Web page that runs an application to analyze your current system settings. Then it recommends updates you can download.

Follow these steps to use Windows Update:

1. Choose Start ➢ Windows Update. A Welcome to Windows Update Web page appears.

2. Click the Product Updates hyperlink.

3. Wait for Windows Update to analyze your system. If you see a prompt asking whether it is okay for Windows to do this, click Yes.

4. A list of recommended updates appears for your system, as in Figure 14.4. Click to place a check mark next to the ones you want.

 NOTE You should always choose to install any critical updates. The others are optional, depending on your interests. For example, if you don't use MSN Messenger Service, you probably don't need the new version of it offered in Figure 14.4.

FIGURE 14.4
Windows Update recommends downloads to keep your system current.

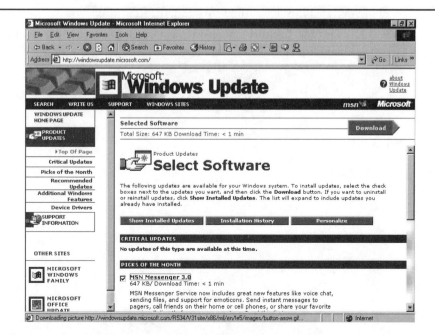

PART

II

Optimizing and Customizing

[Download]

5. Click the blue Download arrow at the top of the screen when you have finished making your selections. A Download Checklist page appears, showing what you have chosen.

[Start Download]

6. Click the blue Start Download arrow.

7. If a license agreement appears, click Yes to accept it. (It might not appear for some updates.)

8. Wait for the updates to be transferred to your PC and installed.

9. If prompted to restart your PC, click Yes.

You can remove or reinstall updates later if needed. Notice the Show Installed Updates button in Figure 14.4. Click that, and the list of updates will expand to include the ones you have already installed.

Some updates can be removed. A Remove hyperlink appears next to updates that fit that description; click it and follow the prompts. Other updates can only be reinstalled; to reinstall an update, reselect its check box.

Using AutoUpdate

When you install Windows Me, an AutoUpdate icon appears in your System Tray. At some point, a Microsoft AutoUpdate box pops up, explaining the feature and asking you to agree to its license restrictions. Click Yes to accept it. This happens only once, and by the time you read this, it has probably already come and gone on your PC.

AutoUpdate automates the work of using Windows Update by periodically checking for updates and downloading them to your computer. Then it notifies you that they have arrived, and asks your permission to install them. It's turned on by default, but you can adjust its settings by doing the following:

1. From the Control Panel, double-click the Automatic Updates icon. The Automatic Updates dialog box appears, as seen in Figure 14.5.

FIGURE 14.5
Configure AutoUpdate here if you want to change the default settings.

2. Select one of the update options:

Automatically Download Updates ... This is the default and the best option for most people.

Notify Me before Downloading Any Updates ... This is for those who are suspicious about things being downloaded to their PCs but who still want to use AutoUpdate.

Turn Off Automatic Updating ... This setting turns off AutoUpdate completely.

3. Click OK.

When an update is available, you will see a bubble over your AutoUpdate icon in the System Tray announcing it. Click the AutoUpdate icon to open the Microsoft AutoUpdate window. From there, click the Install button and wait for the update to be installed. When it is finished, a message to that effect appears; click OK.

Making an Emergency Boot Disk

An emergency boot disk (or a start-up disk) contains the necessary files to start your computer if something is wrong with your hard disk that prevents it from starting up normally. It's a smart idea to always have an emergency boot disk available. This boot disk, in addition to being able to start the PC, contains many helpful utilities—so many, in fact, that they don't all fit on the disk in their uncompressed state. The way that Microsoft has managed this is really very clever. When you boot from the disk, it creates a RAM disk out of some of your system's memory (like a temporary disk that exists as long as the PC is turned on, then goes away when you turn it off). Then it decompresses the utilities onto that RAM disk. When you boot from an emergency boot disk, you have an extra drive letter on your system, and the utilities can be found there.

Not all of the utilities are placed on the RAM disk; a few of them are on the floppy itself. For example, suppose you want to set up a new hard disk and install Windows Me on it. You could boot from the boot disk, use the FDISK program on the floppy to partition the drive, and then use the FORMAT program on the RAM disk to format the drive.

You created an emergency boot disk when you installed Windows Me, but you can create another one at any time. Here's how:

1. From the Control Panel, double-click Add/Remove Programs.

2. Click the Startup Disk tab, and then click Create Disk.

3. Place a blank floppy (or one that contains nothing you want to keep) in your drive, and then click OK.

4. Wait for the needed files to be copied to the disk. If prompted, insert the Windows CD and click OK to continue.

5. When the disk is finished, click OK to close the dialog box.

Windows 95 and 98 included the capability of creating a bootable floppy disk when formatting a floppy. Such bootable disks did not contain any utilities; they merely dumped you into a command prompt (A:\>). Windows Me has removed that feature from the disk-formatting utility, so now the only easy way to create a bootable floppy disk is with the preceding steps.

Correcting System Problems

So far, you've learned about utilities that help you monitor your system and prepare for emergencies. But what happens when problems actually occur? That's the subject of the next few sections. In them, I'll show you how to correct disk errors and how to back up and restore your Windows Registry with System Restore.

Checking for Errors with ScanDisk

Disk errors can result in all kinds of puzzling, tough-to-troubleshoot problems. Fortunately, there is a solution: ScanDisk. It corrects both physical and logical disk errors.

A *physical disk error* is a bad spot on your hard disk. It's usually caused by trauma to the system, such as knocking it off a table. A *logical disk error* is a glitch in the File Allocation Table (FAT), which keeps track of which files are stored in which locations on the disk. Logical errors are usually caused by shutting down your PC improperly (i.e., by turning off the power button instead of using the Start ➤ Shut Down command) or by programs crashing or freezing up. Of the two types, logical errors are much more common.

If you are experiencing lots of error messages in Windows, the first thing you should do is run ScanDisk. When you shut down Windows improperly, ScanDisk runs automatically when you restart it, but you can also run ScanDisk manually, as shown in the following steps:

1. Choose Start ➤ Programs ➤ Accessories ➤ System Tools ➤ ScanDisk. The Scan-Disk window opens.

2. Choose the drive you want to check for errors.

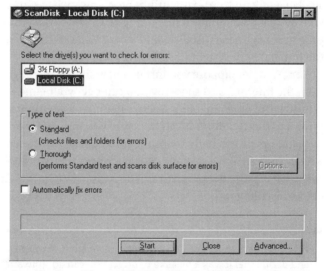

3. Choose Standard or Thorough. Usually Standard is sufficient; use Thorough only if your system has recently had physical trauma or if you are getting Data or Sector Not Found error messages, because a Thorough check can take a long time to run.

4. To correct errors automatically, choose Automatically Fix Errors.

5. Click Start. The testing begins.

6. If you did not choose to correct errors automatically and if ScanDisk finds an error, it reports the error in a dialog box. Click Repair the Error and then OK to continue.

   After correcting an error, ScanDisk might report that it needs to restart; if so, click OK.

7. When testing is complete, a summary box appears. Click Close.

8. Check any other hard disks on your system, or click Close if you're finished.

 WARNING Don't use your computer while ScanDisk is running, because if the drive content changes, ScanDisk starts over from the beginning. If you have problems with Scan-Disk restarting a lot and being unable to finish, make sure all other programs are shut down, including programs running in the System Tray. See Chapter 15 to learn how to manage System Tray programs.

Recovering from Problems with System Restore

System Restore, new in Windows Me, provides a functionality that was previously available only in third-party utility programs such as Go Back. It takes a snapshot of your system configuration (including your Windows settings), makes a list of which programs have been installed, and so on. You can then restore that configuration in the future if your system starts giving you problems.

For example, suppose you install a new shareware program you've downloaded from the Internet, and suddenly you can't get your e-mail anymore. You then try to uninstall the program, but it doesn't help. You can use System Restore to restore your system to the condition it was in before you installed that program.

Windows takes a daily snapshot automatically and keeps it around for about two weeks. You can also take your own snapshots at any time. For example, if you are not sure what a particular program will do to your system, you might take a snapshot right before installing it.

 NOTE System Restore is completely reversible. If you revert to a previous configuration and decide that it was a mistake to do so, you can go "forward" again to the settings you had before you reverted.

Taking a System Snapshot

To take a system snapshot with System Restore, follow these steps:

1. Choose Start ➤ Programs ➤ Accessories ➤ System Tools ➤ System Restore. System Restore opens, as shown in Figure 14.6.

FIGURE 14.6
The opening screen of
System Restore

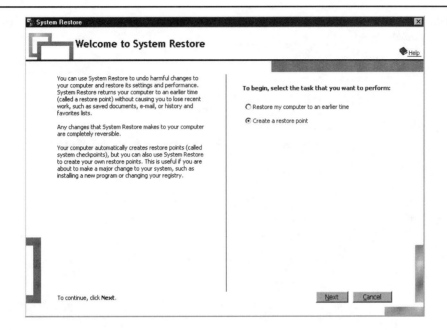

2. Choose Create a Restore Point and click Next.

3. Type a description for the restore point and click Next. Use any description that will help you remember why you created the restore point. For example, you might enter something like **Before Installing New Game**.

4. Click OK.

Restoring a Previous Configuration

If you ever need to go back to a previous configuration, here's how to do it:

1. Choose Start ➢ Programs ➢ Accessories ➢ System Tools ➢ System Restore.

2. Choose Restore My Computer to an Earlier Time, and click Next.

3. Choose the date on the calendar for the snapshot you want to return to. A list of available snapshots for that date appears, as seen in Figure 14.7.

4. Click Next. A confirmation appears; click Next again, and another confirmation appears.

5. Click Restore. The system files are modified as needed, and your computer is restarted.

6. After the restart, the System Restore box reappears. Click Close.

PART
II

Optimizing and
Customizing

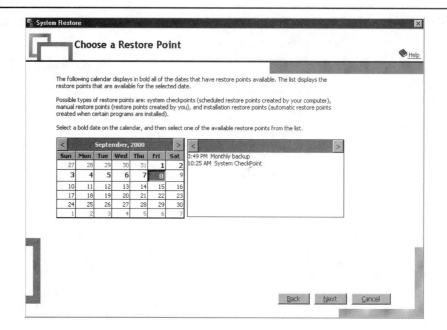

 NOTE Windows Me comes with another great new feature that safeguards your Windows system: System File Restore. It works automatically behind the scenes. If you install a program that overwrites a file that Windows needs to operate, System File Restore automatically reverses that overwriting, ensuring that Windows does not become corrupted by rogue programs installing their own versions of system files.

Troubleshooting Windows Me

Still having problems with your system, even after using ScanDisk and System Restore? Here are some additional tips for troubleshooting common Windows Me computer-system maladies.

Windows Me doesn't start up when you turn your computer on. Here are some troubleshooting tips to try:

- Remember that booting up can take up to a minute or so. Don't assume there is trouble unless there is absolutely no activity on the screen. Sometimes the only movement you'll see is in the little blue cloud-like bar at the screen's bottom.

- Check that the power is connected, the monitor is on, the brightness isn't turned down, the monitor cable is secure, and there's no floppy disk inserted in drive A.

- If the problem persists, press the reset switch or turn the computer off, wait a second, and turn it on again. Let it try to boot again. Windows is pretty good at repairing itself. It notes when a bootup has been unsuccessful, and will try to boot one way or another. It may take some time, grinding away on the hard disk for a while. If there is a problem with the Registry, the Registry Checker may kick in and fix the problem for you at start-up.

- Still no go? If you see the Starting Windows message, you're getting somewhere at least. Press the reset button on your computer, then press and hold the left Shift key while the computer and Windows attempts to boot. This should boot you into Safe Mode (though it might take the better part of a minute or two). Safe Mode uses the most rudimentary of drivers to boot with, to prevent incompatibilities. While booted up in Safe Mode, your job is to discover which setting (such as screen driver) was wrong. Do this using Control Panel, Device Manager, etc. Sometimes just shutting down from Safe Mode and booting again will result in a proper full boot.

- Another means of getting into Safe Mode is to press F8 while Windows is first booting (when you see "Starting Windows" in character mode, before the Windows splash screen appears). This will present a menu of start-up options. Choose Safe Mode.

- If you can't even boot from the hard disk into Safe Mode, insert your emergency start-up disk in drive A and turn the computer off and on again. If you see "Starting Windows Me" but things get stuck after that, restart and hold down the left Shift key. Then choose Safe Mode from the resulting menu and work from Safe Mode to clear up the problem.

You are seeing messages about running low on memory. Here are some things to try:

- Try closing some programs and/or documents.

- Empty the Recycle Bin. Remove any unnecessary programs from the Start-up folder.

- Use Windows Explorer or My Computer to delete some files. Empty the Recycle Bin again.

- Make sure you have at least several (preferably 20 or more) megabytes of free space on your hard disk.

- Let Windows manage your virtual memory settings (use the Control Panel's System applet to set these).

PART

II

Optimizing and
Customizing

• If you have less than 32MB of RAM in your computer, upgrade to at least 32MB, preferably 64MB.

You see messages about running out of disk space.   Try the following:

• Empty the Recycle Bin.

• Delete files you don't need.

• Remove whole components of Windows that you never use, perhaps wallpaper, Exchange, sound schemes, or accessories (some of these consume large amounts of space).

• Purchase a higher-capacity hard disk.

• Right-click your hard disk's icon (for example, from My Computer), click Properties, and click Disk Cleanup.

Printing doesn't work at all.   Here are some tips to try:

• Check that the printer is on, online, filled with paper, and wired securely.

• Try printing a test page by running Help's printer troubleshooter (choose Start ➤ Help ➤ Troubleshooting) or by opening the Printers folder (Start ➤ Settings ➤ Printers), right-clicking the printer, choosing Properties, and clicking Print Test Page. If the page prints, the problem is with your document or application program, not the printer or Windows Me. If the page doesn't print, make sure Properties ➤ Details shows the correct port for the printer (typically LPT1).

• Make sure that you have a good-quality bidirectional printer cable and that it's snugly connected both to the printer and to the PC.

Printing looks wrong.   Here are some troubleshooting tips to try:

• If a partial page printed, check the page orientation. It may be set to Landscape.

• Check the page-layout command in the program you are printing from *and* in the Properties box for your printer (click the Details tab, then Settings). If just the edges of the printout are missing, decrease the margins for your document and try again.

• Make sure the paper size you are using matches the document size you are printing.

• If you get PostScript error codes instead of normal text and graphics, either you are trying to use a PostScript printer driver with a non-PostScript printer or the printer needs to be set to PostScript mode. Add the printer to your computer again using the Add Printer Wizard; choose Start ➤ Settings ➤ Printers ➤ Add Printer (see Chapter 11, "Printers and Printing").

• Make sure that the correct driver is installed for the printer you are using.

- Make sure you are not running low on hard-disk space. Large print jobs are stored temporarily on the hard disk before being sent to the printer, and you need to have several megabytes of free space on your hard disk for that to happen.

Fonts don't print correctly. Try the following:

- Use TrueType or printer fonts whenever possible. Screen fonts—such as MS Sans Serif or System—aren't good choices. Change the font in the document and try printing again.

- If your printer has plug-in font cartridges, you may have the wrong one installed. In the printer's Properties box, click the Fonts tab and ensure that the correct Fonts cartridge is selected. You may have to go to Install Printer Fonts if the cartridge isn't listed.

- If TrueType fonts still aren't printing correctly, as a final resort you can try printing them as bitmaps instead of outlines (select this option from the Fonts tab of the Properties box).

Color printing comes out black and white. Check that you have installed the correct print cartridge by looking inside the printer. In the printer's Properties box, choose Details ➢ Setup to check for a possible cartridge-selection option (it might also be available for the program you're using; select File ➢ Printer Setup).

Printing is slow. Here are some tips to try:

- Open the Properties box for the printer, click the Details tab, and check the spool settings. Spooling should be turned on.

- If you're waiting a long time for a printout to appear, open the printer's Properties box, click the Details tab, and click Spool Settings. Try changing the spool setting from EMF to RAW.

The computer seems "stuck." Try the following tips:

- First, press Esc once or twice.

- If it's still stuck, use Alt+Tab or the Taskbar to switch to another program to see if Windows Me is really dead. (Alt+Tab is the standard keyboard combination for switching from one program to another.)

- If the Taskbar is in Auto Hide mode and doesn't appear, try Ctrl+Esc to bring up the Start list. (This is the standard keyboard combination for keyboards that don't have a Windows key.)

- Use these techniques to get to and save any documents you are working on, then close all programs if possible. If you suspect only one program is having trouble (such as being stuck), press Ctrl+Alt+Del *once*, then wait. In a few seconds a list of programs should come up. Select the program that is listed as not responding and click End Task; repeat for each stuck program.

- Save your work and restart the computer as soon as possible.

Nothing is solving your problem. You're pulling out your hair. Here are some troubleshooting tips to try:

- Check Chapter 8, "Getting Help When You Need It." There you'll find my discussion and explanations of the Help systems used in Windows and in Windows applications, and where to go when Help doesn't help.

- On your computer (if possible), try the troubleshooters that are built into Help (click the Contents tab and double-click Troubleshooting).

- On your computer or another, use Microsoft online Help via a browser and the World Wide Web.

- On your computer or another, read the additional Help text files included on the CD (`network.txt`, `printers.txt`, etc.). You can find them using Explorer; open the file appropriate to your problem (e.g., `printers.txt` if you're having a printing problem). The file will open in Notepad (or Word-Pad if it's too large for Notepad).

CHAPTER 15

Improving System Performance

Windows Me includes a very full set of software tools designed to improve the performance of your system and protect your vital information against breakdowns, damage, theft, or loss. In the preceding chapter, you learned about the tools for protecting and maintaining your system; in this chapter, you will learn about the ones that improve system performance.

NOTE There were several other utilities in Windows 98, but they have been removed in Windows Me. They included Microsoft Backup, DriveSpace, Compression Agent, and FAT32 Converter. I'll talk briefly at the end of this chapter about managing a disk that has already been compressed with DriveSpace in an earlier version of Windows.

Optimizing with Disk Defragmenter

Disk Defragmenter keeps your system performing at its best by detecting and correcting *fragmentation* on the hard disks. The term *fragmentation* sounds a little scary—after all, who wants their hard disk to break into little pieces? Actually, though, it refers to the files stored on the disk, not the disk itself.

When Windows stores information on your disk in a file, it begins *writing* the information onto the first place it can find that isn't already occupied by another file. If the disk already contains a lot of other files, however, that location may not be large enough for the whole file Windows now wants to store. If this is the case, Windows must search for another open spot on the disk for the next section of the file. The process goes on in this way until the entire file has been written to the disk into as many pieces, or fragments, as necessary. Of course, Windows keeps track of the location of all the fragments, and when you need the file again, it can find all the pieces for you without you ever knowing where they are stored.

Actually, this system for breaking files up into fragments when necessary has important performance benefits. If Windows had to stop and find a single section of the disk big enough for each entire file, your system would steadily slow down as the hard disk filled up. Also, you would wind up with less usable disk space. Eventually there would come a time when the disk still had many free areas, but none of them big enough to accommodate a reasonably sized file.

So what's the problem? Well, fragmentation also slows your hard disk down. To access information stored on a disk, the disk drive must move mechanical parts over the location where the information is stored. It takes only a fraction of a second to move these parts, but those fractions add up when a file is broken into many fragments. As more and more files become fragmented, you may begin to notice the slowdown, especially when Windows opens and saves files.

Disk Defragmenter remedies the problem by reorganizing the disk so that each file is stored as a complete unit on a single area of the disk. To do this, it identifies any remaining free areas, moves small files there to open up more space, and uses this newly opened space to consolidate larger files. It continues to shuffle files around in this manner until the entire disk is defragmented. All of this takes place behind the scenes. Though the files have been moved physically on the disk, they remain in exactly the same place logically—in other words, you'll find all your files in the same folders they were in before running Defragmenter.

When Should You Use Disk Defragmenter?

After wading through this long technical explanation, you may feel let down when I tell you that you may not ever really need to defragment your hard disk. Yes, it's true that fragmentation puts a measurable drag on file access if you time the system electronically. But in real life, you'll probably detect a slowdown only if you have very large, very fragmented data files. The reason is simply that today's hard disks are so fast.

 WARNING Also keep in mind that the defragmenting process itself can take quite a bit of time (on the other hand, you can run Disk Defragmenter overnight or while you're out to lunch).

Anyway, the point is simply that you shouldn't worry about a drastic performance loss if you don't defragment your disk regularly.

All that said, here are some tips for deciding when to use Disk Defragmenter:

- Disk Defragmenter itself can help you decide when to defragment. When you run the program, it analyzes the disk to detect fragmentation and offers a recommendation about whether or not to proceed (more on that in a moment).

- The slower your hard disk, the more you'll notice the performance hit caused by fragmentation and the more often you should defragment it. If you're still using a disk with an access time of 25 milliseconds or greater, you'll probably detect an improvement after defragmenting a heavily fragmented disk.

- The greater the percentage of data files (documents, pictures, database files, and so on) on your hard disk—as compared to program files—the more likely you'll need to defragment. After you install your program files, they stay put. Data files, on the other hand, are constantly being revised and saved anew and are much more vulnerable to increasing fragmentation. (If you frequently install and then remove programs, the risk for significant fragmentation also rises.)

Running Disk Defragmenter

To run Disk Defragmenter, complete these steps:

1. Click Start ➢ Programs ➢ Accessories ➢ System Tools ➢ Disk Defragmenter. The Select Drive dialog box appears.

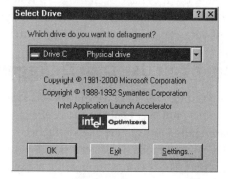

2. Choose the hard disk you want to defragment from the drop-down list.

3. Click Settings to check the settings.

The default settings shown here are good for most situations. Checking the drive for errors is a good idea before the program starts moving data around; if you don't, you could lose some important information in the process of the shuffling. If you want to change the settings for a single instance of running the program, click This Time Only. The first option in the box groups your most frequently used programs together on the disk so they start easily without the drive heads running around too much.

4. Click OK to close the Disk Defragmenter Settings box.

5. Click OK to start defragmenting the drive. If the drive doesn't need defragmenting, you'll be told as much and you can cancel. If it does, the program starts checking the drive for errors. (It does this as a precaution prior to defragmenting.)

If it detects a serious error in the drive, you'll see a report such as this:

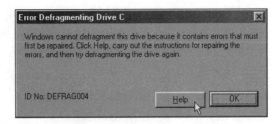

If you see something like that, you'll have to run ScanDisk to repair the error. If there are no errors detected, Disk Defragmenter starts to rearrange the data on the drive. You'll see a progress bar creep across the screen.

The Defragmentation Process

Click Defragment (or Defragment Anyway) in the Defragmentation dialog box to begin the process. You'll see yet another little dialog box informing you of the program's progress:

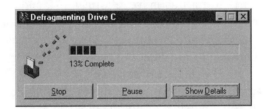

As Disk Defragmenter does its work, the indicator shows you graphically how far along you are in the process, and the percentage complete is displayed as well. Three buttons are available:

Stop Stops the defragmenting process and returns you to a dialog box entitled Are You Sure. The choices are similar to those of the Defragmentation dialog box: You can click Resume to return to defragmenting, Select Drive to pick another drive to defragment, Advanced to set defragmentation options, or Exit to close Disk Defragmenter.

Pause Temporarily stops the defragmenting process. The Pause button appears pushed in while Disk Defragmenter remains paused. To continue where you left off, click it again.

Show Details Displays a large window showing you exactly what's going on during the defragmentation process (Figure 15.1). This window represents the disk contents as a grid of little colored boxes, each of which stands for a single *cluster* (usually 2,048 bytes). The various colors signify the status of each cluster: those containing information that needs to be moved, those that are already defragmented, those that are free (containing no file information), and so on. To see a legend showing the meanings of the block colors, click the Legend button.

PART

II

Optimizing and
Customizing

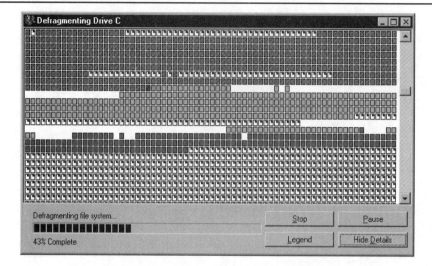

As Disk Defragmenter moves information around, the map gives you a moment-by-moment readout of which clusters are being read and written to, and the resulting disk organization. The bottom of the window displays a progress indicator and readout and includes Stop and Pause buttons. You can close the large map window at any time by clicking Hide Details.

Because Disk Defragmenter continues its work whether or not the program window is visible, you can switch to another program to continue your work. You'll hear the hard disk chattering more or less continuously during the defragmentation process, and your system will probably seem a little sluggish at times when it is waiting for Disk Defragmenter to give it access to the disk. Otherwise, however, you can use Windows just as you normally would.

Deleting Files with Disk Cleanup

How many times have you wanted to install a new program, download some files off the Internet, or save a document and gotten an error message about not having enough disk space instead? You just want a little more room, fast, with no lengthy defragging or compression sessions, and no sleuthing around with Windows Explorer. Disk Cleanup is the right tool for this job. It's a simple system utility that can recover some disk space for you in a jiffy by killing off relatively unimportant temporary files and a few other goblins that tend to grow, munching up precious hard-disk space. You probably didn't even know that some of these files were on your disk; others, like the ones in the Recycle Bin, you did, but had forgotten about.

Here's how to use it:

1. Choose Start ≻ Programs ≻ Accessories ≻ System Tools ≻ Disk Cleanup. A Select Drive dialog box appears.

2. Choose the drive to clean up, and click OK. A report of the space that can be freed up on that drive appears. Figure 15.2 shows an example.

FIGURE 15.2

A sample Disk Cleanup screen

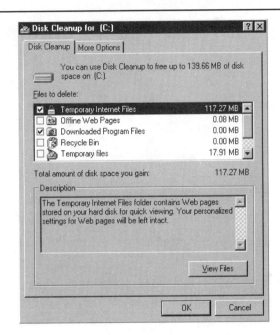

3. Click to place or remove the check mark next to each category of file. You can read a description of each file type in the area under the list by clicking the file item. You can view the individual files in a category by clicking View Files, and from there, you can choose whether to delete them or not individually.

 NOTE When you work with the Web on the Internet, lots of files are downloaded and cached (stored temporarily) on your hard disk to speed up viewing those pages the next time you look at the same Web site. How many Web pages are cached on your hard disk is determined by settings in your browser program. In any case, you can usually free up a bunch of space by cleaning out the cache of temporary Internet files.

4. Once you've selected the file types you want to remove, click OK. The utility does its work and closes, and you're back at your Windows Desktop without further ado.

Finding Even More Space

What? Still not enough space? You need more? OK, click the More Options tab in the Disk Cleanup dialog box. You'll see this box:

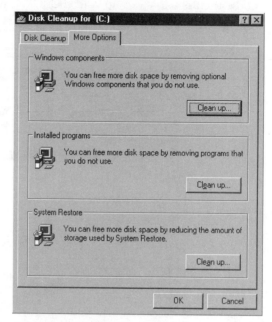

This tab contains shortcuts to three other utilities that you can use to free up disk space on your PC. They are listed below but discussed elsewhere in the book:

Windows Components   Click Clean Up, and the Add/Remove Programs Properties dialog box appears with the Windows Setup tab displayed. You learned how to use this utility in Chapter 13, "Adding and Removing Hardware and Software." This utility removes Windows components that you don't need.

Installed Programs   Click Clean Up, and you're taken to the *first* tab of the Add/Remove Programs Properties dialog box (the option above opened the second tab). Now you can look around for stand-alone programs (as opposed to stuff that comes with Windows proper) that you don't use anymore, as you learned about in Chapter 13.

System Restore   This option opens the File System Properties dialog box, in which you can adjust the amount of disk space used by the System Restore utility. This was described in Chapter 14, "PC Health Features."

Automating Tasks with Maintenance Wizard

Because utilities like the Disk Defragmenter and ScanDisk take so long to run, it's easy to put them off until they're way overdue. Windows Me offers a Maintenance Wizard that can help by scheduling certain important tasks to run at regular intervals without any user intervention. You can set them to run in the middle of the night, for example, or any time when you're not using your PC.

The Wizard ensures that

- Your system is error-free (ScanDisk, covered in Chapter 14)
- Your programs run as fast as possible (Disk Defragmenter)
- You have maximum hard-disk space available (Disk Cleanup)

The following steps show you how to start the Windows Maintenance Wizard:

1. Click Start ➤ Programs ➤ Accessories ➤ System Tools and choose Maintenance Wizard. Depending on how it has been configured, a message may pop up asking you if you want to run Maintenance now or if you want to change your settings. If you do get this message, choose to change your settings.

2. You're given a choice of using Express or Custom settings in the Maintenance Wizard. Choose the Custom option.

3. Follow the instructions for setting the time when tune-ups should happen. Though the suggestion is to leave your computer on all the time, you may not want to do that. After all, it wastes energy, unless you have a computer that is miserly on power consumption. Then again, having the computer tune itself up when you're trying to use it is going to be a disappointment. System performance will degrade past the point of livability. So whatever time you choose for tune-ups, make sure the computer is on and you're not trying to get any work done on it. When you've selected a time, click Next.

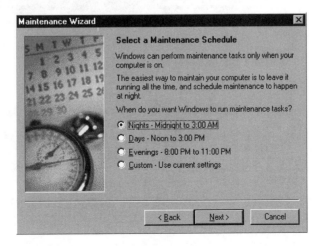

4. The Wizard lists any programs you have in your Startup group and suggests that you can make Windows start up faster by removing them from the Startup group. It's mainly a question of what's convenient for you. Click Next after you make your decision.

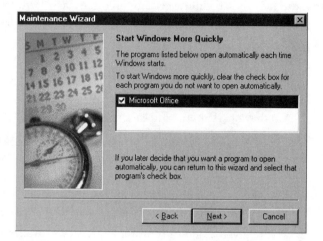

 TIP Later in this chapter, you'll learn about the System Configuration utility, which is a much more powerful means of controlling which programs load at startup.

5. The next two Wizard screens ask if you want to set a schedule for defragmenting your hard disk and running ScanDisk regularly. Follow the instructions to make your choices, and click Next after each window.

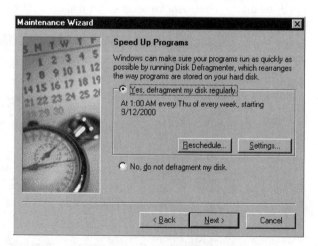

6. Choose whether you want Disk Cleanup to run, and decide which files you want cleaned up. Disk Cleanup doesn't take very long, so it probably won't hurt to go ahead and schedule this one. Click Next.

7. When you're finished setting all of these options, you'll see a summary of what you've selected. Click Finish.

Now you have tasks scheduled to be performed at the times and date intervals you specified.

You aren't limited to just these three programs to schedule, however. Besides using Maintenance Wizard, you can also manually automate other tasks using the Task Scheduler, described in the following section.

More Automation with the Task Scheduler

Task Scheduler lets you set up *any* program to be run automatically at predetermined times. This utility is most useful for running some of the system maintenance programs discussed in this chapter and in Chapter 14. Of course, if you have other programs you want to run, such as batch files or scripts (Windows Me lets you create scripts that run programs), you can do that, too. I'll leave that part up to you.

 WARNING Tasks can't run unless the computer is on. So don't expect to be able to recompress a hard disk in the middle of the night if the computer is shut down, or even if it's in a suspended state.

 NOTE If you upgraded from Windows 95 and had installed the Plus! pack, you already had a similar program called System Agent on your computer. When you upgraded to Windows Me, all of System Agent should have converted over to Task Scheduler.

To set up Task Scheduler, follow these steps:

1. Run the Task Scheduler by clicking Start ➢ Programs ➢ Accessories ➢ System Tools ➢ Scheduled Tasks. You'll see the Scheduled Tasks window. If you have already used Maintenance Wizard, you will have several tasks listed here already.

PART

II

Optimizing and
Customizing

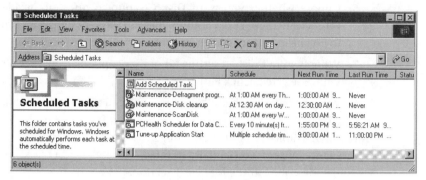

2. Double-click Add Scheduled Task. This invokes a Wizard that walks you through the process of adding a new task. Click Next to begin.

3. Choose the program from the list that Task Scheduler finds, and then click Next. The list contains all programs that Windows recognizes as being installed on your PC.

 TIP Click Browse to locate and select a program that does not appear on the list.

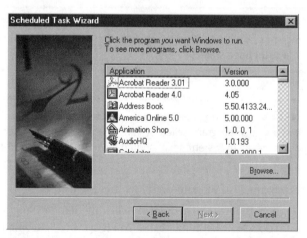

4. Choose how often you want the program run (daily, weekly, monthly, etc.). Then click Next.

5. Specify applicable time options, such as time of day, as required. Then click Next.

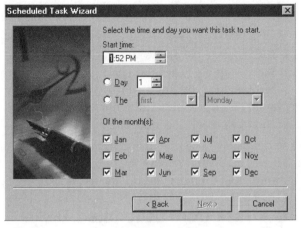

6. Click Finish. It's done, and the task is added to the list. Switch to the Task Scheduler window or double-click the Task Scheduler icon in the Taskbar by the clock, and you'll see the new item in the window.

You may have noticed the button for setting advanced options. It's for setting the options for the program being scheduled. If you missed it during scheduling, you can work with the same options later by right-clicking the task in the Scheduled Tasks window, choosing Properties, and then clicking the Settings tab. Highlights here include specifying whether the task should run if the computer is not idle and whether it should run if the computer is operating on battery power rather than AC (for laptops).

PART

II

Optimizing and Customizing

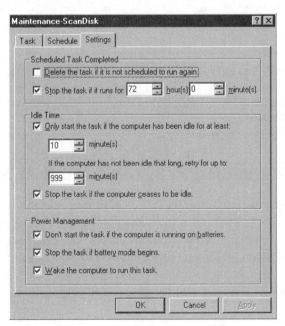

The other tabs in the Properties box for the task also have options you might need:

- The Task tab includes an Enabled check box. You can deselect this to temporarily disable the task on the schedule, without deleting it.

- The Schedule tab allows you to change the schedule for the task. It also has a Show Multiple Schedules check box; when you mark this, a drop-down list becomes available from which you can choose multiple schedules to set. For example, you might want to run ScanDisk in Standard mode every week, but in Thorough mode only once a month.

You can remove a task by right-clicking it in the Task Scheduler window and choosing Delete. This doesn't remove the program from your hard disk, incidentally, so don't worry. It just removes it from the list of tasks to be executed.

Running a Task from Scheduled Tasks

You may want to run one of your tasks immediately. Do this:

1. Open the Scheduled Tasks window.
2. Right-click the task in question and choose Run.
3. You can end the task by clicking the File menu, and then clicking End Scheduled Task.

 TIP Task Scheduler tasks are actually stored in the Windows\Tasks directory. Each file has the extension .job.

 TIP You can view scheduled tasks on a remote computer by opening My Network Places, opening the computer in question, and opening the Scheduled Tasks folder. See the Windows Help file for information if you want to be able to modify the task settings on a remote computer.

Controlling Which Programs Load at Startup

When you start Windows, it takes a minute or longer before you are ready to use your PC. Part of the reason for this delay is that Windows is probably loading one or more utility programs automatically at startup. This can be a good thing because it helps you keep important programs, like virus checkers, loaded without having to remember to load them each time you turn on your PC. But it can also result in a lot of junk being loaded, and your system resources being hogged; that you don't need.

For example, perhaps you have a fax program that loads its driver at startup, but you very seldom send faxes. You could disable it from loading at startup, and then load it manually whenever you need to send a fax.

Sometimes, you can tell which programs are running in the background by examining the contents of the *System Tray* (the area next to the clock in the bottom-right corner). Most programs that run in the background, like virus checkers and fax drivers, have an icon for themselves in the System Tray. You can right-click that icon and choose Exit (or Close, or some other command) to close the program, but it will restart the next time you start your PC unless you prevent it from doing so. The following sections outline various ways to prevent programs from loading at startup.

Removing Programs from the StartUp Menu

Let's try the easy way first. Some programs start automatically at startup because there are shortcuts to them in the StartUp menu. With such programs, you can prevent them from loading by removing the shortcut from there:

1. Choose Start ➤ Programs ➤ StartUp. The programs on the submenu that appears start automatically when you start your PC.

2. To remove one of them, right-click it and choose Delete. This does not remove the program from your system; it simply prevents it from starting automatically.

Disabling Programs through the System Configuration Utility

Windows comes with a utility called MSCONFIG (that's the actual file name that runs it), or System Configuration Utility, that helps you troubleshoot Windows startup problems by disabling certain drivers and programs from loading automatically when you start Windows. But it can also be used (with care) to disable unneeded startup programs.

To use it, follow these steps:

1. Choose Start ➤ Run. Type **MSCONFIG** and click OK. The System Configuration Utility opens.

 TIP Another way to run it is to open System Information (from the System Tools menu) and then choose Tools ➤ System Configuration Utility.

---

2. Click the Startup tab. A list of all the drivers and programs that load at startup appears. See Figure 15.3.

PART

II

Optimizing and
Customizing

FIGURE 15.3
*Disable certain
startup programs or
drivers here.*

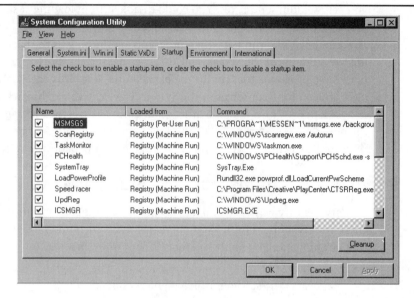

3. Find the program you want to disable, and remove the check mark from its check box.

WARNING Be careful, though; don't disable anything that you aren't sure about because it could be important for Windows operation, or for the operation of one of your favorite programs.

4. Choose OK. You'll be prompted to restart your PC.

5. Click Yes. If you inadvertently disable something that it turns out you need, simply come back to the System Configuration Utility and re-enable it.

Working with a DriveSpace Drive

Windows 9*x* came with a program called DriveSpace that compressed hard disks so that they held more data than they normally could. This technology worked only with 16-bit file systems, however, and most PCs today use the superior 32-bit file system. Therefore, Windows Me has removed the capability of compressing a drive with DriveSpace. However, it still includes a DriveSpace utility for performing maintenance on any existing DriveSpace drives you might have in your system. To access the DriveSpace utility, choose Start ➢ Programs ➢ Accessories ➢ System Tools ➢ DriveSpace.

Most people will never use this utility, so they don't even keep it installed; refer back to Chapter 13 to learn how to remove DriveSpace and free up the space that it takes.

Adjusting Performance Settings

As you were working with the System Properties in Chapter 14 (specifically the Device Manager tab), you might have wondered about the Performance tab in that same box. Well, now it's time to look at it.

The Performance tab of the System Properties is for checking and altering settings that affect the optimal performance of your system. Though Windows Me optimizes as much as it can, you may have need of or simply an interest in knowing what's going on in terms of virtual memory management, disk caching, and other performance determinants. All of these settings now live on this Performance tab, as shown in Figure 15.4. (To get to it, right-click My Computer and choose Properties, then click Performance.)

PART

II

Optimizing and Customizing

FIGURE 15.4
You can set and check system optimization from this page of the System applet.

There are three major performance sections you can examine by using the buttons at the bottom of the dialog box:

- File System
- Graphics
- Virtual Memory

I suggest you examine each dialog box carefully, read the help files, and use the ? button in the dialog boxes to get some tips about each setting before making any changes. Note that in Windows Me, the virtual memory file size is dynamically sized— and is best left that way—rather than being set to a static size. However, if you have multiple disk drives and want to ensure specific amounts of virtual memory on each, or to disable virtual memory swapping altogether, you can.

Other Tweaking Angles

Chapter 2, "Getting Your Hardware and Software Ready for Windows Me," touched on some basic Windows Me software and hardware compatibility issues, some of which will affect system throughput and overall performance. I could write a hundred pages about keeping your hardware doodads up to snuff, your hard disk organized, and other tricks for squeezing the most out of every CPU cycle. But in the end, most people don't bother, and it doesn't really net you much. In reality, there are really only a few truly beneficial performance tricks worth the hassle or price:

- First off, always keep a bunch of free space available on your hard disk. This is essential. You should have at least 20MB (some people say as much as 50MB) free on your disk for use by Windows for virtual memory. If you have too little, you'll start getting messages about running out of memory when you try to switch between programs. If you use only a few small programs at a time, this is less of an issue. Run Disk Cleanup, use the Control Panel's Add/Remove Programs applet (Chapter 13), or some other means to increase your disk space. You can use the Device Manager's Virtual Memory settings to specify a different hard disk if don't want to tie up room on your boot disk for virtual memory.

- Next, you should defragment your hard disk once in a while. Once a month is a good idea. You can use the Task Scheduler to do this if you want.

- If you are unhappy with the performance of your system and it's a pretty fast Pentium or higher already, increase the amount of RAM. You should have at least 32MB for halfway decent performance. Even then, if you run several programs at once, it will bog down and the hard disk will be grinding away, no matter what kind or speed of CPU you have. Move up to 64MB and you'll be much happier.

- If screen redrawing is slow, try reducing the number of colors and/or the resolution you're using. If you're now using 256 or more colors and you can live with only 16 colors, do it. If you're using 16 million colors (High Color) and can live with 64,000 colors, do that. Bump down the resolution a notch (e.g., from 1024×768 to 800×600). With fewer colors and pixels to paint, the Windows graphic subsystem will work much faster. You use the Display applet in the

Control Panel to reduce the colors. Or, if the screen display icon is in the System Tray (near the clock), right-click it and choose from there.

- Do what you can to remove 16-bit drivers from your system. In simplest terms, this means only install and use devices that are recognized and supported by Windows 95 and higher right off the shelf. Network cards, video controllers, CD-ROMs, PCMCIA cards, and the like should all be running with 32-bit drivers. Refer to the installation guide supplied with the product or contact the manufacturer to determine how best to do this. If you're not running DOS programs, you can often safely remove device drivers loaded from those files and let Windows handle all devices, typically loading its own native 32-bit drivers.

PART

II

Optimizing and
Customizing

PART III

Using Windows Me Multimedia

CHAPTER 16

Using the Windows Media Player

If you've used Media Player in Windows 95 or 98, you're probably incredulous that I'm devoting an entire chapter to it in this book. The earlier Media Player was a very simple program, not particularly feature-rich or attractive.

However, the Media Player in Windows Me is a totally different program. The only thing that stayed the same was the name. It's a full-featured multimedia player, capable of playing audio CDs, MP3 music files, and video and sound clips stored in a variety of formats. Here's a rundown of the new Media Player's features:

- You can play media clips—including videos, music, sound effects, and others—in any of dozens of different formats.

- If you have an Internet connection, you can explore an online Media Guide section and download free sound and video clips from your favorite artists.

- If you have an Internet connection, you can listen to hundreds of Internet Radio stations. Some of these are online broadcasts of your favorite stations from around the world; others are Internet-only stations.

- You can play audio CDs on your computer, and use play features like track selection, random play, and so on.

- You can copy tracks from your audio CDs to your hard disk, so you can listen to them while you work without having to insert the CD.

- You can organize your sound clips from various sources into custom playlists, creating your own mixes.

In the following sections, you'll learn how to do all these things.

Starting Media Player

There are a number of ways of starting Media Player. When you insert an audio CD in your computer, it opens automatically and starts playing the CD. You can also start it in any of these ways:

- Click the Media Player icon in the Quick Launch toolbar.

- Double-click the Media Player icon on the Desktop.

- Choose Start ➢ Programs ➢ Accessories ➢ Entertainment ➢ Windows Media Player.

- Double-click a sound or video clip stored on your hard disk.

Windows Media Player has several pages, each represented by a button along the left side of the window. The Media Guide page, shown in Figure 16.1, appears by default if you started Media Player without specifying a clip to open or inserting an audio CD. The Media Guide content changes every day, so yours will look different from the one shown here.

FIGURE 16.1
Windows Media Player opens to the Media Guide page by default.

Click the content to browse it, as with a Web page.

Click a button to use another part of the program.

Using the Media Guide

You might have heard in the news about the illegal distribution of music clips on the Internet. What you might not have heard, however, is that there are also a lot of perfectly legal music and video clips available, including many by big-name artists as well as struggling independent bands.

The Media Guide in Windows Media Player is by no means a comprehensive way of finding clips, but it does include some great features. One is an ever-changing list of featured clips from popular artists. As shown in Figure 16.1, on the day I visited, the artist of the day was Christina Aguilera, with two links to a video clip preview (the 56K for modem connections, and the 300K for faster connections like cable or DSL). Notice the four other smaller features below the main one; each of those is a link to a video

PART

III

Using Windows Me
Multimedia

clip. These range from Hollywood movie trailers to Internet Radio station links, depending on the offerings du jour.

When you click one of those video clip links, Windows Media Player switches to the Now Playing tab and displays the clip, as in Figure 16.2. When you're finished watching it, you can click the Media Guide button to return.

FIGURE 16.2
Media Guide offers up movie trailers for hot new movies, interviews with music and film stars, and other goodies.

Click Media Guide to return to the guide.

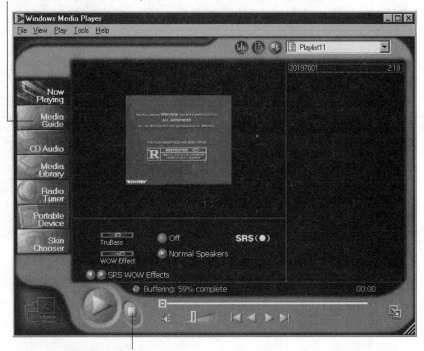

Click Stop to stop the clip early.

In Figure 16.2, take a look at the controls at the bottom of the window. There's a Stop button (which is replaced by a Play button when stopped), a Pause button, a Fast Forward button, and all the other controls you would expect on a cassette tape player, a VCR, or some other real-life media player with which you're familiar. As you'll see in this chapter, that metaphor carries over into all portions of the program.

 NOTE Sometimes when you choose to view a clip, a separate Internet Explorer window pops open with some advertising in it. Close it by clicking its Close (X) button.

As shown in Figure 16.1, the Media Guide page has several tabs across its top. You're seeing the Home tab in Figure 16.1, but you can click any of the other tabs to see similar offerings in the categories of Music, Radio, or Broadband. The Music tab contains links only to music (sound) clips—no Hollywood actors or movies. The Radio tab contains links only to Internet Radio stations. And the Broadband tab contains links to items that take a long time to download on a regular modem connection and are, therefore, best reserved for high-speed (like broadband) Internet users.

The Media Guide also includes a very useful LOOKITUP feature for browsing a large library of clips available for free download. For example, suppose I'm looking for freebies by Bonnie Raitt. I would enter her name in the LOOKITUP box and click Go:

Eventually I'd arrive at a bio of the artist and some hyperlinks to free videos I can download, as shown in Figure 16.3.

FIGURE 16.3
Use LOOKITUP from the Media Guide to locate free videos and music clips from your favorite artists.

Listening to Internet Radio

Never heard of Internet Radio? It's still a fairly well-kept secret, but you can listen to hundreds of radio stations all over the world in static-free glory through the Internet. (A fast Internet connection helps, of course, but is not essential.) Windows Media Player has a whole section devoted to Internet Radio stations.

There are two ways to listen to Internet Radio in Windows Me. The first is to use the Radio toolbar in Internet Explorer. This method was also available in Windows 98. The other is to use the Radio Tuner page in Media Player. Since we're already here in Media Player, let's look at that method first.

Internet Radio in Media Player

Let's jump right in; here's how to tune in an Internet Radio station:

1. Click the Radio Tuner button in Media Player to bring up a searchable list of radio stations.

2. In the Station Finder panel (the right panel), open the Find By list and choose how you want the stations displayed. You can find by format, language, location, call letters, frequency, or any of several other criteria.

3. Another drop-down list appears, based on your choice in step 2. Make your selection from it. For example, if you chose Format in step 2, you might choose Jazz & Blues here.

4. When you find a station you want to try, double-click it. It starts playing, as shown in Figure 16.4.

FIGURE 16.4
Find a station by filtering the list according to format, location, or other criteria.

Information about the chosen station

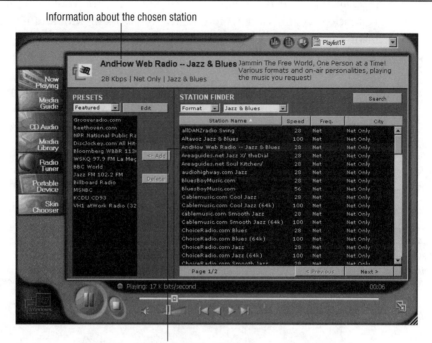

Sort by any of these columns by clicking it.

On a slow Internet connection, such as a regular modem, it may take several minutes before the station begins to play. There might also be some pauses or choppiness in the play on a slow connection. (Cable, satellite, and DSL Internet users should not experience these problems.) A station takes a long time to load, because Internet Radio is a streaming audio format. The music is transmitted to your PC just in time for it to be played in Media Player. On a slow PC, the least little delay can result in a choppy playback, so Media Player creates a *buffer*, a storage area for several seconds of incoming data. That way, if there is a delay in transmission, the music continues to play out of the buffer while your PC catches up, and there is no interruption in the broadcast. The slower your Internet connection, the longer it takes to fill the buffer initially.

NOTE When you double-click a station to play it, a Web page may appear in a separate Window with advertising for that station. You can close this window; the station will continue to play.

To choose another station, simply double-click it, and choose a different filter from the list as needed.

PART

III

Using Windows Me
Multimedia

Internet Radio is considered a WAV broadcast in Windows, so you adjust its volume by changing the Wave setting in your Volume control. You'll learn more about the volume control in Windows in Chapter 18, "Working with Multimedia and Entertainment Hardware."

Setting Radio Presets

Just as on a car radio, you can create presets for your favorite stations. Media Player comes with a list of presets called Featured, which you can see in the left pane in Figure 16.4. You can't edit this list, but you can create your own list of favorite stations by doing the following:

1. Open the Presets drop-down list and choose My Presets.

2. Find a station that you like in the right pane (see the preceding set of steps).

3. Click the Add button to move that station into the My Presets list. See Figure 16.5.

FIGURE 16.5
Add a station to your My Presets list.

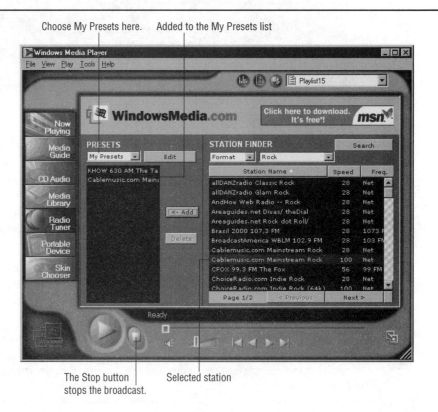

Choose My Presets here.   Added to the My Presets list

The Stop button stops the broadcast.   Selected station

Then to tune to a station on your list, just double-click it. To stop the station from playing entirely (for example, if the phone rings and you need silence while you take the call), click the Stop button at the bottom of the screen.

You can also create new preset lists in addition to My Presets. To do so, click the Edit button in the Presets pane. The Edit Preset Lists dialog box opens. To create a new list, enter a new name in the Add New List box and then click Add.

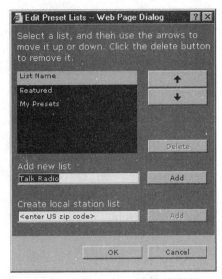

You can also create a Presets list consisting of the radio stations in your area. To do so, enter your zip code in the Create Local Station List box and click Add. Then click OK at the confirmation box that appears. When you are finished, click OK.

 NOTE You can arrange the order of the lists by clicking the Up or Down arrow button in the Edit Preset Lists dialog box. However, the Featured list can't be moved or deleted, and you can't move any other lists ahead of it. That means, unfortunately, that it's the default list that appears each time you open Media Player. It contains stations that have paid a fee to Microsoft to be "featured."

Internet Radio in Internet Explorer

You don't have to start Media Player in order to listen to Internet Radio; instead you can use the Internet Radio controls built into Internet Explorer if you prefer. This is handy when you are already browsing the Web and want something to listen to. It also uses fewer system resources, so it can come in handy if you want to do something else while the radio is playing (like play a processor-intensive game).

To listen to radio in Internet Explorer, first turn on the Radio toolbar. You can then use its controls to find a station. (Once you find a station, you can create a Favorite from it and revisit that station just as you would revisit a favorite Web page.)

PART

III

Using Windows Me
Multimedia

Follow these steps to find and play a radio station through Internet Explorer:

1. Start your Internet connection, and then start Internet Explorer. (See Chapters 20, "Connecting to the Internet," and 21, "Browsing the World Wide Web with Internet Explorer 5.5," for help if needed.)

2. Choose View ➢ Toolbars ➢ Radio. The Radio toolbar appears.

3. Click the Radio Stations button on the toolbar, and choose Radio Station Guide from the drop-down list that appears.

A Radio Station Guide Web page opens in Internet Explorer, as shown in Figure 16.6. Notice how much it looks like the station guide you saw in Figures 16.4 and 16.5.

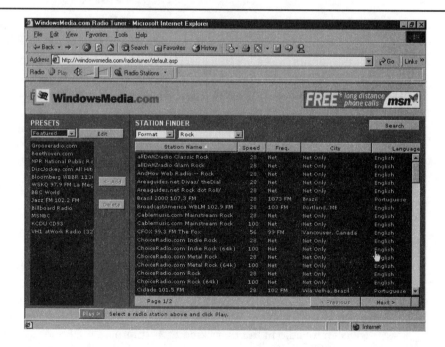

FIGURE 16.6

The Radio toolbar in Internet Explorer lets you listen to Internet Radio without Media Player.

NOTE Your custom presets carry over from Windows Media Player to Internet Explorer, so if you created custom playlists in the previous section, you'll see them here as well.

4. Locate a station to listen to (just as you did with Windows Media Player), and double-click it to start playing it.

5. (Optional) If desired, use the Presets list to add the station to one of your preset lists.

You can also store radio station favorites in Internet Explorer, just like regular Web page favorites. To do so, when listening to a particular station, click the Radio Stations button on the Radio toolbar and choose Add Station to Favorites.

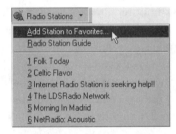

Then enter a name for the station in the box that appears, and click OK.

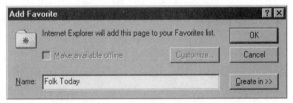

The station will then appear on your Favorites list in Internet Explorer.

In addition, if you reopen the Radio Stations list from the Radio toolbar, you'll see that the station now appears on that menu as well. However, this list is more like a History list of the stations you have played than it is a Favorites list. It shows all the stations you have been listening to, not just the ones you have added to Favorites.

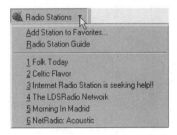

PART

III

Using Windows Me
Multimedia

Playing Audio CDs

When you insert an audio CD in your CD-ROM drive, Media Player launches itself and begins playing the CD.

 NOTE If an audio CD doesn't start automatically, perhaps Auto Insert Notification has been turned off for the drive. Find the drive in Device Manager (see Chapter 13, "Adding and Removing Hardware and Software") and mark the Auto Insert Notification check box in the drive's Properties.

Occasionally you might run into an audio CD that contains some bonus material accessible by a computer. If that's the case, the computer program on the disk will run automatically when you insert the CD instead of Media Player playing the CD. Close whatever program starts running, and open Media Player manually to play the CD.

As the CD plays, you can change to any other tab in the Media Player. It will continue to play. The most common tabs you will want to use during CD play are Now Playing and CD Audio. You can use the Now Playing tab when playing any format (Internet Radio, CDs, digital audio clips, etc.), but I think it's the most fun with CDs.

Working with the Now Playing Controls

The Now Playing tab lists the CD tracks to the right, with a visualization in the center of the player controls at the bottom (see Figure 16.7). Visualizations are patterns, colors, or other moving images that react to the music. You can click the right and left arrow buttons under the current visualization to change it, or choose Tools ➤ Download Visualizations to get more from the Microsoft Web site.

FIGURE 16.7
Use the controls on the Now Playing tab to control the CD play.

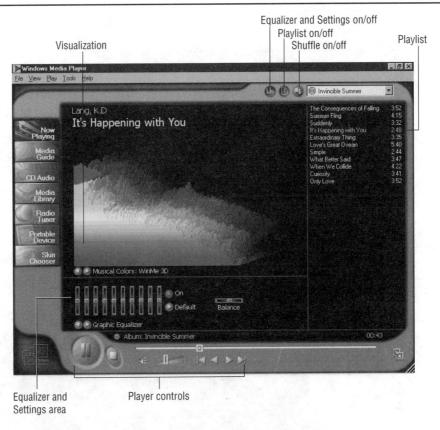

Visualization

Equalizer and Settings on/off
Playlist on/off
Shuffle on/off
Playlist

Equalizer and Settings area

Player controls

First, take a look at the player controls. They work the same as on a regular CD player or cassette deck. You can pause, stop, fast-forward, rewind, and so on.

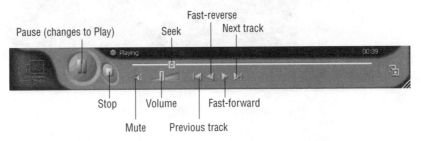

Pause (changes to Play)   Seek
Fast-reverse
Next track

Stop   Volume   Fast-forward
Mute   Previous track

To adjust the volume, drag the Volume slider to the left or right. The Seek slider controls your position within the song being played. You can drag it to jump to a specific spot in the track.

TIP There are equivalent commands on the Play menu for each of the player controls.

Here are some other activities you can do from the Now Playing tab:

- Change to different controls in the Equalizer and Settings area by clicking the right and left arrow buttons under it.

Use these arrow buttons to change what controls are shown.

- Double-click a track on the Playlist to jump to that track.

- Change the visualization by clicking the right and left arrow buttons under it, or choose View ➢ Visualizations and then choose one from the submenus.

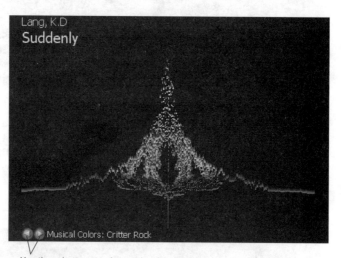

Use these buttons to change the visualization.

- Click the Shuffle button to play the tracks in random order.

Shuffle button

- Resize any of the panes by dragging the divider line between two panes.

- Turn on/off any of the panes with the buttons in the top-right area of the player or with the commands on the View ➤ Now Playing Tools submenu.

Working with the CD Audio Controls

Another important set of controls for playing CDs is found on the CD Audio tab. From here, you can control which tracks play and which do not. You can also copy tracks to your hard disk from here so that you can play them later when the CD is not in the drive, as seen in Figure 16.8.

FIGURE 16.8
The CD Audio tab lets you set additional play options for the CD.

Notice that there's a check mark beside each song on the CD Audio tab, along with details about the track such as time, genre, and artist. If there's a certain track you don't want to hear, deselect its check box and it won't play. You can then go back to the Now Playing tab if you want to use the equalizer or watch the visualization.

You can also right-click a track, choose Edit, and then edit its name. This changes the name as it appears in the playlist but does not affect the CD itself in any way; CDs are read-only.

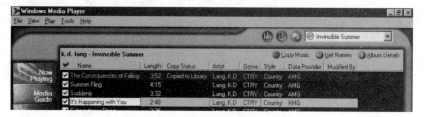

To change the order in which tracks will play, right-click a track and choose Move Up or Move Down.

Copying CD Tracks to Your Hard Disk

If you have a lot of audio CDs that you like to play in your PC, you'll appreciate this feature. Windows Media Player enables you to easily copy selected tracks from a CD to your hard disk so that you can play them without the CD having to be present. That way you can create your own custom playlists, alternating songs from several CDs. (Each track takes up several megabytes of space, however, so make sure you have a large hard disk with plenty of free space.)

Media Player copies each track to your hard disk in WMA (Windows Media Audio) format rather than the more popular MP3 format. That shouldn't be a problem as long as you use Media Player rather than some other player to listen to the tracks.

NOTE You can buy portable devices that play digital audio clips, but the most popular format accepted by these devices is MP3. Some portable media players, however, support WMA format, too, and others allow you to record by hooking them into your sound card or USB port; so the original format of the clip is not an issue. See the documentation for your device to find the best way of transferring CD audio tracks to your portable digital music player.

To copy tracks to your hard disk from a CD, follow these steps:

1. On the CD Audio tab, select all the tracks you want to copy. Remove the check mark next to any you don't want.

2. Click the Copy Music button. The Copy Status column shows the copy progress, as in Figure 16.9, and the button changes to Stop Copy.

FIGURE 16.9
Some tracks being copied to disk.

This track will be copied next.

This track is being copied.

Copy Music/Stop Copy button

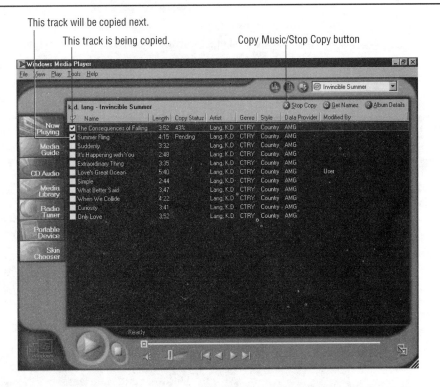

When the tracks have been copied, they appear on the Media Library tab, discussed in the next section. And when you view them on the CD Audio tab, the Copy Status column shows Copied to Library. It's legal to copy your own CDs for your own use like this; it becomes illegal when you distribute them to other people.

PART

III

Using Windows Me
Multimedia

Organizing Clips in the Media Library

On the Media Library tab, you can manage all of the various types of music that are stored on your hard disk. This could include MP3 files, WMA files, WAV files, and files in any of several other formats, too.

The Media Library tab has a folder tree, as in Windows Explorer.

Notice that there are five major sections: Audio, Video, My Playlists, Radio Tuner Presets, and Deleted Items. Let's look at the contents of Audio first:

All Audio   Shows a list of every audio clip. You can sort the list by clicking a column heading (such as Name or Artist). See Figure 16.10.

FIGURE 16.10

All Audio is an unfiltered compilation of all audio clips recognized by Windows Media Player.

Album Shows separate subfolders for each album from which the songs came. (For those of you born after LPs, an "album" is the same as a "CD.") See Figure 16.11.

FIGURE 16.11
Album places clips that are associated with a particular recording in a separate folder.

Artist Shows separate subfolders for each artist.

Genre Shows separate subfolders for each genre (Rock, Country, etc.).

 NOTE How does Windows Media Player know what album a track comes from, or what its artist name and/or genre is? Well, when you copy from CD, as you learned earlier in the chapter, it records that information automatically. You can also right-click the track on the list and choose Edit to edit its information, including its Album setting.

To play a clip, simply double-click it, the same as usual. To remove a clip from the Media Library, right-click it and choose Delete from Library. This doesn't delete the file from your hard disk; it simply removes it from Windows Media Player's listing.

PART

III

Using Windows Me Multimedia

Adding Tracks to Your Media Library

You might have audio files on your hard disk already, independent of Media Player. For example, perhaps you downloaded them from a music Web site like www.mp3.com. To include your existing music clips in the Media Library, do the following:

1. Choose File ➢ Add to Library ➢ Add File. An Open dialog box appears.

2. Locate and select the file you want to add from your hard disk. (Refer to Chapter 5, "Organizing Files, Programs, and Disks," if you need help with file management.)

3. Click Open. The song is added to your library.

Editing a Clip's Information

Depending on the source of a clip, it might not contain full information, such as artist name or genre, or the information might be incorrect. For example, the tracks shown in the preceding figure combined the artist and song name in the filename; that's a common quirk you'll find in downloaded clips from services such as Napster.

You can edit a clip's information to provide the details if you know them. Follow these steps to do so:

1. Right-click the clip and choose Edit. The Name field becomes editable.

2. Type over the current name, or click to move the insertion point into it and edit it.

3. Press Tab to move to the next column (Artist), and type the artist name.

4. Press Tab and continue to the next column, completing all the columns as desired.

5. Click away from the clip to take it out of editing mode.

Automatically Adding Many Tracks at Once

You're probably thinking that adding all your clips to the Media Library is going to be a big chore, right? Wrong. Media Player has a feature that searches your hard disk and automatically adds all the clips it finds.

WARNING Some games come with sound clips for various sound effects in the game, and these will also be added to the Media Library if you go the automatic route described below. You can avoid this by limiting the search to certain folders on your hard disk (the ones where you know your music clips are) or by excluding certain file formats from the search—such as WAV, which is the format that many game sound effect files are in. And you can always remove a clip from the library later if you don't want it there.

To search your hard disk for clips to add, do the following:

1. Choose Tools ➢ Search Computer for Media. The Search Computer for Media dialog box opens.

2. Open the Search for Media In drop-down list and choose the drive on which you want to search (if you have more than one hard drive and if all your clips are on one of them).

3. If you don't want to search the entire drive, click the Browse button next to Beginning In, select the folder in which you want to start, and then click OK.

   This will search the chosen folder and any subfolders within it, ignoring the rest of the drive.

4. (Optional) To omit Windows-supplied WAV and MIDI files from the search, leave the Include WAV and MIDI Files Found in System Folders check box unmarked.

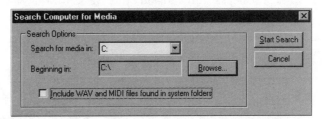

5. When you have selected the search options you want, click Start Search. The search begins.

6. When a message appears that the search is complete, click Close. Then click Close again to close the Search box. The new clips now appear in your Media Library.

PART

III

Using Windows Me
Multimedia

Organizing Clips into Playlists

The full list of your clips can become a bit difficult to manage as you add more and more clips from your CDs and from other sources. That's where custom playlists come in handy. You can create playlists that contain your favorite tracks for various occasions, like "Mellow Music" or "Party Mix," and then load and play those playlists quickly whenever you want them.

To create a playlist, complete the following steps:

1. Click the New Playlist button in the toolbar.

2. Enter the name for the new playlist and click OK.

Now the new playlist appears in the folder tree. Scroll down near the bottom of the folder tree and find My Playlists. Click the plus sign to expand it if needed, and you'll find your new playlist there.

3. Browse the Media Library and select a file that you want to copy to your playlist.

4. Scroll the folder tree pane so that your playlist is visible, then drag the track from the Media Library and drop it onto the playlist.

5. Repeat steps 3 and 4 to add other tracks to your playlist.

Here's another way to add a track to a playlist: Select the track and then click the Add to Playlist button on the toolbar. A menu opens containing all your playlists; click the one you want to add it to. Pretty easy, eh?

To add the currently playing track to the displayed playlist, click the Add button above the listing (looks like a plus sign) and on the menu that appears, choose Add Currently Playing Track.

To move a track around in the playlist, simply drag it up or down on the list or right-click it and choose Move Up or Move Down. There are also Move Up and Move Down arrow buttons above the track listing.

To remove a track from the playlist, select it and press Delete or right-click it and choose Delete from Playlist. There's also a Delete button above the track listing; clicking it opens a menu of deletion options.

Working with Portable Audio Players

If you have a portable MP3 player, you can use Windows Media Player to transfer songs directly to it. (Of course, you can also use the software that comes with the MP3 player if you prefer.)

NOTE An MP3 player is specifically designed to store MP3 digital audio files; it's different from a mini-disc player. If you have a portable mini-disc player, you might be able to hook it up to your PC and record songs by playing them on your PC and capturing the output on the mini-disc with an audio cable, but that's not the same thing as the direct transfer I'm talking about here. Consult the instructions that came with your mini-disc player for details.

Some MP3 players also play music in other formats, such as WMF (Windows Media File). When Windows Media Player copies songs from audio CDs, as you learned to do earlier in this chapter, it saves them in WMF format, not MP3. So if your MP3 player does not play WMF files directly, you will need to use a separate program for conversion. (You can probably find shareware available on the Internet that does this.)

But for the moment, let's assume that you have MP3s on your hard disk to transfer and a compatible MP3 player hooked up to your PC. Here's how to make the transfer:

1. On the Media Library tab, select the folder containing the song(s) you want to transfer.

PART
III

Using Windows Me
Multimedia

2. Click the Portable Device tab. The songs in the chosen folder appear in the left pane (the Music to Copy section).

3. Ensure that your MP3 player is hooked up and turned on.

4. Remove the check marks next to the files that you do not want to copy.

5. Click the Copy Music button. The chosen tracks are copied to your MP3 player.

Changing the Appearance of Windows Media Player

So far in this chapter, you've seen the default Media Player in all the figures, but you can radically change its appearance through the use of a feature called *skins*. When you apply a skin to the player, it works the same as always but the controls look different. Figure 16.12 shows an example of a different skin.

FIGURE 16.12
Skins can make Media Player look different, but it still works the same.

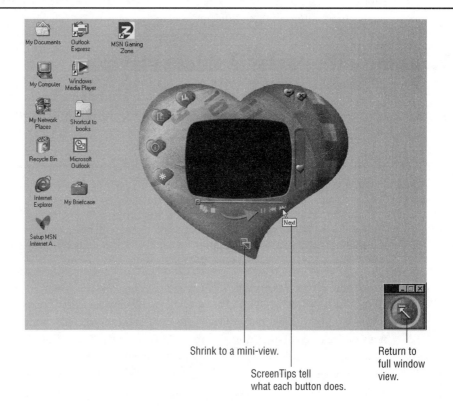

Shrink to a mini-view.

ScreenTips tell what each button does.

Return to full window view.

To select a different skin, display the Skin Chooser tab on the main menu. Pick a skin, and then click Apply Skin.

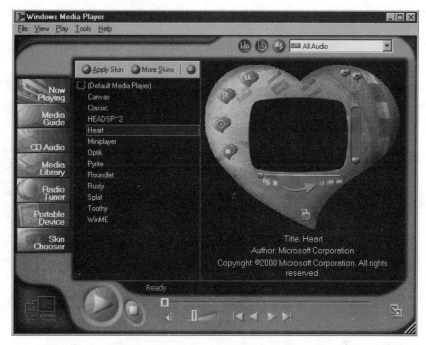

You can get more skins from the Microsoft Web site by clicking the More Skins button. This opens Internet Explorer and displays a page from which you can choose other skins. See Figure 16.13.

PART

III

Using Windows Me Multimedia

Click here to open Internet Explorer to download more skins.

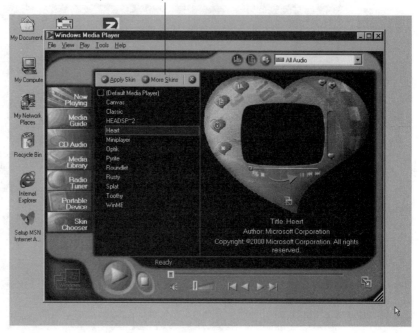

In this chapter we looked at multimedia primarily from an audio perspective. The next chapter covers the other side of the equation: images and video clips. In Chapter 17, "Using Image Acquisition and Movie Maker," you'll learn how to manage scanners and digital cameras in Windows Me and how to create your own movies with Windows Movie Maker.

CHAPTER 17

Using Image Acquisition and Movie Maker

FEATURING:

Playing around with graphics can be great fun in Windows. You can download pictures from the Internet, take pictures with a digital camera, scan photos with a scanner, and receive pictures as e-mail attachments from friends and relatives. And the developers of Windows Me obviously knew how much home users like to do this, because they've included several great new tools and capabilities in Windows Me to make it easier.

In this chapter, I'll show you how to make the most of your scanner and digital camera in Windows Me by using its built-in Scanner and Digital Camera Wizard. I'll also take you through the Windows Movie Maker, a great new utility that enables you to edit video footage and combine it with still photos, soundtracks, and narration to make your own movies.

Working with Scanners and Digital Cameras

In earlier versions of Windows, to run a scanner or to copy pictures from a digital camera, you needed to use the software that came with the device. Windows Me has changed that, however, by providing direct access to many of the most popular scanner and camera models.

 WARNING Not all scanners and cameras work directly with Windows Me. To find out if yours does, go to www.Microsoft.com/hcl. If your device isn't on the list, you can still use it, but you'll need to use the software supplied with the device; you won't be able to use Windows' direct controls for it described in the rest of this section.

If you upgrade to Windows Me from Windows 95 or 98 and you already had a scanner or camera installed with its own software, that software will still be there, and you can continue to use it normally in most cases. But if your scanner or camera is supported, you can also remove the software that came with the device and rely on Windows Me's built-in support. It's strictly a matter of preference. However, most scanners come with software that starts automatically at startup and stays running all the time. Removing that program from the mix can potentially free up some system resources; it's a good thing to do if you have an older computer without a lot of memory.

For some devices, you must go ahead and install the driver software that comes with the device in order for it to work to its best capability. For example, I bought a digital video camera that connected to my USB (Universal Serial Bus) port. When I hooked up the camera to the computer, Windows Me recognized it immediately and it worked. But the image quality was very bad. So I installed the software that came with it, and the image quality got much better.

Because Windows Me handles scanners and cameras differently than previous versions of Windows, you might find that your old scanner or camera driver doesn't work quite right. If that's the case, either you can fall back on Windows' built-in support or you can visit the device manufacturer's Web site to see whether an update or patch is available for downloading.

Testing and Configuring Your Scanner or Camera

First things first: Does Windows Me recognize your scanner or camera? To find out, make sure your camera or scanner is connected to your PC and turned on, and then do the following:

 NOTE Some cameras have a mode switch that determines how they are operating. For example, you might see VCR/OFF/CAMERA or CAPTURE/DOWNLOAD. Make sure that the device is set to Camera (or Download), or Windows won't be able to recognize and use it. Check the camera's documentation if you aren't sure what setting to use.

1. Choose Start ➤ Settings ➤ Control Panel.

2. Double-click Scanners and Cameras. A list of currently installed scanners and cameras appears.

3. If yours appears on the list, double-click it to view its properties.

   If your scanner or camera doesn't appear on the list, see Chapter 13, "Adding and Removing Hardware and Software," for help installing its driver. (Or you can try installing it yourself now by double-clicking Add Device and following the prompts.)

4. If the General tab is not on top, click it to make it so (see Figure 17.1).

PART

III

Using Windows Me
Multimedia

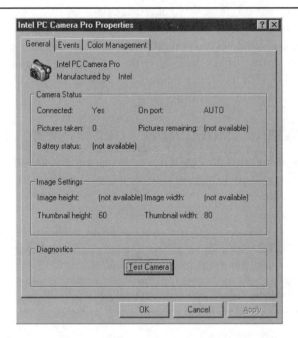

5. Click the Test button. The exact name of the button varies. Depending on the device, it might be labeled Test Scanner or Camera, or just Test Camera, or just Test Scanner. The test takes only a moment, and a box appears telling you whether your device passed.

6. Click OK in the results box. If the device passed the test, you're all set.

If the device didn't pass, check its documentation and its manufacturer's Web site for troubleshooting help.

WARNING There are all kinds of little quirky problems with specific models of computers and specific models of scanners and cameras. Check not only the Web site for the device manufacturer but also the Web site of your PC's manufacturer. For example, my Dell Dimension 4100 doesn't work with the UMAX Astra 2100B scanner under Windows Me for some odd reason.

7. Click the other tabs to see what other settings are available. The settings (and tabs) depend on the device model and type.

   For example, some scanners that have quick scanning buttons on their front allow you to customize the buttons on the Events tab, so you can define what program receives the scan when you press each button. Other scanners and cameras don't allow any such customization here.

8. When you are finished, click OK to close the Properties box.

You're ready to use your scanner or camera! See the following sections for details.

Scanning a Picture

If you have a Windows Me–compatible scanner, you can use the following steps to scan a picture using the Scanner and Camera Wizard. For all other scanners, you must use the scanning software that came with the device, and the steps will be a little different.

 NOTE Some scanners might appear to work with Windows Me (that is, they might show up in the Scanners and Cameras window in the preceding section's test), but they won't work when you actually try to scan something with the following procedure. If that's the case, fall back to using the scanner's own software.

1. Place the picture on the scanner bed and close the lid.
2. Choose Start ➢ Programs ➢ Accessories ➢ Scanner and Camera Wizard.
3. If you have more than one scanner or camera, a box appears asking which you want to use. Click the scanner you want, and then click OK. The Scanner and Camera Wizard runs.
4. Click Next to begin.
5. The Region Selection box appears, and the scanner scans a preview of your picture. It appears in the Preview area, as shown in Figure 17.2.

PART

III

Using Windows Me
Multimedia

FIGURE 17.2
View the preview of the scan and select a region of it for your final image.

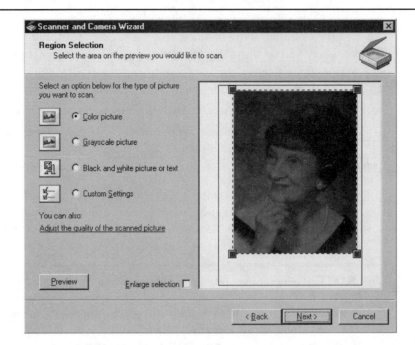

NOTE If needed, adjust the original on the scanner bed and click the Preview button to preview the picture again.

6. Choose an option button for the image type you want: Color Picture, Grayscale Picture, Black and White Picture or Text, or Custom.

7. (Optional) To crop the preview so that only a portion of the image gets scanned, drag the red squares in the corners until only the portion you want to keep is enclosed.

8. (Optional) To fine-tune the scan, click the Adjust the Quality of the Scanned Picture hyperlink. Then make fine-tuning selections in the Advanced Properties dialog box, and click OK to return.

Some of the fine-tuning you can do includes changing the scan resolution (higher is better but results in a larger image file) and adjusting the brightness and contrast.

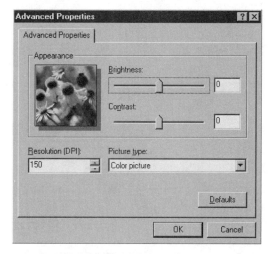

9. Click Next to move on. The Picture Destination box appears.

10. Enter a name for the picture in the Save Picture Using This Name box.

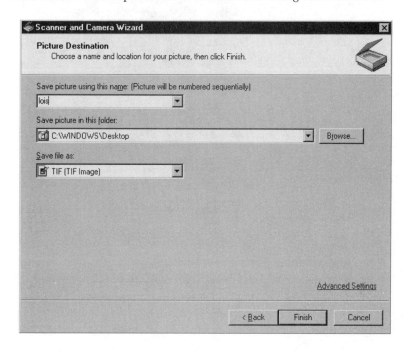

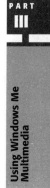

PART

III

Using Windows Me
Multimedia

11. Choose a destination folder for the picture, or leave the default My Pictures selected.

The My Pictures folder is inside your My Documents folder, accessible from the Desktop.

12. Choose a file format for the picture, or leave the default format JPG (JPEG) chosen.

Different programs accept different picture file formats. JPG is a good choice because many programs accept it, including most Web sites, and because it's a compact format that doesn't take up much disk space.

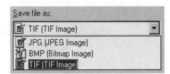

13. Click Finish. The scanner scans the picture (for real this time, not just a preview, so it may take a little longer), and Windows saves it to a file as you indicated.

After scanning a picture, you can import it into any program that accepts pictures, such as Microsoft Word, FrontPage, or Excel, to dress up your work in that program. You can also e-mail the file to a friend to share the picture, print it (making your scanner work like a copier!), or fax it (if you have a fax modem and faxing software for Windows).

Working with a Digital Camera

There are several types of digital cameras on the market today. The term *digital camera* might conjure up one image in my mind and another in yours, so let's review the different types of devices that are all loosely called "digital cameras":

Snapshot cameras   These are similar to the regular go-anywhere 35mm cameras we all know and love. They look and act the same as a regular film-loaded camera except they record the images digitally. Some of them record on floppy disks, and others on removable cartridges. Still others save the images in the camera itself. When the camera gets full, you hook it up to the PC to transfer the images to your hard disk.

Simple video cameras   These remain attached to your PC at all times. Usually they are small (a few inches high, wide, and deep). One brand is shaped like a ball. You can use them for video teleconferencing or for recording video footage near your computer. Since they are always connected to the PC, they have no image storage mechanism in themselves; you always save directly to the hard disk from them.

Handheld, go-anywhere digital video cameras   These look and act like regular camcorders, except they record digitally rather than on a tape. You can hook them up to your PC to transfer the video footage to your hard disk. They can also take still snapshots.

 NOTE   Many digital video cameras require an IEEE 1394 port (a FireWire port) in your computer to connect to. You can buy an interface card for your PC that provides such a connection for about $50. FireWire is similar to (and a competitor of) USB; it is a high-speed interface port for connecting to external devices.

The Scanner and Camera Wizard enables you to

- Transfer stored images from the camera to your hard disk.
- Take new, still snapshots using an attached video camera.

The Scanner and Camera Wizard works only with still images, not motion video clips. If you need to transfer video footage from a video camera to a file on your hard disk, or if you want to capture new motion video footage using an attached camera, see the "Using Windows Movie Maker" section later in this chapter.

Transferring Stored Images from a Digital Camera

If your camera is directly supported in Windows Me, you can use the following procedure to transfer stored images from it.

1. Hook up the camera to the PC if it's not already connected.

2. If the camera requires you to do anything special to it to place it in transfer mode, do so. For example, some camera models require you to flip a switch or turn a dial.

3. Choose Start ➤ Programs ➤ Accessories ➤ Scanner and Camera Wizard.

4. If you have more than one scanner or camera, a box appears asking which you want to use. Click the camera you want, and then click OK.

5. The Scanner and Camera Wizard runs. Click Next to begin. The pictures currently stored on the camera appear in thumbnail (miniature) view.

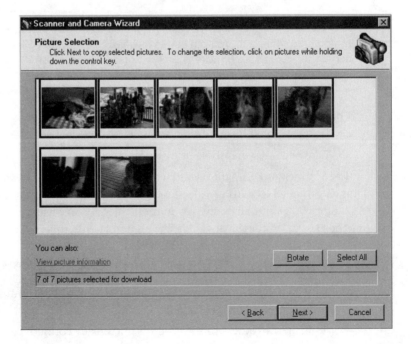

6. Delete any of the pictures that you want to remove from the camera without saving. To delete one, click it and then press Delete on the keyboard.

7. To rotate a picture, click it and then click the Rotate button.

8. Select the pictures that you want to transfer to your hard disk. Selected pictures appear with a dark blue border around them. Click the Select All button to choose them all, or hold down the Ctrl key as you click each one you want.

9. Click Next to move to the Picture Destination box.

10. Enter a name for the pictures in the Save Picture Using This Name box.

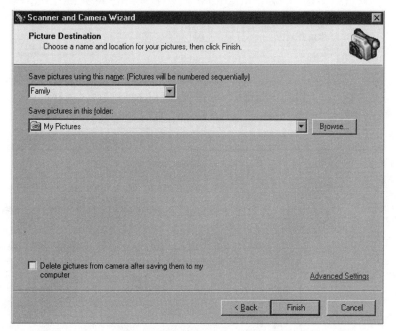

The name you enter can be the same for every picture you scan; Windows will tack on a number to the end of the name so that each picture has a unique name. For example, if you leave the default name here of "Family," the first picture will be Family 001, the second one Family 002, and so on.

11. Choose a destination folder for the picture, or leave the default My Pictures selected.

   The My Pictures folder is inside your My Documents folder, accessible from the Desktop.

12. (Optional) Click Advanced Settings to open a box in which you can choose to create a subfolder within My Pictures. For the name of this subfolder, you can select either today's date or the name that you entered in step 10. Then click OK to return.

PART

III

Using Windows Me
Multimedia

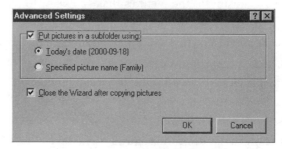

13. (Optional) If you want to remove the pictures from the camera after saving them to your PC, mark the Delete Pictures… check box at the bottom of the dialog box.

14. Click Finish.

The pictures are saved to your hard disk, and the folder in which you saved them appears with thumbnail views of the pictures. You can use the buttons above the preview pane to work with the picture (see Figure 17.3).

FIGURE 17.3
The pictures saved from the camera, now in a folder within My Pictures named with today's date

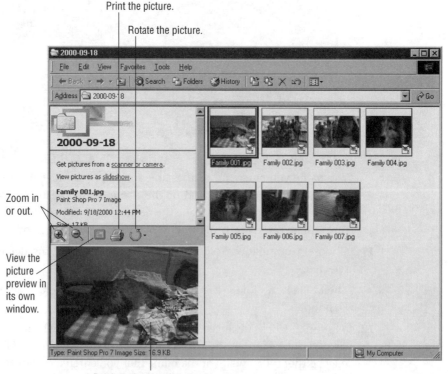

Print the picture.

Rotate the picture.

Zoom in or out.

View the picture preview in its own window.

Preview of selected picture

Taking Snapshots with a Video Camera

If you have a video-type camera that doesn't store pictures, you can still use it with Windows, but you'll do so through the Explore Camera feature instead.

 NOTE To transfer stored motion video footage from your camera, use Windows Movie Maker, described later in this chapter.

1. If you have started the Scanner and Camera Wizard but were told that the camera has no images stored in it, click the Explore Camera (Advanced) hyperlink.

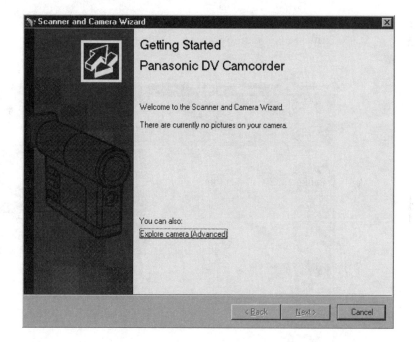

Or, to explore the camera without going through the Wizard, double-click the camera's icon in My Computer.

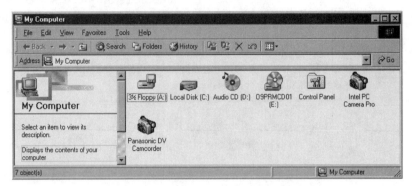

Either way, a window appears with a preview of the camera's video feed in the corner.

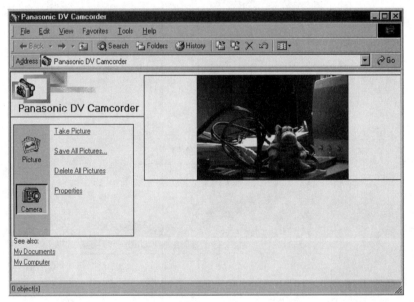

2. To take a still photo with the camera, click the Take Picture hyperlink. The picture appears below the preview pane, as shown in Figure 17.4.

3. To take more still photos, move the camera and click Take Picture again. Repeat as much as you like.

PART

III

Using Windows Me
Multimedia

FIGURE 17.4
*A video camera being
used to take still photos*

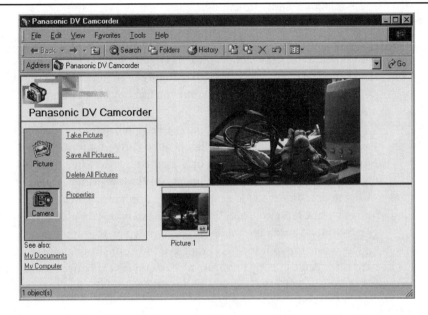

Now you can use the full Scanner and Camera Wizard to save the still pictures you've taken with your video camera. It'll work the same as if you had a real digital camera.

Transferring Images from the Explore Camera Window

If you don't want to bother with the Wizard to transfer the camera's still pictures to your hard disk, you can do the following instead:

1. If you are not already there, double-click the camera's icon in My Computer to open its contents in an Explore Camera window, as in Figure 17.4.

2. Click the Picture icon, changing the list of hyperlinks to those that manage pictures rather than the camera itself.

3. Select the picture(s) you want to transfer.

4. Click the Save in My Pictures hyperlink. The picture(s) are saved there with a default name (Picture 1, Picture 2, Picture 3, and so on) in JPG format, and the My Pictures folder opens.

Using Windows Movie Maker

Windows Movie Maker is another new feature in Windows Me. It helps you organize multimedia clips—that is, pictures, videos, soundtracks, voice narrations, and so on—

into "movies" that you can play on your computer monitor, store on your hard disk, and e-mail to friends and family.

Windows Movie Maker also provides a means for transferring video footage from your video camera to your PC. If you have a digital video camera, all you need is a FireWire connection to plug the camera into. As I mentioned earlier in the chapter, FireWire (or IEEE 1394) is a competitor to USB. It's simply a different kind of interface port. Most PCs don't come with this type of port, but you can buy an add-on circuit card that includes one for about $50.

You can also transfer video footage from a regular, or analog, video camera, but you'll need a special analog-to-digital video converter unit. There are several popular models at around $100 to $200; one is called Dazzle. They usually come with their own software, which you might prefer to Windows Movie Maker.

If you don't have a video camera at all, don't fret. You can use Windows Movie Maker with still photos, too. You can, for example, combine a series of still photographs into an automated slide show, complete with soundtrack.

The music for your movie soundtrack can come from a music clip stored on your hard disk. You can copy one from a CD-ROM (as explained in Chapter 16, "Using the Windows Media Player"), or use a clip (such as an MP3 file) that you have downloaded from a Web site.

If you have a sound card and a microphone to plug into it, you can record voice narration for your movie. This is different from a soundtrack, and plays "on top of" the soundtrack at the same time.

An Overview of Movie Making

First, let's look at the big picture. Here's how to create a movie with Windows Movie Maker:

1. Import the content for the show into Windows Movie Maker collections. These collections are not movie-specific; they can be drawn from over and over.

2. Start a new movie, and arrange the video clips and/or still photos in the order in which you want them.

3. Add a soundtrack if desired.

4. Record voice narration if desired.

5. Preview your movie and then save it to your hard disk.

In the following sections, I'll show you how to accomplish each of these steps. But first, you'll need to start Windows Movie Maker. To do so, choose Start ➤ Programs ➤ Accessories ➤ Windows Movie Maker. Figure 17.5 shows the Windows Movie Maker screen when you first start the program.

NOTE The first time you start Windows Movie Maker, a tour window appears. You can run through the various parts of the tour if you like, or you can click Exit to skip it and rely on the steps in this book instead for your learning.

FIGURE 17.5
Windows Movie Maker. There is no movie content open at this point, and no collections.

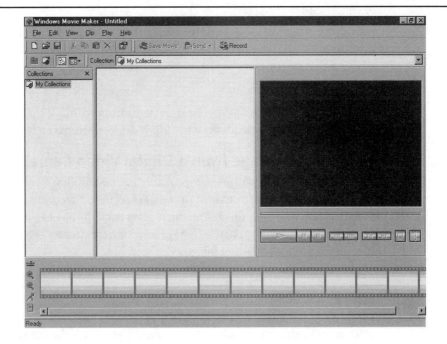

Creating Collections

To start off, you'll create at least one collection and import your content. This gives you some raw material to draw from when assembling the movie.

You can save all your content in the same collection, or you can create different collections for each type of content or for content on particular subjects. Collections are a lot like folders in Windows Explorer.

To create a new collection, follow these steps:

1. Click the collection into which you want to place the new one. (By default this is the top-level collection, called My Collections.)

 2. Choose File ➤ New ➤ Collection, or click the New Collection button on the toolbar.

PART

III

Using Windows Me
Multimedia

3. Type a name for the new collection.

4. Press Enter.

Now, whenever you are recording or importing content in the following sections, simply make sure the desired collection is selected before you record or import.

Recording New Content

You can record new content for your show right from within Windows Movie Maker. The recording process depends on what input devices you have.

Transferring Footage from a Digital Video Camera

If you have a digital video camera, it probably has two modes: Camera and VCR. In Camera mode, it works as described in the next section, "Recording from a Desktop Video Camera." However, in VCR mode, it plays back the already-recorded footage. You can use this mode to save the footage to your hard disk for use in your Movie Maker projects or for any other purpose.

 NOTE If you have a regular (analog) video camera that records onto tape, you'll need some sort of interface device to connect it to your PC. Depending on the model, it might work directly with Movie Maker, or it might require you to use the software that comes with the interface to first save the video to your hard disk. If that's the case, see "Importing Existing Content from Disk" later in the chapter.

Here's how to transfer some video footage from your digital video camera:

1. Start Movie Maker and select the collection into which you want to place the recording.

2. Connect the camera to your PC and turn it on. Make sure it is set to VCR mode.

The following dialog box might appear automatically. If it does not, choose File ➤ Record or click the Record button on the toolbar to make it appear.

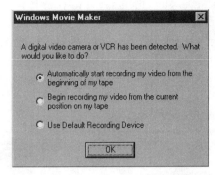

3. To transfer starting at the beginning of the tape, leave the default setting marked and click OK.

The tape rewinds if needed and then starts playing, and Movie Maker starts capturing the video.

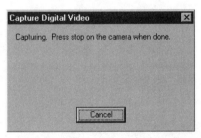

4. When you want to stop recording, press the Stop button on the camera (not in Windows). A Save Windows Media File dialog box appears.

5. Enter a name for the video clip in the File Name box. Windows automatically saves in Windows Media Video (WMV) format.

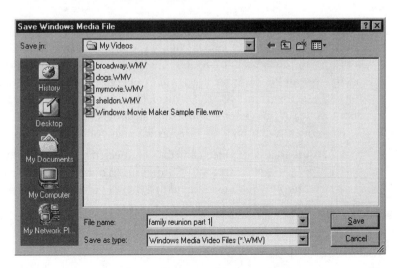

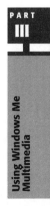

PART

III

Using Windows Me
Multimedia

6. Click Save. The clip is saved to your hard disk and placed in the collection that you chose in step 1.

Figure 17.6 shows the recorded clip. Notice that, because it is selected, a preview of the first frame appears in the preview pane. Notice also that Movie Maker placed the clip in its own subcollection beneath the collection I selected in step 1 (in this case, My Collections).

FIGURE 17.6
A recorded video clip from my digital video camera

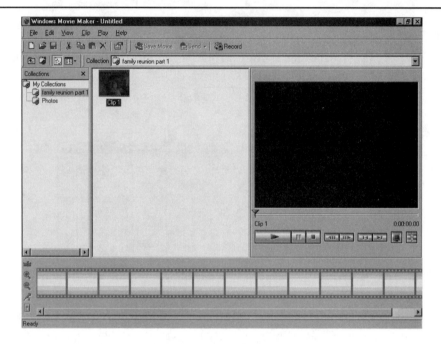

Recording from a Desktop Video Camera

In addition to transferring saved video, you can also use your digital video camera to capture new footage while connected to your PC. If you have a camera that stays connected to your PC full-time, this is your only option unless you want to use the recording software that came with the camera. (The Scanner and Camera Wizard you learned about earlier in this chapter is for still snapshots only.)

To record "live" from a digital video camera, follow these steps:

1. Ensure that your video camera is connected to your PC and that your PC recognizes it. (See "Testing and Configuring Your Scanner or Camera" earlier in this chapter.) If you're working with a digital video camera that has multiple modes such as Camera and VCR, set it to Camera.

2. In Windows Movie Maker, make sure the collection is selected in which you want to place the clip.

3. Choose File ➢ Record, or click the Record button on the toolbar.

4. If the following dialog box appears, choose Use Default Recording Device and click OK. (You might not see it, depending on the type of video camera you have.)

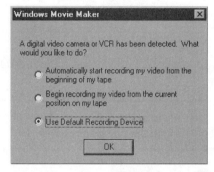

5. The Record dialog box appears. Notice the device listed in the Video Device section.

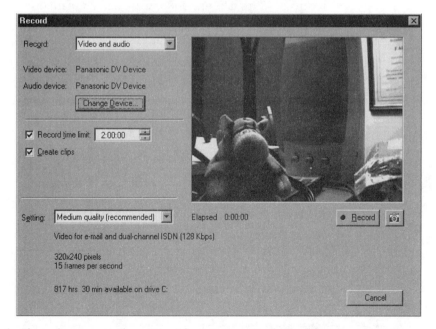

6. If you have more than one video camera attached, and you want to choose one that's different from the one that appears, click the Change Device button. In

the Change Device dialog box, open the Video drop-down list and choose the camera you want. Then click OK.

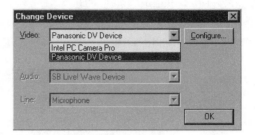

 NOTE Depending on the camera, you might also be able to choose an Audio Device and/ or a Microphone from the dialog box above.

7. In the Record dialog box, change any of the following options as desired:

- Set a Record Time Limit if you want to limit the size of the clip being recorded. (Clips take up a lot of space on your hard disk.)

- Choose Create Clips if you want the video feed broken into separate clips every time it detects a different frame (such as when you turn the camera on or turn off the Pause feature). Otherwise, the entire video feed will be stored in a single clip.

- Choose a quality setting. The default is Medium; higher quality will record more frames per second but will take up more storage space on your drive and will take longer to transmit when you e-mail the movie to someone later.

8. When you are ready to record video, click the Record button.

Or, if you want to take a still photo using your video camera, click the Take Photo button instead and then skip to step 10.

9. When you are finished recording, click the Stop button (in Windows, not on the camera). The Save Windows Media File dialog box appears, in which you can name your clip. (Or, if you're saving a still photo, it's the Save Photo dialog box.)

10. Enter the name you want to use for the clip, and click Save.

 NOTE Video clips are saved in the WMV format; still clips are saved in the JPG format.

The clip now appears in the chosen collection.

More about Clip Splitting

If you chose Create Clips in step 7 of the preceding procedure, Movie Maker may have broken up your video footage into more than one clip, with each one appearing as a separate item in the collection. Movie Maker does this if it detects a new frame (that is, a jump in the action, such as where you paused the recording and then restarted it).

The fact that a clip is split is not a problem because when you assemble the movie, you can place each clip adjacent to one another so that it appears to be one long video piece. Splitting merely adds flexibility to the movie-assembly process.

You can also manually split a video clip into one or more separate clips. To do so, play the clip by double-clicking it, and at the desired split point, click the Split button (the rightmost button in the toolbar beneath the video preview pane).

Recording Sound Clips

Recording a sound clip is just like recording a video clip, except you use only your microphone. To do this, you must either have a built-in microphone on your PC (which is often the case with laptops) or a microphone attached to the Mic port on your sound card.

Follow these steps to record a sound clip with your microphone:

1. Select the collection in which the new clip should be placed.

2. Choose File ➤ Record, or click the Record button on the toolbar. The Record dialog box opens.

3. Open the Record drop-down list and choose Audio Only.

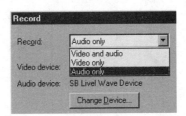

 NOTE If you don't have Audio Only as a choice on the drop-down list in step 3, your digital video camera is probably still connected from the preceding set of steps. Click Cancel, disconnect it or turn it off, and then try again at step 1.

4. If your sound card name doesn't appear next to Audio Device, click the Change Device button, select it, and click OK to return.

5. Set the record quality or any other desired options, as described in step 7 of the preceding set of steps.

6. Click the Record button, and begin speaking or making noise into the microphone.

7. Click the Stop button when finished. The Save Windows Media File dialog box opens.

8. Enter the file name to use. The file will be saved in WMA format.

9. Click Save. The clip is created and placed in the collection.

Importing Existing Content from Disk

If the content that you want to use in your movie is already on your hard disk, you can import it into a collection in Movie Maker. (You must do so if you want to include the content in a movie because movies draw their content only from collections.)

Importing existing content is the same regardless of the content's format. Media Player accepts content in a wide variety of formats, including all popular digital movie formats such as MPG (MPEG), WMV, and AVI. It also accepts many sound and graphic file formats.

To import content, follow these steps:

1. Display the collection into which you want to import.

2. Choose File ➤ Import. The Select the File to Import dialog box appears.

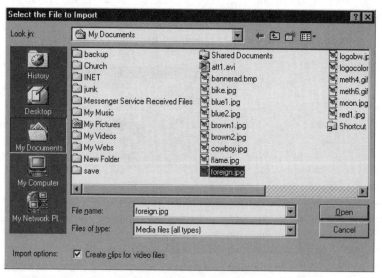

3. Locate and select the file you want to import.

TIP To narrow down the list of files, you might want to choose a file type from the Files of Type drop-down list. By default, all importable files are shown.

4. Click Open to import the file.

If you find that you have accidentally imported the file into the wrong collection, you can easily drag it to another collection, just as you do when managing files in Windows Explorer.

Building a Project

Now that you've imported or recorded the content for your movie, you're ready to start assembling it in a project, which you'll save in Movie Maker.

Is a project the same as a movie? Well, yes and no. The project is the work-in-progress, and the movie is the finished item. After the project is exactly the way you want it, you publish it as a movie, creating a read-only copy that you can never edit again. If you want to make changes to it, you must make the changes to the project and then republish the movie.

You can assemble a project in any order, but I like to start with the visual images (video clips and still photos) and then add the soundtrack. Finally, as the last step, I add the voice narration.

Starting a New Project

A new, empty project starts when you start the program, but you can start a new project at any time by doing the following:

1. Choose File ➤ New Project, or click the New Project button on the toolbar.

2. If prompted to save your changes to the existing project, click Yes or No and save (or not), as appropriate.

You can then assemble your project on the timeline at the bottom of the program window, as described in the remainder of this chapter.

Adding a Clip to the Project

You build your project by dragging clips from your various collections into the timeline at the bottom of the screen.

There are two views of the project: Storyboard and Timeline. Storyboard is useful for assembling the visual elements in the right order, while Timeline lets you add audio clips and match up your audio soundtrack with the video clips.

To switch between Storyboard and Timeline views, you can use the View menu or click the buttons to the left of the project area:

Storyboard

Timeline

NOTE You can add audio clips only to Timeline view. If you attempt to drop an audio clip on the Storyboard, a message will appear, telling you that Movie Maker is switching to Timeline view automatically. Click OK to go on.

Here's a project-in-progress in Storyboard view. Notice that only the pictures and video clips appear.

Click here to switch to Timeline view.

Each clip occupies the same amount of space regardless of length.

The same project viewed in Timeline view shows that an audio soundtrack is also included.

Click here to switch to Storyboard view.

The Speaker icon on clip indicates that it contains audio of its own.

Each clip occupies a space in proportion to its duration.

Soundtrack

To remove a clip from the project, click it on the timeline or storyboard and press the Delete key. To move it around on the project, drag it to the left or right.

Setting Trim Points for a Video Clip

If you want to use only a portion of a video clip, you have a couple of options. You can split the clip and then use only one of the split portions, or you can trim the clip. Trimming is active only for the current project; splitting, however, splits the clip in the collection, so it will continue to be split if you use it later in another project.

To set the trim points for a clip, do the following:

1. Add the video clip to the project, either on the Storyboard or on the Timeline.

2. Make sure the clip is selected (again, on the Storyboard or Timeline).

3. Click the Play button beneath the video preview pane, and when the clip reaches the part where you want it to begin, choose Clip ➤ Set Start Trim Point, or press Ctrl+Shift+←.

4. Allow the clip to continue playing, and when it reaches the part where you want it to end, choose Clip ➤ Set End Trim Point, or press Ctrl+Shift+→.

Everything between the two trim points will appear in the movie; everything else will not.

Changing the Duration of a Still Image

When you import a photo, it is assigned a default duration of 5 seconds to appear on-screen during the movie. You can change the default duration by choosing View ➤ Options and entering a different value in the Default Imported Photo Duration box, shown in Figure 17.7.

FIGURE 17.7
Change the default duration for imported stills here.

 NOTE The photo's default duration is always the setting that was in effect when it was imported. So, for example, if you import a photo when the Default Imported Photo Duration is set to 5 seconds, and you later change that setting to 10 seconds, all photos you imported prior to the change will continue to have 5-second durations.

PART

III

Using Windows Me Multimedia

You can also change a still picture's duration on the timeline, for each individual usage of it by completing the following steps:

1. View the project in Timeline view.

2. Click the Zoom In button to expand the timeline so you can see each item more clearly.

3. Click the picture for which you want to change the duration. Trim handles appear above it.

 NOTE If you don't see trim handles above the picture, as shown above, click the Zoom In button again to zoom in some more.

4. Drag the ending trim handle (the one on the right) to the left to make the picture appear for fewer seconds, or to the right to make it appear for more seconds.

If the picture was not on the end of the timeline, and you increased its duration, the picture to its right might now be partially obscured. Select that picture, and then drag its beginning trim handle (the one on its left) so that the two pictures do not overlap anymore. Continue working your way toward the left until all items are the desired duration.

Creating Transitions

In the preceding section, you saw that it's possible to overlap two objects on the timeline. When you overlap objects, you create a transition effect between them, so that one fades into the other. It's a pretty neat effect, and certainly looks better than simply replacing one image with the next.

To create a transition effect, simply make the clips overlap slightly. You already saw how to adjust the clip's trim in previous sections.

 NOTE Windows Movie Maker doesn't allow you to choose between different transition effects. If that feature is important to you and you're working only with still images, try a program like PowerPoint for assembling your presentation.

Adding a Soundtrack

To add a soundtrack, drag a sound clip onto the workspace. (That sound clip must already be in a collection, so import it into a collection if needed beforehand.) If you're not already in Timeline view, the view switches for you automatically and a box informs you that it's happening.

You can trim the soundtrack the same as any other object. Select it, and then either drag its trim handles or trim it by playing it and setting start and end trim points as you learned to do for videos earlier in the chapter.

Setting Audio Levels

If the video track has its own audio in addition to the audio tracks you are adding, the two can easily conflict with each another unattractively. You can fix this problem by adjusting the project so that one or the other is dominant. To do so, just follow these steps:

1. Choose Edit ➤ Audio Levels, or click the Adjust Audio Level button to the left of the project area.

2. Drag the slider to control the relative volume levels of the two tracks.

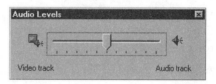

3. Click the Close (X) button on the dialog box to close it.

Recording Narration

After you've finalized the durations of each clip, you're ready to record your narration. You won't want to record it earlier, because if the durations of the clips change, the narration will be off. To record narration, do the following:

1. Prepare your microphone and ensure that it's working. (Chapter 18, "Working with Multimedia and Entertainment Hardware," can help with that if needed.)

PART

III

Using Windows Me
Multimedia

2. Choose File ➤ Record Narration, or click the Record Narration button to the left of the timeline. The Record Narration Track dialog box appears.

3. Set any of the following options:

- If the device and line are not correct as shown, click the Change button and select the correct ones. The device should be your sound card, and the line should be the line into which your microphone is plugged (probably Mic Volume).

- If you want to mute the video soundtrack while the narration is speaking, mark the Mute Video Soundtrack check box. Otherwise, the two will play on top of each other.

- Adjust the recording level using the Record Level slider if desired. Use the meter next to the slider as a guide.

4. When you are ready, click Record. Your presentation begins showing itself in the preview pane.

5. Speak into the microphone, narrating as you go along.

6. When you are finished, click Stop. The Save Narration Track Sound File dialog box appears.

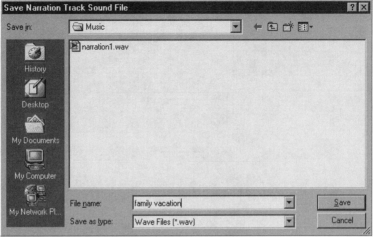

7. Enter a name for the narration track, and click Save. (The track is saved in WAV format.)

If you had a soundtrack, you might find that the narration has forced the soundtrack to move over on the timeline. To have the two of them play simultaneously, drag them so that they overlap.

Previewing the Movie

Before you publish the movie, you'll want to preview it to make sure everything is as you wish it to be. To preview the movie in the preview pane, click the Play button while the first frame of the project is selected in the workspace.

To view it full-screen, click the Full Screen button beneath the preview pane, or choose Play ➤ Full Screen.

Creating Your Movie

Before you create your movie, save your project. Remember, you can't make changes to a published movie; so if you want to change it, you'll need to make changes to the project and then republish the movie. To save your project, choose File ➤ Save, or click the Save button on the toolbar; save as you would any other data file in a program.

Then you're ready to make a movie! To do so, follow these steps:

1. Choose File ➤ Save Movie. The Save Movie dialog box opens, as shown in Figure 17.8.

FIGURE 17.8
*Set the options for the
movie to be created.*

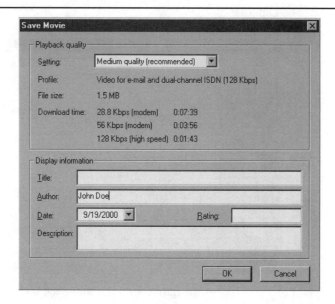

2. Choose a quality from the Setting drop-down list. The default is Medium.

TIP If you you'll distributing the movie via the Internet, set the quality at medium or lower to keep the file size small. If you'll be distributing the movie on a CD or playing it on your own PC, and you have plenty of disk space, use a higher quality. You can check the file size in the Download Time area of the dialog box.

3. Enter any information desired in the Display Information area. All of this information is optional.

4. Click OK. The Save As dialog box appears.

5. Enter a filename for your movie in the File Name box.

6. Click Save. Your movie is saved, and a message appears asking whether you want to watch it now.

7. Click Yes to watch the movie or No to return to Movie Maker.

 NOTE Movie Maker is not a terribly sophisticated program, and there are a lot of "better" video editing programs on the market today that do more sophisticated things, particularly with transitions. If you buy a digital video camera, or a FireWire port for your PC, it might come with its own video editing software that has more features. For example, when I was shopping for a FireWire port card, I ended up buying Studio DV from Pinnacle systems for the same price as I would have paid for a card alone. It included a three-port FireWire port card plus some very good editing software.

Once you've created your movie, you can distribute it on disk or by e-mail to others. The format in which it is saved (WMV) is compatible with Windows Media Player, including older versions of Media Player that came with Windows 9x, so any other Windows user should be able to view your movie on-screen with no additional software required.

In this chapter and the preceding one, you have worked with Windows applications for multimedia. In the next chapter, you'll take a look at some of the hardware-based settings and utilities for multimedia in Windows.

PART

III

Using Windows Me
Multimedia

CHAPTER **18**

Working with Multimedia and Entertainment Hardware

FEATURING:

Windows Me excels at multimedia—that is, combining pictures, sounds, music clips, video, and so on. You've seen that in the last two chapters. This chapter focuses on the hardware that makes all those good things possible: your sound card, your gaming devices, your microphone, and your CD and DVD drives.

Using the Volume Control

If you have a sound card, Windows provides a Volume Control utility for adjusting the volume of the sounds it produces. (If you don't have a sound card, Volume Control is not available.)

The simplest way to adjust the master volume for the whole system is to click the speaker icon in the System Tray. A volume slider appears. Then drag the slider up or down, or click its Mute check box to mute all sound completely.

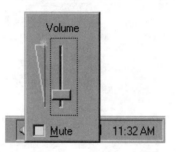

> **TIP** If you don't see a speaker icon in your System Tray, open Sounds and Multimedia from the Control Panel and make sure that the Show Volume Control on Taskbar check box is marked.

Opening the Volume Control Dialog Box

The full version of Volume Control contains volume controls, balance controls, and the like for controlling your sound card. You can get to it by double-clicking the speaker icon in the System Tray or by choosing Start ➢ Programs ➢ Accessories ➢ Entertainment ➢ Volume Control. See Figure 18.1.

FIGURE 18.1

A typical Volume control panel. Yours might look slightly different, and it may have different devices listed.

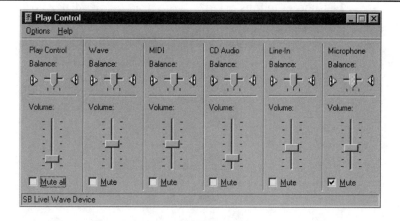

 NOTE The title bar in Figure 18.1 reads Play Control, which means you are looking at the volume and balance sliders for the output portion of the sound card functionality. I'll show you shortly how to control the input (recording) devices.

In Figure 18.1, notice that there is a Play Control column at the far left. Every system has one of these. This controls overall volume for the sound card in general, and everything that runs through it. So, for example, adjusting the Play Control volume would affect your audio CD play, your game play, your system sounds, and so on. To adjust the volume, drag the slider up or down. Or, to mute all system sounds, select its Mute All check box. You can also control the balance between your two speakers with the horizontal Balance slider.

There are other, separate controls for each sound-producing device on your system. You can adjust or mute each of them separately in relation to the overall Play Control volume.

Choosing Which Devices Are Displayed

The devices shown are not necessarily the devices installed on your PC. By default, Windows shows a generic set of volume sliders.

PART

III

Using Windows Me Multimedia

To choose which sliders to show, do the following:

1. Choose Options ➤ Properties. The Properties dialog box opens.

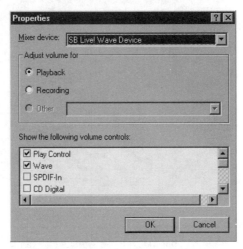

2. In the Show the Following Volume Controls area, place or remove check marks next to the controls to show or hide. You might, for example, choose to hide all the controls that you never use, leaving a much more compact group.

3. Click OK to close. Your volume Play Control window now shows only the controls you chose, as shown here:

Setting the Recording Volume Levels

By default, the Volume Control utility shows the Play controls. If you want to set the volume for input devices such as Line In and Mic, do the following:

1. Start in the Play controls, and choose Options ➤ Properties.

2. Click the Recording button. The list of devices changes to show input devices.

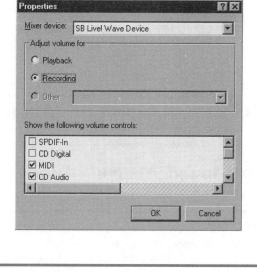

 NOTE Some devices are listed both on the Play and the Recording lists. For example, Microphone appears in both places. The Microphone control on the Play controls adjusts the volume of the microphone feedback coming through your speakers; the Microphone on the Recording controls adjusts the volume of the microphone input.

3. In the Show the Following Volume Controls area, place or remove check marks next to the controls to show or hide.

4. Click OK to close.

When you close the Volume Control and reopen it, the Play controls reappear; you must go through the preceding steps to reselect the Recording controls each time you want to use them.

 TIP If you choose Options ➤ Advanced, the utility turns on an Advanced button at the bottom of the Volume Control box. Then you can click that button to see a few additional sound adjustment controls, depending on your sound card's capabilities.

Working with Sound Schemes

Sound schemes are much like the other schemes you've already dealt with earlier in the book (such as color schemes and Desktop Themes in Chapter 10, "Customizing the Desktop, Taskbar, and Start Menu," and mouse pointer schemes in Chapter 9,

PART

III

Using Windows Me
Multimedia

"Customizing Windows with the Control Panel"). You can assign individual sounds to particular system events, or you can apply an entire scheme. For example, the Musica sound scheme that comes with Windows assigns different little musical ditties to system events such as Exit Windows, Menu Command, and Close Window, whereas the Robotz sound scheme assigns different machinery sounds to those same events.

 NOTE When you apply a Desktop Theme, covered in Chapter 10, you are also applying a sound scheme as part of the big package.

Choosing a Sound Scheme

 NOTE If you don't find the sound schemes shown in the illustrations in this chapter, such as Musica and Robotz, perhaps they are not installed. See Chapter 13, "Adding and Removing Hardware and Software," to learn how to add Windows components and the extra sound schemes to your system.

Follow these steps to choose a sound scheme:

1. Choose Start ➣ Settings ➣ Control Panel, and double-click the Sounds and Multimedia icon.

2. Open the Scheme drop-down list and choose a scheme. See Figure 18.2.

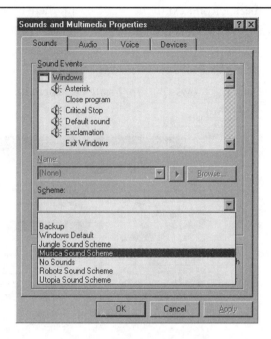

FIGURE 18.2
Select a sound scheme.

3. If a message appears that says that your previous scheme will be lost if you don't save it, click Yes or No.

If you click Yes, a Save As box appears; type the name for the new scheme and click OK.

4. (Optional) Check out some of the individual sounds in the scheme, if desired. To do so, click the event name and then click the Play button.

5. Click OK to accept your new scheme choice.

Your new sound scheme will now be in effect, and any time you do an activity in Windows that has a sound associated with it, you'll hear the assigned sound.

Choosing Individual Sounds

Besides the full schemes, you can also assign sounds to individual events. You can customize the scheme by doing this, even after you've chosen a complete scheme.

To assign an individual sound, do the following:

1. Choose Start ➢ Settings ➢ Control Panel, and double-click the Sounds and Multimedia icon.

2. Click an event on the Sound Events list.

PART

III

Using Windows Me
Multimedia

3. Click the Play button to hear the current sound assigned to it. If there is no speaker icon next to the sound event, there is no current sound assignment.

4. Open the Name drop-down list, and choose a different sound for that event if desired.

or

Click the Browse button, locate elsewhere on your PC a sound file to use, and click OK.

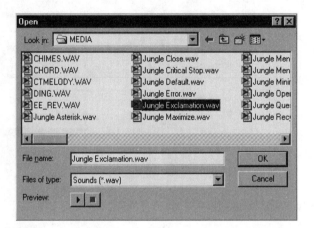

 NOTE Notice that the Open dialog box has its own Play button, so you can preview sounds without leaving the box.

5. Repeat steps 2–4 for other sounds, if desired.

6. Click OK to close the dialog box and apply the sound choices.

Setting Audio Properties

The Audio tab in the Sounds and Multimedia Properties box provides controls for setting up your preferred audio devices. (This used to be in Multimedia Properties in Windows 9*x*.) See Figure 18.3.

FIGURE 18.3
Choose the preferred audio device for recording, playback, and MIDI here.

The Volume buttons in each section open the Volume Control box you worked with at the beginning of this chapter. (The top and bottom ones open Play Control, while the middle one, in the Sound Recording section, opens Recording Control.)

The following sections discuss the other controls.

Setting the Preferred Devices

When you open each of the Preferred Device drop-down lists on the Sounds and Multimedia Properties box, you'll probably find only one device listed: your sound card. If you have only one audio device (your sound card), these "preferred device" settings will not be terribly useful. However, some special situations might necessitate their use.

For example, I have a Sony MiniDisc player that hooks up to my PC using a USB interface. When it's connected, I can play music using Windows Media Player, and the MiniDisc player records it onto a disk. It uses a connection feature called PC Link, and to successfully record to the MiniDisc player, I have to set my preferred audio device for playback to PC Link rather than to my sound card.

Another example: If you hook up a MIDI output device to your system, you will want MIDI playback to be directed to it, rather than to your sound card, so you would set the MIDI Music Playback Preferred Device setting to the MIDI device.

PART

III

Using Windows Me
Multimedia

Setting Advanced Properties

You can also click the Advanced button in the Sound Playback and/or the Sound Recording area to open dialog boxes that let you tweak the settings.

Click Advanced in the Sound Playback section to see this dialog box, for example:

Open the Speaker Setup drop-down list here, and choose the type of speakers you have attached to your PC to adjust the sound to play optimally through that type.

The other tab in this dialog box is Performance:

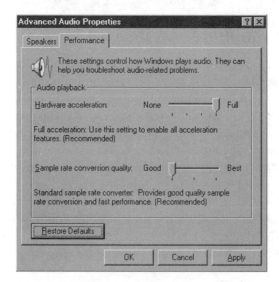

Here you'll find sliders for controlling the hardware acceleration and the sample rate conversion quality. Hardware acceleration should normally be left set to Full unless you are troubleshooting compatibility problems and are directed by a technician to change the setting. The sample rate conversion quality should be left at Good for fastest system performance, but you can bump it up to Best if you have a powerful PC and a need for top-quality sound playback.

Clicking the Advanced button in the Sound Recording section of the Sounds and Multimedia Properties box opens a dialog box that, at first glance, appears to be an exact duplicate of the Performance tab shown previously. However, it is for *recording*, not playback. In most cases, you can leave the default settings alone, as with the playback settings.

Setting Up Direct Voice Support

Direct Voice is a feature in some games that enables you to chat with someone over a network as you are playing an online game that supports the DirectPlay standard. Very few games support it as of this writing, but it's likely going to be all the rage in the coming years. All you need is a microphone (the headphone type is best, since you'll need your hands free to play the game) and a sound card—and, of course, a game or other program with support for the feature.

The Voice tab in the Sounds and Multimedia Properties dialog box offers settings to configure your hardware to work with Direct Voice (see Figure 18.4).

FIGURE 18.4
Set the voice features of your sound and multimedia configuration here.

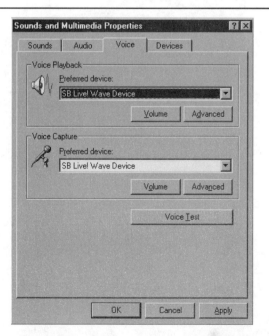

PART

III

Using Windows Me
Multimedia

In the Voice Playback section, you see the same controls as for Sound Playback on the Audio tab. Clicking the Advanced button here also brings up exactly the same Advanced Audio Properties dialog box as you saw earlier. And the Voice Capture section has the same types of controls as the Sound Recording section on the Audio tab. So far, no big surprises.

However, the Voice Test button at the bottom is fairly important. Click it and you'll walk through the Sound Hardware Test Wizard. This Wizard helps you set your audio levels for Direct Voice and confirms that your hardware is usable with that feature. In order to be used, it must be able to record and play back voice at the same time it's playing back sounds (such as from a game). Otherwise, the game sound would cut out whenever you or your network opponent is speaking, and what fun would that be?

To test and configure for Direct Voice, follow these steps:

1. Click the Voice Test button. The Sound Hardware Test Wizard runs.

2. Click Next to begin.

3. Wait for your system to be tested. It takes about 30 seconds. If your system passes the test, you see the following screen:

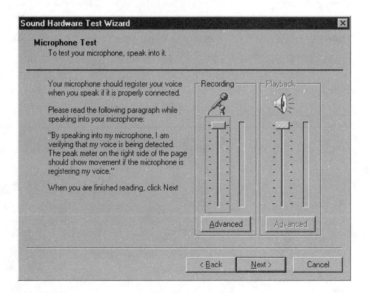

4. Read into your microphone the text shown on screen, and then click Next. The Speaker Test screen appears:

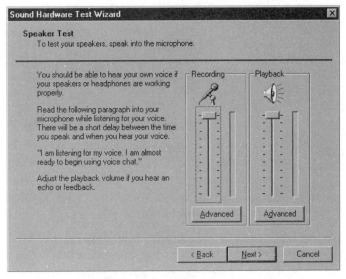

5. Speak into the microphone. You should hear your own voice coming back at you through your speakers, at a one-second delay.

6. Adjust the Playback volume slider, if needed. Then click Next.

7. Click Finish. You're now ready to use Direct Voice in any program that supports it.

 NOTE If you are trying to make Direct Voice work in a game that supports the DirectPlay specification but are having problems with it, go to the Gaming Options applet in the Control Panel, and click the Details button on the Voice Chat tab. This opens a screen explaining the feature more fully, to help you troubleshoot.

Recording Sounds

With Sound Recorder and a microphone, you can create your own sound-effects files to use in Windows. You can assign these sound files to system events, as you learned earlier in the chapter, or you can use them in other programs such as PowerPoint presentations.

You can also record from an audio CD or from any other audio source, using Sound Recorder. Just have that device ready to play, and then record as it is playing.

Here's how to record a sound:

1. Choose Start ➤ Programs ➤ Accessories ➤ Entertainment ➤ Sound Recorder. Sound Recorder opens.

2. If you want to record from a microphone, make sure it's connected and ready. Or, if you're recording from an audio CD or some other source, get it ready. For example, if you have connected your stereo to the Line In jack on your PC, cue up the song on your stereo and press Pause on it. Or, if you're recording from an audio CD on your PC, open it in Windows Media Player and be ready to click Play.

3. In Sound Recorder, click the Record button shown here. Then quickly press Play on whatever input source you're using, or begin speaking into the microphone.

As the sound records, you can watch the line in the Sound Recorder box spike and change, reflecting the sound being recorded.

WARNING Sound Recorder records in WAV format, which takes up a lot of hard-disk space. A typical three-minute song will take over 5MB. This is not the best format for recording entire songs! Use MP3 for that; see Chapter 16, "Using the Windows Media Player," for details about MP3. Sound Recorder is best for recording short clips to be used as system events.

4. When you have recorded the sound, click Stop in Sound Recorder. Then stop the input source (if using one), such as your stereo or Windows Media Player.

5. Choose File ➤ Save, and save the sound file as you would save any other file.

You can play sounds recorded with Sound Recorder right there in Sound Recorder to make sure you got them right; simply click the Play button. You can also play them with Windows Media Player.

Configuring Gaming Devices

Gaming devices are joysticks, flight yokes, gamepads, and other add-on devices specifically designed for playing games on a PC. If you've visited a computer store lately, you've seen the huge variety of such devices that are available.

Most devices come with their own software for calibration, control, and button definition, but in case you don't have access to it or don't like it, you can set up basic functionality with Windows Me's built-in setup and calibration utility for gaming devices.

Installing a Gaming Device

Gaming devices plug into the joystick port on your sound card (or on your PC itself if you have built-in sound). You must plug in a gaming device with the power off, so shut down your PC before connecting the device.

Windows Me might detect your gaming device immediately the first time you turn on your PC after plugging in the device. Or it might need a little help.

To see whether Windows recognizes the device or not, do the following:

1. Choose Start ➤ Settings ➤ Control Panel.

2. Double-click Gaming Options. The Gaming Options dialog box appears, with the Controllers tab displayed.

   If your gaming device appears there, it's installed. If not, you can either run the Setup program that came with it, or you can continue to step 3.

3. Click Add. The Add Game Controller dialog box opens.

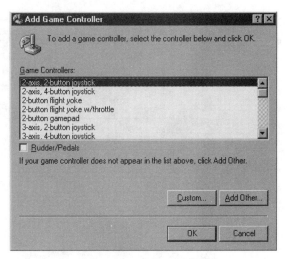

4. Choose the type of controller you have. Scroll down through the entire list; many popular controllers are listed. If you can't find yours, choose one of the generic models at the top of the list, or do one of the following:

   • Click the Add Other button to select from the full list of supported devices. Once you're there, if you don't find your device, you can click Have Disk and select a driver from a disk that came with the controller, if you have one.

- Click the Custom button to define a new set of controller settings in the Custom Game Controller dialog box; then click OK to return.

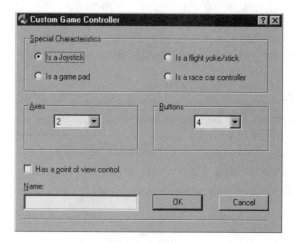

5. Click OK. Windows quickly checks for the presence of the game controller, and if it finds it, "OK" appears in the Status column next to the controller name on the list. See Figure 18.5. Your game controller is now installed.

FIGURE 18.5

A game controller installed in Windows

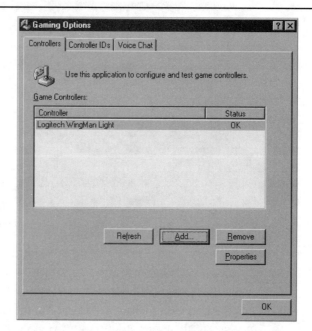

Testing and Calibrating a Gaming Device

Once a gaming device is installed, you can test and calibrate it. *Calibration* means adjustment so that your movements and button presses on the controller correspond faithfully to the actions you want to take in the games you'll be playing.

To test and calibrate a device, follow these steps:

1. From the Control Panel, double-click Gaming Options.

2. Select the controller to calibrate on the Controllers tab, and click Properties. The Game Controller Properties dialog box opens.

3. Click the Test tab if it is not already displayed.

4. If using a joystick, move the joystick all the way to the top, bottom, left, and right, and to each diagonal corner, and observe the movement of the crosshair in the on-screen box. If the crosshair doesn't move exactly to the edges of the box when your joystick is fully moved in a direction, the controller needs calibration.

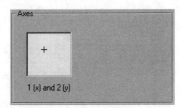

Or, if using some other type of control, use the testing controls provided to test the device. Different types of devices will show different testing controls from the one shown above for a joystick.

5. If the controller has buttons, you'll see numbered circles on the Test tab. Press the buttons on the controller, one after another, and make sure that the numbered circles light up in correspondence with the button presses.

6. If the joystick performed perfectly, click OK. Otherwise, continue to step 7.

7. Click the Settings tab, and then click the Calibrate button. The Controller 1 Calibration dialog box appears. (The "1" might be replaced by another number if you have more than one controller.)

8. Follow the directions that appear in the dialog box to calibrate your device. The exact instructions will vary. Click Finish when you reach the last screen.

9. Click OK to accept your changes to the controller's setup.

Setting Advanced Gaming Device Options

You can have up to 15 separate game controllers in a single PC, and each has a controller ID number. (By default, your controller ID is 1 on a system with a single game controller.) The Controller IDs tab (shown in Figure 18.6) in the Gaming Options dialog box enables you to set a controller ID number for a controller other than its default one, and tells Windows which game port the controller is hooked up to. (On most systems, there is only one game port—the joystick port on the sound card.)

FIGURE 18.6
On systems with multiple game ports and multiple game controllers, you might want to organize them here.

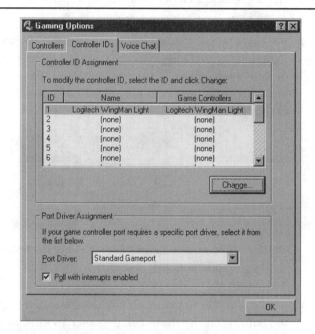

The Voice Chat tab in this dialog box is useful only if you have voice-enabled games installed. You can learn more about Voice Chat, however, by clicking the Details button on that tab to open a dialog box containing some information.

Using DVD and CD-RW Drives

This section talks about some of the fun you can have with multimedia devices like DVD and CD-RW drives. Not everyone has this equipment, of course, but more and more new systems these days are coming with such devices. Even if you don't have some of this stuff, you might still want to read the following sections; they might even make you decide to buy some new hardware!

Playing DVD Movies

DVD stands for Digital Versatile Disk, and it's the latest thing in CD-ROMs. A DVD is like a super CD; it holds lots more data. How much? Enough for over two hours of full-motion video footage. That's why the primary use of DVDs right now is storing and playing movies. DVDs can also hold computer data, but that usage is still in its infancy. Expect to see more and more of it in the coming years, though.

If you have a DVD drive on your PC, it functions just like a regular CD-ROM drive in most respects, all by itself. However, if you want to play DVDs in that drive, you need an MPEG decoder card hooked up to it. Most DVD drives these days come with an MPEG card, but on some newer systems the video card serves as the MPEG card. You might also need to install some DVD software that comes with the card or the drive.

If you have all the right hardware in place, and the drivers are installed, you can simply pop a DVD into the drive and it starts playing.

If your video card supports DVD playback, the Windows DVD player can play your DVD movies. You'll find it on the Programs ➢ Accessories ➢ Entertainment menu if your hardware is compatible with it. But your DVD drive itself probably came with a DVD player of its own; so if you don't find the Windows DVD player on the menu, go with the player designed specifically for your equipment. For example, I have a Creative PC-DVD drive with its own MPEG decoder card, and Windows DVD Player won't work with it; but it plays movies just fine with the Creative DVD player it came with.

Besides movies, you can also play DVD data disks on your DVD drive. These are not that common yet, but some games are beginning to be released on DVDs. For graphic-intensive games, this is a plus because you don't have to swap CDs in the middle of the game.

Making Your Own CD-ROMs

There are various kinds of writable CD drives out there. The original units could write to a blank CD only once; then that blank was permanently written, and nothing could be added, changed, or removed. Those are CD-Recordable (CD-R) drives. Newer ones can do the CD-R thing but can also write to a different kind of disk, CD-Rewritable (CD-RW), which can be changed and erased multiple times. The CD-RW blanks are more expensive, so most people who want to make a CD that won't change use the cheaper CD-R blanks.

Your CD-R or CD-RW drive came with software for making your own CDs; Windows itself doesn't have an application to do that. There are two separate programs—one for CD-R disks and one for CD-RW disks. One popular CD-R program is Easy CDCreator by Adaptec. A limited-functionality version of it comes free with most CD-R and CD-RW drives. Another one is called Nero Burning ROM.

A separate program handles transfer of files to a CD-RW drive using a technology called *packet writing*. This enables you to use the CD-RW disk as though it were a floppy disk—you can drag and drop files to it using Windows Explorer or My Computer.

Making LPs and Cassettes into Audio CDs

If you have a CD-R or CD-RW drive and a sound card with a Line In jack, you can turn your old LPs and cassettes into audio CDs. Some CD-R programs come with software that makes this easy, but even if yours doesn't, you can still do it. The basic process is this: You hook up your stereo system so that the Line Out goes to the Line In on your sound card. At that point, you should be able to hear the stereo play through your computer's speakers. Then you use a program that records sound (such as Sound Recorder, which comes with Windows) to record the stereo playing as a WAV file. Then you use your CD-R program to turn the WAV files into an audio CD.

If you're serious about transferring a lot of LPs and cassettes to CD format, you might want to invest in software that can help you remove some of the pops, hisses, and scratches from the original recordings. Adaptec's Easy CD Creator Deluxe does this, as do several other programs that are available. Such programs take the place of Sound Recorder; they record the input while running it through a filter that improves the quality.

Backing Up Important Files to CD-R or CD-RW Disks

CD-R and CD-RW disks make excellent backup devices. You can periodically copy your important files to a CD-R or CD-RW disk, in case disaster strikes and your hard-disk contents become destroyed.

Windows 98 came with a backup program, but Windows Me doesn't have one. However, there are many good backup programs available for sale in stores, and you can always simply copy the files from your hard disk to a CD-RW drive using Windows Explorer, or periodically create a CD-R containing your most important data files.

One little glitch is that when you copy files, or back them up with a backup program, most hidden and system files are not included, and some of these are essential for your Windows system to operate. So even if you have done what you thought was a complete backup, you might not be able to perfectly restore your hard disk from the backup. The solution? Use a hard disk–copying program such as DriveImage or Norton Ghost. Such programs create an exact duplicate of your hard disk on one or more CD-R or CD-RW disks, and provide a utility for restoring from the backup when needed. Such programs work with both CD-R and CD-RW drives, as well as Zip drives, Jaz drives, tape-backup drives, and other removable media.

Now that you're familiar with Windows' multimedia capabilities, it's time to shift topics. The next few chapters deal with communications, and more specifically, with using the Internet.

PART IV

Communication and Using the Internet

CHAPTER 19

Introduction to Windows Communications

FEATURING:

A few years ago when people bought a new computer, they only planned to do things like word processing, financial record keeping, maybe financial analysis, and of course play some games. They'd tap information into the keyboard, the computer would do its thing, and after a while, it would print the result on a piece of paper or display it on the screen. PCs were typically stand-alone devices, not connected to any other computers. If you needed to exchange data with somebody else, you could use a floppy disk to move files from one machine to the other (a technique that was sometimes called "sneakernet").

But when you start connecting them together, stand-alone computers become extremely flexible communications tools. Relatively early in the development of computer technology, people figured out that it wasn't particularly difficult to transfer information through a wire from one computer to another. As long as the computers on both ends use the same technical standards, you can move messages, programs, text, and video, audio, and other data files back and forth. And when you connect a *lot* of computers together through a network, you can communicate with any other computer on the same network, just as you can reach any other telephone connected to the global telecommunications system from the phone on your desk.

Under the broad category of "communications," your PC can send and receive text, program files, sounds, and images. It can also exchange images of fax pages with a distant fax machine. This data can enter and leave your PC through a modem, a network interface card, or a direct cable connection to another computer.

Communications capability has been part of DOS and Windows since the earliest IBM PCs. Windows Me pushes the limits of today's technology and now includes an extensive set of communications tools that allow you to exchange electronic mail with other computers, potentially look at millions of Web sites, and even use your computer to make international video and audio phone calls for free. This chapter introduces the communications features of Windows Me and tells you how to configure Windows to work with your modem, making it all possible. Once your modem is installed and configured, you can find more specific information about communications applications, such as HyperTerminal, Outlook Express (for e-mail and newsgroups), and Internet Explorer (for browsing the Web), in the subsequent chapters.

 NOTE Another aspect of communications is networking. With Windows Me you can set up your own peer-to-peer network for sharing files, printers, and Internet connections. Networking is covered in Part V.

What's New in Windows Me Communications?

As dial-up communications become more common, there are fewer radical innovations from one year to the next. Between Windows 95 and Windows 98, there were many changes in the communications arena; however, there are very few differences between Windows 98 and Windows Me. That's a good sign—it means that communications is becoming a mature technology area, and we can all be free to put our energy into *doing something* with the data exchanged rather than focusing on the mechanics of the exchange.

Windows Telephony and HyperTerminal, the subjects of the remainder of this chapter, are virtually unchanged since Windows 98.

Windows 98 Second Edition introduced a feature called Internet Connection Sharing, and that's still present in Windows Me. It allows you to share an Internet connection over a network so that one computer with Internet access can provide access to all other PCs in your home. You'll learn about that in Chapter 20, "Connecting to the Internet."

Windows Me offers new versions of Internet Explorer and Outlook Express, but the new versions have only minor improvements over previous versions. You'll learn about Internet Explorer in Chapter 21, "Browsing the World Wide Web with Internet Explorer 5.5," and Outlook Express in Chapter 22, "Communicating with Outlook Express News and Mail."

Windows Me also provides a Home Networking Wizard that automates the process of setting up a home network, as well as configuring Internet connection sharing over it. Part V of the book covers networking. The Internet Connection Sharing Wizard, which was part of Windows 98 Second Edition, is now integrated with the Home Networking Wizard, so you can set up your network and share your Internet connection in a single activity.

The Windows Telephony Interface

Windows Me includes a set of software "hooks" to applications that control the way your computer interacts with the telephone network. TAPI (telephony application programming interface) is an internal part of the Windows Me operating system rather than a specific application program; it provides a standard way for software developers to access communications ports and devices, such as modems and telephone sets, to control data, fax, and voice calls. Using TAPI, an application can place a call, answer an incoming call, and hang up when the call is complete. It also supports things like hold, call transfer, voicemail, and conference calls. TAPI-compliant applications will work with conventional telephone lines, PBX and Centrex systems, and specialized services like cellular and ISDN.

By moving these functions to a common program interface, Windows prevents two or more application programs from making conflicting demands for access to your modem and telephone line. Therefore, you no longer need to shut down a program that's waiting for incoming calls before you use a different program to send a fax.

Unless you're planning to write your own communications applications, you won't ever have to deal directly with TAPI, but you will see its benefits when you use the communications programs included in the Windows Me package—such as Hyper-Terminal, Outlook Express, Phone Dialer, and Remote Access—and when you use Windows-compatible versions of third-party communications programs such as Pro-Comm and WinFax Pro.

Windows Me includes a relatively simple telephony application called Phone Dialer, but that just scratches the surface of what TAPI will support, in the same way that, say, WordPad has fewer bells and whistles than Word for Windows. Phone Dialer is much simpler than some of the other programs that will appear in the near future. Programs from some third parties based on Windows Telephony can now handle control of all your telephone activities through the Windows Desktop. For example, some let you use the telephone company's caller ID service to match incoming calls to a database that displays detailed information about the caller before you answer, or use an on-screen menu to set up advanced call features like conference calling and forwarding that now require obscure strings of digits from the telephone keypad.

The Telephony applet in the Control Panel controls two aspects of Windows Telephony: dialing properties and telephony drivers. The latter is set up automatically for you when you install Windows and your modem, but Dialing Properties must be configured for the PC before you can use your modem. You can set up the dialing properties either before or after installing a modem; if you have not yet set them up, a box will appear, prompting you to do so the first time you use Dial-Up Networking.

Setting Up a Dialing Location

You must set up Windows Telephony for at least one dialing location. If you use a desktop PC, you'll probably never need more than that; but on a laptop PC you might want several dialing locations to choose from, depending on what city you are in at the moment and what building. Some buildings have PBX systems, for example, which require you to dial a 9 for an outside line, and some phone lines have call waiting that you should disable before making a call with your modem.

To set up a dialing location, do the following:

1. From the Control Panel, double-click Telephony. The Dialing Properties dialog box opens (see Figure 19.1).

FIGURE 19.1
*Control how the
modem should dial
from your current
location.*

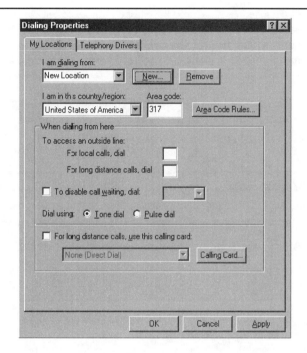

2. (Optional) If you want to create a new dialing location, click the New button, and then click OK at the confirmation box.

3. Open the I Am Dialing From drop-down list, and choose the location you want to set up.

4. (Optional) Change the name of the selected location if desired. For example, if you created a new location, its name is New Location; you will probably want to change the name to something more meaningful, such as Cleveland Office or My Home.

5. Choose a country from the I Am in This Country/Region drop-down list, and enter the local area code in the Area Code box.

6. In the When Dialing from Here section, enter any special numbers you need to dial for an outside line or for a long-distance call. These are used primarily in corporate phone systems. If you have an outside line, leave these blank.

NOTE Don't use the fields in step 6 for the "1" prefix that you dial before long-distance calls. The dialer will add that code automatically.

TIP Insert commas into the phone number to tell your modem to pause before moving ahead to the next digit. On Hayes-compatible modems, each comma results in a two-second pause. At least one comma is necessary when you have to dial a special number to reach an outside line. So **9,** would be a typical entry in the boxes for accessing an outside line.

7. If this line has call waiting, mark the To Disable Call Waiting check box and enter the code to dial in the text box. It's usually something like ***70**, but can vary depending on the phone system.

 NOTE Most people want to disable call waiting before placing a call with the modem because the clicking that signals another incoming call can disrupt data transfer.

8. Choose Tone or Pulse dialing. Almost all modern phone lines are Tone. Tone lines will work with the Pulse setting, but not vice versa.

 TIP If you hear tones when you press buttons on your phone, you have tone dialing. If you hear clicks, you have pulse dialing.

9. If you need to use a calling card for long-distance calls, do the following:

   a. Mark the For Long Distance Calls, Use This Calling Card check box.

   b. Click the Calling Card button.

   c. In the Calling Card dialog box that appears, open the drop-down list and select your calling card (if it appears there).

   d. If your calling card does not appear on the list, click the New button and then fill in the text boxes with the needed information for dialing.

   e. Click OK to return to the Dialing Properties dialog box.

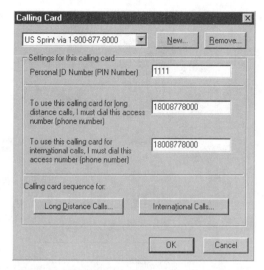

10. Click OK. Your Telephony settings are now configured.

More on Calling Cards

If you were a little confused in the preceding steps about entering your calling card data, here's some more help.

First, before struggling with entering the settings for your card manually, make sure your card isn't on the list of cards. There are a lot of card types listed, even multiple ones for the same company, so be sure to choose the right one.

When you choose a calling card from the menu, the program automatically uses the correct calling sequence for that long-distance carrier. For example, some cards require you to enter your card number first; others want the number you are dialing first. But if you need a special calling sequence, or are manually setting up a card, click the Long Distance Calls button or the International Calls button and choose the sequences for long-distance or international calls in the Dialing Properties dialog box.

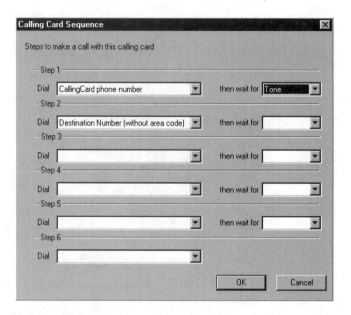

 TIP To enter a specific sequence of digits, choose Specified Digits from the drop-down list for a given field. Then enter the digits in the resulting text box.

You can not only change the sequence of events but also enter any specific numbers or other codes. When you make the call, the events will progress from the top (step 1) to the bottom (step 6).

The Tone option available in the Then Wait For part of the dialog box means to wait for the "bong" tone that you hear after calling the long-distance carrier. Most services require waiting for this tone before you proceed with the dialing sequence and PIN input. If the tone your carrier plays isn't detected by your modem, you may have to use a pause of a second or two instead. Try experimenting with different pause lengths. Typically, you are allowed a few seconds to enter the remainder of the sequence, so the pause amount may not be critical as long as you have waited for the bong to sound.

 TIP If a connection isn't working and you're fine-tuning these events, it sometimes helps to lift the receiver of a phone on the same line and listen (or turn on the modem's speaker), monitoring the sounds. You'll be better able to figure out where a sequence is bombing out.

Advanced users can, if necessary, use the following codes for variables within a calling sequence. Add these to the "specified digits" sequence.

E	Country Code
F	Area Code
G	Destination Local Number
H	Calling-card number
W	Wait for second dial tone.
@	Wait for a ringing tone followed by five seconds of silence.
$	Wait for a calling-card prompt tone (the "bong" tone).
?	Display an on-screen prompt.

For example, the default calling sequence for long-distance calls using an AT&T calling card is 102880FG$H:

10288	Specifies AT&T as the long-distance carrier
0	Specifies a credit-card call
F	Specifies the area code
G	Specifies the local telephone number
$	Specifies a wait for the calling-card prompt
H	Specifies the calling-card number

Telephony Drivers

Windows automatically installs the needed telephony drivers for your modem or other communications hardware, but you can also install additional protocols if needed. For example, in the U.S., TAPI is the most common communications driver, but in Europe, CAPI is popular. You can manage the list of installed telephony drivers from the Telephony Drivers tab in the Dialing Properties dialog box (Figure 19.2). Most people will never need to do this.

FIGURE 19.2
Manage the installed
telephony drivers here.

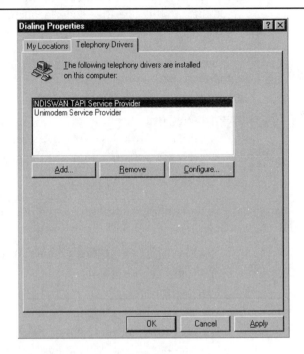

FIGURE 19.2
Manage the installed telephony drivers here.

Installing and Configuring a Modem

For most individuals and small businesses, the most practical way to connect to a remote computer (that is, a computer not physically located in your home or office) is through a dial-up telephone line and a modem. *Modem* is a made-up word constructed out of *mo*dulator-*dem*odulator. A modem converts digital data from a computer into sounds that can travel through telephone lines designed for voice communication (that's the modulator part), and it also converts sounds that it receives from a telephone line to digital data (that's the demodulator part). Using a modem is the most common way to connect to an Internet Service Provider (ISP), as described in Chapter 20. However, non-modem methods such as DSL and cable Internet access are becoming more common.

Choosing a Modem

For reasons of economy, convenience, or simplicity, let's say you've decided to go with an inexpensive connection to the Internet through a modem and a telephone line. What now? If you bought your computer in the last year or two, it probably has an internal modem already. (If you're planning to buy a new computer, the following guidelines will help you find one with a modem that meets your needs.) If you don't already have a modem, go find one.

The *speed* of a modem is the maximum number of data bits that can pass through the modem in one second. Almost all modems sold today run at 56Kbps (that is, 56,000 bits per second). You might see such modems described as V.90, the current communications protocol for communicating at 56Kbps. Older models might be described as K56-flex or X2. Modem speed is much less of an issue nowadays than it used to be because all new modems run at the maximum speed of 56Kbps.

NOTE If you have a 56Kbps modem that can establish a connection only at lower speeds, your phone line might be at fault. If you are several miles from your phone company's switching facility, your connection will be slower than the modem's capability allows. The phone company in your area should be able to provide this information to you.

Modems come in three forms: internal, external, and on a credit-card-size PCMCIA card (also known as a PC card). Each type has specific advantages and disadvantages.

Internal modems Expansion cards that fit inside your PC. They're the least expensive and most common type of modem, and they don't require special data cables or power supplies. To install an internal modem, take the cover off your PC and insert the modem into one of the expansion slots on your motherboard. (Instructions are provided with the modem.)

WARNING When purchasing an internal modem, make sure you don't get one that's marked "for Windows." These Windows-only modems, known as "winmodems," are inferior because they rely on software rather than hardware to do part of their job. Winmodems can be difficult to set up and difficult to troubleshoot when something goes wrong. Look for a modem that can be used with other operating systems, too, such as MS-DOS and Linux—not because you'll ever use one of those operating systems but because such modems are, by definition, not the winmodems that you're trying to avoid.

External modems Separate, self-contained units that are easy to install and move between computers. They cost more than internal modems, and they need a separate AC power outlet. In order to use an external modem, your computer must have an unused serial (COM) connector. Make sure you have an unused COM port before you purchase an external modem, or find a device that lets you share a COM port with two or more external devices. (Typically, this device will be in the form of a switch box with a dial on the front of it.)

PC cards   Small, lightweight devices that fit into the PCMCIA slots on many laptop computers. They're the most convenient modems for people who travel with their PCs, but they're also the most expensive. Some have cell-phone connectors on them. If you have a cell phone and want to send and receive data through it, make sure you get a card that is guaranteed to work with your brand and model of phone! Some cards even come with the cable for your phone already in the box.

 TIP   Cell phones connected to PCMCIA modems must be set to run in "analog" mode, and in the best of circumstances you will only get 9,600bps throughput because of limitations in the cellular technology.

Installing a Modem into Windows

After physically installing the modem in your PC, or attaching it to your PC in the case of an external modem, you are ready to tell Windows about the new device. Most modems sold today are Plug-and-Play (PnP), so when you turn your PC on after attaching the modem, Windows will probably detect the new modem automatically and either install the needed driver or prompt you to insert a disk to do so. If you have a PCMCIA (credit-card-style) modem, simply inserting the card, even while the computer is on, should result in Windows detecting it and loading the appropriate software driver. For details about hardware setup, see Chapter 13, "Adding and Removing Hardware and Software."

Once Windows recognizes your modem, almost all of your Windows-based programs will be able to use it right away, without any special setup in individual programs. That's because Windows Me uses a *universal modem* driver called *Unimodem*. Unimodem is the software interface between all of your computer's 32-bit Windows 9*x*-compatible communications applications (including the ones that use TAPI) and your modem or other communications hardware. It includes integrated control for port selection, modem initialization, speed, file-transfer protocols, and terminal emulation. The modem configuration is handled by Unimodem, so you have to specify setup parameters only once.

If you're using 16-bit communications applications left over from earlier versions of Windows, they'll work with Windows Me, but you'll have to configure their modem settings separately. For example, you'll need to specify what COM port your modem uses, and perhaps enter a setup string that the modem should dial.

If you're using an older modem ("older" means anything that was made before late 1995 and isn't PnP-aware), Windows Me might not detect it. If that's the case, use the following steps to manually set up the modem in Windows.

NOTE If your PC and your modem are both Plug-and-Play compatible but the PC doesn't automatically detect the modem, try running the setup software that came with the modem before going through the following steps. Perhaps there is a setup program. This is especially true with winmodems.

1. Click Start ➤ Settings ➤ Control Panel.

2. When the Control Panel window opens, double-click the Modems icon. The Modems Properties dialog box, shown in Figure 19.3, will appear.

FIGURE 19.3
The Modems Properties
dialog box identifies the
modem(s) currently
installed in your
system.

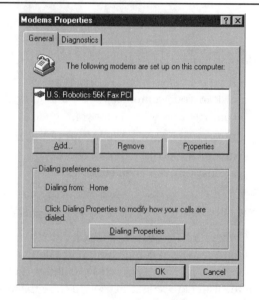

3. If Windows Me has already detected your modem, its name will appear in the Modems Properties dialog box.

   If the correct modem is already listed, close the dialog box and skip to step 6.

   If no modem is listed, or if the name on the list does not match the modem you want to use, click the Add button to run the Install New Modem Wizard.

4. The Wizard runs. Click Next to let Windows try to detect your modem. If it detects it—great. Click Finish to install it. Otherwise, continue to step 5.

5. If you see a message that Windows did not find any new modems, click Next to display a list of modems to choose from.

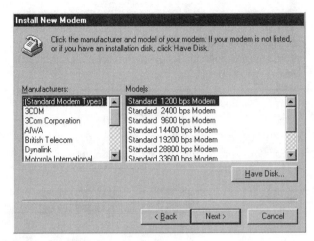

6. Do one of the following:

- If your modem came with a Windows Me or 9x installation disk, put the disk in your computer's drive and click the Have Disk button to load the configuration software for your modem.

- If you don't have a disk, locate and select your modem's manufacturer and model. If it doesn't appear, choose one of the Standard Modem Types to use a generic driver. Then click Next.

7. A list of COM ports appears. Select the port to which the modem is attached, and click Next.

8. Click Finish to complete the modem setup.

When the Wizard completes the installation, it will return you to the Modems Properties dialog box, which should now include the modem you just installed in the list of modems. Click OK to close the Modems Properties box.

NOTE If the list shows more than one modem, you can select the ones you're not using and click the Remove button, but it's not really necessary; Windows Me will identify the active modem every time you turn on your computer. I have two or three modems installed in my system and use different ones with different programs, phone lines, and COM ports. When you create your Dial-Up-Networking (DUN) settings for accessing services such as an ISP, you'll get to stipulate which modem you want to use for that connection.

Testing Your Modem

Before you try to use a newly installed modem, it's a good idea to test it to make sure it can communicate with Windows. The test is very easy to perform:

1. From the Control Panel, double-click Modems.

2. Click the Diagnostics tab.

3. Click the COM port for the modem you want to test.

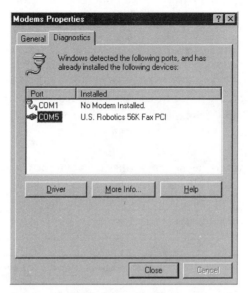

4. Click More Info. After a few seconds, a More Info box appears with output from the modem. If at least some lines report OK, your modem is working properly.

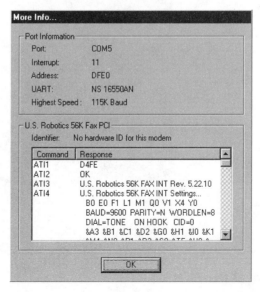

5. Click OK to close the More Info box.

6. Click Close to close the Modems Properties box.

If, in step 4, Windows reports that it can't communicate with the modem instead of displaying a More Info box, you have a problem. Perhaps your modem is not installed correctly, or perhaps there is a resource conflict with another device. See Chapter 13 to troubleshoot device installation problems.

Changing Modem Properties

Once you've installed your modem, all of your Windows Me communications programs will use the same configuration settings. When you change them in one application, those changes will carry across to all the others. The modem properties specify things like the loudness of the modem's speaker and the maximum data-transfer speed.

To change the modem properties, open the Control Panel and double-click the Modems icon. When the Modems Properties dialog box appears, select the modem and click the Properties button to display the Properties box for that modem. Figure 19.4 shows an example.

FIGURE 19.4
Use this Properties dialog box to change your modem settings.

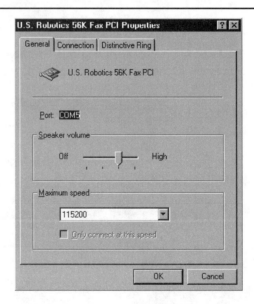

Depending on your modem, you might not have the Distinctive Ring tab shown in Figure 19.4. Also, there might be other tabs, such as Call Forwarding.

General Properties

Let's start with the General tab, shown in Figure 19.4. The General tab has three settings: Port, Speaker Volume, and Maximum Speed.

Port   Use the drop-down Port menu to specify the COM port to which your modem is connected. If you don't have a drop-down list box, there is no choice of port. This will be the case for PCMCIA modems as well as some internal modems.

Speaker Volume   The Speaker Volume control is a slide setting that sets the loudness of the speaker inside your modem. In some cases, you will only have Off and On as options, rather than a variable speaker volume.

Maximum Speed   When your modem makes a connection, it will try to use the maximum speed to exchange data with the modem at the other end of the link. As a rule, if you have a 28,800bps or faster modem, the maximum speed should be three or four times the rated modem speed (e.g., set your modem speed to 115,200) to take advantage of the modem's built-in data compression.

If you don't want to accept a slower connection, check Only Connect at This Speed. This check box will be unavailable if the modem does not support the feature.

Connection Properties

Choose the Connection tab to display the settings in Figure 19.5.

FIGURE 19.5
Use the Connection
tab to change
communication
parameters.

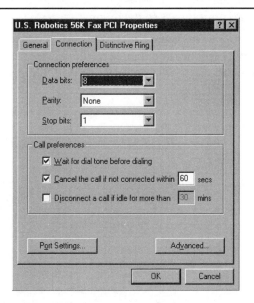

The Connection dialog box has several options:

Connection Preferences   The Data Bits, Parity, and Stop Bits settings must be the same at both ends of a data link. The most common settings are 8 data bits, no parity, and 1 stop bit.

Call Preferences   The three Call Preferences options control the way your modem handles individual calls. Place a check mark in each box if you want to use that option.

Port Settings   Clicking this button brings up the Advanced Port Settings dialog box.

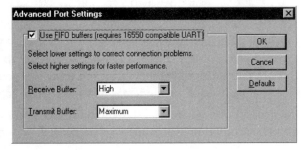

These settings determine how the incoming and outgoing data are buffered (lined up in the queue during transmission) and should probably be left alone unless you have information from your ISP or modem manufacturer to the contrary. If you do experiment and your throughput drops, return to this screen and click Defaults to set the controls back to the original suggested settings.

Advanced Options   The Advanced Connection Settings are options that you will probably set once and then leave alone. They manage error control, flow control, and additional special settings. Figure 19.6 shows the Advanced Connection Settings dialog box.

FIGURE 19.6

Use the Advanced Connection Settings dialog box to specify error control and flow control.

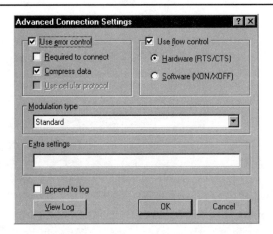

The Extra Settings section is a place to send additional AT (ATtention) commands to your modem. In most cases, you won't need to add any special commands. Because different modem manufacturers use slightly different command sets, you'll have to consult your modem manual for specific commands. If you're using a cell phone with the modem, set the Use Cellular Protocol option on. Cell phones use special data error compression and correction protocols to increase connection speed. The modem will still work with this setting turned off, but turning it on may improve the connection.

Distinctive Ring and Call Forwarding

The two remaining tabs on the Modem Properties box let you set up features that your modem and phone line may or may not have. You might have both of these tabs, one of them, or neither.

Distinctive Ring is a service from your phone company that provides different ring patterns for different kinds of incoming calls. Depending on the kind of modem you have, you can have between three and six numbers, or addresses, for one telephone line. Each number can have a distinctive ring pattern. You can also assign each ring pattern to a specific type of program. For example, if you have two rings assigned for fax calls, any call received with that ring pattern could be automatically sent to your fax program. Some phone companies have distinctive ring patterns based on the duration of the ring rather than the number of rings. Some modems support this scenario. In general, choose the desired number of rings for each kind of incoming call based on settings you get from your phone company. Then check your modem's manual for details on using this feature. Before you can alter the ring settings, however, you'll need to enable the Distinctive Ring feature by clicking the check box.

Use the Call Forwarding tab to tell the computer that your modem line has call forwarding installed. For instructions on how to forward calls from your telephone, contact your phone company. Call forwarding is useful if you are away from your computer and want to receive calls at a different number. The computer can actually activate the call forwarding feature and pass on an incoming data or fax call to another phone number that you specify. Activate the feature with the check box, and enter the necessary codes, supplied by your phone company.

Communicating Using HyperTerminal

The HyperTerminal program supplied with Windows Me lets you and your PC make contact with other computers to exchange or retrieve information. With the advent of the Internet, specialized e-mail programs, and proprietary information service programs like AOL and CompuServe, communications programs such as HyperTerminal are quickly becoming relics of a bygone era. But if you have a need to dial into a BBS (bulletin board system) or make a direct connection with a dial-up service of some sort, you'll definitely be glad it's included in Windows Me. With HyperTerminal and the right hookups, you can communicate with other computers whether they are in your own house, around the block, or on the other side of the world.

 NOTE HyperTerminal is useful for direct PC-to-PC connections only. You can't use Hyper-Terminal to cruise the Web or send e-mail. You need special Internet programs for that. Check the next few chapters for coverage of the Internet, Web browsing, and e-mail. HyperTerminal is also probably not the program you'd use to connect to your company LAN when calling in from a remote site; for that, you'll probably use Dial-Up Networking (see Chapter 22).

Setting Up a HyperTerminal Connection

Before continuing, make sure you have your modem connected to, or installed in, your computer properly, by following instructions in the modem's manual. Incorrect modem installation (most often caused by improper switch settings) is a frequent cause of communications problems. Then, before doing anything else, find the telephone number your modem must dial to connect to the information service, BBS, or computer you're trying to reach. Be sure you have the number for modem communications; in printed material it may be labeled the *modem* or *data* number. *Voice* or *fax* numbers won't work.

While you're looking for the number, see if you can locate any details on the communications setting in force at the computer you want to connect to. Your system must be set up to match, as detailed under "Setting Dialing Properties" later in this chapter.

To access HyperTerminal, begin from the Start menu and choose Programs ➤ Accessories ➤ Communications ➤ HyperTerminal. This will start the HyperTerminal program and display a Wizard for creating a new connection. It's described in the following section.

Once a specific connection has been set up, you'll be able to open it later to reestablish it.

 NOTE To reopen a saved HyperTerminal connection, start HyperTerminal and click Cancel to close the Wizard; then use the File ➤ Open command to open the saved connection.

Defining a New Connection

When you start HyperTerminal, it asks you to define a new connection by walking you through a series of setup dialog boxes. Here's the first one:

 TIP You can also set up a new connection once you're working with the main Hyper-Terminal window by choosing File ➢ New Connection or by clicking the New button on the toolbar to display the dialog box shown above.

Your first step is to give the new connection a name. Keep it simple—something like *MCI* or *The Chem Lab* will do. Then pick out an appropriate icon for the connection from the scrolling list and click OK to go on.

Next, you must supply the phone number your modem should dial to make the connection. HyperTerminal displays the Connect To dialog box, shown here:

Type in the phone number for the new connection. You have your choice of styles. If the phone number for the new connection is local, that's the only number you need to type—Windows has already entered your settings for the country code and area code based on your current Telephony settings. If you're dialing out of the area or out of country, use the first two boxes to set the correct country and area code. And if you have more than one modem connected to your computer, choose the one you want to use for this connection from the list at the bottom of the dialog box.

Click OK when all the settings are correct.

Setting Dialing Properties

Once you've set the phone number, HyperTerminal assumes you want to dial it, and it presents you with the following dialog box:

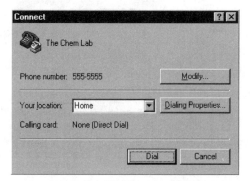

Click Dial to make the connection. See the following section for more information about managing a connection.

Before dialing, make sure the location is correct in the Your Location box. Here, you should select the telephony location. (You learned to set these up earlier in this chapter.) To change any of these properties for the default location or to set up new locations from scratch, click Dialing Properties. This reopens the Dialing Properties dialog box, the same as if you had double-clicked Telephony in the Control Panel.

If you need to adjust the phone number to be dialed (for example, to add a 1 or an area code in front of it), click the Modify button before clicking Dial. This opens the properties for the connection, as shown in Figure 19.7. You can choose a country/region and an area code, and you can choose whether or not to include those codes when dialing. You can also specify whether HyperTerminal should automatically redial on a busy signal, and select a modem to use if you have more than one modem installed. Click OK to return to the Connect box when ready.

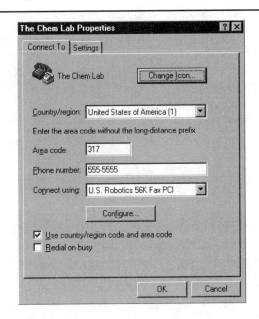

FIGURE 19.7
*Adjust the properties
for this connection if
desired. These settings
affect only this
connection.*

 NOTE For even more settings, click the Settings tab. The settings there are rather specialized, however, and you will probably never need them.

Making Connections

Assuming you've completed all the setup steps properly, the process of actually making a connection couldn't be simpler. All you do is click the Dial button in the Connect dialog box.

 NOTE By the way, if HyperTerminal has displayed the Dial dialog box but you don't want
to make the connection at this time, just click Cancel to go to the main HyperTerminal window. You can reopen the Dial dialog box later by choosing Call ➤ Connect.

When you click the Dial button, HyperTerminal immediately starts the dialing process. You'll see the Connect message window, informing you of the progress of the call.

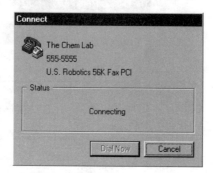

 TIP If you want to stop the dialing process, click Cancel in the Connect window.

Behind the scenes, HyperTerminal begins by sending a series of commands to the modem to prepare it for dialing. These are determined by the settings you've chosen, as detailed in the previous section.

Then HyperTerminal sends the command to dial the number. At this point, if your modem's speaker is on, you'll hear the telephone being dialed. When the phone on the other end is answered, you may hear some high-pitched tones indicating that the modems are "talking" to each other.

If the connection is successful, the message *Connected* will appear briefly in the Status section of the Connect window and you'll hear three quick beeps. The Connect window will then disappear. If you have the status bar visible, you'll see the message *Connected* at its far left followed by a time indicator showing how long your computer has been connected to the remote machine in hours, minutes, and seconds.

At this point, if both modems are set up properly, and depending on how the other computer is programmed, you're likely to see messages from the connection on your screen. From now on, everything you type on the keyboard will be sent to the other computer. You can respond to these messages—or initiate messages of your own—by simply typing whatever you like. And you're now ready to transfer files from disk in either direction.

Sending and Receiving Data

Once you've made a successful connection, you can begin to transfer data between the two computers. What you do now depends entirely on what the other computer expects from you. If you're calling an information service, a BBS, or a mainframe computer, you'll typically have to sign on to the remote system by typing your name and possibly a password. If you're calling a friend's or associate's computer, you can just begin typing whatever you want to say. In any case, once the initial connection is made, there are several ways that you can begin to transfer data between the two computers. The next several sections describe these techniques and how to use them.

Communicating in Interactive Mode

The simplest way to communicate information is directly from your keyboard. As mentioned earlier, once you're connected to the other computer, everything you type is automatically sent to the other end of the connection. Likewise, characters typed at the other computer will be sent to your computer, showing up on your screen. Sending and receiving data this way is called working in *interactive* or *terminal* mode. Communication sessions often begin in terminal mode, with each person typing to the other's screen.

Terminal mode is often used, too, when connecting to many of the information services and e-mail services that are interactive in nature. With these, you type certain commands to the host computer, and it responds by sending you some data. As information comes over the line to your computer, it will appear on the screen, as shown in Figure 19.8. As you type, your text will appear on the screen as well.

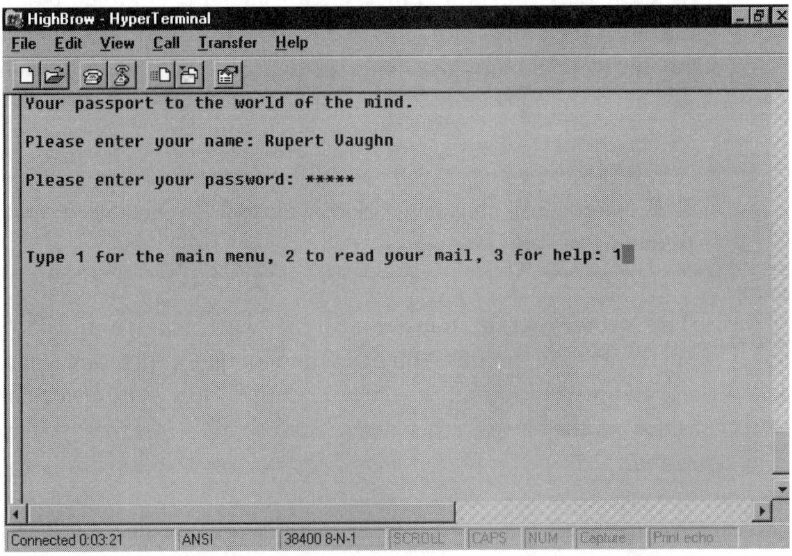

FIGURE 19.8
A typical interactive session. Notice that the user entered the number 1 at the bottom of the screen in response to the prompt from the sender.

There will be times when you'll want to save data you see on your screen while you're working in terminal mode so that you can work with it later. You can *capture* incoming text at any time during a communications session with the Receive Text File command on the Transfer menu and save it in a disk file for later reading, printing, or editing. Here is the basic procedure for capturing text:

1. Choose Transfer ➢ Capture Text.

2. A small dialog box appears, asking you to name the file in which you want the captured text stored. Type in the name (you can use the Browse button to select a new directory) but don't press Enter yet.

3. Click OK. The file will be opened. If the status bar is visible, the Capture message becomes highlighted, indicating the capture is in progress.

4. Continue with your session. All incoming text, along with whatever you type, will be captured in the file you chose. When you want to stop capturing text, choose Transfer ➢ Capture Text again to display a new submenu (only available when a capture is currently in progress). Here, choose one of these options:

    • Stop, to close the file.

    • Pause, to temporarily discontinue capturing text while leaving the file open for more. To resume the capture, choose Transfer ➢ Capture Text ➢ Resume.

Sending and Receiving Documents and Other Files

Most of the files stored on your computer's disks do *not* consist of only text. Instead of simple sequences of characters arranged in lines, the typical file—whether it's a document created by your word processing or spreadsheet program or the program itself—contains all sorts of information in encoded form. This information is perfectly understandable by your computer (with the right software), but it usually looks like complete gibberish to you and me. Such files are called *binary* files.

 TIP Most e-mail programs—including Outlook Express—allow you to "attach" binary files to your e-mail. See Chapter 22 for more about e-mail.

That's why you can't transfer most files with HyperTerminal's Capture Text and Send Text File commands. You need the Send File and Receive File commands instead. These commands transfer the entire document just as it is, without trying to interpret it as text. In the bargain, they detect and correct errors that have crept in during the transfer.

 TIP By the way, it's perfectly okay to send and receive text-only files via the Send File and Receive File commands to get the benefits of error correction. The only drawbacks are that you won't see the text on your screen, and the process will take a tad longer.

It's not uncommon for data transmission errors to occur during the transmission process over telephone lines, particularly from noise or static. In response to this, computer scientists have devised numerous error-detection and error-correction schemes to determine whether errors have occurred in transmission and to correct them if possible. These schemes are referred to as *file-transfer protocols* because they also manage other aspects of the file-transfer process. HyperTerminal lets you choose from several of the most popular of these file-transfer protocols with its Receive File and Send File commands. Although each of the file-transfer protocols has its own characteristics, the critical point is that to send or receive a file successfully, you need to use the same protocol as the other computer.

Sending Files

To send a file, follow these steps:

1. Make sure you're online (connected).

2. Make sure the receiving computer is ready to receive the file. How you do this depends on the computer system, BBS, or information service to which you are connected. If you're sending a file to another PC, you may want to type a message in HyperTerminal mode telling the operator of the other computer to do what is necessary to prepare for receiving the file.

3. Choose Transfer ➤ Send File, or click the Send button on the toolbar. A small dialog box appears:

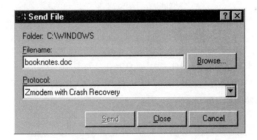

4. Enter the name of the file you want to send (or click Browse, locate and select the file, and click OK to go back to the Send File dialog box). Then choose the error-detection protocol you want (the one in use by the receiving system).

5. Click OK to begin the file transfer.

You'll now see a large window reporting the progress of the transfer, as shown in Figure 19.9. At the top, the name of the file being sent is displayed. Next come several readouts on the error-checking process—these are pretty technical, and you can usually ignore them. If something goes seriously wrong, HyperTerminal will halt the transfer. At that point, you may be able to diagnose the problem by reading the message displayed at LastEvent.

The (slightly) more interesting part of the display is the lower half. Here, Hyper-Terminal shows you graphically and in numbers how quickly the transfer is going. The bar graph at File expands to the right, giving you a quick sense of how much of the file has been sent so far, relative to its total size. Next to the graph, you're shown how much of the file, in numbers, has been sent. Below are counters showing how much time has elapsed since the transfer began, how much time is remaining (assuming all goes well, and if HyperTerminal is able to calculate this), and, in the Throughput area, your current "speed." By clicking the cps/bps button, you can set the display units for throughput speed: either characters per second (cps) or bits per second (bps). Characters per second is actually a measure of the number of bytes (8-bit information units) being transferred each second.

FIGURE 19.9
You'll see a window like this during file transfers.

To cancel a file transfer before it has finished, click the Cancel button at the bottom of the window. If the transfer completes normally, you'll hear a single beep as the window disappears.

 NOTE You can't pause a binary transfer, but you can end it in midstream by clicking Stop or choosing Stop from the Transfer menu.

Let's recap the process of sending binary files: A binary file will arrive just as you sent it, with no modifications (for example, no adding or stripping of line feeds). All types of files, including program files, can be sent and received as binary files. Formatted text as well as program files must be transmitted as binary files, or information will be lost.

Receiving Files

You'll want to use the Receive File command to transfer document and program (non-text) files to your computer from the computer at the other end of the line. The process of receiving such a file is very similar to sending one:

1. After connecting to the other computer, tell the sending computer to send the file and which file-transfer protocol to use in the process. How you do this depends on the computer and program(s) involved. If you're connected to a BBS or information service, you can usually control the process from your computer. If you're connected to another individual's computer, you ask the person at the other end of the line to type in the command to send you the file.

2. Choose Transfer ➢ Receive File, or click the Receive button on the toolbar.

3. The Receive File dialog box appears. Choose the *folder* where you want Hyper-Terminal to store the received file (not the actual filename, which will be set by the other computer). Type in the folder name or use the Browse button to find it. Then select the file-transfer protocol that matches the one used by the other computer. And do all this quickly because the other computer is already trying to send the file. It will wait, but usually not too long.

4. Click OK or press Enter, and the transmission should begin.

Once the transfer is underway, a window that looks and works very similar to the one you see when sending files (Figure 19.9) will appear. See the previous section for details on its use.

 WARNING Depending on the file-transfer protocol you're using, HyperTerminal may not know the size of the file being sent to it. In this case, you won't be able to check to see whether you have enough disk space for the file, and you may run out of disk space while receiving it. This is a real hassle, particularly if you've spent half an hour receiving most of a large file, only to get an error message saying there isn't enough room on your disk for the rest of it. When this happens, HyperTerminal will abort the receiving process. So make sure the disk you choose to store the file on has enough free space on it before you begin the transfer.

Ending a Communications Session

Once you've finished your work (or play) during a session, you should end it by following some simple rules:

1. If you want to save the settings you've made, choose File ➢ Save and name the file.

2. If you are logged on to an information service, e-mail provider, or BBS, follow the system's instructions for signing off. This may be important to free up a

connection for other users or to ensure that the service will cease billing you for connect time.

3. Choose Call ➢ Disconnect.

4. Close HyperTerminal by double-clicking its Control box.

 TIP Despite great strides in the field of communications, mostly due to conveniences spurred by the personal computer market, it is still a bit of a black art. Chances are good that you'll run into some problem or other while transferring files, sending mail, or whatever it is you end up doing with HyperTerminal. The fault will not necessarily lie with HyperTerminal (or you), but much more likely will be the result of improper wiring, faulty modems, noisy telephone lines, incorrect log-on procedures, or incompatible software on the other end of the line. If you're trying to connect to a BBS or information service, don't hesitate to call them (the old-fashioned way) for help. You can also get help from your company's computer expert, your computer store, or an experienced friend.

CHAPTER **20**

Connecting to the Internet

FEATURING:

Before you can use Internet Explorer (or any other Internet application program), you must connect your own computer to the Internet. In this chapter, you will find information about choosing an Internet Service Provider (ISP); making the connection through a modem, a local area network (LAN), or other link; and installing and configuring your system for a TCP/IP connection.

One of the most fascinating features in Windows Me is Internet Connection Sharing (ICS). This allows networked computers to share a single-modem connection to the Internet. Although most business network users have been doing this with proxy-server software for quite a while, ICS makes it that much easier, especially for the growing number of home networks.

If you already have an Internet connection that supports other TCP/IP Internet client programs, you may be able to use it with Internet Explorer, Outlook Express, Net-Meeting, and the other Internet tools discussed in this book. If that's the case, you can skip this chapter. You can also skip this chapter if you are a current user of America Online or CompuServe, since both of these online services provide their own software, including a dial-up connection manager, Web browser, and e-mail program.

 NOTE TCP/IP is the networking software (protocol) established during the 1970s that allows many different kinds of computers to interact with one another regardless of type and operating system. Introduced in 1978 for use on the ARPAnet (the predecessor of the Internet), TCP/IP remains the most widely used network protocol software today, and it forms the basis of the Internet. It is not owned by any one agency or company.

What Kind of Connection?

Choosing a way to connect your computer to the Internet is a trade-off between performance and cost; more money gets you a faster link between your own system and the backbone. (As in the human body, the Internet's backbone forms the core high-speed communications channel on which the Internet is built.) While the difference between file transfers through a modem and a high-speed link can be dramatic, the cost of improved performance may not always be justified. For most home users and many small businesses, a dial-up telephone line and a 56Kbps (kilobits per second) modem is still the most cost-effective choice.

If it's available in your area, you might want to consider ISDN (Integrated Services Digital Network) as an alternative to conventional POTS (Plain Old Telephone Service) lines. ISDN is more expensive and complicated to install and configure, but once it's in place, it offers a substantially faster Internet connection. Your ISP can tell you if ISDN service is available and explain how to order the lines and obtain the necessary interface equipment.

 TIP Microsoft offers an easy means for establishing an ISDN hookup. Go to www.microsoft.com/ and look around or search the site for "Get ISDN." You should find a page with an online Wizard that will find the nearest ISDN provider and let you order service. I used this approach to get my ISDN service, and it was pretty painless.

ISDN is not nearly as popular as it used to be, however, due to the increasing availability of two other technologies: DSL and cable Internet. DSL stands for digital subscriber line, and it's a technology for sending and receiving a high-speed digital Internet signal over an unused portion of a conventional phone line. Cable Internet access uses the same cable as your cable TV signal to send and receive Internet data. There is also satellite Internet connectivity, which works off the same kind of personal satellite dish as satellite television. It is a one-way Internet path only—you can download at very high speeds, but you must also have a regular modem for uploads, which occur at a maximum of 56Kbps.

 NOTE DSL connections are individualized, just like private phone lines, so your neighbor's DSL Internet usage will not affect your own. With cable modems, on the other hand, neighbors share a pipeline to the main office, so if enough of your neighbors get on the Internet at once via cable, you could see a slowdown. However, it is not likely to be as big an issue as the telephone companies (who sell DSL) would like for you to believe.

In a larger business, where many users can share the same link to the Internet, other connection methods—such as dedicated T-1 and T-3 lines—are common. These lines cost rather a lot of money per month ($1,000 or more), but if 500 employees in the company share a single line, the cost per user is actually very reasonable.

If your PC is already connected to a LAN, you should ask your network administrator or help desk about setting up an Internet account; it's likely that there's already some kind of connection in place. If you have just set up a small network in your home or office, you can use ICS to make sharing a connection easier.

What's the best connection type? It depends on your situation. Home users who use the Internet very little should stick with a regular 56Kbps modem. Home users who spend a lot of time on the Internet might find cable the best mix of performance and price. Small business users will probably want DSL because cable modems are typically available only in residential areas. ISDN is more expensive and slower than either cable or DSL, but in some rural areas, it is the only high-speed Internet option available. Satellite Internet access is a last resort for those who have no other high-speed options; it tends to be more expensive and complicated than the other methods.

Table 20.1 lists several types of connections and the speed(s) you can expect from each. The prices are obviously in flux, so make sure to check on them before you decide. Also, don't forget that hardware equipment is needed for all of these solutions. You can buy an analog modem for about $50, but some of the other solutions will cost you hundreds for your hardware or charge you a monthly fee for equipment rental. Some of these solutions, such as satellite hookup, do not include the ISP costs, either. They only supply the hookup to their system, one stop short of the Internet.

TABLE 20.1: POPULAR MEANS FOR CONNECTION TO THE INTERNET

Technology	Speed / Notes	Speed*	Typical cost
Standard 28.8Kbps–56Kbps dial-up service over standard POTS lines	28.8Kbps–33.6Kbps or so. Rarely is 56Kbps achieved due to noise on phone lines.	1x	$20/month + telephone connection charges
ISDN	56Kbps–128Kpbs.	2x–4x	$20–$50/month for your ISP + $50 or so for the ISDN phone line
Satellite	Varies, typically 400Kbps, some as high as 27Mbps.	8x–900x	$20/month + ISP charges of $20 or more
T-3	45Mbps.	1,500x	$16,000/month
T-1	1.54Mbps.	50x	$1,000/month
Frame Relay	Available in 64Kbps increments, up to 1.5Mbps.	Up to 50x	$200–$500/ month, depending on speed
XDSL (includes ADSL, IDSL, SDHL, HDSL, VDSL, and RADSL)	Asymmetrical Digital Subscriber Line (ADSL) can deliver up to 8Mbps over the 750 million existing ordinary "twisted pair" phone connections on earth. Actual speed offerings of these technologies range from 1.5Mbps to as high as 60Mbps on VDSL.	50x–2,000x	$50/month (128Kbps) or $250/month (768Kbps) + ISP service
Cable modem, using existing TV cable systems	10Mbps maximum. In reality, probably about 1.5Mbps with typical number of users. Some systems offer only 500Kbps. Most systems require separate phone line for uplink since they only *receive* data over the cable. Others are bidirectional.	50x	$40/month

* relative to a 28.8 modem (approx)

> **TIP** For a good source of information on high-speed Internet connections and the inside scoop, check this site: `www.teleport.com/~samc/cable1.html`. It's extremely complete.

With that background, let's get down to the job of getting your modem hooked up and maybe even getting you online.

Choosing a Service Provider

As you know, the Internet is the result of connecting many networks to one another. You can connect your own computer to the Internet by obtaining an account on one of those interconnected networks.

Several different kinds of businesses offer Internet connections, including large companies with access points in many cities, smaller local or regional ISPs, and online information services that provide TCP/IP connections to the Internet along with their own proprietary information sources. You can use popular programs, such as Internet Explorer, with a connection through any of these services.

When you order your account, you should request a PPP connection to the Internet. PPP is a standard type of TCP/IP connection that any ISP should be able to supply.

> **NOTE** If you use a cable, DSL, or satellite connection, your choice of ISPs will be limited. For example, with a cable connection, you must use the cable company.

The Information Superhighway version of a New Age gas station, ISPs are popping up all over the country (and all over the world, for that matter). And like long-distance telephone companies, they offer myriad service options. If you're not among the savvy, you may get snowed into using an ISP that doesn't really meet your needs. As with long-distance telephone providers, you'll find that calculating the bottom line isn't that easy. It really depends on what you are looking for. Here are some questions you should ask yourself and any potential ISP:

- Does the ISP provide you with an e-mail account? It should.

- Can you have multiple e-mail accounts (for family members or employees)? If so, how many?

- Does the ISP offer 56Kbps support? If so, which format? It should match your modem.

- Will the ISP let you create your own domain name? For example, I want the e-mail address `bob@cowart.com` rather than something cryptic like `bobcow@ic.netcim.net`. Sometimes creating your own domain name costs extra, but it gives your correspondents an easier address to remember. You can decide if it's worth it.

- Does the ISP provide you with a news account so you can interact with Internet *newsgroups*? It should, and it shouldn't restrict which newsgroups you'll have access to unless you are trying to prevent your kids from seeing "dirty" messages or pictures.

- Do you want your own Web page to be available to other Web surfers? If so, does the ISP provide online storage room for it? How many "hits" per day can it handle, in case your page becomes popular? How much storage do you get in the deal? Do you want the ISP to create the Web page for you?

- What is the charge for connect time? Some ISPs offer unlimited usage per day. Others charge by the hour and/or have a limit on continuous connect time.

- Does the ISP have a local (i.e., free) phone number? If not, calculate the charges. It may be cheaper to use an ISP that charges more per month if there are no phone company toll charges for connecting.

- Does it have many points of presence or a toll-free number you can use to call into when you are on the road?

- Does it have too much user traffic to really provide reasonable service? This has been a major problem with some ISPs, even biggies like AOL. Smaller providers often supply faster connections. Remember that even if you can connect without a busy signal, the weakest link in the system will determine the speed at which you'll get data from the Internet. Often, that weak link is the ISP's internal LAN that connects its in-house computers together, so it's hard to know how efficient the ISP really is. Best to ask someone who's using the service before signing up.

- Is it compatible with the programs you want to use? Can you use Internet Explorer or Netscape Web browsers? Which newsgroups and mail programs are supported?

- Does it have Web access e-mail? If so, then you can check your e-mail when you are on someone else's PC (perhaps while traveling) without having to configure an e-mail program.

 TIP If you have access to the Web, try checking the page www.thelist.com/. You'll learn a lot about comparative pricing and features of today's ISPs, along with links to their pages for opening an account. Another good site is www.boardwatch.com/.

Using a National ISP

The greatest advantage of using a national or international ISP is that you can probably find a local dial-in telephone number in most major cities. If you want to send and receive e-mail or use other Internet services while you travel, this can be extremely important.

The disadvantage of working with a large company is that it may not be able to provide the same kind of personal service that you can get from a smaller, local business. If you must call halfway across the continent and wait 20 minutes on hold for technical support (especially if it's not a toll-free number), you should look for a different ISP.

Many large ISPs can give you free software that automatically configures your computer and sets up a new account. Even if they don't include Internet Explorer in their packages, you should be able to use some version of the program along with the application programs they do supply.

Many local telephone companies and more than a few cable TV companies are also planning to offer Internet access to their subscribers. If it's available in your area, you should be able to obtain information about these services from the business office that handles your telephone or television service. In San Jose, California, for example, a local UHF TV station is using TV broadcasting technology to deliver high-speed Internet service.

Using a Local ISP

The big national and regional services aren't your only choice. In most American cities, smaller local service providers also offer access to the Internet.

If you can find a good local ISP, it might be your best choice. A local company may be more responsive to your particular needs and more willing to help you get through the inevitable configuration problems than a larger national operation. Equally important, reaching the technical support center is more likely to be a local telephone call. Furthermore, in some rural areas, you might find that a local ISP is the only Internet service with a local dial-up number, making it your only option for avoiding long-distance charges while you are online.

But unfortunately, the Internet access business has attracted a tremendous number of entrepreneurs who are in it for the quick dollar—some local ISPs are really terrible. If they don't have enough modems to handle the demand, if they don't have a high-capacity connection to an Internet backbone, or if they don't know how to keep their equipment and servers working properly, you'll get frequent busy signals, slow downloads, dropped lines, and unexpected downtime rather than consistently reliable service. And there's no excuse for unhelpful technical support people or endless time on hold. If a deal seems too good to be true, there's probably a good reason.

To learn about the reputations of local ISPs, ask friends and colleagues who have been using the Internet for a while. If there's a local computer user magazine, look for schedules of user group meetings where you can find people with experience using the local ISPs. If you can't get a recommendation from any of those sources, look back at the previous Tip regarding lists of ISPs on the Web (assuming you already have Web access, which I realize is sort of a catch-22).

 TIP No matter which service you choose, wait a month or two before you print your e-mail address on business cards and letterhead. If the first ISP you try doesn't give you the service you expect, take your business someplace else.

Connecting through an Online Service

If you've decided to go with an online service rather than an ISP, you'll find signup software for some of the major services built into Windows Me. Most online services offer Internet access, as well as their own content, and are an excellent choice for beginners.

The four online services offered are America Online, AT&T WorldNet, Earthlink Internet, and Prodigy Internet. Of these, only America Online is a true "online service" with its own proprietary Web browser and software. The other three are simply national Internet providers. All are easy to sign up with through the Online Services folder on your Desktop and on your Start menu.

If you decide to select one of the online service providers listed in this folder, just double-click the icon for that online service provider to begin setting up your computer for access with that provider. The following steps describe how:

1. Clear the Desktop by clicking the Desktop icon in the Quick Launch bar at the bottom of the screen or by any other method.

2. Look for a folder called Online Services and open it.

3. Double-click the icon of the service you want to check out. A splash screen about the product will appear, or you'll be prompted to insert your Windows CD-ROM or take some other action, depending on the service. You should ensure your modem is on and connected to the telephone line, since a phone call will be made to sign you up. You'll need a credit card number, too, so get that ready.

4. Once signed up, you'll see instructions about what your services will include, how to proceed, and how to connect with the Internet.

 WARNING If you are reading this a year or so after Windows Me came out, there may be versions of America Online available that are newer than the one included in Windows Me. You can use the included version and then download an update after you get connected, but it can be a rather lengthy download. You might prefer instead to use an America Online startup CD you get in the mail or a magazine if it has a newer version on it.

Signing Up for Service

Windows Me includes an Internet Connection Wizard (ICW) that can automate the process of choosing and signing up for an ISP. There are two ways to run it: You can ask ICW for a list of providers available and choose from that list, or you can manually enter the settings for an ISP that isn't on the list. The ISPs on the list are not necessarily the only ones available, nor even the best; they're simply the ones that have paid a fee to Microsoft to appear there.

TIP Have your Windows Me Setup CD handy. The Wizard may need to install some Windows Me files in order to set up your Internet connection.

Signing Up for a Microsoft-Recommended ISP

If you don't have a clue which provider you want and having an easy, automated signup process is important to you, go with one of the providers on the Microsoft-approved list by following these steps:

1. Click Start ➢ Programs ➢ Accessories ➢ Communications ➢ Internet Connection Wizard.

2. Choose the top option, I Want to Sign Up for a New Internet Account (see Figure 20.1). Then click Next.

FIGURE 20.1
*The Internet
Connection Wizard first
asks whether you want
to set up a new account
or use an existing one.*

The Wizard dials in to the Microsoft Referral Service using your modem and retrieves a list of ISPs. Then it hangs up and displays them.

 NOTE If there is more than one phone number available in your area for the Microsoft Referral Service, a list of them appears. You must then choose the one to dial and click Next. If only one number is found, the Wizard simply dials it without prompting.

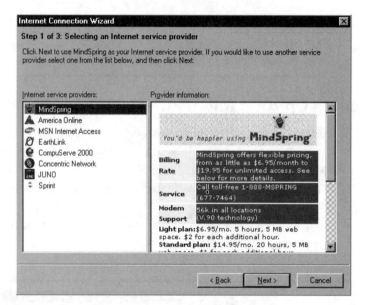

3. Browse through the various ISPs and their offerings. When you find the one you want, select it and click Next.

4. Enter your contact information in the boxes provided and click Next.

5. The remaining steps vary somewhat with the provider chosen. Continue working through the Wizard to get your new account.

Setting Up an Unlisted or Existing ISP

If you want to use an ISP that isn't listed on Microsoft's list or if you already have an ISP account that you want to use on your PC, you can use the Internet Connection Wizard to set it up manually. This isn't nearly as difficult as it sounds! Anyone should be able to do it.

If you want to sign up for a local ISP, find its phone number (voice) and sign up for an account over the telephone. The ISP will send you an information packet in the mail that includes your username and password, the names of the mail servers to use, the phone number your modem should dial, and any other information needed to connect. You'll need to have that information in front of you when you set up the connection with ICW. The same goes for an existing account you are setting up on the PC.

 NOTE If you are using a cable, satellite, or DSL connection, a professional installer probably came to your home and set up everything already, or the equipment came with detailed instructions. Cable, satellite, and DSL connections all work from a network card, and Windows treats them as if you were connecting through a network rather than a modem.

Before running ICW to set up your Internet connection manually, make sure you have the following information:

- A phone number to use for your Internet connection
- Your username (might also be called user ID or login name)
- A dial-up password

Additionally, if your account includes mail service, you must obtain the following information:

- Your e-mail address
- Incoming mail server type (POP3, IMAP, or HTTP) and address
- Outgoing mail server (SMTP) address
- Mail account login name and password

When you've got all that assembled, do the following:

1. Click Start ➣ Programs ➣ Accessories ➣ Communications ➣ Internet Connection Wizard.

2. In the Internet Connection Wizard's initial dialog box (refer back to Figure 20.1), choose the bottom option, I Want to Set Up My Internet Connection Manually. Then click Next.

3. Choose I Connect through a Phone Line and a Modem, and then click Next.

 NOTE If you connect through cable, satellite, or DSL, you would answer I Connect through a Local Area Network (LAN) in step 3, and then the rest of the steps in the process would be different for you. For such connections, certain network settings must be adjusted from Windows's default; contact your ISP to help you with that.

4. Enter the telephone number for your ISP. If you don't have to dial the area code and 1, deselect the Dial Using the Area Code and Country Code check box.

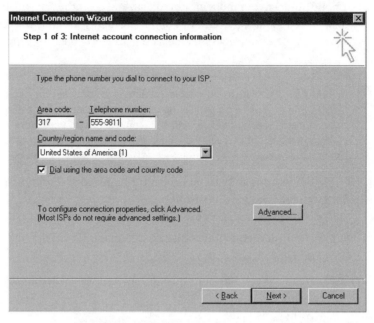

5. If your ISP gave you a specific IP address or DNS address to use, click the Advanced button and enter it on the Addresses tab of the Advanced Connection Properties box; then click OK to return. Most ISPs do not require this.

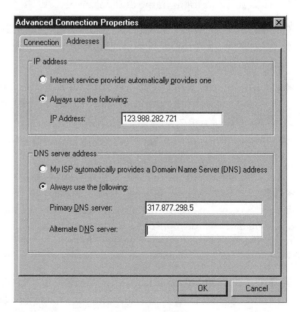

6. Click Next to move on.

7. Enter your username and password in the boxes provided, and click Next.

8. Enter a name for the connection in the Connection Name box. This is a "friendly" name that will appear on lists; it does not have to be the exact name of the provider. Then click Next.

9. Next you are prompted to set up an Internet mail account. Click Yes and then Next.

10. If Windows finds an existing mail account, you're prompted to choose it or set up a new one. Click Create a New Internet Account, and then click Next.

11. Enter your display name in the Display Name box. This is the name that will appear in recipients' inboxes when you send them a message. Then click Next.

12. Enter your e-mail address for sending and receiving messages. Then click Next.

13. Choose the type of mail server you are using from the My Incoming Mail Server Is A drop-down list. The most common type is POP3.

14. Enter your incoming and outgoing mail servers in the boxes provided. Depending on your ISP, these might be two different names or you might enter the same name for both. Then click Next.

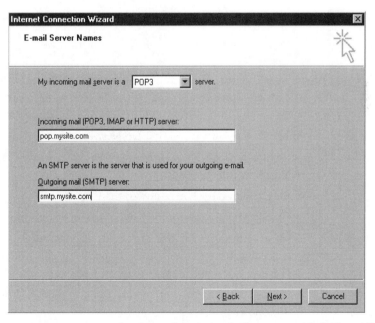

15. Enter your username and password again in the boxes provided. Then click Next.

NOTE Why do you have to enter your username and password again? In step 7, you entered the username and password for establishing the Internet connection; here you're entering them for sending and receiving mail. They are separate because some people use a different service for their mail than they do for their Internet connection.

16. Click Finish. You're done! Windows attempts to connect to your ISP now, using the settings you provided.

By going through the ICW to set up your new account, you accomplished several important things behind the scenes. You installed dial-up networking in Windows if it was not installed already, and you installed TCP/IP as a network protocol. Plus, you created a new dial-up networking connection, which now appears in the Dial-Up Networking folder (Start ➤ Settings ➤ Dial-Up Networking).

If you need to create another dial-up networking connection to the Internet later, such as for another ISP, you can rerun the Internet Connection Wizard, or you can use the Make New Connection Wizard in the Dial-Up Networking folder to create a new connection.

Modifying the Settings for an Internet Connection

If you need to modify the settings for the connection you just created, you can do so from the Dial-Up Networking folder. This might happen, for example, if you are having problems with your connection and your ISP's technical support personnel have suggested that you make certain changes to the connection properties.

Follow these steps to modify a dial-up networking connection:

1. Choose Start ➤ Settings ➤ Dial-Up Networking.

2. Right-click the icon for your connection and choose Properties. The Properties box for the connection appears.

3. On the General tab, change any of the following:

• Change the phone number to dial in the Telephone Number box.

• Select or deselect the Use Area Code and Dialing Properties check box. Generally speaking, leave this off for a local call and turn it on for a long-distance call requiring you to dial 1 first.

• Choose a different modem for the connection from the Connect Using drop-down list.

• Click the Configure button to open the properties for the selected modem and modify them if needed. Click OK when finished to return.

4. On the Networking tab, change any of the following:

- Make sure PPP is chosen on the Type of Dial-Up Server drop-down list unless told otherwise by your ISP. Almost all dial-up Internet connections are PPP.

- Make sure the Enable Software Compression check box is marked.

- Make sure the TCP/IP check box is marked. The other two check boxes, Net-BEUI and IPX/SPX Compatible, can be safely deselected.

- If you need to specify an IP or DNS address to use, or change or remove specific addresses you entered earlier, click the TCP/IP Settings button and enter them. Click OK when finished to return.

5. On the Security tab, change any of the following:

- Modify your username and password if needed.

- Mark the Connect Automatically check box if you want Windows to establish the Internet connection without prompting whenever you open a program that requires access.

- If the Log On to Network check box is marked and you are experiencing delays in connecting, deselect it.

6. On the Dialing tab, change any of the following:

- Select or deselect the This Is the Default Internet Connection check box.

- Change the Retry settings if desired. These determine how many times Windows will redial if the line is busy.

- Select or deselect Enable Idle Disconnect. This automatically disconnects your connection if you do not use it for a specified number of minutes. If you pay by the hour for service, this feature can save you a large bill if you forget and leave the connection running overnight.

7. Click OK to save your changes.

Changing the Default Connection

You saw in the preceding steps that you could set a connection as the default on the Dialing tab. But there's an easier way to choose which connection is your default. Here's how:

1. Open the Control Panel and then double-click Internet Options.

 TIP An alternative to step 1: From Internet Explorer, choose Tools ➤ Internet Options.

2. Click the Connections tab (Figure 20.2).

FIGURE 20.2
You can choose which
connection should be
the default from here.

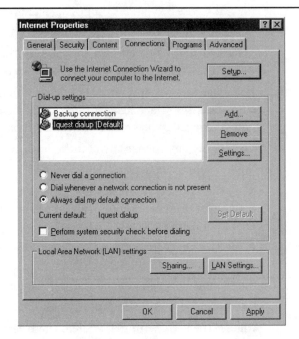

3. In the list of dial-up connections, choose the one that you want as the default and click Set Default.

4. Click OK to close the dialog box.

Telling Internet Programs *Not* to Dial the Phone!

Notice in Figure 20.2 that you can choose to connect via the local area network rather than by a modem. This is intended for workstations connected to a local area network running the TCP/IP protocol and which have a connection to the Internet via a network server or cable or DSL service. But you can use this setting to your advantage, even if you just have a lowly stand-alone computer with a dial-up modem.

Continued ▶

Here's why: It can be annoying when you open your mail program or IE or Netscape and suddenly the phone is being dialed by Windows in hopes of making life easy for you by connecting automatically to the Internet to carry out your wishes. Maybe you're on the phone already, talking to someone, and don't want your modem blasting into your ear. Or you want to ensure that if you're not home but you've left your computer on, your e-mail program doesn't cause Windows to dial the phone and stay online accidentally, racking up connect-time charges.

If you choose Never Dial a Connection in the dialog box in Figure 20.2, running a Web browser or e-mail program will not automatically connect you. You must make your connection to the Internet manually, by double-clicking the icon for your Dial-Up Networking connection from the Dial-Up Networking folder. (You can place a shortcut for it on your Desktop or in the Quick Launch toolbar to make it more convenient.)

This arrangement can give you much more flexibility. For example, when I want to connect to the Internet, I double-click the dial-up networking icon for my ISP. Sometimes I want a fast connection, so I dial up with my ISDN connection. Other times I want to be on all day with minimal cost, so I use my analog Netcom connection ($19.95/month unlimited connect time). The programs I'm using don't know how the connection was made. All they know is that the TCP/IP connection to the Internet is active.

Sharing Your Internet Connection

Personal computers in the home are nothing new. The relatively mature PC market—combined with remarkable price drops on new computers in recent years—means that many homes now have multiple PCs. These multi-PC owners are now seeking to create their own networks to connect all those computers together. The online news source CNET (www.cnet.com) projects that the home networking market will grow from an expected $600 million in 2000 to $5.7 billion by 2004.

Microsoft is doing its best to keep pace with the growing home network market, and Windows Me includes a number of useful tools to make networking worthwhile. Perhaps the most interesting new feature is ICS, which allows computers on your home network to share a single Internet connection. (Actually it existed in Windows 98 SE, too.) This means that two or more computers can access the online world using only a single phone line and modem.

Admittedly, this kind of sharing is nothing new. Networked computers have been able to share Internet access over the network for years using third-party, proxy-server software. The proxy server is usually set up on the network server, and workstations go online through that central connection. By incorporating ICS into Windows Me, Microsoft makes the whole process far simpler.

WARNING ICS can put a real strain on your modem connection, especially if more than one computer is trying to access the Internet simultaneously. As a general rule, assume that each Internet user will require 28.8Kbps of bandwidth. Thus, if you have two computers sharing the connection, it should be capable of 56Kbps transfer rates. With three or more computers on ICS, your best bet is to upgrade to an ISDN, cable, or DSL connection. Otherwise, you may find that even relatively simple actions like downloading e-mail or viewing a Web page is maddeningly slow, if not impossible.

Setting Up Internet Connection Sharing (ICS)

Windows 98 Second Edition came with an Internet Connection Sharing Wizard that you could install and run to set up Internet Connection Sharing on an existing peer-to-peer network. That was great, but you had to have the network set up already.

Windows Me goes one better by providing a comprehensive Home Networking Wizard that not only configures Internet Connection Sharing, but also sets up the home network itself. You'll learn all about the Home Networking Wizard in Part V of the book, "Networking," but for now let's assume you already have your network set up (perhaps it was in place before you upgraded to Windows Me?) and you just want to install the ICS functionality.

First, decide which computer will be used to facilitate the Internet connection. This will be called your Connection Sharing computer. It's the one to which the modem or other Internet access is directly connected. Make sure that the Internet connection on that PC is up and running.

There are two different ways you can install ICS. You can do it from the Home Networking Wizard; but since Part V covers that pretty thoroughly, let's take a look at the other method here, which is to install ICS from Add/Remove Programs in the Control Panel.

Take the following steps to do so:

1. Run the Control Panel and open the Add/Remove Programs applet.

2. Click the Windows Setup tab to bring it to the front.

3. Click Communications on the list, and then click Details.

4. Place a check mark next to Internet Connection Sharing. (If there is already a check mark there, click Cancel and go on to the next section, "Configuring Other Computers in Your Network.")

5. Click OK twice.

6. If prompted, insert the Windows CD in your drive and click OK. Then wait for the Home Networking Wizard to run.

7. Click Next to begin.

8. Choose Yes, This Computer Uses the Following. Then choose A Direct Connection to My ISP Using the Following Device.

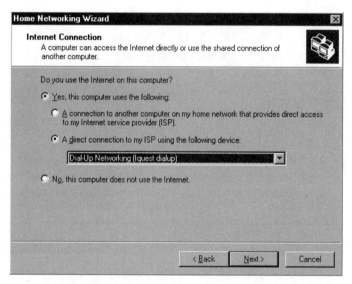

9. Open the drop-down list and choose your Internet connection. It's a dial-up networking connection if you use a modem; it's a network card if you use cable or DSL. Then click Next.

10. You're asked whether you want to share your connection; choose Yes.

11. Open the drop-down list and select the network card to use for the sharing. Then click Next.

12. You are prompted to create a setup disk. If you have PCs on your network that do not use Windows Me, choose Yes. Otherwise choose No and skip to step 15.

13. When prompted, place a blank disk (or one that contains nothing you want to keep) in your floppy drive and click OK.

14. When prompted, remove the disk and click OK.

15. Click Finish.

16. When prompted to restart, click Yes.

17. After restarting, a box announces that Home Networking is set up. Click OK.

Configuring Other Computers in Your Network

Now that your Connection Sharing computer is configured, you need to set up the other computers on your network to utilize the shared connection. Here's how:

1. Do one of the following:

    • If the other PC has Windows Me installed, choose Start ➢ Programs ➢ Accessories ➢ Communication ➢ Home Networking Wizard.

    • If the other PC has Windows 95 or 98, insert the disk you created in the previous steps. Display its contents in My Computer and double-click Setup.exe.

 WARNING The setup disk won't work with Windows NT/2000. But these PCs should work automatically with the connection without special setup, because NT is a more network-aware operating system. If the Internet connection does not work automatically there, run the ICW on that machine and specify that you want to connect to the Internet via a LAN.

---

2. At the opening screen of the Home Networking Wizard, click Next.

3. When asked about Internet connection, choose Yes, This Computer Uses the Following.

4. Choose the option A Connection to Another Computer on My Home Network That Provides Direct Access to My Internet Service Provider (ISP).

5. Click Next.

6. Keep clicking Next to move through the rest of the Wizard, accepting the defaults, until you see a Finish button.

7. Click Finish.

8. If prompted to restart, choose Yes.

The Home Networking Wizard changes the connection setting in your browser so that it looks for an Internet connection over the LAN instead of a dial-up. If the client computer has Internet Explorer 5 or higher, you can view this change by opening the Control Panel and launching the Internet Options applet. On the Connections tab, you will see that Never Dial a Connection has been selected, as shown in Figure 20.3. This is important to note, especially if the client is a computer you plan to remove from the network periodically (such as a laptop). In this case, I recommend you choose Dial Whenever a Network Connection Is Not Present instead.

FIGURE 20.3
*If the client computer
is a laptop or will
be removed from the
network periodically,
consider changing
the settings in this
dialog box.*

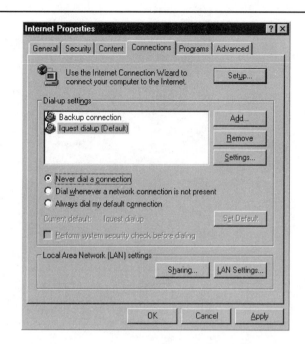

Setting Internet Connection Sharing Properties

Notice on the Connections tab shown in Figure 20.3 that there is a Sharing button.
This wasn't there before you installed Internet Connection Sharing. You can click it to
open a Properties box for Internet Connection Sharing, as seen in Figure 20.4.

FIGURE 20.4

Adjust the properties for Internet Connection Sharing here.

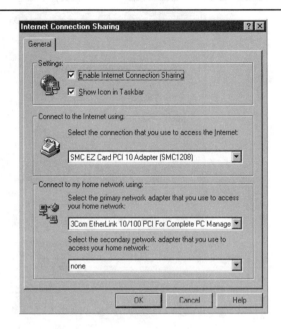

Here's a rundown of the features in this dialog box:

Enable Internet Connection Sharing   If you ever need to temporarily stop sharing your Internet connection, deselect this check box. You might find, for example, that sharing your connection slows down your PC's operation in performing other tasks, so you might disable it while you complete an important, urgent project.

Show Icon in Taskbar   This turns on/off the Internet Connection Sharing icon in the System Tray. When the icon is present there, you can right-click it and choose Options for quick access to this Properties box. You can also right-click it and choose Disable Internet Connection Sharing for quick disabling/enabling.

Connect to the Internet Using   This drop-down list lets you choose a different Internet connection to share. In Figure 20.4, a network adapter is listed because the connection being shared is a cable connection. If you share a dial-up connection, it will be listed here instead.

Connect to My Home Network Using   This drop-down list lets you choose a different network interface card (NIC) in your PC to connect to the PCs that share your Internet connection. Most people will never need to change this.

Now that your Internet connection is up and running, you're ready to do something useful with it! The next chapter, "Browsing the World Wide Web with Internet Explorer 5.5," discusses Web browsing with Internet Explorer, and Chapter 22, "Communicating with Outlook Express News and Mail," covers e-mail and newsgroups.

CHAPTER 21

Browsing the World Wide Web with Internet Explorer 5.5

FEATURING:

Internet Explorer is your window not only to your own computer and network, but also to the World Wide Web and all you'll find there. Although it's really "just a browser," you'll see in this chapter that Internet Explorer does a lot more than simply display pages from the Web. In fact, you'll find that Internet Explorer is now an integral part of Windows, just as the worldwide network called the Internet is now an integral part of our lives.

Inside Internet Explorer

You'll find that Internet Explorer has many similarities to other Windows programs you have used, especially those in Microsoft Office (Word, Excel, Access, and so on). The primary difference between Internet Explorer and other programs is that you use it for viewing files, not editing and saving them. Let's begin by seeing how you can start Internet Explorer.

Starting Internet Explorer

Like almost all Windows programs, Internet Explorer can be started in many ways. You can also run more than one copy of the program at a time, which allows you to view the pages from multiple Web sites or different sections of the same page.

To start Internet Explorer at any time, simply choose it from the Windows Start menu. In a standard installation, choose Start ➤ Programs ➤ Internet Explorer. The program will start and open its *start page*, which is the page Internet Explorer displays first whenever you start it in this way.

 NOTE As with so many other Windows programs, Internet Explorer can be launched in several different ways. Perhaps the easiest is to click the Internet Explorer icon on the Quick Launch toolbar or on the Windows Desktop.

 If the start page is available on a local or networked drive on your computer or if you are already connected to the Internet, Internet Explorer opens that page immediately and displays it.

If you use a modem to connect to the Internet, however, and the start page resides there but you're not currently connected, Internet Explorer opens your Dial-Up Networking connector to make the connection to the Internet.

Here are some ways you can start Internet Explorer:

- Open an HTML file (one with an .htm or .html filename extension) in Windows Explorer, and that file will be opened in Internet Explorer (assuming that Internet Explorer is the default browser on your computer).

- Open a GIF or JPEG image file, which are associated with Internet Explorer, unless you have installed another program that takes those associations.

- While in another program, click (activate) a hyperlink that targets an HTML file to open that file in Internet Explorer. For example, while reading an e-mail message you have received in Outlook Express (as shown below), click a hyperlink in the message that targets a Web site, and that site will be opened in Internet Explorer.

Subject: Some news about Internet Explorer

Take a look at http://www.microsoft.com/ie/ if you'd like to check out the latest on Internet Explorer.

Making Internet Explorer Your Default Browser

If you have installed another browser since installing Internet Explorer, Internet Explorer may not be set as your default browser, and that other browser will be called upon to open any Web pages you request. If you want to make Internet Explorer your default browser and keep it that way, here's how to do it.

In Internet Explorer, choose Tools ➤ Internet Options. On the Programs tab, you'll find an option that reads "Internet Explorer should check to see whether it is the default browser." Select this option and close the Internet Options dialog box.

Now whenever you start Internet Explorer, it will check to see if it is still the default browser. If it finds that it isn't, it will ask if you want it to become the new default browser. If you choose Yes, it will change the Windows settings to make it the default. Now when you open an HTML file—for example, by clicking a hyperlink in a Word document that targets a Web page—Internet Explorer will be the program that opens it. You'll also get the "e" icon on your Desktop for starting Internet Explorer with a double-click.

If you later install another browser that makes itself the default, the next time you start Internet Explorer, it will check to see if it is the default and prompt you accordingly.

To close Internet Explorer, choose File ➢ Close as you would in many other programs. Unlike a word processor or spreadsheet program, when you have been viewing sites on the Web in Internet Explorer, there are normally no files to save before exiting the program.

 NOTE When you started Internet Explorer, it may have caused Dial-Up Networking to make the Internet connection. In that case, when you later exit Internet Explorer, you should be asked if you want to disconnect from the Internet. You can choose to stay connected if you want to work in other Internet-related programs, but don't forget to disconnect later by double-clicking the Dial-Up Networking icon in the System Tray of the Windows Taskbar. Then click the Disconnect button in the dialog box.

The Components of Internet Explorer

Now we'll look at the features and tools that make up Internet Explorer. Figure 21.1 shows Internet Explorer while displaying a Web page. As you can see, the Internet Explorer window contains many of the usual Windows components.

FIGURE 21.1

The Internet Explorer program window contains many components that are common to other windows.

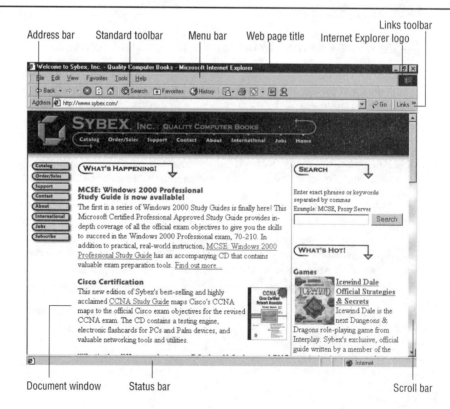

A company or an Internet service provider (ISP) can customize Internet Explorer to make it look and act as though it were its own browser and then distribute it to employees or customers. So if your ISP or your employer gives you a copy of Internet Explorer, it may not look exactly like the one shown in Figure 21.1.

When you want to show as much of the Web page as possible, try the View ➢ Full Screen command, or press F11 on your keyboard. Internet Explorer will be maximized to occupy the entire screen; it will lose its title bar, status bar, two of its toolbars, and even its menu bar. (You can right-click a toolbar and choose Menu Bar to display it again, or press F11 again to toggle back to the standard view.) You can switch back to the normal view by choosing the Full Screen command again. The following list gives the parts of Internet Explorer that are labeled in Figure 21.1:

Web page title   At the top of the window is the usual title bar. It displays either the title of the Web page you are viewing or the document's filename if it is not a Web page. On the right side of the title bar are the Minimize, Maximize/Restore, and Close buttons; on the left side is the System menu.

Menu bar   Beneath the title is the menu bar, which contains almost all the commands you'll need in Internet Explorer. Keyboard shortcuts are shown next to those commands that have them. For example, you can use the shortcut Ctrl+O instead of choosing the File ➢ Open command. The Internet Explorer logo to the right of the menu bar is animated when the program is accessing data.

Toolbars   By default, the toolbars appear beneath the menu bar and contain buttons and other tools that help you navigate the Web or the files and other resources on your computer. The three toolbars are Standard, Links, and Address (refer to Figure 21.1).

Document window   Beneath the menu and toolbars is the main document window, which displays a document such as a Web page, an image, or the files on your computer's disk. If Internet Explorer's program window, which encompasses everything you see in Figure 21.1, is smaller than full screen, you can resize it by dragging any of its corners or sides. The paragraphs in a Web page generally adjust their width to the size of the window.

 TIP   You cannot display multiple document windows in Internet Explorer. Instead, you can view multiple documents by opening multiple instances of Internet Explorer (choose File ➢ New ➢ Window). Each instance of the program is independent of the others.

Scroll bars   The horizontal and vertical scroll bars allow you to scroll the document window over other parts of a document that are otherwise too large to be displayed within the window.

PART

IV

Communication and
Using the Internet

Status bar   At the bottom of the Internet Explorer window is the status bar. It displays helpful information about the current state of Internet Explorer, so keep an eye on it. For example, when you are selecting a command from the menu bar, a description appears on the status bar. When you point to a hyperlink on the page (either text or an image), the mouse pointer changes to a hand, and the target URL (Uniform Resource Locator) of the hyperlink is displayed on the status bar. When you click a hyperlink to open another page, the status bar indicates what is happening with a progression of messages. Icons that appear on the right side of the status bar give you a status report at a glance. For example, you'll see an icon of a padlock when you have made a secure connection to a Web site.

 TIP   You can use the Toolbars and Status Bar commands on the View menu to toggle on or off the display of the toolbars and status bar.

Explorer bar   When you click the Search, Favorites, or History button on the toolbar (or choose one of those commands from the View ➤ Explorer Bar menu), the Explorer bar will appear as a separate pane on the left side of the window. This highly useful feature displays the contents for the button you clicked, such as the search options shown in Figure 21.2. This allows you to make choices in the Explorer bar on the left, such as clicking a link, and have the results appear in the pane on the right. To close the Explorer bar, repeat the command you used to open it, or choose another Explorer bar.

FIGURE 21.2

*When you click the
Search, Favorites, or
History button on the
toolbar, the Explorer
bar opens as a separate
pane on the left side of
the window, where you
can make choices and
see the results appear
in the right pane.*

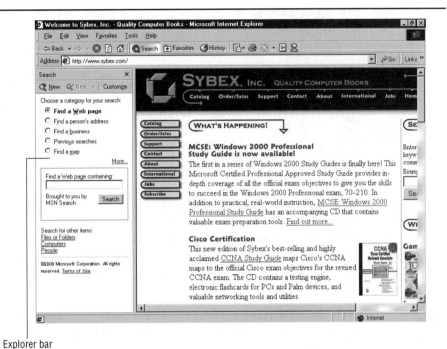

Explorer bar

Some Commands You'll Use Frequently

Here's a short list of the Internet Explorer commands that you might use on a regular basis:

File ➤ Open Opens an existing file (an HTML file on your hard disk) in the current Internet Explorer window.

File ➤ New ➤ Window Opens an existing file in a new Internet Explorer window, while leaving the first window open. You can switch between open windows in the usual ways, such as by pressing Alt+Tab.

File ➤ Save As Lets you save the current document to disk as an HTML file.

File ➤ Properties Displays the Properties dialog box for the current document.

File ➤ Work Offline Lets you browse without being online, as data is opened from your Internet Explorer cache on your local disk.

Edit ➤ Cut/Copy/Paste Lets you copy or move selected text or images from Internet Explorer to another program.

TIP Don't forget that you can access some of these commands from the buttons on the Standard toolbar. Also, try right-clicking an object in Internet Explorer—such as selected text, an image, or the page itself—and see what choices are offered on the shortcut menu.

Edit ➤ Find (on this page) Lets you search for text in the current page, just as you can do in a word processor.

View ➤ Stop Cancels the downloading of the current page. You can also click the Stop button on the toolbar or press Esc.

View ➤ Refresh Updates the contents of the current page by downloading it again. You can also use the Refresh button on the toolbar or press F5.

View ➤ Source Displays the HTML source code for the current page in your default text editor, such as Notepad, which is a great way to see the "inner workings" of a page and learn more about HTML, the Hypertext Markup Language.

View ➤ Internet Options Lets you view or change the options for Internet Explorer (the command is called View ➤ Folder Options when you are displaying the contents of your local disk).

Go ➤ Back/Forward Lets you move between the pages you've already displayed. You can also use the left and right arrow buttons on the toolbar for Back and Forward, respectively.

TIP The Back and Forward buttons have drop-down lists associated with them. You can go back or forward several pages at a time by choosing a page from one of these lists.

Favorites Lets you open a site that you have previously saved as a shortcut on the Favorites menu. The Favorites button on the toolbar opens your Favorites list in the Explorer pane; the Favorites menu lets you choose from the list without opening a separate pane.

Favorites ➤ Add to Favorites Lets you add the current URL to this menu and establish a subscription to the site, if you wish.

Favorites ➤ Organize Favorites Opens the Favorites folder so you can rename, revise, delete, or otherwise organize its contents.

Using the Toolbars

The three toolbars in Internet Explorer (Standard, Links, and Address) are quite flexible. You can change the size or position of each one in the trio, or you can choose not to display them at all. In fact, the menu bar is also quite flexible and can be moved below one or more toolbars, or share the same row with them. Here are some common actions you can perform on the toolbars:

- To hide a toolbar, choose View ➤ Toolbars and select one from the menu; to display that toolbar, choose that command again. Or right-click any of the toolbars or the menu bar and select a toolbar from the shortcut menu.

- To show descriptive text below the Standard toolbar buttons and make the buttons larger, choose View ➤ Toolbars ➤ Customize. In the Customize Toolbar dialog box, choose Show Text Labels in the Text Options list box and then click Close. Open the dialog again to change the display back.

- To change the number of rows that the toolbars use, point to the bottom edge of the bottom toolbar; the mouse pointer will change to a double-headed arrow. You can then drag the edge up to reduce the number of rows or drag it down to expand them.

- To resize a toolbar when two or more share the same row, drag its left edge to the right or left.

- To move a toolbar, drag it by its left edge. For example, you could drag the Links toolbar onto its own row, as shown below.

 NOTE Remember that you'll also find these same toolbars when you are browsing the files and folders on your local computer; the Address and Links toolbars are also available on the Windows Taskbar.

Standard Toolbar

The buttons on the Standard toolbar in Internet Explorer (the toolbar just beneath the menu bar in Figures 21.1 and 21.2) are shortcuts for the more commonly used commands on its menus. For example, you can click the Stop button to cancel the downloading of the current page instead of using the View ➢ Stop command, or click the Home button as a shortcut for the View ➢ Go To ➢ Home Page command.

 TIP Point at a button to see its name appear in a ToolTip.

Links Toolbar

Each of the buttons on the Links toolbar is a hyperlink to a URL (you can also access these links from the Links command on the Favorites menu). By default, they all target Microsoft Web sites that serve as gateways to a wealth of information on the Web (if you received a customized version of Internet Explorer, these hyperlinks may point to other locations).

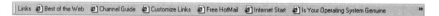

The Best of the Web button displays a useful collection of links to reference-related Web sites where you might, for example, look up a company's phone number, find an e-mail address of a long-lost relative, or find sites that will help you with travel arrangements or personal finance. All the Links buttons are customizable. To customize, do the following:

- To modify a button's target, right-click it, choose Properties from the shortcut menu, and then choose the Internet Shortcut tab.

- To change any aspect of a button, including its display text, choose Favorites ➢ Organize Favorites and then open the Links folder, where you'll see the names of all the buttons on the Links toolbar. Rename a button just as you rename any file in Windows, such as by selecting it and pressing F2. Delete a button by selecting its name and pressing Delete.

- To add a new Links button, simply drag a hyperlink from a Web page in Internet Explorer onto the Links toolbar. When you release the mouse button, a new button will be created that targets the same file as the hyperlink.

- To rearrange the buttons, drag a button to a new location on the Links bar.

Once you've tried these buttons and have a feeling for the content on each of the sites, you can revise the buttons or create new ones that point to sites that you want to access with a click.

Address Toolbar

The Address toolbar shows the address of the file currently displayed in Internet
Explorer, which might be a URL on the Internet or a location on your local disk. You
enter a URL or the path to a file or folder and then press Enter to open that Web site
or file.

 NOTE When you are entering a URL that you have entered once before, Internet
Explorer's AutoComplete feature tries to recognize the URL and displays a list of possible
matches in a drop-down menu. You can either click one of the URLs or continue to type a
new one.

To revise the URL, click within the Address toolbar and use the normal Windows
editing keys. Then press Enter to have Internet Explorer open the specified file. Also,
the arrow on the right side of the Address toolbar opens a drop-down list of addresses
that you've previously visited via the Address toolbar. They're listed in the order you
visited them. Select one from the list and Internet Explorer will open that site.

 NOTE There is one more toolbar available: Radio. You can use it to control the broadcast
of Internet radio. Another way to use Internet radio is through Media Player, described in
Chapter 16, "Using the Windows Media Player."

Getting Help

Internet Explorer offers the usual variety of program help, with a few touches of its
own. Choose Help ➤ Contents and Index to display its Help window, where you can
browse through the topics in the Contents tab, look up a specific word or phrase in the
Index tab, or find all references to a word or phrase in the Search tab.

To see if there is a newer version of any of the Internet Explorer software components, find answers to questions or problems, or add new components, choose Help ➤
Online Support, which is an easy way to keep your software current—immediately and
online.

To work through a basic online tutorial about browsing the Web, choose Help ➤
Tour. Internet Explorer goes online to a Microsoft Web site and opens the Internet
Explorer 5.5 Tour page, where you can click your way through the lessons.

If you'd like to improve your Web-browsing skills, click Help ➤ Tip of the Day to
view short but informative tips for using Internet Explorer. Users familiar with

Netscape Navigator or Communicator can click Help ➤ For Netscape Users to get up to speed on the ins and outs of Internet Explorer.

 NOTE The Microsoft Home Page command is not the same as the Go ➤ Home Page command (or the Home button on the toolbar), which opens your chosen start page.

Moving between Pages

The feature that perhaps best defines the whole concept of browsing in Internet Explorer is your ability to move from page to page, winding your way through the Web. The most common way to do so is by clicking a hyperlink, but this section will also show you some other ways to jump to another page.

Making the Jump with Hyperlinks

You can click an embedded hyperlink (either a text link or a graphic image link) in a page on the Web or your intranet to open the target file of that link. The target can be anywhere on the Web or your local computer. Clicking a link in a page that's on a server in Seattle might open a page on the same server or on a server in London, Tokyo, Brasilia—or maybe next door.

When you point with your mouse to a text or image link in Internet Explorer, the pointer changes to a small hand. Click here to jump to the link destination. Clicking a hyperlink with your mouse is the usual way to activate a link, but you can activate a link in Internet Explorer in several other ways, such as the following:

- You can press Tab to move to the next hyperlink in the page; you'll see a dotted outline around the currently selected link. Press Enter to activate the selected link.

- Right-click a hyperlink and choose Open from the shortcut menu.

- Choose Open in New Window to open the target in a new Internet Explorer window.

- Choose Save Target As to save the target of the link to disk (you will be prompted for a location). In this case, Internet Explorer will not display the target.

- Choose Print Target to print the target of the link without opening it.

You can use any of these methods to open the target of a hyperlink, whether the link is text, an image, or an image map.

In many cases, the target of a hyperlink will be another Web page that will probably have hyperlinks of its own. Sometimes, however, the target will be another kind of resource, such as an image file or a text file that contains no links of its own. In this instance, you'll have to use the Back button to return to the previous page.

Another type of target uses the *mailto* protocol. For example, many Web pages have a link via e-mail to the Webmaster, the person who created or maintains the site. The link target might look like the one shown here on the status bar, where the target uses the mailto protocol.

When you click such a link, your e-mail program, such as Outlook Express, opens a new message with the address of the target already entered in the Recipient field. You can then fill out the subject and body of the message and send it in the usual way.

Other Ways to Move between Pages

Although clicking a hyperlink in Internet Explorer is the usual way to open another resource (a file, such as a Web page or an image), you'll undoubtedly use other means on a regular basis.

Using the Back and Forward Commands

Once you jump to another page during a session with Internet Explorer, you can use the Back and Forward commands to navigate between the pages you've already visited. You can either use those commands on the View ➢ Go To menu or use the Back and Forward buttons on the toolbar.

TIP Alt+Left Arrow and Alt+Right Arrow are keyboard shortcuts for Back and Forward, respectively.

You can right-click either button or click the down arrow to its right to see a menu of the places that button will take you. The first item on the menu is the site you would visit if you simply clicked the larger button. Select any site from the menu to go directly to that site.

NOTE The Back and Forward buttons work exactly the same when you are browsing your local or network drive in an Explorer window. As you display various folders, you can use these buttons to open folders that you have already visited.

Using the Address Bar

As mentioned before, you can also jump to another page by typing its URL in the Address toolbar and pressing Enter. Keep the following in mind when you do:

- Spelling counts! The bad news is that if you do not type in the address exactly right, Internet Explorer will not be able to open the site and will display an error message to that effect. The good news is that the URL you typed might take you to some new and exciting place on the Web. Good luck!

- If you're entering a complete URL including a filename with a trailing file-name extension, watch that extension. Some Web sites use the traditional four-letter extension for a Web page, .html. Other sites may have adopted the three-letter extension, .htm.

> **TIP** One way to take advantage of the Address toolbar is by also taking advantage of the Windows Clipboard. For example, you can copy a URL from a word processing document and paste it into the Address toolbar; after that, all you need to do is press Enter to go to that site.

Choosing from Your Favorites Menu

In Internet Explorer, you can create a list of your favorite Web sites or other destinations, such as folders on your local disk, by adding each one to the appropriately named Favorites menu. You don't need to remember a site's URL in order to return to that site—simply select it from the Favorites menu.

You'll learn more about adding to and organizing the Favorites menu later in this chapter in "Returning to Your Favorite Pages."

Digging into the History and Cache Folders

Internet Explorer keeps track of both the URLs you visit and the actual files that are downloaded. The paths to the storage folders for this content and how this information is used are described below.

History   Internet Explorer keeps a list of the URLs you visit in its History folder; the default location is C:\Windows\History. You can access these URLs in Internet Explorer with the View ➤ Explorer Bar ➤ History command or by clicking the History button on the toolbar. Your past history will be displayed in chronological order in the Explorer bar in the left-hand pane of the Internet Explorer window, where you can select one of the URLs to open in the right-hand pane. Your browsing history is discussed in greater detail later in this chapter in "Using History to See Where You Have Been."

Temporary Internet Files   Internet Explorer saves the files it downloads in a folder on your local drive, which serves as a cache. By default, this folder is C:\Windows\Temporary Internet Files. When you return to a site, any content that has not changed since the last time you visited that site will be opened directly from the cache on your drive. This saves a lot of time when compared to downloading those files again (especially images). You can also open this folder and then open or otherwise use any of the files it contains. Choose View ➤ Internet Options, select the General tab, click the Settings button, and then click the View Files button.

 NOTE When multiple users share one computer, each may have their own History and Temporary Internet Files folders, which will reside within each of their folders within the C:\Windows\Profiles folder.

Browsing Offline

When you have saved a Web page from the Internet to your local hard disk, you can open that page at any time in Internet Explorer; there's no need to be connected to the Internet to do so. However, think about what happens when you click a link in that page. You opened the page itself from your local hard disk, but more than likely, the target file of that link is still back on the Web and not on your disk. To open that file, Internet Explorer needs access to the Internet.

If you have a full-time Internet connection, you might not even notice that Internet Explorer had to go on the Internet to open that file. If you have a dial-up connection, however, Internet Explorer will first have to make the call and connect to the Internet before opening the file, as shown in Figure 21.3.

FIGURE 21.3
When you are not currently connected to the Internet but click a link that targets a file there, you have the choice of connecting or working offline.

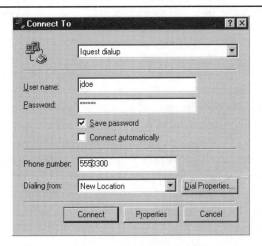

The Dial-Up Networking connector offers three choices:

Connect   Go ahead and connect to the Internet so Internet Explorer can find the targeted file.

Properties   Set the properties for the dial-up connection.

Cancel   Close the dialog box without making a connection.

If you choose Cancel, Internet Explorer will attempt to open and display the specified file from your Temporary Internet Files folder (the cache). Remember that most of the files that are opened while you're browsing the Web are saved in this cache folder, as explained in the previous section, so the requested file might be available offline. If the file isn't found there, however, Internet Explorer displays the dialog box shown below.

As before, you can choose to connect to the Internet to find the file. In that case, the Working Offline icon disappears once you're connected. If you choose to stay offline, the requested file will not be opened because it does not reside locally.

At any time, you can also choose File ➤ Work Offline, which will again display the Working Offline icon on the status bar. Internet Explorer will not attempt to connect to the Internet when you request a file, but will look only in its cache.

 NOTE   Sites you've never visited or haven't visited recently can't be accessed while offline, but chances are good that files for those sites you visit frequently are still in your cache.

 When you're browsing Web pages from your cache in offline mode, you'll notice that when you point to a link in a page whose target file is *not* available locally in the Internet Explorer cache, the mouse pointer changes to the little hand, as usual, but also displays the international No symbol (as shown here). This reminds you that you won't be able to open the target of this link while you are offline.

When you want to return to browsing online when needed, choose File ➤ Work Offline again. The next time you request a file that is on the Internet, a connection will be made in the usual way. You can also click the Connect button in the Connect To dialog box (refer back to Figure 21.3) when you have requested a file that is not available locally. The connection will be made, and you will no longer be working in offline mode.

Being able to browse offline without worrying about Internet Explorer trying to make a connection is especially valuable when you have subscribed to various Web sites and have chosen to have their content downloaded automatically.

With offline browsing, you don't need to go out of your way to return to sites to see if they've been updated, or wait at the keyboard while large files are downloaded, perhaps from a site that is busy during the times you normally access it. Instead, you can set up Internet Explorer to check the sites you want at any time of the day or night, notify you that those sites have been updated, and optionally download any new pages. You can then browse those sites offline and let Internet Explorer load the pages and assorted files directly from your Temporary Internet Files folder (the cache). Not only will these sites load almost instantly, but you can also view them while sitting in your beach chair near the breaking waves.

Returning to Your Favorite Pages

If you've browsed in Internet Explorer for more than a few hours, you've undoubtedly run into what is perhaps the easiest thing to do on the Web—lose your place and be unable to find your way back to a page that you really, really want to visit. Whatever your reasons for wanting to return to a specific page, the Favorites menu offers the best solution for finding your way back.

The Structure of the Favorites Menu

On the Favorites menu, you can store the names of any sites, folders, or other resources that you might want to return to. To visit one again, simply select it from the Favorites menu. Remember that you'll also find the Favorites menu on the Windows Start menu, and you can access your Favorites folder from just about any Files dialog box in a Windows program.

This menu is put together in much the same way as your Windows Start menu. For example, the Favorites menu is built from the Favorites folder within your Windows folder, just as the Start menu is built from the Start Menu folder. The items on the Favorites menu are actually shortcuts that reside in the Favorites folder. You can create submenus on the Favorites menu to help you organize items into relevant categories. The submenus are actually folders within the Favorites folder.

 Don't forget that you can also display your Favorites menu in the Explorer bar. Choose View ➢ Explorer Bar ➢ Favorites, or click the Favorites button on the toolbar. You'll be able to click a link in your Favorites menu in the Explorer bar and see the target open in the pane on the right.

Adding Items to the Favorites Menu

When you browse to a page or other resource that you just might want to return to, the smart thing to do is add it to your Favorites menu. To do so, choose Favorites ➤ Add to Favorites, or right-click anywhere within the page and choose Add to Favorites. You are then presented with the Add Favorite dialog box, shown in Figure 21.4, in which you can do the following:

- Specify the name of the page as it should appear on the menu.

- Choose to place the new item in a submenu on the Favorites menu.

- Choose to make the page available in offline mode. If you select this option, you can click Customize to decide if pages that are linked to this favorite should also be available offline, to set a schedule for updating the page, and to enter a Web site password if one is required. This feature used to be called Subscriptions in IE4, but the whole concept was far too complicated, so it's been simplified here.

FIGURE 21.4

When you add an item to the Favorites menu, you can specify the name that will appear on the menu as well as the submenu (folder) in which it should appear.

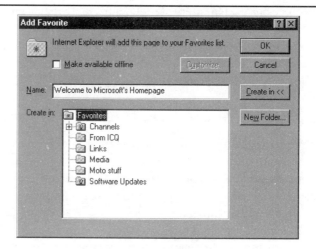

Naming an Item for the Favorites Menu

When you are adding a Web page to the Favorites menu, Internet Explorer by default uses the page's title as its name on the Favorites menu. In Figure 21.4, the page's title is "Welcome to Microsoft's Homepage." If you are viewing a file or folder from your local or network drive, the file or folder name will be used as the default name for the Favorites menu.

In either case, you are free to revise the name to make it more recognizable when you later want to find it on the menu. For example, in Figure 21.4, you could shorten the name to "Microsoft." Not only is this name quite recognizable, but it will also be alphabetized appropriately on the menu.

Try to keep names short and descriptive. Any menu works best when you can quickly scan it to find the item you want. Additionally, the Favorites menu displays only the first 40 characters or so of any long names.

Choosing a Submenu for the New Item

When you add an item to the Favorites menu, it appears on the top-level menu by default so that you'll see that item when you first open the menu. However, this is usually *not* the best place to add new items. In the real world, you'll end up with dozens or, more likely, hundreds of items on your Favorites menu. Opening that menu and finding one long list could soon be less than helpful.

You can avoid this by adding a new item within a submenu so that the item appears "farther down" in the nest of menus. Again, this is the same concept and mechanism as your Windows Start menu.

 TIP Keep at least one submenu that serves as a catchall for items that you can't readily categorize. You can call that submenu something like Temp or Misc. Then, when you can't decide in which submenu to place a new item, don't put it on the top-level menu. Put it in the catchall menu instead, where it will be out of the way so that you can deal with it later when you organize your Favorites menu.

In most cases, when you're creating a new item in the Add Favorite dialog box (as shown earlier in Figure 21.4), you'll want to click a subfolder in the list at the bottom of the box. If the list isn't shown, click the Create In button to make it look like the list in Figure 21.4. Select the folder you want for the new item so that the folder icon appears opened. Then click OK.

If a suitable folder does not yet exist in your Favorites folder, click the New Folder button in the Add Favorite dialog box. Enter a name for the new folder and click OK. The new folder is created within the currently selected folder. You can then select the new folder and add the new item to it.

 TIP If you create a new item in the Links folder, that item appears as a new button on the Links toolbar.

Organizing Your Favorites Menu

When you add a new item to the Favorites menu, you can change its name, place it in a submenu off the Favorites menu (a subfolder of the Favorites folder), or create a new submenu (folder) for it.

The Favorites menu isn't static, however. You can change it whenever the need arises. You can make most changes right from the menu simply by right-clicking a menu item to access its shortcut menu. So if you want to delete an item from the Favorites menu, rename it, or change its target, just right-click it.

If you want to make several changes to the menu, you'll probably find it easier to choose Favorites ➢ Organize Favorites. You'll see the Organize Favorites dialog box, as shown in Figure 21.5. Before you read about the changes you can make to the Favorites menu, you should consider the ways you might organize your menu.

FIGURE 21.5

You can make changes to the files or folders in the Favorites folder with the Organize Favorites dialog box.

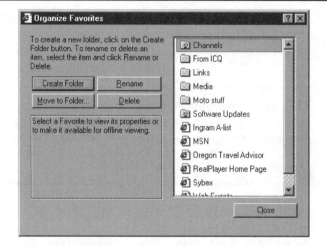

You'll want to organize your Favorites menu every bit as well as you do your day-to-day files on your hard disk. Keeping the things you need well organized, whether they are items on the Favorites menu or files on your hard disk, will make your daily routines much more efficient. So what's the best way to organize your Favorites menu? The answer is "Any way you want."

The trick is to create categories (folders) that are relevant to the types of sites you are collecting and the way you would naturally group them. No doubt you'll be creating new subfolders and rearranging the existing ones on a regular basis. In fact, the more you browse the Internet, the more you'll realize how powerful a well-organized Favorites menu can be.

TIP The menu item named Software Updates in the Organize Favorites dialog box in Figure 21.5 was created so that you can keep on top of the software you have. When you buy new software, you'll probably receive information from the publisher about how to download updates and other useful information from their Web site. If you add those update sites to the Software Updates folder, you will have one central place to check on all of your software quickly and easily.

In the Organize Favorites dialog box, you select items as you always do; you can select multiple items with Shift+Click or Ctrl+Click. You can perform just about any file operation on the selected items, using either the buttons in the dialog box or the commands on the shortcut menu when you right-click a selected item. For example, you can move an item from one menu (folder) to another or delete an item to remove it from the menu. Once you've become familiar with a Web site, you might want to rename its shortcut on your Favorites menu to make it shorter or more recognizable.

Searching the Web

One of the most substantially revised aspects of Internet Explorer 5.5 is its Search feature. Microsoft has incorporated a new Search Assistant into Internet Explorer, starting with version 5.0, that in theory should make searching the World Wide Web easier and more intuitive. The Assistant pools the resources of several different search engines, meaning that whether you're looking for a Web site, an old friend's phone number, or even maps, you aren't limited to the resources of a single search engine. Of course, you may not like this feature if your favorite Internet search engine wasn't included in Microsoft's list. If this is the case, you will have to enter the URL for the search engine in the Address bar and access it that way.

As mentioned before, different search engines work differently. The information in this section will describe how to use and customize the Search Assistant, as well as provide you with a general understanding of how to perform effective Internet searches.

Searching in the Explorer Bar

If you want to search for something on the Internet, the simplest way to begin is to click the Search button on the toolbar. This will open the Explorer bar in the left-hand side of the window, as shown in Figure 21.6. Which search engine is used will depend on your settings in the Search Assistant. See the section "Customizing the Search Assistant" later in this chapter to learn how to change those settings.

Before you can perform a search, you first need to decide exactly what it is you are looking for. As you can see in Figure 21.6, there are five general categories of stuff you can search for. Since Web page searches are the most common, they are listed first. But if you want to look for a person's address, a business, a map, or view a previous search, click the radio button for one of those options. The search window will automatically change depending on which search category you choose.

FIGURE 21.6

The Explorer bar opens with the Search Assistant. Choose a category of information you want to search, and then type the word, name, or phrase you want to look for.

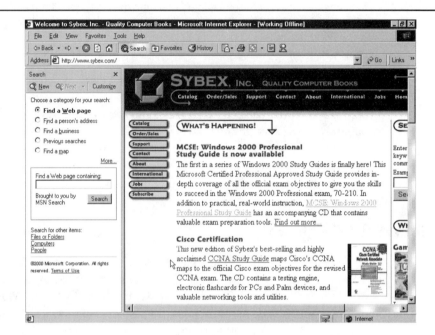

 NOTE   Additional categories are available for searching, including Look Up a Word, Find a Picture, and Find in Newsgroups. Click More in the Search Assistant to view these additional categories.

Type a word or phrase you want to search for. Notice that the search window will say something like "Brought to you by…" and then list a search engine. If you click Search right now, this is the engine that will be used to perform the search. Go ahead and try it. You should see a list of search results similar to those in Figure 21.7.

 NOTE   In the example shown here, I searched for the phrase "expansion theory." Obviously, some of the results match what I'm really looking for better than others. See "Performing Effective Keyword Searches" later in this chapter for more information.

PART
IV

Communication and
Using the Internet

FIGURE 21.7
*The Search Assistant
displays a list of search
results. Click one of
them to visit the page.*

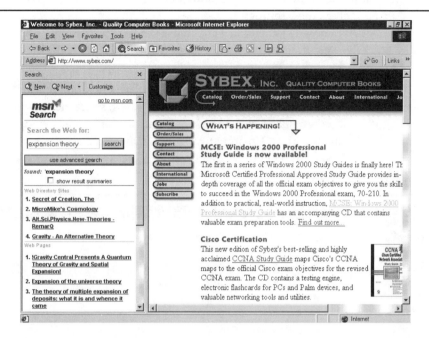

If you don't like the results produced by the current search engine, click the Next button at the top of the Explorer bar. Or better yet, click the down arrow next to the Next button and select an engine from the list that appears. The Search Assistant will automatically forward your search string to that engine and perform a new search. See "Using Common Search Engines" later in this chapter to learn more about using specific engines.

 TIP When you are done searching, click the Close (X) button at the top of the Explorer bar to make more room on the screen for viewing Web pages. Alternatively, you can drag the border of the Explorer bar with the mouse to make it use less space on the screen without closing it.

Customizing the Search Assistant

As mentioned earlier, one of the great features of the new and improved Search Assistant is that it can be customized to work the way you want. For instance, if you want a different search engine to be the first one that appears when you conduct a Web search, you can easily change that here.

To customize the Search Assistant, first open the Explorer bar (if it isn't already open) by clicking the Search button on the toolbar. In the Explorer bar, click Customize. The

Customize Search Settings window opens and should look something like Figure 21.8. Now check these settings:

- Choose whether you want to use the Search Assistant or a single search service every time. If you choose to use a single service, you will be shown a list of services to choose from.

- Under Find a Web Page, place a check mark next to the search engines you want to have available. In the list box on the left, select the search engine you want to access first and click the Move Up arrow to put it at the top of the list. You can use the Move Up and Move Down arrows to place the search engines in order you want them to be used.

FIGURE 21.8

Open the Customize Search Settings dialog box to choose which search services you want to use, and in which order you want to use them.

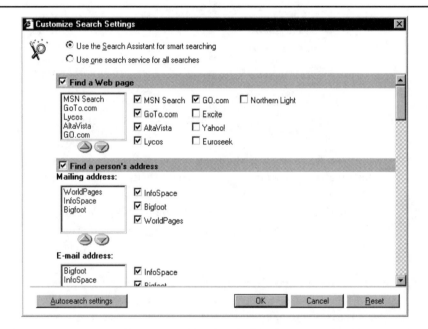

- Choose which directory services you want to use to locate a person's mailing and e-mail addresses. As with Web page searches, you can place the directories in order by your preference.

- Scroll down the dialog to choose directories for conducting business searches. If you don't plan to use this (or any other) category, remove the check mark next to its heading. It will no longer appear in the Search Assistant window in the Explorer bar.

- Select the online mapping services you want to use for finding directions or place names.

- You can access the online dictionaries, thesauri, or encyclopedias listed in Look Up a Word. This can be helpful during that late-night research project where spelling counts!
- Choose a newsgroup search engine under Find in Newsgroups.
- Under Previous Searches, move the categories up or down as you wish. I suggest that you put the category you search on most (probably Web pages) at the top.

When you are done making changes to the Search Assistant, click OK. If you want to return to the default settings for this dialog box, click Reset.

Performing Effective Keyword Searches

If you are searching for Web pages, a common method is a keyword search. A *keyword* is simply a word that represents information you want to find. It is generally a noun, but may also be a verb or some other part of speech. When you use a search engine, you are searching a database for documents that have words that match the keyword(s) you've entered.

 NOTE The most common words, such as conjunctions ("and," "but," etc.), pronouns ("I," "he," etc.), and prepositions ("of," "for," "into," etc.) are ignored by search engines.

Typically, you may enter as many keywords as you want. The engine will search for all the words and find any document that contains one or more of those words. In most search engines, multiple keywords are treated as having an implicit Boolean OR operator. For example, if you entered the keywords **Chevy Impala,** the server would return documents that contain the word "Chevy" *or* the word "Impala." It would, therefore, include pages containing mention of "Chevy Impala," some pages containing mention of "impala" (probably natural wildlife pages, actually, since an impala is an animal), and pages that merely include mention of "Chevy" (without necessarily including "Chevy Impala"). Note that pages containing both words would be ranked higher and appear first in the resulting list.

 NOTE Most search engines ignore the capitalization of your request.

Notice that for the OR search of the preceding paragraph, you did not have to enter the word "OR." To search only for pages that contain *both* Chevy *and* Impala, however, you would have to insert the word **AND** between the two words: **Chevy and Impala**.

NOTE Some search engines infer an "AND" between the words you enter, and find pages that match all the words only. Check the Help information at the search site you're using to find out the syntax for that particular engine.

Even with the AND approach, however, you might still turn up pages that don't mention Chevy Impalas; it's possible you'll turn up pages describing somebody's trip across the country to photograph wild animals (lions, wildebeests, impalas) from the back of their Chevy station wagon. If you wanted to find only pages that contain the words "Chevy" and "Impala" together as a phrase (okay, I admit I should have told you this up front—but, hey, I'm using this example as a teaching tool), then you should put the words together between quotes: **"Chevy Impala".**

See also the discussion later in this section called "Exact Matches"; there are some variations on this approach from one search engine to another.

Combining Criteria

Many engines let you combine criteria in complex ways. Here's a typical example. Suppose you wanted to find pages about child safety that do *not* discuss adolescents. Proper use of the words AND and NOT will help you: **child and safety not adolescents**.

Wildcards

Most engines will let you enter partial keywords by means of *wildcards*. Here's an example. Suppose you were doing research about a car brand and wanted to see any and all pages about it. You might want listings of any occurrences of "Chevy" or "Chevrolet." You could do two separate searches, one for each. Or to be more expedient, you could use a wildcard in your search: **Chev***.

The * character applied at the end of a partial keyword will match all documents that contain words that start with the partial word.

Exact Matches

Often you'll want to search for an exact match of the words you enter. For example, you might want to find pages that contain the entire phrase "Hubble telescope repair." Typically, you would specify that you want an exact match of this phrase by enclosing it with quotes (') or double quotes ("). Some engines, however, want you to use the + sign between the words instead. Thus, depending on the search engine you're using, you may have to try

'Hubble telescope repair'

or

"Hubble telescope repair"

or

Hubble+telescope+repair

One of these should find pages that contain that exact phrase.

 TIP As a general game plan, when you're doing complex searches, start out with a simple search (it's faster and easier), and then check the first ten pages or so of that result to see what they contain. In many cases, this will provide you with whatever you need, and you won't have spent your time concocting a complex set of search criteria. Of course, if too many pages are found and only a few of them are meeting your actual needs, you'll have to start to narrow the search. On the other hand, if no pages are resulting ("no matches found"), you'll have to try again by widening the search.

Using Common Search Engines

Some search engines, such as Go and Yahoo! offer a Browse option as well as a Search option. This means that in addition to being able to search for keywords, you can look through topics by category, such as "business," "entertainment," or "magazines," just to see what is available. This is great if you are interested in seeing what's out there in a general category instead of searching for a specific topic.

This section describes some of the most common search engines on the Web. Some of these search engines are available in the Search Assistant, and some aren't.

Endlessly Indexing the Web

The ability to search the Web for specific sites or files relies on one tiny factor: the existence of searching and indexing sites that you can access to perform the search. These sites are often known as Web spiders, crawlers, or robots, because they endlessly and automatically search the Web and index the content they find.

Search sites literally create huge databases of all the words in all the pages they index, and you can search those databases simply by entering the keywords you want to find. Despite the size of this vast store of information, they can usually return the results to you in a second or two.

This is definitely a Herculean task, because the Web is huge and continues to grow with no end in sight. Plus, a search engine must regularly return to pages it's already indexed because those pages may have changed and will need to be indexed again. Don't forget that many pages are removed from the Web each day, and a search engine must at some point remove those now invalid URLs from its database.

Continued ▶

To give you an idea of just how big a job it is to search and index the Web, the popular AltaVista search site at www.altavista.digital.com recently reported that its Web index as of that day covered 31 million pages from 1,158,000 host names on 627,000 servers. AltaVista also had indexed 4 million articles from 14,000 newsgroups. On top of that, this search site is accessed more than 30 million times each day.

Keeping track of what's on the Web is definitely a job for that infinite number of monkeys we've always heard about!

AltaVista: www.altavista.com   Digital Equipment Corporation's AltaVista claims to be the largest search engine, searching 31 million pages on 627,000 servers, and 4 million articles from 14,000 Usenet newsgroups. It is accessed over 30 million times per weekday.

GO: www.go.com   Combines two powerful search systems, as well as a great news search engine that enables you to search wire services, publications, and more.

Lycos: www.lycos.com   Searches not only text, but also graphics, sounds, and video!

Yahoo!: www.yahoo.com   Started by two graduate students at Stanford, Yahoo! is considered the first search engine and still one of the most comprehensive. If you are looking for the address for a Web site, such as the New York Times Web site, this is a good way to find it.

Excite: www.excite.com   If you can't describe exactly what you're looking for, Excite's unique concept-based navigation technology may help you find it anyway. Excite's Web index is deep, broad, and current: It covers the full text of more than 11.5 million pages and is updated weekly.

Magellan: magellan.excite.com   A different concept in search engines. This one ranks the results using its own independent system in an effort to help you make more refined searches.

CNET: www.cnet.com   This search engine lets you search up to eight search engines at one time. This is a pretty unique and powerful approach to searching. If nothing else, you'll probably get lots of results from almost any search! It's also a good site for linking to other engines.

HotBot: www.hotbot.lycos.com   HotBot is a favorite search engine among many Internet power users, and has been highly rated for its ability to perform powerful and exhaustive Web searches. HotBot now includes a directory system as well.

MyStartingPoint: www.stpt.com   Lets you select a subject area for your search.

WebCrawler: www.webcrawler.com   Offers a speedy Web search engine and a Randomlinks feature to find new and unusual sites. It also features a list of the 25 most visited sites on the Web.

Deja: www.deja.com   Enables you to search through millions of postings to Usenet newsgroups.

BigBook: www.bigbook.com   National Yellow Pages list that covers nearly every business in the U.S., with detailed maps of their locations.

WhoWhere: www.whowhere.lycos.com   This is a comprehensive White Pages service for locating people, e-mail addresses, and organizations on the Internet. WhoWhere intuitively handles misspelled or incomplete names, and it lets you search by initials.

WWWomen: www.wwwomen.com   The premier search directory for women.

Environmental Organization Web Directory: www.webdirectory.com   The categories in this Web directory cover topics such as animal rights, solar energy, and sustainable development.

CNET'S Shareware Directory: www.shareware.cnet.com   This one makes it simple to find trial and demo versions of software. More than 170,000 files are available for easy searching, browsing, and downloading from shareware and corporate archives on the Internet.

The Electric Library: www.elibrary.com   This address searches across an extensive database of more than 1,000 full-text newspapers, magazines, and academic journals, images, reference books, literature, and art. (This is a pay-subscription site, but a free trial is offered.)

Homework help: www.bjpinchbeck.com   This Web site was put together by a nine-year-old boy (with the help of his dad) and provides a comprehensive collection of online information designed to help students with their homework. This excellent reference has won many awards.

 TIP   An invaluable spot for comparing computer prices is www.computers.com.

Using History to See Where You Have Been

Internet Explorer remembers where you have been when you roam the Internet. It keeps track of every single Web site you visit, and makes that information available to you should you need it. This is particularly useful when you want to revisit a Web site, but you can't remember the URL and you didn't add it to your Favorites list.

Your browsing history is organized by day and week, so it is helpful to remember approximately when you last visited the site you are trying to find. The files for Internet Explorer's History are stored in the C:\Windows\History folder on your hard drive. You can access Web pages directly from that folder if you are viewing it using Windows Explorer, but the easier way is to simply view the history in the Explorer bar. To begin, launch Internet Explorer and click the History button on the toolbar.

Your browsing history will open in the Explorer bar, as shown in Figure 21.9. At the top of the list, you will see listings labeled by days of the week and by week. To see the Web sites you visited on a given day, click the day. A list of the Web sites will expand below the day, and each site will have a folder icon next to it.

FIGURE 21.9
Your browsing history opens in the Explorer bar.

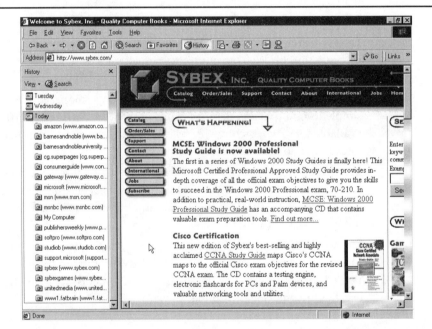

Each Web site is listed as a folder icon because you probably accessed several pages within the site. Click the site listing to see the pages you visited there, and then click a page listing to link to it. In Figure 21.10 you can see that I visited an article about sleep deprivation on MSNBC. I clicked the page listing in the Explorer pane to redisplay that page.

FIGURE 21.10
*Click a Web page listing
to revisit that page.*

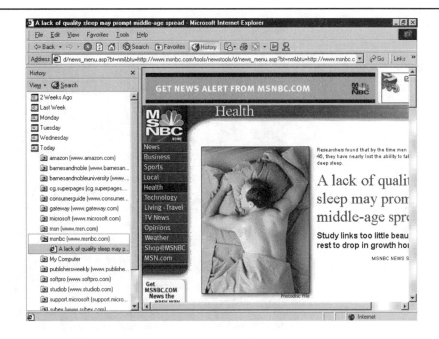

 NOTE Keep in mind that most Web pages change frequently, even ones you might have visited just yesterday. Accessing pages through the History listing links to the page as it appears now, so don't be surprised if the page's contents have changed since the last time you visited. In fact, there is a chance that the page might not be there at all.

When you are done viewing the History listing, click the Close (X) button on the Explorer bar.

Clearing Your History

Useful though Internet Explorer's History listing may be, there is a chance that it can come back to haunt you as well. Anyone who has access to your computer can open the History and see where you have been on the Web. If you value your privacy, this could be a problem, but fortunately it is possible to clear Internet Explorer's History.

To clear the History, open the Internet Options dialog box by clicking Tools ➢ Internet Options. On the General tab you will find several History options as shown in Figure 21.11. You can quickly and easily remove everything in the History list by clicking Clear History. While you're at it, click Delete Files under the Temporary Internet Files field so that others can't view the pages in offline mode.

FIGURE 21.11
Clear Internet Explorer's History here, or change how long the history is kept.

 NOTE Notice that you can also adjust how long the History is kept. The default setting is 20 days, but if you want to be able to go further back in time than that, you might want to change the setting here.

 WARNING If you click Clear History, keep in mind that when it's gone, it's gone. You won't be able to restore the listing later if you decide you really needed something in the list.

Checking Important Internet Explorer Options

Internet Explorer contains a number of important option settings that you should be aware of. They can be accessed via the Internet Options dialog box, which you first saw in Chapter 20, "Connecting to the Internet." Among other things, the Internet Options dialog box controls many aspects of how Internet Explorer works, and it's worth your while to spend a few minutes going through the tabs to see how you can make the settings work better for you.

You can view Internet Explorer options by either opening the Internet Options applet in the Control Panel or clicking Tools ➤ Internet Options from within Internet Explorer. Visit each tab and check the following items:

General   On this tab you can set a new home page if you desire. This is the page that opens first whenever you launch Internet Explorer or when you click the Home Page button on the toolbar. The default home page is the MSN main page, but you might prefer to set this to the home page for your local ISP, a weather or news site, or even your own Web page.

Click Delete Files to clear your disk cache of the Temporary Internet Files that are stored there.

Security   Adjust your Security settings here. For more information, see "Setting Security Levels" later in this section.

Content   On this tab, you can enable the Content Advisor to control access to objectionable material on your computer. Once enabled, the settings are password protected.

Also, if you have certificates to authenticate your identity to certain Web sites, you can view them here.

You can also use this tab to enter personal information about yourself. This might be used to make completing forms on the Internet easier, or to make online shopping more efficient.

Connections   Use this tab to modify settings for your Internet connection. See Chapter 20 for more details.

Programs   On this tab, you can specify the default programs you want to use for editing HTML documents, reading e-mail and newsgroups, making Internet calls, and keeping a personal calendar and a list of contacts.

Advanced   Here, you can review various advanced settings for Internet Explorer. Perhaps the most useful settings here can be found under Multimedia, where you can specify whether Web page elements such as sounds, videos, or pictures are displayed automatically.

Setting Security Levels

Personal security is something you should always be concerned about when you are browsing the Internet. Unscrupulous people are out there, and it is possible to get victimized if you are not careful. Potential dangers abound, and range from having your computer infected with a harmful virus to having personal information or files on your computer compromised.

Internet Explorer makes protecting yourself relatively simple, but you need to make some decisions about how secure you want to be. Inevitably, your decision will probably boil down to a compromise between security and convenience, because in general, tighter security settings will make browsing more difficult.

You can adjust your security settings in the Internet Options dialog box. If Internet Explorer is already open, click Tools ➢ Internet Options, and then click the Security tab (Figure 21.12).

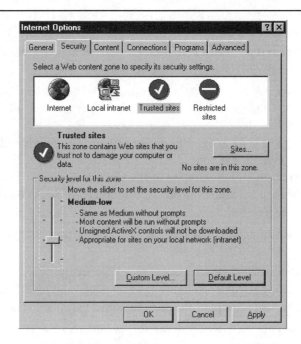

Internet Explorer offers the four basic levels of security, as described in the following list:

High   Offers the highest level of protection. Cookies are disabled, which means you won't be able to view many popular sites.

Medium   The most common setting, it provides a reasonable level of protection from the most insidious hazards, but cookies will be enabled. Possibly harmful ActiveX controls won't run.

Medium-Low   Internet Explorer will warn you against using this setting. Many of the protections available in the Medium level are here, but you won't receive prompts before running ActiveX controls and other potentially harmful applets.

Low   Offering almost no protection, this level is not recommended for free roaming of the Internet.

Of all the levels, Medium generally offers the best compromise of security and convenience. You can also customize security settings, if you wish, by clicking Custom Level. While you're there, consider how you want to deal with cookies. *Cookies* are tiny little files that Web sites can leave on your computer when you visit. They can serve a variety of purposes, such as acting as a counter for how many times you visit a certain Web site, or storing your login name and password for a site. Crafty Webmasters can even use cookies to track the kinds of Web sites you visit, providing them with potentially valuable marketing information.

Cookies have been controversial, to say the least. Many people see them as an invasion of privacy because others can monitor your Web-browsing habits. If you agree, you can disable cookies, but it can make browsing some Web sites very inconvenient. To see what I mean, go ahead and choose Prompt, and then click OK twice to close the dialog boxes. Then visit www.msn.com. Every time the Web site tries to load a cookie, you'll get a warning that looks like this:

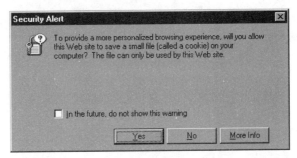

Some Web sites will simply not function if you click No. You'll probably get tired of seeing these warnings every few minutes, but that is the price to pay for keeping your browsing habits a secret.

Security Patches for IE

It seems like every day the news media is reporting another security flaw in Internet Explorer or Microsoft Outlook. To ensure that you always have the most recent security patches, choose Tools ➤ Windows Update, click Product Updates, and allow the utility to check your system. If any critical updates are recommended, follow the prompts to download them.

CHAPTER <u>22</u>

Communicating with Outlook Express News and Mail

Outlook Express is an Internet standards-based e-mail and news reader you can use to access Internet e-mail and news accounts. In this chapter, we'll look first at how to use Outlook Express Mail. We'll then look at Outlook Express News and conclude by showing you how to customize Outlook Express so that it works the way you want to work with your computer.

You can access Outlook Express from your Desktop, from Internet Explorer (IE), and from any program that includes a Go menu. From the Desktop, choose Start ➤ Programs ➤ Outlook Express, click the Launch Outlook Express icon on the Quick Launch toolbar, or click the Outlook Express shortcut on your Desktop. (Windows created this shortcut during installation.) To go to Outlook Express from within IE, click Mail and then choose one of the options from the drop-down menu. From a Go menu, choose Mail or News.

A Quick Tour of Outlook Express

When you first open Outlook Express (OE), you see the window shown in Figure 22.1.

 TIP Before you do anything else, place a check mark next to "When Outlook Express Starts, Go Directly to My Inbox." With this option selected, OE will open to the more useful Inbox instead of the generic Outlook Express screen when you open the programs.

If you click Read Mail, Outlook Express opens your Inbox in Preview Pane view, and you may well have a message or two from Microsoft, as Figure 22.2 shows.

FIGURE 22.1
*The Outlook Express
window*

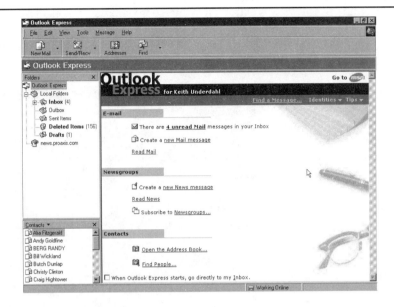

FIGURE 22.2
*The Outlook Express
Inbox window in
Preview Pane view*

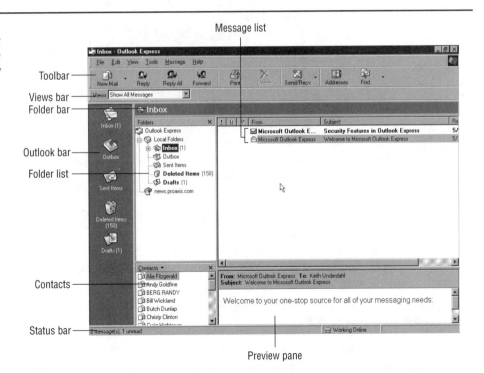

Figure 22.2 shows all the potential on-screen elements for Outlook Express. As you can see, this view is extremely cluttered, so choose a few elements that you want displayed. For instance, when I use Outlook Express, I normally have only the toolbar, folder bar, folder list, contacts, status bar, and message list displayed. You can customize the layout by clicking View ➢ Layout to open the Window Layout Properties dialog box.

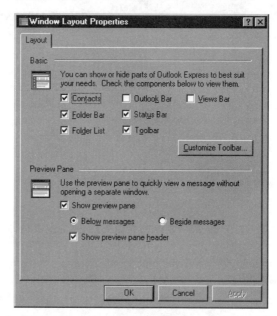

As you can see, in the Basic section of this dialog box, you can choose to display the contacts, folder bar, folder list, Outlook bar, status bar, toolbar, and views bar. In Figure 22.2, they are all displayed.

 NOTE We'll look at the Toolbar section of the Window Layout Properties dialog box later, in the section "Customizing the Toolbar."

You use the options in the Preview Pane section to select how you want to display header information and messages. Check and uncheck these options until the user interface is to your liking and fits the way you like to work when reading messages. You can also adjust the area for the preview pane and the message list by dragging the divider between them.

Moving Around

You can move around in Outlook Express in a variety of ways. Perhaps the easiest way is to simply choose a folder from the folder list. You can also click an icon on the Outlook bar, but since it and the folder list are redundant, I don't recommend displaying both. The folder list displays all of the important locations within Outlook Express.

To move to a different location in Outlook Express, simply click the appropriate listing in the folder list. For instance, if you want to review messages you have sent out recently, click the Sent Items folder. If you want to read new messages that you have received, click the Inbox.

 NOTE Note that unread messages are displayed with boldfaced titles in Outlook Express. Likewise, any folders that contain unread messages will be bold in the folder list as well.

Getting Connected

Before you can actually use Outlook Express to send and receive messages or to read and post news articles, you must set up an Internet e-mail account and an Internet news account. Doing so tells Outlook Express how to contact your e-mail and news servers. You can initially set up one account or multiple accounts, and you can always add more as the need arises.

Establishing an Account with an ISP

To set up an Internet e-mail or news account, you must have an account with an Internet Service Provider (ISP). If you don't have an account with an ISP, getting one may be as simple as checking out the technology section of your local newspaper. Unless you live in a remote area, you may have access to any number of local Internet providers. Chapter 20, "Browsing the World Wide Web with Internet Explorer 5.5," covers all the aspects of acquiring an ISP.

I recently established a new account with a local provider and completed the whole operation in a matter of minutes. I called the phone number listed in the newspaper, told the operator that I wanted an account for mail, news, and Internet access, asked about the charges, gave them my credit card number and told them the e-mail name and password I wanted to use, and within 15 minutes I was online. For unlimited access, I pay about $16 a month.

You can also find ISPs listed in local trade publications, in national publications such as the *Wall Street Journal* and computer magazines, and online. Check out these URLs for a list of ISPs (you can even search by region of the country):

- thelist.com

- www.cybertoday.com/cybertoday/isps/

In general, I've found that local publications are the best source for pointers to local ISPs. The large, online lists don't seem to be as up-to-date.

WARNING Be sure you clearly understand what you are getting and what you are paying for. Some ISPs provide an e-mail account for as little as $5.00 a month. Others charge by the hour for connect time. If you don't have unlimited access, you can rack up some serious charges by surfing the Internet a lot. Additionally, be sure that your provider allows you to connect through a local or toll-free phone number.

You can also use the Windows Internet Connection Wizard to establish an Internet account. To do so, choose Start ➤ Programs ➤ Accessories ➤ Internet Tools ➤ Internet Connection Wizard. The Wizard may ask for your Windows Me CD during this process, so have it handy.

Setting Up an E-Mail Account

Once you have an account with an ISP, you need to have the following information ready to set up an e-mail account in Outlook Express:

- Your e-mail address and password

- Your local access phone number

- The type of server that will be used for incoming mail

- The names of the servers for incoming mail and outgoing mail

When you have this information, you can follow the steps below to start setting up your e-mail account with the Internet Connection Wizard. The first time you start Outlook Express, the Internet Connection Wizard runs to prompt you to set up your e-mail account. If it does this, you can skip step 1.

1. In Outlook Express, choose Tools ➤ Accounts. In the Internet Accounts dialog box, open the Mail tab and click Add ➤ Mail to open the Internet Connection Wizard.

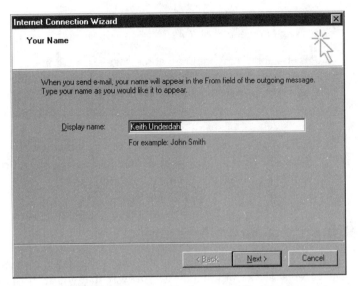

2. In the Display Name text box, enter the name that you want to appear in the From field of outgoing messages, and click Next.

3. In the Internet E-Mail Address text box, enter the e-mail address that your ISP assigned you, and click Next.

4. The Internet Connection Wizard asks you to specify the type of server that will be used for incoming mail and the names of the servers for incoming mail and outgoing mail. Enter this information and click Next.

5. In the Internet Mail Logon dialog box, enter the e-mail address and password that your ISP assigned you. If your ISP requires Secure Password Authentication, click the Log On Using Secure Password Authentication (SPA) button. When you are done, click Next.

6. In the Friendly Name dialog box, enter a name for your e-mail account in the text box, and click Next; then click Finish.

POP3, IMAP, and SMTP Explained

POP3 is an abbreviation for Post Office Protocol 3, a popular method used for storing Internet mail. Many Internet mail applications require a POP3 mailbox in order to receive mail. Your POP mailbox is usually your Inbox.

Continued ▷

SMTP is an abbreviation for Simple Mail Transfer Protocol, the TCP/IP protocol used for sending Internet e-mail. Your SMTP mailbox is usually your Outbox.

IMAP is an abbreviation for Internet Message Access Protocol, the protocol that allows a client to access and manipulate e-mail messages on a server. It does not specify a means of posting mail; that function is handled by SMTP.

You have now set up an Internet e-mail account and can send and receive messages. By default, the new account is set to use any dial-up connection available. If you want the account to use only a specific connection, see "Customizing Mail and News Options" later in this chapter to learn how.

Setting Up a News Account

Before you can read newsgroups, you have to connect to a news server. You set up a news server account in much the same way that you set up a mail server account.

Before you set up a news account, you must have already established an account with an ISP and obtained the name of the news server(s) you plan to use. Also, ask your ISP if you need a username and password to log on to the news server. After you do this, you can follow these steps:

1. Start Outlook Express and choose Tools ➤ Accounts.

2. In the Internet Accounts dialog box, select the News tab and then choose Add ➤ News to open the Internet Connection Wizard.

3. In the Display Name field, enter the name that you want to appear when you post an article or send an e-mail message to a newsgroup, and then click Next.

4. In the E-Mail Address field, enter your e-mail address and click Next.

5. Now, in the Internet News Server Name dialog box, enter the name of the news server that you received from your ISP (typically something like News.Myisp.com). If you have to log on to this server with an account name and password, check the My News Server Requires Me to Log On check box. Click Next, and then click Finish.

You have now set up an Internet news account, and you can read, subscribe to, and participate in newsgroups.

Do You Want to Use Your Real Name or an Alias?

If you want to remain anonymous while cruising newsgroups, you can enter a fake name in the Display Name field in the first Internet Connection Wizard dialog box. You can use anything you want, but we suggest that you let the limits of good taste guide you. Remember: If you can use a fake name, so can anybody else.

If you want to be even more anonymous, enter a fake e-mail address as well. Some ISPs have policies about this; so check to be sure that entering a fake name does not violate these policies.

Reading and Processing Messages

Now that your e-mail account is set up, you are ready to begin sending and receiving messages. If you still have the welcome message from Microsoft in your Inbox and if you still have the preview pane displayed, you'll see the header information in the upper pane, and the message in the lower pane.

 NOTE If you have a different configuration, double-click a message header to read the message. The message will open in its own window.

After reading a message, you can do any of the following:

- Print it.
- Mark it as read.
- Mark it as unread.
- Move it to another folder in the Outlook Express bar.
- Save it in a folder.
- Forward it to someone else.
- Reply to it.
- Delete it.

For some of these tasks, you use the File menu, and for some of them you use the Edit menu. In addition, you can take care of some tasks by simply clicking a toolbar icon.

PART
IV

Communication and
Using the Internet

Receiving Mail

Before we get into all the neat things you can do with your messages, let's look at the many ways in which you can retrieve your e-mail:

- Choose Tools ➤ Send and Receive ➤ Send and Receive All.
- Choose Tools ➤ Send and Receive, and click the account you want to retrieve mail from (if you have more than one mail account).
- Click the Send and Receive icon on the toolbar, which works the same as choosing Tools ➤ Send and Receive ➤ Send and Receive All.

Received messages are placed in your Inbox or in other folders that you have specified using the Inbox Assistant. You can also choose to display only newly received messages. To do so, choose View ➤ Current View ➤ Unread Messages.

You can now begin processing your mail, as described in the following sections.

Printing, Marking, and Moving Messages

Printing, marking, and moving messages are simple, straightforward tasks, so we'll start with them.

Printing Messages

On occasion, you may want a paper file of e-mail messages that you have sent or received. For example, you might work on a large project that involves some people who aren't using e-mail, or you may want to maintain paper files as a backup. To print a message, open it and place your cursor in the message; then either click the Print tool, choose File ➤ Print, or press Ctrl+P.

Marking Messages

When you first receive a message, a closed envelope icon precedes its header, which is in boldface.

After you read the message, Outlook Express marks it as read by changing the icon to an open envelope and changing the header from bold to lightface type. If, for whatever reason, you want to change a message from Read to Unread, select the message header and choose Edit ➤ Mark As Unread. If you want, you can change it back to Read if you want by selecting it and choosing Edit ➤ Mark As Read. (You might want to do either of these to call attention to a message that you want to review.) To mark all messages as read, choose Edit ➤ Mark All As Read.

Saving Messages

With Outlook Express, you can save messages in folders you created in Windows Explorer, and you can save messages in Outlook Express folders. You can also save attachments as files.

To save messages in Windows Explorer, follow these steps:

1. Select the header of the message you want to save.

2. Choose File ➤ Save As.

3. In the Save Message As dialog box, select a folder in which to save the message. Outlook Express places the subject line in the File Name box. You can use this name or type another one.

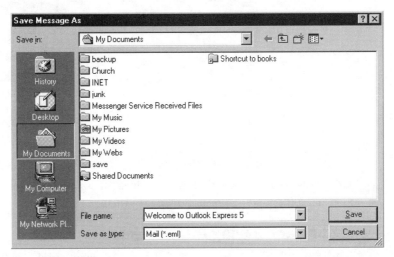

4. You can save the message as e-mail (with the .eml extension) or as text (with the .txt extension). Select the file type, then click Save.

Saving Messages in Outlook Express Folders

Although Outlook Express saves messages in the Deleted Items, Inbox, Outbox, and Sent Items folders, you can create your own folders in which to save messages. Once you have created new folders, you can easily move messages from one folder to another by dragging and dropping. You can also right-click messages and choose Move to Folder to open the Move dialog box and select a new location.

To create a new folder in Outlook Express, follow these steps:

1. Choose File ➤ New ➤ Folder.

2. In the Create Folder dialog box, type a name for the new folder and click OK.

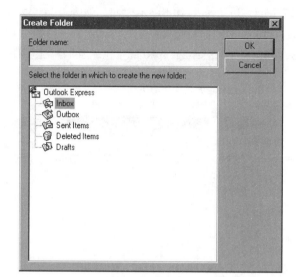

You now have a new folder in your folder list, and you can drag any message from any other folder to it—or from it to any of them.

Reading and Saving Attachments

An attachment is a file that is appended to an e-mail message. You'll know that a message has an attachment if the header is preceded by the paper clip icon. When you open the message, you'll see an attachment icon at the bottom followed by the name of the file and its size.

To read an attachment, simply double-click its icon (if the attachment is a text file). To save an attachment, follow these steps:

1. With the message open, choose File ➢ Save Attachments.

2. Click the filename to open the Save Attachment As dialog box.

3. Select a folder and a filename, and click Save.

A Word about E-Mail Viruses

You have no doubt heard about the phenomenon of e-mail viruses. In April 1999, the Melissa virus received widespread media attention, causing many e-mail users to become more paranoid than ever.

Continued ▶

The Melissa virus propagated itself via e-mail attachments. It came as a Microsoft Word document with the `.doc` file extension, and it could infect the user's machine only if the file was actually opened, and if the user had Word 97 or Word 2000. An Excel version followed, as well as a version with the more generic `.rtf` extension. The virus then proceeded to disable macro protection on the victim's machine and send document files via e-mail to people in the user's Outlook or Outlook Express Contacts list. Recipients saw that the message came from someone they knew (even though the sender was unaware that all of this was happening), so they assumed that the attachments were safe to open.

Then in 2000, an e-mail virus struck again—this one called "I Love You." Similar situation, except this virus, even more insidious, deleted graphics files from the victim's hard disk and in some cases caused other damage, too.

What does this mean for you? Although the subject of computer viruses could fill a book, the salient point for us to understand here is that the only practical way for a virus to infect your computer via e-mail is through an attachment. Infection requires conscious action on the part of the victims—in this case, opening a file attachment. The easiest way to protect yourself from this kind of damage is to be *extremely* careful about opening e-mail attachments. If you weren't expecting to receive an attached file, or you are not absolutely sure who the sender is, don't trust it.

Backing Up Your Message Files

In the likely event that the only messages you will lose are those most important to you, back up your message folders regularly. Here are the steps:

1. Select a folder, and then choose File ➤ Folder ➤ Compact. Doing so decreases the amount of disk space that each folder requires.

2. Find the files on your computer that have the extensions `.idx` and `.mbx`.

3. Copy the files to a backup disk.

To compact all folders, choose File ➤ Folder ➤ Compact All Folders.

Replying to a Message

When a message is selected, you can reply to it in the following ways:

- Click the Reply to Sender icon in the toolbar.

- Click the Reply to All icon in the toolbar (if the message has carbon-copy or blind-copy recipients or multiple recipients).

WARNING If there were blind copy recipients, and you choose Reply to All, those recipients get a copy of your reply too, but you don't get to see who they were. This can be very dangerous if you are replying with sensitive information!

- Choose Message ➤ Reply to Sender (Ctrl+R) or Message ➤ Reply to All (Ctrl+ Shift+R).

By default, Outlook Express Mail includes in your reply all the text of the message to which you are replying. If you don't want that message included, follow these steps:

1. In the Outlook Express window, choose Tools ➤ Options to open the Options dialog box. (The Options dialog box will be discussed in more depth later.)

2. Select the Send tab, and remove the check mark next to Include Message in Reply.

3. Click Apply, and then click OK.

To include only selected portions of the message in your reply, leave the Include Message in Reply option checked and follow these steps:

1. Click the message header to open the message.

2. Click the Reply to Sender icon. You'll see the message header and the text of the message to which you are replying. The message is now addressed to its original sender.

3. In the body of the message, edit the message so that the portions you want are retained and then enter your response.

4. Click the Send icon on the toolbar to send your reply. (Sending messages will be discussed in more depth later.)

Forwarding a Message

Forwarding an e-mail message is much easier than forwarding a letter through the U.S. mail, and it actually works. To forward a message, follow these steps:

1. Open the message.

2. Select Forward in one of the following ways:
   - Click the Forward icon on the toolbar.
   - Choose Message ➤ Forward.
   - Press Ctrl+F.

3. Enter an e-mail address in the To field. (You can also add your own comments to the message, if you choose.)

4. Click Send.

Deleting a Message

You can delete a message in three ways:

- Select its header and click the Delete icon on the toolbar.

- Select its header and choose Edit ➤ Delete.

- Open the message and click the Delete icon.

The message is not yet permanently deleted, however; Outlook Express has simply moved it to the Deleted Items folder. To delete it permanently, follow these steps:

1. Select the Deleted Items folder.

2. Select the message you want to delete.

3. Choose Edit ➤ Delete or click the Delete icon.

NOTE As you'll see in the "Customizing Mail and News Options" section later in this chapter, you can also specify that all messages in the Deleted Items folder be deleted when you exit Outlook Express Mail.

WARNING Outlook Express has no Undelete command, so be sure you really want to delete a message when you delete it from the Deleted Items folder.

Creating and Sending Messages

By now, you must be champing at the bit to create and send your own messages, so let's do that next. In a later section, you'll explore the many options you have when composing messages. In this section, you'll compose a simple message and send it.

Composing Your Message

You can begin a new message in a couple of ways:

- Choose Message ➤ New Message (Ctrl+N).

- Click the New Mail icon in the toolbar.

When you begin a new message, Outlook Express displays the New Message window, as shown in Figure 22.3.

FIGURE 22.3
You have a blank canvas on which to compose your message.

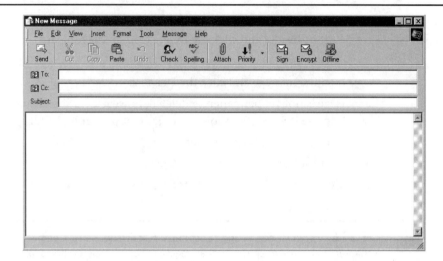

Header Information

The header section of the New Message window has four fields:

- From (available only if you have multiple mail accounts)
- To
- Cc
- Subject

The only field that you must fill in is the To field. All recipients can see the addresses you enter in the Cc, or carbon-copy, field.

The From field allows you to choose which e-mail account you want to use to send the message if you have more than one account. (You won't see the From field unless you have more than one mail account configured in OE.) This is a useful feature, especially if you want to specify that a message be sent from your work account or personal account. The e-mail address shown in the From field is the address to which replies will be sent.

If you don't fill in the Subject field, Outlook Express displays a message box asking if you really want to send the message with no subject line. When Outlook Express saves your message in a folder, it uses the subject line as the filename.

Creating Your Message

To enter header information and compose your message, follow these steps:

1. Enter the e-mail address of the primary recipient in the To field. If you are sending a message to more than one primary recipient, separate their addresses with semicolons.

NOTE If you have addresses in your Contacts list, you can click the little address book icon next to the word To or Cc and select an address rather than typing it. We'll look at how to use Contacts in detail in a later section.

2. Optionally, enter e-mail addresses in the Cc (carbon-copy) field.

3. Enter a subject line for your message.

4. Enter the text of your message. You can create e-mail messages in Plain Text or Rich Text (HTML) format. (We'll look at this in detail later.)

You can also set a Priority for your message. By default, the Priority is set to Normal. To set it to High or Low, choose Message ➢ Set Priority, and select from the submenu. You can also use the Priority button on the toolbar.

If you set the priority to High, an exclamation mark precedes the message header in your recipient's mailbox. If you set the priority to Low, a down arrow precedes the message header.

Your message is now complete, and you are ready to send it.

Sending Your Message

You can send your message in several ways:

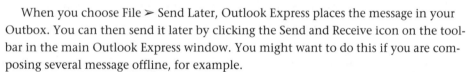

*   Click the Send icon on the toolbar in the New Message window.

*   Choose File ➢ Send Message or File ➢ Send Later.

When you choose File ➢ Send Later, Outlook Express places the message in your Outbox. You can then send it later by clicking the Send and Receive icon on the toolbar in the main Outlook Express window. You might want to do this if you are composing several message offline, for example.

Sprucing Up Your Messages

Now that we've covered the basics of reading, responding to, creating, and sending messages, let's look at some bells and whistles you can employ.

To see some of the possibilities available to you, compose a new message. Click the New Mail icon to open the New Message window, and then choose Format ➢ Rich Text (HTML). You'll see the screen shown in Figure 22.4. Notice the Formatting toolbar, which contains many of the same tools you see and use in your Windows word processor. You'll also see the Font and Font Size drop-down list boxes that are present in your Windows word processor.

 TIP One tool that you may not see in your word processor is the Insert Horizontal Line tool. Click this tool to insert a horizontal line that spans the width of your message.

FIGURE 22.4
*The New Message
screen ready for Rich
Text formatting*

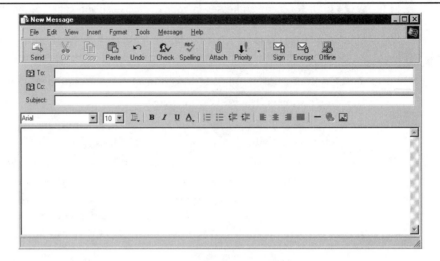

FIGURE 22.4
*The New Message
screen ready for Rich
Text formatting*

As you create your message, just pretend that you're using a word processor, and use the formatting tools to apply emphasis to your message.

You can format an e-mail message in the same ways that you format any other document. All the usual design rules apply, including the following:

- Don't use too many fonts.

- Remember, typing in all capital letters in e-mail is tantamount to shouting.

- Don't place a lot of text in italics. It's hard to read on the screen.

- Save boldface for what's really important.

NOTE If you send an HTML message to someone whose mail program does not read HTML, Outlook Express prompts you to send the message as plain text.

Using Stationery

In addition to the formatting you've just seen, you have another way to add some class or some comedy to your e-mail messages: stationery. While composing a message, choose Format ➤ Apply Stationery. You'll see a list of predesigned formats, including the following:

- A party invitation

Continued ▶

- A holiday letter

- A formal announcement

- An Ivy border

Play around with these a bit, and you'll probably think of occasions for which they would be really useful.

Adding a Signature to Your Message

Unless you're new to e-mail, you are probably in the habit of signing your messages in a particular way. If you want, however, you can create a signature that will be automatically added to all messages that you send. To do so, follow these steps:

1. In the main window, choose Tools ➢ Options to open the Options dialog box. Click the Signatures tab to bring it to the front.

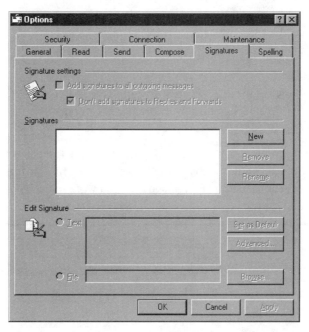

2. Click New, and type a signature in the Edit Signature box.

3. Click to place a check mark next to Add Signatures to All Outgoing Messages. You can also choose whether you want your signature placed in replies.

Adding a Picture to Your Message

Many of the picture-editing features of Microsoft Office 2000 are included with Outlook Express. You can insert pictures, size them, and move them around. Figure 22.5 shows a message that has a picture from Microsoft Office Clip Art inserted into it.

FIGURE 22.5
An e-mail message containing a picture from the Clip Art file

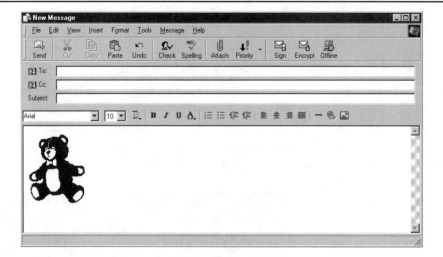

You can insert a picture into a message in two ways:

- As a background over which you can type text

- As a piece of art

To insert a picture as a background, choose Format ➤ Background ➤ Picture. Outlook Express Mail displays the Background Picture dialog box shown in Figure 22.6. Enter the filename of an image that you want to use as background, and click OK.

FIGURE 22.6
The Background Picture dialog box

To insert some decorative art in your message, follow these steps:

1. Place the cursor in the body of your message, and click the Insert Picture icon on the Formatting toolbar to open the Picture dialog box.

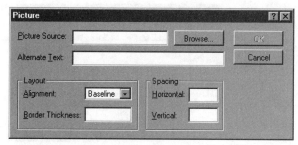

2. If you know the name of the file you want, enter it in the Picture Source box. If you don't know the filename, click Browse and select an image.

3. If you are sending this message to several recipients, some of whom may not be able to view the image, type text to substitute for the image in the Alternate Text box.

4. Specify layout and spacing and click OK.

Adding a Background Color to Your Message

To apply a color to the background of your message, choose Format ➢ Background ➢ Color, and select a color from the drop-down list. The screen in the message body is filled with the color you selected.

Now type something. Can you see it on the screen? If not, you have probably chosen a dark background and your font is also a dark color—most likely black if you haven't changed it from the default.

To make your text visible, you need to choose a light font color. To do so, click the Font Color icon and choose a light color. Now type something else. You should see light-colored letters against a dark background. Impressive for an e-mail message, huh?

Attaching Files to Your Messages

In Outlook Express Mail, sending files along with your messages is painless and simple.

To attach a file to a message that you are sending to a recipient who has an Internet e-mail address, follow these steps:

1. In the New Message window, choose Insert ➢ File Attachment. Or, click the Attach icon in the toolbar.

2. In the Insert Attachment dialog box, select the file you want to attach, and click Attach. (You can select multiple files to attach, but be aware that some recipients' e-mail programs might not be able to handle multiple attachments.)

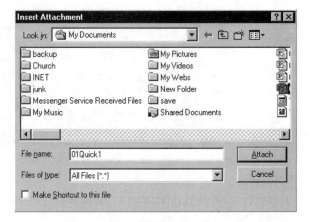

Your message now contains an icon indicating that a file is attached, the name of the file, and its size.

 NOTE As an alternative to the Insert ➢ File Attachment approach, you can drag and drop files from any folder window into the message pane.

 TIP If you accidentally attach the wrong file, select the attachment icon, and press Delete.

In addition to attaching a file, you can insert part of a file's text in a message, which is a handy way to avoid retyping something that you already have stored on your computer. To insert only a portion of a text file in your message, follow these steps:

1. In the New Message window, choose Insert ➢ Text From File.

2. In the Insert Text File dialog box, select the file you want, and click Open. A copy of the text file opens in the body of your message.

3. Edit the file so that your message contains only the text you want.

Setting Up and Using Your Contacts List

Before you get too far out in e-mail cyberspace, you'll want to set up your Contacts list. It's the repository for all sorts of information that you can use online and offline:

- E-mail addresses

- Voice, fax, modem, and cell phone numbers
- Home and business addresses
- Home page addresses

 TIP You can print out your Contacts list and take it with you.

Once an e-mail address is in your Contacts list, you no longer need to type it in the To or Cc fields. You simply click the Select Recipients from a List icon and select the address you want.

In addition, you can use your Contacts list to look for e-mail addresses in ISPs' address books, and you can use it to create distribution mailing lists.

One thing you may find confusing is that Outlook Express uses at least three different names to refer to your Contacts list. In some places it's referred to by its old name, Address Book, and on the OE toolbar it's called simply Addresses. Rest assured, they all refer to basically the same thing.

If you already have a Windows Address Book, Outlook Express Mail uses it. If you have an Address Book (or messages) in any of the following, you can import them:

- Eudora Pro or Light Address Book (through version 3)
- LDIF-LDAP Data Interchange Format
- Microsoft Exchange Personal Address Book
- Microsoft Internet Mail for Windows 3.1 Address Book
- Netscape Address Book (version 2 or 3)
- Netscape Communicator Address Book
- A text file that has comma-separated values

To import one of these address books, follow these steps:

1. Choose File ➢ Import ➢ Address Book.
2. In the Address Book Import dialog box, select the file you want to import, and click Open.

Accessing Contacts

You can open Contacts in the following ways:

- Choose Tools ➢ Address Book (press Ctrl+Shift+B).
- Click the Addresses icon on the toolbar.
- From a New Message window, click the address book icon next to To or Cc.

Adding Contacts

If you don't currently have a Windows Address Book or an Address Book that you can import, you can create one from scratch. If you're thinking that typing in all that information from your organizer would be a monumental task, you're right. But you don't have to do it all at once, and, in fact, you'll soon see an easy way to add to your Contacts as you receive messages.

Open the Address Book now, and let's get started. You'll see the Windows Address Book window, as shown in Figure 22.7. Addresses have already been entered in this Address Book, but if you haven't entered any in, obviously the lower-right portion of this window will be empty.

FIGURE 22.7
The Windows Address Book window

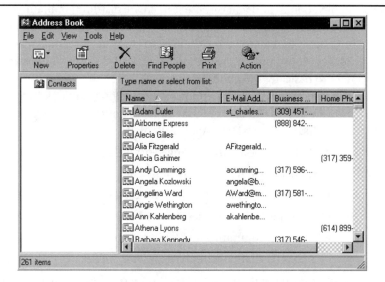

You can add a name to your Address Book in two ways:

• Choose File ➢ New Contact (Ctrl+N).

• Click the New icon on the toolbar and select New Contact from the menu that appears.

Regardless of the method you use, Windows displays the Properties dialog box.

Entering Personal Information

As you can see, the Properties dialog box has seven tabs. When you enter new contact information, the Name tab is selected by default. To enter information, follow these steps:

1. Enter the person's first, middle, and last names.

 TIP Press tab to move from one field to another. As you enter names, they appear in the Display field.

2. Now enter the person's e-mail address and press Enter. If the person has more than one e-mail address, click Add and continue entering addresses.

 TIP To make one of multiple e-mail addresses the default, select it and click Set As Default. If the person has only one e-mail address, it is automatically the default.

If you make a typing mistake, click Edit and fix the address. Or, if you change your mind altogether, get rid of the address by clicking Remove.

If this is all the information you want to store for now, click OK. You'll now see the information for this person listed in the Windows Address Book window, and you can simply click the Action ➤ Send Mail icon if you want to compose a message to them.

If you want to continue entering more information about this person, however, you can select one of the other tabs in the Properties box. For our purposes here, let's select the Home tab.

Entering Home-Related Information

When you select the Home tab, you'll see the window shown in Figure 22.8. Enter as much or as little information as you need.

FIGURE 22.8
The Home tab of the Properties window in Address Book

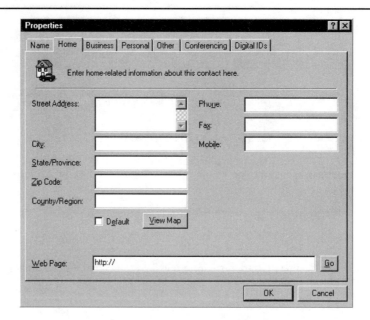

If this person has a personal Web page, you can enter the URL in the Personal Web Page text box. If you are connected to the Internet, you can then click Go to open this contact's home page in a browser window.

Now let's also assume that you want to enter some business-related information for this person.

Entering Business-Related Information

Select the Business tab (shown in Figure 22.9), and enter as much or as little information as you think you need. Remember, you can always come back to this tab and change, delete, or add information.

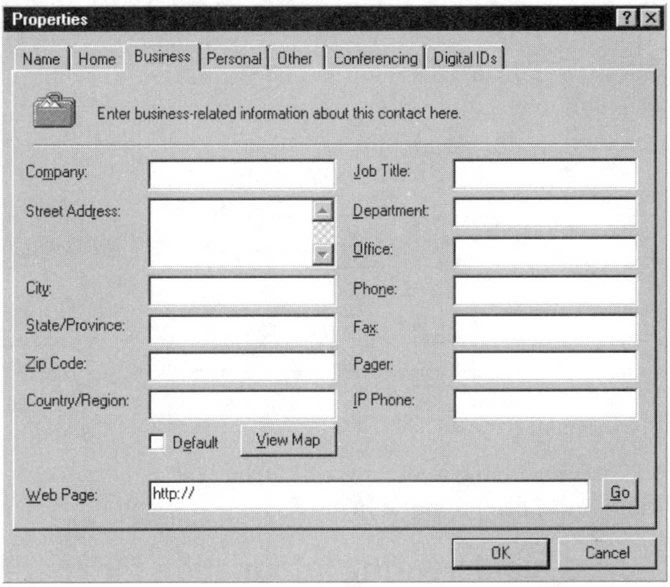

FIGURE 22.9
The Business tab of the Properties dialog box for the Address Book

If this person has a business Web page, you can enter the URL in the Business Web Page text box. When you are connected to the Internet, you can then click Go to open this home page in a browser window, just as you can with a personal Web page address.

Making a Note about This Person

Do you also need to store some information for which you haven't yet seen a convenient spot? Perhaps, for example, you want to enter the names of a client's spouse and children or make some other comment that's important to remember about the client. You can put this on the Personal tab, as shown in Figure 22.10.

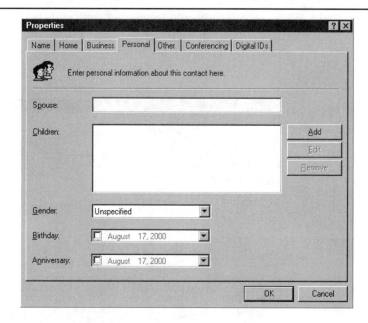

The Other tab is another good catchall place for miscellaneous information if you can't find a place to put it here.

Adding Conferencing Information for Your New Contact

If you know that you'll be getting together with this person via NetMeeting, you can enter contact information in the Conferencing tab, as shown in Figure 22.11. Enter the person's conferencing address and server here.

FIGURE 22.11

*The Conferencing tab
of the Properties
dialog box of
Address Book*

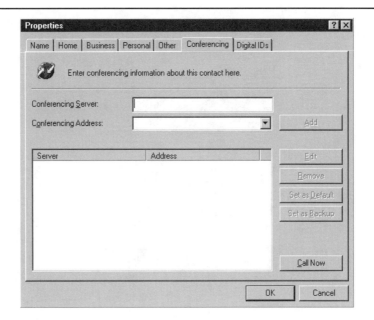

 TIP See Appendix C for details about NetMeeting.

Adding, Removing, and Viewing Digital IDs for This Person

You use a digital ID (certificate) when you want to show that you wrote a message, to
show that the message has not been tampered with, and to prevent others from signing your name to messages that you did not write.

When you use a digital ID, you encrypt your message. Only a person who also has
your certificate can read your message. If you want another person to have your certificate, you usually send it as an e-mail message attachment. When you send e-mail to a
contact who has the certificate, that person uses the certificate to decrypt the message.

You use the Digital IDs tab to add, view, and remove certificates (see Figure 22.12).

If you are entering information about someone in your Address Book and you
receive a certificate from that person, the certificate will be in a file on your computer
and will probably have the extension .pub. To enter it on this tab, click Import.

 TIP You obtain a digital ID from a qualified certifying organization such as the Internet
security company VeriSign. For more information about digital certificates and for information about applying for one, see VeriSign's Web site at www.verisign.com.

FIGURE 22.12

The Digital IDs tab of the Properties dialog box of Address Book

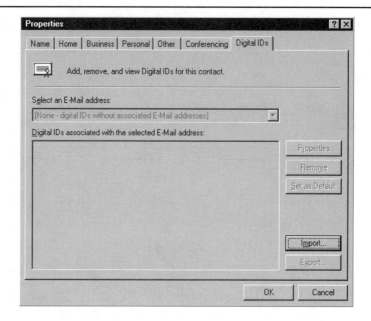

Now that you've seen how to add information about an individual to your Address Book, let's look at how to set up a group.

Setting Up a Group of Contacts

When you use a group, you can send the same message to several people at once; in other words, it's a distribution list.

You might set up a group for any number of purposes. For example, you might want to remind the Thursday night duplicate bridge club in your office that this week you'll be playing at Joe's house and that it's BYOB. Or you might set up a group that consists of the staff in your department.

To set up a group, open Address Book and click the New ➤ New Group icon on the toolbar. You'll see the Group tab of the Properties dialog box, as shown in Figure 22.13.

To create a group, follow these steps:

1. In the Group Name box, type a name for the group.

TIP Be sure to make the name descriptive so that you know exactly which people are getting what. You probably don't want to invite the entire sales department to a baby shower for someone in your aerobics class.

FIGURE 22.13
The Group tab of the Properties dialog box of Address Book

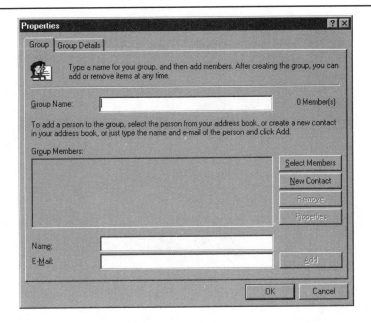

2. If you want to add to the group a person who is not yet in your Address Book, click New Contact to open the Properties dialog box.

3. Click Select Members to open the Select Group Members dialog box.

NOTE On the Group Details tab, you can enter comments. For example, if you're setting up a group named New Products Task Force, you might make a note that this group meets every Wednesday at noon over lunch.

4. To place members in the group, select the person's name and then click Select. The names of the members begin to accumulate in the Group Members section.

5. When you have selected all the names you want, click OK. Outlook Express again displays the Properties dialog box for the group you are creating. If the list is to your liking, click OK.

You will now see the name of the group you just created in the Windows Address Book window. To send mail to the group, select the group name and choose Action ➤ Send Mail.

Customizing Your Address Book Window

If you have entered several contacts, you might notice that in the Address Book window they appear in the order in which they were entered. This is probably not the most useful way to maintain this list, especially if you have many contacts and many groups.

To change the order, choose View ➢ Sort By. You'll see the options shown below.

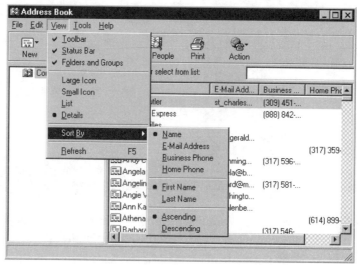

Click an option, and Outlook Express sorts your list accordingly.

But you have still other ways to customize this window. You can choose Large Icon, Small Icon, or List view. If you choose View ➢ List, you'll see only the names, not the e-mail addresses and phone numbers.

Printing from Your Address Book

On occasion, you may need a printed copy of your Address Book. For example, you might want to take a printed copy on a trip. To print the entire contents of every contact in your Address Book, follow these steps:

1. Open Address Book.

2. Choose Edit ➢ Select All.

3. Click the Print icon.

4. In the Print dialog box, click the Memo option button (if it isn't already selected), and then click OK.

You'll get a printed copy showing the name of each contact (in alphabetic order by last name), followed by that person's information (both home and business).

To print only business-related information about a single contact or your entire list, click the Business Card option. If you want to print only names and phone numbers, click the Phone List option.

Using Outlook Express News

If you've subscribed to any of the commercial ISPs, you've no doubt browsed online newspapers and magazines and seen a news flash when you sign on to the service. That's not what we're talking about in this section.

This section concerns *newsgroups,* collections of articles about particular subjects. Newsgroups are similar to e-mail in that you can reply to what someone else has written (the newsgroup term for this is *posted),* and you can send a question or a response either to the whole group or to individuals.

To read newsgroups, you need a *newsreader,* and that is what Outlook Express News is. But before we get into the nuts and bolts of how to use Outlook Express News to read newsgroups, we want to look at the kinds of newsgroups that are available and give you a bit of background about how they work, what they are, and what they are not.

 WARNING If you are new to newsgroups, be aware that they are uncensored. You can find just about anything at any time anywhere. No person has authority over newsgroups as a whole. If you find certain groups, certain articles, or certain people offensive, don't go there. Later in this chapter, you'll see how you can filter out such articles. But remember that anarchy reigns. Forewarned is forearmed.

You can start Outlook Express News in any of the following ways:

- From the Outlook Express opening screen, click Read News. (Remember, to get back to the opening screen, click Outlook Express at the top of the folder tree at the left.)
- Click News in the Outlook bar.
- Choose Tools ➢ Newsgroups.

Downloading a List of Newsgroups

Before you can access newsgroups, you need to download a list from the ISP's news server. Connect to your ISP and open Outlook Express. In the Outlook bar or folder list, click the icon for your news server to open this dialog box:

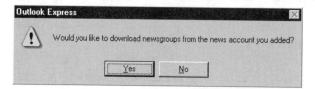

Click Yes to download a list of the newsgroups available on your news server. While this takes place, you'll see a message similar to the following:

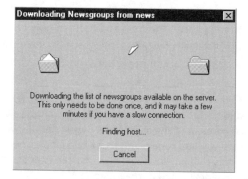

Depending on the speed of your connection, this downloading process should take only a few minutes. Watch as the counter increases—you'll be amazed at the number of newsgroups.

Once this list is downloaded, your newsgroups dialog box will look similar to this:

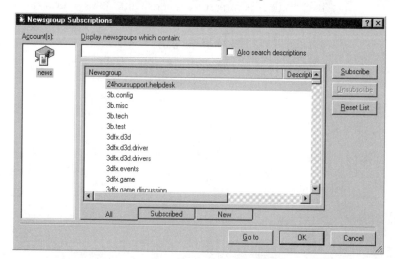

TIP   Only the names of the newsgroups are downloaded to your computer; their contents remain on the news server. Periodically, you can update this list by clicking Reset List.

Searching for an Interesting Newsgroup

Well, now that you have all this at your disposal, how do you find something that you're interested in? It reminds us of having to go to a department store to select what we're going to wear to work every morning. With so many choices, how can you decide (if money's no object, of course)?

You can select a newsgroup to read in two ways:

- You can scroll through the list (this could take some time).

- You can enter a term to search on.

Just for the sake of doing it, scroll the list a bit. As you can see, it's in alphabetic order by hierarchical categories. Now let's assume you don't see anything right away that strikes your fancy. Not to worry—you can search for something. To search for a topic, enter the word or words in the Display Newsgroups Which Contain box.

WARNING   Type your entry and then don't do anything! Wait a second, and groups containing what you entered will appear in the Newsgroup area. You don't need to press Enter, click OK, or do anything else. Just wait a nanosecond.

I entered the word **internet**, and Figure 22.14 shows the results.

FIGURE 22.14
A list of newsgroups that appeared when I searched on the word "internet"

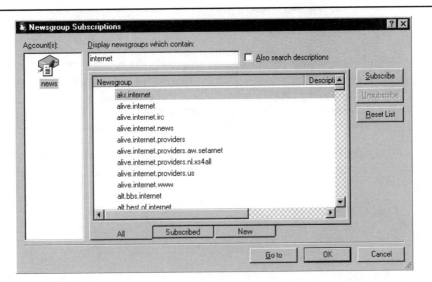

Reading a Newsgroup

Now you can select a newsgroup to read. To do so, follow these steps:

1. Click the name of the newsgroup.

2. Click Go To.

I chose to read `microsoft.public.internet.news`, and Figure 22.15 shows what I got.

FIGURE 22.15
A message from the selected newsgroup appears in the preview pane.

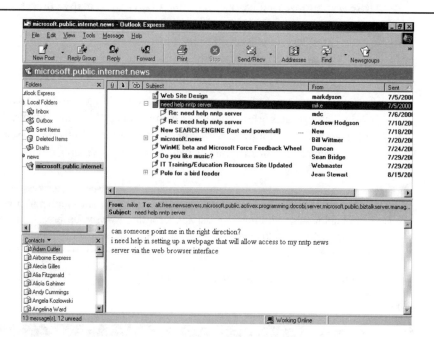

 NOTE Unfortunately, Outlook Express News doesn't maintain the list that your search found in the Newsgroup dialog box. If you want to select another newsgroup that was in the found group, you have to repeat your search.

To read an article, simply click its header. You can also double-click the message header to open it in a separate message window.

Replying and Posting

While you're reading a newsgroup, you can respond to an individual author of a message or you can reply to the entire group. Choose the method most appropriate to the topic and the subject of the newsgroup.

> **TIP** You'll occasionally see requests for responses be directed toward the individual and not the group; you should honor these requests.

To respond to an individual author, follow these steps:

Reply

1. Click the Reply tool button.

2. In the message window, type your message.

3. Click Send.

Reply Group

To reply to the whole group, click the Reply Group tool button. The name of the group will appear in the To field.

New Post

To post a new message to a group, click the New Post tool button. To reply both to the author and to the newsgroup, choose Message ➤ Reply To All. You can also use the Message menu to forward articles and to forward articles as attachments.

Subscribing and Unsubscribing to Newsgroups

When you read a newsgroup, it appears as a subfolder in your News folder. When you exit Outlook Express, these folders are deleted from the folder list.

When you *subscribe* to a newsgroup, it also appears as a subfolder in your News folder. When you exit Outlook Express News, however, this folder is retained in the folder list. The next time you access your news server, you can simply click this folder to open the newsgroup.

You can subscribe to newsgroups in the following ways:

- In the Newsgroup Subscriptions dialog box, select a group and click Subscribe.

- With the newsgroup open, right-click the newsgroup's listing in the folder list and choose Subscribe.

When you no longer want to subscribe to a newsgroup, follow these steps:

Newsgroups

1. Click the Newsgroups tool button.

2. In the Newsgroup dialog box, select the Subscribed tab.

3. Select the name of the newsgroup, and click Unsubscribe.

While viewing a newsgroup, you can unsubscribe by right-clicking the newsgroup's listing in the folder list and choosing Unsubscribe.

Rules for Posting to Newsgroups

Although newsgroups are not controlled by any single entity, there are some established rules for using them:

- Lurk before you post; get a sense of the group's culture and style.
- Never forget that the person on the other side is human.
- Don't blame system administrators for their users' behavior.
- Never assume that a person is speaking for their organization.
- Be careful what you say about others (as many as three million people may read what you say).
- Be brief.
- Your postings reflect upon you; be proud of them.
- Use descriptive titles.
- Think about your audience.
- Be careful with humor and sarcasm.
- Post a message only once.
- Summarize what you are following up.
- Use Mail; don't post a follow-up.
- Be careful about copyrights and licenses.
- Cite appropriate references.
- Don't overdo signatures.
- Avoid posting to multiple newsgroups.

Filtering Out What You Don't Want to Read

As we've mentioned, most newsgroups are not censored in any way. Outlook Express News, however, provides a way that you can be your own censor. You can choose which newsgroups appear on the message list and are downloaded to your computer.

 NOTE Some groups are moderated—that is, someone is in charge of the newsgroup and reads posts and replies. That person applies certain specified criteria, and only those messages that meet these guidelines appear in the newsgroup. When a newsgroup is moderated, you'll see a message to that effect when you open the newsgroup.

Selecting newsgroups and messages that you don't want to appear on your computer is called *filtering*. You might choose to filter groups and messages for any number of reasons, including the following:

- To avoid scrolling through messages on topics that don't interest you

- To screen out messages that have been around a long time

To filter newsgroups and messages, follow these steps:

1. Choose Tools ➢ Message Rules ➢ News to open the New News Rule dialog box.

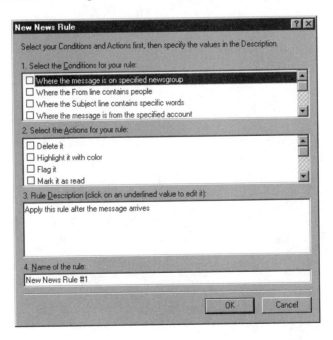

2. In section 1, place a check mark next to each rule you want to use.

3. In section 2, place a check mark next to the action you want taken.

4. In section 3, click the blue links as needed to provide more specific information.

5. Click OK when you are done making rules.

How you ultimately use this dialog will depend on the rules you're making. For instance, if you want to delete any messages that contain objectionable words in the subject line, choose Where the Subject Line Contains Specific Words in section 1. In section 2, choose Delete It. In section 3, click the blue link that says Contains Specific Words, and enter the words you find objectionable.

Viewing, Marking, and Sorting Messages

As is the case with Outlook Express Mail, by default your preview pane is split horizontally, with header information in the top pane and messages displayed in the bottom pane. To change this format, choose View ➢ Layout to open the Window Layout Properties dialog box. In the Preview Pane section of this dialog box, select the options that correspond to the way you want to display messages.

You can also choose to display only certain messages. Choose View ➢ Current View, and then select an option from the drop-down menu.

You can choose to display the Subject, From, Sent, Size, and Lines fields in headers. Follow these steps:

1. With a newsgroup displayed, choose View ➢ Columns to open the Columns dialog box.

2. Place a check mark next to only the columns you want displayed.

3. When the display is to your liking, click OK.

 TIP To return to the default display, click Reset.

Browsing for Messages

You can look for messages using the scroll bar, and you can go to certain messages by choosing View ➤ Next and selecting from the drop-down menu.

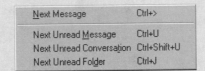

Next Message	Ctrl+>
Next Unread Message	Ctrl+U
Next Unread Conversation	Ctrl+Shift+U
Next Unread Folder	Ctrl+J

As you can see, you can choose the next message or choose the next unread message, thread, or newsgroup.

When reading a message, you can click the up and down arrows at the top of the message to go to the previous or next message in the newsgroup.

Interpreting the News Icons

When you view a newsgroup, you'll notice that some messages are preceded by a plus sign (+). This means that this message is part of a thread. To view the thread, simply click the plus sign. The message that is part of the thread is displayed. It may also be preceded by a plus sign if it is part of a further, ongoing thread.

When you click a thread to display the further messages, it becomes a minus sign (–). Click the minus sign to once again collapse the thread.

For an explanation of the many, many other news icons, choose Help ➤ Contents and Index, select the Contents tab, select Tips and Tricks, and then click Message List Icons for Outlook Express.

Terminology

Here are a couple of terms that will prove helpful when you are working with messages:

Header The information displayed in the message window. The header may contain information such as the name of the sender, the subject, the newsgroups to which it is posted, and the time and date the message was sent or received.

Thread An original message and any posted replies. If you reply to a message and change the title, however, you start a new thread.

Marking Messages

Although Outlook Express marks messages as you read them and indicates which messages you have not read, you can manually mark messages. As you'll see in the section "Customizing Mail and News Options," you can use the Read tab of the Options dialog box to have Outlook Express automatically mark all messages as read when you exit a newsgroup. You can also mark messages using the Edit menu.

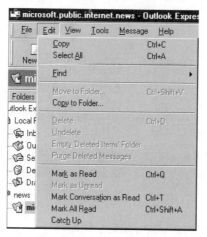

Select a message header, click Edit, and select one of these options.

Sorting Messages

By default, Outlook Express displays messages in ascending alphabetic order by subject. For example, in a software engineering newsgroup, a message header about Hungarian notation appears before a header containing "IBM Kasparov vs. Deep Blue."

You can change the order in which messages are displayed. Choose View ➤ Sort By, and then choose an option from the drop-down menu

To display the most recently sent messages first, choose View ➤ Sort By ➤ Sent. To display the list so that all messages by any one sender are grouped together, choose View ➤ Sort By ➤ From. (Sorting and grouping headers can make for some interesting reading.)

Setting Key Mail and News Options

You can customize many aspects of Outlook Express so that it works the way you like to work. For example, you can place buttons for the tasks you most commonly perform on the toolbar, and you can choose not to display those you rarely need. Also, you can establish all sorts of rules for Outlook Express to follow while you are composing, sending, and receiving messages.

Let's look first at the ways you can customize the toolbar.

Customizing the Toolbar

When you first install Outlook Express, the toolbar in the main window looks like this:

To add or delete buttons or to rearrange them, choose View ➤ Layout to open the Window Layout Properties dialog box, and then click Customize Toolbar.

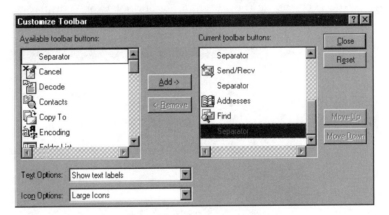

From the Customize Toolbar dialog box, you can add or delete buttons. To add a button, follow these steps:

1. Select the button in the Available Toolbar Buttons list.

2. Click the Add button.

3. Click Close.

4. In the Window Layout Properties dialog box, click Apply, and then click OK.

The button now appears on your toolbar.

TIP You can return your toolbar to its original format at any time. In the Customize Toolbar dialog box, choose Reset and then Close. Then, in the Window Layout Properties dialog box, click Apply and then click OK.

Customizing Mail and News Options

You can use the Options dialog box to establish your preferences for both Outlook Express Mail and Outlook Express News. Let's start by looking at the General options.

 NOTE Depending on your installation of Internet Explorer, the default settings may differ. Before you start using Outlook Express extensively, take a moment to see which options are checked by default on your system.

The General Tab

When you choose Tools ➤ Options, Outlook Express displays the Options dialog box with the General tab selected.

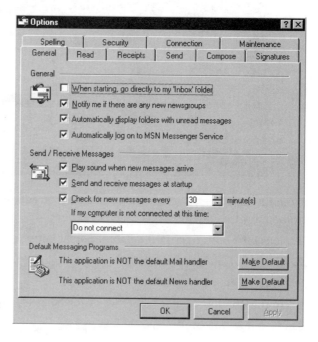

Table 22.1 shows the options that you can set up in the General tab.

Option	What It Does
When Starting, Go Directly to My "Inbox" Folder	Check this item to go immediately to your Inbox when you start Outlook Express.
Notify Me If There Are Any New Newsgroups	Check this option if you want Outlook Express to check for new newsgroups and download their names when you access a news server.
Automatically Display Folders with Unread Messages	Check this option if you want to display only unread messages.
Automatically Log On to MSN Messenger Service	Mark this if you use MSN Messenger and want to be connected every time you go online.
Play Sound When New Messages Arrive	Of course, this works only when you are connected to your e-mail server. If you don't want to be notified when new mail arrives, uncheck this option. You can customize the sound via Control Panel ➢ Sounds.
Send and Receive Messages at Startup	With this option enabled, Outlook Express will automatically send unsent messages and check for new mail when you start the program.
Check for New Messages Every x Minutes	Check this item and then click the spinner-box arrows to select a time interval.
If My Computer Is Not Connected at This Time	If your computer is offline when it becomes time to check for new messages, do you want it to connect or not? Choose an option in the drop-down list here to decide.
Default Messaging Programs	If Outlook Express is not already set as your default mail and/or newsreader, click one of the buttons here to set it.

Reading Mail and News

Select the Read tab, and Outlook Express displays this dialog box:

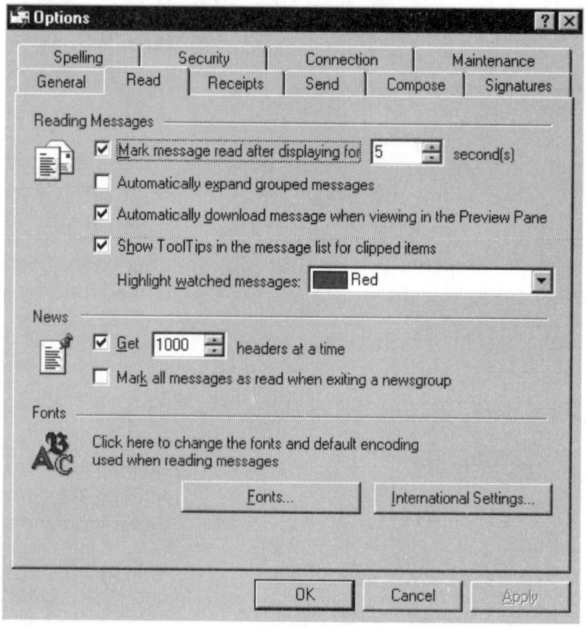

Table 22.2 shows the options in the Read Tab.

TABLE 22.2: THE OPTIONS IN THE READ TAB

Option	What It Does
Mark Message Read After Displaying for x Second(s)	You can change the number of seconds, and you can uncheck this option to manually mark messages as read.
Automatically Expand Grouped Messages	If you select this option, threads and all replies are displayed when you open a newsgroup.
Automatically Download Message When Viewing in the Preview Pane	If you uncheck this option, select the header and then press the spacebar to display the message body.
Show ToolTips in the Message List for Clipped Items	With this enabled, if you hold the mouse pointer over a clipped item, a tooltip will appear showing the name of the attachment.

Continued

TABLE 22.2: THE OPTIONS IN THE READ TAB (CONTINUED)	
Option	**What It Does**
Get *x* Headers at a Time	Set at 300 by default. You can set this option to a minimum of 50 and a maximum of 1,000. (Would you really want to download 1,000 headers?) If you uncheck this option, all headers in the newsgroup are downloaded, regardless of the number.
Mark All Messages as Read When Exiting a Newsgroup	When you select this option, you choose to read only messages marked as unread when you return to this newsgroup.

You use the Fonts section of the Read tab to change the fonts used when reading messages. When you install Outlook Express, messages you read are formatted in the Western Alphabet using Arial as the proportional font (when you are using the HTML format), using Courier New as the fixed-width font (when you are using the Plain Text format), and a medium font size. To change any of this, click the Fonts button. Outlook Express displays the Fonts dialog box, as shown in Figure 22.16. Click the down arrows to survey your choices.

FIGURE 22.16
The Fonts dialog box

Mail Receipts

To set preferences for mailing receipts, click the Receipts tab.

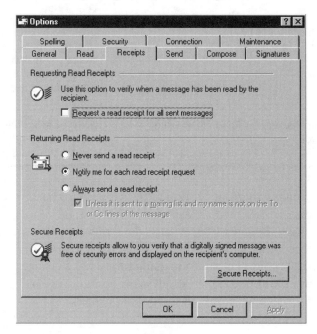

Here you can request a read receipt so that a message returns to you letting you know the recipient has opened your message.

You can also specify how you want to handle requests for read receipts that come from others. Note that because of this capability, you might not always get a receipt when one of your recipients reads a message if they have this setting set to Never Send a Read Receipt.

Finally, you can set up secure receipts, which work with digital signatures to ensure that the intended recipient got the message, and not some interceptor.

Sending Mail and News

To set your preferences for sending mail and news, select the Send tab.

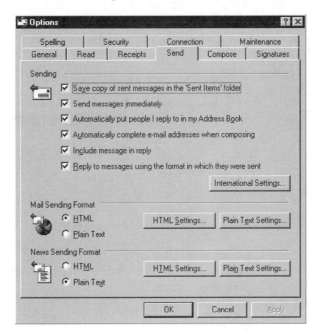

In the upper half of this dialog box, you can choose to include messages in replies and specify when messages in the Outbox should be sent.

In the Mail Sending Format section of the Send tab, you specify whether you want to send mail in HTML or Plain Text format. If you want all messages composed and sent in HTML, check this option and click the HTML Settings button to open the HTML Settings dialog box.

In the Encode Text Using drop-down list box in the MIME Message Format section, you have three choices:

- None
- Quoted Printable
- Base 64

These are the available bit and binary formats for encoding your message. Quoted Printable is selected by default.

The Allow 8-Bit Characters in Headers check box is unchecked by default. This means that foreign character sets, high ASCII, or double-byte character sets (DBCS) in the header will be encoded. If this check box is checked, these characters will not be encoded.

When you select Plain Text as your mail sending format and click Plain Text Settings, Outlook Express displays the Plain Text Settings dialog box.

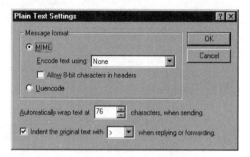

In the Encode Text Using drop-down list in the Message Format section of this dialog box, you have three choices:

- None

- Quoted Printable

- Base 64

None is selected by default.

 NOTE Unless your system administrator or ISP instructs you to do so, don't change these settings.

By default, when you send messages in Plain Text format, lines wrap at 76 characters. To change this format, click the drop-down list arrow and select a greater or lesser number of characters. Also by default, the original text of a message to which you reply is preceded by an angle bracket. To select another character, click the drop-down list arrow.

In the News Sending Format section of the Send tab, you can choose whether to post articles in HTML or Plain Text. Selecting Plain Text is a wise choice if you are posting to a widely read newsgroup. Most newsreaders cannot display articles in HTML. Selecting either HTML or Plain Text and clicking the Settings button opens the Settings dialog box for that selection. In either case, you'll see the same dialog box that opens when you select that option for sending mail.

Table 22.3 lists and explains the other options in the Send tab.

TABLE 22.3: ADDITIONAL OPTIONS IN THE SEND TAB

Option	What It Does
Save Copy of Sent Messages in the "Sent Items" Folder	This is handy for verifying that you really sent a message that you intended to send. If it is unchecked, you can still keep a copy by including yourself on the Cc or Bcc line.
Send Messages Immediately	If you check this item, messages are sent when you click the Send button rather than being saved in your Outbox until you send them.
Automatically Put People I Reply to in My Address Book	Check this option if you want the names and e-mail addresses of everybody you reply to in your Address Book.
Automatically Complete E-Mail Addresses When Composing	If you check this option, Outlook Express completes the e-mail address you are typing as soon as it recognizes a series of characters, if this address is in your Address Book.
Include Message in Reply	If you check this option, you can edit the message to which you are replying so that it retains only the pertinent sentences or paragraphs. This device comes in handy when you are responding to a sender's questions.
Reply to Messages Using the Format in Which They Were Sent	To send a message in a different format, uncheck this item.

Checking Spelling

If you send and receive lots of e-mail, you're probably used to seeing and, for the most part, ignoring typos. In the early days of e-mail, the only way to check what you were sending was to stop, read it over, and, with minimal editing features available, fix your errors.

This was a time-consuming task associated with a powerful time-saving application, and most people just didn't (don't?) bother. If you're simply communicating with colleagues down the hall or buddies in your bowling league, maybe it doesn't matter. But if you're sending a trip report to your boss or posting a major announcement to a newsgroup, it matters. You want to appear professional, and you certainly don't want to embarrass yourself with a couple of transposed letters.

 NOTE Outlook Express uses the spelling checker that comes with Microsoft Office 95, 97, or 2000 programs. If you don't have one of these programs installed, the Spelling command is unavailable.

Using the spelling checker, you can quickly give your messages the once-over before they wend their way to the outside world. Click the Spelling tab to display your options.

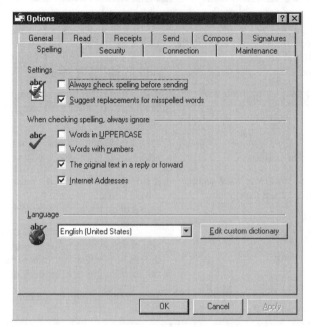

Table 22.4 shows the options available in the Spelling tab.

TABLE 22.4: THE OPTIONS IN THE SPELLING TAB

Option	What It Does
Always Check Spelling before Sending	Check this option if you want Outlook Express to quickly look for typos before a message is sent.
Suggest Replacements for Misspelled Words	With this option checked, Outlook Express checks your spelling as you go along and suggests replacements.
Always Ignore Words in UPPERCASE	When this option is checked, words entirely uppercased are ignored in the spelling check.
Always Ignore Words with Numbers	When this option is checked, words that include numeric characters are ignored in the spelling check.

Continued ▶

TABLE 22.4: THE OPTIONS IN THE SPELLING TAB (CONTINUED)	
Option	**What It Does**
Always Ignore the Original Text in a Reply or Forward	When this option is checked, only your message is spell-checked, not the message you are forwarding or to which you are replying.
Always Ignore Internet Addresses	If you've ever had your spell checker come to a halt every time it reaches a URL, you'll want to keep this option turned on.

By default, your messages are checked against a U.S. English dictionary. If you want to choose British English, click the Language down arrow. To create or change a custom dictionary, click Edit Custom Dictionary.

Enhancing Security

You use the Security tab to establish security zones and to specify how Outlook Express handles digital certificates (also know as digital IDs).

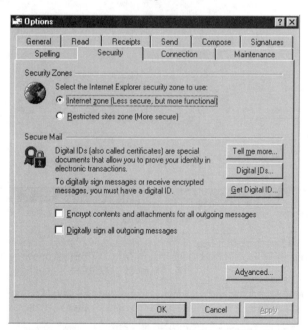

With Internet Explorer, you can assign Web sites to zones that have varying levels of security. If you have a digital certificate (as discussed earlier in the "Adding, Removing, and Viewing Digital IDs for This Person" section), you can add it to all outgoing messages by using the options in the Secure Mail section of this tab.

To obtain a digital ID, click the Get Digital ID button in the Secure Mail section. Or for more information, click the Tell Me More button.

Your Connection Options

As we mentioned early in this chapter, we are assuming a dial-up connection to the Internet. You use the options in the Connection tab to specify how you connect to your ISP when you start Outlook Express.

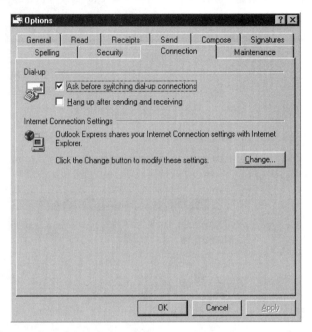

Table 22.5 lists and explains these options.

TABLE 22.5: THE OPTIONS IN THE CONNECTION TAB

Option	What It Does
Ask before Switching Dial-Up Connections	If you have separate Internet connections for your various accounts, this makes Outlook Express prompt you before it hangs up an existing connection and dials a new one.
Hang Up after Sending and Receiving	When this option is selected, Outlook Express automatically disconnects from your ISP after sending, receiving, or downloading.
Outlook Express Shares Your Internet Connections Settings with Internet Explorer	Clicking the Change button opens the Internet Properties dialog box. See Chapter 11, "Printers and Printing," to learn more about those settings.

The Maintenance Tab

You use the options in the Maintenance tab to determine how your local message files are stored.

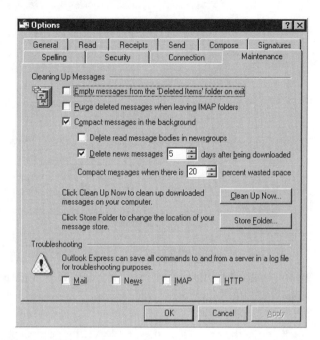

Table 22.6 lists and explains these options.

Communication and
Using the Internet

TABLE 22.6: THE OPTIONS IN THE MAINTENANCE TAB	
Option	**What It Does**
Empty Messages from the "Deleted Items" Folder on Exit	Messages are placed in this folder when you select a message and choose Delete. Check this item if you want the Deleted Items folder emptied when you exit Outlook Express.
Purge Deleted Messages When Leaving IMAP Folders	Deleted messages are purged when you leave folders on the IMAP server.
Compact Messages in the Background	Contains suboptions to help preserve hard-disk space. Set at 20 percent by default. You can choose a minimum of 5 percent and a maximum of 100 percent.
Troubleshooting	You can choose to have a log file recorded for the different protocols listed to aid in troubleshooting problems.

Now let's look at the Clean Up Now button on this tab. When you click this button, Outlook Express News displays the Local File Clean Up dialog box.

In this dialog box, first specify the files you want, and then click the appropriate buttons to do the following:

- Compact the files.

- Remove the message bodies but leave the headers in the files.

- Remove all messages, headers, and bodies from the files.

- Reset the information stored for the selected newsgroups so that you can download messages again.

CHAPTER **23**

Publishing on the Web

The Web is a very democratic environment. Unlike newspaper and TV, on the Web everyone can have a voice. All you need to do is create a Web page and upload it to a Web server, and suddenly millions of people all over the world have access to your ideas, opinions, and products/services for sale.

There are entire books written about creating Web sites (that is, collections of Web pages), and I can't hope to make you an expert in a single chapter here. However, I'll review the basic concepts of Web page creation, show you how to create them in Notepad and Microsoft Word, and help you choose a Web server on which to publish your pages. I'll also point you toward some resources for making your Web pages more sophisticated when you're ready to take that next step.

Understanding Web Publishing

One of my favorite things about the World Wide Web is that it was not created by a marketing person; no one with an MBA thought up this business model and then set out to make millions by building a worldwide ad agency. Instead, the Web was created by a group of physicists in Switzerland because they wanted to share their technical diagrams with other scientists. Prior to the Web, most of the information on the Internet was text, and it wasn't even formatted (no fancy fonts, no colored text, not even bold and italics). The creation of the Web in the early 1990s changed all that, making it possible to display images and—later—sound, animation, and video on the Internet. But the Web still suffers from the fact that it was born as a practical solution to a scientific problem—and even its creators could not have predicted its impact.

Today, the Web is the fastest growing part of the Internet and the most dynamic; it's a place where you can create information and make it available to nearly everyone else on the Internet. This brings me to an important distinction that often confuses people. The Web is not the Internet—it's part of the Internet, just as e-mail is part of the Internet. What makes e-mail and the Web so important is that they are the most universally accessible parts of the online world.

Another important thing to understand is that no one "owns" the Internet. It works as a cooperative arrangement among an international group of private and public organizations and individuals. The two organizations that come closest to acting as governing bodies for the Web are the Internet Network Information Center (InterNIC), which manages *domain name* registration, and the World Wide Web Consortium (W3C), which sets HTML standards.

NOTE The World Wide Web is still in its infancy. Design rules and even the language used to create Web pages are continually changing and evolving. To stay abreast of the latest technical standards, keep an eye on the World Wide Web Consortium at www.w3c.com.

Web Publishing Terminology

Let's start out by reviewing some terms that may or may not be familiar to you from your previous exposure to the Internet. You learned in Chapter 21, "Browsing the World Wide Web with Internet Explorer 5.5," about Web pages, Web sites, and hyperlinks. You also learned how you can jump from page to page using hyperlinks or enter Web addresses directly into your Web browsing program. Here are a few more key concepts:

HTML Stands for Hypertext Markup Language. This is the file format for most Web pages. Depending on the program you use to create your Web pages, you may have the choice between saving in HTML format or Web Page format; they are the same thing.

NOTE There are other, more sophisticated, page formats that some Web browsers can display, such as CGI, XML, MHT, and XPML. They are primarily for professional Web designers creating online stores and secure database and ordering systems, however. As a beginning Web page artist, you will work with HTML format.

Web server A computer that's connected to the Internet full-time and whose job it is to provide access to Web pages stored on it. Your ISP has a Web server, and you probably are allowed a certain amount of free space on it. However, there may be limitations on it, such as no business use or no more than a certain number of visitors per day.

Web host A company that specializes in renting Web server space. Your ISP might also function as a Web host, but you are free to contract with a Web hosting company separate from your ISP to host your Web site if your hosting needs exceed those provided for free by your ISP.

URL Stands for Uniform Resource Locator. It is the unique address pointing to a particular Web site and usually includes the address of the Web server on which the page is stored. For example, if your ISP's domain name is Iquest.net and you're using the free space provided with your account, your Web page's URL might be http://www.iquest.net/members/~yourname.

Domain name A unique Web address such as www.something.com. You can buy the rights to a particular domain name for about $70 for two years. You don't need your own Web server in order to have a domain name; when you contract with a

Web hosting company, they will take charge of your domain name and redirect users to your Web site on their server automatically. Using a domain name is optional; it makes more sense for businesses than for individuals.

Other Uses for HTML Documents

As you learned in Chapter 21, HTML is a document format consisting of plain text plus coding that applies formatting to it. This makes it an ideal format for sharing documents across different kinds of computers, like among Macs, PCs, and UNIX machines. Increasingly, people are beginning to use HTML as a word processing format when compatibility is important. Most modern word-processing programs, such as Microsoft Word, Corel WordPerfect, and Lotus WordPro, can seamlessly open and save HTML files. Other programs, too—not just word processors—can save in HTML format; so you can create content in programs such as Microsoft PowerPoint or Microsoft Excel and then share that content in HTML format with others who don't have those programs installed on their PCs.

HTML has also become a popular format for sending formatted e-mail messages. Most e-mail programs these days can display HTML coding in an e-mail message; in fact, when you format e-mail in Outlook Express, the formatting is a variation of HTML called MHT (which stands for mail HTML).

Choosing Your Web Page Creation Program

If you're just starting out with Web page creation (and I'm assuming that's the case in this chapter), you will probably not want to go out and spring for a $500 Web site creation program. Instead, you'll want to ease into the process by creating a few pages with a program that you already have.

There are two types of Web page creation programs: text editors and WYSIWYG (what you see is what you get).

You can use any text editor to create an HTML file, including Notepad. Just create a plain text file and save it with an .htm extension. You type the text, enter the coding in angle brackets, and off you go. Unfortunately, you need to be a real programmer in order to do this because it requires knowledge of the HTML language. You have to know precisely where all those codes and brackets go.

More popular and practical for the nonprogrammer is a WYSIWYG program, in which you apply formatting just as you would in a word processor. Then when you save, it converts all that formatting to the needed HTML coding automatically for you.

Do you already have a WYSIWYG Web page creation program? Probably. As I mentioned earlier in the chapter, almost all programs these days have a "Save as HTML" or "Save as Web Page" feature. That means you can use a word processor, a desktop publishing program, or even a spreadsheet or database program to generate Web content.

If you have Microsoft Office, you have Microsoft Word, the leading word processor in the world, which happens to create very nice, amateur-quality Web pages. I'll show you how to use it for Web page creation later in this chapter. Microsoft Publisher 2000 also does a good job of creating Web sites; it can't open HTML files, however, so you must reopen the site in Publisher format and resave it in HTML every time you want to make a change to it.

Some versions of Microsoft Office also come with Microsoft FrontPage, a very powerful tool for creating professional-quality Web sites. If you are fortunate enough to have this program available, you might want to explore its capabilities. There's more to FrontPage than I can tell you about here, but you might like to read *Mastering Microsoft FrontPage 2000* by Daniel A. Tauber and Brenda Kienan with Molly E. Holzschlag (Sybex, 1999) or *Microsoft FrontPage 2000: No Experience Required* by Gene Weisskopf (Sybex, 1999).

NOTE Windows 98 (the original version, not 98 SE) came with FrontPage Express, a stripped-down version of FrontPage designed for creating simple Web pages. However, Windows Me does not include it.

Some Web professionals turn up their noses at FrontPage, however, for two reasons. One is that in order to use the Web sites created with FrontPage, the server that hosts them must support FrontPage extensions. This is usually not a big deal, since most Web hosts offer this capability. The other reason is that FrontPage, in its push toward making formatting simple for the nontechnical user, internalizes a lot of the formatting and layout functions, thus creating nonstandard HTML that an expert user can't fully control. For example, in a normal HTML document, all the formatting is controlled by text codes in angle brackets such as <b> and <i>. But in FrontPage, formatting is applied through themes (similar to the themes in Windows Me), and the individual formatting of a particular theme is not easily editable. That's why people who are real experts with HTML don't like FrontPage.

When you're ready to move up to the Web site creation tools that professionals use, consider Macromedia DreamWeaver. It creates "pure HTML" files that Web experts prefer and is the top choice of the people who create the sites for large corporations.

Creating a Web Page in Word

Since so many people have Microsoft Word as their word processing program, I'd like to spend a little time looking at it as a Web page creation device, even though it's not, strictly speaking, a part of Windows Me. With Word 2000, you can even create a multi-page site, in which all the pages are connected by a navigation bar containing links to each of the other pages.

Starting a New Web Page in Word 2000

Let's begin with something very basic: a simple, one-page Web site in Word. You can start with a blank page, or you can use one of the Web templates supplied with Word that provide preset formatting and placeholder text. In the following steps, just for example purposes, I'll show you one of the templates.

1. Choose Start ➢ Programs ➢ Microsoft Word.

NOTE If you don't see it there, perhaps Microsoft Word is not installed on your PC. If that's the case, you can try to create a Web page in whatever word processor you have installed; abandon these steps and give it a try on your own.

2. Choose File ➢ New. Click the Web Pages tab, and then double-click Right-Aligned Column.

A sample Web page appears, ready for your customization, as shown in Figure 23.1.

FIGURE 23.1
A Web page template
in Word

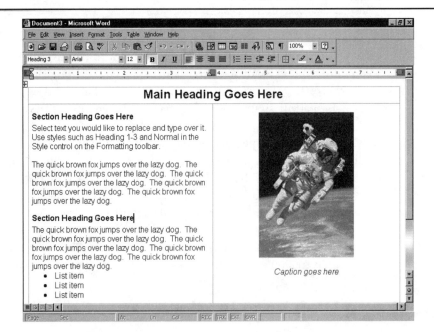

You can do several different things:

*   Replace the picture with an image of your own (select it and use the Insert ➢ Picture ➢ From File command).

*   Delete the existing text and type your own.

- Use the formatting commands and toolbar buttons in Word to add different fonts, boldface and italic, bulleted lists, different text alignments, and so on.

- Change the sizes of the panes by dragging the gray lines. (The particular layout in our example uses a Word table to organize the text into multiple panes.)

Creating a Multipage Site

If you want a Web site that contains multiple pages linked together, use the Web Page Wizard instead of one of the other templates when creating your new document in Word. This creates several pages, and adds a navigation bar to link them. Figure 23.2 shows such a site created and ready for your customization.

PART IV

Communication and Using the Internet

FIGURE 23.2
A multipage Web site created in Word

Navigation bar

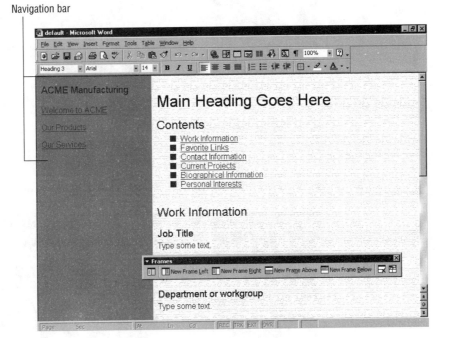

To use the Wizard, follow these steps:

1. In Word, choose File ➢ New. Click the Web Pages tab, and double-click Web Page Wizard.

2. Click Next to begin.

3. Enter the title for your Web site in the Web Site Title box. This name will appear in the title bar when people use a Web browser to view your site.

4. Confirm the name shown in the Web Site Location box. The last part of it should match the name you entered in step 3. Then click Next.

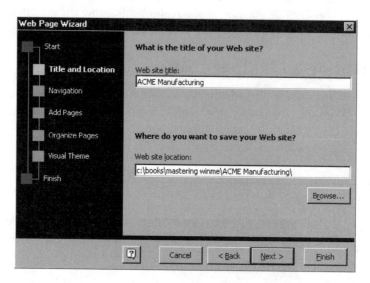

 TIP Make a note of the full path; you will need to know it later when you are ready to transfer the Web site to a server.

5. Choose the type of navigation bar you want for the site, and then click Next.

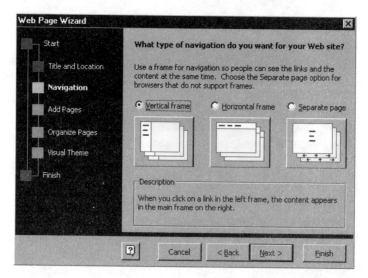

6. If you want more pages in the site than currently appear, add them to the list.

• To add more blank pages, click Add New Blank Page as many times as needed.

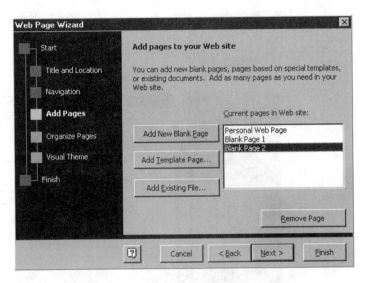

• To add a template page, click Add Template Page and choose the template you want. The names of the templates appear in a dialog box, and behind it, a preview of the selected template page appears.

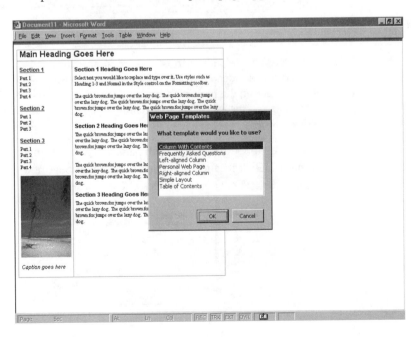

- To add an existing file as a page, click Add Existing File and choose the file you want to use; then click Open.

7. To remove a page from the list, select it and click Remove Page.

8. When you are happy with the number of pages, and the template for each one, click Next.

9. Next, arrange the order of the pages. Click a page, and then click the Move Up or Move Down button to move it on the list.

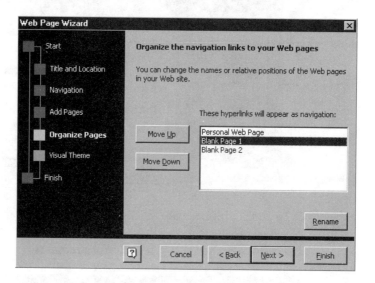

 NOTE Since Web site pages can be viewed in any order, it isn't critical to arrange all pages in a sequential order. However, the order you choose in step 9 will be the order in which pages appear on the navigation bar; so if you have a preference in that regard, set it here. The top page on the list will be your starting page, also known as your home page.

10. You will probably want to give each page a more meaningful name than the template name. Click it, and then click Rename. Type a new name in the Rename Hyperlink dialog box, and then click OK.

11. When you are finished arranging and naming pages, click Next.

Next, you're asked about a visual theme. These are like the Desktop Themes in Windows; they apply a set of formatting to your site.

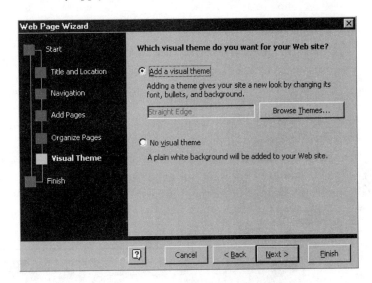

12. Choose No Visual Theme if you don't want one. Or, to apply a theme, click the Browse Themes button. Then select a theme in the dialog box that appears and click OK to return.

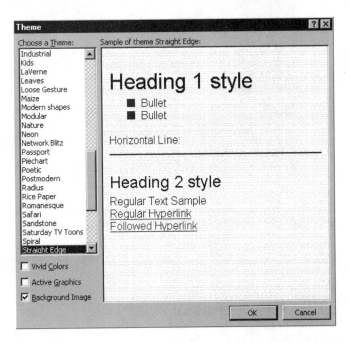

13. Click Next, and then Finish. Your Web site is created in Word.

14. Customize it by adding your own text and formatting. Then see the next section to save your work.

Saving in Web Format

If you create a Web page (or multipage site) using one of Word's Web templates or the Web Page Wizard, you can simply click the Save button on the toolbar or choose File ➤ Save. Word will automatically display the Web-enabled version of the Save As dialog box.

You can also save any existing Word document in Web format by using the File ➤ Save As Web Page command.

From the Save As dialog box, shown in Figure 23.3, you save the same as with any other document, except for one extra feature: the Change Title button. Click it and enter a title if desired (for the title bar). This will already be filled in correctly if you used the Web Page Wizard.

FIGURE 23.3
Saving as a Web page is similar to saving in any other program.

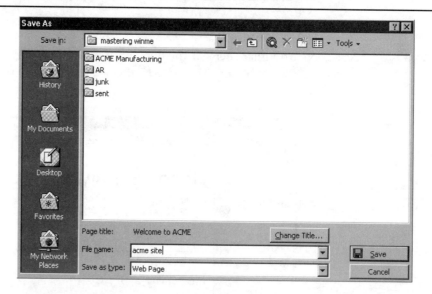

If you need to save with any special options, such as greater backward compatibility with old Web browsers prior to Internet Explorer 5.0, click the Tools button in the Save As dialog box and choose Web Options from the menu that appears. In that dialog box, you can fine-tune the Web format in which your work is saved.

Formatting Text on a Web Page

Formatting text on a Web page is about as easy as formatting text in a word processor. You have similar options, too, such as boldface and italic, indenting, creating lists, and changing size and alignment.

Besides the normal formatting, there are a few formatting capabilities that are especially valuable when working with Web pages in Word. The following sections outline them.

Applying a Visual Theme

You saw earlier when using the Web Page Wizard that you can select a visual theme for formatting your Web page/Web site in Word. But you can also apply these visual themes at any time, to any Web page, even ones that you have created from scratch or by saving existing Word documents in Web format. To do so, choose Format ➤ Theme. The same Theme dialog box appears that you saw earlier. Choose the theme you want and click OK.

Not all of the themes are installed by default when you install Microsoft Word. If you choose a theme that is not yet installed, an Install button will appear instead of a preview of the theme. Have your Word or Office 2000 CD ready in your drive, and then click Install and follow the prompts to install it.

Applying Web Styles

Most formatting on the Web is based on styles. For example, there's a Heading 1 style, a Heading 2 style, and so on. If you want to make a particular paragraph into a heading, rather than manually apply a certain formatting to it, you can simply apply a Heading style. To do so, follow these steps:

1. Position the insertion point within the paragraph you want to apply a style to.

2. Open the Styles drop-down list on the Formatting toolbar (the left-most list) and choose a style.

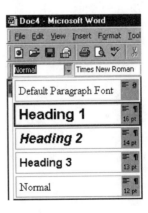

TIP Only a few styles appear on the list by default. There are many more HTML-based styles you can apply. To see them, hold down the Shift key when you open the Styles drop-down list.

Creating Graphical Bulleted Lists

A popular and attractive trend on Web pages is to use little graphics as bullet characters instead of the traditional round, plain bullets.

To set this up, do the following:

1. Select the paragraphs that you want to make bulleted.

2. Choose Format ➤ Bullets and Numbering.

3. Click the Bulleted tab, and then click the Picture button. The Picture Bullet dialog box appears.

4. Click the graphical bullet you want to use. A palette of four icons appears.

5. Click the top icon (Insert Clip) to choose that bullet character. It is applied to the selected paragraphs.

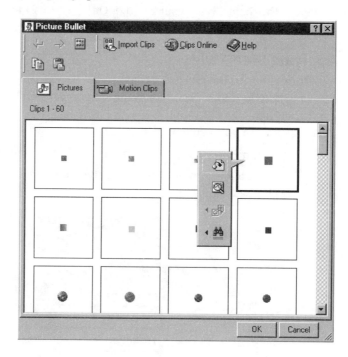

For your added convenience, the next time you click the Bullets button on the toolbar, the bullet you just chose will be the default one to appear until you start a new document or choose a different bullet character.

Adding Images to Web Pages

No matter how compelling your text is, the images on your Web page almost always get the most attention. You can add pictures to a Web page the same way you add pictures to a regular word processing document.

1. Place your cursor in the area of your Web page where you want your image to appear.

2. Choose Insert ➢ Picture ➢ From File.

3. Locate and select the picture you want to use.

4. Click Insert.

You can also use artwork from Word's extensive Clip Gallery instead of your own pictures if you prefer. To do so, choose Insert ➢ Picture ➢ Clip Gallery. Choose the clip you want, and then insert it by clicking it and clicking the Insert Clip button as you did when choosing a graphical bullet character in the preceding section.

Creating Hyperlinks

The magic of the World Wide Web is the interactive feature known as *links* (sometimes called *hyperlinks*). Links enable a viewer to move from one piece of information (a section of text or an image) to another at the click of a mouse. You can set links to other pages within your Web site or to other Web sites on the Internet.

You can have either text or graphical hyperlinks. Text hyperlinks are underlined; graphical hyperlinks look like any other graphic. But when you hover your mouse pointer over them in a Web browser, the mouse pointer turns to a hand, indicating that clicking the item will take you somewhere else.

Click here for the church's monthly calendar of activities

To insert a hyperlink, do the following:

1. Choose Insert ➢ Hyperlink, or click the Insert Hyperlink button on the toolbar. The Insert Hyperlink dialog box appears.

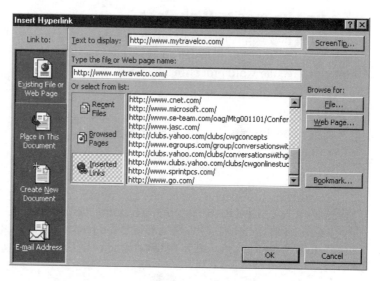

2. To create a hyperlink to a Web page, enter its URL in the Type the File or Web Page Name box. Or, to browse for it, click the Web Page button under Browse For. This opens Internet Explorer. Locate the page using IE, and then switch back to Word and the address will be entered automatically.

3. The text in the Text to Display box is the text that you highlighted before selecting the command (if any). If you would like to change it, make your change here.

4. (Optional) If you want certain text to display when the user hovers the mouse pointer over the item, click the ScreenTip button and enter the text for that purpose; then click OK to return.

5. Click OK. The hyperlink is created.

Choosing Where to Host Your Pages

As I mentioned at the beginning of the chapter, you'll need a way to put your Web pages online. Unless you work at a big company with its own site or are at a university that provides access to its Web server, you'll probably need a commercial service provider to host your site. The ISP that you use for your Internet connection might provide a limited amount of Web hosting space for free. If you're not sure if your account includes this feature, you should be able to find out by visiting your ISP's Web site or by calling the ISP's technical support or sales office.

However, the free space provided by your ISP might be subject to some limitations. For example, you might not be able to post commercial material there, or you might not be able to use your own domain name if you have one. Therefore, you might find yourself shopping for a Web hosting company in addition to your ISP. There are thousands of companies out there who would like your Web hosting business.

If you just want to post a few personal pages (or even a few dozen), you don't need much server space, so price will probably be the overriding factor in your decision. However, if you want to post an ambitious commercial venture that you expect will draw millions of visits, you'll need to be more particular. (Of course, if you're creating such a site, you are doubtless working with a professional Web designer who will likely have some suggestions as to good Web hosting companies.) The following sections outline some things to look for when choosing.

NOTE If you want to find a server anywhere in the world, the site called The Directory lists more than 10,000 Internet Service Providers and bulletin board services in 120 countries. Check them out at this URL: www.thedirectory.org.

1. How much do they charge?

Comparing the pricing among service providers is like comparing long-distance telephone companies. They don't all charge for their services in the same way, so finding out who really has the best deal for you can be hard. Before you choose a service provider, get a good start on your development plan so you know what kinds of services you'll need. Then look around for the provider that offers the best combination of services for the best price. (Your answers to the other questions in this section will help you understand your options.) You may decide, for example, that 24-hour technical support is worth a little more per month. On the other hand, if you don't plan to sell any products online, you won't want to pay the extra cost for a server that supports secure transactions.

Charges vary dramatically from as little as $5 per month to hundreds per month. Why should you pay that much? You shouldn't, unless you need tons of space for your site and you are attracting hundreds of thousands of visitors. (If you start getting that kind of attention to your Web site, you should be able to afford to move to a more expensive server; but you probably don't need to start out on one that costs that much. Remember, you can always upgrade later.)

Two basic charges are commonly associated with leasing Web space on a commercial server. The first is based on how much space you want; the second is based on how much traffic you attract (sometimes called *throughput*). The first charge is pretty straightforward. For the base rate of, say, $20 per month, you might get 10MB of space. If you decide later that you need another 5MB, that will probably cost you about $5 more per month. It's a little like renting an office: the more square feet, the more it costs.

NOTE Ten or twenty megabytes of space on a Web server may not sound like much in a world where new computers come with two- or three-gigabyte hard drives. But on the Web, you want all your files to be as small as possible so they load as quickly as possible for your users; and a site with a few hundred pages and graphics may still be less than 10MB if it's done well. The one exception to this is if your site features software programs for viewers to download or large images, video, or sound files. These types of files are inherently larger and will require more disk space. As a general rule, you should be able to start with minimal server space because you can always add more space later. Just make sure you've made arrangements with your service provider to add more space as you need it.

Moving to a New Server

As you consider which service provider is best for you, remember that you can always move to a new server later if your situation changes. Transferring your Web site to a new service provider is usually a simple and painless process unless you haven't registered a domain name or you use CGI (Common Gateway Interface) scripts (programs that are installed on the server to add interactivity to your Web site, such as online discussion areas, forms, and shopping systems).

One of the biggest advantages of having a domain name is that you get a permanent address, which means that if you move your site to a new server, you keep the same domain name and therefore the same Web address. This is an advantage because viewers will always use the same address to find you, even if you move to a new server on the other side of the country. If you don't have a domain name, your Web address will include the name of your service provider; and if you ever change service providers, you'll have to change your address, too.

Moving to a new service provider generally involves these tasks:

- Setting up an account at a new service provider

- Notifying InterNIC (the organization responsible for registering domain names) that your name should be assigned to the new server. If you don't have a domain name, you'll have to notify all your viewers. (I hope you never have to do that. In case you haven't figured it out, I strongly recommend getting a domain name.)

- Uploading the HTML pages, images, and other files that make up your Web site to your new service provider.

- Closing your account with your old server after everything is up and running at the new one.

Continued ▶

After paying about $30 to $50 (the setup cost at most service providers), you're ready to settle into your new home—that is, unless you use CGI scripts. Unlike HTML pages and images, which can be moved easily from one server to another, CGI scripts usually have to be tailored to work on each new server. If the systems are very similar, this may not be a big deal, but if you move from one kind of server to another (say, from Windows NT to Unix), you may have to pay a lot of money to have all your CGI scripts reworked. If you plan to use lots of interactive features that require CGI scripts, be more selective about your server, because moving will be complex and probably more expensive.

There are additional charges you may face as well, such as paying more to use your own domain name. You almost undoubtedly have to pay more if you want a Web server that supports secure commerce transactions. Security is a complicated issue on the Web, but mostly it deals with *encryption* (a process of encoding and decoding messages so they are harder to intercept). The more secure the system, the more it usually costs. Getting clear on the kinds of services that are important to you, such as secure transactions, will make sorting through the pricing structures used by different service providers easier.

2. Do they provide technical support?

Technical support can be crucial. Each server has different features and limitations, and knowing how to use the service can be hard if you can't reach anyone who can explain it. Some service providers have knowledgeable technical support people on call 24 hours a day; others may never answer the phone. A good test is to call several service providers you are considering and see how long it takes them to respond to your initial questions. If you have trouble finding out how to buy their services, you'll probably have even more trouble getting help after they have your money.

Technical support is also often available by e-mail. It's best if the service provider offers it both ways (that is, phone and e-mail). Some questions (especially as you get more experience) are easily and conveniently handled by e-mail. At other times, you will want a person to talk you through a problem. E-mail is also important if the service provider is not local, because it saves long-distance phone charges. Most service providers also have a FAQ (frequently asked questions) page, a great place to get answers to common questions and find out the common problems users are having.

TIP Although you should expect your service provider to give you basic assistance, such as helping you understand the specific aspects of its system and how to log on to its server, very few will provide help with HTML development or CGI scripts unless you pay extra. A service provider that employs lots of people to answer your questions may be more expensive than it's worth. Hiring your own consultant to help you sort out how to build your Web site could mean you can choose a cheaper service provider and save money in the long run.

3. How reliable are they?

Your site is up and running. Thousands of people are visiting every day, ordering products, and chatting in the online discussion area. Then, all of a sudden, *crash!* The entire system goes down, and no one can get to your Web site.

This scenario is almost inevitable. Computers crash; systems fail. Don't panic, but keep in mind that some systems crash more frequently than others and some take a lot longer to get up and running again. Ask your service provider about its track record. How often does its system fail? How long does it usually take to get back online? Does the hosting company have technical staff on call 24 hours a day to fix the things that go wrong in the middle of the night? If reliability is important to you, make sure you check out the company's reputation for staying up and running.

Try to ask some of the company's other customers how happy they are. But be aware that running a Web server is a relatively new business, and it's not an easy one. Most service providers suffer growing pains. I've seen this happen with many companies. A new service provider opens up; it gets great equipment, a friendly staff, and a fast connection to the Internet; and it quickly becomes the favorite in town. Then it gets swamped. The service attracts new customers too quickly to keep up with the demand. For a while, the service goes down the tubes: It can't answer all its phone calls, its systems crash too often because it's overloaded, and everyone complains. Then the company catches up, hires more staff, adds phone lines, and gets better equipment, and the service improves dramatically. This is a common scenario. The challenge is to make sure you come in after the company has upgraded and not while it's in the middle of growing pains. Ask around and see how the company is doing, but be sure to check with current customers, not just old ones who may have left before things were improved.

Be sure to talk to more than one customer, especially those you know. Some people will complain about anything. If, for example, the person complains that "it's too slow," ask them to be more specific. Is it that their Web pages take too long to download, or is it that the technical staff are too slow in returning phone calls? Then ask what tests the customer did to determine the cause of the problem. Remember, your goal is to find the best system for *your* needs. Assessing the validity of someone else's complaint can help you determine if you'll have the same problems.

4. How many Web sites do they serve, and how much traffic do they attract?

Viewers on a Web server are like cars on a freeway: The more people on the road, the longer it takes to get home. Service providers put as many as 100 Web sites on one server, sometimes more. But even if the server has only one other Web site, the entire system may slow down if that one site gets heavy traffic.

A Web server may have a fast connection to the Internet, but if the server hosts too many Web sites or if the sites attract a lot of traffic, you may find that it takes longer to download your Web pages, especially at peak times. If the service gets too busy, you may not be able to view your site at all; instead, you'll get an error message stating that the server is too busy and you should try again later. I hate to admit I learned this the hard way. I was in a demo with a client once and couldn't show them one of my Web sites because the service provider was overloaded. Once in a great while this may be understandable, like the day Princess Diana died—there was so much activity on the Internet that service suffered in most places. But if your site is unavailable on a regular basis, you should definitely consider moving to a better Web hosting company.

On the other side of this issue, be aware that your service provider may charge you much higher rates if your Web site attracts too many viewers and slows down the system. Ask your provider about usage charges, and be prepared to upgrade in a hurry if you expect a large number of users.

A good way to test the speed of a server before you sign on is to visit a few of the Web sites already on the provider's server and compare loading times with other service providers. Note that the size of graphics and other files also affects speed, so try to compare similar HTML pages on each server to make a fair comparison. Most service providers feature a list of their customers, which makes finding sites on their server easy.

5. What kind of backup systems do they have in place?

Backup systems can be crucial on the Internet. Technical problems are common, and servers go down regularly. Many providers are not established well enough to have an alternate computer, an on-call technical staff, and an emergency power supply. But if you *must* ensure that your Web site is always available, then you must pay for a high-end server with backup systems in place.

Moreover, you should always keep a backup of your own Web site yourself. You can do this simply by keeping a copy of the Web site files on your hard drive (something you may already be doing if that's where you created them). If other people are working on your site, always get copies of their work in case you need it again. You can also create a backup by downloading the new pages and images to your computer, using an FTP program such as WS_FTP.

6. Do they provide CGI scripts and/or limit the use of your own scripts?

Many service providers offer common CGI scripts (image maps and basic forms, for example) to all their Web site clients and enable you to use your own scripts to add other functions to your Web site. Other providers may limit your use of scripts or may charge you to test them before they put them on the server. These providers are concerned about security issues and about the fact that a poorly written script can slow down the server and even cause it to crash. If programmers will be working on your site, ask them to check out the service provider to ensure that it accommodates the kind of Web site you want. If you don't have a programmer on staff, you may be especially interested in a service provider that provides the use of common scripts for setting up your own guest book or e-mail forms on your site. Ask the service provider what it has available, or check out its Web site for more information.

 NOTE CGI scripts are special programs that provide greater levels of interactivity than basic HTML. Features such as order forms, guest books, online discussion areas, and shopping systems are made possible by CGI scripts. These scripts are usually written in sophisticated programming languages such as Perl, C, or C++. Writing CGI scripts is much more complicated than creating HTML pages.

7. How fast are the servers' connections to the Internet?

The speed of a service provider's connection to the Internet affects how quickly your pages and graphics get to your viewers. The faster the connection, the better the server should perform. For example, a T-1 line is faster than a T-3 line, but the speed still depends on how many users are being served. Some service providers have more than one connection, allowing them to balance the traffic on their servers.

8. Do they provide security?

A secure server is called secure because the data being transmitted between the client and the server is *encrypted*. The level of encryption varies, depending on the type of service you use. Some common protocols include Secure Socket Layer (SSL), used by Netscape servers, and Pretty Good Privacy (PGP), used by Mosaic servers. Expect to pay considerably more for your Web space if you want a secure server. The current range is about $60 per month to $1,000 per month, and that only gets you the secure *server* software. If you want password access, for example, you probably have to do your own custom programming (with CGI scripts) to set it up. If you want to offer credit card transactions that will be verified online, you need a processing service such as Cybercash to handle the actual transaction.

Ask your service provider how much support you can expect with a secure server account. Are there trained staff people who can help you set up secure transactions? Do they recommend any consultants? Has the company made any special deals with other vendors who can process online transactions? If your provider has established a relationship with a company such as Cybercash or Checkfree, setting up your Web site may be easier and less expensive. Find out what kinds of support the company offers, whether any discounts come with its service, what exactly the company includes with its monthly rate, and what other costs you should expect to pay to set up the system you want.

9. Do they recommend consultants?

If you need a consultant to help with some or all of the development of your Web site, you may benefit from a service provider that recommends consultants or provides staff members who can help you. Finding a good consultant can be a challenging process and will be easier with a service provider that includes a referral service or staff to help you.

If you are planning to hire a consultant, it's great if you can consider the consultant's recommendations in your decision about where to put your Web site, but be sure you don't choose a service provider just because a consultant recommends it. Some consultants get commissions and other perks from service providers that may taint their judgment about what's best for you. A good consultant will research and recommend two or three service providers that meet your needs and then let you decide which is best for you.

10. Where are they located?

As you look for a server, keep in mind that unlike your dial-up connection—in which there's an advantage to having a local phone number, because it saves you long-distance phone charges—your Web server does not need to be in the same geographic location as you are. You can send files anywhere on the Internet, so your Web site can be almost anywhere. If you are in a small town or an isolated area with limited options, you may want to look beyond your neighborhood to find a better deal.

If you have the opportunity, however, check out the company's office. Visiting a service provider's facility is one of the best ways to assess how reliable that service may be. (It's impossible to determine if someone is running a server from a closet or from a large office just by viewing a Web site online.) Legitimate, reliable service providers should be open to letting you see their offices and equipment.

Publishing Your Web Pages to a Server

There are several ways to place your Web pages on the Web server that you chose in the preceding section. If the program that you use to create the Web pages allows it, you can save directly to the server. If not, you can transfer your pages using an FTP program, or using the Web Publishing Wizard in Windows Me.

Before starting, check with the Web hosting company you are using to find out what method they recommend. You will also need a user name and password for access to the Web server, and if you're transferring the pages via FTP, you'll need an FTP address plus a separate FTP user name and password.

Saving Directly to the Server

Professional-quality programs like Microsoft FrontPage have a Publish feature that you can use to automatically transfer your pages (and any changes in the future) to the Web server of your choice. Check the program's documentation for the specifics; in FrontPage 2000 the command is File ➤ Publish Web.

In Microsoft Office programs such as Word, PowerPoint, Publisher, and Excel 2000, you can save directly to the server via the Save As dialog box. It allows you to transfer either via the Web or via FTP. The Web method is easier, but because not all servers allow this type of transfer, some of you might be stuck with the FTP method.

As an example, let's look at how to save directly to a Web server in Word 2000.

1. Choose File ➤ Save As Web Page.

2. Open the Save In drop-down list and choose My Network Places.

3. Click the New Folder button in the dialog box. The Add Network Place Wizard runs.

4. Enter the URL for the Web site address to which you want to publish. Then click Next.

5. An Enter Network Password box appears. Enter your username and password for the Web server, and then click OK.

6. Click Finish. A folder opens, showing the content of your area of the Web server, just as if it were a folder on your own hard drive.

7. Switch back to Word using the Taskbar, where the Save As dialog box is still open. Notice that now a shortcut to that new Web folder is listed.

8. Double-click the shortcut for the Web folder. Its content appears in the Save As dialog box.

9. Click Save to save your Web page there.

In the future, you can skip a lot of this, because the shortcut will have already been set up; perform only steps 1, 2, 8, and 9.

Saving via FTP within an Application

If the above steps didn't work for you, then perhaps the Web host you are using doesn't support this type of transfer. If that's the case, try the FTP method instead. If you are using a Microsoft Office application or another application that supports direct network access, you can use the following steps:

1. Choose File ➢ Save As Web Page.

2. Open the Save In drop-down list. If your FTP location already appears there, choose it and skip to step 8. Otherwise, choose Add/Modify FTP Locations.

3. Type the FTP site name in the Name of FTP Site box.

4. Click the User button, and enter your username in the User text box.

5. Enter your password in the Password box.

6. Click Add, and then click OK.

7. Double-click the FTP location you just created.

8. On the FTP server, navigate to the folder where your Web host has instructed you to save files.

9. Click OK.

Using an FTP Program

If you have created your Web pages in a program that doesn't support direct transfer to the Web host, you can use an FTP program to transfer them. There are many FTP programs available as shareware, but one of my favorites is WS_FTP. You can download it at www.wsftp.com.

Each program works a little differently, but in WS_FTP, there are two file panes. The one on the left shows your local hard disk, and the one on the right shows the Web server to which you are connected. (You have to connect first, of course, using the FTP username and password provided by your Web hosting company). Then you click the right-pointing arrow button to transfer the files. Figure 23.4 shows an example.

FIGURE 23.4
WS_FTP is a popular
FTP program used for
transferring Web
content to a server.

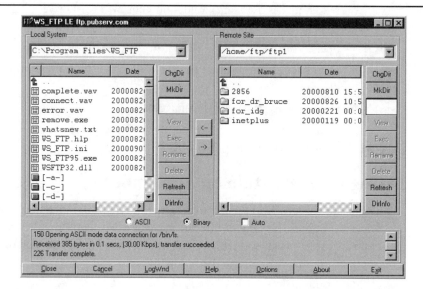

 WARNING If you transfer via FTP, make sure you get all the associated files, too (graphics, etc.), not just the files with the .htm extensions. Otherwise, your pages will lack their graphical content. Usually all the associated files will be in the same folder as your HTML pages, or perhaps in a subfolder.

Using the Web Publishing Wizard

The Web Publishing Wizard helps you transfer files or folders to a server. It's not the quickest method, but it's nice to have if the other methods aren't working for you. You can transfer only one file or folder at a time, so it's easiest if you place all the files you need to transfer into a single folder beforehand.

If the feature is installed, you can start it with Start ➣ Programs ➣ Accessories ➣ Internet Tools ➣ Web Publishing Wizard. If it's not installed there, install it with Add/ Remove Programs, as described in Chapter 13, "Adding and Removing Hardware and Software."

The Web Publishing Wizard walks you step by step through the file transfer. (It's really easy and self-explanatory, so I won't belabor it here.)

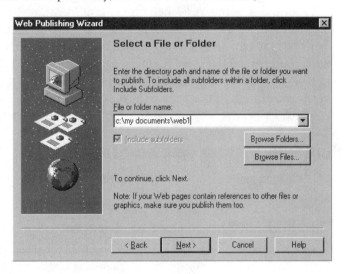

Advanced Web Design Techniques

The World Wide Web is evolving to become a more dynamic and entertaining place, thanks to the addition of multimedia to many Web sites. Teaching you how to add multimedia content to your Web site is well beyond the scope of this book. I can, however, give you an overview of the kinds of multimedia features you could add, and direct you to informative Web sites where you can learn more about the technologies that appeal to you.

Animated GIFs

By far the most universally supported animation format is the animated GIF. These files are simply a series of GIF images run together to create the illusion of motion. Animated GIFs can be created in programs such as Microsoft's GIF Animator or BoxTop's GIFmation, a more powerful tool that retails for around $30.

Other technologies offer integrated video and sound as well as interactivity (all great features you can't get from an animated GIF), but these advantages come at a price. The main drawback of many of the following technologies is the requirement that your users have the most up-to-date software—the newest browsers or plug-ins.

Until recently, most nonanimated GIF technologies for animation delivery also required that the entire animation file be downloaded by the Web surfer before it could be viewed, which slowed things down even more. This is now rarely the case. All the technologies described in the following sections transmit frames in playable order, so as soon as the first few frames arrive on your browser, the animation begins to play. This is referred to in the industry as *streaming technology*.

All streaming technologies aren't necessarily identical, however. Animated GIFs, for instance, begin to play as soon as the first frame arrives. Technologies geared toward the delivery of more movie-like presentation (frame rates in excess of 12fps and non-looping animations in excess of a few seconds) tend to hold the first frames in a buffer until enough frames have arrived to allow the entire movie to play smoothly. That means you can still notice a delay when the animations first load; still, they start playing much sooner than if the entire file had to be downloaded.

Multimedia Technologies for the Web

The following sections provide brief descriptions of the most popular technologies for delivering multimedia Web content.

Macromedia Shockwave for Director

Shockwave enables you to put Director files on a Web page. This is a big deal because Director is the most popular program around for creating CD-ROM multimedia titles, which means the program already has a large following and many people know how to use it. It also means you can create complex multimedia files, using animation, sound, video, and lots of interactive functionality.

Shockwave for Director has proven to be one of the most popular plug-ins on the Web (more than 12 million people have downloaded it). The problem is bandwidth. Most files created for CD-ROMs are huge by Web standards, and consumers are spoiled by the quality and speed of CD-ROMs. Because of the bandwidth limitations on the Web, developers who create with Shockwave for Director are still limited to very simple projects.

To learn more about Shockwave for Director, visit Macromedia's Web site: www .macromedia.com.

 TECH TIP Macromedia lumps all the player plug-in technologies for its products under the name Shockwave, but there are Shockwave plug-ins for five different Macromedia programs: Director, Flash, Freehand, Extreme 3D, and Authorware. Each plug-in is designed to handle the kind of files created by its corresponding program. For example, Shockwave Freehand can be used to display images created in the illustration program Freehand. The advantage is that if viewers use the plug-in, you don't have to convert your images to GIF or JPG (JPEG) format but can keep them in the richer, more versatile Freehand file type. Viewers can download each of these plug-ins separately or get all of them in one large plug-in package (approximately 2MB).

Macromedia Flash

Flash won acclaim because it creates animations that download really quickly. It also produces scalable, interactive animations with synchronized sound. All that, and you still get smaller file sizes than with any other animation technology on the Web. Flash files are dramatically faster to download because Flash images are vector-based. The term *vector-based* means the images are made up of coded instructions to draw specific geometric shapes, filled with specific colors. This takes far less space than the data needed for a *raster* image, such as those used by animated GIFs or JPGs. As a result, Flash files can be significantly smaller than other types of images and animation files. An animated GIF that is 200K and takes about a minute to download on a 56K modem might be only 20K when recreated as a Flash animation.

Flash is hampered by the same problem that keeps many of these other technologies from reaching the masses: the need for a plug-in for viewing them. But Flash has a better chance than most of overcoming this obstacle because on the one hand it creates files well suited to the bandwidth-strapped Web, and on the other it's part of the Macromedia Shockwave suite, which is already one of the most popular plug-ins on the Web.

You can find out more about Flash at Macromedia's Web site: `www.macromedia.com`.

Apple QuickTime

QuickTime is a cross-platform format that enables you to create digital, real-time video content with synchronized sound for the Web. Because QuickTime content can include almost all types of popular multimedia formats (still images, sound, 3-D virtual reality, and QuickTime VR), it's one of the most versatile delivery platforms for the Web. QuickTime content can now also be interactive. The latest version enables you to set links within a QuickTime file that can take users to a different segment of the movie or to a different Web address.

To learn more about QuickTime, visit `www.apple.com/quicktime`.

Java

Unless you've been hiding under a virtual rock, you know Java is not coffee on the Web. What makes Java special is that programs created in it can be run on any computer system. Usually, if you create a program in another programming language, such as C or C++ (from which Java was derived), you have to create one version for the Macintosh, another for the PC, and a third for the Unix operating system. But Java, created by Sun Microsystems, is a platform-independent programming language that can be used to create almost any kind of program, even something as complex as a word processing or spreadsheet program, and it will work on any type of computer. Java applets can be embedded in Web pages, used to generate entire Web pages, or run as stand-alone applications.

To learn more about Java, visit `www.sun.com`.

JavaScript

JavaScript is a subset of Java that was created by Netscape. JavaScript can be embedded into HTML pages to create basic animations and other interactive features. You won't get the complex functionality of Java, but JavaScript is a lot easier to create and can be used to deliver animated and interactive content over the Web without requiring plug-ins. Unlike Java, JavaScript doesn't produce stand-alone programs. JavaScript is often used in combination with other multimedia features, such as images or sound files, to add greater levels of interactivity.

For more on JavaScript, check out the JavaScript Guide in the developer's section at the following Web site: `www.netscape.com`.

Dynamic HTML and Cascading Style Sheets

Essentially, Dynamic HTML (D-HTML) is HTML with a kick. That kick comes from the power of adding scripting languages (usually JavaScript). Adding the power of a scripting language makes it possible to dynamically change the attributes of elements on a page without involving the server, which means features can change quickly because they don't require entire page reloads to take effect.

D-HTML and its subsets—features such as Cascading Style Sheets (CSS), Layers, and Filters—will provide great design power on the Web in the future. Unfortunately, today these features are supported only by the latest browsers and even then, don't display the same way on, say, Netscape Navigator as they do on Internet Explorer. As a result, this is a great technology to watch but not one that makes much sense to use today.

A great place to learn more about D-HTML is at this Web site: `www.projectcool .com`. You can also find information about D-HTML at `www.dhtmlzone.com`.

Let's wrap up our discussion of the Internet now, and move on to the next major topic in the book: Networking. In the next few chapters, you'll learn how you can set up your own peer-to-peer network with Windows Me.

PART V

Networking

CHAPTER 24

Building a Peer-to-Peer Network

In addition to local area networks (LANs) in the workplace, small networks are becoming increasingly popular in the home. Affordable PCs have been around long enough that many homes are already on their second or third computer, and it stands to reason that many people want to connect those multiple boxes together to share resources. Hardware producers, such as Diamond Multimedia, 3Com, and a host of others, are rushing to sell packages designed specifically to make home networking easy.

Windows Me has all the features necessary to make it the perfect network citizen. Right out of the box—with no additional software required—your PC and Windows Me are capable of connecting to 32 Windows 9x/Me workstations. And setup is easy, because Windows Me comes with a Home Networking Wizard to automate the process of installing and configuring the network drivers.

Because the networking features are truly integrated parts of Windows Me, you can access drives and printers located on the network from any Windows application—always in the same way, regardless of the computer you are connected to.

In this chapter, I'll introduce you to some networking basic concepts, and then I'll walk you through setting up a simple peer-to-peer network of Windows Me workstations. You'll learn how to obtain and install networking hardware, and then you'll learn how to use the Home Networking Wizard to install the needed drivers and protocols and to set up your files and printers for sharing and security.

Windows Me Network Overview

Windows Me is positioned as an operating system for homes and very small offices. Microsoft strongly encourages users who connect to large corporate networks to move to Windows 2000, which has much more robust and flexible networking capabilities.

However, that said, Windows Me is still a very capable network-aware operating system. You can use it to connect to Windows NT, Windows 2000, Novell NetWare, or Banyan network servers, and you can also use it to create serverless peer-to-peer networks among Windows Me PCs.

Additionally, Windows Me can act as either a Dial-Up Networking client or as a host so that you can use regular phone lines to extend the reach of your network. This allows you to dial into your office network while you are on the road (or at home, or anywhere) and still have the same resources available as if you were sitting right at your desk.

NOTE   When Windows Me was in beta testing, it was announced that Windows Me would not provide support for Novell and Banyan networks. The public outcry was so strong, however, that those features were put back into the final release product. There are still news articles circulating on the Internet regarding Windows Me's lack of that connectivity, but such articles are outdated.

Client/Server versus Peer-to-Peer Networks

There are dozens of types of networks out there, but they can all be broken down into two large categories: those with servers (client/server networks) and those without (peer-to-peer networks).

A *server* is a PC that's dedicated to the task of running the network; nobody uses it as a workstation. Most large corporate networks employ at least one server. A server takes the network processing workload off the client PCs so that they are completely free to go about the daily business of their owners (running applications, managing files, and so on).

In a home or small office, however, there might not be an extra PC to spare to function as a server, or there might not be money in the budget for the software that runs the server (such as Windows 2000 Server). In that case, a peer-to-peer network is the best choice.

Peer-to-peer refers to the fact that each station on the network treats each other station as an equal or a peer. There is no special station set aside to provide only file and print services to all the other stations. Instead, any printer, CD-ROM drive, hard drive, or even a floppy drive located on any one station can (if you wish) share access with all the other stations on the network. When you share a resource, such as a disk drive or printer, the computer that shares the resource becomes the server, and the computer that accesses the shared resource becomes the client. In a peer-to-peer network you can both share resources and access shared resources equally. In effect, your computer can be both a server and a client at the same time. Figure 24.1 illustrates a peer-to-peer network arrangement.

PART

V

Networking

FIGURE 24.1
A typical peer-to-peer network topology: Notice that no particular station is designated as a stand-alone server.

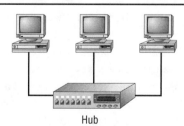

Hub

Of course, there are security features as well, which will allow you to grant or remove access to shared resources on your computer. But first let's get the network up and running.

 NOTE Amazingly, with Windows Me, it is possible to set up a peer-to-peer network of two computers with no additional hardware except a $5 cable! By installing the Direct Cable Connection (DCC) network driver supplied in Windows Me and by connecting a cable between available printer or serial ports on two PCs, you can quickly set up a simple, yet full-featured, two-station network, actually sharing drives and printers just like the bigger networks. See "Using Direct Cable Connection" at the end of this chapter for details.

Most Windows Me users contemplating setting up a network will want a peer-to-peer network rather than one that employs a server. Why? Because Windows Me is marketed primarily at the home and small-office person, and such users typically have very modest networking needs. Those who need large corporate networks with servers will probably gravitate toward Windows 2000 Server to run the server and Windows 2000 Professional for the individual PCs (the *clients*) on the network.

However, Windows Me PCs are perfectly capable of hooking into an existing client/server network, and they can function as clients on networks in which the server is running Windows NT, Windows 2000 Server, Banyan Vines, or Novell NetWare. The process of setting up to connect to a server-based network is essentially the same as that to connect to a peer-to-peer network (see "Running the Home Networking Wizard" later in this chapter).

If you need to set up a peer-to-peer network, the remainder of this chapter can help you with that.

Understanding Protocols

A *protocol* is a set of rules and conventions for accomplishing a specific task. In the case of computer networking, a protocol defines the manner in which two computers communicate with each other. As an analogy, consider the protocol you use to place a phone call. Before you dial, you first make sure no one else is using the phone line. Next, you pick up the phone and listen for a dial tone. If you are at your office, you might have to dial 9 and again wait for a dial tone. Then you can dial either a seven-digit number for a local call or a 1 followed by a 10-digit number for a long-distance call. You then wait for the other person to answer. But if you do not follow this protocol correctly—for example, if you do not dial a 9 for an outside line when at the office—you will be unable to place your phone call.

In the world of computers, a protocol works exactly the same way. If a client does not structure and send a request in the exact manner in which the server expects it—and we all know how particular computers can be—it will never establish the connection.

When you first activate the networking component on your computer, Windows Me installs the TCP/IP protocol by default. Besides this one, Windows Me allows you to install several other protocols that—depending on the design of your network and type of applications you run—might provide better performance or other advantages, such as NetBEUI. (In Windows 98, NetBEUI was installed by default, as a matter of fact.) On a small peer-to-peer network, NetBEUI is great because it's a very efficient protocol. It can't be used on larger networks, however, because it's not routable (that is, it can't be used on a network that contains routers, which are a type of connector box for connecting subnetworks).

Windows Me gives you a choice of several transport protocols. These protocols fall into two broad groups. First, open-systems protocols such as NetBEUI and TCP/IP allow you to connect to several vendors' networks. With them you can communicate over a Windows Me peer-to-peer network or over another vendor's network. The second type of transport protocols are the proprietary protocols used to support specific vendors' networks such as Banyan Vines and DEC Pathworks.

Here are a few basics about the open-systems protocols that come with Windows Me:

- TCP/IP is the default protocol for Windows peer-to-peer networks. It's also often used over wide-area networks, for Internet Connection Sharing, and for communicating with computers running some flavor of the Unix operating system.

- IPX/SPX is the protocol used to connect to Novell NetWare file servers.

- IPX/SPX with NetBIOS adds support for the NetBIOS application programming interface (API) to the standard IPX/SPX protocol.

- Microsoft 32-bit DLC (data link control) and Microsoft DLC (16-bit) are for communicating with IBMs or other mainframes. DLC provides an interface between Windows Me machines and mainframes as well as network printers. Network managers handle this type of protocol.

- NetBEUI is a protocol originally developed by IBM and used by Windows 3.11 for Workgroups and LAN Manager. It's also a fast, efficient protocol that all versions of Windows understand, and great for small peer-to-peer networks.

- ATM Call Manager, ATM Emulated LAN, and ATM Lan Emulation Client are for large company use. ATM stands for Asynchronous Transfer Mode. Some companies use ATM for their data transmission backbones. You need an ATM card in your PC to take advantage of this high-speed networking option. If you are using ATM, no doubt you'll have a network administrator who will have explicit instructions about how to install it.

- Fast Infrared Protocol allows you to network with other devices and computers using IrDA (infrared) ports. Some "wireless" networking devices use infrared transmission for this purpose.

PART
V

Networking

Don't worry if all those specs make your head swim. For most people using Windows Me, all this talk about various protocols is merely academic. If you're building a peer-to-peer network, the Home Networking Wizard will automatically install appropriate protocols for you (IPX/SPX, and perhaps TCP/IP), and it will configure your PC to use them.

Buying Your Network Hardware

When you go shopping for home networking equipment at your local computer store, you might be surprised at the variety of schemes available. There are wireless networking kits, networking cards that use your home telephone wires instead of network cables, and more. Don't let the plethora of options available intimidate you. All of these networking schemes work more or less the same within Windows. The main differences involve the type of cabling used, and if you buy a kit, it'll automatically come with the right cable type.

Regardless of the network type, each computer in the network needs a network interface card (NIC). Typically, this is an ISA or PCI card that fits into a slot in the motherboard, but on a laptop PC, it could be a PCMCIA (PC Card) device. This way, the network cable plugs into that card. The traditional type of network card is *Ethernet*. There are various flavors of it, including 10Base-2, 10Base-T, and 100Base-T (listed here from slowest and cheapest to fastest and most expensive). Of these, 100Base-T is the fastest, but 10Base-T is more economical and probably more than fast enough for the average home network. If you can get a decent price on a NIC that supports both, all the better.

Typically, the other end of the network cable plugs into a hub. The hub is like a town square—all the cables from all the networked PCs plug into it, and all the traffic passes through it on its way to its destination. With some wireless home networking kits, there might not be a hub, so be sure to read the directions that come with your hardware.

 NOTE The hardware I'm describing here is for a simple peer-to-peer network; networking hardware can get much more complex as you move into the server-based type.

Assuming you have not bought a networking kit for some special type, such as wireless or telephone-line networking, here's a shopping list of networking equipment you will need:

- One 10Base-T NIC for each station you want on the network.
- One Ethernet (RJ-45) twisted-pair cable for each workstation to be connected. Cable-length requirements will be based on the distance between the computer

and the hub, usually somewhere between 6 and 50 feet, up to 328 feet at the maximum.

- A hub. This is a must if you plan to network three or more computers. Two computers can be networked without a hub, but you need to purchase a special cable (called a crossover cable) made specifically for that purpose.

 TIP Look in your local computer store for an Ethernet network starter kit. The kit should include everything you need, aside from the computer, to get your network up and running: two software-configurable network cards, about 25 feet of cable, a hub, and complete instructions. You can purchase additional add-on kits that include another network card and more cable, or you can simply buy more network cards and cable separately. If you are buying a kit for a wireless network, the hardware in the kit will probably differ from what is listed here.

Figure 24.2 shows what a typical NIC looks like. The card in Figure 24.2 has two kinds of connectors: RJ-45 and BNC. The RJ-45 one is the important one for a simple peer-to-peer network of the type we're constructing in this chapter; you don't need the BNC connector. (The BNC connector is used for a different kind of network cabling system than the one you'll want for your small peer-to-peer network.) Simple RJ-45 10Base-T network cards cost around $35 at the time of this writing.

FIGURE 24.2
This is a typical Network combo-card, sporting both RJ-45 and BNC thin coax connectors.

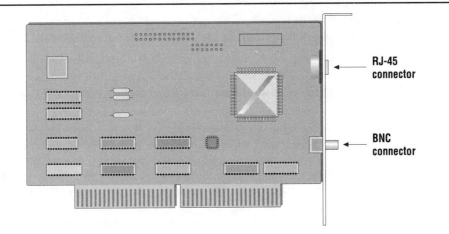

RJ-45 connector

BNC connector

As for the hub, there are very inexpensive models that accept four or five RJ-45 connections. If your network will consist of four or fewer computers, such a hub is your best choice. An 8- or 16-port hub is only a little bit more expensive. (In general, plan on spending around $10 per port.)

There's nothing special you need to know about buying the cables, except to look for RJ-45 on the packaging and to make sure that the cables are long enough (with some to spare) to reach from Point A to Point B.

Installing Your Network Hardware

In this section, I'll describe how to install and connect the basic hardware elements of your peer-to-peer network—the NIC and the cables.

Installing the Network Interface Card (NIC)

All modern network cards you buy in stores today are Plug-and-Play and jumperless (or have a jumperless operation option at least). Windows will assign resources to the card automatically. *Jumpers* are little black blocks that fit down over pins on the circuit board to change a configuration setting. Back before Plug-and-Play was popular, most circuit boards included jumpers for setting the desired interrupt request (IRQ) and memory address to use.

In the unlucky event that you are working with a network card that still requires jumpers to configure it, you have a little work to do. First, open the card's manual to where it shows how to set the jumpers or switches to configure the card's settings. For now, don't make any changes, but do write down the current IRQ number, direct memory access (DMA) channel, and memory address because you will need these to configure the driver.

Next, physically install the card. Follow these steps to do so:

1. Make sure the PC's power is turned off—unplug it to be really safe—and remove the PC's case. If you have questions about how to remove your computer case, refer to your owner's manual for a complete description.

 WARNING Don't forget to unplug your PC from the AC outlet before opening up the cover. This ensures you have the PC's power turned off, plus it reduces the chance of electric shock. Having come this far, I don't want to lose you. Also, before you install the network card, be sure to ground yourself by touching the metal case of the computer or by using a grounding strip to eliminate the possibility of static electricity zapping your network card.

---

2. Remove the screw that holds the thin metal slot cover behind the connector you intend to use for your card. Don't drop the screw into the machine! If you do, you must get it out one way or another, such as by turning the machine over.

3. Insert the card gently but firmly until it is completely seated in the slot. You may have to wiggle the card a bit (from front to back) to ensure it seats firmly into the connector.

4. Store the metal slot cover somewhere for future use and screw the card in securely (this can be a hassle sometimes because the screw may not line up with the hole very well).

WARNING After installing your network card, it is imperative that you take the time to put the screw back in the bracket and tighten the card down securely. If you don't, once you have the network cable attached to the card, a little tug on the cable could easily uproot the NIC, damaging it and your computer's motherboard (if the power is on). This is not fun. So take the extra time to put the screw back in.

If the PC in question is a laptop computer or a desktop that accepts PCMCIA cards, your chores are much easier. Simply plug the card into an available PCMCIA slot. Your computer (and Windows Me) can even be running while you do this. (You might want to verify this first, however, by reading the manual or asking the salesperson since there are a few early PCMCIA cards that should only be inserted when the unit is off.) And, of course, it won't hurt to insert the card before turning on the laptop. If the card is in the next time Windows Me starts up, the appropriate driver will be loaded immediately. But the ability to insert the PCMCIA card *while* Windows is running is Plug-and-Play at its finest. If all goes well, network drivers appropriate to your card will get automatically loaded when you insert the card and unloaded when you remove it. The first time you plug the card in, however, you may be prompted to insert the Windows CD-ROM (or one of the disks) to load the correct network card driver.

NOTE Some network cards may come with updated Windows Me drivers included on a disk. Read the documentation that came with your card (or call the manufacturer) to determine whether this is the case, and if it is, insert this driver disk into your drive when you are prompted to do so.

Repeat the above process with each PC you intend to network. When finished, place each PC's cover back on, but do not put all the screws back into the case yet—anyone who's done this before will tell you that screwing the case back on before making sure everything works is the best way to ensure that things will *not* work. Unfortunately, even with Plug-and-Play network cards, you may still end up having to get back inside your PC to reconfigure that Sound Blaster or some other card that happens to be using a needed IRQ or DMA channel and is not itself Plug-and-Play compatible. (In my experience, sound cards are the most frequent problem.)

Setting Up the Hub

A hub has its own power supply, which you plug into an electrical outlet. When you do so, a light on the hub should illuminate, indicating that it is ready for use. (Check the documentation for more info.) Now you're ready to install the cables.

Installing the Cables

Connect the cables to the back of each network card. The connectors work in a similar manner to telephone cables. Connect the other end of each cable to the hub. If you are networking two computers and have decided to forego a hub, you will probably have just one cable that strings from one network card to the other. Remember, a hubless 10Base-T network requires a crossover cable, or else the computers won't recognize each other.

With a network card installed in each of your stations and each card connected to the hub, you are now ready to install and configure your Windows Me software for networking. If all goes well, the hard part of your job is already complete.

Setting Up the NIC in Windows

If you've just finished installing the NIC in the PC, turn the PC on and let Windows start up. One of three things will happen:

- Windows will automatically detect the network card and automatically install the needed driver for it.

- Windows will detect the network card and prompt you for a driver disk. In this case, you'll insert the disk that came with the NIC and follow the prompts.

- Windows will not immediately detect the network card. See Chapter 13, "Adding and Removing Hardware and Software," for help in making Windows recognize a new piece of hardware.

If you are not sure whether Windows has set up your network card correctly, you can check it in the Control Panel. Choose Start ➢ Settings ➢ Control Panel and double-click Network to open the Network Properties dialog box, as shown in Figure 24.3. If your network card is listed, you're ready to go on to the next step.

Networking

FIGURE 24.3
*The Network Properties
dialog box*

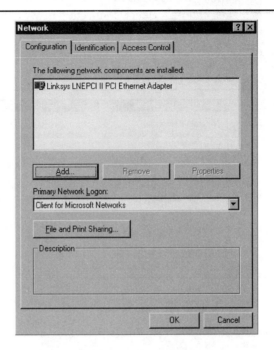

PART
V

NOTE If Windows Me did not detect your NIC, make sure you have a driver disk for the card, and then see Chapter 13 for help installing new hardware that Windows does not automatically detect.

Running the Home Networking Wizard

In earlier versions of Windows (9x), you had to manually configure a network card and install the needed protocols and clients through the Network applet in the Control Panel. You can still do it that way, but the Home Networking Wizard in Windows Me makes it much easier to do the same thing. The Home Networking Wizard can also automatically install the needed protocol to share an Internet connection across your network with multiple PCs.

Follow these steps to set up networking on your PC:

1. Choose Start ➤ Programs ➤ Accessories ➤ Communications ➤ Home Networking Wizard. At the introductory screen, click Next.

2. When prompted, indicate whether this PC is connected to the Internet, and in what manner (see Figure 24.4).

For example, if this PC has a modem, choose Yes, This Computer Uses the Following. Then choose A Direct Connection to My ISP Using the Following Device, and select the Dial-Up Networking connection from the drop-down list.

Choose Next when you have made your selections.

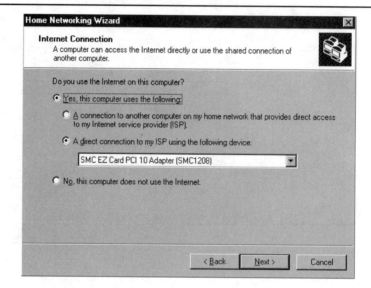

FIGURE 24.4
Specify the Internet connection for the PC, if any.

3. Depending on your answer in step 2, you might be asked whether you want to share the Internet connection. Choose Yes or No. If you choose Yes, choose the network adapter to use to share it (that is, the NIC that's hooked up to your home network). Then choose Next.

4. Enter a name for the computer in the Computer Name box. This will be the computer's name on the network, the name by which other computers will know it (see Figure 24.5).

FIGURE 24.5
Specify a name and a
workgroup.

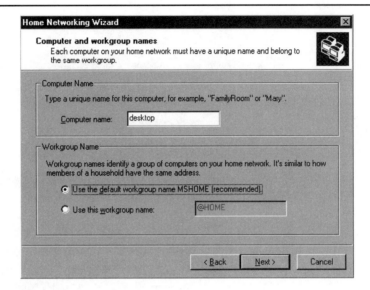

Home Networking Wizard

Computer and workgroup names
Each computer on your home network must have a unique name and belong to the same workgroup.

Computer Name
Type a unique name for this computer, for example, "FamilyRoom" or "Mary".

Computer name: desktop

Workgroup Name
Workgroup names identify a group of computers on your home network. It's similar to how members of a household have the same address.

○ Use the default workgroup name MSHOME (recommended).

○ Use this workgroup name: @HOME

< Back   Next >   Cancel

5. Accept the default workgroup name, or click Use This Workgroup Name and enter a different workgroup name.

All the computers on your home network must use the same workgroup name for them to communicate, so it is best to accept the default name unless you already have a network set up with a different workgroup name and you are merely adding a new computer to it.

 WARNING If you have a cable or DSL Internet connection through a network card in your PC, you must use the computer name and the workgroup name specified by your ISP; otherwise your Internet connection might not work.

6. Click Next. The TCP/IP Properties screen appears. See Figure 24.6.

PART
V

Networking

FIGURE 24.6
*Choose whether to
share certain folders
and printers on this PC.*

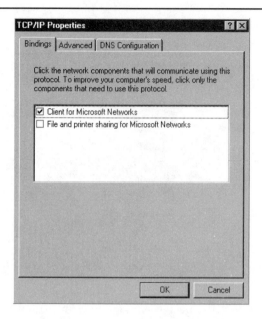

7. Set your file sharing options, and then click OK:

   • To share My Documents, leave the check mark in its box.

   • If you would like to set a password for sharing My Documents, click the Password button. Enter the password to use, type it again to confirm it, and then click OK.

   • To share a printer, make sure the check box next to the printer's name is marked.

NOTE On a home network on which you have no private data that you need to hide from anyone, you might choose not to use a password for sharing. If you don't specify a password, a warning appears when you click Next. You can Click OK to acknowledge it and then Next again to proceed without a password.

8. Click Next. You are asked whether you want to create a setup disk. If you will have any Windows 9x PCs on your network, click Yes and then Next to create the disk. Then follow the prompts to create it.

   On the other hand, if the other computers are already set up on the network, or if the other computers are running Windows Me or Windows 2000, you do not need the setup disk, so click No and then Next.

NOTE The setup disk you create contains a streamlined version of the Home Networking Wizard.

9. When you reach the Completing the Home Networking Wizard screen, click Finish. The needed files are copied.

10. When prompted to restart your computer, click Yes to do so. The computer restarts, and a network logon box appears.

11. Log on to the network by entering your username and password. (Just make them up, using something you will remember, if you don't have them already). Then click OK. Your computer is now connected to the network.

 TIP If you do not want to be prompted to log in at startup, do not enter a password in step 11.

Manually Adding Network Drivers

If you need to add additional protocols for networking, or you simply prefer to go on your own, you can install the needed networking components yourself by following these steps:

1. From the Control Panel, double-click Network.

2. Check the list of components on the Configuration tab. If you do not see Client for Microsoft Networks, do the following:

   a. Click Add, then click Client, then click Add. A list of Microsoft-provided clients appears.

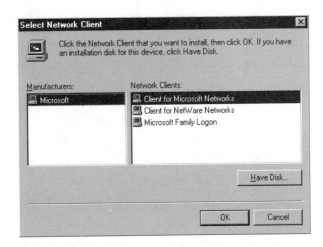

PART

V

Networking

b. Click Client for Microsoft Networks, and then click OK.

c. If prompted to insert the Windows disk, do so and click OK.

3. You need at least one protocol. The most common one is IPX/SPX-compatible. If it's not already there, or if you need to add another protocol, do the following:

a. Click Add, then Protocol, then Add. The Select Network Protocol dialog box opens.

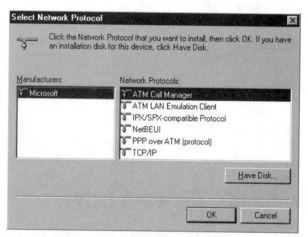

b. Click the protocol to install, and click OK.

c. If you are prompted to insert the Windows CD, do so and click OK.

4. Open the Primary Network Logon drop-down list and choose the client for the network (for example, Client for Microsoft Networks).

5. You will also want to set up file and printer sharing if you want others on your network to be able to use this computer. To do so, click File and Printer Sharing. The File and Print Sharing dialog box opens.

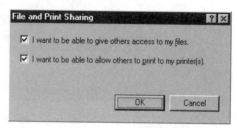

6. Make sure that both check boxes are marked to share both files and printers. Then click OK.

7. Click OK. If prompted to restart, click Yes.

Networking with Windows NT/2000

Microsoft's modular approach to networking in its operating systems has made internetworking Windows Me with Windows NT and Windows 2000 quite simple. This section discusses some of the unique features of an NT/2000 network, and describes how to make your Windows Me machines fit in.

 NOTE If you have a simple home network only, and aren't a part of a large corporate Windows NT/2000 client/server network, you can skip this section altogether.

Workgroups

As you saw when you went through the Home Networking Wizard earlier in the chapter, each PC is a member of a particular workgroup. On a simple peer-to-peer network for home networking, typically, there is only one workgroup, but larger networks running on Windows NT/2000 might have many different workgroups. Usually, PCs are assigned to one workgroup or another according to job function, department, or physical proximity—whatever makes the most sense in a given situation. Subdividing the full group of network users into workgroups keeps things simple for the average user, and makes it easier for them to locate the PCs belonging to people with whom they work most closely. And where security is needed, passwords can be assigned within the workgroup on a per-resource or per-user basis (a single password can even be used by a group of users).

Small networks—say those with a total of 50 or fewer workstations—might find that the workgroup approach is a sufficient and easy enough means for subdividing and organizing the network resources and users, assuming they're subdivided into multiple workgroups. But with very large networks, workgroups are not adequate because there's no way to oversee all the different workgroups. Managing the centralized networking resources on larger networks requires being able to access and configure user accounts and other network resources in a way that transcends the boundaries of individual workgroups.

Domains

For ease of organizing and managing large networks, Microsoft came up with the idea of *domains*. Domains are similar to workgroups but provide the ability to group all users in a single user *database*. This database resides on the Windows NT Server *domain controller* (and, optionally, in NT 4.0, on *backup domain controllers*). When you log on to a domain from the Windows Me logon dialog box, you are authenticated as a specific user with specific access rights. These access rights are the basis for your ability to use shared resources on the network, such as a shared directory or printer.

PART

V

Networking

For more specific information on NT Server, take a look at my book on NT called *Windows NT Server 4.0: No Experience Required* (Sybex, 1997).

Protocols Required

To allow your Windows Me stations to communicate with an NT/2000 server, you must make sure they are using one of the protocols used by the server. In most cases, this will probably be either NetBEUI or IPX/SPX—or if you have a really big network, you may be using TCP/IP. On a small Windows-only network (where no connections to Novell or other systems are needed), NetBEUI will be your fastest protocol. Again, you just need to make sure the Windows Me PCs are talking the same language as your server.

Adding a Windows Me PC to an NT/2000 Server Network

The Home Networking Wizard can set up a Windows Me PC to operate as part of a client/server network the same way that it sets up for a smaller network. Go ahead and run it, as described earlier in the chapter. This will set up your printers to be shared if desired, as well as your My Documents folder. If you want to share additional folders, or entire drives, or set security restrictions for the sharing, see "Sharing Resources on the Network" later in this chapter.

 NOTE To employ user-level or group-level access rights, you must be part of a Windows NT domain or you must be using pass-through authentication with a Novell NetWare server.

If the NT server is a domain server, you will also need to create a user account on the NT server for each Windows Me user that will be needing access to resources on the NT server. Use NT's User Manager for Domains, or in Windows 2000, use Active Directory Users and Computers to create these accounts, and then set any desired file restrictions using NT's File Manager or Windows Explorer, and any desired printer or printing restrictions using NT's Print Manager. (If you are an end user on a corporate network, your network administrator might handle this himself.)

If you are using NT Workstation, simply make sure you have the same workgroup name specified on the NT workstation as you do for each Windows Me station that will be part of this workgroup. The Home Networking Wizard should take care of this.

However, if you are using NT Server, you must set the Windows Me PC to log on to the NT domain and enter the correct domain in the domain field at each station. To do this, open the Network Properties from the Control Panel, and double-click Client for Microsoft Windows Networks. Click the Domain check box and type in the name of your NT domain (see Figure 24.7).

FIGURE 24.7
*Configuring a Windows
Me station to log on to
an NT/2000 Server
domain*

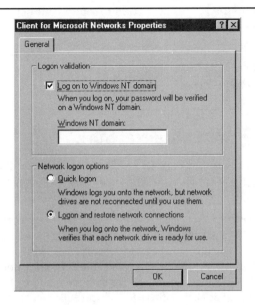

After performing these steps, you should be able to open My Network Places on any Windows Me stations in the workgroup (or domain) and see an icon for the NT server. Also, when using the server browsers in either NT's Print Manager or Windows Explorer, you should now see your Windows Me stations appear as additional servers in the workgroup (or domain).

NOTE If your office has one or more Novell NetWare print servers and you are running NT Server, you can use the NT Printers folder to share NetWare print servers. You must first install and configure the NetWare Gateway Services software (supplied with NT Server) and then connect to the NetWare print queue before trying to share it. In this way, Windows Me and 9*x* stations (and even DOS, Windows 3.1, and Windows for Workgroups stations) will not need Novell-specific network drivers loaded in order to print on the Novell print queue. However, you will need to use a printer driver for each printer you use.

Working with Network Resources

Start up Windows Me on each of your PCs. You should now see the My Network Places icon on each Desktop. Double-click the icon, and you should see, at the minimum, three icons:

Add Network
Place

Add Network Place A Wizard that walks you through the process of creating a shortcut to a certain computer, drive, or folder on the network.

Home
Networking
Wizard

Home Networking Wizard   Reruns the Home Networking Wizard that you used in the preceding section to set up your network; you can use it to make changes to the network configuration.

Entire Network

Entire Network   Browses all the computers and shared drives/folders and printers on the network.

Browsing the Entire Network

Let's start with Entire Network. Browsing with it is like working with My Computer, except that it shows your whole network instead of the drives on your local PC.

> **NOTE**   Each PC on your network should appear in Entire Network. If any are missing, or worse, if you do not have a My Network Places icon on your Desktop, you'll have to do some troubleshooting. The most common problem, aside from missing protocol(s) and incorrectly configured network cards, will be that one or more of your stations are not set to the same workgroup as all the others. See Chapter 25, "Network Security and Troubleshooting" or use the Network Troubleshooter built into Windows Help.

Double-click Entire Network, and a list of workgroups appears. For a home-based network, there will be only one workgroup.

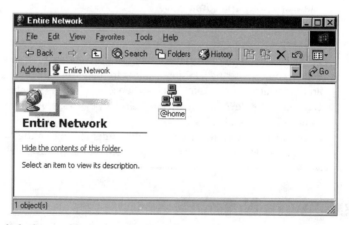

Double-click the workgroup, and a list of computers on that network that have shared resources appears. Any computers that do not have any drives, folders, files, or printers shared will not appear.

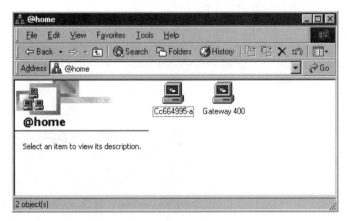

Double-click the computer you want to browse, and a list of shared drives, folders, and printers appears.

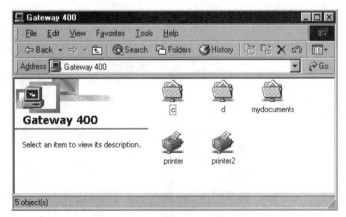

From there, double-click a printer icon to see the printer's queue (refer back to Chapter 11, "Printers and Printing," for details about print queues) or double-click a drive icon to browse the shared files there, just as you would when browsing a local drive.

Creating a Network Place

The level-by-level browsing you saw in the preceding section works great if you don't know exactly what you're looking for. However, if you frequently need to access a certain drive or folder on a remote PC, you might want to create a shortcut for it. Such shortcuts are known as *network places*. You create network places in the My Network Places folder (no surprise there), but you can also create shortcuts to them anywhere else that you place shortcuts, such as on the Desktop.

PART
V

Networking

To create a network place, do the following:

1. In the My Network Places window, double-click Add Network Place. The Add Network Place Wizard runs.

2. Click the Browse button. A Browse for Folder dialog box opens.

3. Click the plus signs to expand the tree to locate the drive or folder to which you want a shortcut, and select it.

4. Click OK. The network path to that resource appears in the text box.

NOTE Network paths are always preceded by two slashes: \\. The full network path to a resource includes the computer name, a slash, the drive name, and if it's a path to a folder, another slash and the folder name. It's not necessary to include the workgroup name unless it's in a different workgroup than the computer creating the shortcut. By the way, this naming convention is called UNC (Universal Naming Convention).

5. Click Next.

6. Type a descriptive name for the network place. This text will appear under its icon.

7. Click Finish. The new Network Place shortcut appears in the My Network Places window.

From then on, whenever you want to use this network resource, you can simply open the My Network Places window and double-click the shortcut icon.

 TIP You can put the shortcut you created on your Desktop by holding down the Ctrl key and dragging the icon from My Network Places to where you want it on your Desktop.

Mapping Windows Shared Drives

Most Windows-based programs are *network-aware*, which means you can browse My Network Places the same way you browse other folders when you are saving and opening files. However, some programs, especially older 16-bit programs, don't offer direct network support. If you want to save and open files on a network drive from one of these programs, you must map the network drive to a drive letter. Then your system sees the network drive (or a folder on a network drive) as a new local drive letter on your own PC.

For Windows Me PCs, the fastest and easiest way to map a network drive is to locate the drive or folder in My Network Places, right-click it, and choose Map Network Drive. The Map Network Drive dialog box appears.

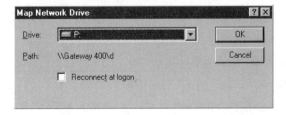

Choose the drive letter you want to use, choose whether to reconnect this mapping automatically when you start the PC, and then click OK. The drive or folder's contents appear in a folder window for browsing. You can work with it, or close it if you don't have anything you need to do with it right now. Notice before you close it, however, that its title bar now indicates its new drive letter assignment:

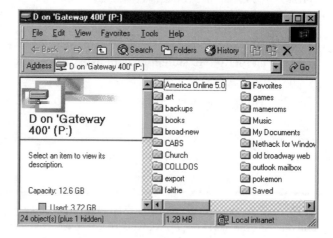

 NOTE Note that the Reconnect on Logon option is enabled by default; this is probably what you want. With this option on, whenever the PC in question is booted up, it will automatically log in the remote drive and map it to the desired logical drive.

Using Shared Printers

To use a shared printer on the network, you must set up that printer on your own PC as a network printer. After that, you can print to the network printer as easily as you print to any local one, simply by choosing it from the Printer list in the Print dialog box of the program from which you are printing.

To set up to print to a network printer:

1. Choose Start ➢ Settings ➢ Printers.

2. Double-click Add Printer.

3. Click Next to begin.

4. Click Network Printer, and then click Next.

5. Click the Browse button; then locate and select the printer on the list of network resources. Click plus signs to expand lists, just as you do with drives and folders in Windows Explorer.

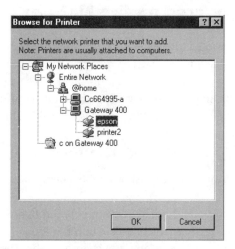

6. Click OK to return to the Add Printer Wizard.

7. Choose Yes or No to indicate whether you print from MS-DOS programs, and then click Next.

8. Enter a name for the printer. This name will appear under its icon on your Printers folder and on lists of printers in Print dialog boxes.

9. Choose Yes or No to indicate whether you will use this printer as your default printer. Then click Next.

10. Click Yes or No to indicate whether you want to print a test page.

11. Click Finish. The files needed for shared use of the printer are copied from the printers network location to your own hard disk, and the printer appears in your Printers folder.

Printers that you share on the network have a slightly different icon in the Printers folder from the local printers. This window shows both local and network printers installed.

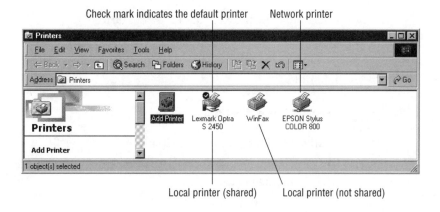

Check mark indicates the default printer   Network printer

Local printer (shared)   Local printer (not shared)

Sharing Resources on the Network

Being connected to the network and sharing other PCs and printers does not necessarily mean that your own drives and printers are shared. When you went through the Home Networking Wizard, you indicated whether or not you wanted to share your My Documents folder, as well as each of your local printers. But there are more sharing options than those simple ones, as you'll see in this section.

Setting Up File and Print Sharing

File and Print Sharing must be enabled before you can share files or printers on your network.

If you chose to share My Documents through the Home Networking Wizard, file sharing is already enabled; if you didn't, it probably isn't. The same goes for printers; if you chose to share a printer when running the Home Networking Wizard, print sharing is already set up.

To check, and to turn sharing on if needed, do the following:

1. From the Control Panel, double-click Network. (A shortcut: right-click My Network Places and choose Properties.)

2. Click the File and Print Sharing button.

3. Make sure both check boxes are marked.

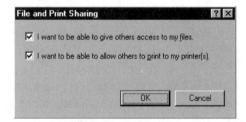

4. Click OK.

5. Click OK to close the Network Properties box.

6. If prompted to restart your PC, click Yes to do so.

Now overall file and print sharing is enabled, and you can share individual folders, drives, and printers.

Sharing Drives and Folders

To share a drive or folder, do the following:

1. Right-click it and choose Sharing. The Properties dialog box for the item appears with the Sharing tab displayed.

2. Click the Shared As option button. The rest of the dialog box's controls become available (see Figure 24.8).

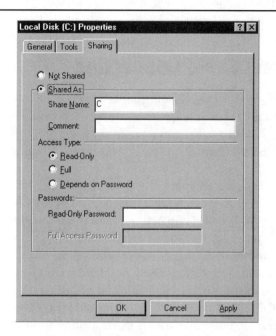

3. (Optional) Enter a more meaningful name in the Share Name box. For example, if you are sharing a drive that contains backup files, you might call it Backup.

4. Choose one of these three access types:

- The default is Read-Only, which only allows other users to open and view the contents but not to change them.

- The Full option lets anyone on the network both read and make changes to this folder. Keep in mind, by the way, that sharing a drive or folder shares all the subfolders below it as well.

- Depends on Password lets you make the resource available to some people with full access and to others with Read-only access, depending on the password they use.

5. Enter the password(s) to use in the Passwords section. To allow password-free access, leave these fields blank.

6. Click OK. The item is now shared, and its icon appears with a little hand under it to indicate that fact.

Sharing Printers

Sharing a printer works just like sharing a drive or folder. Right-click it and choose Sharing. Then choose the Shared As option button and fill in the other fields as desired, just as you did in the preceding steps.

Using Direct Cable Connection

Windows Me's Direct Cable Connection (DCC) is a wonderful little utility that lets you have a fully operational network connection between any two PCs, connected only by their serial or parallel ports.

If you have network interface cards in your computers already, you can forget about DCC. It's only a boon if you don't want to get into the hassle of setting up a network, or if you have a computer that *doesn't* have a network card in it. Since a network card can transfer data much faster than the DCC will (the slowness is due to the limitations of serial and parallel ports), you'll want to use the LAN option whenever possible. Even a relatively "slow" 10Mbps Ethernet card is super fast compared to a measly parallel port (and *super*-super fast compared to a serial port).

If you're one of the growing numbers of laptop users, you probably appreciate having the mobility of the laptop but still find times when you could really use a Zip drive, or a CD-ROM drive, or just wish you could copy files up to the network or down to your laptop faster than with floppies. Using DCC, you can very easily connect that laptop to any other computer running Windows Me (or Windows 9x, since it works on those operating systems too) as long as you have either a serial-to-serial or a parallel-to-parallel cable designed for data transfer between two computers (LapLink-style cables). There's a place where I live that sells nice long parallel cables for only $5, and if you find a similar deal, I'd recommend buying a few. It is really simple to connect the cable to the printer port on your laptop and to an office PC, start DCC on both PCs, and within seconds, actually have a network connection, which allows you to access any shared resources on whichever PC is configured as the host.

To set up Direct Cable Connection, complete the following steps:

1. Make sure the feature is installed. Choose Start ➤ Programs ➤ Accessories ➤ Communications. If Direct Cable Connection is not there, use Add/Remove Programs to add it from the Windows CD, as described in Chapter 13.

2. To start up the DCC applet, click Start ➤ Programs ➤ Accessories ➤ Communications ➤ Direct Cable Connection.

   When you start up DCC for the first time, it will ask you to select whether this PC will be configured as a Guest PC or as the Host PC, as shown in Figure 24.9. Choose one and then click Next.

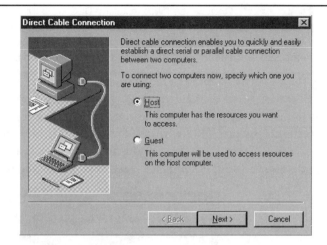

3. Select which port you want to use with DCC (see Figure 24.10). Then click Next.

If at all possible, you should use a parallel port. Not only is it quite a bit faster than the alternative (a serial port), but usually it will also be easier to find a parallel port available on the computers you'll be connecting to.

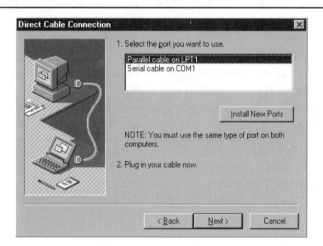

PART

V

Networking

TECH TIP   Once, when I was installing DCC, no parallel ports showed up in the Ports list. After checking out my Device Manager list in Control Panel ➢ Devices, I discovered that the parallel port was disabled because it conflicted with a sound card. After reconfiguring the sound card to a different IRQ, the printer port showed up in DCC's list of available ports.

Now that you've configured one PC, you need to do the same on the other one, of course making sure you choose the same port type (either serial or parallel), and remembering which one you've decided to set up as Host and which one as Guest. Then, connect your cable between the two ports, click Listen on the host PC, and click Connect on the guest PC. After a few seconds, you should see a message similar to this:

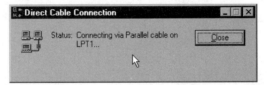

If you've entered a password (on both sides), next you will see the message "Verifying User ID and Password," and then the connection will be established. Once the connection has been established, you can minimize the DCC Status dialog box on both PCs to get them out of the way.

At this point, you will be able to access the host PC from My Network Places and thus you can map drives, install a printer driver corresponding to any printers on the host side, and so on—just like we did earlier in the chapter.

 TIP   If you will be using DCC frequently on a particular PC, you may want to drag the DCC icon from the Accessories ➢ Communications folder onto your Desktop for easy access. Or, if you prefer, drag and drop the DCC icon onto your Start button or Quick Launch bar.

By now, you should have a good understanding of the many options that Windows Me gives you for interconnecting (networking) your computers. In the next chapter, I'll discuss troubleshooting and security for network connections.

CHAPTER **25**

Network Security and Troubleshooting

FEATURING:

The preceding chapter helped you set up a peer-to-peer Windows Me network based on a "best-case" scenario—that is, a situation in which security is only minimally an issue and in which all the hardware works exactly as advertised right out of the box. For the majority of home networks, that'll be the case. However, if you're reading this chapter, I'll assume that you are either interested in more security and monitoring for some reason or having a problem getting your network up and running.

This chapter is a quick read because I know you're in a hurry to get your security concerns and operational problems resolved and get on with the business of networking.

Network Security in Windows Me

Sharing a resource on the network doesn't have to be an all-or-nothing proposition in which you put your important files out there for a free-for-all. The security settings in Windows Me's networking component allow you to specify exactly *what* you want to share and *how* you want it shared.

Password-Protecting a Resource

One of the most basic types of security for Windows Me network sharing is password usage. Back in Chapter 24, "Building a Peer-to-Peer Network," when you were running through the Home Networking Wizard, you were given the opportunity to specify a password for access to your shared resources. You also learned how to manually set passwords for Read-Only and Full access to an individual resource through its properties. This is called *share-level access control* because you are controlling the security as you share the resource.

Let's quickly review that procedure for assigning a password to a shared network resource (that is, a drive, folder, or printer):

1. Right-click the resource's icon and choose Sharing.

2. Choose the level of access you want:

    Read-Only Appropriate for drives or folders containing files that others can look at but not modify. Past financial records, for example, would be useful for others to see, but you would not want anyone to change or delete them.

    Full Appropriate for printers and for drives/folders that you want others to use to store their work, or to get input or collaboration on data files from several people on the network.

    Depends on Password Lets you have the best of both worlds. You can assign two different passwords to the resource (or assign a password only to

Full), so that everyone may see the resource but only people with the correct password may modify it.

3. Enter the password(s) for the access level(s) you chose to have. See Figure 25.1.

4. Click OK to accept the change.

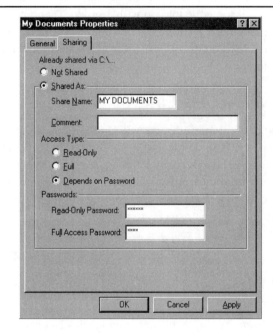

Obviously, any such security is only as good as the confidentiality of the passwords. If security is of more than passing interest to you, you should encourage proper choice of user passwords. There are several good computer security books that discuss guidelines for selecting difficult-to-guess passwords.

Please bear in mind that Windows Me was not designed to be a really secure operating system. If you do need something more secure, strongly consider using Windows 2000— it's one of only a few operating systems that has security incorporated in it at every level, earning it a C2-level security rating.

Hiding Share Names

Here's a little-known but very useful strategy. In any Shared As name (when you right-click a resource and choose Sharing), if you add a dollar sign ($) to the end of the share name, that resource becomes invisible but still accessible to those who know of both its existence and its name. For example, if you want to make your CD-ROM drive accessible anywhere on the network but not have everyone using it, you might type **CDROM$** as the drive's share name. Then, whenever you need to access this drive from another station, you would need to specify the machine name and the share name to map to the drive or otherwise access it. The access path would look similar to this: \\CD_Station\CDROM$. Obviously, this technique is only as secure as the knowledge of the resource's share name (and location).

You may want to combine share-name hiding with share-level passwords. In this way, even if someone logs on with a stolen ID and password, he or she may not know that a particular resource exists. I wouldn't count on this, but on the other hand, I wouldn't discredit or overlook even small additional layers of security where they are called for.

User-Level Access Control

Although the simple effectiveness of the two methods above might be all that's needed on smaller networks, eventually you'll need to consider *user-level* access control. This more-sophisticated security relies on Windows Me verification of users by their logon password. In other words, you specify exactly which users and groups of users are to have access to a given network resource, and then those users, once they have logged in, automatically gain access to that network resource.

For Windows Me to make use of user-level access, it must use a Windows NT Server user database, so you can't set up this kind of security on a Windows Me peer-to-peer network.

If you're connected to a client/server network, do the following to set up user-level access control:

1. From the Control Panel, double-click Network.

2. Click the Access Control tab.

3. Choose User-Level Access Control.

4. In the text box provided, enter the computer or network domain where the master list of users is stored. Check with the network administrator to get this information.

5. Click OK.

6. If prompted to restart your PC, click Yes.

 NOTE To employ user-level or group-level access rights, you must be part of a Windows NT/2000 domain or be using pass-through authentication with a Novell NetWare server. Since this is not the case for most small-business and home networks, most users of Windows Me will never have the opportunity to use this feature.

Using Net Watcher

Net Watcher is a program that allows you to monitor resources you have shared on your LAN. You'll want to run this program if there is heavy traffic on your shared items, such as files or printer. For one thing, it lets you know what the consequences might be if you need to shut down your computer. You'll see who is attached to your resources and what they are using. Secondly, it can help you analyze your LAN traffic flow, and possibly determine why your computer is acting a little sluggish (lots of folks are using the contact database!).

You cannot see only who is currently using resources on your computer, but you can also disconnect them from specific files if need be, or easily share new folders. To use Net Watcher, follow these steps:

1. Start Net Watcher by clicking Start ➢ Programs ➢ Accessories ➢ System Tools ➢ Net Watcher. The program appears:

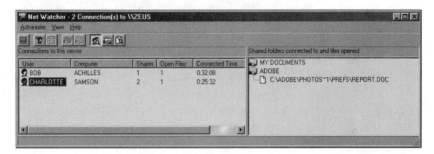

Notice that there are two users using stuff on my machine now, Bob and Charlotte. Clicking a person in the left pane displays (in the right pane) what they are using.

2. Clicking the Shared button will show what you currently have shared (they aren't necessarily being used):

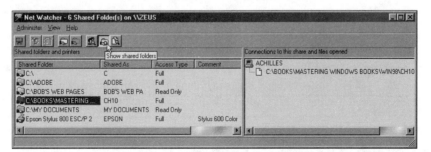

3. Click the Open Files button or choose View ➢ Open files to see a listing of open files, who is using them, and what the share status is.

TIP If you don't have Net Watcher on the System Tools menu, it's not installed. You'll have to go to Control Panel ➤ Add/Remove Programs ➤ Windows Setup and add it from there. You can find Net Watcher under System Tools.

To stop sharing a file or resource, click the resource and click the Stop Sharing button in the toolbar (or choose Administer ➤ Stop Sharing Folder). You'll be asked to confirm. To disconnect a specific user, choose the user display mode, click the user, and click the disconnect user button (or choose Administer ➤ Disconnect User). You'll be advised that this could spell trouble for the user.

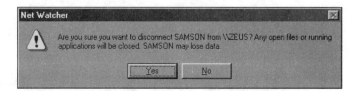

Checking Resources on Another Computer

In case you're administering other computers on a LAN, you can also check out the activity on another's computer workstation. First, make sure the remote computer is set up for remote administration. Secondly, ensure that you're set up as an administrator (given access permission). You do these things from the Control Panel ➤ Passwords applet. After this has been done, follow these steps:

1. Double-click My Network Places.
2. Click the name of the computer on which you'd like to view shared resources.
3. On the File menu, click Properties.
4. Choose Tools ➤ Net Watcher.
5. On the Net Watcher View menu, click the type of information you want to see. You'll be asked to supply a password since remote administration always requires a password.

 TIP If Net Watcher is already running, you can choose Administer ➤ Server and enter or browse to the server you want to remotely administer.

Network Troubleshooting

Not only are networking problems sometimes difficult to track down, but typically, they also require a quick resolution because frequently a network problem means downtime for one or more network users. When you first learn of a problem, it helps to assign it a priority by taking into account criteria such as the following:

- How many users are (or will be) affected?
- What type of work (emergency, critical, or lower priority) is affected?
- How difficult does the problem appear to be?
- Does the problem have a known solution (at your organization), or are you dealing with something new?

 TIP It is a very good policy to always log problems as they occur. Include the time and date, who reported the problem, initial prognosis, and estimated time to resolution. And, most important, be sure to add a detailed description of both the problem and the steps taken to fix it. While such a log requires a certain time (and discipline) investment, it can pay off significantly the next time a similar problem occurs. Be sure to make frequent backups of your log, including regular printed copies. (Keeping it on the computer gives you the ability to do quick searches.)

Dealing with networking problems—and with computer problems in general—is largely a matter of deduction, eliminating possibilities through questioning, trial and error, and adverting to past experience. This is why keeping a problem-and-resolution log can be so effective. If someone else is reporting the problem to you, write down what they say and ask questions while the situation is still fresh in their memory. Almost always, the first thing you should ask is, "When was the last time this equipment [or software or whatever] worked correctly?"

The second most helpful question to ask—assuming someone else is explaining the problem to you—is, "What were you doing when you noticed the problem?" (Avoid giving this question an accusatorial tone—you just want to know what led to the problem.) Besides helping to narrow your focus, these questions sometimes point you directly to the root cause of the problem. Sometimes, for example, users will try tightening the keyboard or mouse cables and end up loosening the network cable. Perhaps they turned off the computer without first shutting down. About half the time, the problem was caused by operator error; but if so, rather than chastising the user, show them how to avoid this problem in the future. As much as you may enjoy using computers, don't forget that to some users, computers are probably a mystery and even an object of fear. Try to pass on your appreciation of computers whenever possible. A thorough and positive introduction to the computer and occasional user training can go a long way toward eliminating accidental damage to cables, keyboards, and other hardware and software.

Troubleshooting is also helped by having a good memory (or a good set of notes). When was the software on this station upgraded? Which network adapter (and drivers) is it using? When was this cable run? Again, knowing what to look for greatly reduces the number of possibilities you need to look at.

Certain applications may indirectly cause extra troubles for your organization. Maybe an older communications program insists on using an earlier version of WinSock, thus conflicting with Windows Me's built-in version of WinSock. Perhaps some application is opening files in exclusive mode, preventing other users from opening the same files.

Has a new piece of hardware or software recently been added to the station? If so, this is a good place to start looking. Until every system is fully Plug-and-Play aware and has only Plug-and-Play components installed, interrupt and I/O address conflicts will be an ongoing source of problems. The best weapons against such conflicts are these: using identical hardware for all workstations, using the same interrupts and I/O addresses for the same devices in each workstation as much as possible, documenting the card settings on a sheet of paper taped inside each computer, and lastly, making use of a POST (power-on self test) diagnostics card.

Such a card fits into the bus of a problem PC and can perform a large array of tests on the computer, reporting the results via LEDs on the card. The Discovery Card from JDR Microdevices costs about $99 and can find IRQ- and DMA-related conflicts, while a more complex card may cost $1,200 to $1,500 and can identify all devices set to the same IRQ, bad SIMMs, and errors on the motherboard, as well as problems with the power supply, serial and parallel ports, and so on.

Such errors might otherwise take half a day or longer to diagnose, besides the productivity time wasted while the system is down. I have seen completely configured systems delivered with two serial ports configured to the same address, a network card conflicting with video memory, and even two parallel port adapters, both configured to LPT1, in the same PC. Obviously, whoever configured these systems was not using a POST diagnostics card.

In the rest of this chapter, I'll look at some of the most common problems that can plague your Windows Me network and how you can resolve them most efficiently.

 NOTE You can also find some limited assistance in the Windows help system, which is described in Chapter 8, "Getting Help When You Need It."

Diagnosing Cable Problems

One of the nicest things about small peer-to-peer networks is the relative ease of diagnosing and fixing cable problems. If one PC is having a problem, check that PC's NIC (network interface card) and cable connection. If all PCs suddenly lose their network connection, you should check out your hub.

If none of the cable connections have pulled loose, try swapping in a different hub. If the stations now connect to the network again, you've found the problem. You can see the practicality of keeping a spare hub around—ideally one that's identical to what's in use so that you can immediately replace the hub if it ever becomes necessary. For diagnostic purposes, though, even a hub with a small number of ports lets you try connecting a few stations. If it works, you know there's a problem with the other hub.

Other types of networks, however, pose greater troubleshooting challenges. On a network using thin coax cabling (such as a 10Base-2 network), it's much more likely for the whole network (or segment of a network, if on a large one) to go down, because of the nature of the connection. Typically, what you'll have to do then is perform *binary searching* for the location of the cable break by splitting the network segment in half, seeing which half still works when you connect it to the server, then splitting the bad subsegment in half and repeating this process until you locate the offending cable portion.

When single stations lose their connection on a star-type client/server configuration, again the problem-solving process is much easier. The first thing to do (obvious, but frequently effective) is to check that both ends of the cable are connected tightly. If this doesn't take care of the problem, try connecting the hub end of the cable to a different jack on the hub.

 NOTE One thing I really appreciate about Windows 9x/Me and NT/2000 is their ability to auto-reconnect when a connection is temporarily broken. This may seem like a small thing, but it's nice not to have to reboot the station each time; I can just double-click My Network Places or reopen a folder on a network drive.

If you still aren't able to establish a connection, try whichever of these is less trouble: either swap in a different cable or connect a different PC to the end of the existing cable (use a PC known to have no trouble getting on the network). Using these two tests, you can determine either that the cable is bad (if the new cable worked or the new PC did not) or that the original PC has a network-card problem (if the new PC worked, but the new cable did not work with the original PC). If you determine that the cable is the problem, you might try replacing the cable connector if you are adept at this and think it's a quicker solution than running a new length of cable.

Finally, if you're able to connect to the network, but transferring data across the network seems as slow as molasses, you're likely dealing with an poor-quality (or damaged) network cable. Remember, nowadays you want level 5 cable, if possible (or at least level 3); otherwise, you can expect all sorts of problems with throughput on your network.

Diagnosing NIC and Driver Problems

If you have reason to believe a network card may not be functioning properly, here are several things you can try—in the order in which you'll most likely want to try them. First, if Windows Me is already running, go into Control Panel ➢ Networks and check that all network components that should be installed actually are. If not, add them, shut down and restart Windows Me, and again try to get on the network. If this doesn't work, then just to get everything working, you could remove any network (software) components other than these three:

- The driver for the installed network card

- The protocol(s) you need to get on the network

- The appropriate client service (for example, Client for NetWare Networks or Client for Microsoft Networks)

The most important thing is to verify that the card settings match those configured on the driver. To do this, double-click the network card in Device Manager (from System from the Control Panel). This should bring up the network card's properties box (see Figure 25.2). Click the Resources tab and verify that the settings are correct. Also write down these settings in case you need to pull your network card later to verify that its settings correspond to these.

 NOTE You can also view the network card's properties through the Network applet in the Control Panel, but the Resources tab is not available from there. Therefore, in this case, you must go through the Device Manager.

FIGURE 25.2
Verifying and configuring network-card settings

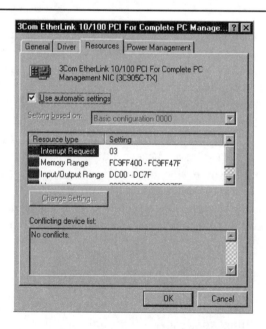

Next, check out the Driver Type. To do this, open the Network applet from the Control Panel, click the Configuration tab, and double-click the NIC on the list; then click the Driver Type tab, which is shown in Figure 25.3.

FIGURE 25.3

Make sure you are using the Enhanced Mode (32 Bit and 16 Bit) NDIS Driver.

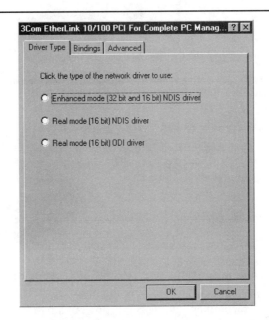

In almost all cases, you'll want to select the first radio button, Enhanced Mode (32 Bit and 16 Bit) NDIS Driver; the only reason you ever need real-mode drivers is if you happen to be using a network card for which you cannot find Windows Me protected-mode drivers or if you want to test network-connectivity problems. For instance, when attempting to solve a connectivity problem, you can install an NDIS 2.0 (real-mode) driver, boot Windows Me to a command prompt using your emergency boot disk, and then try to log on to the network with a Net Logon command. If that works, but the NDIS 3.1 (protected-mode) driver failed, at least you have identified the problem and you can begin troubleshooting the protected-mode driver installation. In any case, make sure the setting matches what you need.

Also, click the Bindings tab and verify that a check mark is placed next to the protocol(s) you will need to get on your network. For example, if your network is based on the IPX/SPX-compatible protocol, make sure that the check box for it is marked (see Figure 25.4).

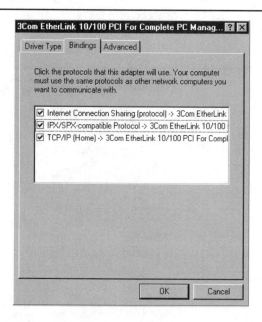

If you notice any incorrect settings, after changing them, you'll want to restart Windows Me and see if you are now able to connect to the network. Otherwise, the next thing I'd recommend doing is printing out a handy list of equipment and resource settings, which can be done by going to Control Panel ➤ System ➤ Device Manager and clicking Print.

If your network card is one that lets you software-configure the IRQ and I/O address with a DOS-based program, open a DOS window and run this software now. If the settings match what they should be, good. Otherwise, adjust them accordingly.

NOTE Some cards that let you run a software-configuration utility also have one or more jumper settings that need to be set before your configuration software can work; otherwise, it won't run at all, or when you try to make changes, they won't stick. In this case, refer to your card's documentation for information on enabling the software-configuration option.

If your network card is not software configurable, you'll need to remove the network card to visually inspect it and possibly make changes to it. Again, first print out the system summary report, as it will definitely be helpful in setting your card. Next, shut down Windows, turn off the PC and unplug it, remove the PC's cover, and take out the network card. If you're lucky, the network card will have the jumper settings silk-screened near the jumper pads. Otherwise, dredge up your card's documentation and flip to the jumper-settings diagram. Verify that the settings match what your driver is configured to. If not, make changes to the jumpers.

If your network card settings match your network driver settings and you are *still* not able to connect to the network, it's likely that either the IRQ or the I/O address conflicts with another card. If this is the case, refer to your system configuration report and select a different (unused) IRQ and I/O address for your network card. To see a list of IRQs and other potentially conflicted system resources, go to Control Panel ➢ System, and click the Device Manager tab; then double-click Computer. You'll see a dialog box listing lots of goodies to help you, as shown in Figure 25.5.

FIGURE 25.5
To help you determine resource conflicts, go to the Device Manager and double-click Computer.

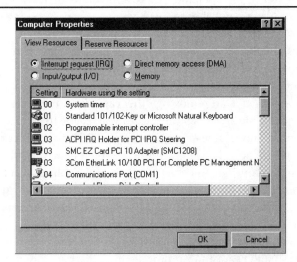

When you've got your network card configured, gently reinstall it and tighten down the edge bracket with a screw. Replace the PC's cover (you don't want to replace all the screws holding the cover just yet—wait until your network card is verified as operational). Then turn the computer back on and make any changes to the network-card driver to synch it with the changes you've made to the card. If you're prompted to shut down and restart Windows Me, do so.

PART
V

Networking

NOTE When attempting to get network support operational, you may want to start Windows in *safe mode with networking support*. This disables other drivers that may conflict with your network card, reducing the number of factors that can interfere with initially connecting with the network. To boot Windows Me in this mode, press the F6 key when the computer is first starting (when you see the Starting Windows Me prompt), before you see the logo screen. (On a fast computer, you may have to act quickly, as the window of opportunity between "starting" and the logo is very small.) If the F6 approach doesn't work, try holding down the Shift key during bootup.

If you've got any patience left, and you're *still* not able to talk to the network at this point (you're probably a saint!), you might try swapping this network card into a PC that is talking to the network—and perhaps swap that PC's card into the problem PC. This, finally, will tell you one way or another what you need to know. Either the NIC from the bad PC will now work in the good PC, meaning there's still a conflict with another card in the bad PC, or the bad card will also refuse to work in the good PC. If it's a conflict, start removing other cards from the bad PC one by one, bringing up Windows Me after each time, until you're able to get back on the network. If your organization is large enough to have a POST diagnostics card, you will have put it to use before now, I'm sure. Otherwise, you'll be wishing you had one at this point.

If you continue to have no success after fooling with IRQs and I/O addresses some more, try installing a different network card, preferably from a different vendor. If the first card was a jumpered card, do yourself a favor and try a newer card. By the time you're reading this, just about any new network card should at least be software configurable, if not fully Plug-and-Play. Just choose one of the top five or six brands, and you should be up and running again in no time. If not, your problems are way outside the scope of this book and you certainly deserve a prize of some sort for having come this far.

The next chapter deals with remote networks. If you telecommute from home, you will likely need to dial into a corporate network, for example, to exchange files with your coworkers. You'll learn all about Dial-Up Networking in Chapter 26, "Extending Your Reach with Dial-Up Networking."

CHAPTER 26

Extending Your Reach with Dial-Up Networking

In the past few years, the number of mobile computer users has increased dramatically, as advances in computer technology and changes in the business climate have made it easier to use a computer on the road. Improved manufacturing techniques have allowed miniaturization only dreamed about 10 years ago—clearly, there would be far fewer mobile users if everyone still had to carry around a 17-pound Compaq luggable. And improved communication interfaces have allowed users to access other computers without having to memorize obscure Unix or AT modem commands.

On the business side, the near-universal reliance on computers, coupled with the downsizing and reengineering trends that have forced users out of the office and into their home offices or onto the road to visit client sites, has created a demand for remote access. This has happened at about the same time that advances in computer technology have provided the means.

Mobile users are everywhere. Because computer-toting travelers are ubiquitous these days, few self-respecting motels and hotels now fail to provide RJ-11 data jacks on their phones. I no longer ask if a hotel is modem-friendly; I simply assume that one of the reasons they are still in business is that they provide data jacks. Although I still carry a telephone patch cable with alligator clips on one end, it has been more than a year since I stayed in a hotel in which I actually had to splice their phone cord to be able to use it with my modem.

You don't have to be a laptop owner to need remote connectivity, however. More and more people are telecommuting from home, which often means connecting remotely to the company's server from a desktop PC.

In this chapter, I'll first cover the options that Windows Me provides for remote connections and help you choose the best one for your particular circumstance. Next, I'll examine the hardware requirements for effective remote commuting over phone lines and take an in-depth look at Dial-Up Networking. Then, I'll cover specific issues you need to address when using remote access, such as security.

Remote Access—What Is It?

Since remote use of computers has become so prevalent, Microsoft has seen to it that remote access is seamlessly integrated into the Windows Me operating system, giving you simple access to essential system resources. Think of it this way: When you're in the office using your computer that's attached to the local area network (LAN), Windows Me takes care of the details when you want to print to a network printer or use some data stored on a hard disk somewhere across the network. The details of this process are handled smoothly by the Windows Me networking architecture, system calls, and the user interface.

When you're using a Windows Me computer away from the office, the operating system attempts to find other solutions when you ask for access to one of your office network's resources such as a printer. This is possible because Windows Me supports multiple network protocols and adapters, as discussed earlier in this part of the book. If you've set up your computer correctly, Windows Me will attempt to reach the office LAN using Dial-Up Networking (DUN), essentially replacing the LAN cable and network interface card (NIC) with telephone wires and modems.

As in the case of normal Windows Me LAN connections, Dial-Up Networking supports a broad base of network protocols. Using DUN, you can remotely connect to systems running TCP/IP (such as the Internet), NetWare-based servers, and NetBEUI-based servers.

 TIP One of the most popular uses for Windows Me's DUN is connecting to the Internet. As explained in Chapters 19, "Introduction to Windows Communications," and 20, "Connecting to the Internet," almost everyone who uses a Windows Me machine to connect to the Internet for e-mail or Web access will use DUN to do it. (Exceptions would be cable or DSL Internet users, or those on a corporate network that provides Internet access.) See those chapters if all you want to do is get connected to the Internet.

Connections to Novell NetConnect servers via the NRN protocol or NT servers using the RAS (Remote Access Services) are automatic. Industry-standard PPP (Point-to-Point Protocol) and the newly added PPTP (Point-to-Point Tunneling Protocol) are supported as well. Other protocols are easily added. All a software vendor has to do is write its code to support the Windows Me Remote Accesses API. Microsoft, for example, supplies a SLIP (Serial Line Internet Protocol) as part of the Windows Me Resource Kit.

Remote Control versus Remote Node

Let's look at the other side of the equation for the moment: Suppose you are in charge of the network, and other people need to dial into it from remote locations. If you need to allow off-site users to connect to your network, you essentially have two choices: remote *control* or remote *node*.

- *Remote-control* programs use standard telephone lines and provide on-demand connections. Remote control works just as you would expect from the name. You sit down at the remote computer, it dials into a host computer, and then you can actually control the computer you dial into from the computer you have dialed in from. The leading remote-control products include Norton pcAnywhere, Carbon Copy, and Co-Session. When you type or move the mouse on the remote computer, the software sends the keystrokes and mouse movements to the host computer for processing. In turn, the software transmits any screen updates such as dialog boxes or drop-down menus from the host back to the remote computer for display. If the user wants to run an application, they launch the application on the host computer.

- *Remote node* works on an on-demand basis just like remote control, but rather than taking over the host computer, the remote computer uses the host computer as a *server*. This places the remote node directly on the network. In other words, the phone line becomes an extension of the network cable. This allows the user to request file and print services just as if they sat right next to the file server. When a user starts an application, it runs on their local computer, not on the host computer as it would when using remote-control systems.

Remote control and remote node both provide network connectivity, but they use two entirely different approaches to providing remote access. The primary difference between these two types of remote-access software is that remote-control software actually takes over complete control of the host system, while remote-node software just uses the modem to provide a network interface to the host system.

Setting Up Dial-Up Networking

As explained earlier, a mobile user can use Dial-Up Networking to seamlessly connect remote resources. While early versions of Windows included a version of DUN called *Remote Access Services* (RAS), it was clearly an add-on feature. To use it, you had to start it separately before accessing shared resources on a remote computer. Installing DUN in Windows Me places the remote-node software directly into the core operating system, so you can access remote resources just as you can local ones.

Whenever you try to open a remote file (whether through the File ➢ Open dialog box or by double-clicking the file), Windows Me automatically starts DUN and establishes the remote connection with the host computer. You've probably seen this in action if you use DUN to connect to the Internet. If you start Internet Explorer when your Internet connection is not active, a Connect dialog box appears, prompting you to enter your password and to dial up your ISP. (Or, if you have IE set to automatically dial the connection, it dials your ISP without asking.)

 TIP   If DUN is not installed, go to the Control Panel and choose Add/Remove Programs ➢ Windows Setup ➢ Communications ➢ Dial-Up Networking. You can also install it by running the Internet Connection Wizard and configuring your PC to connect to the Internet using a dial-up Internet connection.

DUN and TAPI

Dial-Up Networking uses the Telephone Application Programming Interface (TAPI), Microsoft's proposed standard for integrating telephones and computers. Because TAPI allows multiple applications to share a single line, one application can wait for a call while another dials out.

"What is the point?" you may ask. After all, when one application dials out, the line is busy, so waiting applications can't receive a call anyway. Well, suppose, for example, you have a fax program waiting to receive incoming faxes and you want to use DUN to download a file from a computer in a satellite office. In some earlier versions of Windows, you would have had to shut down the fax software before you could use the modem for any other purpose. Because DUN uses TAPI, however, you can leave your fax program running in the background as you connect to a remote computer. As soon as you finish with DUN, the fax program will pick up any incoming faxes.

Another benefit of TAPI is its support of multiple telephony location profiles, which allows you to separate a DUN connection from a particular dialing location. That means you can use the same DUN connection with different telephony profiles to, for example, dial "9" for an outside line or not, dial "1" and the area code or not, and so on. You learned about setting up dialing locations in Chapter 19.

Along with its support of TAPI, Windows Me further simplifies DUN by supporting the *Unimodem* infrastructure. You can think of Unimodem as the modem equivalent of the Windows printer subsystem. As you may recall, rather than require each application to manage its own printing, Windows 9*x*/Me allows an application to send a print job to the printer subsystem, which then passes the job to a printer driver specifically designed for the printer in use. Unimodem does the same thing: It provides a single interface for any application requiring communication services. When an application wants to access a modem, it sends a packet, or "communication job," to Unimodem, which then passes the packet off to the modem-specific driver.

Planning Your Connection

Any time you want to connect to a remote computer, you must keep three questions in mind. First, what type of server or host do you want to connect to? Second, how will you connect with it? And third, what communication protocol will you use? Luckily, Windows Me supports the majority of the options available. Better yet, Dial-Up Networking will negotiate with the host and automatically configure itself using the best set of options that both it and the host support.

What Type of Server or Host?

Windows Me supports the following remote-node servers:

- Windows 9*x* or Me Dial-Up Server (one incoming connection only)

- Windows NT 3.*x* and 4.*x* RAS (up to 256 incoming connections possible)
- Windows 2000
- Novell NetWare Connect
- Microsoft LAN Manager Remote Access Servers
- Windows for Workgroups 3.*x* RAS (if you have the separate WFW RAS server installed)
- Shiva NetModem or LanRover (and compatibles) dial-up router
- Third-party PPP and SLIP servers, including Internet access providers

How Will You Connect?

If you are like the vast majority of Windows Me users, you'll use standard modems to establish asynchronous connections over "plain old telephone service" (POTS)—residential and business phone lines. To accommodate users with additional requirements, DUN also supports the following:

- PBX modems
- Integrated Services Digital Network (ISDN), including aggregation of ISDN lines to gang two B channels for 128K throughput on internal ISDN adapters
- Parallel port or null modem over a serial connection

Which Protocol Will You Use?

Just as you may have a choice of protocols when plugging directly into your local area network, you may have a choice of using one of the following protocols with DUN:

- NetBEUI
- TCP/IP
- IPX/SPX

If your network has either an NT/2000 server or a NetWare server, Windows Me will fully support user-based security, allowing you to grant different users varying levels of access to your computer and the rest of the network. Additionally, if your server is running NT, Windows Me supports domain-trust relationships and centralized network security administration.

Installing Dial-Up Networking

Dial-Up Networking may already be installed on your PC. If you use a dial-up Internet connection, it's almost certainly installed. To check, choose Start ➤ Settings and look on the menu. If Dial-Up Networking appears, you're all set. If it's not, install it using Add/Remove Programs, as you learned in Chapter 13, "Adding and Removing Hardware and Software."

Creating a New DUN Connection

Once you have the Dial-Up Networking component installed, you need to set it up correctly for your particular use. To do so, you'll create a new Dial-Up Networking connection:

1. Choose Start ➢ Settings ➢ Dial-Up Networking. The Dial-Up Networking folder opens.

2. Double-click Make New Connection. You'll see the screen below.

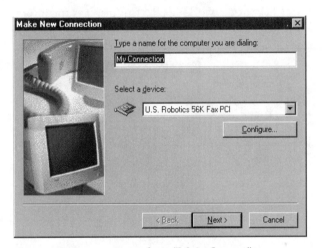

3. Give your connection a name, such as "Main Server."

4. If you have more than one modem, select the modem you want to use.

5. Click Next. This leads you to the screen where you enter the particulars for this connection.

6. Enter the area code and phone number.

7. If necessary, change the country code.

8. Click Next.

9. Click Finish to save the connection.

Now that you've set up DUN, whenever you open up the Dial-Up Networking folder, there will be two icons: the connection you just created—Main Server in my example—and Make New Connection. If you double-click the new icon, Windows Me will open a Connect box so you can dial your new connection.

If you need to set any special properties for the dial-up connection, right-click its icon and choose Properties. Chapter 20 touched on this, and the following section discusses it further. If you are dialing into a corporate server, the network administrator there might have some specific settings you should adjust.

PART

V

Networking

Setting DUN Connection Options

For a successful Dial-Up Networking connection, you must ensure that the correct server type and other options are chosen. In most cases, the default settings will work fine, but in case you're having problems with a DUN connection, follow these steps to adjust its settings:

1. Open the Dial-Up Networking folder (Start ➢ Settings ➢ Dial-Up Networking).

2. Right-click the connection you want, and select Properties.

3. Click the Networking tab. This displays the information shown in Figure 26.1.

FIGURE 26.1

Set the server type and other options here.

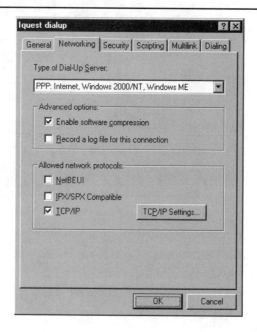

Obviously, you can configure a bunch of stuff here. Let's look at the most important ones.

Type of Dial-Up Server Windows Me will connect to four types of DUN servers:
- NRN (NetWare Connect)
- PPP (such as Windows 9*x*, Windows NT/2000, and Internet access providers)
- SLIP (used by Unix systems) or a compressed variant called CSLIP
- Windows for Workgroups and NT Server 3.1

Whenever Windows Me establishes a Dial-Up Networking connection, it assumes the computer on the other end is a PPP server. If it isn't, Windows Me cycles through the other possibilities until it succeeds in making a connection or fails on all four. If you know the type of server to which you will connect (and you probably do), you will reduce your connection time by selecting the proper type in this field. A warning, however: If you change the default PPP setting and select the incorrect type of server, Windows Me will not cycle through the other options. Rather, it will give up after trying your selection.

Enable Software Compression   As a rule, data compression will increase the effective data-transfer rate. These days, most modems support compression themselves, so you can have either the software (your computer) or the hardware (the modem) compress the data for you. For almost all types of data, software compression will provide superior performance to hardware compression. As you probably know, data compression works through a pattern-recognition algorithm that reduces redundancies in the data. Because Windows Me provides more memory for storing patterns than your modem does, software compression has a better chance of recognizing complex patterns and thus of compressing the data as much as possible. The only time data compression does not increase performance—and in fact might reduce it—is when you transfer already highly compressed data such as Zip files. If you plan to transfer Zip files in a given Dial-Up Networking session, turn off software compression. Along the same lines, if you choose to use software compression, be sure to turn hardware compression off.

Record a Log File for This Connection   This is a troubleshooting feature. If you check this box, Windows Me will create a text file containing all the messages generated when connecting, including which portions of the initial handshaking were successful and which were not.

Allowed Network Protocols   I briefly covered network protocols in Chapter 24, "Building a Peer-to-Peer Network," but let's revisit them here. The computers on both ends of the connection must be running the same protocol. If you're connecting to the Internet, that will be TCP/IP. As a rule, I disable all nonapplicable protocols whenever possible. This should increase security and possibly increase speed when using this connection. If you're using TCP/IP, typically you must set the TCP/IP settings (click the TCP/IP Settings button) to match those of the host computer. That information is available from the system administrator or Internet Service Provider you're dialing into.

Establishing a Dial-Up Networking Connection

With Windows Me, you have three ways to establish a remote connection:

Explicit   You double-click the icon for the DUN connection, and it connects.

Application-initiated   An application that requires a remote resource, such as a Web browser needing to display a Web page, causes an automatic connection to occur.

Implicit   Windows initiates the connection when it can't find a particular resource locally or on your physical network.

Explicit Connections

Connecting to a remote computer with an explicit connection is very similar to creating a RAS connection with Windows for Workgroups 3.11 or Windows NT.

When you create an explicit connection, you manually dial up the remote computer and log on. Once you've done this, the remote computer and all its share points show up in My Network Places. You can manipulate these resources just as you would any other computer's resources—except that it's much slower.

 TIP   If, once you are connected, no remote resources show up, or if you get an error message about not being able to browse the network and you know everything on the server side of the connection is set up correctly, then you most likely have a problem with the networking protocols set for your local computer. You're probably using different protocols on the two ends of the connection. For the connection to work, all machines must be using the same protocol, just as with a LAN connection. The setting of protocols is accomplished via the Control Panel's Network icon. Other chapters in this part of the book explain the installation of protocols.

To use Windows Me Dial-Up Networking to explicitly connect to a remote computer, follow these steps:

1. Open the Dial-Up Networking folder (Start ➤ Settings ➤ Dial-Up Networking).

2. Double-click the icon you created for the DUN connection. This will bring up a Connect To dialog box like the one shown in Figure 26.2.

FIGURE 26.2
*Connecting to a
remote network*

Connect To	
	Iquest dialup
User name:	jdoe1
Password:	******
	☑ Save password
	☐ Connect automatically
Phone number:	7133301
Dialing from:	Home Dial Properties...
	Connect Properties Cancel

3. Enter the password, if any, for this resource. If you are connecting to a computer with user-based security, enter your login name and password.

4. (Optional) Change the dialing location if needed by selecting one from the Dialing From drop-down list. If you don't have multiple dialing locations defined (see Chapter 19), this will be unavailable.

 NOTE When you initiate a dial-up connection, you can select a dialing location each time you establish a connection. Whenever you change locations, your location selection remains in effect for only that one connection. The next time you connect, it will revert to your current location (as set in the Telephony applet in the Control Panel, which you can change as you travel about).

5. Click the Connect button.

Windows Me will now initiate a process that will result—if all goes well—in a connection to the remote computer. As the negotiation between the two computers progresses, Windows reports the connection status.

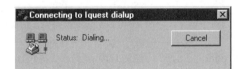

Now that you have manually initiated the connection, you will remain connected until you click the Disconnect button (or until you "time out" your session connection—that is, until you let the connection run without input for a period of time that surpasses the timeout value that is set from the Connection tab on the DUN connection's property sheet).

A dialog box appears to inform you that you are connected; click Close in it to close the dialog box. This does not terminate the DUN connection.

An icon will appear in the System Tray (near the clock in the Taskbar) to indicate when you are connected and online.

Dial-Up Networking icon

When you are ready to disconnect, you can right-click the icon and choose Disconnect. Or you can double-click it to display a Status window that reports the number of bytes transferred, and then click the Disconnect button from there.

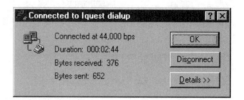

Application-Initiated Connections

Windows Me also allows application developers to create programs that will establish DUN connections themselves rather than forcing the user to initiate the session manually.

A DUN-enabled application will take responsibility for automatically connecting to a DUN server as needed. The application uses Windows Me's Remote Access Session API to select a server, initiate a connection, and later disconnect the session. Besides allowing applications to initiate their own connections, the Remote Access Session API also reports the status back to the calling application. This way, if the server is unavailable for some reason (like the line being busy), the application can try again later.

The Outlook Express client provided with Windows Me serves as an excellent example of an application that takes advantage of the Remote Access Session API. If you have configured Outlook Express for remote access, it will automatically use Dial-Up Networking to connect to your mail server any time you try to access your mailbox.

You can change Outlook's connection method by selecting (from within Outlook Express) Tools ➢ Options ➢ Connection ➢ Change and choosing the desired DUN connection. As soon as it is connected to the mail server, Outlook Express will send all your outgoing mail, retrieve any new messages, and then disconnect.

TIP For more information on using Outlook Express, see Chapter 22, "Communicating with Outlook Express News and Mail."

Implicit Connections

Establishing a Dial-Up Networking implicit connection to a remote computer is just like connecting to that same computer in the office: Simply double-click the network object. Depending on the type of object you clicked, Windows Me may try to automatically create an implicit connection; that is, it's automatic, but it is initiated by Windows Me itself, not a specific application. Whenever you have Dial-Up Networking installed, the following circumstances will cause Windows Me to establish an implicit connection:

- You click a link pointing to a remote resource.

- You try to use a network resource while disconnected from a network.

- Either you or an application you're using specifies a resource using a universal naming convention (UNC) name (that is, *server_name**share_point*), and Windows Me cannot find it on the local area network. Windows Me references printers via their UNC names (*server_name**printer_name*), so printing to a remote printer will also trigger an implicit connection.

- You try reconnecting to a remote OLE (object linking and embedding) object (also known as a DCOM object) not located on the local network.

- An application tries to connect to a named pipe.

Whenever you try to access such a resource either by clicking it directly or through an application request, Windows Me first tries to find it locally on your computer or out on your LAN. If it fails to locate the resource, Windows gives you the dial-in dialog box shown in Figure 26.3, asking if you want to connect to the resource through Dial-Up Networking.

PART
V
Networking

FIGURE 26.3
Windows Me asks the user if it should connect to a remote resource via Dial-Up Networking.

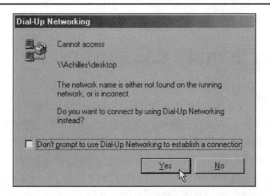

It then checks the Registry for the Dial-Up Networking entry for the server associated with the object. If it finds a server, it establishes the connection automatically. If it cannot find a server associated with the object, it prompts the user to either select the proper Dial-Up Networking connection for the object or enter a new one. With this information, Dial-Up Networking tries to establish a connection to the server.

If it succeeds and successfully establishes a Dial-Up Networking connection, Windows Me stores the name of the connector in the Registry so that the next time you click the object or enter its name in a File ➢ Open dialog box, it doesn't have to prompt you to select the server.

Deciding on Your Connection Mode

The decision concerning which of the three connection modes (explicit, application-initiated, or implicit) you should use most often depends on the type of work you do. If you are a network manager and your job requires you to manage several remote networks, you'll probably find yourself using explicit connections most often, as they give you the greatest amount of control over your remote session. Less-technical users will probably rely on implicit connections because they are less of a hassle. Whether you use application-initiated connections depends on whether you're using any remote access–enabled applications.

 TIP I often establish remote connections myself rather than relying on a remote access–enabled application to do it for me. Why? Because once I have a connection to a remote server, I can do several tasks online rather than having each connection-enabled application simply hang up when it is done with the first task. How you tell an application to let you make the connection manually rather than doing it for you varies with the program. You'll have to read its documentation (ugh). In some cases, such as with Outlook Express, you use the Connect Using the LAN setting rather than telling it to dial up by itself. Some recent programs from Microsoft have options such as Let Me Make My Own Connection to the Internet, which makes a little more sense to the novice.

Using Your Remote Connection

Once you have connected to a remote computer, you can use any of its shared resources, be they files, printers, or other modems (for faxing), just as though you were in the same office building and connected with Ethernet or Token Ring.

Besides the resources on the single computer you're dialed into, you may also use the services of any other computer in the work group (or the NT domain)—assuming you've been given access. In other words, if you dialed into your office computer from home, you could copy the files from any computer that your office computer can see, or print a report on any printer your office desktop can access. Of course, an administrator can restrict access to specific machines and resources, so a caller doesn't necessarily have access to all machines on the LAN.

As noted earlier, DUN allows you to leverage the near-universal reach of the phone system to extend your computer network; all your networked computers need is a phone line. But just because you *can* does not mean you *should*. You'll need to exercise some caution when using remote resources over a dial-up connection because your connection is much slower than a normal network connection. While you might not think twice about transferring a very large file over a LAN connection, trying this over a DUN link will produce a very disappointing performance. The same goes for starting up applications that reside on the remote computer. In both cases, the cause of the poor performance is the same: DUN must transfer the entire application file over the phone link. For example, starting FoxPro from a remote computer requires the transfer of the entire 2.5MB executable file. Instead of taking a few seconds to load from a local hard disk, it takes about five minutes over a 56Kbps modem connection!

 TIP Whenever you want to run an application during a DUN session, make sure you have the application on your local hard drive *and* in your DOS search path. This will ensure that you run the local version instead of passing the entire executable across the wire.

If you do need to run actual programs across a dial-in link, you should use a program designed for this purpose, such as pcAnywhere, from Symantec. It's surprisingly responsive and intelligent. You can dial directly into another computer's modem to make the connection, or even use the Internet as the intermediary link for long hauls. Such remote-control programs (there are others on the market, too, such as Remote Control) actually let you see exactly what is on the remote computer's screen and interact with it to transfer files and run programs. You can even use it to remotely examine and adjust settings on the remote machine. This is a perfect tool for remote administration of systems by computer consultants and the like.

Dial-Up Networking and Security

Whenever you allow dial-in access to your network, you open it up to everyone who has a modem. Before you set up a Dial-Up Networking host, you need to take a good look at the risks involved and design your security model to minimize them. Some network managers go so far as to forbid dial-up access to any of their machines, regardless of the circumstances. While this is a draconian step, you do need to give security some thought.

Before setting up a DUN server, your first level of network security was not the user accounts and logins but the more difficult hurdle of gaining *physical* access to your network. DUN effectively removes this major (and probably most effective) deterrent because the outside world is now physically connected to your network (or single-PC server). Anyone with the right skills may be able to break into your server.

For a system with remote access, your first line of defense becomes the relative obscurity of your modem's phone number. Before anyone can gain remote access to your network (at least through the telephone lines), the would-be hacker must know your data phone number. Accordingly, you should keep a tight grasp on who knows this number. You cannot, however, keep your modem number a secret. Hackers can (and will) set their modems to dial every number in a given prefix just to look for modems.

The next level in your security model is supplied by the user accounts and passwords. Regardless of how open your company is with its data, instituting a policy of secure logins and passwords on any network is a good precaution. This becomes essential when physical access is no longer a requirement for logging on to your network. How you implement this varies based on server type.

You can add security to your network by using Dial-Up Networking's callback feature. When using a Windows Me DUN server with the callback facility turned on, as soon as the server authenticates a user, Windows Me drops the line. It then calls the user back at a prearranged phone number. The obvious advantage to this feature is that simply figuring out the modem number and guessing the login and password combination is not enough to gain access to your network. An unauthorized user must also be at the prearranged phone number, which is not so likely.

This scenario also has an obvious drawback: It will not work for users who move around and thus do not have a consistent phone number, such as members of your sales force. There is also a less obvious security hole: The phone system is not all that secure, and talented phone hackers (phreakers) can reroute a phone call to any location.

 NOTE Many companies implement RAS callback features primarily as a means of controlling phone costs. Callback enables you to control who pays for the call and therefore provides a means of tracking costs. With callback, companies are able to centralize their telecommunications costs to one line (or a group of lines) so they can easily tell how much money they are spending to provide their free-spirited users with ready access to corporate resources. Additionally, callback allows them to route calls through the least-expensive channels available, whether they are WATS lines or lines purchased though a reseller.

On top of these security measures, you can use several third-party security devices such as random-number generators and encrypted-access modems with DUN to further bolster your security.

The best method for maintaining a secure environment is to regularly monitor your network's activity—not only the dial-in portion, but *all* activity. When you notice something unusual, such as repeated (yet unsuccessful) login attempts or abnormally high traffic at strange times, investigate it at once to find out the cause. While the answer may be simply an employee working late or someone who forgot their password, it may also be someone trying to break into your system.

Security and Internet DUN Connections

Finally, a little tip about settings for file sharing. Obviously, for a DUN connection to be used by, say, outside employees, you'll want to enable file sharing; otherwise, a remote user won't be able to gain access to information on the server's hard disk. But when your DUN connection (*from* the server, not *to* it) is specifically for making a connection to an ISP (for the purposes of getting e-mail, surfing the Web, doing FTP transfers, etc.), you will *not* want to have file sharing turned on. Why not? Because it leaves a major gap in security for someone to break into your computer while you're sitting there connected to the world's largest network. Get used to thinking of the Internet as a huge LAN, with millions of users on it, any one of whom could break into your system if you're not careful. Windows Me may warn you of this danger if you have installed the TCP/IP protocol with file and printer sharing turned on. Or it might not. This is something you should manually check if you're using your TCP/IP modem connection only for Internet work. Here's how:

1. Open the Control Panel and choose Network. Click the Configuration tab if it's not already on top.

2. Choose TCP/IP → Dial-Up Adapter, and then click the Properties button. (Click OK to accept the resulting warning about your TCP/IP settings.)

3. Click the Bindings tab.

4. Make sure the File and Printer Sharing option is not enabled (i.e., make sure the check mark is cleared from the check box), as shown in Figure 26.4.

5. Close the dialog boxes and reboot.

PART

V

Networking

FIGURE 26.4
*Ensuring that file
sharing is turned off for
TCP/IP over the dial-up
adapter can help
protect your computer
when you are
connected to the
Internet.*

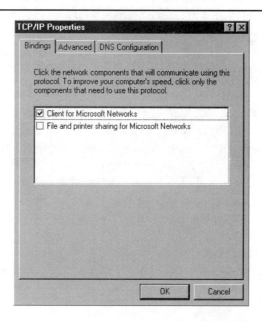

 NOTE   Remember, you can share a DUN connection with other workstations on your LAN using the Internet Connection Sharing feature. See Chapter 20 to learn about configuring and using a shared connection.

CHAPTER 27

Advanced Networking

Networking computers together used to entail thousands of dollars worth of software and hardware, weeks of training, and enough headaches that most individuals would never think of trying it, and small companies would have to hire a small army of consultants to get a network going and keep it going. Extending networks to other cities was even more difficult and expensive! Now you can practically buy network cards at the grocery store, and the software for connecting your computer to the Internet is free (and, thanks to America Online, so are floppy disks).

While the cost barrier has all but disappeared, the complexity of networking remains just under the surface, barely disguised by Setup Wizards and fervent hopes of "plugging and playing." Here we're going to look under the covers, so to speak, of Windows networking so that you can exercise your choices with a little more information.

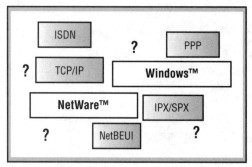

The choices you make in installing and maintaining a network become more complex when you need to work with computers running software other than just Windows Me. If NetWare, Windows NT Server, Macintoshes, or Unix computers are part of your networking environment, you have to make some difficult choices. These choices can have a great impact on the ease of maintaining your network in the future. As the ambassador used to say, "It's all a matter of protocol."

Network Protocols

Human beings all make the same sounds, but we put them together differently into languages, and it's important for all parties of a conversation to pretty closely agree on what these sounds are going to mean. For computers, "pretty closely" isn't quite good enough: They have to agree exactly. While you and I can understand questions put in many different and even vague ways, computers can't. *Protocols* are the very precise languages, or instructions, that computers use to communicate over networks to convey your requests and ensure that your data gets where it's supposed to, without errors or omissions along the way.

Windows supports many networking protocols. The most common protocols used between PCs and other computers worldwide are described in Table 27.1.

TABLE 27.1: COMMON PC NETWORKING PROTOCOLS	
Protocol	**Description**
NetBEUI	Developed by Microsoft and IBM for the first PC networks, and commonly used in simple PC networks
IPX/SPX	Developed by Xerox and Novell for their PC networking software, and used in the majority of medium and large corporate PC networks
TCP/IP	Developed two decades ago for the U.S. Defense Department's ARPA research network, and now the basis of the global Internet
AppleTalk	Developed by Apple Computer for Macintosh networking

Let's take a look at how the components of Windows networking work together. As my Grandpa used to say, "If you got your bindings, you're halfway there." (Well, he never actually said that, but it sounds like a Grandpa saying, doesn't it?)

What Are Bindings?

No, bindings have nothing to do with skiing. Modern networking software allows you to pick and choose which protocols, which network cards, and whatever file-sharing services you want. Each of these items is run by a separate little bit of software, and *bindings* are what we call the connections between them. The connection from a high-level application like Internet Explorer to a protocol interpreter to a network card is called a *protocol stack*. In Windows, your protocol stacks can be connected any which way, depending on what services need to use which protocols, and which networks are connected to which network cards (see Figure 27.1).

PART

V

Networking

FIGURE 27.1
Protocol stacks in Windows networking

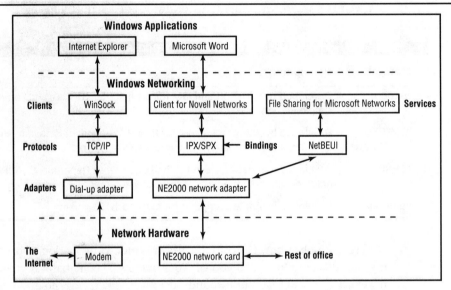

You could call these software bits *drivers,* but in Windows we refer to them by names that tell you where they fit in the stack:

Clients   Connect to file-sharing services on other computers through the stacks below them, and present virtual disk drives (like R: on \\Main_Server) to Windows applications.

Protocols   Manage the transferring of data in an orderly manner between clients on different computers, by transferring data to and from adapters.

Adapters   Transfer data between protocols, through a physical network of cards, wires, modems, routers, fiber-optic cables—hardware, in other words.

Services   Offer your computer's resources, like disk drives and printers, to clients on other computers.

You may recognize these categories as the choices on the Network applet's Add dialog box (access this from the Control Panel). *Bindings* are the connections between these pieces. Bindings are set in the Control Panel's Network applet by selecting a network component, clicking Properties, and selecting the Bindings tab (see Figure 27.2). Each component allows you to set check boxes to enable bindings to the components *above* it in the protocol stack. For example, Adapters list bindings that can be made to protocols; Protocols list bindings that may be made to services and clients. Clients and Services don't have bindings properties since they're only connected from below.

FIGURE 27.2

Setting bindings in the Control Panel's Network applet

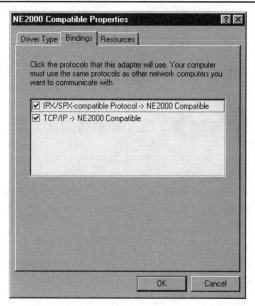

Look at Figure 27.1 again, and trace the connections made in this particular computer:

- Internet Explorer is using a dial-up connection. Internet Explorer always uses the WinSock client and the TCP/IP protocol, which here is connected to the Internet through the dial-up adapter and a modem. Meanwhile, ...

- Microsoft Word is editing a file on a Novell file server. It's using a network drive, which is handled by the Client for Novell Networks, using the IPX/SPX protocol, bound to a NE2000 network adapter.

- Someone elsewhere in the office can use a drive shared by this computer. Their "Client for Microsoft Networks" talks to this computer's "File Sharing for Microsoft Networks," using the NetBEUI protocol, which is using the same NE2000 network card over the same wiring.

It all looks very orderly, doesn't it? It is, and it's taken about 20 years for it to become so. As my father used to say, ... (Oh, you're getting tired of this, aren't you? Let's get on to the details.)

TIP There are some nasty computer buzzwords and acronyms coming up. If you don't know what they mean and don't have a network administrator who makes these choices for you, that's actually a good sign: It means the issue at hand probably doesn't apply to you, so you can safely ignore it. However, you can find exhaustive definitions of these and other technical terms on the Web at www.webopedia.com.

Choosing Network Protocols and Services

If you are just sharing files or printers in a small network of computers running only Microsoft Windows, you can pretty much choose either NetBEUI or IPX/SPX with a toss of a coin. You probably already did this when you installed peer networking in Chapter 24, "Building a Peer-to-Peer Network." You can stop reading this chapter right here, lucky you.

If you need to connect computers running different operating systems, however, or you want to use a shared connection to the Internet, then you have to make an informed choice. Here are some of the factors to take into consideration:

- Internet access
- Types of file servers whose shares you'll be using
- Types of computers that will be using the files *you* share
- Size of your network
- Security issues if your network is connected to the Internet

You want to install as few network protocols and components as possible, and to have each bound to as few of the others as necessary. The trick is to find the combination of the fewest components that will work.

I suggest making a list of the types of file servers and client computers on your network, then making a list of possible services and protocols. Circle the ones you must provide and cross out the ones that are not usable. With what's left, you can make an educated choice.

Let's discuss each of the factors that we listed above.

Internet Access

If you'll be using Internet or Web applications, you must install the TCP/IP protocol.

 NOTE On a small peer-to-peer network of computers using Windows Me as well as Windows 2000, 9x, or NT, you'll still need to add either NetBEUI or IPX/SPX in addition to TCP/IP. There is a bug in the networking software, which prevents the list of computers from appearing in My Network Places if only TCP/IP is installed.

Types of File Servers Whose Shares You'll Be Using

If you need to use files shared by NetWare or other non-Windows operating systems, you'll need to install the particular protocol(s) used by these file servers. Your network administrator can help you choose the protocols you'll need. To use a NetWare file server, you'll most likely want to install the Microsoft-manufactured IPX/SPX-compatible protocol as well as the Client for Novell Networks. For all other cases, use the client manufactured by your network vendor.

If you are using Windows-based file servers (for example, files shared from other computers running Windows 2000, 9*x*, NT, or Me), use whichever protocol those servers are using for file sharing: TCP/IP, NetBEUI, and/or IPX/SPX.

But as I noted above, networks that use Windows 95 and/or 98 computers as well as Windows Me computers don't work properly with just TCP/IP alone. My Network Places will not show any computers. You should install either NetBEUI or IPX/SPX as well as TCP/IP on *all* your computers on a network that mixes versions of Windows.

Types of Computers That Will Be Using the Files You Share

If you are going to install a file-sharing service, consider who is going to be using your shares. For example, to share your drives and/or printers with DOS computers that connect to Novell file servers, you must install the File Sharing for Novell Networks service and the IPX/SPX-compatible protocol. That's all the DOS computers will be able to use. Similarly, if you have DOS-based clients that use Microsoft networking, you'll have to install the NetBEUI protocol. (In this day and age, this is an unlikely scenario!)

If your office network consists primarily of Windows computers, and you want to share files or printers, install File Sharing for Microsoft Networks and the protocols used by the computers that will be using your drives. You must install Windows for Workgroups DOS network drivers (provided with Windows NT Server) on any DOS machines that will use the shared drives.

There is no direct way to share your files or printers to Macintosh computers from your Windows Me computer. For that, you have to get Windows NT Server or Windows 2000 Server for its File Services for Macintosh feature, *or* get additional software for your Macs so that they can use Windows file sharing.

 NOTE For more information on internetworking Windows and Mac computers, check out Virtual PC from Connectix (www.connectix.com), or DAVE from Thursby Software Systems (www.thursby.com). Mac OS X may offer some additional networking options when a Samba server is made available.

Size of Your Network

The choice of protocol can make a big difference in the manageability of your network:

- NetBEUI requires no configuration once it's installed. However, it's not terrific with large networks of more than 100 computers or so since its packets can't be routed. It can be passed via MAC-layer bridging, but this is inefficient over large networks or wide area networks. (If you haven't seen these terms before, it just means your network isn't large enough to worry about this!)

- IPX/SPX requires no configuration. It can be routed over wide area networks, which makes it a strong choice for networks that are connected via data or phone lines.

- Administering a TCP/IP network is the most work since each computer must be assigned an IP number, network mask, and DNS, WINS, and/or DHCP server addresses. However, it's also the most efficient protocol and can be easily routed, especially over the Internet, either in raw form or encrypted and tunneled; thus it's easy to join TCP/IP networks. Networks with Windows 2000 Server always use TCP/IP.

Security Issues If Your Network Is Connected to the Internet

If you use the Internet via a direct or dial-up connection and file sharing is bound to the TCP/IP protocol, then anyone in the world can attempt to use your shared drives! Of course, this may be exactly what you intend; if so, bind TCP/IP to file sharing to enable this. Otherwise, eliminate the possibility of an unwanted break-in on your computer and *un*bind file sharing from TCP/IP to prevent Internet access of your shared drives. Use a different protocol for file sharing. I recommend NetBEUI.

 WARNING This bears repeating: If you connect to the Internet and don't need to offer file sharing over the Internet, don't bind TCP/IP to file sharing. Use a different protocol for file sharing.

In any case, if your computer is connected to the Internet, even just intermittently via Dial-Up Networking, you should have passwords set for *all* shared resources on your computer.

Putting It All Together

Phew, that's a lot to consider. Well, remember that back in Grandpa's time, it took weeks of training to get even this far. Remember also that you only have to worry about this when you're working with different types of computers on the same network.

If your network uses Windows NT or Windows 2000 Server, your NT network administrator will make this decision about the protocol for you. In the absence of any compelling reasons, use just the NetBEUI protocol for Windows file sharing and unbind TCP/IP from file-sharing services.

Here's one last thing to consider: If you are sharing drives and want to use user-level security for them, you *must* use the file-sharing services corresponding to the type of server that provides your network's user authentication. In other words, you must use Novell file sharing if your network validates its users and passwords through a Novell server, and you must use Microsoft file sharing if you are part of a Windows NT Server domain.

Installing and Configuring Network Components and Bindings

Choosing types of network services and protocols is the hard part and probably takes longer than finally installing them, thanks to Windows Me's quick-and-easy Network applet on the Control Panel. It's just a little more complicated than the peer-to-peer network installation I described in Chapter 24. In this chapter, I'll assume you're already familiar with the steps for installing basic networking. I'll just add the details for the more complicated settings you'll need to make. Remember, most of the settings listed below, except those for hardware, can be left at their default values. You can usually get a complex network going just by adding the components and clicking OK, but for best performance, removing unnecessary bindings will make the network faster and more secure, and will consume less memory.

Hardware

Install the physical network cards and/or modems as instructed by the manufacturer, and described in Chapter 24. If you make any jumper settings, do write these down. In the unlikely event that you use non–Plug-and-Play hardware, you can view the interrupts and I/O addresses that are already in use by choosing Start ➢ Programs ➢ Accessories ➢ System Tools ➢ System Information. It has an Explorer-like display that lists in-use resources. Any interrupts or I/O addresses that are not in use are available for your network hardware.

PART

V

Networking

Clients

Install the clients you need: Microsoft, Novell, and/or other clients as required for your particular network. In the Network applet on the Control Panel, click Add, then highlight Client and click Add. Select the manufacturer and the client name, and click OK. Then configure the properties, which vary depending on the clients you install. Table 27.2 details the specific properties to be set for Microsoft Networks, and Table 27.3 details the specific properties to be set for Novell Networks.

Repeat the procedure of the previous paragraph to add any additional clients.

TABLE 27.2: CLIENT FOR MICROSOFT NETWORKS PROPERTIES SETTINGS

Client for Microsoft Networks Properties	Settings
Logon Validation	If your network contains a computer using NT Server as a domain controller, check Log On to Windows NT Domain and enter the name of the domain server. This enables you to use any of the domain's resources with just your login password. (If you are connecting to a Windows 2000 Server, enter the down-level domain name provided by your network administrator.) Do not enter your Internet domain name here. Enter your Windows networking domain name. There should be no dots and no .com!
Network Logon Options	If you use network drives and mark them Reconnect at Login, then every time you start up Windows Me, your computer will reestablish the network connections. This can take some time, especially if one or more of the servers is down or is being reached by dial-up networking. You can save some time at startup by checking Quick Logon. The downside is, if a server is unreachable, you won't find out until you try to use it.

TABLE 27.3: CLIENT FOR NOVELL NETWORKS PROPERTIES SETTINGS

Client for Novell Networks Properties	Settings
Preferred Server	Enter the name of the main file server you use for logging in; this will be the server that Windows uses to verify your username and password. (If user-level sharing is enabled, this is the server that will be queried to check the names and passwords of other users attempting to use your shared drives.)

Continued ▶

TABLE 27.3: CLIENT FOR NOVELL NETWORKS PROPERTIES SETTINGS (CONTINUED)

Client for Novell Networks Properties	Settings
First Network Drive	Enter the lowest drive letter to use for mounted Novell shared volumes. Most people familiar with Novell networking expect this to be F.
Enable Logon Script	If this option is checked, Windows Me will read and execute your processing logon script stored on the Novell file server when you first log in to Windows Me. Novell commands such as map will be honored, and external programs run with # will be executed, but TSR programs loaded during logon will not be loaded into your DOS-prompt windows. Your network administrator will tell you if you should set this feature. It's unlikely that you will need it.
Advanced: Preserve Case	If set to Yes, the case of filenames sent to and received from Novell file server will not be altered; instead, the files will appear as the Novell server displays them. If set to No, filenames will be changed to lowercase. Leave this set to Yes.

NOTE If you use Novell-specific network software or programs that depend on directly accessing Novell's Directory Services, you will need to use the Novell Client rather than Microsoft's Client for Novell Networks. The reason for this is that Novell's version makes the full NetWare API (Application Programming Interface) available to programs, while Microsoft's version provides only a minimal subset of Novell functions.

NOTE You can get the most recent Novell Client and installation instructions at www.novell.com. Experience has taught me that the Novell Client tends to have more bugs than the Microsoft Client does. Whether this is Microsoft's fault or Novell's, I can't tell you. In any case, my advice is to use the Novell version only if your software absolutely requires it.

NOTE If your Novell network uses NetWare Directory Services, be sure to add the Service for NetWare Directory Services, discussed in the "Services" section. (Just how many more times could we use Services in one sentence?)

PART

V

Networking

Adapters

Adapter driver software is usually installed automatically when Windows detects the added hardware. If, however, your adapter is not a Plug-and-Play device, use the Add New Hardware applet on the Control Panel to install its driver, as discussed in Chapter 24. Then, from the Network applet (also on the Control Panel), configure each adapter's properties as detailed in Table 27.4.

TABLE 27.4: ADAPTER PROPERTIES

Adapter Properties	Settings
Driver Type	Leave this set to Enhanced Mode unless instructed otherwise by the manufacturer or your system administrator. The 32-bit drivers work best with Windows Me.
Bindings	Leave the bindings alone during this step of the installation. We'll come back and set the bindings after all the protocols have been entered.

Advanced Adapter Properties

Adapters have varying resources; the most common ones are listed in Table 27.4. In Table 27.5, I list some of the more interesting advanced resources. When it comes to these settings, you'll usually do best by leaving them at their original settings.

TABLE 27.5: ADVANCED ADAPTER PROPERTIES

Advanced Adapter Properties	Settings
Record a Log File (dial-up adapter)	Records a log file detailing the negotiation and sign-on when remote dial-up connections are made. This may be used to debug connections that fail.
IP Packet Size (dial-up adapter)	Controls the size of TCP/IP (Internet) data packets passed through the dial-up adapter. If your Internet transfer rates are *much* lower than you expect, you might try adjusting this parameter. It's normally set to Automatic; you might try setting the value to Small if you find your throughput is very low. Larger packets can slow transfers due to fragmentation. Normally, the best packet size is determined automatically. Windows Me has been improved greatly over Windows 9*x* in this respect.
Resources	These properties control hardware settings such as interrupts, I/O address, and memory transfer addresses. PnP hardware will self-configure. Manually set hardware must be set here. If you've already installed the hardware, enter the IRQ and I/O values you used; otherwise, choose IRQ and I/O values from the available choices that do *not* show a * (an asterisk) indicating a conflict, note the values, and then install the hardware when Windows restarts.

NOTE Advanced users who have previously used network-tweaking software to change the TCP/IP window size will be happy to know that it should no longer necessary to do so with Windows Me. The TCP/IP software in Windows Me was borrowed from Windows 2000, and this new version adjusts the window size automatically.

Dial-Up and Virtual Private Networking

If you will use a modem or a Virtual Private Networking (VPN) connection to connect to a remote network, be sure that the required components are installed. Check your Network applet's component list for Dial-Up Adapter, Dial-Up Adapter #2 (VPN Support), and Microsoft Virtual Private Networking Adapter. If they're not present, follow these steps:

1. Open the Add/Remote Programs applet on the Control Panel and view the Windows Setup tab.

2. Highlight Communications and click Details.

3. Be sure that Dial-Up Networking and/or Virtual Private Networking are checked. If they're not, check them and click OK. You may need to insert your Windows Me installation CD-ROM.

Protocols

Now add the required protocols. In the Network applet on the Control Panel, click Add, select Protocols, and click Add again. Follow the same procedure you used to add clients and adapters to select the protocols you will need. As discussed earlier, I suggest that you use TCP/IP and NetBEUI unless your circumstances dictate otherwise.

Services

If you wish to share your drives and/or printers on the network, or to enable special remote-management functions, add the required services:

- File and printer sharing for Microsoft Networks

- File and printer sharing for Novell Networks

  These first two options let you share folders or whole drives and printers with other computers on your network. We discussed making the choice between Microsoft and Novell-type sharing earlier.

  To add either service, click Add. Select Services and click Add. Highlight the required service and click OK.

  Click the File and Print Sharing... button and check either or both boxes as appropriate.

- Service for NetWare Directory Services

  This service is used on NetWare 4.0 LANs; your administrator will advise you if you should install it.

 NOTE If you were planning to install Microsoft's remote administration services, you might be surprised to find that they're missing from Windows Me. Read about the "Late, Great Zero Administration Initiative" later in this chapter.

Set Bindings

Go through the list of installed components in the Network applet on the Control Panel and select the first entry that lists a protocol and an adapter together. This might look like NetBEUI → Dial-Up Adapter. Click Properties and select the Bindings tab. Remove any unnecessary bindings by clearing their check marks. If you're not sure if a binding is necessary, leave it checked. Repeat this procedure with each protocol/adapter pair.

 WARNING If you're using NetBEUI for file sharing, I suggest that you unbind File Sharing for Microsoft Networks from each TCP/IP protocol entry. This will prevent Internet attackers from viewing or damaging your shared files. This may not be an option on a corporate network, but I strongly advise this for home users.

Set Protocol Properties

Now go back through the protocols listed as installed components in the Network applet on the Control Panel, and select and configure any properties required for each. When you have installed more than one adapter, each protocol will appear once for each adapter to which it is bound. You should set the properties for each protocol-adapter binding according to the network to which the particular adapter is connected.

 NOTE Do not configure the properties page for "TCP/IP → Dial-Up Adapter." You'll do this in the Dial-Up Networking application since the properties for each dial-up connection will be different.

I have listed the properties you'll need to set for each protocol in Tables 27.6, 27.7, and 27.8.

TABLE 27.6: TCP/IP PROPERTIES SETTINGS

TCP/IP Properties	Settings
IP Address	If your network has an NT or Windows 2000 server with DHCP, or other DHCP server, select Obtain an IP Address Automatically. Otherwise, enter an IP address assigned by your network administrator. If your network uses TCP/IP for file sharing and is not connected directly to the Internet, you can use the address 192.168.0.*x*, where you replace *x* with a number between 1 and 254. Use a different number at each computer. Keep a list of the names you assign to each computer and their IP numbers. (You can still use this scheme if you connect to the Internet by Dial-Up Networking.)
	Networks with Windows 98 and Windows Me computers only can use Obtain and IP Address Automatically even without a DHCP server, but I don't recommend this.
	Leave Detect Connection to Network Media checked.
Subnet Mask	If you specified an IP address, enter the network mask assigned by your network administrator. If you used the addressing scheme above, enter 255.255.255.0.
WINS Configuration	If your network administrator gave you a WINS server address, check Enable WINS Resolution. Enter the address (minding the dots), and click Add for each server. Otherwise, disable WINS resolution.
Gateway	If your network is directly connected to the Internet or other networks, you must enter the addresses of the primary routers on your network here. Without direct connections to other networks, omit this. (Again, your administrator will know what to enter here.)
DNS Configuration	If your network is connected to the Internet or has non-Windows hosts that are not named by the WINS system, you must enter DNS server addresses for Windows to convert *machine.domain*.com-type addresses into IP addresses. See the "Entering DNS Server Addresses" sidebar nearby for an explanation of how to enter these addresses.
Bindings	Windows normally binds everything to everything on installation. If any bindings are not necessary, as determined earlier, uncheck any that are not needed. For example, if you use TCP/IP for Internet access and Net-BEUI for file sharing, you can uncheck File and Printer Sharing for Microsoft Networks on the TCP/IP properties page.
Advanced	If you are using NetBEUI for file sharing, check Set This Protocol to Be the Default Protocol on the NetBEUI Advanced Properties page *only*.

PART

V

Networking

Entering DNS Server Addresses

On the TCP/IP properties page, the DNS Configuration setting may require you to enter a DNS server address in order for Windows to convert *machine.domain*.com-type addresses into IP addresses. Your network administrator will give you this information. There will usually be two or more addresses to enter here. For each one, follow these steps:

- Click Enable DNS.

- Enter the IP numbers of each DNS server, and click Add for each.

- Enter the DNS name for your computer under Host and your Internet domain under Domain. For example, my Web server computer is named "www" and the domain is "cowart.com." Do *not* enter your Windows NT/2000 domain name here. Enter your Internet domain name.

If you frequently use machines in one or two other domains, and there are no machines with the same name in your domain, you might enter the other domain names in "domain suffix search order." If, for example, I entered berkeley.edu in the Domain Suffix list and I asked Internet Explorer to display http://baker, Windows would first look for a server named "baker.cowart.com" (my domain), and then "baker.berkeley.edu" before giving up. This could save me time if I used "baker" frequently.

TABLE 27.7: IPX/SPX PROPERTIES SETTINGS

IPX/SPX Properties	Settings
NetBIOS	If you use the IPX/SPX protocol for Windows file sharing (either client or service), check this box. Windows file sharing requires NetBIOS software support. Also, if you want to perform remote administration of this computer via an IPX/SPX network, you must also enable NetBIOS support.
Advanced Properties	
Frame Type	Leave set to Auto. However, Windows may fail to connect to versions 2 and earlier of NetWare file servers with this setting. If you're unable to connect to an older Novell file server, try changing this setting to Ethernet 802.3.

Continued ▶

TABLE 27.7: IPX/SPX PROPERTIES SETTINGS (CONTINUED)	
IPX/SPX Properties	**Settings**
Network Address	Windows normally determines the IPX network number automatically, with this parameter set to 0. If the network usually has no Novell file servers present but will be using routers, or will be dialing into a network with Novell routers, it may be necessary to set this. Your network administrator can tell you if this is necessary.
Bindings	Windows normally binds everything to everything on installation. If any bindings are not necessary, as determined earlier, uncheck any that are not needed. For example, if you use TCP/IP for Internet access and IPX/SPX to connect to Novell file sharing, you can uncheck Client for Microsoft Networks.

PART

V

TABLE 27.8: NETBEUI PROPERTY SETTING	
NetBEUI Property	**Setting**
Bindings	Windows normally binds everything to everything on installation. If any bindings are not necessary, as determined earlier, uncheck any that are not needed.

Networking

 NOTE Each protocol's Advanced Properties tab contains a check box labeled Set This Protocol to Be the Default Protocol. If you have more than one protocol installed, you can check this box on the protocol that is your primary one for file-sharing services. It's not terribly important that you do, however.

NetWare Servers and Long Filenames

Novell NetWare servers can coexist quite well on a network with Windows Me computers. Microsoft considers smooth integration with NetWare networks to be so important that it developed its own NetWare driver software, and includes it with Windows Me. However, versions of NetWare prior to version 4 can have difficulty with the long filenames used by Windows. If you have a NetWare file server on your network, you should know about the steps required to support long filenames, and the potential problems you may encounter. The problems differ depending on the version of NetWare. In this section, I offer some important advice for NetWare network administrators that I found buried in Microsoft's Web site.

Versions 4 and 5

NetWare version 4 and 5 servers store long filenames without problems.

Version 3.12

By default, NetWare version 3.12 servers store only the short "eight-dot-three" file-names that are a carryover from the old days of DOS. However, they can be told to make room to store Windows Me's long filenames, if you wish. Just follow these steps:

1. At the NetWare server console prompt, type the following two lines:

   ```
   load os2
   add name space os2 to volume sys
   ```

2. Add the following line to the `startup.cnf` file:

   ```
   load os2
   ```

3. Shut down the file server. Then copy the file `os2.nam` from the NetWare distri-bution disks or compact disk to the same disk and directory that contains `server.exe` on the NetWare file server (that is, the directory from which the NetWare server loads on its DOS partition).

4. Restart the NetWare file server.

With long filename support installed, there are a few strange side effects you should be aware of:

- If a DOS computer user opens, edits, and saves a file that had a long filename when they started working with it, they might not even know that it had a long filename because all that they will see is a truncated version of it. Worse, all they'll save is the truncated version. From that point on, the long name will be lost, and the file will go by the shortened, mangled 8.3 name that the DOS user saw. For example, `Trip Planning Spreadsheet.XLS` might be seen by the DOS user as `TRIPPL~3.XLS`; and after saving the document, the file will appear as `TRIPPL~3.XLS` to Windows Me users as well.

- In an MS-DOS Prompt box in Windows Me, you can't alternate between short-ened directory names and long names as you type `dir` and `cd` commands. Mys-teriously, the DOS box wants to use one or the other, but not both. If you use Explorer, this is not an issue. If you use the DOS prompt a lot, you might try to avoid using long folder names on the Novell server so that this issue doesn't come up.

Wide Area Networks

When you connect your LAN to another LAN, you create a wide area network (WAN). What makes a WAN a WAN isn't really how widespread the computers are, but that the connection between the networks is generally slower than LAN speed, usually by a factor of 10 or more. High-speed data connections can be expensive, so you would generally use the cheapest (and slowest) means that are sufficient for your requirements, balancing the need for speed with the need to conserve money. These long-distance connections are made using special hardware and/or software systems called *routers*. The job of a router is to listen to all the data on a network to determine which data is destined for computers on networks located elsewhere, and to send it there.

Tying networks together is becoming much more economical than it was in the past. There are several reasons:

- The Internet has become an effective way of tying LANs together. The cost of using the Internet is not distance-sensitive. You pay only for the hardware required and a monthly fee to an Internet Service Provider. The monthly fee is usually based only on the speed of your connection and how long you stay connected, rather than on how far data gets transferred and how much you actually send.

- Router hardware has become much less expensive simply because networking has become so widespread.

- High-speed data services provided by telephone companies, such as DSL, Frame Relay, ISDN, and ATM, are more economical than older leased-line services. The technology used as the basis of the global telephone network itself is now all digital and based mostly on very high-speed fiber-optic cable, so it's become relatively inexpensive to "piggyback" data connections along with telephone conversations.

It's beyond the scope of this book to describe how to install and manage a WAN. We'll just note here that it's now possible for small offices to connect their LANs together for a few thousand dollars of hardware plus a few hundred dollars a month, or even less. For the adventurous, routers can even be constructed from older 386 PCs with commercial or shareware routing software for just a few hundred dollars.

Active Directory

If your Windows Me computer is part of a Windows 2000 Server network, you should install Microsoft's Active Directory add-on client software so that you can take advantage of Windows 2000's enterprise-wide searching capability.

For information about installing and using Active Directory, see the following sections of Chapter 28, "Internetworking Windows Me with Windows NT/2000": "Joining a Windows 2000 Server Domain" and "Searching Active Directory."

PART

V

Networking

Internet Printing Protocol

If you're a road warrior, you might be excited to know that Windows printing services are now available across the Internet, using a new service called the *Internet Printing Protocol (IPP)*.

IPP was designed by the software and printer manufacturing industries to provide a standard way of sharing printers over the Internet and TCP/IP networks. IPP services can let you send output to a printer at your home office while you're away. IPP is also designed to let service bureaus, hotels, and copy shops offer printing services to travelers. For example, you could use IPP to print presentation slides from your hotel room directly to a nearby Kinko's, using nothing but standard Windows printing tools. Nifty!

Windows 2000 Professional and Server support printing via IPP. A growing list of printer models and service companies also offer IPP services. All you need to know is the URL of the remote printer.

If you have IPP printers available to you, here's how to set up Windows Me to take advantage of them. First, install IPP support. This is a one-time setup procedure:

1. Insert your Windows Me installation CD-ROM. If the Setup program appears, select Browse the CD-ROM. Otherwise, open My Computer and browse into your CD-ROM drive.

2. Browse to the \add-ons\IPP folder and double-click the ipp.txt icon. Read this file for Microsoft's comments on IPP. You may want to print these notes. (Better do this at home before you need the IPP printer!) Close Notepad when you've finished reading the notes.

3. Double-click the wpnpins.exe icon. The installation is quite fast.

4. Windows will ask to restart the computer. Click Yes.

Then, to add an IPP-based printer to your Printers folder, you can use either of two techniques.

If the printer is based on a Windows 2000 computer running Internet Information Services, you can view its available printers from Internet Explorer via a built-in Web page:

1. If the computer is on your LAN, enter the URL http://name/printers, where *name* is the host name of the Windows 2000 computer.

   OR

   If the computer is on the Internet, enter the URL http://*name.domain*.com/printers, where *name.domain*.com is the Internet name for the computer.

2. This will display a list of available printers on a Web page. Click the desired printer to view its status page, as shown in Figure 27.3.

3. Click Connect to install the printer in your Printers folder.

FIGURE 27.3
Viewing a printer shared via IPP from a Windows 2000 computer

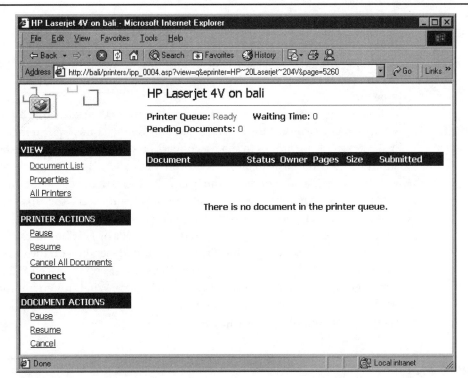

You can also install the printer using the normal "Add Printer" method if you know the URL for the printer. Your service bureau or network administrator will give you the URL and specific installation instructions for Windows Me. The instructions will go something like this:

1. Open your Printers folder and double-click Add Printer. Click Next.

2. Select Network Printer and click Next.

3. Enter the URL for the remote printer, e.g., **http://boston.ma.company.com/ printers/ColorFilm/.printer**, and click Next.

4. You may be asked to supply the location of driver software for the printer if the IPP service cannot automatically obtain it over the Internet. Your print service provider will provide you with instructions in this case.

5. Continue with normal printer installation by choosing a name and selecting whether or not to print a test page. (Before choosing Yes, be sure you won't be charged for the test page!)

Once the printer is installed, you can select and use this printer just as you would any Windows printer. As long as your network or Internet connection is up, the printer is available.

Getting Your LAN on the Internet

One particular instance of wide area networking is connecting your network to the Internet, which could be considered a global WAN comprising millions of computers. If you work in an office or home with several computers with modems, you've probably noticed that they are rarely all busy at once. So why can't everyone just share one modem?

That's exactly what this section is about. But rather than share one modem among a group of people who can use it in turn, but only one at a time, the Internet is designed to make it possible for groups to share a connection *simultaneously*. Imagine being able to surf the Internet from any computer on your network, at any time, without worrying about Dial-Up Manager or dial-up anything. It's easier than you might think.

For the speed-hungry corporate network with many users, the answer lies in a combination of a high-speed data connection and router hardware (see Figure 27.4). A full-time, always-on connection to the Internet at speeds of 128Kbps to 1Mbps in the U.S. costs anywhere between $50 and $1,000 a month, depending on the technology used. Installing data lines and purchasing routing hardware costs between $150 and $2,500. Elsewhere in the world it can cost much, much more. What this buys is Internet access without dialing, without delays, and without any hardware at each workstation, other than the network wire already in place.

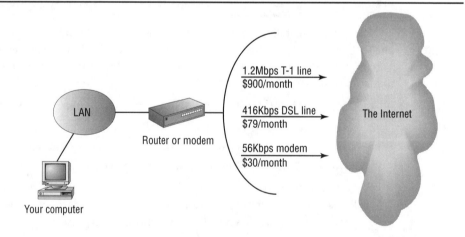

FIGURE 27.4
Costs of connecting a
LAN to the Internet

Sharing a DSL or Cable Internet Connection

If you have DSL or cable Internet service available, small, inexpensive "DSL/cable sharing routers" are available at a cost of about $150. These devices let you use an inexpensive, single-user DSL or cable Internet modem to connect your whole LAN! Besides providing routing and connection sharing, they offer a built-in firewall (security) function to prevent hackers on the Internet from reaching your computers.

These devices use a network function called *network address translation,* or *NAT*, to manage all Internet transactions using a single IP address, as illustrated in Figure 27.5.

FIGURE 27.5
A NAT router can use a standard single-user account for the whole network

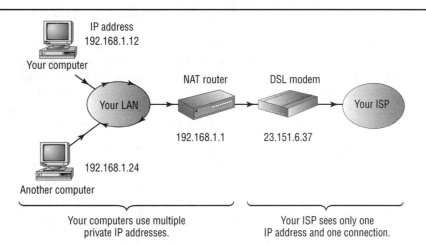

These NAT routers stand between your network and the Internet and carry out the network data conversations on your behalf. When you send a request to a remote computer, the router sends the request on with its own IP number in place of yours. When data comes back from the Internet, the router knows that the data is yours and forwards it to your computer. This lets the entire LAN communicate to the outside world with just one IP address.

There are some pluses and minuses to using a NAT router to connect to the Internet. Here are the pluses:

- IP numbers on your LAN are private, and you can assign them any way you want.

- Incoming connections can be directed to a specific computer or rejected outright. This boosts your network's security.

- The latest router models support the *PPPoE* logon protocol used by many DSL service providers.

There are a couple of minuses:

- Some network protocols will not work with NAT, which is best suited for plain e-mail, FTP, and Web access. Protocols that include your IP address as part of the data (such as the video part of a NetMeeting connection) won't work because the router is unable to determine which computer on the network should receive the data coming back from the server.

- If everyone on the NAT router is trying to use the Internet at once, transfer rates can drop as several people share the data rate of a single connection.

NOTE I recommend these devices as the best approach to connecting your small LAN to the Internet. If you can get DSL or cable Internet service and aren't planning to host public Web or mail servers on your LAN, this is definitely the way to go. My favorite product is the BEFSR41 model manufactured by LinkSys (www.linksys.com). It even includes a four-port 10/100Mbps Ethernet hub.

 NOTE You could also use Microsoft's Internet Connection Sharing to connect your DSL/ cable service to the rest of your LAN, by installing two network adapters. However, I do not recommend this practice. The cost of a hardware-sharing device (about $120) is well worth the added security it offers. Don't think twice about it.

ISPs can also set you up with a more expensive router and multiple IP addresses for your LAN, usually at an additional cost per month. Use this approach if you need to host Web or mail servers on your LAN, since each will need a unique, fixed IP address.

Sharing a Dial-Up Connection

You can use Windows' built-in Internet Connection Sharing to connect your LAN to the Internet via modem or ISDN. In this scenario, one computer is set up with a Dial-Up Networking connection to your ISP, and the other computers on your LAN send their Internet requests to this one computer, as shown in Figure 27.6. It will dial your ISP automatically when *any* user on the LAN wants to use the Internet, and will automatically hang up after a few minutes of non-use.

FIGURE 27.6
Internet Connection Sharing uses one computer to establish a dial-up connection for the whole LAN

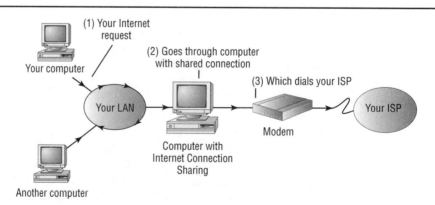

Commercial software products such as WinGate perform the same function, and there are even some hardware devices that do this.

Dial-up connection sharing, like the DSL/cable sharing devices, uses NAT, so it has the same pluses and minuses that I described for shared DSL/cable service. An additional limitation is that the computer that will establish the connection must be left turned on in order for other LAN users to reach the Internet.

A *big* additional minus for software-based connection sharing is that there is no firewall effect for the computer that makes the dial-up connection. It's still exposed to the Internet, and this is a security risk.

Finally, shared dial-up service doesn't keep your LAN connected to the Internet full-time, so it's not appropriate for making your own Web server available to the world. But if you don't have Web servers (or e-mail or other servers) that you want to make available, and if security is not a big worry, this can be a very attractive and inexpensive way of getting hooked up.

 WARNING I prefer hardware NAT solutions because they offer greater protection from hackers. When you use Microsoft's Internet Connection Sharing, the computer that makes the dial-up connection is exposed to hackers. If you use Microsoft's software approach, do not enable File and Printer Sharing on the computer that establishes your connection.

Despite its limitations and security risks, setting up a shared dial-up connection is pretty simple. Here's how:

1. Choose one Windows Me computer to share the connection. If at all possible, this computer should *not* have File and Printer Sharing enabled. Perform the remaining steps on this computer.

2. Set up and test the dial-up connection to your ISP on this computer. Don't proceed until it's working.

3. Open the Add/Remove Programs applet on the Control Panel and select the Windows Setup tab. Highlight Communications and click Details. Be sure that Internet Connection Sharing is checked. If it isn't, check it to install it now. You may need to insert your Windows Me CD-ROM and restart Windows. If the component is already there, close the Control Panel.

4. Open My Network Places and start the Home Networking Wizard.

5. Step through the Wizard to the Internet Connection page. Check Yes, This Computer Uses the Following. Check A Direct Connection to My ISP Using the Following Device. Select the appropriate Dial-Up Networking connection entry. Click Next.

6. Click Yes under Do You Want Other Computers... to Use the Connection.... Select the LAN adapter that connects your computer to the others on your LAN. Click Next.

7. On the Establishing Internet Connection page, check Yes, and enter the username and password for your ISP account.

8. Heed the warning about Automatic Updates initiating connections, and disable Automatic Updates on *all* your LAN computers if you want to avoid these connections.

9. Click Next repeatedly to finish up the Wizard. Create a Home Networking Wizard disk if you have Windows 9*x* computers on your LAN.

10. Open the Network applet on the Control Panel, select the TCP/IP entry for your LAN adapter, and select Properties. On the IP Address tab, select Obtain an IP Address Automatically. Close the Control Panel.

11. Restart this computer.

Then on each of your other computers, follow these steps:

1. Open the Network applet on the Control Panel, select the TCP/IP entry for your LAN adapter, and select Properties. On the IP Address tab, select Obtain an IP Address Automatically. Close the Control Panel.

2. Run the Home Networking Wizard.

3. Step through the Wizard to the Internet Connection page. Check Yes, This Computer Uses the Following. Check A Connection to Another Computer on My Home Network.... Click Next.

4. Click Next repeatedly to finish up the Wizard.

5. Restart each computer after reconfiguring it.

Now, as long as the computer with the shared connection is booted up, *any* computer on the LAN should be able to access the Internet, one at a time or simultaneously.

Network Security

The information on your computer is valuable property. When you are connected to a network, it's possible for other people to get into the files on your computer and read, modify, or delete them. Usually, that's the *purpose* of networking! But it can also be a source of much unhappiness if the person reading, writing, or deleting is not supposed to be doing those things.

If you just share files on a network in your own small office, you can probably worry less about security since you probably trust the people you work with not to act inappropriately. But in larger companies, with computers connected to the Internet, or on computers containing sensitive information on payroll, personnel, or other secrets, you should take precautions to prevent unauthorized people from reaching into your computer, invisibly, through the network wiring.

Basic Issues

The first line of defense is the simplest. Since you don't have to protect something that isn't exposed, you can take steps to hide your resources:

- Don't share any drives or folders you don't have to.

- Don't connect a computer with sensitive information to any networks you don't have to.

- Don't enable the network bindings between file sharing and TCP/IP unless you need to.

This way you can eliminate the risk to some drives and computers outright, and then focus on protecting the rest.

For resources that *are* connected to the outside world (be it the Internet, or your corporate LAN, or your brother-in-law's computer next door), you can take these simple precautions to make it harder for your security to be compromised:

- Use good passwords (not your last name, your spouse's name or your telephone number) on every shared drive. The best passwords have combinations of letters and numbers or punctuation and can't be guessed by just trying common words. Words like *cheese* might be guessed, but who would think of trying *riceball202*?

- Use user-level security, if possible, so that each remote user has their own password and you can directly control which users have access to which resources. I'll explain how to enable this in the next section. User-level security is *essential* if you install Personal Web Server and want to allow remote users to publish or post files to your computer.

- Share lower-level directories for general users, if possible, rather than entire disk drives. Of course, for remote backup, you may need to share whole disk drives. If you do, assign these shares different passwords from other shares, and/or permit only administrator-type users to read them.

- If your network is directly connected to the Internet, use a firewall to limit the network services and connections that may be made through your Internet connection. A *firewall* is a computer that divides your network from the incoming Internet connection, and denies access to specific network services that you don't want to be made available over the Internet. Firewall software is available for NT computers and for most routers used in Internet connectivity. Or you can use commercial firewall software such as Black Ice Defender, ZoneAlarm, and others. If you use a NAT router for your Internet connection, that router is a darned good firewall itself.

NOTE For more information on personal firewall software, visit www.pcworld.com and search for "Personal Firewall Software."

User-Level Security for NT and NetWare

If your network includes a NetWare or Windows NT Server file server, you can use user-level security on the network to help protect your shared files. These file servers contain a database of user names and passwords that all of the other computers on the network query to determine if users are valid. These file servers take over the job of checking usernames and passwords for all the computers on your network.

However, there is a slight catch: If you have both NT and NetWare servers on your network, you must choose just one to be the security reference. In a Windows NT Server domain, this job might be shared by several NT servers, and you need not specify which. With NetWare, on the other hand, you must specify one particular NetWare file server to be the reference.

 WARNING If you have neither type of file server on your network, you can't use user-level security in Windows Me, and this in turn means that if you connect to the Internet, you should not enable Web-based publishing from Personal Web Server.

This is a catch because Windows Me File Sharing for Microsoft Networks can use only an NT domain for security references, and File Sharing for Novell Networks can use only a Novell server. You have to choose just one of these types of file sharing, and that locks you into the choice of your security source—that is, if you want to have user-level security. To enable user-level security, do the following:

1. Bring up the Network applet on the Control Panel.
2. Click the Access Control tab (see Figure 27.7).
3. Select User-Level Access Control.
   - If you are using File Sharing for Microsoft Networks, enter your Microsoft domain name.
   - If you are using File Sharing for NetWare Networks, enter the name of the NetWare file server that will be used to validate user names and passwords.
4. Click OK.

FIGURE 27.7

Setting user-level security in the Network applet on the Control Panel

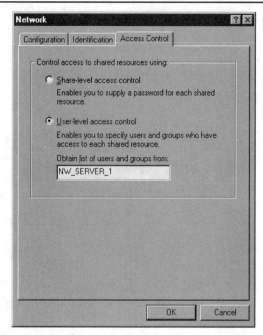

If you are using a Novell 3.*x* file server for validation, you must have an account on the NetWare server.

If you don't have a user account on the Novell file server, you must create a special user account on this server so that Windows can inquire about the validity of usernames and passwords. To create this account, do the following:

1. Create a user named WINDOWS_PASSTHRU with no password. Set all the following account restrictions to No: Account Disabled, Account Has Expiration Date, Limit Concurrent Connections, Allow User to Change Password, and Require Password.

2. Delete all group memberships for this account, including the group EVERYONE.

3. Delete all trustee rights for this account.

4. Delete any station or time restrictions that might exist on this account. Be sure to check the Time Restrictions property and enter an asterisk (*) for any time periods that are disabled by default.

This will let Windows attach to the server with this login name just to validate passwords, but it will prevent anyone from accessing any files on the file server using this unguarded account.

When you restart Windows, user-level security will be enabled. Now, the sharing properties on drives and folders will have an area in which to list users and groups and

PART

V

Networking

their access rights. By default no one can read or write to a share unless you assign specific rights to users and/or groups of users. Click Add to assign rights to a share (see Figure 27.8).

FIGURE 27.8
Assigning users rights in sharing properties

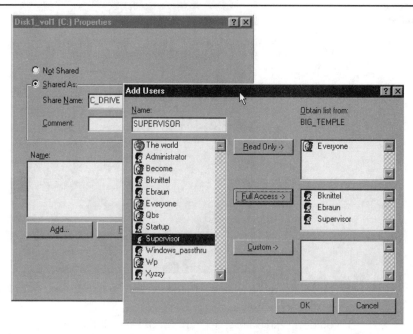

On the left of the Add Users dialog box, Windows lists the user and group names it found on the file server you entered when you enabled user-level security. "The world" signifies any user of any computer without a login name. Names with a single-face icon stand for individual users on the network, and names with a two-face icon stand for groups of users. A user will get share access rights that consist of the sum of his or her user rights plus the rights of all groups that the user is a member of. To assign rights, do this:

1. Highlight a user or group name in the Name list and click Edit.

2. Click one of three buttons:

   • Read Only Access Rights, to allow the user the privilege of listing directories and reading files but not modifying anything

   • Full Access Rights, to allow the user all read, write, delete, and modify access rights

   • Custom Access Rights, to assign specific access rights for this share

3. Enter all names and groups you wish to permit to have access to this share, and click OK.

I suggest that you not grant any access at all to "The world" since no login name or password is required to use the share if you do grant "world" access.

If you've selected "Custom" rights, a second dialog box will appear (Figure 27.9) for each user with Custom access. This box lets you check which access rights you wish to grant. The options are described in Table 27.9.

FIGURE 27.9

Assigning custom access rights

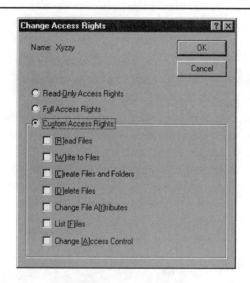

TABLE 27.9: ACCESS RIGHTS FOR CUSTOM ACCESS

Access Type	Lets Remote User . . .
Read Files	Read the contents of a file, if the user knows its name
Write to Files	Write to a file
Create Files and Folders	Create new files and/or folders
Delete Files	Delete files
Change File Attributes	Change read-only, archived, hidden, and other file attributes
List Files	List the contents of the shared folder and its subdirectories
Change Access Control	Change these access rights for themselves and other users(!)
Read-Only Access	Works like Read Files, plus List Files

Custom Access Rights let you create folders with special properties. For example, Create Files without Read Files, Write to Files, or Delete Files, would let a user create a

PART

V

Networking

data file in your shared drive but not remove it, view it, or modify any existing files; this would be good for a directory into which people could drop off files for you, because nobody could snoop into or change what was there.

You can modify a user's or group's rights later by displaying the folder's Properties page, clicking Sharing, selecting the username, and clicking Edit.

You can right-click Properties of any subfolder of a shared folder or drive, and view the Sharing properties for the subfolder. It will be marked "Already shared via…" and will show the name of the containing shared folder.

You can do the following:

- Share this subfolder as a separate share, if you wish.

- Set different user access rights for the subfolder. These will apply to users using this folder via *any* share.

When you change a folder's user rights, it makes sense that the same rights ought to apply to any folders inside this folder. So Windows asks you whether you want to apply the rights you just edited to all subfolders, whether to leave the subfolders alone, or whether to ask you folder by folder, as shown in Figure 27.10.

Normally, you'd apply the changes to all subfolders. However, if you've granted special, greater permissions to one of the subfolders, you might not want to have the current folder's access rights carried down.

FIGURE 27.10
You can specify whether your security settings should apply to all or only some of the subfolders.

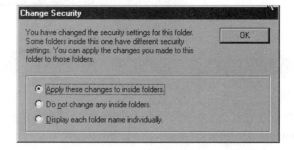

The Late, Great Zero Administration Initiative

Microsoft gave network managers a set of remote management tools as part of its Zero Administration Initiative for Windows 9*x*. These Windows versions came with extra tools to assist network managers in configuring and maintaining computers on an enterprise network:

- A Policy Editor, which let administrators hide many Control Panel settings and options from regular users.

- Remote Registry editing and Remote Management services, which let managers repair problems from a centralized location.

- Instrumentation software, which management could use to measure network performance, bottlenecks, and so forth.

- An extra-cost Windows 9x Resource Kit, which consisted of detailed additional documentation and a heap of "tweaking" software tools for setup, maintenance, and management.

These tools together allowed large organizations to lock down and maintain large numbers of Windows-based computers. The end result might not have been quite "zero" administration, but at least it offered the potential for *minimal* administration.

All this has changed with Windows Me. Microsoft has removed the remote administration tools from the Windows Me CD-ROM and will not offer a Resource Kit. This is most likely a strategy to pressure large organizations into moving from Windows 9x to Windows 2000 as their primary end-user operating system.

If you depend on these tools to maintain your organization's network, you can upgrade to Windows 2000, of course, or you can try to get by with older versions of the missing software components until you're ready for the big upgrade. Some suggestions for evading Microsoft's squeeze play are listed in Table 27.10.

TABLE 27.10: WHERE TO GET THE MISSING ADMINISTRATIVE COMPONENTS

Feature	Workaround
Remote Administration	Remote administration of file sharing is still built into Windows Me. Enable it from the Passwords applet on the Control Panel.
Remote Registry	Can be installed from a Windows 98 or 98 Second Edition disk.
Policy Editor	You can use the Windows 98 Second Edition Policy Editor, but there is no guarantee that all policies (which are really registry entries) will work since Microsoft has changed some of the organization of Registry entries in Windows Me.
SNMP Agent	Can be installed from a Windows 98 or 98 Second Edition disk.

The following sections offer some tips for installing and using the administrative services.

Administrative Tools

Here is a summary of the administrative tools available to network managers. Some of these tools have to be obtained from a Windows 98 installation disk, as described in the previous section.

PART

V

Networking

Remote Administration

The Remote Administration service allows remote computers to connect to the "insides" of Windows networking, to view and change shared printers and folders. Since this is a powerful feature, it is enabled only for users and/or groups with Remote Administration privileges.

To enable Remote Administration, you must follow these steps:

1. Install file-sharing services.

2. Open the Password applet on the Control Panel, select Remote Administration, and check Enable Remote Administration of This Server.

3. If you are part of a Windows NT domain and are using user-level network security, click Add to add users and/or groups that are to have Remote Administration privileges. Be sure to add only bona fide network administrators to the list.

4. Click OK to close the Passwords Properties dialog box.

   If you are using share-level security, enter a password for Remote Administration.

 WARNING Remote Administration privilege is a very powerful feature: It lets a user view or alter any file on your computer regardless of file-sharing security settings! Be very restrictive in the users to whom you give this privilege. Microsoft documentation says: "Remote Administration privilege gives that person full access to all shared resources on the system regardless of other user-level security settings, including the ability to add and remove other remote administrators."

Remote Registry

The Remote Registry service allows a remote computer to edit the Registry settings of the Windows Me computer. Since this is a very sensitive part of Windows, Remote Administration privileges are required, and user-level security on an NT server or NetWare network is also required.

 NOTE As I discussed at the beginning of this section, the Remote Registry service is *not* provided as a part of Windows Me. If you want it you have to obtain a Windows 98 installation CD-ROM.

To install the Remote Registry service, follow these steps:

1. Enable Remote Administration as described in the previous section.

2. In the Network applet in the Control Panel, click Add.

3. Select Service and click Add.

4. Insert a Windows 98 or 98 Second Edition installation CD-ROM into your computer and click Have Disk.

5. In the Install from Disk dialog box, click Browse and locate the \Tools\ Reskit\Netadmin\Remotreg directory on the CD-ROM.

6. Select regsrv.inf, and click OK.

7. Close the Network applet on the Control Panel.

The Remote Registry service must be installed on *both* the computer whose Registry is to be edited and the remote computer doing the editing. (It's installed by default on Windows NT and Windows 2000.) You must also have file sharing and user-level security installed, using a Windows NT server for password verification. Also, both computers must have a networking protocol in common.

 WARNING The Remote Registry service is a powerful and potentially dangerous doorway into your computer. You should install it only if necessary, and only behind a firewall if your computers are connected to the Internet.

Microsoft SNMP Agent

Remote monitoring of your computer's network functions via SNMP (Simple Network Management Protocol) is used in many corporate networks.

 NOTE As I discussed at the beginning of this section, the SNMP agent is not provided as a part of Windows Me. If you want it you have to obtain a Windows 98 installation CD-ROM.

To install the Windows SNMP Agent, do the following:

1. In the Network applet on the Control Panel, click Add.

2. Select Service and click Add.

3. Insert a Windows 98 or 98 Second Edition installation CD-ROM, and click Have Disk.

4. Browse to \Tools\Reskit\Netadmin\Snmp and select snmp.inf. Click OK.

5. Close the Network applet.

WARNING Do not install the SNMP Agent unless your organization requires it and you have a firewall in place to block SNMP traffic from the Internet. SNMP can reveal significant security information to remote viewers.

Policy Editor

Policies are special Registry entries that are set when Windows is installed and which allow managers to restrict what users can do with their computer. For example, you can prevent them from adding new software, from changing network or security options, and so forth. Although this wouldn't sit well with you as a home computer user, in a large corporate setting, it might be the only way to avoid the total chaos of thousands of "user-customized" or "user-mangled" computers. Policy settings may be stored on a central Windows NT or NetWare server and automatically downloaded by Windows Me computers as part of each user's "profile."

Microsoft has stated that it will *not* provide a Policy Editor tool targeted for Windows Me. You can try to use the Windows 98 Second Edition Policy Editor and policy files, but there is no guarantee that they will work with Windows Me. Most policies probably will work, but you should test your setup thoroughly. You can install the Policy Editor from a Windows 98 Second Edition installation CD-ROM from directory \Tools\Reskit\Netadmin\Poledit.

For the Policy Editor to apply policy changes to users' computers on its network, the client computers must have Remote Administration and Remote Registry services installed.

NetMon

The NetMon network monitoring application lets remote administrators monitor network traffic on a workstation, gather statistics, and even capture and view network data. To install the NetMon Agent, follow these steps:

1. In the Network applet on the Control Panel, click Add.

2. Select Protocol and click Add.

3. Select Manufacturer Microsoft and Protocol "Microsoft Network Monitor Driver."

4. Click OK.

5. Close the Network applet.

 WARNING Do not install the NetMon Agent unless your organization requires it.

Windows Me does not come with the NetMon system tool for viewing captured network traffic. The viewing component is part of Microsoft Systems Management Server.

Net Watcher

The Net Watcher utility, run from Start ➢ Programs ➢ Accessories ➢ System Tools ➢ Net Watcher, lets you view shared folders, connected users, and currently open files on the local computer or a remote computer. With this tool, you can also add or remove shared folders, disconnect users, or close files on a remote computer.

 NOTE If Net Watcher doesn't appear in your System Tools folder, run Add/Remove Programs from the Control Panel, choose the Windows Setup tab, and check the System Tools box. Click OK to install these additional programs.

 NOTE To work with a remote computer, Net Watcher requires that the remote computer have Remote Administration enabled and that you have Remote Administration privileges on that computer.

System Monitor

System Monitor, described in Chapter 14, can measure the performance of various components of a remote computer, such as CPU utilization and network traffic. Remote system monitoring requires user-level security, Remote Administration, and Remote Registry services.

PART

V

Networking

CHAPTER 28

Internetworking Windows Me with Windows NT/2000

FEATURING:

As you connect more stations to your Windows Me peer-to-peer network, sooner or later you will want to interconnect with one or more Windows 2000 or NT workstations or servers. Windows NT/2000 provides you with an array of powerful options and tools that can help maximize the usefulness and productivity of your Windows Me workstations—especially in the areas of security, performance, and network administration. If you are working in a corporate environment, you probably already have Windows NT/2000 servers on your network. In this chapter, my goal is to show you how to use Windows Me stations with one or more Windows 2000 or NT stations, which will function as servers for files, printers, and applications.

 NOTE Windows 2000 is based on Windows NT version 4.0; in fact, it was originally named NT 5.0. For simplicity's sake I'll write "Windows NT/2000" when I mean *both* operating systems. When I need to discuss differences between the two, I'll use "Windows NT 4.0" and "Windows 2000" to make the distinction clear.

Some Networking Philosophy

In Chapter 24, "Building a Peer-to-Peer Network," you saw how each networked peer showed up in My Network Places as a computer icon. Each station's shared printers and folders were available to anyone who double-clicked a particular computer or created a map to one of the shared drives or printers. This is great as far as it goes, but consider how it would be if you had two hundred, a thousand, or even several thousand stations on the network all appearing in My Network Places. Clearly, this would become very confusing to use, and a *nightmare* for the network administrator. What is needed, then, is a way to organize these stations into groups, and perhaps groups of groups, so that visualizing and working with the stations becomes both more manageable and efficient: thus the concept of *workgroups*.

Workgroups

First introduced in Windows 3.11 (Windows for Workgroups), the subdividing of Windows workstations into workgroups helps free the members of each workgroup to maintain, support, and use only those resources needed by their workgroup. All other network resources may still be *physically* connected, but the workgroup sees and makes use of only those resources directly relevant to its area. From the user's vantage point, 95 percent of the clutter is removed from My Network Places, and lumping all computers together into My Network Places becomes a reasonable approach once more. And where security is needed, passwords can be assigned within the workgroup on a per-resource or per-user basis (a single password can even be used by a group of users).

Small networks—say, those with a total of 50 or fewer workstations—might find that the workgroup approach is a simple and sufficient enough means of subdividing and organizing the network resources and users, assuming they're subdivided into multiple workgroups of 10 or fewer stations. But with very large networks, workgroups are not adequate because there's no way to oversee all the different workgroups. Managing the centralized networking resources on larger networks requires being able to access and configure user accounts and other network resources in a way that transcends the boundaries of individual workgroups.

Domains

One significant limitation of the workgroup concept is that users' logon names and passwords are stored independently in each computer on the network. When a new user appears or a user wants to change their password, this new information has to be entered separately into *each* computer the user might want to access, either directly or through the network. Imagine how much time it would take to set up 20 users on 20 computers! Faced with this much effort to set up and maintain user accounts, users would probably want to forgo using passwords at all.

So, in order to make organizing and managing larger networks easier, Microsoft came up with the idea of *domains*. Domains are similar to workgroups but provide the ability to store names and passwords for all users in a single user *database*. This database resides on the Windows NT/2000 Server *domain controller* (and, optionally, on other *backup domain controllers*). When you log on to a domain from the Windows Me logon dialog box, you are authenticated as a specific user with specific access rights. Your ability to use shared resources on the network, such as a directory or printer, is based on these access rights.

 NOTE It's important to point out that this use of the word domain is similar to, but not identical to, its use with the Internet. Microsoft Network domain names and Internet domain names are like postal zip codes and telephone area codes: They both serve the purpose of dividing up large networks, but they're unrelated.

For more specific information on NT Server, take a look at my book on NT called *Windows NT Server 4.0: No Experience Required* (Sybex, 1997).

PART

V

Networking

Workstation versus Server

Windows NT/2000 comes in a confusing number of flavors. They are categorized as "workstation" versions or "server" versions:

Workstation Versions	**Server Versions**
Windows 2000 Professional	Windows 2000 Server
Windows NT 4.0 Workstation	Windows 2000 Advanced Server
	Windows 2000 Data Center Server
	Windows NT 4.0 Server
	Windows NT 4.0 Server Enterprise Edition
	Windows NT 4.0 Terminal Server

The workstation versions are intended mainly for use by individuals as their personal computer operating system, while the Server versions are intended for use on industrial-strength file server and data processing center computers. The server versions permit unlimited client connections, come with lots of additional networking and administrative software, and cost more. The Workstation/Professional versions limit incoming network connections to 10 at most, but they cost much less.

NOTE Professional, Workstation, whatever! Why Microsoft had to change their naming system, I'll never understand. It may help their marketing department, but it sure doesn't help customers (or book authors). For the remainder of the chapter, when I say "NT/2000 workstation," I mean "Windows 2000 Professional or Windows NT 4.0 Workstation." When I say "NT/2000 Server," I mean "one of the Windows 2000 Server or Windows NT 4.0 Server versions."

Although I will be concentrating primarily on Windows NT/2000 in its capacity as a file server in this chapter, remember that NT/2000 can also be used as a workstation and as a file-sharing peer with Windows Me and Windows 9x.

Why, you may wonder, would a regular user want to use NT/2000 on a desktop computer? There are various reasons to choose Windows NT/2000 over Windows Me:

- You want NT/2000's improved reliability, as well as its management and software installation support.

- You plan to run NT/2000 series software or certain high-end graphics software.

- You need Windows 2000's network and file encryption support.

- You need beefed-up security or support for non-FAT file systems.

Business users, software developers, CAD (Computer Aided Design) users, and scientists doing math-intensive work might need or prefer Windows NT/2000 over Windows Me for a combination of these features. Some programmers, for example, have both Windows Me and Windows NT/2000 installed on their stations, and they can boot to one operating system or the other as needed in order to develop and test their software.

Let's look at the differences between the workstation and server flavors. The workstation version (Windows 2000 Professional or Windows NT 4.0 Workstation) has the following limitations when compared to the corresponding server version:

- It cannot function as a domain controller.
- It has a maximum of 10 simultaneous client connections.
- It does not support Roaming User Profiles.
- It does not provide gateway services to Novell NetWare.
- It does not provide network services for Apple workstations.
- It has a limit of two CPUs (for "symmetric multiprocessing").

Let me clarify these briefly.

It cannot function as a domain controller. First, and perhaps most notably, the workstation version cannot act as a centralized user database for the network. Although NT workstations cannot be used as a domain controller, they *can* log on to a domain and can function as an additional file- and printer-sharing server within an existing domain.

 NOTE Despite its domain controller limitation, I do want to emphasize that NT/2000 workstations can perform very ably as servers for a workgroup of Windows Me stations. Thus, when cost is an issue and the 10-client limit is not a problem, Windows 2000 Professional or Windows NT 4.0 Workstation might well be a good choice.

It has a maximum of 10 simultaneous client connections. The 10-connection limit does not prevent NT workstations from having more than 10 user accounts or from recognizing more than 10 other stations on a network. It simply means that no more than 10 other workstations or servers can be *simultaneously* connected to its disk and printer resources. This same limitation applies to Windows Me and 9*x*, and limits their usefulness as a central file-sharing resource for larger networks.

It does not support Roaming User Profiles. The Server versions of NT/2000 can store your user preferences and home directory information on the central server so that your preferences, software settings, and network file mappings will appear to "follow" you, no matter which networked computer you use. Windows 2000 Server can even place your My Documents folder directly on the server so that your saved documents will always be available to you no matter which computer you use.

It does not provide gateway services to Novell NetWare. If your network uses Novell NetWare servers, any Windows version can *use* resources on the NetWare servers if the NetWare client support is installed. But Windows NT/2000 server versions provide a *gateway service,* which makes Windows resources available to NetWare clients and vice versa, allowing a more transparent type of mixed network.

It does not provide network services for Apple workstations. Windows NT/2000 server versions also offer an Apple-compatible gateway service. If your network has a mixture of PC's and Macs, Windows 2000 Server or Windows NT 4.0 server will let your Mac and Windows users share files and printers transparently.

It has a limit of two CPUs (for "symmetric multiprocessing"). If you have a server computer with more than two CPUs, you will need NT Server to take advantage of this extra horsepower.

 NOTE The above differences between NT/2000 Server and Workstation are by no means the only differences, but they are the main points to keep in mind if you're considering buying NT/2000. For the rest of this chapter, I'll be discussing the Server version unless otherwise mentioned. Also, due to the similarities between Windows 95, 98, and Me, all references to Windows Me in this chapter also apply to Windows 95 and 98 unless otherwise mentioned.

NT/2000 Server, as opposed to NT Workstation/Windows 2000 Professional, provides for centralized administration because all of the user accounts and groups reside on the domain controller rather than on each individual NT workstation. NT/2000 Server can also be set up with this "domain server" feature turned off. In this mode, it essentially works just like NT Workstation, but it does so with unlimited user connections, and it still includes the rest of the NT Server functionality, like the Novell Gateway Service and Macintosh Services. In this mode it's called a stand-alone or member server.

Windows NT 4.0 versus Windows 2000

Windows 2000 is an advanced version of Windows NT—in fact, it was originally named Windows NT 5.0 before some marketing hotshots decided that an operating system with so many new, more powerful features needed a new, more confusing name.

Windows Me shares some of the advancements: System File Protection, a more friendly Desktop, excellent power management features, and improved installation/setup Wizards. Beyond that, Windows 2000 has much greater reliability, strong network and file encryption, and many additional features made possible by the addition of Microsoft's Active Directory network management service.

Active Directory and Windows 2000 Server

If you're part of a Windows 2000 Server network, you'll discover that its network services really outshine those of Windows NT 4.0 Server. One of Windows 2000 Server's great advantages is *Active Directory*, a database of network information that goes far beyond just usernames and passwords. Active Directory provides information about the following:

- Network users and passwords
- Group and subgroup membership
- User names, addresses, locations, telephone numbers, employees, and managers
- Shared printers, with information about printer capabilities and location
- User rights, permissions, and restrictions
- Software available for automatic installation
- Home directory location
- And much, much more

In a nutshell, Active Directory is an "all-in-one" network management database that makes Windows 2000 Professional and Server networks much more manageable than Windows NT 4.0 domains. Windows 2000 Professional users can take full advantage of Windows 2000's features.

Windows Me and 9*x* users can still use a Windows 2000 Server network, but of all the most advanced features, only the powerful user- and printer-searching functions are available. I'll discuss Active Directory searching later in this chapter.

Adding Windows Me Workstations to the Network

For the remainder of this chapter, I am assuming that you've already set up your workstation for networking, as I discussed in Chapter 24.

To allow your Windows Me stations to communicate with an NT/2000 server, you must make sure that your stations are using at least one protocol in common with those used by the NT/2000 server. While you almost certainly have already installed TCP/IP for Internet access, for security purposes, some network managers use a different protocol for file sharing. Because of this you may need to install either NetBEUI or IPX/SPX as well.

Your network's administrator can tell you which protocol(s) you need.

 TIP If you have only TCP/IP installed and find that My Network Places (Network Neighborhood on Window 9*x*) comes up empty, try installing the NetBEUI protocol as well and restart your computer. In practice, this often fixes the problem.

PART

V

Networking

Adding Workstations to an NT/2000 Server

Your Windows Me stations need to be told how to log on to the network, and the method differs depending on whether your network is a domain or a simple workgroup.

After you join your workstation to an NT/2000 server by one of the following three methods, you should be able to open My Network Places on any Windows Me station in the workgroup (or domain) and be able to see an icon for the NT/2000 server. Also, when you are using the server browsers in either NT/2000's Print Manager or File Manager, you should now be able to see your Windows Me stations appear as additional servers in the workgroup (or domain), at least, those Me stations with file and/or printer sharing enabled.

Joining a Windows 2000 Server Domain

If your Windows Me or 9x computer is part of a Windows 2000 Server domain, you should install the Active Directory client so that you can take advantage of Active Directory's searching capabilities. (You won't get Windows 2000 Professional's management benefits, but you'll be able to find out how many color laser printers your company has in Japan, if you care to know.)

Generally, if you're part of an organization large enough to use Windows 2000 Server, you'll have a network administrator or support department to do this setup work for you. If you have to handle it yourself, though, here's what to do.

To install the Active Directory Client, you'll need to get a Windows 2000 Server CD-ROM disk. Then follow these steps:

1. Insert the Windows 2000 Server installation CD into your Windows Me computer's CD-ROM drive. When the Setup program asks if you would like to upgrade to Windows 2000, click No.

2. Click Browse This CD. Open the CLIENTS folder, then WIN9X.

3. Double-click DSCLIENT.EXE and click Next until the Wizard finishes.

4. When asked to restart the computer, remove the CD-ROM and click Yes.

When the Active Directory client has been installed, you must configure your Windows Me station to use the domain controller to validate usernames and passwords. To do this, follow these steps:

1. Open Control Panel ➢ Network (or right-click My Network Places and select Properties), then double-click Client for Microsoft Windows Networks.

2. Click the Log on to Windows NT Domain check box and type in the name of your NT/2000 domain in the Windows NT Domain text box (see Figure 28.1). Your network manager will tell you what your domain name is—you want the so-called "downlevel domain name."

NOTE Your network's downlevel network domain name will *not* be the same as your company's Internet domain name. It will not end in .com. In fact, it should not have any dots in it at all. Entering the domain name incorrectly is a common source of network logon problems. Be careful here!

3. Click OK.

4. Select the Identification tab and enter your network's downlevel domain name again under Workgroup. Then close the Network applet of the Control Panel and let Windows restart the computer.

FIGURE 28.1
Configuring a Windows Me station to log on to a Windows 2000 Server or Window NT Server domain

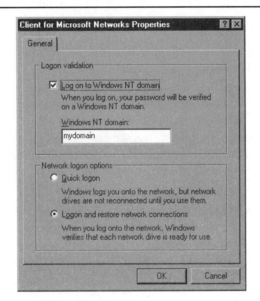

Do this on *each* of your Windows Me stations.

Joining a Windows NT 4.0 Server Domain

If your network is managed by Windows NT 4.0 Server, you don't need the Active Directory client. Otherwise, the procedure for setting your workstation to use the domain for network logons is similar to that for Windows 2000 Server. Follow the second set of steps 1 through 4 in the preceding section to set your network's domain name in each of your Windows Me stations.

Joining a Windows 2000 or NT Workgroup

If your network has no Windows NT/2000 servers—or if you have NT/2000 servers configured to be member servers and none is a domain controller—you just need to be sure you have the same workgroup name specified on the NT workstations as you do for each Windows Me station that will be part of this workgroup.

Do not check Log on to a Windows NT/2000 Domain under Client for Microsoft Networks Properties.

Sharing Resources on the Network

Once you're properly a member of the network, you can share resources with the rest of the network, and you can use shared resources from other computers.

Sharing Resources from Windows Me

Sharing resources from your Windows Me computer on a domain network is almost as easy as I described in Chapter 24.

First though, you should decide how you want to specify who has permission to use resources shared from your Window Me computer. Choose one of the following:

- Use share-level protection to assign a single password to each of your shared folders and/or printers. Any users wishing to use your shared folder will need to know the password. The password will be the same for all users. This is the only choice on a workgroup network, and you can leave the password blank on any type of network to grant unlimited access to everybody.

- Use user-level protection to let the Windows NT/2000 domain controller provide a list of users and groups so that you can specify which individuals can access your shared folders. Their own private network login and password will serve to identify them automatically. This is the best choice on a domain network if you want to use any sort of access control.

 NOTE To employ user-level protection, you must be part of a Windows NT/2000 domain or you must be using pass-through authentication with a Novell NetWare server.

To tell Windows which method you wish to use, open the Network applet on the Control Panel and select the Access Control tab. Select Share-Level Access Control to specify individual passwords, or User-Level Access Control to specify user/group access. If you choose user-level control, enter your network domain name as the source of valid user and group names (see Figure 28.2).

FIGURE 28.2
*Configuring Windows
Me to use user-level
access control*

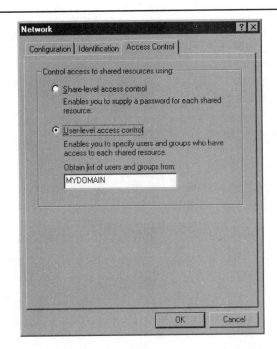

When you are finished adding user or group names, click OK. Then, use the instructions in Chapter 24 to share any drives, folders, and printers you want your Windows Me stations to access.

If you are using share-level access control, enter a password to protect each shared item. If you are using user-level access control, you'll see a new dialog box when you create a new network share, as shown in Figure 28.3.

FIGURE 28.3
User-level access control lets you specify which domain users/ groups can access the network resource.

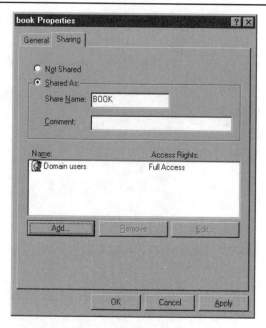

When you create a new network share, click Add. This will take you to the Add Users dialog box where you can specify which users and/or groups to grant read-only or full read-write access (see Figure 28.4). To specify users, select a name in the left-hand list, then click Read Only or Full Access. Add any additional names, then click OK. (For more information on setting file-sharing permissions, see "User-Level Security for NT and NetWare" in Chapter 27, "Advanced Networking.")

FIGURE 28.4
Adding access for Users and Groups

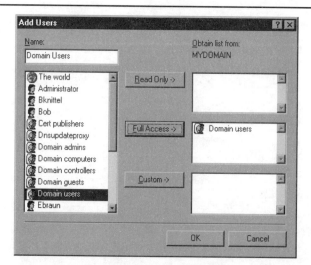

What user and group names would you select from the list on the left? Here are the most useful ones:

- Domain Users gives access to anyone in your organization with a valid login and password.
- Domain Admins gives access to network administrators.
- Specific group names limit access to validated members of a group, (e.g., Accounting or Engineering).
- Specific user names can be used to limit access to just the people you name.
- The World gives access to anybody with or without a password. Use this for folders you wish *anyone* to be able to see and for printers you'd let *anyone* use.

 WARNING If you grant The World access to shared folders, use Read-Only access. Don't add The World at all if you share your entire hard drive—just grant access to specific folders.

Sharing Resources from Windows NT/2000

When you are sharing resources from Windows NT/2000 workstations or servers, you'll use the standard Windows NT/2000 sharing procedures. Here they are in a nutshell:

1. Use Windows Explorer and right-click Sharing to share folders you want Windows Me stations to access.
2. Use NT/2000's My Computer ➢ Printers folder to share any printer(s) you want your Windows Me stations to access.
3. You will need to create a Windows NT/2000 user account for each Windows Me user who will need access to resources on an NT/2000 server or workstation. On an NT/2000 domain, use NT/2000's User Manager for Domains to create these accounts on the domain controller. On an NT/2000 workgroup, create a user account for *each* Windows Me user on *each* NT/2000 workstation that shares folders. Then set any desired user-level file restrictions using NT/2000's File Manager or Windows Explorer, and any desired printer or printing restrictions using NT's Print Manager.

PART

V

Networking

NOTE If your office has one or more Novell NetWare file or print servers and you are running NT/2000 Server, you can use the NT/2000 Printers folder to share NetWare print servers. You must first install and configure the NetWare Gateway Services software (supplied with NT/2000) and then connect to the NetWare print queue before trying to share it. In this way, Windows 9x/Me stations (and even DOS, Windows 3.1, and Windows for Workgroups stations) will not need Novell-specific network client software or drivers to use the Novell print queues or shared folders.

Using Shared Printers

One of the major benefits of using Windows NT/2000 or Windows Me is that they both provide the ability to connect to a network printer without installing a printer driver. Windows has the ability to automatically install printer drivers over the network when you first use a shared printer. When the printer is shared from a like operating system, your computer will automatically download the required printer drivers, making setup a snap. In addition, Windows 9x/Me users can automatically receive the correct drivers from Windows NT/2000 computers if they've been installed on the Windows NT/2000 computers as Alternate Drivers.

 NOTE Be sure that the administrators of the Windows NT/2000 workstations and servers install Windows Me and 9x Alternate Drivers on their computers so that you can take advantage of this automatic driver installation. This is done on the NT/2000 printers' Sharing properties page.

Mapping Windows Me and Windows NT/2000 Shared Drives

At this point, you might also wish to establish *persistent* drive mappings for the drives that are offered for share on either the NT/2000 server or your Windows Me stations, or both. This will allow you to always have the same drive letters assigned to shared drives (or folders).

In my opinion, the fastest and easiest way to map to any shared drive is to right-click the My Network Places icon (or Network Neighborhood, for Windows 9x and NT 4.0 users) and select the Map Network Drive option. In this dialog box, open the drop-down Drive list and select the drive letter you want the remote drive to map to (i.e., how the drive appears in your Explorer window). Then, in the lower box, enter the actual pathname of that drive as it appears on the network; thus, you must enter it in network drive syntax, which includes the computer name, in the format shown here:

  *machine_name**share_name*

For example, you might type **\\achilles\C** (no colon) if you are mapping a drive that is shared from a machine known as "achilles" on the network and whose C drive is shared by the name "C".

 NOTE Note that the Reconnect on Logon option is enabled by default; this is probably what you want. With this option on, whenever the workstation in question is booted up, it will automatically log in the remote drive and map it to the desired logical drive.

If you don't know the exact network pathname of the resource you are trying to map (for instance, if you want to map a shared folder rather than an entire drive), don't fret. My Network Places makes it easy to browse to and map a shared folder or drive. Try this approach:

1. Open My Network Places, either in Windows Explorer or from the Desktop. Drill down into Entire Network to find the desired computer.

2. Open the computer whose drive or folder you want to map for your use.

3. Now you'll see the list of folders and drives that the workstation has made public (i.e., has offered for sharing). Right-click the one you want to map, and choose Map Network Drive.

4. You'll see a box like the one shown below (in this example, I've mapped the drive from Windows Explorer):

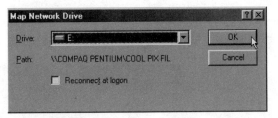

5. By default, the drive letter that is already entered for you is the next available letter; you can change it to another letter using the drop-down list.

PART

V

Networking

6. Enable the Reconnect at Logon check box if you want this mapping to be made automatically each time you boot up your machine. (This works only when the remote computer is already running.)

 NOTE If and when you ever need to disconnect from the remote drive, you can do it quite easily. Open My Network Places ➤ Tools ➤ Disconnect Network Drive, or right-click the mapped drive in Windows Explorer and choose Disconnect.

Using Windows Me on a Windows NT/2000 Network

Assuming your NT/2000 station is going to function primarily as a server, you will probably place some or all of your workgroup's most frequently accessed data on the NT/2000 station. You would do this to free up your workstations' loads somewhat and also to get the best performance because you now have a dedicated server. Just keep in mind that NT Workstation can only provide 10 simultaneous connections, so using it as a dedicated server will only work well for modest networks.

If your network uses Windows NT/2000 Server, when you start up Windows you'll be asked to enter your username and password *and* your domain name. Be sure to enter the correct Windows NT domain name when you log on.

Also, if you have Windows 2000 Server or Windows NT/2000 Server, your network administrator can also enable Roaming User Profiles. This feature stores your user settings and preferences (technically, for those of you who care: the HKEY_CURRENT_USER Registry hive) on the server, so that they appear the same on any computer you use. You can also have a Home Directory folder permanently mapped to a server location. Use this folder to store important files so that they'll always be available to you no matter which of your network's computers you use.

Searching Active Directory

If you are a member of a Windows 2000 Server network with Active Directory, you'll find two nifty additions to your Start button's Search menu: Printers and People.

To search for people in your organization, choose Start ➤ Search ➤ People. Under Look In, select Active Directory. Type in a name or e-mail address, then choose Find Now (see Figure 28.5).

FIGURE 28.5

Searching for a person in the organization using Active Directory

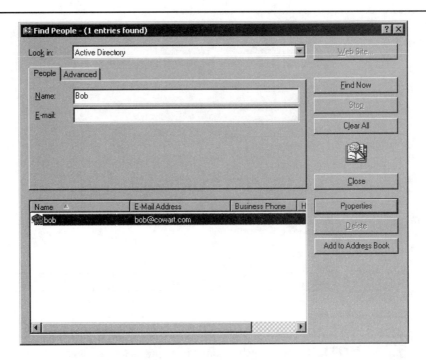

You can use the Advanced tab to set very specific search criteria like last name, phone numbers, etc.

To search for printers in your organization, choose Start ➤ Search ➤ Printers. Enter criteria for the specific type of printer you need, and choose Find Now, as shown in Figure 28.6.

FIGURE 28.6

Searching for a printer using Active Directory

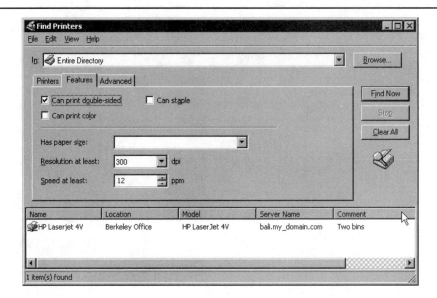

 NOTE If your searches turn up empty, select a different part of your organization's domain structure under In, at the top of the Find Printers dialog box. Sometimes searches don't work correctly when you choose Entire Directory.

If you find a printer you'd like to use, right-click it in the list of found printers and select Connect. Windows will automatically start the Add Printer Wizard to install it into your Printers folder.

CHAPTER 29

Advanced Dial-Up Networking

We've seen how to use Dial-Up Networking to connect to the Internet or to a corporate LAN (local area network), but we can do more than just that. Many connectivity options that used to be the domain of expensive, proprietary corporate set-ups are now simply built into Windows Me. It's all because of the desire for more speed, more connections, and more flexibility. Now, we expect to be able to use a laptop computer on the corporate LAN at work, and then take it home and dial into the Internet, or the office, or the computer next door. We expect Windows to take care of all of this for us. Plug-and-Play, tote and dial; it's all supposed to be effortless. And it is! (Well, almost.)

New Internet connection technologies such as cable modems (which connect through your television cable system), xDSL telephone, wireless, and satellite are spreading and changing daily. Most telephone and cable companies are aggressively deploying these high-speed Internet services throughout the country. These technologies will eventually completely replace Dial-Up Networking, but for the time being, modems are still useful for some important tasks.

In this chapter, we'll look at the following advanced dial-up connection topics:

- How to use ISDN (Integrated Services Digital Network) data service

- Using multiple modems for faster transfers

- Allowing another computer to dial in to yours

- Using Virtual Private Networking for secure, private networking over the Internet

- Creating scripted logins for unusual dial-up situations

Using ISDN Data Service

ISDN is a telephone technology that lets one telephone line carry up to two calls at once, with each call carrying either voice or data at 64Kbps in each direction. It also permits these channels to be combined into a single data connection at 128Kbps. How does ISDN differ from xDSL service? xDSL data service is usually run along a standard telephone line, over the same pair of wires that your telephone uses. The DSL (digital subscriber line) digital signal "rides" on top of the analog telephone voice signal. ISDN service, on the other hand, is entirely digital, whether it's carrying voice, data, or both. ISDN is a special type of service—standard telephones can't be plugged into this type of line—and is usually more expensive than an ordinary phone service.

When it was first introduced, the telephone industry thought that ISDN would take over the world, but it turned out to be too expensive for them to support and there wasn't enough demand to justify spreading it everywhere. Now the much faster and cheaper xDSL technologies have come along, so ISDN's role will remain limited to providing dial-up networking for businesses and providing Internet access for people too far from their telephone company's central office to use xDSL.

So, while ISDN is a waning technology, if you typically do heavy-duty data transfers and cable or xDSL service isn't available in your area, ISDN might be just what you need.

If you decide to look into ISDN service, you'll quickly find that using it is not as simple as installing and using an ordinary telephone and modem. As I first discussed in Chapter 20, "Connecting to the Internet," ISDN is a complex technology, and at first, it can be a bit daunting. Many telephone companies that offer ISDN service have formed partnerships with ISPs (Internet Service Providers) in their area to let you do one-stop shopping and setup. Your ISP might be able to order your phone line, deliver your equipment, and talk you through setup.

What Is ISDN?

ISDN stands for *Integrated Services Data Network*. An ISDN telephone line carries information strictly in digital form, in the same manner as the wire between your computer and your printer. An ISDN telephone turns your voice into digital information and sends it over the phone line to the phone company's office. An ISDN adapter doesn't need to convert a computer's binary information into sounds (like that screechy ordinary modem you have); instead, it can send the information directly as a digital signal.

The data stream between your house and the telephone company is broken into three parts, called *channels*, which can be used to carry on multiple connections. A basic ISDN line can carry two 64Kbps channels, called *B* or *bearer* channels, and one 16Kbps channel called the *D* or *data* channel. The B channels can carry transmissions that started out as analog or digital signals; that is, they can carry such transmissions as a voice conversation or a fax (analog), or they can carry a computer connection (digital). The D channel is used only to communicate information *about* the incoming and outgoing calls, and it is used just between the ISDN adapter and the telephone company.

How do they get three channels into one telephone wire? Well, imagine yourself at Disneyland, waiting for a roller coaster train, and there are three lines of people waiting to get on. Now imagine that the train has alternating rows of red and blue seats, with a row of green seats just every so often. The train conductor fills the red seats from one line, the blue seats from the second line, and the green seats from the third line. In just this way, the ISDN equipment sends bits of data for the three channels *B1*, *B2*, and *D* back and forth, like this:

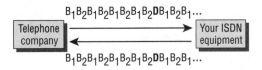

Since there are fewer green rows, the line for the green seats moves more slowly than the other two. If one of the lines becomes empty, the conductor just leaves the corresponding seats empty.

When the car stops at the other end of the ride, the conductor there sends the three groups of people out through three separate exit gates according to the color of their row. Similarly, the ISDN equipment at each end sorts the bits out as they arrive, keeping the three channels separate.

ISDN service can offer many additional features like caller ID, multiple phone numbers per incoming line, selective ringing of different telephone extensions, call transfer, and low-speed, always-connected data communication over the D channel.

An ISDN telephone line has two types of phone numbers: ordinary telephone numbers (seven digits plus area code) and *SPIDs (Service Profile Identifiers)*. There are typically two SPIDs per ISDN line. A SPID is a special ISDN telephone number, and in some cases, it can be used to select one particular extension telephone from several that are connected to the same phone line. You'll need to know both numbers to install your ISDN card.

Choosing the Equipment

Windows Me includes full support for most ISDN adapters on the market. Be sure to choose an ISDN adapter that has Windows Me support.

Which type of adapter should you choose? There are four questions you should consider when choosing an ISDN adapter: (1) Do you need a POTS jack? (2) Should you use a U or S/T interface? (3) Do you need an internal or external adapter? and (4) Is what you choose going to be compatible with your ISP's and phone company's equipment?

POTS Jack

Some ISDN adapters contain a jack into which you can plug a piece of ordinary telephone equipment, like a phone or fax. This is called a *POTS (plain old telephone service)* jack (see Figure 29.1 for a diagram of how this works). The adapter provides an analog signal to let the phone use one of ISDN's two B channels for phone calls.

FIGURE 29.1

An ISDN adapter with a POTS jack gives you an extra voice or fax line

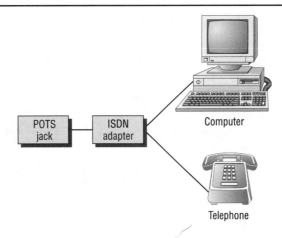

POTS jack — ISDN adapter — Computer — Telephone

If you're using this ISDN line for a home office, it might make sense to have a POTS jack to give you access to an extra voice or fax line. Since your ISDN adapter will probably *never* receive calls (unless you're setting it up as a *dial-up server*, which I will describe later in this chapter), you can put a fax machine on the POTS jack and give out the phone number for your ISDN's second channel for fax callers. In this way, you'll be getting a "free" phone line in addition to your data line. Even if you're using both data channels at the time a call comes in, the ISDN software should temporarily close one down, without interrupting your data connection, so that the incoming call can come through. (This is way cool!) One potential disadvantage, though, is that the ISDN adapter must be powered up for the phone to work.

U versus S/T Interface

ISDN wiring is done with ordinary telephone cable, but the equipment comes in two flavors: the "U" system uses one pair of wires, and the "S/T" system uses two pairs (Figure 29.2). With S/T wiring, you can plug more than one ISDN device into the same line, like extensions on an ordinary telephone line. But the wire coming from the telephone company is U, and converting the U wiring to S/T requires a device called an NT-1 (network terminator). The NT-1 requires AC power and costs close to $150. Plus, you need to worry about line length and termination resistance with S/T wiring. If you have only one ISDN device to plug into your line, the best bet is to get a U interface device. Look for an ISDN adapter that says it has a U interface, or one that says it has a built-in or internal NT-1.

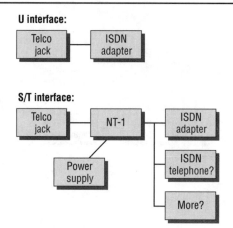

FIGURE 29.2

Comparing the U interface and the S/T interface

Internal versus External

ISDN adapters or modems, (or, to be technically precise: terminal adapters or TAs) like regular analog modems, come in two varieties: internal and external. On the one hand, external adapters have an edge over internals in that they are portable. On the other hand, external ISDN adapters use one of your computer's COM ports, so there could be data loss if the port doesn't use up-to-date electronics or a special high-speed serial card. Ordinary COM ports on PCs can have a hard time keeping up with data transfers at the speed of an ISDN adapter, which can transfer data at a rate up to 128Kbps, or even faster with compression enabled. If you choose to use an external IDSN modem, check the documentation for your computer's COM ports to be sure that they can handle data over 128K. You want to see that the motherboard or serial card has a 16550 or 16660 UART chip. If not, you'll need to get a new high-speed serial card at your computer store.

Also, there is a fundamental difference in the way Windows treats internal versus external ISDN adapters. External adapters are treated as ordinary modems, and they are expected to handle *all* of the details of communicating with the data communication equipment on the other end of a data phone call. Multilinking (using both data channels for higher speed), phone company configuration, compression negotiation, and connection management are all done by the adapter and are out of Windows' purview. This is an advantage for external adapters, because they can automatically add or drop the second B channel as your data transfer rates rise and fall, and you can install, set up, and use them just as you would an ordinary modem, as covered in Chapter 26, "Extending Your Reach with Dial-Up Networking."

Internal adapters, on the other hand, are treated as if they were LAN cards. While these can be trickier to install, Windows handles all details of configuring the card, managing its data channels, and so on. Windows' management of the second B channel is not as elegant as with an external adapter because Windows will not automatically add or drop the second channel. But Windows can manage voice calls on the adapter using Windows Telephony software. Finally, an internal adapter is plugged right into the computer's bus, doesn't use a COM port, and has no transfer rate problems. So, while external adapters are easier to configure and install, internal adapters have a slight edge in the extra features they can make available.

Compatibility

Most ISDN adapters allow you to use both of ISDN's 64Kbps B channels at the same time, for a throughput of 128Kbps (or more, with compression). The way that your adapter negotiates for this extra channel must be compatible with the ISDN equipment on the other end. The adapter box or specifications will list the protocol it supports. You will see this described as Bonding, MP, MPP, RFC1717, etc. Make sure your ISP supports the same one. Also, see if your ISP supports compression over the ISDN line, and make sure your adapter supports the same compression type. Most adapters advertise either *Stac* or *Ascend* compression. You'll need to ask your ISP what kind of equipment they use, and you should check with the adapter vendor to make sure that they guarantee that the adapter will work with your ISP's equipment because there seem to be many compatibility problems with compression. Also, some ISPs will not enable compression because their service is priced for ISDN's base data rate and they don't want you to exceed that.

Discuss all of these features with your ISP before purchasing your adapter. When you set up your ISP account, you will need to get the following information:

- The dial-in number for ISDN service
- Your login name and password
- The compression type (if any)
- Whether multilink (or "2B," meaning both-B-channel) service is supported and any extra charges it incurs
- The B channel data rate: 64Kbps or 56Kbps

Getting ISDN Telephone Service

An ISDN phone line is a very different animal than a regular phone line (or a POTS line, in telephone company jargon). Getting one ordered and installed can be a real headache! There is a confusing variety of classes of service that determine whether your line will be using one or two high-speed B channels and whether these channels will carry voice, data, or both. It's best to work with your ISP to coordinate the installation of your line; many ISPs can handle the ordering process for you at no additional charge. Unless there's a reason to do otherwise, you will probably get *2B+D voice and 64K data* service.

When the line is installed, the telephone company will send an ISDN-experienced installer to set up and test your line, but only to the point where the line enters your house. You're responsible for getting the line from there to your computer. One pair of a standard twisted-pair phone cables will work for U wiring. The line must end in an eight-conductor modular jack. If you have someone else install the inside jack for you, be sure they are familiar with ISDN.

 NOTE IMPORTANT! There is no dial tone on an ISDN line, just a DC voltage. (Even telephone company repair people have thought that an ISDN line was broken because of this!) If you plug an ordinary phone into an ISDN jack, you won't hear anything.

Be sure to clearly label the jack *ISDN ONLY*. It's also a good idea to mark the telephone company's demarcation box, and red-tag the line on any punch blocks in wiring closets.

When your line is installed, be sure that your telephone company installer gives you the following information:

- Switch type (for example, ESS5 or DMS 100)
- SPID numbers for each B channel
- Telephone number(s)
- Circuit number, or frame or loop identification
- Service/repair phone number for ISDN problems

Write all that information down and keep it handy. You'll need the first three pieces of info to install your adapter, and the other two are handy if there is ever trouble with the line.

Installing an External ISDN Adapter

An external adapter is treated just like an ordinary modem as far as Windows is concerned. Install it just as you would any other modem for Dial-Up Networking. Use the Add New Hardware applet on the Control Panel to install the adapter, using the instructions that are provided by the manufacturer. When you define a Dial-Up Networking connection, enter the ISDN phone number provided by your ISP.

Installing an Internal ISDN Adapter

An internal ISDN adapter is installed like a network card. First, install the hardware following the manufacturer's instructions. Most ISDN adapters are Plug-and-Play compatible, so jumper settings probably won't be needed. Then, follow the software setup instructions provided by your manufacturer. The procedure will go something like this: When you've inserted the card and restarted your computer, Windows will detect the new hardware and install any needed driver software. If this doesn't happen (as it doesn't with my ancient US Robotics Sportster ISDN card), you may need to use the Add New Hardware applet (from the Control Panel), and from the dialog box that opens, you will need to click the Have Disk button to install the drivers.

You may need to choose between one of several similar drivers for your ISDN terminal adapter, depending on the type of data protocols used in your country and/or by your ISP. The choices usually involve choosing between PPP, V.120, and X.75 for the protocol; and between U.S. and European ISDN signaling standards. If your adapter offers such a choice, your ISP will be able to tell you which to use. In the United States, PPP is almost always used.

Then, if Windows doesn't automatically start up the ISDN Configuration Wizard (Figure 29.3), start the Wizard using Start ➤ Programs ➤ Accessories ➤ Communications ➤ ISDN Configuration Wizard.

PART
V

Networking

FIGURE 29.3
The ISDN Configuration Wizard's Switch Type choices

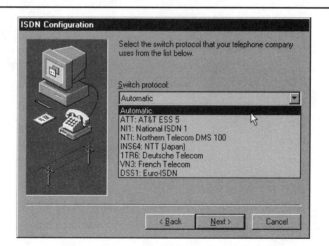

The ISDN Configuration Wizard asks for the information provided by the telephone company (as described at the end of the previous section). If you didn't get it from your phone company installer, your ISP might be able to give you this information and be able to tell you exactly what to enter for Windows Me. You might be successful leaving the Switch type set to Automatic, which means the ISDN software will attempt to determine what kind of equipment the telephone company is using. The second Wizard screen (see Figure 29.4) asks for the telephone numbers and SPIDs. Sometimes the adapter can automatically determine them, so you might not need to type them in. But if you do, just enter whatever the installer gave you. Generally the installer gives you two phone numbers and two SPIDs; the SPIDs will be very similar to the phone numbers.

TIP Sometimes the telephone company doesn't use phone numbers, just SPIDs, for configuring ISDN connections. So it may be that you won't need to enter phone numbers here. However, some adapters need you to enter the phone numbers anyway in order to have the software automatically determine the switch type and the SPIDs.

FIGURE 29.4
The ISDN Configuration Wizard's telephone and SPID entries

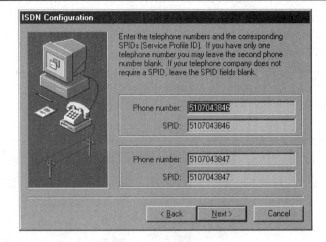

The next Wizard screen just contains a Finish button. When you press this, Windows will restart after completing the installation. If you also have a LAN connection in your computer, you might want to remove any unnecessary bindings between different network protocols and your LAN and ISDN adapters. See Chapter 27, "Advanced Networking," for more on this.

 NOTE Once the ISDN adapter driver is installed, it will appear as an installed network component in the Network applet on the Control Panel, not as a modem in the Modems applet. Nevertheless, it will be available as one of the devices you can choose to use when making a new Dial-Up Networking connection.

If you need to change the ISDN parameters after installation, you can run the ISDN Wizard again from Start ➢ Programs ➢ Accessories ➢ Communications.

TIP If your ISDN card came with software that includes a diagnostic test program, try running it now. Since there is no dial tone and no modem noise with ISDN, it's impossible to tell by ear what's wrong if your dial-up connection doesn't work. Without the diagnostic program, you won't be able to tell for sure whether it's the line, the card, the software, the phone number, or the password. A diagnostic program will check everything all the way up to the ISP to verify that everything's working.

Now, in Dial-Up Networking , select Make a New Connection. You will see that two dial-up devices have been added to your system; these correspond to the two available 64Kbps B channels on the ISDN card.

1. Select the first B channel on your card as your device (Figure 29.5).

FIGURE 29.5
*Selecting the ISDN card
for Dial-Up Networking*

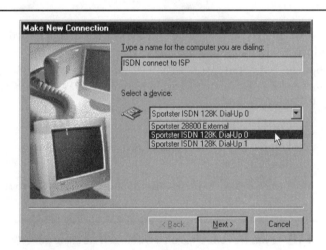

2. Your ISP will tell you if you should connect at 64Kbps or if your service is limited to 56Kbps (some phone companies limit ISDN calls that go through more than one central office to 56Kbps). If you are limited to 56K, click Configure and select 56K Data as the speed preference. Otherwise leave it at 64K.

3. Click Next. Enter the area code and telephone number of the ISDN connection. Your ISP will give you this information.

4. Click Next, and then click Finish to save the new connection.

Now, select the connection. Windows will display the Connect To dialog box, as shown in Figure 29.6.

FIGURE 29.6

The Connect To dialog box for ISDN

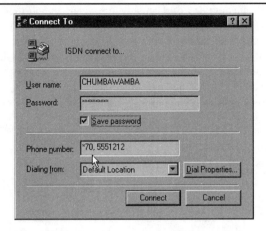

I've entered my username and password, but look: My dialing properties setup has added *70 to the phone number to disable call-waiting! This is great for regular modems but doesn't work with ISDN. If you have call-waiting on your regular modem line, enter a new dialing location for your ISDN calls, *without* call-waiting. To do this, follow these steps:

1. Click Dial Properties and New.

2. Enter **ISDN** as the I Am Dialing From location, and uncheck the Call Waiting box. Click OK.

Now the Connect To box will not add *70. Click OK to test your ISDN connection.

TIP If you are connected on a LAN to servers using the IPX or NetBEUI protocols when you make the dial-up connection, the dial-up manager may inform you that these servers will not be available during the dial-up connection. These protocols don't tolerate multiple simultaneous connections. NetWare LANs have this limitation, for example. If they are not needed, you can unbind these protocols from the dial-up adapter to prevent this from happening; see Chapter 27 for more information on this.

If your ISP account permits you to have 128Kbps access using two B channels, and you want to use this feature (usually it comes at an extra cost), you can use *multilinking* to get that extra speed. In the next section, we'll explain how this works, but here's the bottom line for ISDN:

1. In Dial-Up Networking (Start ➢ Settings ➢ Dial-Up Networking) select the dial-up connection and right-click Properties. Click the Multilink tab.

2. Click the Use Additional Devices radio button.

3. Click the Add button.

4. Under Device Name, select the second channel of the ISDN card. Under Phone Number, enter the ISDN telephone number of the dial-in server again. Click OK.

Bingo, you should now have 128Kbps access.

Multilinking Modems

I'll bet you still have a 1200 baud modem in a drawer somewhere, which was a godsend at the time you got it. Finally, you could transfer e-mail faster than you could read it. Now you have the latest 56K baud modem and it's not fast enough! You want more speed! You *need* more speed! There are faster technologies available, like ISDN, cable modems, satellite downlink, and xDSL, but they can be expensive to install and use. How about just using more modems? Don't laugh: It's possible! This process is loosely referred to as *ganging modems*, and uses a protocol called *Multilink Channel Aggregation (MCA)*.

Managing an Internet connection with multiple modems is actually a complex problem. Internet data is sent between computers using an addressing scheme known as *IP numbering*. Each computer on the Internet has an IP number that is used as a data delivery address, just as a street address is used to deliver mail. When you connect to an ISP, your modem is given an IP number for the duration of your call. Using this IP number, the Internet can deliver data to your computer from anywhere in the world. Now, if you simply installed two dial-up adapter modems and used each to call your ISP (as shown in Figure 29.7), the two dial-up adapters would each have a different IP number (here, I called them 1.2.3.4 and 1.2.3.5).

If you were using Internet Explorer to download the latest demo program from Microsoft, Internet Explorer could use only one IP-number-to-IP-number connection to get a given file, and so it could use only one of the two modems. At the same time, although it *could* use the other modem to download a different file, it would have to be programmed specifically to try this, and it still would not speed up the download of just a single file.

What MCA does is make both modems share one IP number, and it then uses both to send data simultaneously (see Figure 29.8). Your programs don't need to even know this happens. But do remember that this does require the other end of your modem connection to be in on the arrangement as well.

The software in your computer and at the Internet provider have to know that data arriving through either modem is for the same IP address (1.2.3.4 in this example). Both ends use whichever modem is free at a given moment to send the next data packet.

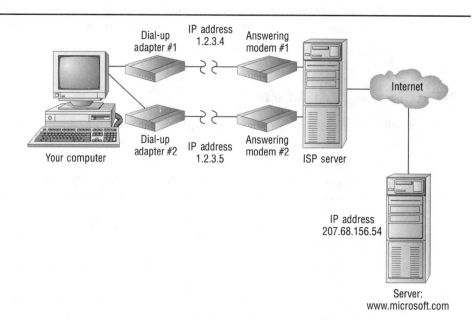

FIGURE 29.7
Using two dial-up adapters: close but no cigar

PART
V

Networking

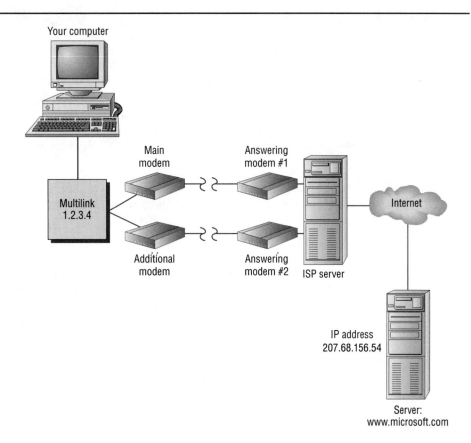

FIGURE 29.8
Multilinked modems share the load

Your computer

Main modem

Answering modem #1

Multilink 1.2.3.4

Additional modem

Answering modem #2

ISP server

Internet

IP address 207.68.156.54

Server: www.microsoft.com

The tricky part is that when your computer makes the *second* call, it must communicate to the other side that it wishes to add a modem to an existing connection, rather than to establish an ordinary connection with a distinct IP number. This is what the Multilink Channel Aggregation Protocol (IETF standard RFC 1717) does. It extends the Point-to-Point Protocol (PPP) to allow a dial-up server to negotiate this new type of connection. The extended protocol allows any number of connection devices to be multilinked, and it allows either end to request that connections be added and dropped as communication needs change.

Bound to Get Better

If you are familiar with ISDN networking, you may remember that even older ISDN software allowed both of ISDN's data channels to be *bound* into one high-speed connection. However, the negotiation procedure was unique to each vendor's software. Several protocols were developed, but only the Multilink Protocol (MP) has emerged as the common standard that is supported by all vendors. MP is designated RFC 1717 by the international Internet Engineering Task Force (IETF).

MP generalizes multilinking to *all* types of connections, including combinations of ISDN, leased lines, and standard analog modems connected to the same dial-up server.

Not many ISPs use equipment with the necessary software to provide MCA service with ordinary analog modems, but some do. If you are calling a Microsoft Windows NT/2000 Server dial-up server, it *does* have the ability to make this type of connection. Microsoft says that, using four 33.6K modems, you can transfer at 134Kbps! (If you're paying for four telephone lines at each end of this type of connection, this might not be as economical as ISDN.) Of course, ISPs will charge you for multilinking since you'll be utilizing two of their incoming phone lines.

If you have determined that multilinking is available for the service provider you use, it's a snap to install.

First, verify that the protocol that your remote connection server supports is the RFC 1717 Multilink access. Get the telephone numbers of the remote access server line(s) you will be using from the system administrator. All of the multilink connections must be made to the same server because the data packets must be collated within one router before being forwarded on to other IP addresses. Then follow the appropriate set of steps below.

Multilinking Analog Modems

To set up Multilink operation for a standard dial-up connection, follow these steps:

1. Install and test an ordinary dial-up connection using one modem, as described in Chapter 26.

2. Install an additional modem using the Add New Hardware applet on the Control Panel.

3. Click Start ➤ Settings ➤ Dial-Up Networking. Select the tested dial-up connection, and right-click Properties.

4. Click the Multilink tab (Figure 29.9). Set the Use Additional Devices option, and click the Add button.

5. Select the secondary modem from the list of installed modems. Enter the appropriate telephone number for the second modem in your target dial-up server (this will be the same as the original modem if your dial-up provider uses a "rollover" telephone bank). Click OK.

FIGURE 29.9
Adding a second modem for a dial-up connection

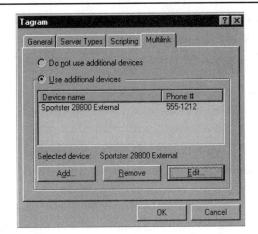

 TIP You can actually add as many modems as you like (and as your dial-up provider will allow).

Multilinking External ISDN Adapters

External ISDN adapters manage multilink connections by themselves, without Windows even knowing about it. If your adapter and ISP support multilink connections (the use of both B channels together), your adapter's instructions will tell you how to configure a multilink connection. In some cases, all you need to do is enter your ISP's telephone number twice as the number to dial.

 TIP If your ISP and/or local telephone company charge quite a bit more for a two-B-channel connection, here's a way to manage your spending. Set up two connections in Dial-Up Networking: Name one of them **One Channel** and configure it for just one B channel (that is, using just one phone number), and name the other **Two Channels** and configure it for two B channels. Then you can use the One Channel connection whenever you want to be sure you're not spending the extra fees for a higher-speed connection.

PART
V

Networking

External ISDN adapters can *dynamically* add or drop a second connection as your data transfer rates rise and fall. Because phone companies charge a certain amount to establish a call and then charge by the minute, it's best for the adapter not to make and drop the second connection too frequently—you could end up paying more in "first minute" charges than you save in overall connection time. The adapter will probably be installed with sensible default settings, but the software that accompanies the adapter may let you adjust the timing, if you wish. There are two settings you should be able to change. Here's how to compute the best values to use:

Time before making second connection, when data rate exceeds 64K (carrying capacity of one channel)   You can leave this at the default setting. If your main use for Dial-Up Networking is transferring large files, you might shorten it to no less than 10 seconds.

Time before dropping second connection, when data rate falls below 64K   Compute the following number:

- The number of cents charged for the *first minute* of an ISDN call

- Minus the cents per minute charged by the ISP for the second channel

and multiply that difference by 60. Then divide that product by the following number:

- The cents that would be charged for an *additional minute* of an ISDN call

- Plus the cents per minute charged by ISP for the second channel

If the resulting quotient is zero or negative, use the lowest allowable value for this setting. If the quotient is positive, enter it as the number of seconds to wait before dropping the second connection.

Multilinking Internal ISDN Adapters

To set up Multilink service for an internal ISDN adapter, follow these steps:

1. Install the ISDN card and configure a dial-up connection as described in Chapter 26. This will make connections only through the card's first B channel. Test the ISDN connection this way first.

2. In Dial-Up Networking, select this dial-up connection and right-click Properties.

3. Click the Multilink tab. Set the Use Additional Devices option, and click the Add button.

4. Under Device name, select the second channel of the ISDN card. Under Phone Number, enter the ISDN telephone number of the dial-in server again. Click OK.

If you have two ISDN cards, you can add two more entries for the second card as well. This could give you up to four B channels, or 256Kbps data service. You can actually mix a combination of multiple ISDN and/or standard modems as long as they are all supported by and connect to the same connection server. Your network administrator or dial-up provider can tell you if this is possible.

That's it. Now, when you select this dial-up connection, your computer will dial through the first modem and establish the first channel and then the second. You can manually disconnect either or both "channels" using the Dial-Up Connection control in your Taskbar's System Tray.

 TIP Internal ISDN adapters do not offer the "dynamic control" that is offered by external adapters (described earlier). External modems have a distinct edge here.

Setting Up a Dial-Up Networking Server

Windows Me contains a Dial-Up Networking Server component that lets you enable an installed modem to *receive* Dial-Up Networking calls. A calling computer will have access to files and printers you have shared on your computer using file sharing for Microsoft or NetWare networks. You can use this feature to dial in to your office computer from home, for example. From there you can transfer files, connect to your office network's servers, or use remote-control software to run applications on other computers (Figure 29.10).

However, it does *not* support TCP/IP networking, so you can't use it to access the Internet or an intranet, your Personal Web Server, or any other network resources available solely through the TCP/IP protocol. (If you had visions of using this to set up your own ISP business, you're out of luck. You'll have to buy Windows 2000 Server do to that.)

FIGURE 29.10
*Using Dial-Up
Networking and Dial-
Up Server to connect to
a Windows Me
computer*

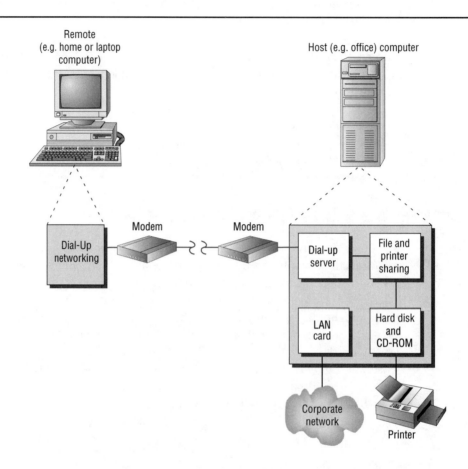

Although the host computer needs to be using Windows Me, the remote computer does not. It can use any operating system with IPX or NetBEUI over PPP or Windows RAS support, such as Windows for Workgroups, Windows 9x, Me, or Windows NT/2000, or some third-party routers called "remote access servers."

 WARNING If the computer you propose to use as your host is connected to a company LAN, be sure to check with your network administrator to see if your company permits users to set up dial-in access to their computers! In some companies, you could be fired for compromising established security policies. At the very least, your network administrator might want to confirm that your computer is properly protected by passwords.

Setting Up the Dial-Up Server

To establish a Dial-Up Networking server, you must have already installed Dial-Up Networking and configured at least one modem. Then follow these steps:

1. In Control Panel, start Add/Remove Programs and select the Windows Setup tab.

2. Highlight Communications and click Details.

3. Scroll down the list of components and be sure "Dial-Up Server" is checked. If it isn't, check it. Close the dialog boxes and Control Panel. Windows may ask you to insert your Windows Me CD-ROM and restart.

4. Select Start ➤ Settings ➤ Dial-Up Networking.

5. Select Connections ➤ Dial-Up Server from the menu.

6. The Dial-Up Server control dialog box will appear (Figure 29.11). If you have more than one modem installed, click the tab for the modem you wish to use to receive networking calls.

7. Enable Dial-Up Server by clicking Allow Caller Access.

8. If you wish to protect your computer from remote access by unauthorized users (and you should), click Change Password. Invent a password and enter it in the New Password and Confirm New Password boxes. Click OK. (This password will be used just to decide whether to permit a remote caller to make a connection to your computer. In addition, the caller will be required to supply any other required usernames and passwords to use any shared drives or printers on your computer or your office network.)

PART

V

Networking

FIGURE 29.11
Dial-Up Server
configuration

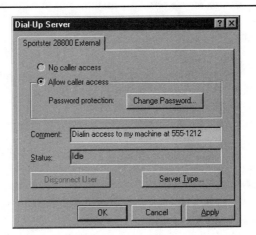

WARNING Be sure that you have also set passwords for any drives and printers you've enabled for sharing! Anyone with your modem's phone number will be able to dial in to your computer!

9. Click Server Type. Then check out the following situations for any that apply to you:

  • If you will be using Windows 98, Me, or NT/2000 to dial in, click Server Type and select Default. (Enable Software Compression and Require Encrypted Password are selected by default, and you should leave them checked.)

  • If you will be calling this computer from a computer running Windows for Workgroups or Windows NT 3.1, click Type of Dial-Up Server and select the appropriate entry. This mode does not permit software compression or encrypted passwords.

  • If you will be using TCP/IP networking and/or file sharing using Windows Me or Windows NT/2000, leave the Server Type set to PPP.

  • If you will *only* be using some version of Microsoft Windows 9*x*, Me, or NT/2000 to dial in, you can improve security by checking Require Encrypted Password.

10. Click OK to close the Server Types window, then OK again to close Dial-Up Server.

 Windows will now test the modem and tell it to answer calls from remote computers. A small icon will appear in your Desktop System Tray, showing that the dial-up server is active. It will remain active even if you close Dial-Up Networking, and will restart every time you reboot your computer. Double-click this tray icon to bring up the Dial-Up Server dialog box at any time.

 NOTE The dial-up server will remain active until you use the Dial-Up Server dialog box to check No Caller Access.

The modem will now answer all calls on its telephone line. Unless you're using an ISDN line, be sure no other devices, such as fax machines or answering machines, are plugged into the same line; otherwise more than one of them might answer your remote computer's calls! If you need to share an analog phone line with a fax machine, get yourself a device called a *fax switch* (about $60 U.S.) to answer and route calls to the appropriate device. (These devices cannot be used for ISDN lines. If you are using an ISDN adapter that provides a POTS jack, you can leave a fax machine plugged into the

POTS adapter with no problems because the POTS line uses the second ISDN telephone number while the modem answers only the first.)

Connecting to the Dial-Up Server

To connect to your computer's dial-up server, the caller needs to know the modem's telephone number and file-sharing usernames and passwords for your computer.

If your computer uses user-level security for its file sharing, the caller should use their normal Windows username and password to connect to your computer. Windows will check their username against the network's login list.

If your computer uses share-level security, they can use any login name, but must use the password you assigned to the dial-up server.

Managing the Dial-Up Server

You can display the dial-up server status at any time by selecting the Dial-Up Server icon in your Taskbar's System Tray. Under Status, Windows will say Monitoring while it's waiting for a call, Answering while it's negotiating a new remote connection, and Connected when someone is using the dial-up connection. You can force them off your machine at any time by clicking the Disconnect User button. You can turn off dial-up access by selecting No Caller Access.

Scripting Your Connections

When you establish a dial-up connection, it's usually necessary to identify yourself to the computer on the other end of the call. It's necessary for security and maybe billing purposes. Windows Dial-Up Networking asks you for a username and password when you make a dial-up connection. There are standard protocols for passing this information on, and Dial-Up Networking can usually communicate them properly to the equipment on the other end. Windows NT/2000 Remote Access Service, Windows Me Dial-Up Server, and most Internet PPP servers will work "right out of the box."

However, you might run into a situation where the built-in protocols simply don't work to get the connection going. This can occur, for instance, in some older dial-up server systems that require a human-readable sign-on process for the login and password, and only then permit PPP to start. These may be called *shell accounts*, may just be due to old equipment or software, or may occur when special national or international data carriers are used, such as CompuServe, Tymnet, or Interspan.

If you find that your dial-up connections fail after the modems have made a proper connection because Windows can't continue through the authentication procedure, you might be running into one of the situations described in the previous paragraph. If that's the case, contact your network provider for detailed login instructions. Ask if

PART

V

Networking

they have a Windows Me *dial-up script* (SCP file). If they can provide one, you're set... just copy it into a folder on your computer and then, in Dial-Up Networking, do the following:

1. Right-click Properties on the Dial-Up Networking connection.

2. Select the Scripting tab (Figure 29.12).

3. Enter the path and filename for the script file, or use the Browse button to find it and click Open.

4. If you want to watch the sign-on procedure the first few times to see if it works, uncheck the Start Terminal Screen Minimized option.

5. Click OK.

Then try the connection again. If it fails, you will see what the remote computer and your computer sent to each other, and you can report this to your network provider for assistance. You can also check the Step Through Script option to watch each script step occur one at a time.

FIGURE 29.12

Enabling a dial-up script

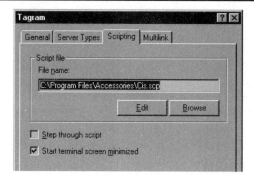

Writing a Dial-Up Script

Instructions for writing a script are beyond the scope of this book. However, if you're familiar with such things, you can look at the sample script files provided with Windows Me. The scripts included with Windows Me are in \Program Files\Accessories; they're listed here in Table 29.1.

TABLE 29.1: DIAL-IN SCRIPTS INCLUDED WITH WINDOWS ME

Name	Description
Cis	Logs in to CompuServe using the specified username and password, then establishes a PPP Internet connection
Pppmenu	Logs in to a menu-based Internet provider and activates PPP
Slip	Logs in to a SLIP protocol server
Slipmenu	Logs in to a menu-based Internet provider and activates SLIP

These four scripts demonstrate how to look for remote prompts, reply to them, send names and passwords, and retry in the case of failures. It's likely that you can modify one of these scripts to meet your needs.

There is online documentation for dial-up scripting commands. Use WordPad to open \Windows\Script.doc. Note that the documentation is only a reference and assumes you already understand how to write this kind of script program.

When you encounter a system that requires a script to manage its connection sequence, my recommendation is to connect manually the first time, and write down the prompts the remote system gives you and the responses you must make. (Let's hear it for the high-tech pencil-and-paper recording system!) Only then should you try to write a script to handle the connection sequence.

An Example Script

To show you what is possible, here is one of the scripts supplied with Windows, with comments describing what it does. This PPPMENU.SCP script is used to connect to an ISP whose equipment requires you to log in and select from a menu. In networking lingo, this is often called a *"shell account."* Since you don't want to have to manually navigate through this menu every time you connect, you can use this script to read the menu and make the choices for you.

PPPMENU.SCP

This script file demonstrates how to establish a PPP connection with a host that uses a menu system. If you wanted to, you could use the following lines of code in sequence and have a working script (that is, after you replaced the prompt strings and the connect string with appropriate ones of your own). However, it's not meant to serve as a tutorial on how to write a script; rather, I want to demonstrate some of the types of things you can do with a script. For example, they can send strings, look for strings, use "if...then" and looping statements, etc.

Part V — Networking

Every script file must have a main procedure. All script execution starts with this main procedure:

```
proc main
```

Next we set up a counter to limit the number of attempts to get the menu, and variables to hold the prompts we expect from the called equipment. nLoginTimeOut is the number of seconds to wait for the login prompt:

```
integer nTries = 3
string szLogin = "username:"
integer nLoginTimeout = 3
```

This is the password prompt we expect, and a typical timeout value:

```
string szPW = "password:"
integer nPWTimeout = 3
```

This ISP prints a menu list like this once your password is verified:

```
1              : Our special GUI
2              : Establish slip connection
3              : Establish PPP connection
4              : Establish shell access
5              : Download our software
6              : Exit
  Choose:
```

This is the prompt once your password is verified:

```
string szPrompt = "Choose:"
```

This is the command to send to establish the connection. "^M" means Control-M, which is the Enter key.

```
string szConnect = "3^M"
```

SLIP is an older protocol; you shouldn't use it if you can help it. Use PPP if at all possible.

```
boolean bUseSlip = FALSE
```

Here goes...

Delay for 2 seconds first to make sure the host doesn't get confused when we send the two carriage returns:

```
delay 2
transmit "^M^M"
```

Attempt to log in at most nTries times:

```
while 0 < nTries do
```

Wait for the login prompt before entering the user ID, time out after *x* seconds:

```
        waitfor szLogin then DoLogin
            until nLoginTimeout
TryAgain:
```

Hit Enter again to request the menu:

```
    transmit "^M"
    nTries = nTries - 1
endwhile
```

We have failed. Let the user try manual connection:

```
goto BailOut
```

DoLogin:

We get here after we see the login prompt. At this point, we send the $USERID string, which is your login name. (You entered your UserID and password when you started the Connection process. Dial-Up Networking makes them available to the script as $USERID and $PASSWORD):

```
    transmit $USERID, raw
    transmit "^M"
```

Wait for the password prompt:

```
    waitfor szPW until nPWTimeout
    if FALSE == $SUCCESS then
        goto TryAgain
    endif
```

Send the password:

```
    transmit $PASSWORD, raw
    transmit "^M"
```

Wait for the menu prompt:

```
    waitfor szPrompt
```

Send the Establish PPP Connection choice:

```
    transmit szConnect
    if bUseSlip then
```

The SLIP protocol must get the IP address from a text message sent by the remote machine (this is one reason why SLIP is not desirable):

```
        set ipaddr getip 2
    endif
```

Connection should be established now. The script is finished:

```
    goto Done
```

In case something did not respond, we must halt the script and let the user log in manually. Hence, this final section is appended:

```
BailOut:
    set screen keyboard on
    halt
Done:
endproc
```

Using Point-to-Point Tunneling to Create a Virtual Private Network

If you've set up a dial-up server on your computer, you've probably worried about unauthorized or even malicious people calling into your computer and doing...well, who knows what! When a computer is accessible from the outside world, security becomes a very serious concern. Modems are bad enough, but connecting to the Internet provides a direct wire through which hundreds of millions of people can get at your computer. Although very few would probably be interested in my computer, or maybe yours, for larger companies, the risk is much greater since there could be sensitive information at stake. *Virtual Private Networking* can protect a network from intruders while still allowing access by authorized users via modem or over the Internet.

How Tunneling Works

Suppose you have a large office building and you're worried about receiving fraudulent or insulting mail. Anyone can drop a letter with your address into any mailbox, and as long as they've taken the trouble to spend 33 cents on a stamp, the postal service will deliver it to you. If all your workers work inside, you could protect them by simply not permitting any mail to enter the building at all. Now *that's* security! But suppose you have a sales force working all over the world. You need to let them send their orders in, so you have to let the mail service deliver mail. But by permitting the post office to deliver mail to your office, you allow other people to send you mail as well.

A network like the Internet works the same way: A data packet can be sent from any IP address to any other. If you want to let trusted people communicate, you expose your network to the entire population on the Internet.

Here's a solution using ordinary mail. Your outside salesperson takes a letter she wants to send to you, puts it inside a big red envelope, seals it with a lock, and then mails it. At your office, a guard stands at the door of the mailroom. The guard accepts only letters in these special red envelopes and discards all other mail outright. Then the locks are opened with the secret key. If the key works, then the inside letters are removed and passed into the building. Outgoing mail is handled the same way: Every letter is locked inside a red envelope and mailed. The outside staff knows that any letter in one of these special envelopes came from the office and can be trusted if their key opens the lock.

The *Point-to-Point Tunneling protocol* (PPTP) does exactly this with network data. Every data packet destined for a secured network is encrypted with a digital key and sent inside a special tunneling protocol packet. After the Internet delivers this packet to the protected network, a *gateway* computer decodes the enclosed data, verifies that it is from an authorized user, and if so, passes it through to the protected network. Only the gateway computer is connected directly to the Internet, so the computers on the protected network can only be reached through the gateway, and only through properly encrypted packets.

While these protected computers are invisible to the outside world, a computer using PPTP can send data in to them, and in fact has an IP number that makes it *part* of the protected network. We say that the outside computer has a *tunnel* to the protected network. While part of the connection is through the public Internet, both ends of the tunnel are, for all practical purposes, inside the private network. So, this is called a *Virtual Private Network*, or *VPN*. Figure 29.13 shows how a VPN looks in use.

When the tunnel is connected, the VPN software in the remote computer is assigned an IP number from the protected network (here, 192.168.0.121). This IP number is not part of the worldwide Internet—in fact, it's an illegal number on the Internet. The dial-up connection through the ISP, though, is addressed as 209.5.73.62. The dial-up adapter on the remote computer can send and receive anywhere in the world using this address. At the protected network, only the gateway connection 205.149.0.33 is visible. The protected computer's 192.168.0.35 is not. The gateway computer would simply discard any packet arriving from the Internet addressed to 192.168.0.*anything*, as it could not possibly be legitimate.

FIGURE 29.13
*A Virtual Private
Network using Point-to-
Point tunneling*

Computer using VPN:

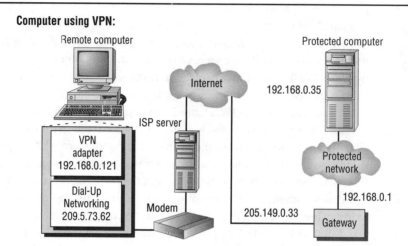

Works as if it were:

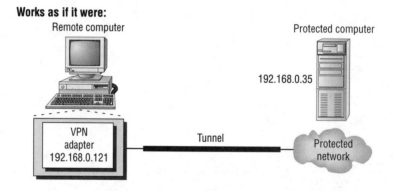

Figure 29.14 shows how a packet travels from the remote computer to a host on the private network. When the tunnel is connected, the remote computer thinks its IP number is 192.168.0.121. It sends data through the VPN adapter addressed to host 192.168.0.35 on the private network. The VPN adapter packages it up for delivery over the Internet—it's now a packet from 209.5.73.62 to 205.149.0.33. This packet can be transported over the Internet, safe from prying eyes. The gateway verifies that the packet is valid, decrypts it, and it's now once again a packet from 192.168.0.121 to 192.168.0.35. This packet is passed through the private network to the host.

If all this sounds complex, well, it is. But, as it turns out, *using* tunneling from the remote computer is simple with Windows Me. You simply need to tell Windows the name or IP address of the gateway computer. All other negotiation for IP private addresses, encryption passwords, etc., is handled entirely by the software.

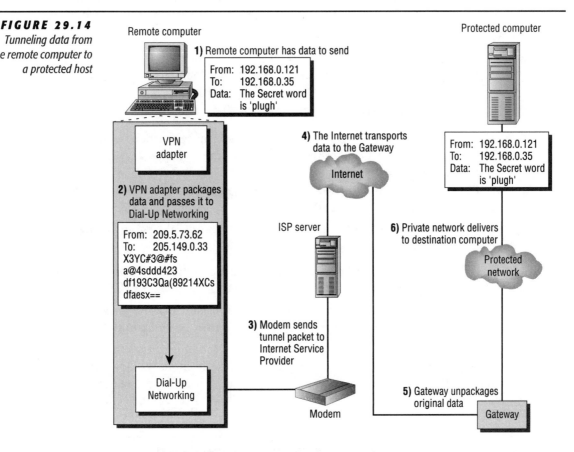

FIGURE 29.14
Tunneling data from the remote computer to a protected host

The setup of the gateway is more complex. It's handled by the administrator of the protected network using Windows NT/2000 Server or a compatible router and, thankfully, is not our concern here.

Installing the VPN Client Software

Before setting up tunneling, your computer should already be set up and tested for networking with the required LAN card and/or dial-up adapter and modem.

To install the VPN tunnel software, complete the following steps:

1. In Control Panel, start Add/Remove Programs and select the Windows Setup tab.

2. Highlight Communications and click Details.

3. Scroll down the list of components and be sure Virtual Private Networking is checked. If it isn't, check it. Close the dialog boxes and Control Panel. Windows may ask you to insert your Windows Me CD-ROM and restart.

4. Open the Network applet in the Control Panel. Be sure all protocols required by the network on the other end of your VPN connection are installed. If necessary, add any required protocols.

5. Click OK on the Network dialog box.

Windows will install the software and restart your computer.

Connecting to a Private Network

If you will reach the remote gateway through a modem connection, set up your Internet connection via Dial-Up Networking, as described in Chapter 26. Check the connection to make sure it works.

Even if your tunnel is reached through a LAN rather than a modem, you will use Dial-Up Networking to connect the tunnel. To do so, follow these steps:

1. Start Dial-Up Networking from Start ➤ Settings ➤ Dial-Up Networking.

2. Click Make New Connection.

3. Enter a name for the connection, for example, **Office Network via Tunnel**. In the Select a Device list, choose Microsoft VPN Adapter. Click Next.

4. Next to VPN Server, enter the host name or IP address of the gateway computer, for example, **vpn_gateway.mycompany.com**, or **205.149.0.33**. Click Next, then Finish.

Select the new connection to begin the tunnel connection. Windows will display the standard Dial-Up Networking login dialog box, except that instead of a phone number it will have a space for the VPN Server name (as shown in Figure 29.15).

FIGURE 29.15

Establishing a VPN tunnel connection

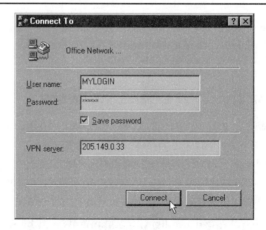

Click Connect to make the connection. The tunnel will be set up using your LAN or a standard dial-up connection, if you use dial-up Internet service. In the latter case, the dialer will automatically start and you will see the Connect To dialog box again to sign in to your ISP.

 TIP If you are connected on a LAN to servers using the IPX or NetBEUI protocols when you make the tunnel connection, the dial-up manager may inform you that these servers will not be available while you are connected through the tunnel. These protocols don't tolerate multiple simultaneous connections. (For example, NetWare LANs have this limitation.) Unbinding these protocols from the dial-up adapter, if they are not needed through the tunnel, may prevent this from happening; see Chapter 27.

One or two Dial-Up Manager icons will appear in your Taskbar, one for the tunnel and one for the modem dial-up connection, if applicable.

Once the connection has been established, you can use Explorer to locate and use remote servers just as if they were part of your local network. If the remote network does not have a Windows NT/2000 server, however, you may not see all of the computers in My Network Places. You might have to type their names explicitly to view and use them in Explorer.

Select the Dial-Up Manager icon(s) in the Taskbar to view the status of the connection and to disconnect when you are finished using the remote network.

 NOTE You can configure your VPN connection to automatically disconnect after a period of disuse. Right-click the VPN connection and select Properties. View the Dialing tab and check Disconnect When Connection May Not Be Needed.

Routing Issues

While the tunnel connection is established, network routing is changed according to the protocols that are bound to the VPN adapter. Table 29.2 lists the situations you might run into, depending on which protocols are being used.

TABLE 29.2: CHANGES TO VPN-BOUND NETWORK ROUTING ACCORDING TO PROTOCOL

Protocol	Effect of VPN on Network
NetBEUI	Servers using NetBEUI on a local LAN are not available. If a Windows NT/2000 server is on the remote network, you will be able to see all remote servers in My Network Places.
IPX/SPX	Servers using IPX/SPX on a local LAN are not available. If NetBIOS over IPX is enabled, you will be able to see remote servers in My Network Places.
TCP/IP	All file servers and Internet access should be normal, for both local and remote addresses.

PART

V

Networking

APPENDIX A

Installing Windows Me on Your Computer

Chances are good that your computer came installed with Windows Me already, in which case reading this appendix isn't necessary for you. On the other hand, if you are still using Windows 3.x, Windows 95, or Windows 98, or you have no version of Windows on your computer at all, you'll want to read this appendix. If at some point after you install Windows you discover that you are missing some of the components discussed in this book, you can install them later from the Windows Control Panel's Add/Remove Programs applet, as explained in Chapter 9, "Customizing Windows with the Control Panel."

There are several basic scenarios when installing Windows Me:

- Installing on a new or newly formatted hard disk
- Installing over Windows 3.x
- Installing over Windows 95
- Installing over Windows 98

Within each scenario, there are subscenarios, based on the source of the installation programs:

- Local CD-ROM or hard disk
- Installation files copied to your hard disk
- Network CD-ROM or hard disk

It's highly likely that you'll be installing from a local CD-ROM drive, over an existing Windows installation.

 NOTE If you have a previous version of Windows on your computer, you can install from a command prompt, but Microsoft recommends installing from within Windows.

Although I don't recommend it, you can choose to install Windows into a directory other than the existing Windows directory. This lets you install a "clean" version of Windows Me, with no settings pulled in from the earlier installation. Although this assures you of having a fresh Registry, and might make you feel safer about trying out the new version, it will be a hassle in the long run. What I *do* recommend is upgrading *over* your existing Windows directory, by which I mean installing into the same directory; typically this would be C:\Windows. Besides, when you install over an existing version of Windows, you are offered the option of saving your old system files; so you can effortlessly revert to the old system if you want. (But be forewarned that if you're currently running Windows 9x, it can take as much as 110MB of additional space to perform this save.)

When you opt to install over an existing Windows version (that is, 3.*x* or 9*x*—see the note below about Windows NT), various important settings—such as program INI settings, file locations, program associations, program groups, and so forth—are transferred into your new version. The most important advantage of this approach is that you won't have to install all your applications (such as Microsoft Office) again for Windows Me. (If you install to a separate directory, things get pretty complicated because with two separate versions of Windows on the same computer, the changes you make in one version don't carry over to the other.)

TIP If you are installing on a computer that has Windows NT or 2000 on it, read the NT/2000 section at the end of this appendix. You cannot install over NT or 2000, although Windows Me can coexist with NT or 2000 on the same system, and you can choose which one you want at each startup.

Microsoft has done a laudable job of making the Windows Me installation process pretty painless, thanks to the Setup Wizard, which provides a pleasant question-and-answer interface. It's been made even simpler than in Windows 98 by asking only a few questions up front, and then doing the rest of the work on its own without your intervention. Therefore, I'll spare you the boredom of walking you through *every* step here on paper. Rather, I'll get you going and discuss some of the decisions you'll have to make along the way.

TIP Setup requires approximately 210MB of hard disk space to complete. The exact amount will vary depending on the setup options you choose, as well as on the configuration of the hard drive you are installing Windows on. For additional information about space requirements, see the file \Win9x\setup.txt on the Windows Me CD-ROM before you begin installation.

WARNING Microsoft strongly suggests that you back up any important existing data and programs before you install Windows Me, just to be safe. Also, be sure to take the Setup program's advice about making a new startup disk. Startup disks that you may have created with earlier versions of Windows are not compatible with some features of Windows Me.

Easiest Approach: A Full Upgrade from an Earlier Version of Windows

First off, you'll need to decide whether you are going to install from CD-ROM or your local area network. I highly recommend using a CD (or networked CD or hard disk if one is available). If you choose to copy the installation files to your hard disk, see \Win9x\setup.txt on the Windows Me CD-ROM for special instructions.

Before beginning, make sure you have at least 210MB of free hard-disk space on the drive you're going to install Windows on. You can use Windows Explorer or the DOS dir command to check this.

When you insert the Windows Me CD-ROM into a Windows 9x computer in which AutoInsert Notification is turned on (the default), a message appears asking whether you want to upgrade to the newer version of Windows on the CD.

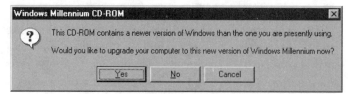

You can click Yes to start the Setup program right away, or No if you want to browse the CD-ROM first. For example, you might want to read the text files readme, setuptips.txt, and setup.txt on the CD-ROM beforehand, for the latest information about certain hardware compatibility issues and setup options. The first two are found in the root folder on the CD-ROM; setup.txt is in the Win9x folder on the CD-ROM. To view these, locate them in a file listing (Windows Explorer or My Computer) and double-click them.

NOTE When you upgrade over an earlier version of Windows, the same accessory programs are installed as were in your previous installation. You can change which programs are installed later through Add/Remove Programs in the Control Panel (see Chapter 9).

If you chose to read the text files first, you can either double-click setup.exe on the CD-ROM when you are ready to run Setup, or you can remove and reinsert the CD-ROM in the drive to again get the message offering to upgrade you.

TIP As I mentioned earlier, if you're using the CD, the CD-ROM drive needn't be on your local computer. Furthermore, you can install over a local area network or dial-up connection from a shared directory or drive that contains the CD (or a copy of all its files). You simply switch to that directory (via File Manager in Windows 3.*x* or Windows Explorer in Windows 9*x*) and run `setup.exe`.

If you're in Windows 3.*x*, or if AutoInsert Notification is turned off for your CD-ROM drive, you won't get the automatic message that offers to run Setup. In Windows 3.1, you'll need to switch to the File Manager or Program Manager, open the File menu, and choose Run. If you're running Windows 9*x*, go to Start ➤ Run. Then enter whichever of the following commands is appropriate for your circumstance (i.e., depending on whether you're installing from a CD-ROM, hard disk, or network):

- If installing from a CD, enter **d:\win9x\setup**.
- If installing from a network, click Browse and navigate to the network computer and CD-ROM drive where the disk is located.

(You may have to replace d: in the above statement with the appropriate drive letter for your machine.) Alternatively, in File Manager or Windows Explorer you can look around for `setup.exe` and double-click it.

The Setup program checks your disks for errors and checks to make sure no other programs are running. This is because Setup might bomb, in which case any work you have open in those programs could be lost. Switch to any program in which you have open work, save the work, close the program, and switch back to Setup.

Then it displays the Welcome screen shown in Figure A.1.

NOTE If you install from the DOS prompt instead of from Windows, you'll have more questions to answer than the ones you're asked from this series of screens, relating to your choice for the destination directory for Windows and concerning which components to install. If you're interested in this approach, see the following, "Installing Windows Me from a Command Prompt."

APP
A

Installing Windows Me on
Your Computer

FIGURE A.1

FIGURE A.1

The first Welcome screen when installing over an existing version of Windows

Next, you'll see a license agreement. If you agree to the terms, click I Accept the Agreement, then click Next. You'll be prompted to enter the Product Key, which is a 25-digit number you should have received with your Windows Me CD. After you enter it, click Next again.

Setup now checks out what hardware is in your computer and initializes the system's Registry file. It will check for installed components if you are upgrading from a previous version of Windows, and it will check to see that you have enough hard disk space. Assuming there is enough disk space (you checked for that earlier, didn't you?), you won't see any error messages about that. If you do, see the "Removing Uninstall Files to Free Up Disk Space" section later in this appendix.

At this point, you'll also be asked if you want to save your "system files." This is so that you can uninstall Windows Me if it doesn't work, or if you decide you don't like it, or if for some other reason you want to be able to go back to your old operating system. (See the "Reverting to the Previous Operating System" section later in this appendix.) Click Yes or No. If in doubt, click Yes. Then click Next. If you have more than one hard drive, you will also be asked which disk you want the uninstall files saved on.

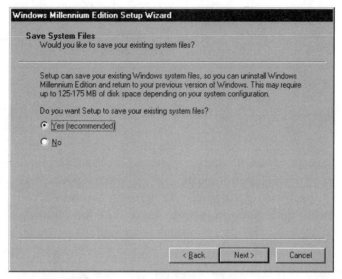

Your current system files will be backed up to a hidden, compressed file. If doing that would leave too little space for installation of Windows Me, you'll be alerted and given the option of skipping the backup in order to save disk space.

At this point, Setup offers the opportunity to create an emergency startup disk. This is for starting your computer in case the hard disk is damaged or some system files get lost or corrupted. Since these are problems that could happen on even the best of machines, it's a good idea to make such a disk and keep it in a readily accessible drawer near your computer. This disk is also necessary for uninstalling Windows Me in case the installation bombs.

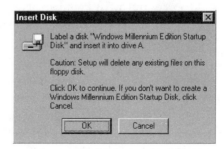

You'll be prompted to insert a floppy disk in the disk drive and click OK to make the disk. Anything on the floppy disk will be erased, so don't use one with something important on it. You can skip this procedure by clicking Cancel, but I don't recommend it. When the disk is finished, you're prompted to remove it and click OK to continue.

APP
A

Installing Windows Me on
Your Computer

TIP For reasons given earlier, it's a very good idea to proceed with the creation of the startup disk now. However, if you don't have a floppy with you, you can cancel this process for now and continue with the rest of the installation. You can always make a startup disk later using Add/Remove Programs in the Control Panel. However, if Setup crashes for some reason, you could be left with a computer that won't boot.

Now click Finish, and you'll move on to the main stage of the installation process: the copying of files from the source to your hard disk. This is the portion that takes the most time. A status bar keeps you abreast of the progress of the file-copying operation.

At some point, your computer will reboot. Remove the floppy disk, if you haven't already, and let the computer restart. If nothing happens for an extended period, you may have to turn the machine off and then on again. It *should* pick up where it left off.

From here on, the process is completely automated. Your PC will restart itself one or more times and will copy various drivers for the hardware it detects. Just let it do its thing, and 30 to 40 minutes later, Windows Me will be ready to roll.

Installing Windows Me from a Command Prompt

You may prefer to install Windows Me from a command prompt if one of the following conditions exists:

- You have no version of Windows on the machine.

- You have an existing version of Windows on the machine but want to keep that version and set up Windows Me too. Then, by changing folder names or using some third-party utility program such as Partition Magic or BootCom, you can choose which version boots up. (This option is for confident, advanced users.)

- You want to control what components of Windows get installed or in what folder the Windows files are placed. You don't get to make those choices when upgrading over an existing version.

If you have Windows 9*x* on the PC, create an emergency boot disk (choose Add/Remove Programs from the Control Panel and use the Startup Disk tab to do so). Then boot from that disk. If asked, choose to start with CD-ROM support.

 NOTE If you are upgrading from Windows 95, the boot disk won't provide CD-ROM support. In that case, either you can manually create config.sys and autoexec.bat files on the boot disk that loads the CD-ROM driver or you can copy the Windows Me setup files (basically the Win9*x* folder on the CD-ROM) to your hard disk beforehand and then install from there instead of from the CD.

So boot your system using your emergency boot disk, and when you arrive at the A:\> prompt, type **E:** and press Enter (or whatever letter your CD-ROM drive is). Or, if you have copied the setup files to your hard disk, type **C:**, press Enter, and then change to the folder in which you copied them (CD *foldername*).

Then type **setup** and press Enter to start the Setup program. You'll see a message that ScanDisk is going to run; press Enter again to allow it.

ScanDisk checks the hard disk media. Assuming that all is okay (see the following section if it's not), exit ScanDisk by typing **X** (for Exit) when prompted. Setup will proceed, temporarily in character mode, then in a GUI mode with graphics, blue background, and mouse functionality.

Work through the Setup step-by-step, clicking Next to move from screen to screen. Just as with an upgrade, you are prompted to accept the license agreement and to enter your 25-digit Product Key.

After that, you'll be given the option of choosing a hard disk folder for your Windows Me installation. The default will be the existing Windows folder if there is one, but you can create a different folder at this point by typing a name for it.

Next, you're given the opportunity to save your existing system files (if you are not installing on a PC that had no Windows version on it previously). Choose Yes or No, just as you would when upgrading.

Next, you're prompted to create a boot disk, as with upgrading. Insert the disk, click OK, wait for the files to be copied, and then remove the disk. Click OK to continue.

Depending on whether or not you are installing in the same folder that you used for a previous Windows installation, you might see some or all of the following questions and options:

- Choose which set of Windows Me components to install: Typical, Portable, Compact, or Custom (your choice).

- Provide your name and company name.

- Select specific components.

- Provide or verify your network ID: computer name, workgroup, and workstation description.

- Choose your country and/or time zone.

 TIP Just fill in the blanks and keep clicking Next, and you'll be done in no time flat. If you have a situation that requires additional Setup options—for example, you may be a LAN administrator and want remote Setup capabilities—refer to the Microsoft Windows Me Resource Kit.

APP
A

Installing Windows Me on
Your Computer

Reverting to the Previous Operating System

Assuming you opted during your Windows Me Setup to save your previous version's system files, you can revert to that version of Windows in case of a failed or unappreciated installation. (For exceptions to the "Saving System Files" scenario, see the upcoming sidebar.)

To uninstall Windows Me and completely restore your system to its previous Windows version, follow these steps:

1. Choose Start ➢ Settings ➢ Control Panel.

2. Double-click Add/Remove Programs.

3. On the Install/Uninstall tab, click Windows Millennium Edition, and then click Remove.

If you can't even get to the Start menu to begin the steps above (because of problems starting Windows), use your startup disk to start your computer and, from a command prompt, type **a: UNINSTAL**, and then press Enter.

Here are a few notes to be mindful of when running Uninstal:

• The Uninstall program needs to shut down Windows. If your computer starts to run Windows again on reboot, try booting from the emergency boot disk you created during Windows Setup.

• If you saved your files on a drive other than C, you can use the /w option to specify the drive where the files are located. For example, if your system files were saved to drive E during installation, type **Uninstal /w e:** to access them on that drive.

Why You Can't Always Save Your System Files

The option of saving your system files for a future uninstall is not always offered during Setup. Here are two situations where Setup doesn't offer the option:

• You are installing to a new folder. (In this case, you don't need to revert to your previous version; instead, you can simply boot to the previous version's folder to run that version.)

• You are running a version of MS-DOS earlier than 5.0. (In this case your system is automatically updated with the version of DOS that is used in Windows Me.)

Continued ▷

In most other situations, you are given the option of saving your system files. When you choose this option, Setup saves your system files in a hidden, compressed file on your local hard drive. (They cannot be saved to a network drive or a floppy disk.) If you have multiple local drives, you will be able to select the one you want to use.

If you are not in one of the above exception situations but you see a message during Setup about not being able to save your system files, refer to the "Setup Error Messages" section of the setup.txt file in the CD's Win9x folder.

Removing Uninstall Files to Free Up Disk Space

If you want to free up an additional 50MB to 100MB of disk space, you can remove the Uninstall files. Please note, however, that without the Uninstall files, you will no longer be able to uninstall Windows Me. In short, save this operation until you're sure you're going to keep Windows Me.

Here are the steps for removing the Uninstall files. Note that Windows Me must be running to perform this operation.

1. Choose Start ➤ Settings ➤ Control Panel.

2. Double-click Add/Remove Programs.

3. On the Install/Uninstall tab, click Delete Windows Millennium Uninstall Information, and then click Add/Remove.

How to Install Windows Me to a Machine Running Windows NT or 2000

Although you can install Windows Me to a machine that is already running Windows NT or Windows 2000, you must install it to a separate partition—you cannot install Me *over* NT, or vice versa. (You may remember that you could install NT over Windows 3.*x* and share settings, associations, and so forth; Windows Me does not work this way.) As a result, though, you can have NT or 2000 and Windows Me on the same computer and boot either operating system as you like; they won't share INI settings, installed applications, or other settings. This may change in the future, but in the meantime, it's simply an annoyance because you'll have to install most applications twice—once for NT and once for Windows Me.

If you're configured to multiboot MS-DOS and Windows NT or 2000
Boot to MS-DOS, and then run Windows Me Setup from either MS-DOS, Windows 95, or Windows 98. You won't be able to install Windows Me to a partition with a shared Windows 9*x*/Windows NT configuration; you'll need to install Windows Me to a different partition.

APP
A

Installing Windows Me on
Your Computer

If you're not configured to multiboot MS-DOS and Windows NT or 2000   You must first configure your computer to multiboot MS-DOS/Windows and Windows NT. Then follow the instructions above.

If you were planning to boot to MS-DOS from a floppy disk and then run Windows Me Setup   This approach permits you to install Windows Me as you wish; however, you will no longer be able to boot to Windows NT or 2000. You can *restore* Windows NT, however, by booting from the Windows NT boot/repair disk and then selecting the Repair option.

 NOTE Windows Me Setup will not run on OS/2. You need to boot to MS-DOS and then run Setup from the MS-DOS prompt. For more about installing over OS/2, see the `setup.txt` file on the Windows Me CD in the \Win9x folder.

Multibooting Windows Me with Linux

If you currently have a version of Linux installed on your computer and want to be able to multiboot Windows Me, you must install Windows on its own DOS partition. Create the partition using Disk Druid, and then run a normal MS-DOS prompt installation of Windows as described earlier.

When the installation is complete, reboot using your Linux boot floppy. The Windows Me Setup program erased LILO (the Linux Loader program), so you'll have to reinstall it by running `/sbin/lilo`. LILO can then be configured to ask you which operating system you want to boot during startup.

APPENDIX B

Windows Me Accessibility Features

Accessibility means increasing the ease of use or access to a computer for people who are physically challenged in one way or another. Many people have difficulty seeing characters on the screen when they are too small, for example. Others have a disability that prevents them from easily typing on the keyboard. Even those of us who hunt and peck at the keyboard have it easy compared to those who can barely move their hands, are limited to the use of a single hand, or are paralyzed from the neck down. These people got the short end of the stick for some time when it came to using computers, unless they had special data-entry and retrieval devices (such as speech boards) installed in their computers.

Microsoft has taken a big step in increasing computer accessibility for disabled people in Windows Me by including features that allow many challenged people to use Windows programs without major modification to their machines or software. (Accessibility add-ons for older versions of Windows have been available for some time, but as add-ons.) For more information about Microsoft's ongoing advancements in accessibility support and for API information, please see www.microsoft.com/enable.

There are two Accessibility components in Windows Me: Accessibility Options and Accessibility Tools. The *Accessibility Options* are the features you can set up through the Control Panel's Accessibility applet; these control special uses for the keyboard, display, mouse, and system sounds. The *Accessibility Tools* are stand-alone applications such as a magnifier, high-contrast mouse pointer schemes, and an Accessibility Wizard (which walks you step-by-step through the process of setting up the Accessibility Options in the Control Panel).

 NOTE These options and tools are not installed by default. To install them, use the Windows Setup tab in Add/Remove Programs (see Chapter 13, "Adding and Removing Hardware and Software").

Setting the Accessibility Options

To access the Accessibility Options, double-click the Accessibility icon in the Control Panel. This opens the Accessibility Properties dialog box, containing several tabs. The following sections outline the options on each tab.

 TIP To set up all these options at once according to your needs, run the Accessibility Wizard, described later in this appendix.

Keyboard Accessibility Settings

For people with limited mobility, holding down a key while pressing another (for example, pressing the Shift key to make a capital letter) can be a challenge. The Keyboard accessibility settings, shown in Figure B.1, help with this problem and others.

FIGURE B.1
The Keyboard settings control several special-purpose keyboard features.

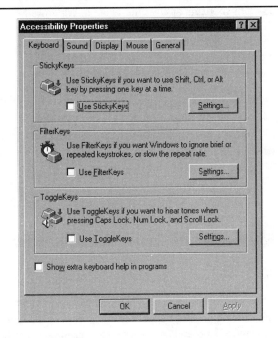

To adjust the Keyboard settings, follow these steps:

1. Click the Keyboard tab (if it's not already selected). There are three basic setting areas:

    StickyKeys   Keys that in effect stay pressed down when you press them once. Good for controlling the Alt, Ctrl, and Shift keys.

    FilterKeys   Lets you filter out quickly repeated keystrokes in case you have trouble pressing a key cleanly once and letting it up. This prevents multiple keystrokes from being typed.

    ToggleKeys   Gives you the option of hearing tones that alert you to the Caps Lock, Scroll Lock, and Num Lock keys being activated.

2. Click the box of the feature(s) you want your Windows Me machine to use.

3. Note that each feature has a Settings button from which you can make additional adjustments. To see the additional settings, click the Settings button next to the feature, fine-tune the settings, and then click OK. The most likely setting changes you'll make from these boxes are to turn on or off the shortcut keys.

4. After you've made all the keyboard changes you want, either move on to another tab in the Accessibility Properties box or click OK to return to the Control Panel.

 TIP You can turn on any of these keyboard features—StickyKeys, FilterKeys, or Toggle-Keys—with shortcuts at any time while in Windows Me. To turn on StickyKeys, press either Shift key five times in a row. To turn on FilterKeys, press and hold the right Shift key for eight seconds (it might take longer). To turn on the ToggleKeys option, press the Num Lock key for five seconds.

When the StickyKeys or FilterKeys feature is turned on, a symbol will appear on the right side of the Taskbar indicating what's currently activated. For example, in the graphic below I have both StickyKeys and FilterKeys set on. StickyKeys is indicated by the three small boxes, representing the Ctrl, Alt, and Shift keys. FilterKeys is represented by the stopwatch, illustrative of the different key timing that goes into effect when the option is working.

FilterKeys indicator

StickyKeys indicator

 TIP Turning on FilterKeys will make it seem as if your keyboard has stopped working. You have to press a key and keep it down for several seconds for the key to register. If you activate this setting and want to turn it off, the easiest solution is to use the mouse or switch to the Control Panel (via the Taskbar), run the Accessibility applet, turn off FilterKeys, and click OK.

You can disable StickyKeys from the Settings dialog box, or you can turn it off by pressing two of the three keys that are affected by this setting. For example, pressing Ctrl and Alt at the same time will turn StickyKeys off.

Sound Accessibility Settings

There are two Sound accessibility settings, SoundSentry and ShowSounds (see Figure B.2). These two features are for the hearing impaired. What they do is simply cause some type of visual display to occur in lieu of the normal beep, ding, or other auditory alert that the program would typically produce. The visual display might be something such as a blinking window (in the case of SoundSentry), or it might be some kind of text caption (in the case of ShowSounds).

FIGURE B.2
*The Sound
accessibility settings*

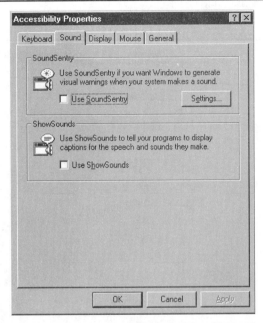

The Settings button for SoundSentry lets you decide what will graphically happen on screen when a program is trying to warn you about something. For example, should it flash the window, flash the border of the program, or flash the whole screen? If you really don't want to miss a beep-type warning, you might want to have it flash the window. (Flashing the whole screen doesn't indicate which program is producing the warning.)

NOTE Not all programs will work cooperatively with these sound options. As more programs are written to take advantage of these settings, you'll see more *closed captioning*, wherein sound messages are translated into useful captions on the screen.

Display Accessibility Settings

The Display accessibility settings pertain to contrast. These settings let you set the display color scheme and font selection for easier reading. This can also be done from the normal Display setting, described below, but the advantage to doing it here is that you can preset your favorite high-contrast color scheme, then invoke it with the shortcut key combination when you most need it. Just press Left+Alt, Left+Shift, and then Print Screen. This might be when your eyes are tired, when someone who is sight impaired is using the computer, or when you're sitting in an adverse lighting situation. Figure B.3 displays the dialog box.

FIGURE B.3
The Display accessibility settings

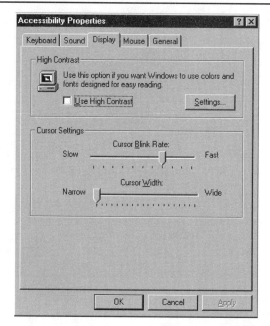

To change the Display accessibility settings, follow these steps:

1. Turn on the Use High Contrast option box if you want to improve the contrast between the background and the characters on your screen. When you click Apply or OK, this will kick in a high-contrast color scheme (typically the Blue and Black scheme), which will put black letters on a white work area. (You can't get much more contrast than that!)

2. Click the Settings button if you want to change the color scheme that will be used for high contrast or if you want to enable or disable shortcut key activation of this feature. This option may come in handy because some of the schemes have larger fonts than others and some may show up better on your screen than others.

TIP You can experiment more easily with the schemes in the Display applet than here. If you wish, you can even create your own custom color scheme with large menus, title bar lettering, and dialog box lettering. I explain how to do all this in Chapter 10, "Customizing the Desktop, Taskbar, and Start Menu."

3. To adjust the cursor settings, drag the sliders to the left or right. For example, to make the text cursor in a text box wider and easier to see, drag the Cursor Width slider toward Wide.

4. Click Apply if you want to adjust more settings from the other tab pages, or click OK to return to the Control Panel.

Mouse Accessibility Settings

If you can't easily control mouse or trackball motion, or simply don't like using a mouse, this dialog box is for you. Of course, you can invoke most commands that apply to dialog boxes and menus throughout Windows and Windows programs using the Alt key in conjunction with the command's underlined letter. Still, some programs, such as those that work with graphics, require you to use a mouse. This Accessibility option turns your arrow keys into mouse-pointer control keys. You still have to use the mouse's clicker buttons to left- or right-click things, though. Here's what to do:

1. Click the Mouse tab in the Accessibility Properties dialog box. You'll see the box displayed in Figure B.4.

FIGURE B.4
The Mouse accessibility settings

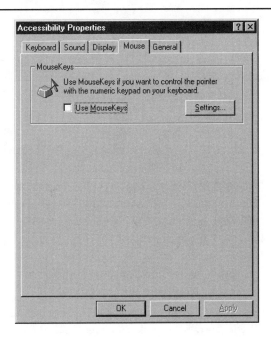

TIP This is a great feature for laptop users who are on the road and forgot the mouse. If you have to use a graphics program or other program requiring more than simple command choices and text entry, use the Mouse accessibility tab to turn your arrow keys into mouse-pointer keys.

2. Turn on the MouseKeys option if you want to use the arrow keys in place of the mouse. You'll probably want to adjust the speed settings for the arrow keys, though, so that the pointer moves at a rate that works for you. The Settings button brings up the box shown in Figure B.5. Note that you can also set a shortcut key sequence to activate MouseKeys.

FIGURE B.5
The MouseKeys settings

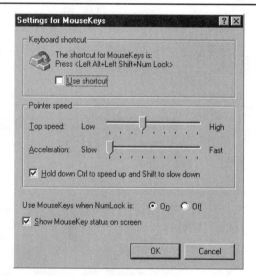

3. Play with the settings until you like them. The Top Speed and Acceleration settings are going to be the most important. And note that you have to set them, click OK, then click Apply in the Mouse dialog box before you can experience the effect of your changes. Then go back and adjust your settings if necessary. Notice that one setting lets you change the tracking speed on the fly while using a program, by holding down the Shift key to slow down the pointer's motion or the Ctrl key to speed it up.

4. Click Apply in the Mouse dialog box if you want to make more settings from the other tab pages, or click OK to return to the Control Panel.

TIP The pointer keys that are used for mouse control are the ones on a standard desktop computer keyboard's number pad. These are the keys that have two modes, Num Lock on and Num Lock off. These keys usually have both an arrow and a number on them; for example, the 4 key also has a ← symbol on it. Most laptops don't have such keys because of size constraints. However, many laptops have a special arrangement that emulates these keys, providing a 10-key numeric keypad (and arrows when Num Lock is off).

Other Accessibility Settings

The last tab in the Accessibility Properties box is called General (see Figure B.6).

FIGURE B.6
*The General
accessibility setting*

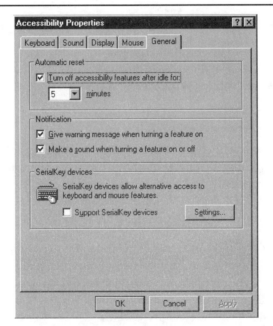

This box is divided into three sections pertaining to these subjects:

- When Accessibility functions are turned on and off. Notice that you can choose to turn off all the settings after Windows has been idle for a period of time.

- How you are alerted to a feature being turned on or off. You have the choice of a visual cue (a little dialog box will appear) and/or a sound.

- Acceptance of alternative input devices through the serial (COM1 through COM4) ports on your computer.

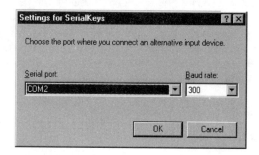

Using the Accessibility Tools

The Accessibility Tools, if installed, are on the Start menu: Start ➢ Programs ➢ Accessories ➢ Accessibility. There are three tools:

- Accessibility Wizard
- Magnifier
- On-Screen Keyboard

Let's look briefly at each one. If these features don't appear on the Accessibility menu, or if there is no Accessibility menu, you need to install the Accessibility features (see Chapter 13).

Running the Accessibility Wizard

The Accessibility Wizard walks you step-by-step through the process of setting the Accessibility Options you learned about in the preceding sections of this appendix. It asks you questions about your abilities, and based on the answers, it turns certain accessibility features on or off. To run it, choose Start ➢ Programs ➢ Accessories ➢ Accessibility ➢ Accessibility Wizard.

I won't belabor each step of the process because it's fairly self-explanatory. Figure B.7, for example, shows the part where you choose which font size you are most comfortable with. Simply follow the prompts.

FIGURE B.7
The Accessibility Wizard provides an easy way to set up accessibility features.

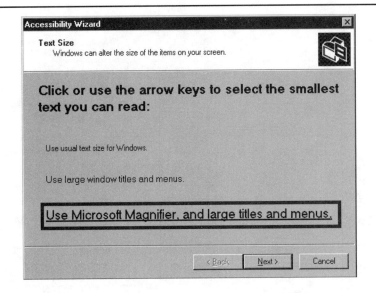

NOTE The Magnifier feature mentioned in Figure B.7 is described in the following section.

Using the Magnifier

The Magnifier enlarges whatever the mouse pointer touches in a pane at the top of the screen. For example, in Figure B.8, the pointer is over Windows Media Player. To turn on the Magnifier, choose Start ➢ Programs ➢ Accessories ➢ Accessibility ➢ Magnifier.

FIGURE B.8

The Magnifier at work

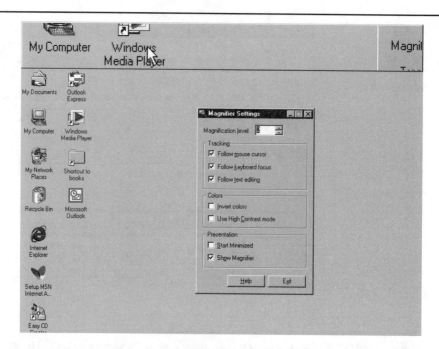

The Magnifier is in operation for as long as the Magnifier Settings dialog box remains open. If desired, you can minimize it to get it out of your way. Click Exit to close it altogether and stop using the Magnifier.

Using the On-Screen Keyboard

This utility displays a keyboard in a window on screen, and you can type by clicking the key buttons on screen. To turn it on, choose Start ➤ Programs ➤ Accessories ➤ Accessibility ➤ On-Screen Keyboard.

Then, to use the keyboard, click in the window in which you want to type, and position the insertion point where you want to start typing. Then click the buttons in the On-Screen Keyboard window to type letters. For example, Figure B.9 shows Microsoft Word being used with the On-Screen Keyboard.

FIGURE B.9

*Using the On-Screen
Keyboard*

The On-Screen Keyboard window stays on top.

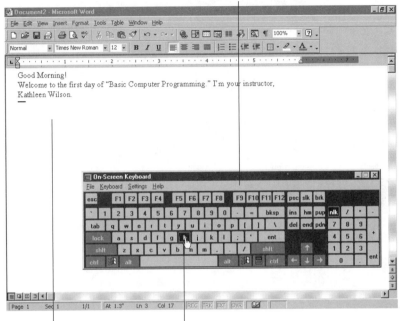

The Word window is active.   Mouse pointer over a key

NOTE Don't click the title bar of the On-Screen Keyboard window, bringing it to the foreground. It's designed to work with other programs, and so you can type with it only when
another program's window is active. The On-Screen Keyboard window will remain on top
even when it's not the active window.

APPENDIX <u>C</u>

Using NetMeeting

Microsoft NetMeeting is a real-time, Internet-based, telephone and application-sharing program that lets multiple people connect with one another over the Internet to get work done in an ingenious manner. It's sort of like bringing several people into the same room, where they can work on documents together (through interactive applications), write on a blackboard they all can see (only in this case, the term is whiteboard), and talk to each other—all at once. They can even see each other if they happen to have a compatible video camera. NetMeeting includes support for international conferencing as well as domestic hookups, and incorporates international standards. It provides true multiuser application-sharing and data-conferencing capabilities.

 NOTE Unfortunately, as far as the telephone aspect of NetMeeting goes, I should mention that, as with most Internet phone applications, the voice quality isn't quite up to what you're probably used to on a real telephone. Utility and software companies have been working seriously, however, to provide higher quality Internet telephony as of this writing.

One way of describing NetMeeting is to say it takes the power of your PC running some powerful applications and adds the power of the video telephone and the global reach of the Internet. Although I'm risking sounding too much like a Microsoft advertisement, I will say it could actually transform the way telecommuters do their everyday work, the way clubs hold meetings, and the way schools present instructional material.

The newest version of NetMeeting, version 3.01, operates in much the same way as earlier versions of the program. The big change is in its directory service. Rather than forcing users to connect to large, generic Internet locator servers (ILSs), NetMeeting 3.01 is now based around MSN Messenger Service's address book. This seems a very natural extension because MSN Messenger Service is a simple, text-only service that provides much the same basic functionality as the more business-oriented NetMeeting.

 TECH TIP Some of the companies in the videoconferencing field that have created add-ins or competing products include Creative Labs, Inc.; Intel; PictureTel; VDOnet Corp.; and White Pine Software, Inc.

NetMeeting Uses

Supporting one or more people over the Internet or over a corporation's intranet, Net-Meeting provides an effective way to communicate and collaborate in real time. (*Real time* means there is little or no delay, as there is with e-mail.) NetMeeting uses existing standards of *multipoint data conferencing* to let you accomplish the following:

- Talk to others on a speakerphone or headset (half or full duplex, depending on your sound card)
- See each other while talking (limited to a pair of users), or just see one party
- Share an application that you have on your machine with people who don't have it on theirs
- Collaborate with others, using the shared application to create and revise a document together
- Transfer files back and forth as you talk
- Write and display pictures on a shared whiteboard
- Type to each other from the keyboard in chat mode

 TIP Don't confuse the term *application sharing* under NetMeeting with the way the term is used in the context of LANs. In the world of LANs, the term only means letting people use the same program without having it on their local machine, by making it available on a server computer that they can all access. In the context of NetMeeting, application sharing takes on the additional meaning of people actually editing the same documents on those applications—while being able to see each other's changes in real time! Even if the application isn't a true "multiuser" program, NetMeeting lets multiple people run the program and work on the same documents simultaneously.

Consider how most of us normally work with our computers now. You're probably limited to using your PC pretty much for getting your work done on your local drive, maybe printing over a network, and sending copies of your files to lots of people. When you really have to collaborate with one person or a group of people, it comes down to picking up the phone, "doing lunch," or "taking a meeting." Rarely are people patient enough to crowd behind your desk and crane their necks over your shoulder while you try to show them something complicated on your computer screen. With NetMeeting you have a fistful of new options. Imagine these benefits:

> **Technical support,** allowing support organizations not only to *see* the scenario or situation on a remote user's computer but also to be able to *correct* a problem during a support call without having to physically go to the remote PC.

Virtual meetings, allowing users to be in different locations and conduct meetings as though everyone were in the same room.

Presentations, allowing one expert to use a graphing or spreadsheet program to demonstrate different what-if scenarios to a group of remote users, while driving home his or her points by drawing diagrams on the whiteboard.

Document collaboration, allowing users to collaborate on documents or information in real time.

Telecommuting, allowing users to extend their presence beyond file sharing or e-mail while on the road or in remote branch offices.

Customer service, allowing users to communicate directly with customer service from a Web site or to be able to see graphic information as part of a telephone call.

Distance learning, allowing presentations to be made or information to be disseminated to numerous people at the same time over the Internet or intranets.

Deaf or hard-of-hearing individuals can use NetMeeting to communicate more effectively in real time with others in the workplace, the classroom, and the home—gaining substantial benefits over using traditional TTY devices.

As mentioned, NetMeeting has *multipoint capability*. This means that, unlike most of the phone and video toys running around on the Internet, which are point-to-point, a group of folks can interact all at once, and not just with their voices. I don't mean to downplay the usefulness of the Internet phone products that have been introduced in the last couple of years. They are actually great for letting you converse at virtually no cost (other than your connect time over the Internet) with anyone around the world who is similarly equipped, and they can be an incredible boon for families with members in foreign countries, or even for businesses with remote offices. They're not so good for the long-distance carriers, but that's another story. NetMeeting can earn its keep pretty quickly even if used only for this purpose.

It should be obvious how NetMeeting can improve the productivity of users in a corporate environment by extending the telephone call to include data-conferencing capabilities. Now imagine the effect that integrating NetMeeting into Web pages could have. Until you have NetMeeting, you're limited in how you can interact with companies or individuals via their Web pages. Sure, you can read stuff, fill in some fields asking for data (essentially interacting with databases), order products, and leave e-mail. But, as mentioned earlier, the SDK (software development kit) for NetMeeting lets developers and Web site producers put rich data-conferencing capabilities into their pages. Web site creators can program conferencing capabilities directly into a Web page using the NetMeeting ActiveX control for conferencing. Web sites and ISPs (Internet Service Providers) can also create communities through conferencing services, by providing a directory of users with common interests via an Internet locator server (more on this later in the chapter).

System Requirements and Platform Compatibility

If your computer is capable of running Windows Me, it is also capable of NetMeeting. I'm giving you the following specs primarily because you might want to communicate with other people who have less-powerful computers than yours and who might be running other versions of Windows. Anyone with a system meeting these requirements can download NetMeeting for free from www.Microsoft.com/netmeeting.

These are the minimum and recommended system requirements for NetMeeting version 3.01:

- Pentium 90 or higher personal computer.

- 16 MB of RAM.

- Windows 9x, Me, or NT/2000. (To run any of the foreign-language versions of Microsoft NetMeeting, users must be using the same language version of Windows.)

- Internet Explorer 4.01 or later.

- 14,400bps modem (minimum) or LAN. Microsoft recommends at least a 56Kbps connection speed. If you're among the rich or lucky, you'll want one of these high-speed connections: T-1, TV-broadcast, or cable-modem. You'll notice that screen redraws, video picture updates, and sound will be smoother with ISDN or faster connection.

- Sound card, speakers, and microphone. (Required for real-time voice.)

- Video camera. (Required for transmitting video, but not for receiving it.)

 TECH TIP Since NetMeeting supports any video capture card or camera that supports Video for Windows, you have a wide range of products to choose from. Prices start from as low as around $99 for some tiny video cameras, such as the Intel Digital Camera ProPack that mounts on top of your monitor or clips on your laptop screen. Some newer ones aimed specifically at Windows 98 and higher connect quite easily to the USB port; they don't tie up your parallel printer port or require you to open the computer and plug in a card or anything nasty like that.

Windows Me comes bundled with NetMeeting 3.01, so you don't have to worry about downloading it unless you desire a newer version that may become available after this writing. If it's not installed yet, see Chapter 13, "Adding and Removing Hardware and Software," to add it to the installed Windows components.

One requirement you may have to consider relates to whether you plan to use NetMeeting for data only or for data plus voice and/or video. Data-conferencing features of Microsoft NetMeeting work with a 14,400bps or better modem connection, 32-bit

APP
C

Using NetMeeting

TCP/IP networks, and IPX networks. Real-time voice and video are designed for TCP/IP networks only (such as the Internet and corporate LANs).

NetMeeting supports more than 20 language versions, including Brazilian Portuguese, Chinese (simplified), Chinese (traditional), Czech, Danish, Dutch, Finnish, French, German, Greek, Hungarian, Italian, Japanese, Korean, Norwegian, Polish, Portuguese, Russian, Slovenian, Spanish, Swedish, and Turkish.

Installing NetMeeting

Before you can begin using NetMeeting, you have to install it (or make sure it is already installed). If you have Windows Me, you can install it as you would any Windows component. NetMeeting also comes with Windows 2000. You can tell whether you have it by clicking Start ➤ Programs ➤ Accessories ➤ Communications and looking for Microsoft NetMeeting (see Figure C.1).

 NOTE   On non-Windows Me PCs, NetMeeting might be installed somewhere else; look in the Internet Tools submenu or directly on the Programs menu itself.

FIGURE C.1
Determining whether you have NetMeeting installed

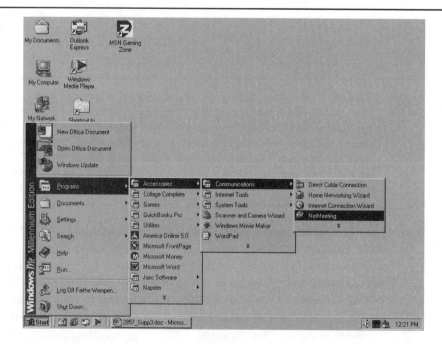

If you need to install NetMeeting on a PC that doesn't have Windows Me (or Windows 2000), do the following:

1. Open your Web browser and go to www.microsoft.com/netmeeting.

2. Click the Download button. A page appears with download options.

3. Click the NetMeeting 3.01 hyperlink.

4. Accept the default language (English Language Version) and click Download Now.

5. Choose Run This Program from Its Current Location, and then click OK.

6. Wait for the setup file to transfer to your hard disk.

7. When the Setup program starts, follow the prompts to install NetMeeting.

Running NetMeeting for the First Time

The first time you use NetMeeting, you are prompted to register yourself and to configure your microphone and other settings. Here's how it goes:

1. Choose Start ➢ Programs ➢ Accessories ➢ Communications ➢ NetMeeting. A box appears touting the cool features of NetMeeting. Read it if you want.

 NOTE If you acquired NetMeeting from a download rather than having it installed with Windows Me, it might not be in the location specified in step 1; look on the Programs menu for a NetMeeting shortcut.

2. Click Next.

3. Now you'll see the dialog box shown in Figure C.2. Fill in your name and other information asked for in the box. Then click Next.

FIGURE C.2

*Filling in your
identification
information*

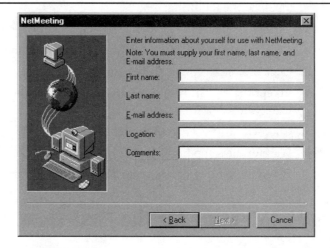

4. Next, you're asked whether you want to log on to a directory server when Net-Meeting starts. By default this check box is marked, as is the Do Not List My Name in the Directory check box. Deselect either if desired; then click Next.

 NOTE A *directory* is a listing of other users; it's sort of like a big waiting room where people gather to wait for meetings to start or to network with one another. The default one is Microsoft Internet Directory, and that's probably the only one you'll have on your list unless you are part of a corporation that maintains its own directory for NetMeeting. You must be a MSN Messenger Service user to access the Microsoft Internet Directory; later in the chapter I'll explain the signup process for that.

5. Depending on your connection, you might be asked what your connection speed will be. Choose your speed and click Next. (You might not see this.)

6. Two more check boxes (both marked by default) specify that shortcuts for Net-Meeting should be placed on your Quick Launch toolbar and on your Desktop. Deselect either or both if desired, and then click Next.

7. Click Next again to move on to sound settings. Now you'll be asked to set the Play volume and to try recording some sound (see Figure C.3). Make sure your microphone is set up, then click the Test button and adjust the volume.

FIGURE C.3
Record a few seconds of sound in order for the computer to adjust the record level.

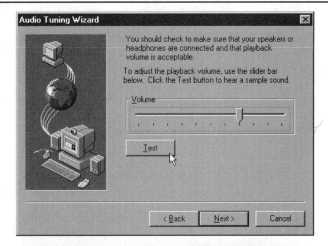

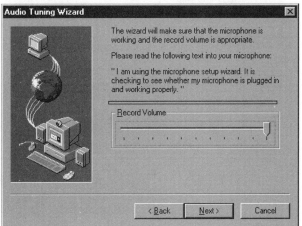

8. Click Next, read the test sentence aloud into your microphone, and then click Next again. Presumably you successfully recorded some sound and the sound level was set automatically. If it didn't take, you'll be told about it and advised what to do. You can return to the previous dialog box by clicking Back, and then you can try again, once you've plugged in your mike, fixed your sound card, or whatever.

TECH TIP Some sound cards are capable of full-duplex sound, letting you talk and listen at the same time, as on a normal telephone (as opposed to half duplex, which switches back and forth from transmitting and receiving, like a CB radio). Full duplex gives a more natural feeling to the conversations that you may have over NetMeeting. If you use NetMeeting a lot for voice communication, you should look into upgrading to a full-duplex sound system. Depending on the kind of card you now have, you may be able to just purchase an additional half-duplex sound card. In other cases, you'll have to remove or disable your current card and replace it with a full-duplex card.

9. Click Finish. In a second or two, NetMeeting will appear, ready to roll, as you see in Figure C.4. A new icon appears in the System Tray. It simply indicates that NetMeeting is running. Double-clicking it brings up the NetMeeting window if it's not in view.

If you're not connected to the Internet, you'll be prompted to do so. Then move to the next section.

FIGURE C.4
NetMeeting ready to roll

TIP For a listing of sound and video cards, as well as other NetMeeting-compatible products, check the NetMeeting site www.microsoft.com/netmeeting/prodguide. There's a whole lot of stuff listed there that's compatible with NetMeeting, including a dozen or so cameras, lots of audio gear such as headsets, group conferencing add-ons, conferencing servers and bridges, call center integration, and more.

Setting Up Directory Access

To find someone to have a NetMeeting with, you must either invite them directly or choose them from your Contacts list in MSN Messenger or from a directory server. MSN Messenger takes its data from the Microsoft Internet Directory server, which is the default server in NetMeeting. However, there are many NetMeeting directories all over the world, including many maintained by private corporations for the exclusive use of their employees. Sometimes, you might hear one referred to as an ILS.

The Microsoft Internet Directory is a free-to-use directory server maintained by Microsoft, but to use it, you must sign up for MSN Messenger, Microsoft's Internet chat program. That's because the Microsoft Internet Directory and MSN Messenger are integrated, as of version 3.01 of NetMeeting.

Previous versions of NetMeeting allowed you to browse everyone who was connected to large Internet directory servers such as ils1.Microsoft.com and ils2.Microsoft.com. The newest version of NetMeeting doesn't work like that anymore, however. Instead, you have access only to the people you have set up on your Contacts list in MSN Messenger. That makes signing up for MSN Messenger Service all the more important.

Using a Specific Directory Server

Most people will probably use the default Microsoft Internet Directory server for NetMeeting. However, if you have a specific Internet directory you want to use with NetMeeting, here's how to set that up:

1. Choose Tools ➢ Options.
2. On the General tab, enter the address of the server in the Directory box. Many Internet directory services begin with "ils" (short for Internet locator server).
3. Click OK.

Now the chosen directory will be your default, and you can skip the whole MSN Messenger setup procedure in the next section.

APP
C

Using NetMeeting

Here are some Web pages that provide information and access to other directory servers:

- www.netmeet.com
- www.visitalk.com
- www.vidwatch.com

Signing Up for MSN Messenger

MSN Messenger is a totally free instant-messaging program that you can use to communicate with friends all over the world one-on-one. It's a text-only service, where you type something, then they type, and back and forth like that. (NetMeeting, in contrast, is like a super version of MSN Messenger, complete with audio and video feed and application sharing.)

Have you noticed a pattern in Microsoft's behavior? They give away all kinds of cool programs and services, but you have to sign up for them (and provide your personal data such as name and address). That's the case with MSN Messenger Service, too. To use it, you must either be a Hotmail user (a free, Web-based e-mail service from Microsoft) or sign up for a Microsoft Passport. Either way, Microsoft gets your contact information so they can market future products to you.

If you don't have a Hotmail account or a Microsoft Passport, see the following section to get a Hotmail account. Otherwise, skip to the next section, "Setting Up MSN Messenger."

Signing Up for a Hotmail Account

The easiest way to get rolling is to sign up for Hotmail, a Web-based e-mail system. Accounts are free (funded by advertisers). It never hurts to have an extra e-mail address, as you never know when it will come in handy.

To sign up for Hotmail, do the following:

1. Open Internet Explorer and go to www.hotmail.com.

2. Click the Sign Up Now! hyperlink. Read the terms of service, and click I Accept.

3. The Hotmail Registration screen appears, asking for information about you. Enter it into the fields provided.

   Part of this includes choosing a user ID for yourself. This will form your e-mail address. For example, if you choose johndoe as your user ID, your Hotmail e-mail address will be johndoe@hotmail.com.

4. Click the Sign Up button at the bottom of the page.

   If the name you chose is already taken, you'll be prompted to select another; if your name is accepted, you'll see a Sign Up Successful! screen.

5. When you get to the Sign Up Successful! screen, close your Web browser. You are now signed up.

Setting Up MSN Messenger

Now that you have a Hotmail ID, you're ready to sign up for MSN Messenger:

1. Choose Start ➢ Programs ➢ MSN Messenger Service. A Welcome dialog box opens.

2. Click Next, and then Next again. (Since you already have a Hotmail account, you do not have to bother with getting a Microsoft Passport.)

3. Enter your sign-in name. This is either your Hotmail account ID (minus the @hotmail.com part) or your Microsoft Passport ID.

4. Enter the password for that ID in the Password box.

5. Open the Provided By drop-down list and choose either hotmail.com or passport.com, depending on which you are using.

6. Click next, and then Finish. MSN Messenger opens and logs you on. You're connected! See Figure C.5.

FIGURE C.5
*MSN Messenger
Service, at your service*

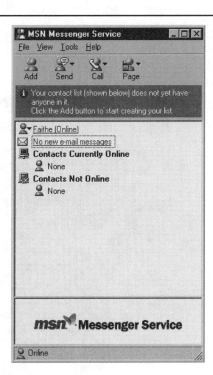

NOTE You can leave MSN Messenger running as you use NetMeeting, or not, as you choose. To use the directory in NetMeeting, however, you must be logged into MSN Messenger. (You'll be prompted from within NetMeeting to connect as needed, so you don't have to start MSN Messenger ahead of time.) By default, MSN Messenger sets itself up so that it runs automatically whenever you are connected to the Internet. To turn this off, from within the MSN Messenger window, choose Tools ➢ Options, and on the Preferences tab, deselect the Always Run This Program… check box.

Adding Someone to Your MSN Messenger Contact List

The easiest way to start a NetMeeting with other folks is to invite them by choosing their names from your Contacts list. You set up the Contacts list from MSN Messenger, and then it becomes available in both programs. You can invite someone to participate in a NetMeeting from within either program. (More on that shortly.)

To add someone to your Contacts list, that person must be signed up for the MSN Messenger Service, too. If you know the person's Hotmail address, you can add them to your Contacts list directly. If not, you can search the MSN Messenger directory. People can opt out of the directory, so it's possible the person you're seeking is not listed; but it's worth a try if you don't know the exact ID.

1. From within MSN Messenger, click the Add button. The Add A Contact dialog box opens. See Figure C.6.

FIGURE C.6
Set up your friends and coworkers in the Contacts list so you can invite them to NetMeetings later.

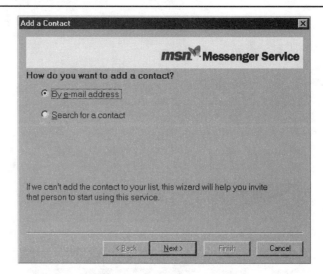

2. Choose one of the following options, and follow these instructions:

By E-Mail Address Choose this if you know the person's e-mail address. Then click Next, and you are prompted to enter it. Do so, and click Next again.

MSN Messenger looks up that e-mail address in its database. If the person has a Hotmail account or a Passport, you see a Success! message. Continue to step 3. However, if the person does not have either type of account, a message appears to that effect. Continue to step 3 anyway, and make sure you choose Yes in step 3 to send the person a message explaining how to get one.

Search for a Contact   Choose this if you don't know the e-mail address. Then click Next, and a form appears in which you can enter a name and country. Enter what you know about the person, and click Next to search for matching entries in the Hotmail member directory. A list of matching persons appears; select the one you want and click Next. Then continue to step 3.

3. A message offers to send an e-mail to the person explaining how to install MSN Messenger. Click Yes to send the person instructions or No to skip it if you know the person is already an MSN Messenger user; then click Next.

4. To add another contact, click Next and return to step 2. Otherwise, click Finish.

Now the people you entered appear on your Contacts list. There are two separate listings: people currently online and people currently not online. Figure C.7 shows one person in each list.

APP
C

Using NetMeeting

FIGURE C.7
One of my contacts is online and the other isn't.

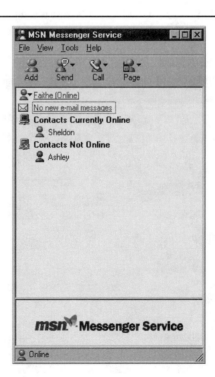

Inviting Someone to a NetMeeting

You can invite someone to a NetMeeting either from within NetMeeting or from within MSN Messenger. I'll show you both ways.

Selecting Someone to Invite from the NetMeeting Directory

You can invite someone to participate in a NetMeeting from the Directory window in NetMeeting itself. If you are using the Microsoft Internet Directory as your default server, your MSN Messenger Service Contacts list appears, and you choose a person from there. If you have set up some other server to use instead, a list of the users logged on to that server at the moment appears. In this appendix, I'll focus primarily on the former.

1. From within NetMeeting, choose Call ➢ Directory. The Microsoft Internet Directory window opens.

2. If prompted to log on to MSN Messenger Service, click the hyperlink to do so. When you're logged on, you'll see your MSN Messenger contacts, as shown in Figure C.8. Notice how much it looks like the Contacts list in Figure C.7. It's the same list—just presented in a different place.

FIGURE C.8
Choose one of your MSN Messenger contacts to invite to a NetMeeting.

3. Click the name of the person you want to invite. A Waiting for Answer indicator appears next to the name.

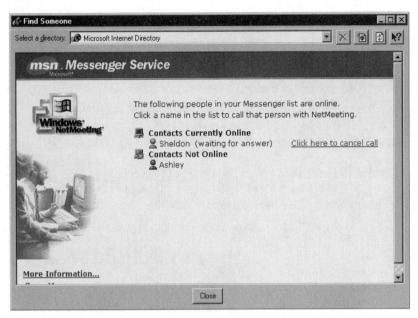

Meanwhile, on the recipient's screen, a box like this appears. The recipient clicks Accept to accept your invitation.

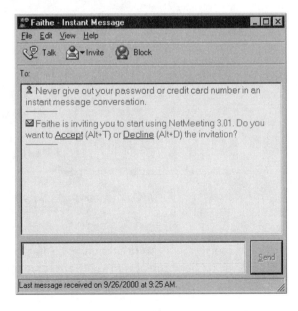

Then a "phone" starts ringing on the recipient's computer, and the following box appears. When the recipient clicks Accept here, the NetMeeting connection is established.

4. Switch back to the Find Someone box, and either invite someone else or click Close to begin meeting with the current participants.

Inviting Someone from MSN Messenger Service

If you're already in MSN Messenger Service but you haven't started NetMeeting yet, you might find it easier to invite one of your contacts there to a NetMeeting connection and start NetMeeting automatically at the same time. To do so, follow these steps:

1. In MSN Messenger, locate the person you want to invite on your Contacts list.

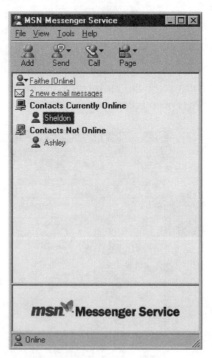

2. Choose Tools ➢ Send An Invitation ➢ To Start NetMeeting 3.01 ➢ *name* where *name* is the name of the person you want to invite.

A message appears on that person's screen, with hyperlinks to Accept and Decline.

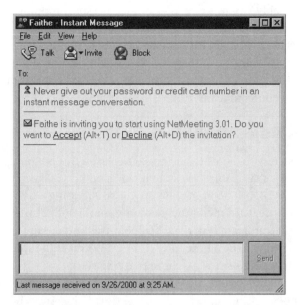

If the recipient clicks Accept, NetMeeting runs on both PCs and an Incoming Call box appears on your screen. (Notice that this is different from when you invited the person via NetMeeting, in the preceding set of steps. In that situation, the following box appeared on the remote user's screen instead of your own.)

3. Click the Accept button in this box, and the NetMeeting connection begins.

Hanging Up

I know, you haven't done anything yet in your meeting, but let's take care of a few housekeeping matters before getting into that. When you've finished with your call, don't forget to hang up. Of course, you should say good-bye first, either on the Chat board or with your voice. When you're ready to finally terminate the call, click the End Call button on the toolbar.

Adjusting Your Audio and Video

Invariably you're going to have to make some modifications to your sound and video setups. As unexciting as it is, many conversations start with some replay of the old Alexander Graham Bell conversation over the first telephone. I always seem to end up doing 10 minutes of "Can you hear me?" before we start having a real conversation or getting useful work done. Likewise, video often takes some adjusting as well. Here are some points to remember.

Sound Adjustments

To start with, adjust your speakers or use a headset, and make volume adjustments that are reasonable. The system works best if you keep your local volume turned fairly low. Well, not booming, anyway. If you're using a half-duplex system, earphones are best since, with them, the incoming sound doesn't trigger your microphone to turn on. The program is fairly good about this and doesn't trigger super easily, but this is something to be a little careful about. With a full-duplex system, callers may hear an echo of their own voice through the speakers.

You can control the speaker volume from a couple of places. My speakers have a volume control right on them, so I usually just turn the knob down a little bit. I also turn down the bass a little and bring up the treble a bit. This makes the voice more intelligible on my system. Yours may be different. You can also use the Volume Control in Windows (by double-clicking the speaker icon in the system tray).

While you're in the Volume Control, you should check the Microphone muting option. Make sure the Microphone's Mute check box is marked. Muting prevents the mike from playing through your speakers and producing feedback.

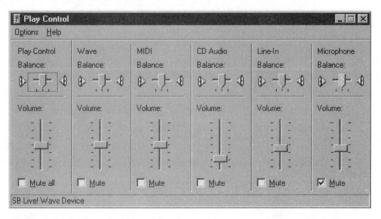

NOTE If you don't see the Microphone control in the volume controls, choose Options ➢ Properties; make sure that there is a check mark next to Microphone on the list of controls to display.

 The other place you can adjust volume is through NetMeeting itself. To display the volume controls, click the Adjust Audio Volume button in the NetMeeting window. The participant list box disappears and is replaced by two sliders, as shown here:

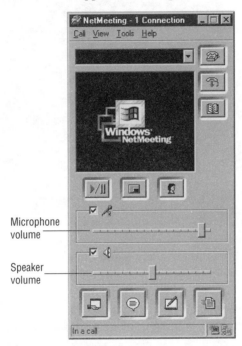

You might need to try adjusting the microphone slider a bit if people say either that you're coming in distorted or that you're too quiet. Test your settings with a number of people, though, before you make the definitive decision about your volume setting. It might just be that the other person's speakers are set too low or high!

Finally, the biggie is the microphone silence detection, which you get to from the Tools ➤ Options ➤ Audio tab.

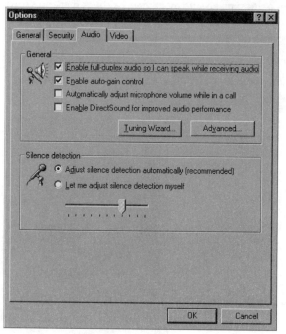

This control determines how loud your voice has to be in order to switch your microphone on. If set too high, any sound in the room will trigger your transmission, in effect drowning out the other people in the conversation, unless you all have full-duplex cards.

You'll have to mess a bit with this setting. First, click the Let Me Adjust Silence Detection Myself button. Then start dragging the slider a bit. You want it as low as possible, but still high enough to switch on when you start talking. Try different settings, but not drastically different from the way the slider was set. The Wizard probably did a fairly good job at setting this originally. As a rule, talk fairly close to the mike and try to keep the sensitivity down. Then adjust the mike volume as needed so people can hear you loudly enough.

Video Adjustments

You'll probably make some of your video adjustments through software that comes with your camera. For example, my system (the Phillips Easy Video card) has a couple of control programs to fine-tune my video capture. If you have a Connectix camera, you'll have a different set of controls, and so forth. Refer to the documents that come with your system for possible suggestions about appropriate NetMeeting settings.

If all is well, when you make a call to someone with a camera, you'll see their image in the NetMeeting window. You can also choose to have a mirror image of your own video displayed as well.

Here are some video settings you can adjust:

- You can click the Pause and Play buttons at the bottom of each video window to pause or restart the video you are sending and receiving. Pausing video input and output can improve the sound if the voices are starting to break up. This is because the video consumes large amounts of data bandwidth, often causing the audio to be delayed or lost.

- Right-click on a video window, and you'll see a number of settings, including Properties, which brings up a bunch of settings to play with, as shown in Figure C.9.

- As a rule, the smaller the display size, and the fuzzier the image you send (faster video), the less data you have to transmit per frame of video. So if things are getting bogged down, try the small image size.

- If you don't mind having strangers see your image before you see theirs, turn on the Automatically Send Video check box as well as the Automatically Receive Video check box (which is on by default). Then the participant and you will see each other when you make or receive a video call.

FIGURE C.9
A few video settings to play with. The defaults are probably the best bet.

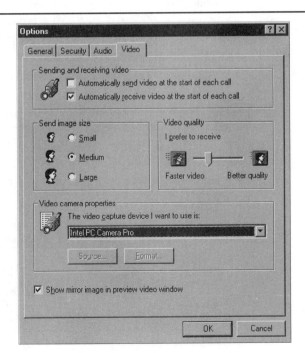

Communicating with Other NetMeeting Participants

There are two ways to talk with other meeting participants. If you both have a video camera and a microphone, you can carry on a normal conversation through those media as though you were in the same room. This is called video teleconferencing.

However, most people don't have video cameras, and the microphones may be a little iffy as well. Therefore, most people rely on the text-based communication ability of NetMeeting, known as Chat.

Using Chat

Chat provides a text-based mechanism to communicate with participants in a conference. Chat always seems to work. Thus, it's a good way to get started talking to someone in case your sound (and possibly video) isn't working. You can use Chat by itself, if you want, to communicate about common ideas or topics with fellow conference participants; or you can use it to augment your conference proceedings, as you would record meeting notes and action items to distribute later as the minutes of your meeting.

To use Chat, just do this:

1. Click the Chat button at the bottom of the NetMeeting window, or choose Tools ➤ Chat. You'll see a window with two sections.

2. Type a message into the bottom (Message) section. If you wish, you may now edit your message in the usual ways. After typing and editing, click the Send button next to the text entry area. Your message is now sent, at which point you'll see your message appear below your name in the upper window.

You can see in Figure C.10 a chat I had online while I was testing NetMeeting.

FIGURE C.10

A chat window. Type into the bottom of the window and click Send to send your message.

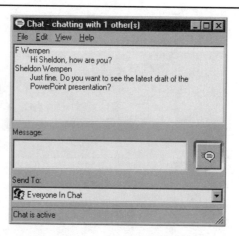

Using the Whiteboard

Need a visual aid to make your point? Use the Whiteboard feature to draw a picture that the other people in the conference can see. You can paste onto the whiteboard from another application, copy an active window, or copy any portion of the screen and drop it into the whiteboard. Several people can even draw on the picture at the same time. It also sports a few drawing tools, so you can sketch diagrams, organization charts, and flowcharts; or you can display other graphic information and share it with other people in a conference. Since the program is object-oriented (versus pixel-oriented), you can move and manipulate the contents by clicking and dragging with the mouse. A cute little remote pointer (in the shape of a pointing finger) and a highlighting tool can be used to point out specific contents or sections of shared pages. This is a great tool for ad hoc collaborations!

NOTE The Whiteboard works a lot like the Paint applet that comes with Windows. See Chapter 6, "WordPad and Paint Basics," to learn more about the various tools and techniques you can use here.

To use this feature, click the Whiteboard icon at the bottom of the window or choose Tools ➤ Whiteboard. The whiteboard appears on both your and your participants' screens. Any time any one of you makes a change to the whiteboard, it is transmitted to the others. Figure C.11 shows a whiteboard with a diagram and some notes on it.

APP
C

Using NetMeeting

FIGURE C.11
The Whiteboard is great for group discussions that involve graphic concepts.

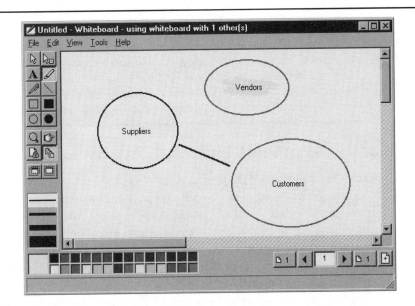

If you want to copy something to your whiteboard (such as a picture or the contents of a window) do this:

1. Open that item in another window. If it's a picture, for example, open it in a drawing or graphics-viewing program.

2. Switch to the Whiteboard program and choose Tools ➢ Select Area (or click the Select Area button in the toolbar, on the left side of the Whiteboard window).

3. Switch to the program displaying the stuff you want to display on the whiteboard. Notice that you now have a crosshair cursor. Select the desired area by clicking and dragging with the crosshair, releasing the mouse button when finished. Now everything in the boxed area you just selected appears on the whiteboard, which means the other folks can see it, too.

Anyone in the conference can point to stuff on the whiteboard by clicking the pointing finger in the toolbar on the left side and then clicking in the screen. You can also move the hand around—but you have to intentionally drag the pointer hand and drop it before the other folks see the effect.

You can also highlight stuff with the highlighter pen tool in the toolbar—second column, second row. Very useful. Don't forget to try the Zoom control, too, from the View menu, when you want a close-up.

You can create multiple pages of stuff to share. If the whiteboard gets full with material that you don't want to erase just yet, simply create a new page by clicking the Insert New Page button (looks like a page with a plus sign on it). Then work from there. If you don't care about what's on a page and are running out of room, just clear the page by choosing Edit ➢ Clear Page.

TIP   Let's say you're working with a colleague and you have to sign off. It's the end of the workday, or you have lunch waiting. You can save a page or pages for later use in your next session. Just choose File ➢ Save As, and name the file. It gets a .wht extension on disk. You open it later by opening the Whiteboard, choosing File ➢ Open, and browsing for the document. By default it goes in My Documents\Work In Progress.

Sharing Documents and Applications

You can actually share the programs running on your computer with other people in a conference. NetMeeting works with existing Windows-based programs that you already have, and you don't need any special knowledge of conferencing capabilities to share them. You just run any old program normally, and then share it. Other people you're connected to (in "conference" with) then see your actions as you use that program, such as editing a document. They see your cursors as you edit content, scroll through information, and so forth. In addition, if you're running the program, you can choose to allow others to *collaborate*, so others in the conference can take turns editing or controlling the application.

The amazing thing is, everyone can collaborate on a document even if only one person has the program that's being shared! So, for example, if I want an architect and my partner to help out on an AutoCAD drawing of a house we're working on, as long as each of us has NetMeeting on our machines and one of us has AutoCAD on our system, we're set.

Here are some examples of how the application-sharing capability in NetMeeting can be used to improve productivity:

- You could share a Word or other word processing program so that multiple people could collaborate on editing a document.

- Two or more programmers could share a programming language, working together to create a new program.

- Several people could share a spreadsheet program to work together on verifying and updating information.

Here's how to get NetMeeting to share your running applications, so that others in the conference can see what you're doing:

1. Start the application you want to share. The program does *not* have to know how to be NetMeeting "aware." Any program will do; it could be Word, it could be Photoshop, it could be the Calculator, etc. Also, it's not necessary for each person to have the application on their computer—it only has to be on the computer that is sharing it.

2. Switch back to NetMeeting. Click the Share Program button (the leftmost button at the bottom of the NetMeeting windows) or choose Tools ➤ Share Application. The Sharing dialog box opens, listing all the currently running programs.

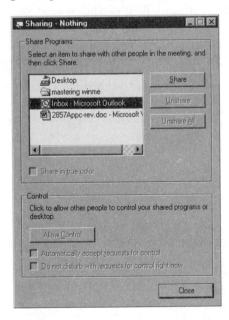

3. Select the program to share and click Share. Then click Close.

4. Start working in the application you have shared—for example, typing numbers into Calculator.

When you share an application, by default it's shared in Work-Alone mode, which means that only *you* can work in it. If you want, you can let others work with you to get things done more quickly. You do this by collaborating, as follows:

1. Click the Share Program button again in the main NetMeeting window. The Sharing box reopens.

2. Select the shared application and click the Allow Control button.

3. If you want others to be able to take control without your permission for each application, mark the Automatically Accept Requests for Control check box.

4. Click Close.

5. Return to the shared application.

If you ever need to end collaboration—that is, to regain and *keep* control of the program—press Esc on your keyboard.

TIP It's always good to issue a voice or chat warning that you want to take control of the mouse. Otherwise, it becomes a free-for-all, with people trying to get the mouse control away from each other.

NOTE To share the document that results from this collaboration, you must send the final file to the participants in the meeting. See "Doing File Transfers to Other Participants" later in this chapter.

On the other end, the person who will be assuming control of the application can choose Control ➤ Request Control from the shared window. After waiting for the owner to click Accept (if needed—see step 3 of the preceding procedure), control passes to the requester, and they can use the application just as though it were on their own PC.

When a participant is finished taking a turn with the program, they can allow someone else to take control by choosing Control ➤ Release Control from the shared window.

Sharing Your Clipboard

Here's another nifty feature. Two or more people can quickly share the contents of their Clipboards (remember, you put stuff on the Clipboard by using the Cut or Copy command from an application) regardless of whether they're set up to share applications.

You just have to be connected to someone else using NetMeeting. This "sharing" via the Clipboard protects you from being vulnerable to the other person(s) with whom you're connected. If you haven't shared an application per se, but only your Clipboard, you may share only as much of a document as you wish, by copying it to your Clipboard; there is no danger of someone seeing all of your document unless you want them to.

Here's how this feature is used:

1. Get into the program containing the information you want to "share" with another.

2. Using your Edit menu, the right-click menu, or other appropriate function in the program, cut or copy the information you want to share. This will put it on your Clipboard. Interestingly, this also puts the information on the Clipboard of people you are sharing applications with. It's as though you've taken over their Windows Clipboard without even knowing about it. (They can do the same thing to your Clipboard, so a little communication about what you're doing might be the polite way to go about this.)

3. Now the other people you're connected with can use an Edit ≻ Paste command in any application they have on their local machine to paste the material into their own documents. (And, of course, you can do the same with applications on your machine.)

4. Until someone else copies or cuts something new to their Clipboard, the earlier material remains on each participant's Clipboard, and each person can paste the material elsewhere in as many places as they want.

 NOTE Clipboard sharing also happens automatically if you have set up an application to share or collaborate on.

Doing File Transfers to Other Participants

While you're in a meeting with folks, it's often useful to be able to send files to one another, or to disseminate files to everyone in the meeting quickly. You can do this in NetMeeting. It's effortless. In fact, since NetMeeting is being used as a social meetinghouse on the Internet, I've seen lots of people sending pictures of themselves to each other, or utility programs, or resumes, using this approach. Since the file transfers happen in the background, you can keep right on talking or chatting while the files are being transmitted. The intended recipients have the option of accepting or declining receipt of a file being sent to them—an important consideration since files could be carrying viruses. As usual, plan to do a virus check on every file you accept via NetMeeting.

To transfer a file to someone, follow these steps:

1. From the NetMeeting window, choose Tools ➤ File Transfer, or click the Transfer Files button at the bottom of the NetMeeting window. The File Transfer dialog opens.

2. Click the Add Files button, and browse to the files you want to send. The Select Files to Send dialog box opens.

3. Select the file(s) on your PC that you want to send, and click Add. The file appears on the File Transfer list.

4. When you are finished adding files, click Send All. The transfer begins.

   On the participants' screens, a box appears reporting the file transfer. Each participant can choose to Open or Delete the file, or to Close the box without interacting with the file at all.

TIP NetMeeting is an OLE-compliant program, so you can drag files from an Explorer window (any folder window or from Windows Explorer proper) and drop them onto the conference window. All participants of the conference (excluding yourself) will then receive the files.

INDEX

Note to the Reader: Throughout this index **boldfaced** page numbers indicate primary discussions of a topic. *Italicized* page numbers indicate illustrations.

A

G

J

K

O

P

X

Y

Z